A History of the Modern Middle East

A History of the MODERN MIDDLE EAST

RULERS, REBELS, AND ROGUES

Betty S. Anderson

Stanford University Press
Stanford, California

Stanford University Press
Stanford, California

Printed in the United States of America on acid-free, archival-quality paper

Library of Congress Cataloging-in-Publication Data

Names: Anderson, Betty S. (Betty Signe), 1965– author.
Title: A history of the modern Middle East : rulers, rebels, and rogues /
Betty S. Anderson.
Description: Stanford, California : Stanford University Press, 2016. |
Includes bibliographical references and index.
Identifiers: LCCN 2015050232 | ISBN 9780804783248 (pbk. : alk. paper)
Subjects: LCSH: Middle East—History—1517—Textbooks. | Middle
East—Politics and government—Textbooks.
Classification: LCC DS62.4 .A63 2016 | DDC 956—dc23
LC record available at http://lccn.loc.gov/2015050232

ISBN 9780804798754 (electronic)

Designed by Bruce Lundquist

Typeset at Stanford University Press in 10/15 Sabon LT

Contents

Boxes

Illustrations

Maps

Preface

This book begins with Turkic migrants moving from Central Asia to the Middle East because they were pivotal for the founding of the Ottoman (14th century) Empire and instrumental to the establishment of the Safavid (16th century) Empire. From there, the book proceeds to the current day. I chose to start with the founding stories of these empires because the governmental structures their leaders established and the relationships forged between state and subjects provide valuable background information for the changes wrought in the more traditionally defined modern era of the late 18th century forward. The Ottoman Empire influenced societal and governmental relationships throughout most of the Middle East for centuries and even for years after its dismantlement in 1923; Safavid strengths and weaknesses both became issues to be tackled by the Qajar (1796) and Pahlavi (1925) successors and integral parts of Iranian national and governmental identity. The text focuses on Egypt, Israel-Palestine, Jordan, Saudi Arabia, Lebanon, Syria, Iraq, Turkey, and Iran within the region while recognizing the changing roles that Britain, France, Russia/the Soviet Union, and the United States have played in these countries for centuries.

In examining these empires, their many state successors, and their foreign influences, I address the term "Rulers" that appears in the book's subtitle. To determine how rulers over many centuries and within different kinds of state structures came to power and maintained it, I analyze the bases for the rulers' authority, the institutions that implemented the leaders' policies, and the groups and people who became stakeholders in the state systems because they worked for the state and believed in the legitimacy of the leadership. I foreground state governance as the core thread connecting the narrative across centuries and borders, while illustrating the integrated nature of the relationships that has existed between the governors and the governed since the founding of these empires many centuries ago.

The recent upheavals throughout the Middle East provide the other side of the historical bookend for this text and open a window onto who the "Rebels and Rogues" of the subtitle are. On February 14, 2005, former Lebanese prime minister Rafiq Hariri died in an enormous explosion. Over the next months, Lebanese citizens massed in demonstrations against the Syrian government for its alleged complicity in the attack and for remaining in occupation of portions of Lebanon since 1976. Even with followers of Hizballah supporting a continuing Syrian presence in Lebanon, Syria withdrew from the country by the end of April 2005. In June 2009, millions of Iranians took to the streets to protest the reelection of President Mahmoud Ahmadinejad and the fraud that accompanied it. Before the election, dramatic actions such as a "human chain" of 150,000 people circled Tehran in support of candidate Mir-Hossein Mousavi. After the government issued the election results, protesters began with silent demonstrations for four days, as people stood together but did not yell out any slogans. Within days Ahmadinejad and his police and security agencies successfully repressed the movement, and Ahmadinejad began his second term; as many as 150 people died in the clashes with police. This movement came to be called the Green Revolution because of the prevalence of green banners among the protesters in support of Mousavi's campaign and the democratic slogans ringing out.

The events of the Arab Spring were sparked on December 17, 2010, when Tunisian Mohamed Bouazizi immolated himself and died the following day from his injuries. His act was a protest against the dire economic conditions he faced in Tunisia and the stark gap between rich and poor arising around him. His death triggered massive, countrywide demonstrations against the government of Zine El Abidine Ben Ali, who had been in power since 1987 and was now forced to flee to Saudi Arabia on January 14, 2011. Similar demonstrations erupted in Tahrir Square in Cairo on January 25, 2011, and when these demonstrations also became countrywide over the next 18 days, President Husni Mubarak resigned on February 11, 2011, and turned executive authority over to the Supreme Muslim Council of the Armed Forces (SCAF), led by Defense Minister Field Marshal Hussein Tantawi.

On February 27, 2012, President Ali Abdullah Saleh of Yemen stepped down after 12 years as president of a united Yemen and 22 years earlier as president of North Yemen. Like dominoes, surrounding states faced similar upheavals, with a Syrian uprising beginning in the southern town of Dar'a in March 2011. Muammar Qaddafi's 42-year tenure as leader of Libya ended under bombardment from NATO; he died at the hands of rebels on October 20, 2011. The governments of Jordan, Saudi

Arabia, and Bahrain faced repeated demonstrations that these leaders were able to quell but not eliminate completely. On May 28, 2013, protesters came out into Gezi Park in Istanbul, a former Armenian cemetery and one of the last green spaces in the city, to oppose the government's urban development plans. The next year saw the demonstrations spread across the country and expand to include broader denunciations of corruption in the office of Turkish prime minister Recep Tayyip Erdoğan.

The shifts in power and the attempts at transforming governmental leadership all came at the hands of diverse and often massive demonstrations against state leaders and their policies. The participants did not join because of one particular grievance or as members of one particular interest group. They protested against the lack of job opportunities for secondary and university graduates, rising levels of economic inequality, the poor quality of services provided by their governments, state brutality by police and security services, discriminatory water policies, and foreign support for the dictators that led their state governments. They did so with overlapping identities, as youth, nationalists, Islamists, secularists, women, government employees, and workers.

Some wanted more state control over the economy; others wanted more privatization. Some wanted reform; others sought the complete overthrow of their governing structures. In Bahrain Shi'a wanted participatory rights in the government. In Egypt, the protesters deemed President Mubarak an unfit ruler over their government but recognized the legitimacy of the military to hold power in his stead; in Tunisia, a transformation of government has been undertaken that could dramatically change the relationship between state and citizenry. All the protesters could stand beside each other in the streets, regardless of their differing demands, because they agreed that collectively they had the right to demand change and that their governments could not be trusted to take the lead.

The leaderless nature of the protests in 2010 and 2011 allowed for many different avenues for politicization and mobilization, generating enormous numbers of participants, but this phenomenon worked poorly once governments had fallen and elections occurred. While Islamist associations such as the Muslim Brotherhood were able to quickly shift into political-party organizing for elections, other new political parties found it difficult to establish national organizations and successfully lobby for votes. The Egyptian military was still powerful enough to wage a coup in summer 2013 against the Muslim Brotherhood–dominated government that came to office after Mubarak's ouster.

Meanwhile, Jordan's King Abdullah, whose leadership has survived the protests, plays what some scholars call the "reform game," whereby he moves prime ministers and cabinet officials into and out of office so that he appears to bring change but does not alter the state's power structure. Erdoğan faced demonstrations that spread far beyond Gezi Park and involved months of accusations of corruption within his government. However, he retained enough support in the country to become Turkey's first directly elected president on August 28, 2014. Syria's uprising has evolved into a brutal civil war with no discernible end in sight.

While the events taking place from Iran to Turkey to the Arab world in the last 10 years were unprecedented in the number of participants and their cross-border nature, they were nonetheless not unique to the history of the region. The organizational structures established by the participants, the wide-ranging demands made on governments, the questions about state legitimacy, and even the failed attempts at wholesale governmental change have occurred in the past.

To address the many times these events have taken place, I distinguish between the "rebels and rogues" of Middle Eastern history. Rebels, over the centuries, completely opposed the leadership and systems of governance ruling over them. For example, a diverse group of rebels appeared throughout the Middle East in the years immediately after World Wars I and II because in those moments it was unclear in every area covered in this book what type of government would result from the shifting events. The rebels wanted, at the least, control over their own local domains, while others took a wider view and sought leadership over the new nations being formed. Rebels are also the Kurds, the Armenians, and the Palestinians who continually rejected the national claims of the governments ruling them. Junior military officers came into the halls of government via military coups. Starting with Muhammad ibn 'Abd al-Wahhab (1703–1792) and his rebellion against the religious leadership of the Ottoman sultan, many groups and individuals have challenged their leaders' right to usurp the authority of God.

I build on a concept of rogues that Karen Barkey defines in *Empire of Difference: The Ottomans in Comparative Perspective* (2008) when she says of the Celali protests against Ottoman governance in the 17th century that they "were not interested in rebellion but concentrated on trying to gain state resources, more as rogue clients than as primitive rebels." From this starting point, I designate as rogues those actors who challenged their leadership to reform state governance or who used their challenges as the means for gaining positions within the state. Rogues were those who did not directly rebel against the Ottoman Empire as it weakened in the 18th century but who nonetheless took advantage of the political openings to devise tools for strengthening their military, political, and economic positions in relation to the central government.

In the 1920s and 1930s, rogues were those students, professionals, and workers who frequently went out into the streets to protest against European colonialism and the hold old notables held over governmental posts. They posited that the Arab world would be stronger if the borders of the new states drawn after World War I were erased, but they did not organize to overthrow their governments in the interwar years. Instead, they advocated for reform of government agencies so they would be more representative of the diverse voices of the citizenry and so old notables could be replaced. Most protesters of the Green Revolution, Arab Spring, and Gezi Park events did not want to reinvent their governmental structures but to make them more accountable to their citizenries. They wanted to force from power those who stood in the way of such change and who had monopolized positions of power for decades. They wanted their governments to be more responsive to the economic crises so many people faced.

To be able to meld these rulers, rebels, and rogues into a holistic narrative of Middle Eastern history, I incorporate the academic monographs I used in my classes over the years as supplements to the political histories usually presented in textbooks. And while no book of a mere 500 pages can truly do justice to the wonderful work my colleagues have produced, I hope I have done so by giving them pride of place in a large narrative of Middle Eastern history. In keeping with the conventions of the textbook format, the book contains no citations to locate the source for a specific piece of data. I have included all of my sources for this text in the bibliography.

While benefiting from the richness afforded by my colleagues' close studies of their subjects, I have also taken advantage of the broad geographical and chronological sweep that a textbook project allows so that I could locate patterns across regions and times. I found commonalities of practice between bandits in the Balkans at the turn of the 19th century and the institution-building project that Mehmet Ali undertook in Egypt at the same time. I examined the governmental structures established after World War II—from Iran to Turkey and through the Arab world—in order to construct a common schema for governance for that period.

I followed educational practices across history to analyze why schooling could produce stakeholders for the states but also graduates who were their states' most consistent critics. Thus, the text pivots between general representations of governing practices—focusing on shared patterns across borders—and deeper studies of the actions and motivations of individual groups located in the academic monographs of my colleagues.

Too often, the media available to students of the Middle East allow country names ("Egypt," "Saudi Arabia"), stereotypes ("terrorist," "militant," "Shiʿa," "youth"), or politicians ("Erdoğan," "ayatollahs") to represent the actions and belief systems of millions of people. The region can appear as an area of unchanging opinions and prejudices, a place of implacable instability, as the wars and sectarian crises of the contemporary period seem to indicate. It is impossible to understand developments in the region over time or to analyze the tumultuous events of the last few years through such narrow lenses. These categorizations fail to explain the complex relationships that have been forged and the overlapping identities, grievances, and desires that the peoples of the Middle East have held and continue to express.

My goal from the beginning of this project has been to integrate both large and small political players into the narrative of Middle Eastern history, to complicate how the governors and the governed have interacted throughout history. Political leaders never completely governed separately from the peoples under their control; nongovernmental actors could not ignore the state institutions in their lives. I examine the many types of rulers wielding power in the Middle East alongside societal groups that rarely appear in textbooks and other media venues, usually left out because their influences are more difficult to measure than those of the political leadership. I return century to century, decade to decade, to the actions and ideological positions proffered by monarchs and presidents, and also by slaves, religious clerics, provincial notables, urban merchants, students, professionals, workers, peasants, and army officers as examples of how rulers, rebels, and rogues forged Middle Eastern history together.

A History of the Modern Middle East

MAP 1. Modern Middle East.

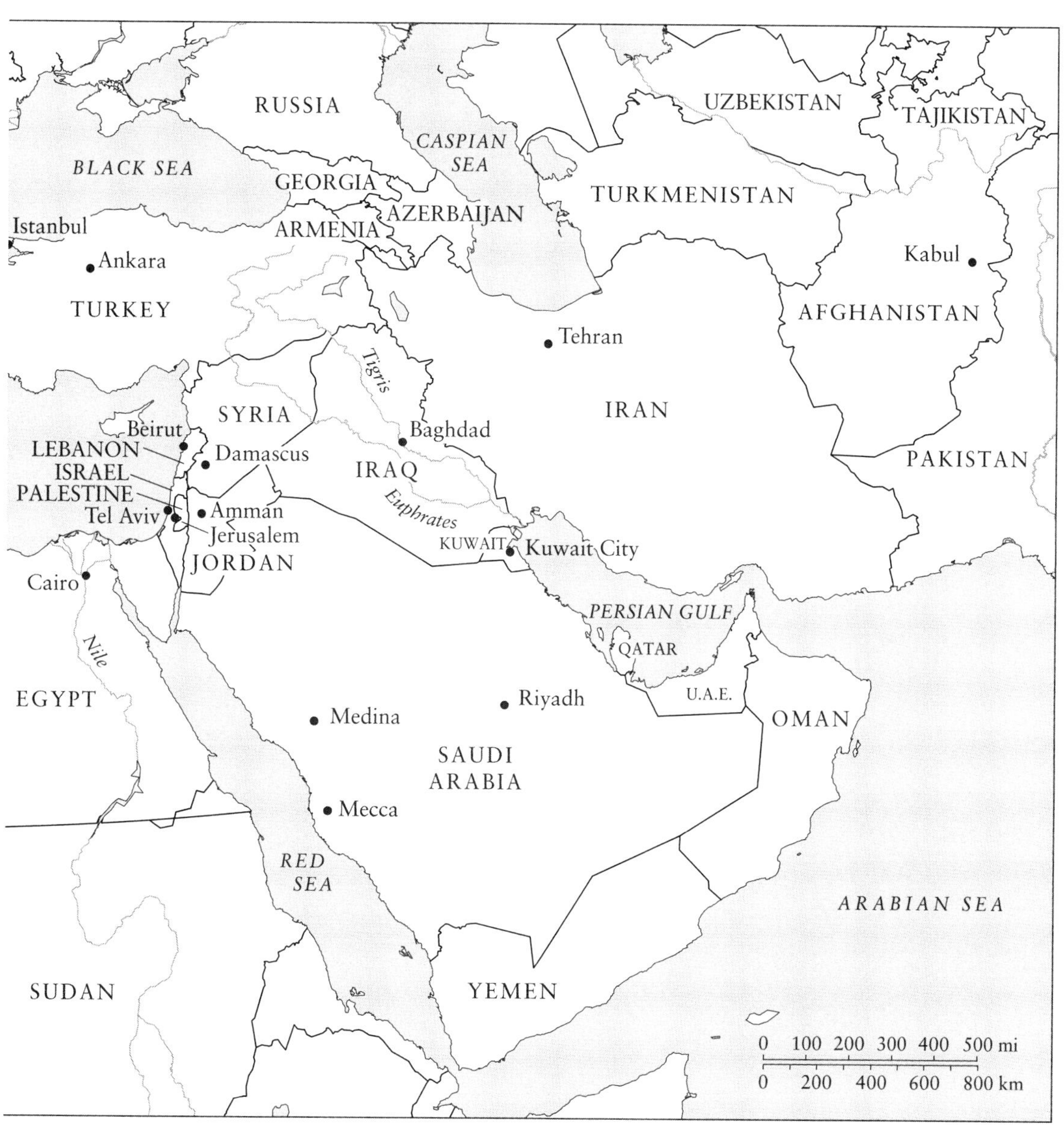
RUSSIA
UZBEKISTAN
TAJIKISTAN
CASPIAN SEA
BLACK SEA
GEORGIA
TURKMENISTAN
AZERBAIJAN
ARMENIA
Istanbul
Ankara
Kabul
TURKEY
AFGHANISTAN
Tehran
Tigris
SYRIA
IRAN
Beirut
Baghdad
LEBANON
Damascus
ISRAEL
IRAQ
PAKISTAN
PALESTINE
Euphrates
Tel Aviv
Amman
Jerusalem
KUWAIT
Kuwait City
JORDAN
Cairo
PERSIAN GULF
Nile
QATAR
U.A.E.
EGYPT
Riyadh
Medina
OMAN
SAUDI ARABIA
Mecca
RED SEA
ARABIAN SEA
SUDAN
YEMEN
0 100 200 300 400 500 mi
0 200 400 600 800 km

PROLOGUE

Islam and the Prophet's Successors

THE ANGEL GABRIEL SPOKE TO MUHAMMAD (ca. 570–632) in the year 610, in a cave in the Arabian Peninsula outside the town of Mecca in the region of the Hijaz. He told Muhammad to "recite" and thus began Muhammad's Prophethood. Soon thereafter Muhammad spoke of the revelations he was receiving, and as he began to attract followers, he faced persecution from the Quraysh, the most powerful tribe in Mecca and guardians of the icons of polytheism collected in the center of the town at the Ka'ba. In 622, Muhammad and his followers left Mecca for Medina to avoid persecution. This migration, or hijra, marks the beginning of the Muslim calendar because in Medina at this time, Muhammad expanded the number of his followers and began the process of building the institutions that would come to define the Islamic faith and the state ruling over the believers.

While in Medina, Muhammad built up an army to fight his way back to Mecca and did so successfully in 630, when the Quraysh surrendered the town to him. Muhammad immediately went to the Ka'ba to destroy all the icons of polytheism, leaving only the black stone of Abraham because Muslims believe it is the last piece of the altar Abraham left behind when he lived in Mecca. Muhammad then returned to Medina for the last two years of his life; the Masjid al-Nabawi, the Mosque of the Prophet, stands on his burial site. Mecca and its Ka'ba are considered the holiest site in Islam; Medina is the second holiest because of its ties to the Prophet and its importance for developments in early Islam.

Muhammad initially preached that he was bringing together all the monotheists under one banner because God had presented the same message to all the Prophets who had come before him. Muslims believe that the complete message and word of God as presented to his Prophets has been preserved in the Quran. As conflicts broke out with the Jewish tribes of Medina, Muhammad began to develop institutions and rituals for a third monotheistic faith, separate from Judaism and Christianity. Muslims still revere all the Prophets who received God's message before Muhammad and consider Jews and Christians as "People of the Book" who require special legal and religious protections within Islamic states. These protected peoples (dhimmis) follow their own laws and their own leaders as long as they accept the supremacy of Muslim rule over their lives. Those who believe there is only one God whose message was preserved in the Quran through his last Prophet are Muslims, those who submit to God following the faith of Islam.

Within 500 years of the Prophet's death, Islam had become the dominant faith in the Middle East, but Christian and Jewish denominations and communities flourished under the protection accorded them by Muslim rulers. In succeeding years, new sects of Christianity joined those that formed after the crucifixion of Jesus Christ and when the Roman and Byzantine Empires accepted Christianity as the state religion in the 4th century. Arabic became the predominant language in the Arabian Peninsula, the Levant, and North Africa, while Persian maintained its dominance in Iran and throughout much of Central Asia.

Five acts, or pillars, make up the core of the faith of Islam; in performing them, Muslims show reverence for their God while also recognizing that they are doing it collectively, at the same time of day or the same time during the course of a year or lifetime. None of the pillars requires a person to separate himself or herself in a sacred institution; they can all be done in private or in public together with other worshippers. The practice of these pillars requires no equivalent to priests, rabbis, ministers, or liturgical councils; a Muslim speaks directly to God.

The shahada, or declaration of the faith, is the central concept in Islam that lays out the core elements in Muslim belief: There is no God but God, and Muhammad is his messenger. The essence of Islam is this oneness of God (the tawhid) and the Muslim belief that his divinity cannot be divided or shared in any way. God, or Allah in Arabic, sent Prophets throughout history with the message of his oneness. Muhammad is considered the last Prophet because Muslims believe the revelations from God were recorded correctly and completely in the Quran. The second pillar, salat, requires that all Muslims pray five times per day, facing Mecca and the Ka'ba at its center. At designated times throughout the day, the call to prayer rings out and Muslims cleanse themselves and perform the prayer.

The third pillar requires all Muslims to give charity (zakat) in keeping with Muhammad's message in Mecca and Medina that believers must be responsible for each other. The fourth pillar, the pilgrimage to Mecca (the hajj), must be carried out by every Muslim—man or woman—in his or her lifetime, if he or she is capable of doing so. Pilgrims follow the route of Muhammad as he destroyed the icons in the Ka'ba in 630 and reenact events in the life of Abraham and his family. The last of the pillars is fasting during the month of Ramadan, the month when Muhammad first heard the revelation from God. During Ramadan, Muslims must refrain from eating or drinking during daylight hours.

Upon his death in 632, the Prophet's followers decided a successor had to be found who could guide the Muslim community into the future. The consensus of the community was that the Prophet's successor, or his deputy, the caliph, needed to be of sound mind and body and knowledgeable about the revelations passed on and interpreted by the Prophet. The first of them, the four Rashidun caliphs (the Rightly Guided Successors)—Abu Bakr (632–634), 'Umar (634–644), 'Uthman (644–656), and 'Ali (656–661)—were all related to the Prophet via marriage. Each had personally seen how he led the community and thus had special insight about the message delivered to him. They succeeded in keeping the community together, expanding its territorial reach, and bringing more believers into the fold. They thus established a community of believers (an umma) connected through faith in the revelations and Muhammad's Prophethood. The Rashidun period showed that the community could live on beyond Muhammad, that Islam was not merely a cult following a man. The Rashidun caliphs constructed a world and a state where people followed the faith and the protectors of that faith, not whoever might be the strongest military shaykh at the moment.

But the Rashidun period was not without its conflicts. 'Umar and 'Uthman were both assassinated by enemies within the community. The

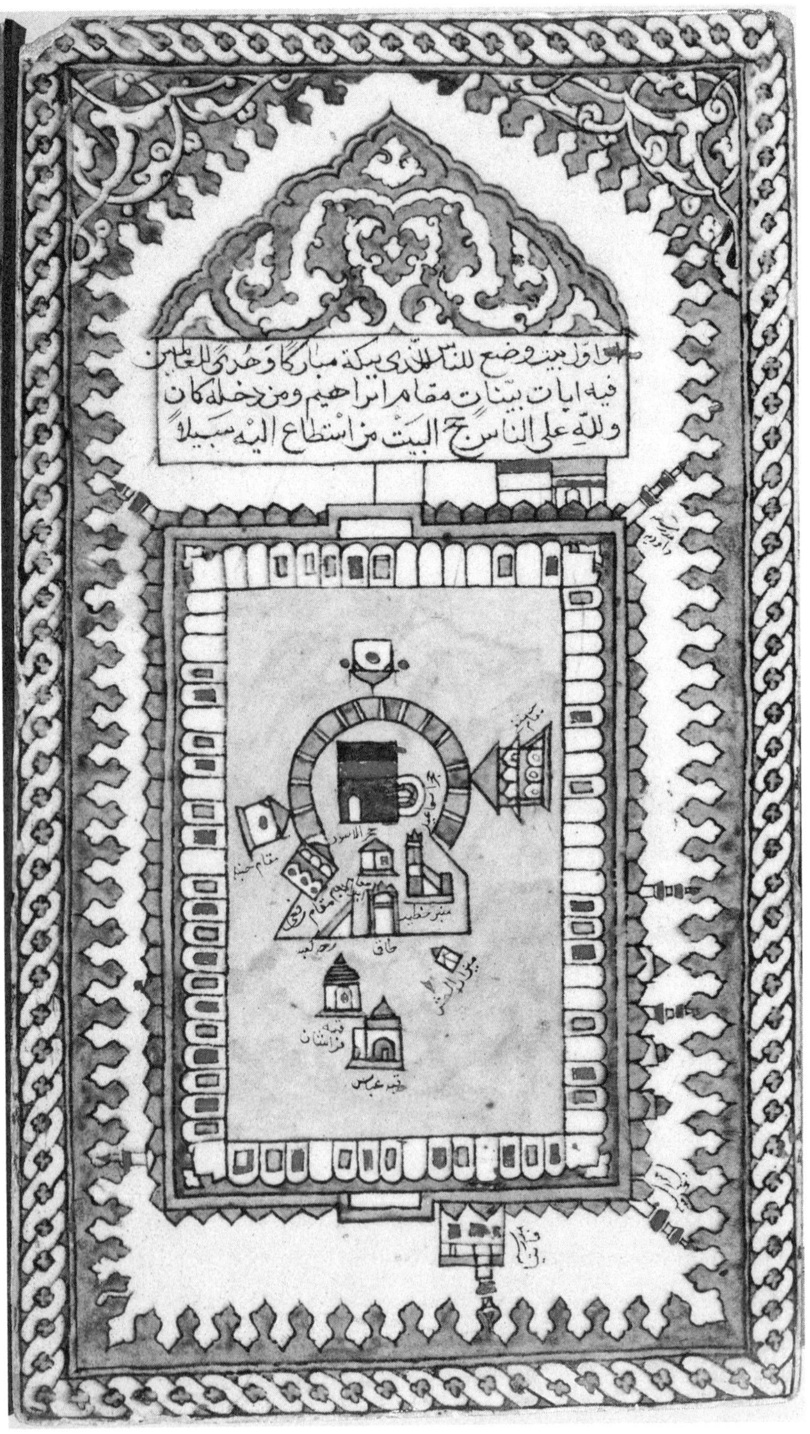

FIGURE 0.1. Tile depicting the Great Mosque of Mecca. The three lines of Arabic writing in the upper part of this large, ceramic wall tile are from the third chapter of the Quran and exhort the Muslim faithful to make the pilgrimage to Mecca.

choice of ‘Ali as successor brought about the first schism in the faith because his designation highlighted the factionalism within the society. ‘Ali, a cousin of the Prophet, was also married to the Prophet’s daughter Fatima, and their children and descendants have carried the line of the Prophet into the next centuries. Many groups in Mecca and Medina opposed his caliphate and went to war against him. ‘Ali set up his forces in Kufa, in southern Iraq, and immediately found himself in a civil war within the community. He successfully defeated a number of opponents but then faced a strong army fronted by the Umayyad family, who had gained influence because they controlled Damascus, the capital of present-day Syria. During the fighting, Kharijites (“those who go out,” so-called because they walked out on ‘Ali) killed ‘Ali and thus helped the Umayyads defeat ‘Ali’s forces and establish a new dynasty in Damascus (Umayyad Empire, 661–750). Refusing to recognize the legitimacy of Umayyad rule, ‘Ali’s son Hussein launched a new military campaign against the Umayyads, but he was defeated at Karbala, located in southern Iraq today. Hussein and almost every male member of the family were killed, but his sister Zaynab managed to save Hussein’s son Zayn al-‘Abidin, which allowed the Prophet’s family line to continue.

The schism in Islam between Sunni and Shi‘a arose from conflicting opinions about the proper qualifications for the Prophet’s successors and the battles that ‘Ali, Hussein, and the Prophet’s family waged in Kufa and Karbala against their many opponents in the Umayyad Empire. Shi‘a believe that leadership should have gone only through the line of the Prophet, through ‘Ali and Fatima, because the family itself held special interpretive powers and rights, second only to those of the Prophet himself. They consider the first three caliphs illegitimate for this reason. Sunni Muslims consider the consensus decisions made by the earliest Muslim community as valid and thus accept the legitimacy of all four of its caliphs. They represent almost 90 percent of all Muslims today.

Amid these conflicts, the Rashidun period brought Arab armies across the Arabian Peninsula, where they destroyed the Sasanian Empire (224–651), the latest in a long line of Persian empires in Iran, and captured substantial Middle Eastern territory from the Byzantine Empire based in Constantinople (330–1453). Under Umayyad rule, Muslim-Arab armies marched across North Africa and reached Spain in 711. But the conflicts over leadership were not resolved as the years progressed, and the Umayyad Empire witnessed repeated challenges to the family’s authority over the Muslim world. In 750, the Abbasid family succeeded where others had failed and established the long-lived Abbasid Empire based in the newly constructed city of Baghdad. The family ruled from this center, with only a few interruptions, until the Mongols destroyed the city and dissolved the empire in 1258. The surviving members of the Umayyad family forged a Muslim dynasty in Spain; successors maintained Muslim rule in the Iberian Peninsula for more than 700 years.

In the first 150 years of Abbasid rule, the empire they fronted was the central civilization of the world, with ideas and products moving into and out of it from around the world. This was a cosmopolitan civilization that encompassed peoples from throughout the region—including Arabs, Persians, Turks, Muslims, Christians, and Jews—who all contributed elements to cultural and scientific progress. Patrons at the Abbasid court and throughout the cities prompted scholars, artists, and doctors to write some of the most important philosophical, poetic, and medical treatises of the medieval period. Trade and artisan crafts flourished when the Abbasid court flourished, with goods coming from as far away as China and moving through the Middle East toward Europe, and from Africa to Central Asia.

Poets wrote odes to their patrons, to love, and to God; they compiled lengthy epics to Arab, Persian, and Turkish greatness. In the process, these poets also refined and expanded the means of expression in the Arabic, Persian, and Turkish languages as they competed for patrons and sought the favor of as large an audience as possible. Greek philosophical and medical texts entered the Abbasid canon when works initially written in Greek were translated into Syriac during the Byzantine Empire and then into Arabic in the medieval period, a task largely undertaken by Christians. The data and ideas contained within these texts helped fuel a medical revolution as scholars throughout the empire added to Greek medical knowledge.

Scholars also directed their attention to how the Quran's message could be translated into their everyday lives. A prolonged debate took place between self-appointed Islamic scholars (ulama) about the evidence to be used by believers to reason out solutions to new faith-based questions. The goal was to place all human acts into the context of Islamic piety; this meant adjudicating every aspect of a person's life, from the length of a beard to the terms of a marriage to the judicial power of a caliph. At the same time, the ulama also wanted to bring all older laws from the region into accordance with Islamic values and precepts.

From this study came the process of codifying the shari'a (Islamic law), which is not a revealed law but a divinely inspired one because the ulama undertook the process of ijtihad, of struggling to understand the faith through independent reasoning. The shari'a incorporates the Quran as the word of God while also recognizing that the Prophet should be emulated because he could have lived his life only in accordance with God's precepts; his actions flowed from God's commands. His interpretations of God's revelations, recorded as hadith, have a sacredness because of his Prophetic designation by God. The process of compiling the hadith established the sunna, the established practice or custom of the Prophet. The ulama also included a provision, analogy (qiyas), that allowed for a comparison between the Quran and the hadith when new questions arose that neither text addressed directly. Through this process, a doctrine emerged that designated the ulama with the role of determining the consensus of the community (ijma'), binding on all Muslims because it was sanctioned by God in accordance with the Quran and hadith.

This work took place in several areas throughout the Muslim world simultaneously in the 9th and 10th centuries, with scholars influenced by differing legal traditions practiced across their disparate regions. The result was the codification of four schools of jurisprudence, madhhabs (the chosen ways), within Sunni Islamic law. Sunni Muslims consider all of them—Shafi'i, Maliki, Hanafi, and Hanbali—equally legitimate, but their associated judges weighed the accepted elements of shari'a differently.

When this process was completed by the 10th century, the scholars involved declared the gates of ijtihad closed because a consensus had been accepted concerning the process and custom of Islamic law. From that point forward, the shari'a was not supposed to be an instrument of debate and negotiation but an understandable and effective system that comprised a set of rules for determining a legal ruling in any circumstance. The closing of the gates did not preclude any judge or scholar from tackling new questions and finding new answers, but no future scholar was supposed to debate the process necessary for adjudicating legal decisions. Islamic rulers then established school systems to train judges and court systems for adjudicating cases presented to them, based on the shari'a.

But the Abbasid caliphs found it difficult to maintain centralized control over their enormous territory for successive centuries. New dynasties emerged that came to control segments of the region. The Fatimids (909–1171) conquered most of North Africa and established Cairo as their capital; while they followed Shi'ism, they did not impose that sect of Islam on the predominantly Sunni communities they ruled. Between

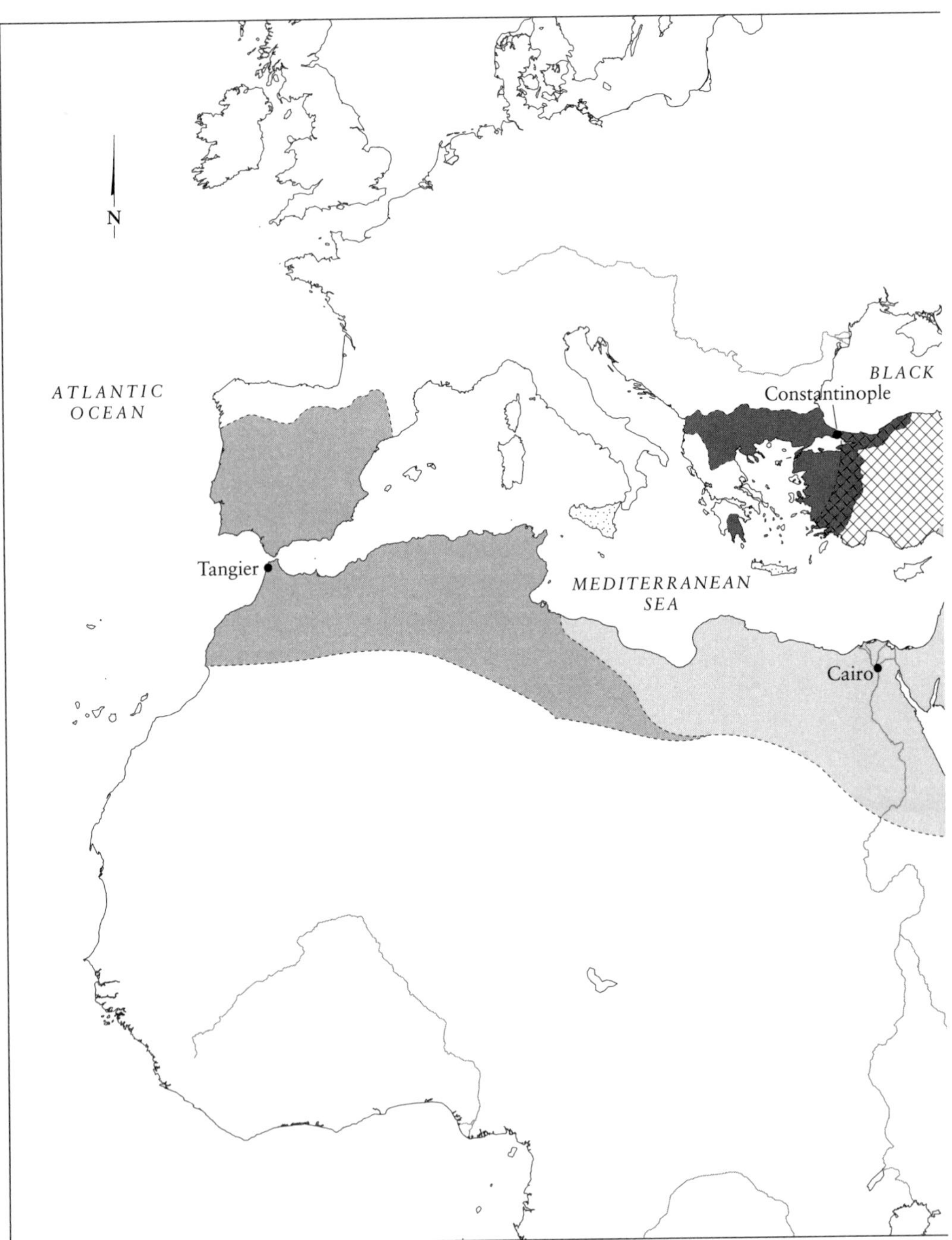

MAP 2. Islamic Empires, 7th to 16th Centuries. This map portrays territory of the pre-Islamic Middle East, the Umayyad Empire (660–750), the Abbasid Empire (750–1258), and successor empires.

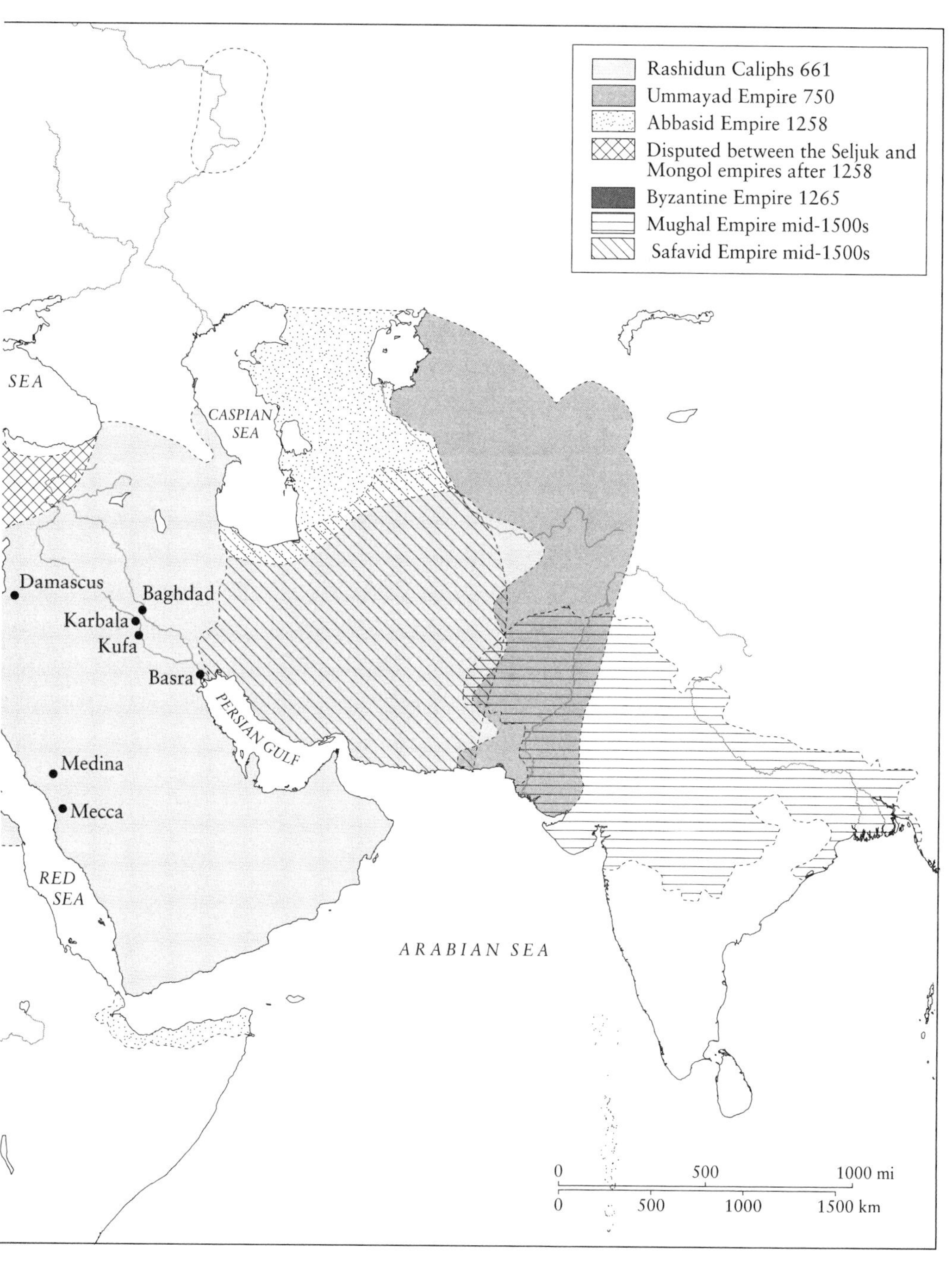

Rashidun Caliphs 661
Ummayad Empire 750
Abbasid Empire 1258
Disputed between the Seljuk and Mongol empires after 1258
Byzantine Empire 1265
Mughal Empire mid-1500s
Safavid Empire mid-1500s
SEA
CASPIAN SEA
Damascus
Baghdad
Karbala
Kufa
Basra
PERSIAN GULF
Medina
Mecca
RED SEA
ARABIAN SEA
0
500
1000 mi
0
500
1000
1500 km

1099 and 1199, European Crusaders ruled Jerusalem and the Holy Land; their state ended when a Kurdish official to the Fatimid court, Salah al-Din al-Ayyubi (Saladin, ca. 1138–1193), defeated them militarily. Salah al-Din used the legitimacy accrued to him by this victory to overthrow the Fatimids and establish the Ayyubid Empire in Cairo (1171–1250), including within its territory all of modern-day Egypt. This empire did not survive for long after the founder's death. His sons were defeated by their own slave army (Mamluks), which ruled Egypt and the Levant via a series of shifting political confederations until the Ottomans conquered the territory in 1517. The rest of North Africa fell to diverse confederations of families and tribes until the Ottoman military conquered these territories during the course of the 16th century. On the northern borders of the Abbasid Empire, the caliphs had to contend with new migrants moving in from Central Asia, whose successors defeated the empire in 1258.

BIRTH OF EMPIRES 1

The Ottoman and Safavid Empires through the 18th Century

STARTING AS EARLY AS THE 6TH CENTURY but accelerating thereafter, Turkic and Mongol tribes migrated from the area roughly situated at the crossroads of today's Russia, Mongolia, Northern China, and Kazakhstan. Over the centuries, successive waves marched through present-day Uzbekistan, Afghanistan, Pakistan, and India, establishing a series of Turkic and Mongol dynasties along the way, the last of which was the long-lived Mughal Empire in India (1526–1857). Turkic tribes also traveled southwest, across the Iranian plateau and into Anatolia and the Middle East. In 1055, the Turkic Seljuks conquered the Abbasid capital of Baghdad. Although they became the de facto rulers, calling themselves sultans (derived from the Arabic word for authority), they retained the Abbasid caliphs as titular heads of the empire.

In the face of internal dissension and threats posed by the arrival of new and stronger Turkic confederations, the Seljuks could not maintain cohesion; in 1194 the empire disintegrated, and the Abbasid Empire as a whole fell to the Mongol descendants of Genghis Khan (ca. 1162–1127) in 1258. The region between Anatolia and India came under the control of the empires of the Ilkhanid Mongols (1256–1335) and the Timurids (1370–1507). During the rise and fall of these many empires, the Byzantine Empire continued to rule from Constantinople. Its territories in the Levant and North Africa were lost to the Muslims, and Anatolia became a battleground as Turkic Muslim leaders pushed their way west. The defenses around the capital city slowly weakened.

Birth of the Ottoman Empire

It was in these conditions that the Ottoman Empire arose and came to rule territories from the European Balkans through Anatolia, to the Levant, the Arabian Peninsula, and North Africa between the 14th century and the empire's demise in 1923. Originating from the Oghuz tribe and taking the name from the family's founder, Osman I (r. 1299–1326), the family migrated from Central Asia, worked for a time in service to the Seljuks, and then began to acquire power independent of any other tribe in the region. During the 14th century, the Ottomans became the preeminent Anatolian power and in 1346 captured the first of the wealthy, fertile lands of the European Balkans. In 1453, Sultan Mehmet II (r. 1444–1446; 1451–1481) captured the Byzantine capital of Constantinople at the head of a military force that was arguably the most powerful military in the world. From this base in the renamed Istanbul, the Ottomans established an empire that lasted for centuries.

FIGURE 1.1. Diorama depicting the conquest of Constantinople by Sultan Mehmet II in 1453.

The Ottoman waves of conquest from the late 13th to the 16th centuries peaked under Sultan Süleyman the Magnificent (the Lawgiver, r. 1520–1566), when his army stood at the gates of Vienna in 1529. While his army could not bring down the walls of the Hapsburg imperial capital, the Ottoman army was still strong enough to hold new territories in Greece and the Balkan provinces between Istanbul and Vienna and to extend its conquest to North Africa and the Arabian Peninsula over the following years. Nonetheless, the defeat did signal that the Ottoman advance was slowing; by the end of the 17th century it had stopped completely. The Russians defeated the Ottomans at the northern shore of the Black Sea in 1670, and another attempt to capture Vienna in 1683 failed. In the 1699 Treaty of Carlowitz, the Ottomans ceded much of Hungary to the Austrians after yet another defeat. The Ottoman era of military expansion was over although the empire would survive more than two centuries before it came to an end in the aftermath of World War I.

Birth of the Safavid Empire

Shaykh Safi al-Din (1252–1334) established the Safavid Sunni Sufi order in the province of Azerbaijan in northwestern Iran and attracted followers in areas from Egypt to India in the 13th and 14th centuries. In the quest for an empire in the 15th century, the family allied with a confederation of tribes called Qizilbash, named for the distinctive red turbans worn by the warriors, and converted to Shi'ism. In 1501, Shah Isma'il (r. 1501–1524) and the Qizilbash established the Safavid Empire by successfully capturing the Azerbaijani capital of Tabriz and conquering the rest of modern-day Iran and most of Iraq. But attempts to expand farther were thwarted to the west by the superior army of the Ottomans, leading to the Safavid defeat at the Battle of Chaldiran in 1514 and the eventual loss of Baghdad to Ottoman rule. To the east, the Safavids continued to battle the Uzbeks for land along their shared frontiers and the Mughals for the city of Qandahar.

The height of Safavid power occurred under Shah Abbas I (r. 1588–1629). The shah monopolized revenues collected along the major trade routes that traversed Iran and from his new capital in Isfahan presided over a centralized administrative structure. However, his successors struggled with economic problems and could not maintain an armed force sufficient for fending off invaders. As a result, the Safavids fell under the sway of an Afghan tribe in 1722, and in 1736 all pretense of Safavid rule was eliminated when Nader Shah Afshar (r. 1736–1747) removed the Safavid puppet shah from the throne. Iran remained fragmented geographically and politically until the Qajar dynasty from Azerbaijan chose Tehran as its capital and established its rule across Iran in 1796.

Ottoman and Safavid Differences and Similarities

The Ottoman and Safavid Empires differed in many respects, from the religious institutions they propagated to the relationships they negotiated with power brokers in their regions. The Ottoman sultans represented themselves as the protectors of orthodox Sunni Islam, especially after their conquest of Mecca, Medina, and Jerusalem in the early 16th century. The Safavid shahs imposed Shi'i Islam on Iran, established a clerical establishment to oversee it, and inextricably connected the religion to the ruling powers.

The Ottomans created a governing structure led by specially trained officials at the imperial center complemented by a host of intermediaries tasked with representing the sultan's interests in the provinces. The system, characterized by complex sets of dependent relationships, largely destroyed the independence of the tribes and princes who had aided the Ottoman conquest and of the Muslim and non-Muslim religious clerics who had held comparable influence before the Ottoman rise.

The Safavids succeeded in building a centralized state structure under Shah Abbas I that weakened the Qizilbash tribesmen as independent players. But the state struggled to counter the independent power of their newly established Shi'i clerical institution and the autonomy of the many tribes in the provinces.

SUFISM

Simultaneously with the work done to codify the doctrines of the Sunni and Shi'i sects, those who came to be called Sufis (named possibly after the wool of the simple cloaks many early Sufis wore) were studying the Quran to find a mystical connection to God. Some meditated over the 99 names of God (dhikr), others danced (dervishes), and still others brought their breathing down to the lowest possible level, all so they could feel God's love inside them. Once Sufis had perfected their path to God, they passed it on to their followers, who slowly began to create permanent brotherhoods training successive generations of followers. The process paralleled that of scholars focusing on the elements of Islamic law. Recognizable Sufi brotherhoods began to form across the Muslim world in the 11th century. These brotherhoods guided their followers in the proper rituals, and their leaders and prominent families frequently became local influential political players.

The Ottomans presided over a diverse, wealthy economy that could withstand fluctuations in the world economy, whereas the Safavids stood on a more precarious economic foundation. Extensive irrigation works needed to be maintained for crops to grow on the Iranian plateau, and all revenues from export products had to be monopolized by the state to support the empire's military and administrative structure.

Nevertheless, these two empires had many elements in common, from their Turkic tribal origins to the governmental structures they established and the paths to royal legitimacy they articulated. The Ottomans were a Turkic tribe leading the conquest across Anatolia, and the Safavids required support from the Qizilbash, a confederation of Turkic tribes, in their quest for empire. Both leaderships spoke Turkish yet glorified Persian as the language of arts, architecture, and culture. In both empires, the religious creed associated with the ruling family had been a heterodox, flexible amalgamation of religious ideas during the time of conquest but became an orthodox faith with a hierarchical structure based on shari'a law once the polity had become settled. The Safavid family was perceived as legitimate rulers because of their long-standing leadership over the Safavid Sufi order, as well as the family's many blood ties with renowned Turkic tribes and the Byzantine royal family. In the first years of the empire, the family also came to claim descent from 'Ali and the Shi'i imams, thus adding an element of divinity to their already illustrious family line. The Ottomans had no such lineage, but they spent the first 100 years of their rule writing one into existence so that they could represent themselves as equals of the many eminent dynasties that had preceded them.

None of these elements could have been successful, however, if the early Ottoman and Safavid leaders had not been adept at negotiating the many alliances required to construct an armed force sufficient for achieving their imperial goals. The sultans and shahs had to earn their allies, even in the case of the Safavids, who had a built-in group of supporters for their Sufi order. They did so primarily by winning battles and distributing wealth and influence to those who chose to fight alongside them. Anatolia, Azerbaijan, and the Iranian plateau were filled with tribes and princely rulers with the potential for establishing dynasties under their own names. Through military prowess and strategic alliances both the Ottomans and Safavids succeeded in defeating the strongest of them and incorporating the rest into their military force.

The leaders of the Ottoman and Safavid Empires proved equally skillful at locating the types of allies they needed to govern a settled polity. The Ottomans transitioned the Turkic tribal allies of the conquest phase into provincial government officials; simultaneously, they elevated specially trained officials to their administration and the elite corps of their military. The Safavids worked to undermine the power of the Qizilbash tribal allies by centralizing power within a governmental administration led by Persian administrators. In this process, Persian administrators became the new intermediaries connecting shahs to subjects and resources.

The Ottomans and Safavids were victorious in both conquest and governance because they combined effective narratives of legitimacy with practical negotiating skills that enabled them to secure the services of useful allies. By offering expertise to their sultans and shahs in return for a measure of influence over their respective realms, thousands of military leaders, tribal shaykhs, urban merchants, clerics, officials, and administrators became stakeholders in the systems of Ottoman and Safavid governance. The largesse flowing from the imperial centers, and the skills proffered by these intermediaries in return, kept the complex imperial gears oiled and in motion.

Ottoman Legitimacy

The centuries of Islamic and Turco-Mongol rule throughout Central Asia and the Middle East had established lineage as a key element in any claim to governance. The Abbasids attracted followers because of their descent from the Prophet's family; the Ilkhanids, because of their descent from Genghis Khan; and the Mughals, from Timur (r. 1370–1405) of the Timurid dynasty. Lineage was important because it limited the number of possible claimants to the throne, making it difficult for upstarts from new families to challenge those already established as rulers throughout the region. It was nevertheless possible for a new family to rule, provided it had the military might and was able to coax a member of a legitimate ruling family to act as a figurehead. For example, when the Seljuks conquered Baghdad in 1055, they could not rule in their own name because they had no lineage granting them the independent right to do so. Instead, they received accreditation from the Abbasid caliphs to rule in the Abbasid name. Even Timur, who would come to rule over the powerful Timurid Empire, which produced many other dynasties in the region, had to rule from behind a member of Genghis Khan's family for a few years before he and his successors could rule on their own. Once in power, all of the ruling families bolstered their legitimacy by claiming they ruled in

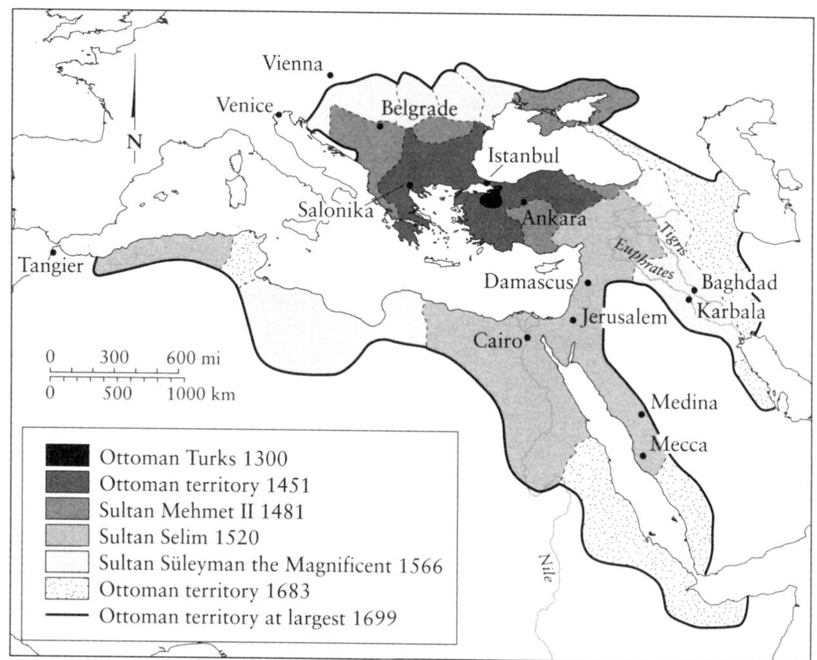

MAP 3. Ottoman Expansion, 13th to 17th Centuries. This map portrays the rise of the Ottoman Empire as it conquered Anatolia, the Balkans and Constantinople (1453) and as it reached its largest extent in the 16th century.

order to protect the Islamic faith and its believers; they also built grand mosques, tombs, and schools and provided security for the ulama as they adjudicated shari'a law.

Anatolia in the late 13th and early 14th centuries was a mélange of Turkic and Christian principalities loosely overseen by the Byzantine emperor. The Ottomans came to the military fore because they cleverly married into families of Muslim and Christian faith—and even into a faction of the Byzantine ruling family—as part of their gambit to become the strongest power broker in the region. From the earliest days, the Ottoman leadership also constructed a narrative that provided the family with a lineage tailored for ruling an empire. The sultans commissioned historical works of the family's ancestors that, in various chronicles, tied the Ottomans back to the oldest son of Oghuz Khan, who conquered much of Central Asia, or to the last Seljuk sultan, who designated an Ottoman leader as his official successor. These stories, however fictitious, designated the Ottoman family as standing among the small group who could demand allegiance because of their connections to great conquerors of the past.

Religious Mandate

From the beginning of their Anatolian enterprise, the Ottomans attracted followers because they presented themselves as divinely guided warriors for Islam (ghazis) fighting against the Christian infidel princes and the Muslim Turkic tribes who refused to follow their lead. But by the time of the conquest of Constantinople in 1453, the Ottoman sultans were turning away from this fervid charisma-based militancy and began to represent themselves as protectors of Sunni orthodoxy. The story of heterodox frontier warriors new to Islam and lacking in religious legitimacy gave way to the Ottomans as uniquely qualified to oversee the affairs of the Sunni faith. They had defeated the Eastern Orthodox Byzantine Empire in the name of Islam and, as of the early 16th century, presided over Mecca, Medina, and Jerusalem, the holiest sites in Islam. To strengthen this perception, sultans built grandiose mosques and schools, necessary emblems of religious overlordship and, simultaneously, proof of the exceptional wealth and power the Ottomans wielded since no other family could build such architectural gems. Chronicles of this era also manufactured stories of Ottoman ancestors who served the major figures of monotheism, such as Abraham and Muhammad.

Governance Mandate

The Ottoman sultans presented themselves not only as guardians of the faith but as the purveyors of just governance for their subjects. The Ottomans dispersed authority among many stakeholders throughout the empire so that no one group could grow too powerful or abusive over those they ruled. The sultan's subjects were obligated to fulfill their duties to him; in return he protected them from the worst depredations of those in power. To establish this system, the Ottomans promised to guarantee security along the trade routes for merchants large and small; protection for urban artisans producing the manufactured goods of the empire; and at least a subsistence level of living for the peasants, the largest group of the sultan's subjects. A concomitant element of this concept of just governance touched on the protection role the Ottomans claimed for themselves over the Sunni faith. The state provided the stability that allowed the ulama to adjudicate the Islamic faith and for the followers to feel secure in practicing its tenets.

When the system worked well, revenues flowed into the central treasury and social harmony was maintained. Rebellions erupted when the carefully designed balance of power required recalibrating; these events occurred when the Ottoman central treasury lacked sufficient funds to meet its obligations or when intermediaries failed to fulfill their part of the bargain with the sultan. Throughout the centuries of Ottoman rule, such rebellions broke out repeatedly and were put down with force by the Ottoman army or stanched by replacing the most abusive of the intermediaries. While this structure rarely worked perfectly, the Ottoman family was never threatened by another family challenging its lineage. Until the last century of the Ottoman Empire's reign, the sultan faced no internal military force superior to his own and the system of just governance proved an effective governing tool. There were few credible calls for overthrowing the system because the Ottomans provided the stability and security that enabled most groups to subsist and a large number of people to flourish.

Ottoman Contracts in the Military and Provincial Administrations

The Ottomans dispersed power among their many intermediaries by carefully delineating the services each of the sultan's military, provincial, and religious leaders would perform for the state and by limiting the terms of their tenure. The sultan achieved this by negotiating different types of contracts with them according to their particular skills. These contracts established the intermediaries as the sultan's delegates to the peasants working the land, the artisans producing the goods, the cavalrymen calling up his army, the bandit leaders gathering mercenary soldiers, the religious clerics ruling over their flocks, and the collectors bringing in the taxes. The Ottomans interacted with a relatively small proportion of the population and regarded the vast majority of their subjects as corporate entities under the control of the contract-bound intermediaries.

A signed document did not always mark these exchanges. In many cases, such a document did exist because it represented official recognition of the intermediary's obligation to the sultan. But whether or not there was a signed paper, these relationships were contractual in the sense that both sides laid out the services each brought to the relationship. Their terms also contained protections for all parties: the sultan, the intermediaries, and the subjects ruled by both. The contracts, however negotiated, always contained language about termination; the tenure of the contract could be as short as the months required for the annual fighting seasons or for the lifetime of the contract holder. Other parts of the contract specified how much revenue or influence a contract holder could accrue during the terms of the contract. The system did not always work as designed, and not every contract holder met his obligations even in years of strong enforcement from the sultans. Nonetheless, it opened official avenues for the ambitious to acquire wealth and influence and provided protections for the most vulnerable of the sultan's subjects. The sultan had the ultimate power to break a contract and replace an abusive tax collector or an inefficient military officer.

Sipahis and the Timar System

Warfare in the early years of the 14th and 15th centuries rewarded the victors well; the Ottomans and their allies repeatedly conquered fertile lands, with multiple resources to exploit and disperse. In order to engage a trained cavalry for conquest across Anatolia, Greece, and into the Balkans, the Ottoman sultans made alliances with the Turkic nomads and settled Christian notables living throughout these regions. Turkic, Anatolian, and European cavalrymen (sipahis) contributed the soldiers, animals, and retainers necessary for repeated seasonal military campaigns. In return, they received a portion of any assets captured during the fighting. In this exchange, the sultans received allies for the conquest, and the sipahis augmented their own influence through an alliance with a rising military power.

But as the pace of conquest slowed in the mid-15th century, sipahi officers slowly transitioned into provincial leaders rather than members of the military vanguard. There was a diminishing amount of profit available from warfare and a growing need to consolidate provinces already under Ottoman sovereignty. To address these circumstances, the Ottomans made new contracts with the sipahis. They granted them rights to collect revenue on a specified parcel of land and to exploit that land and its peoples in exchange for agreeing to fight in the Ottoman army when required. This arrangement was an adaptation of the timar system, which had been used in the Middle East as early as the Abbasid era. The individuals (sipahis, generally) who held the rights to revenue under this system were called timariots.

The timar structure set up a permanent system for keeping the sipahis loyal to the sultans in years of less profitable warfare and during their tours of seasonal fighting, while also limiting their ability to amass power and wealth. The revenues from the land were intended to provide sipahi officers with sufficient funds for equipping themselves to fight for the Ottomans whenever called on. A successful campaign could mean increased land for a sipahi, but with this came an obligation to outfit additional soldiers. If a sipahi failed to appear for seasonal warfare or performed poorly, the sultan could take away his right to the land and give it to another cavalryman more useful to the sultan's army. Furthermore, the timariots could not pass the land on to their sons; those sons had to prove their battle readiness before receiving a contract from the sultan and taking control of such revenues for themselves.

In the early years of conquest, these relationships between the Ottomans and the sipahis had been largely one of equals. As the Ottomans became the dominant military power in Anatolia, Greece, and the Balkans by the end of the 15th century, the sultans came to wield much more leverage in the negotiating process because they could impose harsher penalties for noncompliance. In this transition, timariots became subordinate to their monarch rather than leaders of independent military forces. By the 16th century, most of this territory was ruled by timariots who rarely fought for the sultan but instead primarily performed the work of collecting taxes and enforcing Ottoman governance in the provinces. At times, the sultans appointed timariots as governors of their provinces, but more often they were appointed as subgovernors and lower-level officials working on behalf of the governor sent from Istanbul or the equally powerful Ottoman-appointed religious cleric. To perform their duties, these timariots assembled local military forces that were sometimes called up for the imperial army. But usually these militias simply served as defense forces for the provinces. So long as the taxes were remitted to the treasury and the region remained stable, the timariots could do as they pleased locally and the sultan could claim to have fulfilled the promise of just governance.

Iltizam

After the Ottomans conquered the Arab provinces in the 16th century, the iltizam, a tax-farming structure, became the dominant tax-collection system in the region. In this system, the Ottoman authorities held annual auctions so local leaders could bid for contracts to collect taxes from given areas or industries for a set period of time as mültizam (a person who holds an iltizam). In 1695, when the sultan altered the system to allow for life-term tax contracts (malikanes) to be purchased, he opened the auctions to high officials based in Istanbul and to new strata of local notables who could afford the large buy-in amount. The Ottoman treasury benefited from the infusion of large cash payments from the auctions. Also, the longer-term leases allowed for more intensive development on the land and more tax revenue to be collected. The local notables who held malikanes enhanced their local positions but in return were required to keep the peace in the territories under their control. The malikane holders living in the capital were eligible to purchase these tax farms because they could be trusted to maintain the sultan's writ in their territories.

In the same era, European feudal lords held their lands through hereditary rights. They intermarried with other aristocratic families in the region to cement strategic alliances, and they frequently used their power to challenge the monarch. However, by retaining ownership of the land and selling only the right to collect the revenues from it, the Ottomans prevented the establishment of a landed aristocracy. Neither timar nor iltizam holders had hereditary rights to land that would have enabled them to establish enough of a lineage or consolidate enough force to threaten the empire. Families could accrue great wealth through trade and manufacturing or the production and exchange of movable property, but the division of property among all legal heirs required by Islamic heritance laws negated the possibility of maintaining the wealth over many generations. Finally, the contracts protected the sultan by requiring reaccreditation on a regular basis. Even when malikanes became hereditary in the 18th century, they were held by a small number of elite officials dependent on the Ottoman state for their privileges and not willing to challenge its power structure.

The system in all its elements encouraged competition rather than cooperation among the power seekers. For all these groups, accreditation by the sultan as a contract holder was lucrative and influential enough that rebellion usually proved unprofitable. A rebellion would occur when a new player wanted to gain accreditation, not because an existing leader wanted to overthrow the Ottoman system.

Peasants

The peasants working the timar and iltizam land were free; the institution of serfdom did not exist in the Ottoman Empire except in territories where the sultans found it difficult to impose a rotating leadership system. The typical peasant holding was a çift-hane, an area as large as a pair of oxen could work. Over time, most peasants became hereditary tenants on their lands and could lose their right to tenancy only if they failed to cultivate the land for three consecutive years. Because these peasants were free, they could leave the land when poor harvests occurred or when there were opportunities for seasonal fighting with the Ottoman army.

Furthermore, the system of just governance provided an element of protection against the most abusive treatment by revenue collectors. Timariots and other local representatives of the sultan wielded a great deal of independent power year to year, but they could lose that status if they failed to keep their realms quiet and obedient. Peasants under their purview had an avenue for protest under these terms of the contract system. The peasants could rebel to receive better local treatment or obtain imperial aid in times of economic crisis; the sultan stood as guarantor for their livelihoods. As did the competition over the positions in local governance, these rebellions usually ended when the worst of the abuses subsided and the perpetrators had been removed. They did not threaten the imperial center at any time in the empire's history.

Ottoman Contracts and Religious Authority

Since the first days of Ottoman military expansion at the end of the 13th century, the Ottoman rulers had presented themselves as leaders of the Muslim faith. The Ottoman sultans made the successful transition from leadership reflecting a popular and heterodox interpretation of Islam to installing themselves as the primary guardians of Sunni orthodoxy. Henceforth, they followed the lead of their many imperial predecessors and built the monuments to the faith that would serve as grand symbols of their power and religiosity. Through such magnificent mosques as the Süleymaniye Mosque in Istanbul, the Ottomans established a uniquely Ottoman architectural legacy for their rule that made it impossible for any other challenger to attain a comparable status because of the immense resources required. By providing safe escort of the annual caravans to Mecca and back, the Ottomans proved they had the military power to protect one of the pillars of the faith, the hajj pilgrimage.

To officiate over Islam, the Ottomans established an elaborate religious bureaucracy under their name. Most sultans also took on the title of caliph, harking back to the tradition and legitimacy of the Abbasid dynasty, and the sultans adjudicated their rule and their subjects through shari'a law. Shari'a law applied to all Muslims of the empire, with Hanafi law the dominant school of jurisprudence within its borders. The sultan appointed the Şeyhülislam (shaykh al-Islam), who served as head of the Islamic bureaucracy within the empire, tasked with appointing all the judges (qadis) in every town and issuing the most important legal opinions (fatwas) on behalf of the sultans' actions. He also sat on the sultan's

Imperial Council along with the ministers overseeing the secular branches of government. Schools trained men for their service to the faith and to the sultan; graduates became employees of the Ottoman state. Muslim clerics brought Ottoman administration over the faith into every corner of the realm; at the Friday noon prayer in the mosque, clerics reverently recited the name of the sultan as caliph.

Ulama

All education for religious scholars, the ulama, began at one of the thousands of kuttab schools built around the empire, instructing students in how to memorize the Quran, a revered skill in Islam and the foundational element in religious education. At a higher educational level, a smaller number of madrasas offered instruction in topics such as Arabic grammar, Quranic interpretation, jurisprudence, sources of the law, and didactic theology. For further study, a few students enrolled at al-Azhar University in Cairo, founded in the 10th century by the Fatimid dynasty, or the elite Ottoman religious schools in Istanbul, such as the six schools attached to Süleymaniye Mosque. Graduates were hired for the Islamic schools and courts and for posts in the administration. The vast majority of such trained ulama worked as teachers at all levels in schools in the empire; graduates of the madrasa system also served as members of the Ottoman scribal class, or "Men of the Pen," taking on the duty of transcribing and transmitting the laws and dictates of the state.

The religious clerics of Sunni Islam always maintained a degree of independence from Ottoman control. Their leverage came from the crucial religious legitimacy they bestowed on the Ottoman sultans. Most members of the ulama were employees of the Ottoman state, but many others were independent, working in towns and villages without the imprimatur of the Ottomans backing them. Both groups came to control a large percentage of local revenues because of the rules in Islam setting out the means by which donations could be made to build and sustain Islamic institutions. In Islam, individuals may set up a religious endowment (waqf) for anything associated with practicing the faith, including the building of mosques, schools, hospitals, and tombs; the resulting revenues are exempt from state taxation in perpetuity. And the waqf were not subject to accreditation or review by the sultan but remained within the exclusive purview of the ulama and their donors. Unlike the timar and iltizam systems, waqf revenues could not be taken away from the Muslim clerics if services were not continued or the executor or donor died; successors carried on their works. This was a relationship between the donor, the ulama, and God: it did not include the Ottoman sultan.

Millet System

When the Ottomans ascended to the leadership of much of the Muslim world, they accepted the Quranic injunction to protect the "People of the Book." The sultans allowed Christians and Jews much autonomy to follow their own laws as long as they remained obedient to the Ottoman state. While granting more privileges to Muslims than to Christians and Jews, the system worked for centuries, as evidenced by the fact that the kind of sustained, violent religious upheavals that plagued Europe did not occur under Ottoman aegis. However, in terms of religious relations within the empire, the system can be defined as one of tolerance based on an acceptance of diversity of belief rather than one of equality between the believers. As long as no one individual or group among the People of the Book attempted to challenge its position in society or governance, the status quo harmony that the Ottomans constantly sought to maintain could prevail.

As in other aspects of his realm, the sultan's key to maintaining harmony among the disparate non-Muslim groups was to find and work with effective intermediaries. The system for governing the non-Muslim communities of the empire came to be called the millet system (the word translates to "nation" or "community" but came to mean, in Ottoman terms, a corporate religious group). Although its elements evolved over the centuries, in general the millets worked in much the same way as the timar system in that the sultans accredited non-Muslim religious leaders to serve as delegates to their respective sects. The Ottomans initially accredited the Eastern Orthodox, Armenian, and Jewish communities as formal millets, allowing their respective religious and lay leaders to maintain autonomous power over their communities in terms of tax collection, education, and law as long as they respected the authority of the sultans and kept their co-religionists obedient to sultanic rule.

The first relationship the Ottomans negotiated was with the Eastern Orthodox community. Its members constituted the largest group of people living on the lands conquered in Anatolia, Greece, and the Balkans in the early years, and the Ottomans needed to find the easiest way possible to incorporate them into the governing structure. Under Byzantine rule, the head of the Greek Orthodox Church, the patriarch, had held relatively little power in relation to the emperor. The Ottoman sultans granted him a privileged position within the new Ottoman ruling class by giving him the right to collect taxes from all the Eastern Orthodox Christians, not only from Greece but also Anatolia and the Balkan areas of Bulgaria, Romania, Macedonia, and Serbia. The patriarch used this position to establish extensive networks of churches, schools, trading houses, and agricultural lands through which he collected revenues and adjudicated Christian legal issues. While this accreditation expanded the patriarch's authority exponentially, the sultans kept the patriarch's power in check by requiring that all new patriarchs buy a decree (firman) from the Ottoman state legitimizing their positions. This reconfirmed on a regular basis that the patriarch served at the pleasure of the sultan and not as an independent actor within the Eastern Orthodox community.

No such central leadership structure equivalent to the Greek patriarch existed among the Armenian and Jewish groups of the empire. The Armenian community was divided between the Christian Apostolic and Catholic Churches, and while these sects had strong religious leaders, no one person or institution among them could represent all Armenians to the Ottoman court. The Ottomans dealt with this situation by appointing Armenian patriarchs presiding in Istanbul and Jerusalem, with the former the far more influential of the two. The Jewish community was also too geographically and organizationally diverse to follow one rabbinical leader. Given this situation, the Ottomans agreed to work with local Jewish councils and synagogues in Istanbul and throughout the towns where a substantial Jewish community lived. Armenian and Jewish leaders collected taxes from their local members and presided over their legal issues, yet none acquired the power of the Greek patriarch, the wealthiest and most influential contract holder within the millet system.

Non-Muslim Merchants

Non-Muslim communities also served a complementary purpose in facilitating trade between the Ottoman Empire and Europe. Non-Muslims comprised the largest group of sailors and merchants exchanging Ottoman and European products in the empire from the 1453 conquest of Constantinople to the middle of the 19th century. They opened trading houses throughout the port cities of Europe and moved goods on their ships. The old Byzantine-era foreign quarter of Istanbul in Galata grew in size as European merchants took advantage of the wealth of the Ottoman Empire and the opportunities for trade. European merchants established trading zones along coastal regions throughout the empire, in areas such as Izmir and Salonika, where they traded primarily with non-Muslim merchants. These exchanges positioned the empire's non-Muslim subjects as vital conduits in the economic relationship between the empire and European states.

Although the majority of Armenians were peasants and petty merchants in the eastern provinces of Anatolia and in the coastal cities along the Mediterranean coast, the small number who established themselves in Istanbul formed a financial backbone for the empire. The most powerful merchants, the Armenian Amira group of bankers, provided finances for the Ottoman state and maintained much of the overland trade from Europe through Iran and India and north into the Russian Empire. They served as bankers to the central government and many provincial governors; prominent families dominated the positions of director of the Imperial Mint, chief imperial architect, and superintendent of the Gunpowder Mills. Within the Armenian millet, they provided financing for the Armenian patriarchs and served as financiers funding education and philanthropic projects throughout the empire and with the Armenian diaspora community abroad. They brought their expertise and contacts in banking, finance, and world trade into service of the Ottomans; in exchange they became wealthier and more powerful because of their service on behalf of the Ottoman state. To a lesser extent, Jewish merchants provided contacts between Europe and the merchants and products of the Ottoman state, led by Jewish migrants from Italy, known as Francos. In both the Armenian and Jewish cases, Italy and Venice in particular became pivotal centers for their worldwide trading networks.

Phanariots

In the 18th century, the most powerful group of Christian merchants was the Greek Phanariots, so named because they maintained their base in the Phanar neighborhood of Istanbul. They grew wealthy because they were the leading traders with Europe from ports along much of the Ottoman coastline; they turned this wealth into political power within the Eastern Orthodox millet by becoming the primary financial supporters for the Greek patriarch and the extensive religious networks he operated. In service to the Ottoman Empire, the Phanariots became the sultans' chief diplomats to Europe and the formal liaisons between the Ottoman government and the patriarch. Their dominance over shipping throughout the Mediterranean, Black, and Aegean Seas also ensured that Phanariots were frequently appointed as translators for the Ottoman fleet. Before long, being appointed translator meant being made the chief Ottoman administrator for the islands and coastal cities of the region as well. The Phanariots had much to offer the Ottoman sultans; the sultans, in turn, gave them formal accreditation to expand their trading and financial networks even further.

This relationship proved so fruitful that the sultans expanded the realms into which the Phanariots could provide services. In the Danubian provinces of Wallachia and Moldavia, local revolts persisted decade after decade and provided opportunities for the Austrians and Russians to intervene into Ottoman affairs. The Ottomans resolved the problem by appointing Phanariots to serve as governors when the local notables refused to acquiesce to Ottoman control. The first to serve in Moldavia arrived in 1711; in Wallachia, he took up his post in 1716. Upon appointment, they and their successors went from Istanbul to the provinces amid elaborate processions so that all along the route people could see the Phanariots as symbols of Ottoman power. These governors took charge of all administrative tasks within the principalities for the Ottoman state and the patriarch, while also defending the borders against Russian and Austrian aggression. The local landowning elite, the boyars, agreed to this arrangement because they retained their power, which included maintaining peasants in serflike conditions working their land. The Phanariot governors and the boyars held their positions by appointment of the sultan; that accreditation could be withdrawn if any of their subordinate networks proved disloyal to the state.

Ottoman Imperial Slave Elite

Sipahis, mültizam, ulama, patriarchs, and Phanariots, by contractual arrangement, could wield considerable power within the local domains they were allowed to govern on behalf of the sultan. But they had no access to positions at the imperial core. For the top imperial positions, the Ottoman sultans trusted only those completely beholden to them personally. To fill the top imperial positions, the government brought slaves to Istanbul and trained them to serve the sultan.

Devşirme

The Ottomans incorporated prisoners of war into their army from the beginning of their rise to military preeminence, but the system was truly perfected after Mehmet II conquered Constantinople in 1453 and moved to sideline the sipahis in favor of a standing army and administration.

The devşirme (child levy) required that Christian families in the Balkans and Central Asian regions provide a quota of boys for Ottoman service. The boys typically entered the system between the ages of 7 and 20, and a sophisticated recruitment process identified the most talented boys for the most rigorous and prestigious training. They were converted to Islam as part of their training. Simultaneously, slave guilds brought the most beautiful young Circassian girls from the northern Caucasus region to the Ottoman harem; from at least the mid-15th century, these concubines became the mothers of all future sultans.

Those who entered into the structure were technically not allowed to maintain contacts with their birth families because the Ottoman world was meant to serve as their new family alliance system. Furthermore, these slaves were prohibited from receiving any source of revenue other than from the sultan; their livelihoods came only through their connection to him. They could not marry or set up a household of their own until granted permission to do so by the sultan. When they died, they could not pass on their accumulated wealth to their sons and daughters; their property was returned to the sultan. These policies were designed

SLAVERY

Islam prohibits Muslims from enslaving other Muslims but allows enslavement of non-Muslims. Provisions in the Quran mandate that slaves not be treated with deliberate cruelty; manumitting them is applauded as a meritorious act. The Ottoman sultans did not invent the concept of slavery as a training ground for elite corps; rather, the system can be traced back to the Abbasid quest to replace the nomadic Arab armies with a regular standing army once they consolidated their position in Baghdad. The Abbasids initially incorporated prisoners of war into their army but then turned to levies of non-Muslim young men and boys they could train as soldiers for this standing army. This practice was also adopted by the short-lived Ayyubid Empire (1171–1250) in Egypt, which was then overthrown by its own slave army (Mamluks) who established their own rule in Egypt in 1250.

As a result, under the Abbasids, the Ayyubids, and the succeeding Islamic empires, slave armies served as the most influential military forces. Elevating slaves to top military positions meant that rulers did not have to rely on the subject peoples for military service. Instead, these slave armies--and the administrative cadres who came to office via the slave guilds--were professional units serving at the behest of their rulers and with little connection to the population at large. The members were beholden solely to the leaderships and loyal to each other because of the unique training they had received collectively. For the members themselves, service in these armies was an established means for upward social mobility.

to guarantee that no member of the devşirme or the harem could use birth families or any outside aid to forge an alliance against the Ottoman throne. In the same way that the contract system prohibited mültizam from establishing hereditary rule, the slave structure allowed an individual to acquire power and property in his or her lifetime but without the right to pass it on to heirs.

This arrangement was not Islamic as much as it was uniquely Ottoman; the Ottoman leadership adapted the Muslim concept of slavery to fit the needs of its changing state institutions. This system provided the Ottoman government with regular cadres of talented young men and women, molded over succeeding years to be their personal professional military and administrative officials as well as the mothers of the sultans' heirs. The system, when it worked well, rewarded merit and thus allowed a great deal of social mobility within its ranks because the participants were among the best educated in the empire. Among the free-born, only Muslim clerics had a comparable opportunity, and even among them only a small minority could influence imperial policy. Most recruits of the devşirme reached no higher than the middle ranks of their particular field, and the women brought into the harem via slave guilds usually married men who graduated from the system along with them. A privileged few, as a result of their talents, could rise to the highest reaches of the government and military; a small number of the concubines became the mothers of sultans. They were connected to each other by their privileged training; concomitantly, they were physically and socially alienated from the majority of the sultan's subjects.

Language and Culture

Ottoman Turkish, as well as the elite culture that arose around it, defined and placed boundaries around those being included; only those with access to the proper training and with reason to use the language spoke it. Written in a modified Arabic script, the language combined Turkish grammar with sophisticated and nuanced Persian and Arabic words to form a unique entity. The Ottoman Turkish language symbolized the separation in training between those of the devşirme ranks and the rest of the empire's population. The civilization and its language were not connected to a specific ethnicity or religion as much as to the privilege and power accorded to members of an exclusive Ottoman club. Ottomanism as a culture had no popular variant because elites made no effort to bring the mass of the population into this identity structure. The slaves brought into governance received specialized training in this language and culture; many of the contract holders throughout the provinces also spoke the language in order to perform their state functions. Few other groups spoke Ottoman Turkish or understood the unique culture that arose around it. Even the Turks in Anatolia were not privileged in this system, for they spoke a number of Turkish vernaculars that had little in common with Ottoman Turkish. As a result, the term "Ottoman" refers to the family at the core of this empire, the elites owned by the sultan directly, the state itself, and the provincial revenue collectors who constituted the local elites.

Topkapi Palace

Mehmet II began construction of Topkapi Palace in Istanbul, which epitomized the separation of the sultans and their slaves from their subjects. Its organization into courtyards delineated who had the right to approach the sultan physically; access defined a subject's power. Earlier sultans had lived in a palace in Edirne because that European city had served as the Ottoman capital between 1365 and 1453. After the conquest of Constantinople, Mehmet II made Topkapi the home for the family household and the imperial government.

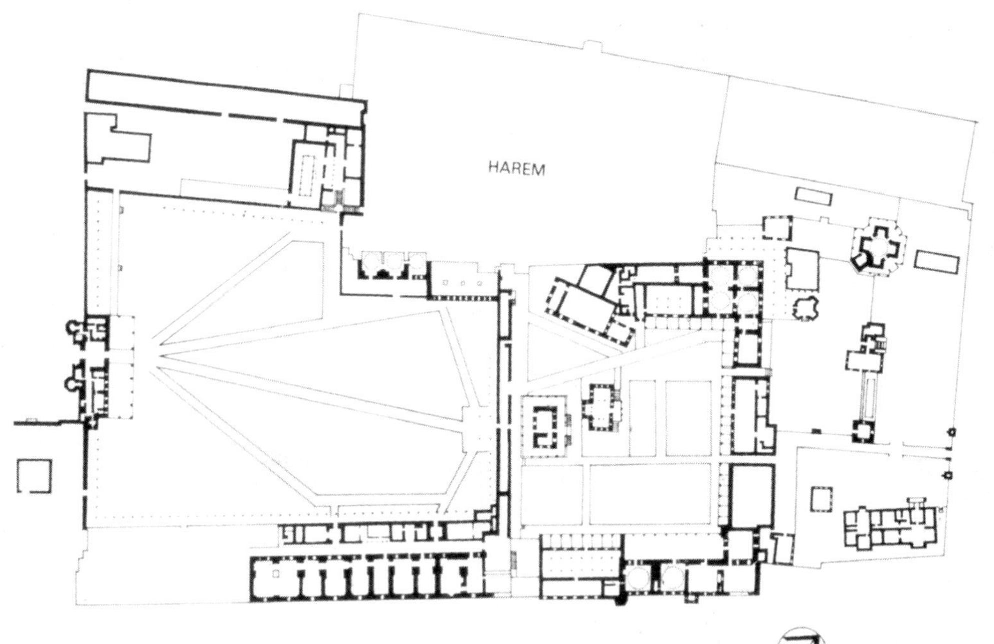

FIGURE 1.2. Plan of Topkapi Palace in Istanbul. The large first courtyard is displayed to the left, the second courtyard in the middle, and the harem along the top.

The architectural design of the palace regulated access to the sultan and the most important officials in the realm. The first courtyard of Topkapi was open to the public with few impediments to entrance but with no avenue for interacting with the empire's power brokers. The second courtyard provided a protected place for the governing elite who had varying degrees of power depending on their right to interact with the sultan or his chief representatives. In this zone, foreign ambassadors met with high government officials and the daily business of imperial governance took place. The third courtyard contained the inner household of the sultan, where all members were either directly related by blood to the sultan or had been brought in as slaves and thus had become his property. At its peak, hundreds if not thousands of concubines, sons and daughters of the sultan, and eunuchs lived in the harem at Topkapi Palace, supervised by the mother of the sultan (the valide sultan).

The boys of the devşirme most esteemed for their intelligence and beauty attended the Palace School at Topkapi Palace in the third courtyard, where as pages they were groomed to ascend to the highest levels of the administration and military upon graduation. For those boys chosen for Topkapi, the training kept them isolated within the walls until graduation, with access into the city only rarely and only when duty called. The eunuchs of the palace strictly supervised them during the day and as they slept at night to forestall any potential disobedience. Their studies included Ottoman, Persian, and Arabic literature; Islam; shari'a codes; history; music; mathematics; and physical and vocational training. Upon graduation, pages took positions within the palace; the most talented attended the sultan in the Royal Chamber and moved into the top ranks of the administration and military corps. A second cadre of boys attended the Galatasaray, a preparatory school outside the walls

HAREMS

Stories from the Prophet's life indicate that his wives were at times secluded from the public because of their special place in the new Islamic society. The Abbasid elite adopted this rule for the women of their family and adapted the Sassanid urban and royal traditions of establishing a formal location in the palace reserved for the women of the family so they could be protected from men unrelated to them. Mothers, wives, sisters, aunts, concubines, children of the caliph, and female servants lived in this area, with the entrances supervised by eunuchs. Wealthy imperial and provincial officials created formal harems in their own homes, while even poor families separated the women from the men as best they could in the space in which they lived.

FIGURE 1.3. Sultan Mehmet III (r. 1595–1603) sitting on the Ottoman throne and attended by two Janissaries. Turkey, ca. 1600.

of the palace; others deemed less qualified received mentorships with sipahis in Anatolia. How difficult their training was depended on where the boy was placed, whether in the more elite schools in the capital or out in the provinces for more practical training, while the level of skill they displayed during their training determined their position within the elite ranks upon graduation.

The imperial officials trained through this slave recruitment system worked in the capital for the central government and as governors and administrators in the provinces. From the 15th to the 17th centuries, almost all top government posts were held by those trained within the devşirme, including the grand vizier (chief minister), who was the highest official in the Ottoman government and the primary implementer of the sultan's wishes. Of 47 grand viziers holding office during the peak years of the devşirme system in the 16th and 17th centuries, only five were of Turkish origin, meaning they were free-born, while the rest were Christian Albanians, Greeks, and Slavs coming through its slave ranks. The grand vizier presided over the Imperial Council, the highest institution of government, and functioned out of his office, the Sublime Porte, situated just outside the gate of Topkapi Palace.

Military

The Ottoman sultan's formidable army was likewise composed of Palace School graduates who entered the officer ranks of the Janissary corps (Yeniçeriler, or the "new soldiers"). A greater number mentored with the sipahis and went on to fill the army rank and file. All of these soldiers received standardized training specifically designed to make them a uni-

JANISSARIES

The Ottomans trained slaves to serve as Janissaries, the most elite wing of the Ottoman army, and in the highest posts in the government. After they were selected as part of the devşirme, their training included conversion to Islam and study of Islamic law, Ottoman Turkish, and military strategy. The graduates of the program stood in the ambiguous position of being Muslims, so they technically were no longer slaves, but their property remained in the hands of the sultan and they could not marry or have children unless he granted permission. Upon their deaths, their property did not pass to their heirs but was returned to the sultan. Their sons, as free-born Muslims, could not follow them into the Janissaries or into most government positions because those positions remained exclusively in the hands of those who passed through the devşirme and its specialized training.

fied fighting unit. With this new army, the Ottoman Empire became the premier "Gunpowder Empire" of its day. The Janissaries were actually a relatively small force of possibly 30,000 infantrymen between the 15th and 16th centuries, but they adopted gunpowder weapons more effectively than any other European or Asian force at the time and were so highly disciplined at the peak of their power that their exploits extended well beyond their size.

The devşirme system, overall, constructed a professional military and administrative elite whose members were beholden to the sultan and connected to each other but who had few connections to the subjects over whom they ruled. Istanbul rotated governors and Janissary regiments into and out of the provinces on a regular basis, forestalling the possibility that they could establish close links with the populations under their rule.

Ottoman Succession Policies

The Ottomans followed the Turco-Mongol tradition that recognized all male members of the ruling family as possible claimants to leadership. In practice, the reigning leader typically chose his successor before his death: an oldest son, a younger one, or a brother deemed more able to rule. When the leader died, however, the successor still had to prove he was worthy of the throne, despite this advantage. More often than not, one or more of the many family contenders waged war against the designated successor, claiming that he was not fit to rule. Since Ottomans eschewed the Central Asian practice of dividing the sultan's property among all the heirs, the winner, in any given Ottoman succession struggle, took the throne and all of the territories and wealth of the former sultan.

Fratricide

When an Ottoman sultan died, all the sons rushed to the capital to enter into the struggle for succession. The sons, who had been sent into the conquered provinces to gain political and military experience, had established households of military retainers loyal to them personally. They had the means to mount bloody campaigns. Between 1362 and 1595, almost every succession was marked by not only a battle between the claimants but the massacre and maiming of all those who failed to attain the throne. This system of fratricide may have been a brutal training ground for the sultans who came to the throne, but it produced leaders with the desire and capability to expand Ottoman imperial reach. By choosing not to divide the family wealth, generation to generation, the Ottomans also ended the territorial fragmentation that had followed the death of leaders in the Turco-Mongol tradition. Ottoman sultans could build on the work of their predecessors and lost less time to the battles of consolidation that their forebears had been forced to undertake.

Seniority

At the beginning of the 17th century, the family discontinued fratricide as the primary method for choosing a new sultan. All sons of the Ottoman family henceforth lived their lives inside the harem, or the "Golden Cage," waiting for their moment to ascend the throne, with the oldest living male of the family granted the honor. While a sultan lived, these males remained in perpetual legal childhood because they could not marry or sire children of their own. They were not allowed to set up households of retainers unless they became sultan themselves, which meant they could not build up the loyal cadres of administrators, military men, and sons their predecessors had used to battle for the throne. Once he gained the throne, a sultan began at once to build up his personal household, but he was at a disadvantage because of the years when he was forbidden to acquire such retainers. Occasionally, strong sultans emerged from this system, but more often, grand viziers and Janissary leaders stepped into the power vacuum, exercising their mastery over the intricacies of palace politics.

Succession through seniority also meant that brothers followed brothers to the throne more often than sons followed fathers. This shift diminished the importance of the father-son relationship because a sultan had no way of guaranteeing that a particular son would succeed him. Under these circumstances, mothers became increasingly important because they were the only constant in a man's life inside the harem.

Mothers of the Sultans

At the beginning, and during most of the expansionist phase of imperial conquest, marriage alliances matched those being made on the battlefield; Ottoman sons married princesses of the lands being conquered and with whom the sultans were allying their forces. Once they became the undisputed military power in Anatolia, Greece, and the Balkans, the Ottomans no longer gained any advantages by these alliances, and they no longer needed to extend legitimacy to families who could potentially oppose their rule.

Slaves then took the place of princesses, and the marriages that continued to take place with women of notable families produced no children.

Concubines were brought to Topkapi by slave guilds and trained in much the same way as the boys of the devşirme. These young Circassian girls lived in strictly supervised dormitories and received an education in the principles of Islam and those skills deemed necessary for social refinement, including sewing, embroidery work, dancing, singing, reading, and the playing of musical instruments. The women moved up the ranks of the harem as they proved their merit, receiving salaries for the positions they held. The salaries they earned could be invested in businesses outside the walls.

Despite being secluded in the harem, the women nonetheless had glimpses of the outside world, since women teachers, seamstresses, singers, and peddlers brought their products inside the harem walls; the chief black eunuch who supervised the harem served as a business agent for the mothers who commissioned tombs and other such monuments to themselves and their sons. In addition, a secret passageway from the harem led to a window onto the Council Hall so the women and eunuchs could follow the great political debates of the realm.

The most coveted position was that of favorite of the sultan and the potential mother to his son. Only those concubines who produced a child for the sultan remained in the harem their entire lives. Once a woman became pregnant by the sultan, she received her own apartment in the harem and a high salary. The mother of a potential sultan served as the sole member of her son's household during his childhood, working to guarantee that he was the oldest living male relative on the day the sultan died and that once he took the throne he would have allies willing to govern on his behalf. To accomplish this feat, the mother had to spend years making alliances with grand viziers and palace eunuchs and at times even resorted to poisoning other possible contenders. After her son attained the throne, the valide sultan served as one of the most important people in the empire because of her influence over him and because of the many alliances she had formed to secure his position.

The rest of the women trained in the harem married the pages as they left the third courtyard for administrative work in the capital and around the empire; daughters of the sultan married men such as the grand viziers. The joint training and marriage system of administrators and their potential wives created intertwined networks of officials beholden to the sultan for their positions.

The sultans who came to the throne from within the Golden Cage system made fewer and fewer decisions about the day-to-day affairs of state. Delegates implemented the sultan's wishes while rarely consulting him directly. As a result, by the late 17th century, sultans reigned rather than ruled; they stood as the chief symbols of Ottoman sovereignty but wielded relatively little military or administrative power despite the vast apparatus functioning in their names. As a vivid symbol of this shift, the sultans retreated to their old palace in Edirne for extended periods of time in the 17th and 18th centuries, leaving Topkapi open to those who now held power, including the grand viziers, the Janissaries, and the eunuchs; only at the end of the 18th century did the sultans return to Topkapi on a full-time basis.

Celali Rebellions

The goal of the Ottoman system of contracts with intermediaries and reliance on an imperial slave elite was to ensure that the sultan's intermediaries and officials received their position, pay, or promotion from the sultan alone and that they could not form any kind of alliance of elites, families, or religious figures that could threaten Ottoman power and royal legitimacy. At no point did the contract and slave system work perfectly, but it was sustained for centuries in its original design because enough people became its stakeholders. A number of sultans were deposed during the 17th century at the hands of Janissaries and grand viziers, and many more sons of sultans died long before becoming sultan, but none of the rivalries within the inner courtyard of Topkapi Palace tried to bring down the Ottoman throne or institute a new royal lineage. The mothers, the grand viziers, the Janissary officers, and the harem eunuchs struggled among themselves to find sultans more beholden to the wishes of their own palace factions. The timariot, mültizam, Amiras, Phanariots, and clerics of the recognized religions all competed with one another for a share of Ottoman wealth and influence, but none conspired to overthrow the entire system.

The so-called Celali rebellions of the late 16th and early 17th centuries in Central and Eastern Anatolia provide an example of a local breakdown in the Ottoman system of just governance, but they also illustrate how the intricate network of relationships provided a fail-safe protection for the Ottoman leadership. Named after an early 16th-century rebel who fought for the Safavids against the Ottomans, these rebellions arose when the Ottoman economy could not sustain repeated seasons of warfare by the late 16th century and the state appeared to be weakening as a sovereign power because of military losses to the Europeans. The Celali rebellions took place all over Anatolia and lasted for three decades between the late 16th and early 17th centuries. No coordination took place between rebel bands, so at no point did the Ottoman army have to contend with a mass uprising. The rebellions were locally based, and the leaders demanded local power and accreditation from the sultan rather than a wholesale transformation of the empire's governance.

Since the beginning of the Ottoman conquest, sultans had arranged to supply nomads and mercenaries with armaments and food whenever they needed them to fight in seasonal campaigns. The urban unemployed from all areas of the empire, especially those from Western Anatolia, dominated the mercenary ranks in most years; in the Balkans, the Ottomans hired roaming Christian bandits from the earliest days of their conquest. The result after many years of Ottoman rule was that thousands of men served the imperial and provincial government through a series of seasonal and temporary contracts.

These auxiliary armies always outnumbered the Ottoman standing army, increasing in number even more rapidly after the Battle of Lepanto in 1571 when the Holy League, a coalition of the Catholic states of southern Europe, handed the Ottoman navy a massive defeat. In the aftermath, the Ottomans had to recruit thousands of irregulars to replace the archers and musketeers lost in battle. But the contracts duly negotiated could be upheld only if the two sides fulfilled their obligations. In the late 16th century, military and economic conditions made the Ottoman promise of just governance difficult to maintain.

With the shift away from cavalry armies, the sipahis had been almost completely sidelined in favor of the infantry units of the Janissaries and mercenaries. Many controlled local timars, but others had been left unemployed and without resources outside their seasonal contracts with the Ottoman army. They resented their loss of influence and the powerful positions the Janissaries held in terms of Ottoman military power. Because all of these groups were contract soldiers, they were not paid in the off-season so suffered through months of deprivation without alternative resources to tap. They were joined by peasants and urban workers who lost their livelihoods to famines and droughts throughout Anatolia because of what one scholar calls a little ice age. These groups rebelled in areas across Anatolia during the late 16th and early 17th centuries.

At their core, these Celali rebellions were not challenges to the Ottoman system as much as gambits by local regiment leaders and notables to acquire Ottoman government positions in the provinces. These positions were appealing because they opened doors for holders to gain access to tax farms and local militias so they could establish themselves as powerful provincial stakeholders in the Ottoman Empire. The Celali leaders could be described as rogue clients rather than as rebels since the rebellions they led were not meant to undermine the Ottoman system but to gain the influence that came with Ottoman governmental positions. Even as the Ottoman Empire had begun to weaken in relation to Russia and Austria, gaining accreditation as an Ottoman provincial intermediary still accorded the holder a great deal of local power. The Celali rogue leaders rose up so the sultan's government would reward their military prowess with government posts. They took advantage of the poor economic situation to recruit bandits, mercenaries, and peasants into their rebel militias so they could provide sufficient leverage against the sultan.

Ottoman leaders understood the motivation behind this rogue demand and granted a number of the Celali leaders local government positions as a way of ending their rebellion and bringing them into the system. The Ottoman army of Janissaries and loyal local sipahis successfully subdued with military force those who did not receive such recompense and continued the fight. The Celali rebellions ended when the most powerful leaders had been incorporated into the Ottoman system as stakeholders and the weaker ones were defeated by the Janissaries and former rogues fighting to maintain their newly won posts as Ottoman intermediaries.

Competition for Ottoman resources became a hallmark of the 17th and 18th centuries throughout the realm, as provincial soldiers, officials, and officers of the devşirme system sought to gain more influence. With the economic situation deteriorating and the military balance shifting in favor of European powers, the Ottoman sultan had few resources to distribute. Under these conditions, many of the state's officials pushed against the limits of their contracts so they could collect resources from alternative sources. Instead of relying on the dispersion of resources from the imperial center, imperial officials and provincial leaders took the initiative and collected resources from previously untapped realms throughout the empire. They kept those revenues under their own control and passed on little to the central treasury. The imperial system itself stayed intact, but the networks and incentives for the intermediaries evolved.

Even when the Ottoman imperial government was weak, accreditation as an Ottoman official remained a valuable means for garnering local authority and wealth. As were their Celali predecessors, these administrators were rogues rather than rebels against the system, since many chose to maintain their Ottoman accreditation as government officials and tax farmers. Many others competed to join their ranks. But when the Ottoman Empire moved into the 18th century, these officials had to work on both the Ottoman and global political stages, as European military and economic pressure impinged on Ottoman sovereignty. For Ottoman intermediaries, these new conditions presented both challenges and opportunities.

Ottoman Governmental Adaptations

When Sultan Süleyman the Magnificent stood at the walls of Vienna in 1529, he commanded the most powerful military in Europe and ruled a vast territory of fertile lands and wealthy manufacturing centers. Most products traversing the world, from raw agricultural goods to the most sophisticated of Chinese porcelain, passed through his lands and added to Ottoman coffers because the Middle East served as a bridge connecting the world's shipping and caravan lanes. But the power relationship between Ottoman and European powers was about to make a significant shift. Portuguese ships had navigated around the Cape of Good Hope at the end of the 15th century and entered the Indian Ocean from Europe for the first time, followed by British, French, and Spanish ships over the next century. Now new pathways competed with the Mediterranean, Arabian, Silk Road, and sub-Saharan trade routes that had enriched Ottoman subjects and the state's central treasury.

Along the coasts of the Indian Ocean and the Persian Gulf, western European powers established trading posts so they could gather and ship the world's goods. The Dutch in the 17th century and the British in the 18th commanded the largest navies in the world, triggering a European competition to improve shipping technology and move goods around the world as quickly and profitably as possible. The French established a special relationship with Christian merchants in the eastern Mediterranean, intensifying a competition for Mediterranean trade that already included Spanish, Italian, and Ottoman merchants.

Meanwhile, the 17th century saw Peter the Great reform and strengthen the Russian Empire; its expansion over the next century threatened the northern borders of the Ottoman Empire. A second attempt to conquer Vienna in 1683 failed, and turmoil continued to rage along the Austrian-Ottoman border. Population increases, manufacturing innovations, and shipping improvements increased competition for land and products around the world, with Ottoman goods and lands as part of the spoils. European merchants expanded contacts with the primarily non-Muslim traders, merchants, and sailors, such as the Greek Phanariots, Armenian Amiras, and Jewish Francos.

Capitulation Treaties

Merchants could compete for Ottoman trade through a series of commercial and military Capitulation treaties between the Ottoman and European powers. The first treaty was signed with France in 1569, when the Ottomans needed military aid to combat Spanish attacks in the Mediterranean, and eventually included 17 states. The treaties included provisions for a military alliance between the signers, rights for importing European goods into the empire at relatively low tariff duties, and allowances for increased Ottoman exports to Europe.

While the military provisions lasted only as long as the military conflict that had prompted the treaty, the economic terms continued to dictate relations between European and Ottoman merchants. In particular, European merchants received special protections and immunities from Ottoman law that allowed them to conduct their business with rights accorded them by their own state governments. This immunity was further expanded to Ottoman citizens trading with European powers in the Treaty of Küçük Kaynarca, signed in 1774 after an Ottoman military loss to Russia. The treaty granted Russia the right to protect the Eastern Orthodox communities of the Ottoman Empire. France soon received a similar right of protection over the Roman Catholics, and Britain and other European countries, for their agents. This meant that the Europeans could grant extraterritorial rights to the non-Muslims working in their trading networks.

The Capitulation treaties and the Treaty of Küçük Kaynarca created fissures in Ottoman sovereignty because entire segments of the population looked to other countries for legal and economic protection. As virtual citizens of Russia and France, then Britain and the Austria-Hungary Empire, they were no longer subject to the economic provisions binding the subjects of the Ottoman Empire. They received economic revenues disconnected from Ottoman state largesse and control and paid lower tariff duties, in line with those of their European allies. In contrast, Muslim merchants who dominated internal trade paid taxes several times while moving goods around the empire. European merchants and their non-Muslim agents paid only one tax when their goods arrived on the Ottoman coast.

Inflation and Corruption

When the Spanish and Portuguese began to colonize the Americas in the 16th century, they brought into world circulation a wealth of gold and silver dug out of the mines of Mexico, Bolivia, and Brazil. On their ocean-going ships, the Spaniards, Portuguese, and then the Dutch, English, and French moved goods at unprecedented rates while expanding the cash economy around the world. The Ottoman Empire's economy was not diverse or flexible enough to absorb the influx of gold and silver that arrived so was beset by high inflation as early as the 16th century. The Ottoman government exacerbated the problem by frequently resorting to debasing the currency and by continuing the traditional policy of paying fixed salaries. The incomes of administrators and military men could not keep pace with the increasing cost of goods and services.

Because of the dwindling revenues supplied by the sultans, corruption seeped into the administration and military, running rampant as the 18th century dawned. Unqualified applicants bought administrative and military posts and then took bribes to recoup their initial payments; all demanded extraordinary fees for any type of services rendered. Breaking all the rules that had ensured devşirme loyalty to the sultan, the members of the administration no longer waited until the sultans declared they were free to marry and start their own households. Instead, they married when they chose, made economic alliances with provincial leaders, and became holders of timars and iltizams without permission from the sultan. Thus, by ending their seclusion from the people of the empire, the former devşirme recruits became inextricably linked to urban and provincial elites, merchants, religious clerics, and tax farmers.

The administrative leadership built power structures more beholden to themselves and their allies and less so to the sultans personally. Starting in the late 16th century with decreasing numbers of recruits destined for the administrative ranks and then with the last devşirme levy for the Janissary force in 1703, the sultans no longer had a full-fledged slave administration and military force. While the sultans still brought Circassian women into the harem as concubines, grand viziers and other top officials fashioned their own personal households by inducting their sons into their units and regiments while also purchasing slaves and contracting with free Christians and Turks.

No longer was it imperative to be physically close to the sultan to accrue imperial power; grand viziers wielded power over networks of subordinates loyal to themselves. Provincial governors and Janissary regiments no longer moved around the provinces on a regular basis but stayed in one place for periods long enough to establish local power bases. As a result, the path to success for many new recruits in the 18th century was to find a powerful patron among the administrative or military grandees. The actual occupant of the Ottoman throne was immaterial by this time since the state effectively represented the sultan with little to no input from the sultan himself. The intricate work undertaken to establish the foundation for Ottoman legitimacy—in terms of lineage and religious and political authority—meant that the system was able to function well even when weak sultans sat on the throne.

Janissaries

After the abolition of the child levy in the early 18th century, the Janissaries recruited internally from within the empire, bringing their slaves and their own sons into the upper ranks alongside them. In the process, the Janissaries transformed from a peasant-based slave army looking outside the empire for recruits to one filled with the urban unemployed. Soldiers acquired new revenue streams by serving as paid protectors for provincial economic enterprises, particularly those of the many artisan and merchant guilds functioning throughout the empire. Other members of the Janissary corps worked as artisans or owned their own coffeehouses, because they continued in their livelihoods after their induction or bought their way into these businesses after they joined the corps. Despite their alternative occupations, the Janissaries refused to disband as a military force; their status as representatives of the sultan and his state gave them more influence than they could achieve independently. By the 18th century, the Janissaries were a large, expensive group for the imperial government to support but provided little real work in return for their pay. They were, in fact, more of a menace than anything resembling an effective fighting force.

Tax and Waqf

By the late 17th century warfare was no longer a profit-making enterprise but an increasingly burdensome expense, as evidenced by the events surrounding the Celali rebellions and by the losses of territory to Russia and Austria. The Ottoman Empire tried to summon resources by raising custom tariffs and other duties, but the economy was not profitable enough to bring in the necessary additional revenues. The largest source of all tax receipts for the entire span of the empire's existence had come from agriculture; however, the political vacuum at the center allowed provincial leaders and timar and iltizam holders to keep an increasingly larger amount of the tax receipts at home.

Agriculture remained organized on small farms, cultivated by peasant families and under control of the timariot and mültizam. Techniques remained simple, with energy provided by animals and humans. Individual timariots, mültizam, and peasants initiated a shift to cash cropping in a few areas and accrued profits as a result of the European demand for raw materials such as cotton. However, little revenue made its way to the central treasury in Istanbul. The move to cash cropping was fragmentary and uneven across the empire so did not represent a large-scale shift in agricultural priorities. Small-scale manufacturing took place in every town and city of the empire, but only some industries were geared toward production for export. The European powers took advantage of an expanded definition of the Capitulation treaties to buy more raw goods while selling back increasing amounts of manufactured products. As a result, the Ottoman economy as a whole fared poorly in its competition with the industrializing European powers, although a few local notables increased their wealth through trade arrangements with the Europeans.

The practice of endowing religious institutions as waqf became equally as corrupt as those services associated with the administration and military. Many donors still set aside property for religious purposes, but many others established waqfs as a way to shelter their properties and profits from the tax rolls. One calculation estimates that about 20 percent of all the land in the Ottoman Empire transitioned over to waqf property during the course of its existence, diminishing the revenues available to the treasury but providing an avenue of independence for the ulama and donors. As a result, top religious officials grew quite wealthy because of their right to supervise waqf endowments.

Despite European military and economic pressure and the corruption of many elements of the Ottoman governing structure, the 18th century saw the empire hold, in large measure because its institutions were flexible enough to adapt to the new conditions. Innovation took place at all levels of government, from the center to the periphery, as the old members of the devşirme and the new types of contract holders experimented with what autonomy could grant them individually. When salaries from the central treasury were no longer sufficient, the sultan's officials and intermediaries who had the wherewithal could avail themselves of many other avenues in the diverse Ottoman economy.

The Ottoman army by this point was composed in large measure of mercenaries, bandits, and the local militias of the contract holders. The Russian and Austrian armies, each in the process of being reformed and modernized, were not particularly effective on the battlefield. Though the Janissaries had weakened as an imperial military force, the Ottoman Empire could periodically regain land from Russia and Austria in the 18th century, but more often during this time the Ottomans lost land along the northern borders.

Thus, the Ottoman Empire in the late 18th century was in a weak position economically and militarily but secure in its territorial and governmental control because no group or coalition desired its destruction. The basic elements of the system—legitimacy of the Ottoman royal family and pragmatism and flexibility in the contracts negotiated with the many power brokers around the empire—maintained the empire intact. The power had merely shifted away from the sultan and into the hands of his imperial officials and the local intermediaries who ruled in his name in the provinces.

Safavid Empire

Whereas Ottoman governance relied on a combination of contracts and a slave elite, the Safavid Empire was founded on the twin pillars of religious charisma and tribal military prowess. Shah Isma'il was born into a lineage through which he could build strong alliances, unlike the Ottomans. He descended from a number of important Turkic tribes and could even claim a Byzantine emperor as a grandfather. His leadership over the Safavid Sufi order gave him a charisma that attracted many tribes

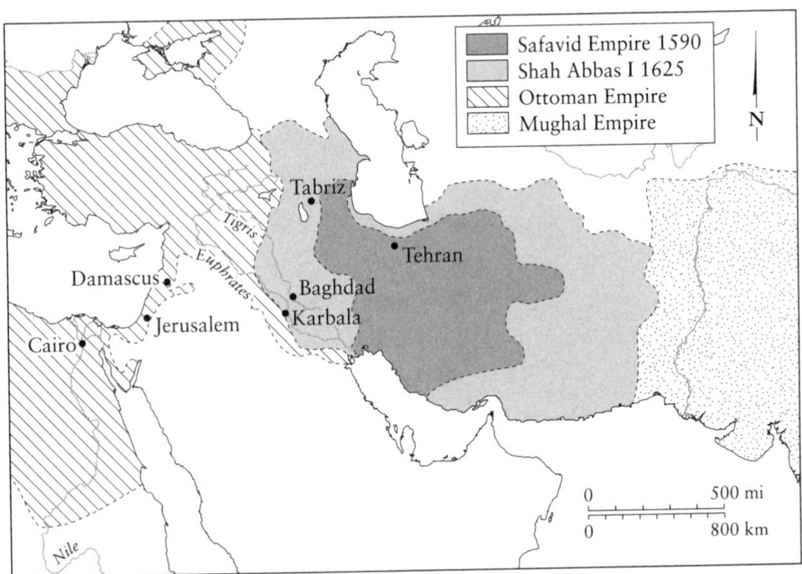

MAP 4. Safavid Expansion, 16th to 17th Centuries.

FIGURE 1.4. Folio from the *Tarikh-e alam-ara-ye Shah Isma'il* (The world adorning history of Shah Isma'il) depicting the battle between Shah Isma'il and Abul-khayr Khan, painted ca. 1688.

کنون از پیام آن سخن برکشم / دو بن سرو کان مرغ دارد بشم
جو زو بازگردد بماهی شود / بدان تیرگی و سیاهی شود
بر و مرغ بران جو خورشید دان / جهان را بد و بیم و امید دان
بهین شارسان این سرای سپنج / که هم ناز و گنجست و هم درد و رنج
برآید یکی باد با زلزله / ز گیتی برآید خروش و غلغله
کسی دیگر از رنج ما بر خورد / نپاید برو نیز هم بگذرد

زبرج بره تا ترازو جهان / همی تیرگی دارد اندر نهان
دو سرو آن دو بازوی چرخ بلند / کز اویم شاد و زو با گزند
دگر شارسانی بر کوه سا / سرای درنگست و جای شما
همی دم زدن بر تو بر بشمرد / همو بر فزاید همو بشکرد
همه رنج ما ماند با خارسان / گذر کرد باید سوی شارسان
چنین رفت از آغاز یکسر سخن / همین باشد و این نگردد کهن

اگر توشه مان نیک نامی بود / روانها بدان سر گرامی بود

from his home region of Azerbaijan. Shah Isma'il undoubtedly played on this charisma and his family's long residence in the district to attract fervent support from tribesmen who came together in the Qizilbash confederation.

In addition, Shah Isma'il retained support of his army because he made a point of distributing to all of his followers the extensive assets captured with each defeated town and fort as they moved out from Azerbaijan and across the Iranian plateau. While this policy appealed to the tribesmen fighting on his behalf, he also attracted seasoned military officials since he was willing to defer to their military expertise as he gradually learned how to lead an army on his own. As a result, Shah Isma'il could rely on support because of his leadership over a respected Sufi order, but his pragmatic decisions concerning how to wage battle against Iran's many power centers proved just as important in the successful establishment of the Safavid Empire in 1501.

FIGURE 1.5. (*opposite*) *Zal Expounds the Mysteries of the Magi* from the *Shahnama* of Shah Tahmasp. The *Shahnama* made for the Safavid ruler Shah Tahmasp (r. 1524–1576) is the most luxurious 16th century copy of this poem about the legendary kings of Iran. It took more than 20 years to complete and involved two generations of the best Safavid artists, including Qadimi, painter of the scene here. In this painting, the hero Zal seeks advice on his wish to marry Rudaba from the wise Magi, seated at the foot of his throne.

Persian Roots

Although the Safavid family could have been Persian, Azeri Turkish, or Kurdish, they had been settled in Azerbaijan for such a long time by 1501 that they could make a valid assertion to being rightful rulers over a Persian land. The first Safavid shahs augmented this perception by frequent references to the *Shahnama* (Book of kings, 1010) of Abu al-Qasem Ferdowsi (ca. 920–1020), which celebrated the epic history of kingship in Iran from its earliest days. Ferdowsi began his tale with mythical, fantastic stories about the ancient Iranian kings and then progressed through the kings who reigned in the centuries before the Arab-Islamic conquest of Iran in 651. The *Shahnama* provided such a strong guide for potential Iranian leaders because it described the rituals necessary for a king to be recognized and revered by his people. Using this paradigm, Shah Isma'il presented himself as the reincarnation of a succession of Iranian heroes from the *Shahnama*.

Starting with Shah Tahmasp (r. 1524–1576), all the Safavid shahs established sophisticated libraries and artistic centers called ateliers that were odes to such institutions that had been established in the Timurid capitals of Herat and Samarkand in the 15th century. In those years, these cities had been the cultural center of the Persianate world, producing immaculate miniature paintings, distinctive religious and palace architecture, and sophisticated Persian poetry. By reinvigorating the Persian arts, exalting their connection to the heroes of the *Shahnama*, and highlighting their long-standing residence in the region of the Iranian plateau, the Safavid shahs made a valid claim for leadership over the Persianate world.

Religious Cohesion

The Safavids established their right to rule partly based on their leadership of the Safavid Sufi order. Their establishment of a Shi'i religious hierarchy enabled them to centralize and control Iran. Initially, the religion of Shah Isma'il had little institutional structure but contained elements of Sufism, Sunni and Shi'i Islam, Christianity, and the local religion of Zoroastrianism, established in Iran in the 5th century BC. He mobilized an enthusiastic following among the Qizilbash by playing on their desire as frontier warriors to battle against the tribes of Azerbaijan that were trying to curtail their independence and mobility. Shah Isma'il also proclaimed himself descended from 'Ali and the Shi'i imams, conferring on himself the divinity that came through the imam's line.

In 1501, when Shah Isma'il established the empire, he forced his new subjects to convert to Shi'ism; some left the country, but most stayed

SHI'ISM

Shi'ism began to take concrete form when the Shi'a formally broke with the Abbasid caliphs in the 8th century. It developed further under the Safavids of Iran (1501–1722) and in the shrine cities of Qom in Iran and Najaf and Karbala in southern Iraq in the 18th and 19th centuries. In Sunni Islam, the role of interpreting the faith passed to the ulama as representatives of the community; in Shi'i Islam that power is designated to the familial successors of the Prophet, the imams. The imam must lead the Muslim community because only he has the legitimate power of interpretation; in each generation there must be an imam who has sovereignty over the Muslim world.

Twelver Shi'ism, the dominant group within Shi'ism, recognizes 12 legitimate successors to the Prophet, beginning with 'Ali. The Isma'ilis split off from the Twelvers in the 8th century over disputes about the line of succession within the Prophetic family of imams. However, both branches believe that the last imam went into hiding (occultation) and that the Mahdi (the righteous one, or the Hidden Imam) will return at the end of days to bring the Kingdom of God on earth. In the meantime, interpreting the faith fell to the Shi'i ulama, deputized by the community to serve as jurists until the imam returned. Mujtahids (interpreters of the faith) and later ayatollahs (signs of God) came to serve as the foremost religious leaders for this task.

The Shi'i sects also distinguished themselves organizationally by compiling their own canons of religious doctrine. Shi'i scholars began collecting hadith from the Prophet and the imams during the 10th century, matching the work begun earlier by the Sunni ulama.

and accepted the situation. Local Sunni clerics also converted to Shi'ism, guided by the arrival of Shi'i clerics from places like southern Lebanon where an organized Shi'i structure already existed. Uniquely Shi'i celebrations became opportunities for tying Shi'a to the state and for differentiating Shi'ism from Sunni Islam. The yearly pageants commemorating the killing of 'Ali at Najaf and Hussein at Karbala reenacted the betrayals perpetrated against the Prophet's family and Shi'a more broadly, calling on participants to publicly flagellate themselves in punishment for their predecessors' failure to support these men in their time of need. These events gave entrée to the faith for the popular classes in the society while also showing that the shahs stood as protectors of the faith and the faithful.

But in Shah Isma'il's transition from a Sufi leading a tribal army to a shah presiding over a settled empire, the pillars of religious faith changed. In the conquest of Iran, Shah Isma'il could rely on reverence for his leadership over the Safavid Sufi order and his reputed ties to the imams. A pivotal moment occurred when he lost a number of battles after the conquest of Tabriz and the Iranian plateau in 1501, diminishing his religious charisma and his ability to keep the Qizilbash in line behind his policies. In their place, his son and successor, Shah Tahmasp, undertook to establish a Shi'i hierarchy. This helped spread Shi'ism throughout Iran and gave formal legitimacy to the Safavids as the protectors of orthodox Twelver Shi'ism, not just a leadership based on charisma and popular rituals. As a sign of their power, wealth, and reverence for the faith, the shahs patronized major Shi'i shrines, tombs, and mosques throughout Iran, especially in Shah Abbas's new capital of Isfahan after the move there in 1598. This hierarchy helped standardize Safavid rule throughout Iran and push the Qizilbash from the central circles of power.

This faith was not the heterodox, fluid religion of the pre-empire Safavid Sufi order; rather, it was based in shari'a law and disseminated by trained officials. To cement the foundations for such an orthodox faith, clerics collected hadiths from the Prophet, the imams of the Prophetic line, and those mujtahids who had served in their stead since the Hidden Imam had gone into occultation in the 9th century. The sayings and writings of Shah Isma'il also joined the canon because of his claims to being part of the Prophetic line. Schools and court systems trained and passed out judgment based on the precepts of Shi'ism being enunciated under Safavid rule. In the process, a Twelver Shi'a orthodoxy became the Safavid state religion.

But this reliance on an orthodox Shi'i hierarchy as a cornerstone of Safavid legitimacy ultimately worked against Safavid power when the shahs who ruled after Shah Abbas proved too weak to govern efficiently. In the political vacuum that resulted, the Shi'i establishment became more prominent as protectors and adjudicators of the faith than the shahs and thus independent of Safavid leadership. The Safavid government appointed top officials such as the imam jom'a (leader of the chief Friday prayer of each city) and court judges, but the officials in these posts were not the most influential Shi'i clerics. Independent mujtahids and their students, followers, and employees had a much greater influence over people's faith and the directions Shi'ism took. They did not claim to be infallible like the imams, but they professed a great degree of authority for interpreting the faith, an authority the shahs could not override, having lost their religious supremacy.

A division of labor of sorts developed as the religious clerics and the state claimed different elements of power. The mujtahids presided over the shari'a courts while the state held jurisdiction over 'urf, or customary law. No clear-cut division lay between these two systems, but the former dealt primarily with personal status and commercial issues while the latter concerned itself with any kind of relationship involving the state. Very importantly, the Shi'i clerics gained control over vast waqf properties throughout the country, giving them an independent economic power base and protecting those revenues from state taxation and control. They also collected the charity (zakat) required of all Muslims, keeping it out of the hands of Safavid government leaders and officials. With these resources, combined with the claim to authoritatively pass judgment on matters of faith, the mujtahids grew in number and influence throughout the Safavid period.

Military and Administrative Power

The Qizilbash had followed Shah Isma'il because he represented a rebellion against the tribal powers then ruling Azerbaijan and the Iranian plateau and because he had religious aura. In the first years after 1501, they served as the primary military force and as provincial governors for a Safavid dynasty in the process of expanding its territory. During his reign Shah Tahmasp played off the different clans in a divide-and-rule strategy that brought one clan into imperial power for a time only to be replaced by another when the first accrued too much influence. As a result, some Qizilbash leaders continued to hold sway at the court, but most found few positions within the new, centralized Safavid polity. Their religious views did not accord with the orthodox Shi'ism gaining prominence, and their loyalty to the Safavid family waned when repeated military defeats diminished their ability to take control over new territories.

When he came to the throne in 1588, Shah Abbas accelerated the weakening of the Qizilbash tribes. He followed the Ottoman lead by training a permanent slave infantry army from among the Christian populations in the region, with numbers reaching 10,000 soldiers and 3,000 bodyguards at the peak of their strength. When they confronted the power of the Ottoman Janissary troops armed with guns and cannon, the Safavids similarly equipped their army and distanced themselves from the outmoded cavalry of the Qizilbash. Shah Abbas also worked to transition autonomous land in the provinces into government-controlled land so that the revenues could be shifted from the Qizilbash commanders into the vaults of the central treasury. Those tribes who refused to submit to Shah Abbas's centralized rule were exiled to the empire's frontiers. They included Qizilbash in the northwestern and Arab and Baluch confederations in the southern and southeastern parts of Iran. These acts marginalized the tribes as a military power in the empire at the same time governance shifted from one dominated by a tribal confederation to a central bureaucracy.

The consolidation of Safavid administrative structures facilitated the shift from reliance on nomadic Qizilbash shaykhs and tribesmen to a settled bureaucracy led by Persian officials. Persian administrators, descendants of those who had served all the many dynasties ruling over Iran since the fall of the Sassanid dynasty in 651, came to take their place in the capital and in the provincial governorates. As they had done for the previous dynasties, these administrators standardized the implementation of Safavid ordinances throughout the provinces.

Shah Abbas and Isfahan

The height of Safavid administrative and economic power occurred during the reign of Shah Abbas, who increased the revenues brought into the central treasury by expanding the road and caravansary system so that Persian cotton, spices, silks, rugs, and ceramics could more easily travel overland between Mughal India and Ottoman Istanbul. To further facilitate such trade, Shah Abbas successfully captured the port of Hormuz from the Portuguese and established there the port of Bandar Abbas, where the British quickly became the dominant foreign trader from their perch in India. Shah Abbas moved the capital to Isfahan in 1598 so he

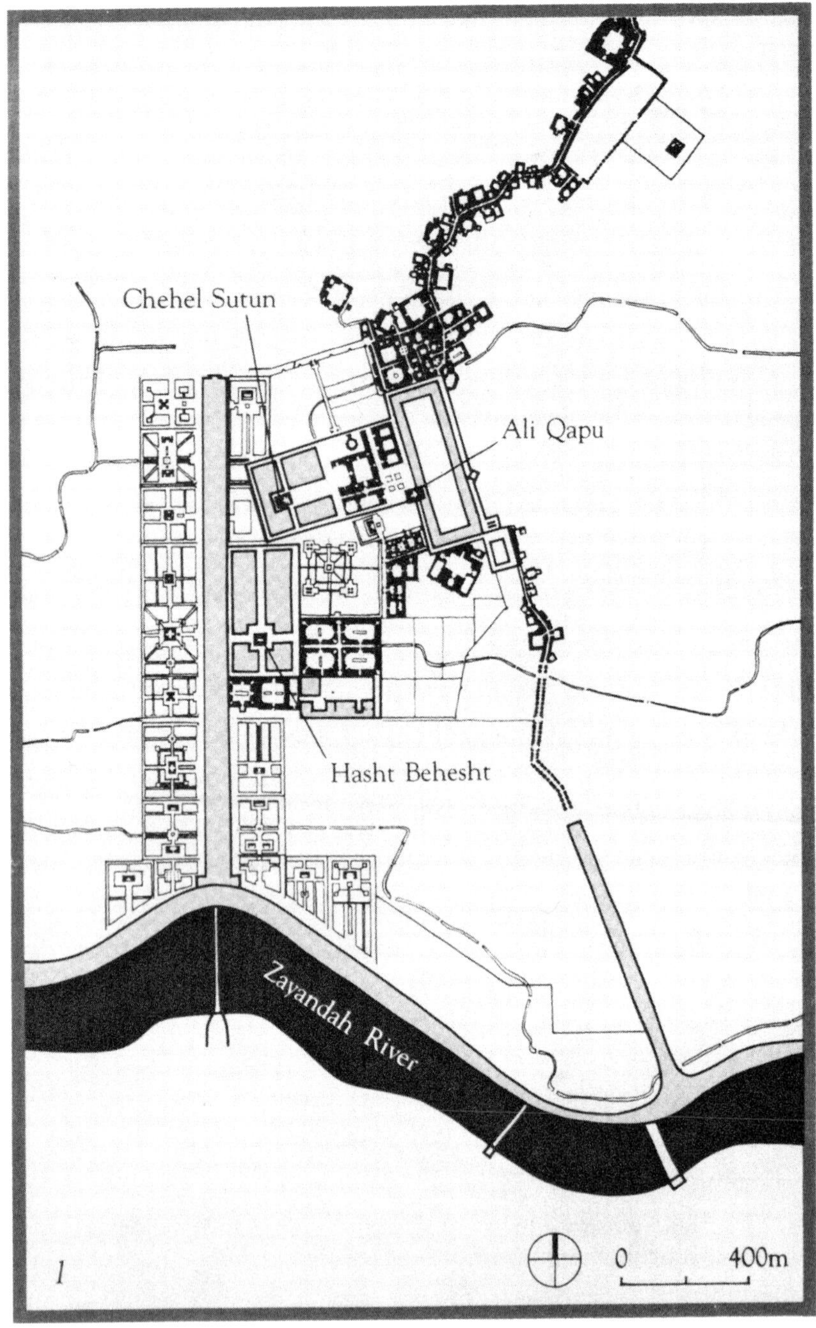

FIGURE 1.6. Plan of the Maydan-e Shah Palace complex in Isfahan, largely built by Shah Abbas. Chahar Bagh Boulevard and its surrounding palace gardens extend from the river to the north. Ali Qapu served as the gatehouse to the Maydan-e Shah grounds; and Chehel Sutun and Hasht Behesht, as palace pavilions. On this plan, the bazaar extends from top of the Maydan-e Shah Palace, and the Masjed-e Shah (mosque) stands alongside the bottom wall, angled toward Mecca.

could build it up as a central hub for manufacturing and trade and as the focal point for Safavid architectural majesty.

The Ottomans could afford to seclude themselves in Topkapi because of their reliance on a dependent retinue; the Safavid shahs had to remain out in public because too many independent power brokers continued to function under their sovereign rule. The Safavid shahs had to continually display their wealth, superior position, and might so the many power brokers in the realm would submit to them and consider them indispensable to the maintenance of their own power. They had to constantly negotiate with these autonomous power brokers so they would continue to implement imperial policies.

Just as Topkapi epitomized Ottoman modes of sovereign authority at the cornerstone of Ottoman imperial power, Shah Abbas's newly enhanced capital of Isfahan represented the elements most representative of Safavid royal practice. The palace complex included a royal square and a mansion-lined boulevard designed for public processions. The shah ordered the commanders of his slave army to build identically gated mansions along the boulevard as a symbol of his power over the Safavid state and their subservience to him. Near the palace complex were the communities that Shah Abbas transplanted to Isfahan, including close advisers from the original capital of Tabriz and Armenian merchants whom Shah Abbas had forced to move to the suburb of New Julfa so he could better collect the revenues from the silk trade they dominated. Housing them near the palace complex indicated their indebtedness to the shah for the wealth and influence they had accrued under his tutelage.

The complex also included a bustling bazaar symbolizing Isfahan's position as a pivot point for world trade. Open to all the city's residents, the open areas throughout the complex were available for sporting matches, military parades, and holiday processions. Shah Abbas and his successors, unlike the Ottoman sultans, held frequent councils during the week for their subjects to present their grievances and for their advisers to consult them about policy decisions. Shah Abbas also frequently walked the streets of the city, greeting his subjects and engaging in the many public events taking place.

Safavid Decline

This level of wealth and centralized power could not be maintained after Shah Abbas's death in 1629 because his successors were less qualified for the tasks facing the throne. They were also encountering the same economic pressures weakening the Ottoman Empire by the 17th century. Increases in world ocean shipping in the 18th century decreased overland trade along the Silk Road that traversed Iran, weakening the Iranian economy, which was so dependent on transit dues. To avoid future succession battles, Shah Abbas had instituted the Ottoman policy of keeping all the male heirs in the harem until their time to ascend the throne. As a result, shahs took over leadership having had little political experience. By the early 18th century, the Safavid rulers no longer had control over the tribes, and their administrative effectiveness deteriorated. The economy suffered when it had little cohesive support from the state. The expensive irrigation systems necessary for production in the Iranian plateau fell into disrepair, decreasing the tax revenues to be obtained from previously productive agricultural lands.

These economic difficulties, combined with deteriorating charismatic and military legitimacy, allowed powerful religious and tribal leaders to challenge the shahs' authority. Shah Abbas's successors largely failed to maintain a military force that could withstand a concerted attack. The Janissary-like slave army required a constant infusion of revenue to maintain its strength and the soldiers' loyalty, but economic crises had dramatically diminished the funds available to them. The Qizilbash tribes, which the shahs had marginalized, were no longer at their service for the empire's defense. In 1722, the Ghilzai Afghans laid siege to Isfahan and with a relatively weak army succeeded in breaking the power of the Safavids. Until 1736, a nominal Safavid shah remained on the throne, but when Nader Shah Afshar took control over Iran, that pretense was eliminated and the Safavid Empire ended its reign. The tribes that Shah Abbas had exiled to the frontier regions returned to their original territories and regained a large measure of the autonomy the Safavids had taken from them. The Zand dynasty (r. 1751–1795) emerged as a large confederation of tribes that ruled in central Iran until the Qajars from Azerbaijan defeated them in 1796.

Conclusion

In its most basic form, Ottoman governance worked through contracts, whereby the contractees provided valuable services to the sultan and thus enabled the Ottomans to rule over large swaths of territory with relatively few officials functioning in the sultan's name. From the Ottoman perspective, the contract system in its ideal setting provided divide-and-rule aspects that kept contractees from working together against the sultan's wishes or of finding ways to establish a lineage or a royal claim that could threaten the Ottoman throne. These contractees were Ottoman stakeholders because they grew wealthy and powerful within the parameters of their contracts; they needed the Ottoman Empire to continue to exist so they could maintain their positions of influence.

Filling imperial positions with slaves enabled the sultans to literally own the officials designated to implement their wishes. The slaves brought in through the devşirme and the slave guilds received the best educations in the empire and became, in the process, a select group standing above and outside society, separated from the population by their acculturation process. Most of the slaves in the system did not achieve great acclaim, wealth, or power, but they were all part of an elite unit granted privileges few others could obtain. Through such a process, the Ottomans constructed another set of stakeholders who were willing and able to play power politics but were also aware that they needed the Ottoman family in order to keep their positions. Until the end of the 18th century, none of these stakeholders actively sought to overthrow or appreciably change the system; they merely pushed against the limits of their contracts and positions to see how flexible they could be.

Although an Afghan tribe defeated the Safavids, the shahs centralized Iran as no empire had been able to do for centuries. The institutions they established came to define Iranian religion and governance from that point forward. They made the successful claim that they were the next in a long line of Persian kings in the mold of the *Shahnama* while adding Shi'ism as a defining Persian element. Orthodox Twelver Shi'ism reigned over Iran, with mujtahids and ulama attaining even more influence in the 18th century when the political leadership shifted between different tribes and no centralized administration governed them. In the midst of this chaos some clerics moved to the southern Iraqi pilgrimage cities of Najaf and Karbala but continued to have a strong influence over events in Iran.

Persian administrators persisted as the glue keeping all the systems of governance together, regardless of which tribal dynasty ruled over the largest amount of territory. The tribes regained a large measure of the autonomy they had lost under Safavid rule; one such confederation, the Qajars, gained control of the country in 1796. In establishing their right to rule, the Qajars claimed succession from the Safavids. In fact, the Qajars adopted the Safavid sword and crown (with its four plumes symbolic of Safavid control over Afghanistan, India, Turkestan, and Iran), using them in all their ceremonies. In this way, the Qajars presented themselves as a Persian dynasty carrying on the work of their Safavid forebears.

The Ottoman and Safavid systems both relied on familial legitimacy and pragmatic negotiation with the many power brokers under their control to maintain hegemony over their territories. No family challenged the Ottomans as the rightful leaders of the realm. The Safavids were so successful in establishing the cornerstones of rulership that the Qajars used the symbols of Safavid rule as legitimizing elements when they took control. The stakeholders in both these realms shifted over the decades and centuries, and their share of power, as well as the share held by the ruling families, changed, but the ruling structures remained largely unchanged. The systems worked for as long as they did because people recognized the legitimacy of the ruling families and understood that power could be accrued through accreditation by the state.

REFORM AND REBELLION

2

The Ottoman Empire, Egypt, and Qajar Iran in the 19th Century

THE QAJARS AND OTTOMANS faced the dawn of the 19th century in different positions governmentally and militarily. The Qajars took the throne in 1796 and spent the next decades trying to recentralize the state after almost a century of autonomous rule by tribes and Shi'i clerics. The Ottomans entered the era challenged by a new set of rogue clients and exposed to intensified economic and military pressures from the Europeans. The Russians and Austrians continued to push against the northern borders, and the western European states increased their trade throughout the Mediterranean. In reaction, both the Ottoman sultans and the Qajar shahs initiated reforms during the course of the century aimed at centralizing control over the states' resources and staving off further European intervention.

The most successful models of military preparedness and economic power available to the Ottoman and Qajar rulers were those of the British, French, and Prussians. The means chosen to stop European pressures were to institute European-style training regimens for the armies, open European-style schools for the administrators, standardize law codes for Muslims and non-Muslims alike, and reform property laws to better collect taxes and control the resources being grown and produced.

The Ottoman reforms were premised on shifting away from the sultan's personal guarantee of just governance for all his subjects to a state in which all citizens, not just the intermediaries, received rights in return for fulfilling new types of obligations to the state. The Qajar shahs initiated reforms as a means for uniting the country's many fractious groups. Both leaderships, to different degrees, presented themselves as bringing Western-style modernity to Middle Eastern governance and society.

When these new policies were implemented, old stakeholders lost their influence while new intermediaries and subjects attained or were forced into positions that had never existed before. The states coerced peasants into their armies, forced farmers to grow products for export, displaced merchants as intermediaries in foreign trade, and weakened the hold religious clerics held over schooling and the law. To facilitate such changes, the states trained new military and administrative officials to design the new policies. They recruited new local leaders in the provinces to implement them.

Despite these efforts, the Ottoman and Qajar governments did not succeed in protecting their realms from European penetration. Instead, paying for the new institutions forced them into debt to European bankers, the British and French colonized North Africa, and the Russians and British entered into a competition for Qajar resources. Centralization also proved difficult to achieve as Greece and the Balkans broke away from Ottoman sovereignty and as new stakeholders demanded more say in government decision making when their state leaders failed to forestall debt and colonization. Furthermore, the leaders' claims that they represented modernity failed to win over their subjects: by the end of the 19th century, new Ottoman stakeholders criticized the sultan and his allies for failing to fully reform governance; and Qajar constituents, in defense of Iranian national sovereignty, mounted enormous protests against economic concessions to the Europeans.

Rogues and Rebels in the Ottoman Empire

In the last quarter of the 18th century in the Ottoman Empire, rogues and rebels found innovative ways to benefit from loose Ottoman political control and increased European economic and military interest in the region. Most of their acts were no different from those perpetrated by the leaders of the Celali rebellions in the 16th and 17th centuries. As in the earlier events, rogue clients took advantage of a weak Ottoman government to increase their local authority. However, a small number of rebels did directly oppose Ottoman sovereignty. Neither set of actions imperiled the empire, but their combined effect weakened the Ottoman sultan's control over his subjects while helping Russia, France, and Britain intervene more directly into new arenas within the empire. The Ottoman military put down all these different types of revolts, but in contrast to the situation in the 17th century the status quo ante was not reestablished in the aftermath. Instead, the Ottoman sultans and a new Ottoman governor of the province of Egypt, Mehmet Ali, engaged in a wholesale reformation of military and government institutions that would irretrievably alter the bases of legitimacy for the Ottoman government and its subjects' relationship with it.

Entrepreneurs of Jabal Nablus

The province of Jabal Nablus in Palestine represents an example of an area that was always filled with rogue clients. Its local leaders exploited the opportunities of the 18th century to become powerful and wealthy by combining the influence of government positions with the economic innovations they instituted on their land and in their factories. Over the centuries of Ottoman rule, the merchants and tax farmers of Jabal Nablus always welcomed the Ottoman offer of governmental positions. The Ottomans repeatedly confirmed and reconfirmed their appointments as subdistrict chiefs and district governors, and during the annual caravan to Mecca for the hajj, Nablus merchants made a great deal of money by trading with the pilgrims. Their permanent government positions and those connections they attained during the hajj added to their local legitimacy and to the wealth they acquired by their economic exploits. But they rarely paid their taxes on time and often functioned autonomously of the Damascus government tasked with supervising their region.

In the 18th century, Nablus merchants, peasants, and tax farmers moved into commercialized agriculture and turned their surplus into investment in manufacturing, particularly with anything produced from olives. They sold these raw and processed materials to the Europeans and other Ottoman provinces such as Egypt. They built on the credibility accorded them by their government positions while taking advantage of new agricultural and manufacturing opportunities provided by European merchants. Newly wealthy families henceforth made money from all possible realms, most of which were new or expanded zones in the 18th century. They continued to offer fealty to the Ottoman sultan while

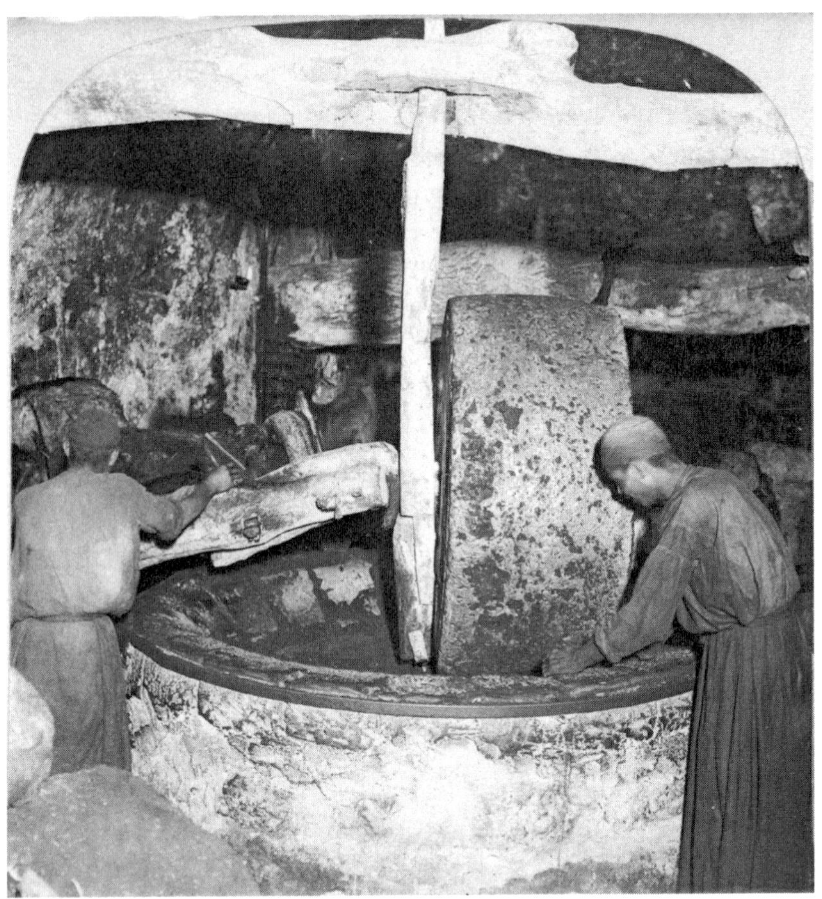

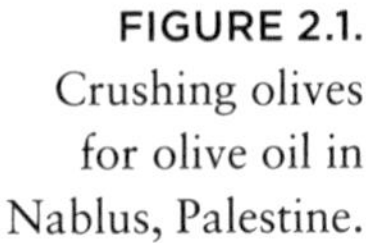

FIGURE 2.1. Crushing olives for olive oil in Nablus, Palestine.

negotiating the terms of their economic relationship with European merchants outside the realm of Ottoman supervision and largely beyond the reach of the Ottoman treasury.

Zahir al-'Umar and the Levantine Coast

Zahir al-'Umar (ca. 1690–1775) of Akka (Acre) used military skill and economic innovation to preside over the Levantine coast for decades. He began his political career as an Ottoman tax collector in the Mediterranean coastal city of Sidon; from that post he militarily captured the port of Akka in 1746. Over the next two decades, he came to control not only Sidon and Akka but much of the hinterland surrounding them. There he pressured farmers to grow cotton for export and monopolized its sale to French merchants, signing trade agreements as if he were a sovereign power rather than a subject of the Ottoman sultan. These policies were a dramatic change from the past when the mültizam had done little to direct the types and amounts of produce grown, content merely to collect revenues from the peasants' labor. The existence of a free peasantry in most areas of the empire militated against such domination over the actual products to be cultivated.

As did many an Ottoman functionary before him, he recognized that a high provincial posting could augment his local authority. When his lobbying efforts in this regard failed, al-'Umar allied with a group of Mamluks from Egypt to lead a military force against the Ottoman regiments in Damascus. In 1770, al-'Umar rebelled against the sultan in large part because his request to be appointed governor of Damascus had been repeatedly denied. While this effort ultimately failed and he died during the Ottoman siege of Akka in 1775, his actions provided a blueprint for how a provincial leader could grow both militarily and economically strong by forging new relationships with European merchants and by transforming cultivation and production to supply foreign markets with new goods.

Pasvantoğlu Osman Pasha and the Balkans

The end of the 18th century opened on a Balkan population heavily exploited by Ottoman officials. Against sultanic dictates, the Janissary troops, who collected the revenues from their iltizams in the region where they were stationed, abused the peasantry on whose labor they relied. In reaction to these abuses, ambitious local leaders formed irregular military bands of peasants to attack the institutions of Ottoman power. Pasvantoğlu Osman Pasha formed one such unit in Bulgaria in the region of Vidin. He began life as a bandit like his father had been before him, served in the Ottoman army from 1787 to 1792, and then returned to banditry when his military service ended. He was able to gather around him large numbers of disaffected renegades, peasants, and Janissaries and grew so powerful he unilaterally took over the pashalik (governorate) of Vidin, refusing to wait for Ottoman accreditation for his action. When in 1795 he declared independence from the Ottoman government, many more men rallied to his cause because of the power he represented. He managed to remain in power in Vidin until he died in 1807 because the Ottomans could not field a military unit strong enough to unseat him.

. . .

While these rebellions and rogue actions proved costly to the Ottoman treasury, with tax revenues diverted away from Istanbul and military

FIGURE 2.2. Nablus, Palestine, 1857.

regiments called up, they did not seriously threaten the empire as a whole because they were largely fought within the bounds of the Ottoman contract system. None of the leaders tried to overthrow or destroy the empire; they merely pushed the limits to augment their own power or revolted against particularly abusive Ottoman officials. They were not building long-term institutions to establish a new type of governance for themselves or to pass on to their heirs; they were merely working with the opportunities presented to them at the moment.

Zahir al-'Umar rebelled so the sultan would appoint him governor of Damascus. Men like the merchants of Nablus and al-'Umar showed how economic innovation could allow access into the new global trading system but without directly challenging Ottoman sovereignty. When the promise of just governance failed, the peasants of the Balkans were able and willing to join the band of a leader who allowed them to attack those symbols of abusive power the Janissaries represented, just as their Celali predecessors had done two centuries earlier. Pasvantoğlu Osman Pasha did not appreciably weaken the Ottoman hold over the Balkans, but he did tap into the frustrations felt by many in the region.

Two exceptions were the actions undertaken by a Saudi-Wahhab alliance in the Arabian Peninsula and a revolt that culminated in Serbian autonomy in 1817. These were outright rebellions against Ottoman legitimacy and rule. Nevertheless, their influence remained local, which meant they did not pose a radical challenge to Ottoman governance in Istanbul, at least in the short term.

Saudi-Wahhab Alliance

Muhammad ibn 'Abd al-Wahhab (1703–1792) formed a group in the Arabian Peninsula in the 18th century calling themselves Muwahhidun, or believers in the oneness of God, the tawhid. 'Abd al-Wahhab derided the Ottomans for putting their resources into elaborate tombs and shrines and for fronting grand celebrations on such events as the Prophet's birthday instead of looking to the true faith embedded in the core documents. He denounced all forms of idolatry and popular beliefs about Islam that the Ottomans had encouraged, calling these acts jahiliyya, referring to the Age of Ignorance Muslims identify as the pre-Islamic era in Arabia. Instead of advocating blind obedience to Ottoman dictates on religion, 'Abd al-Wahhab preached a return to the Quran and the sunna of the Prophet as the sole guides for the faithful. He designated jihad, or holy war, a requirement for all Muslims forced to live under a leadership that was un-Islamic like the Ottomans. In this call, jihad would defeat the Ottoman Empire and bring into being a true Islamic state in its place.

'Abd al-Wahhab joined forces with Muhammad ibn Saud (d. 1765), leader of an Arab clan of Najd in central Arabia, to achieve his religious goals through military conquest. Together, they conquered and settled areas of the Arabian Peninsula and put into practice their interpretation of the Quran and the Prophet's message, while warring against those who did not favor the same path to Islam. Muhammad ibn Saud's son Abdul Aziz (r. 1765–1803) continued his father's conquests and led attacks against the Hijaz. In 1803, he occupied Mecca and Medina, and on arrival, he and his tribesmen destroyed the Ottoman tombs and shrines they considered un-Islamic. Henceforth they prohibited Ottoman subjects from undertaking the pilgrimage. Attempts by the Ottoman military to recapture the region failed over the next years. By capturing the holiest sites in Islam and rationalizing their action with a religious philosophy in opposition to the Ottomans', the Saudi-Wahhab fighters posed a serious challenge to Ottoman religious legitimacy. But in this instance, the alliance made no military attempt to move beyond the Arabian Peninsula, and the revolt did not bring about any similar revolts even though the conquest of the Hijazi besmirched the sultan's claim to protecting the Islamic faith.

Serbian Revolt

A revolt that erupted in Serbia in 1804 against Janissary exploitation brought together tens of thousands of disgruntled peasants. In 1817, Miloš Obrenović took up the leadership of the revolt. With an army of 20,000–30,000 bandits and Russian support, he forced the Ottoman government to grant him a provincial governmental appointment. Obrenović became prince of a semi-autonomous region under Russian protection; in 1830, the Ottoman sultan declared this position hereditary, and Obrenović's family subsequently held the Serbian throne for most of the 19th century.

The revolt began because of anger at Janissary and landholder exactions; the leaders did not immediately work toward the larger goal of political autonomy from Ottoman rule but for better local conditions for the peasantry. The shift came when the Russians adopted the Serbian program as another tool for weakening the Ottomans along the Black Sea and into the Balkans. This action did not present an immediate threat to Ottoman sovereignty, but it did provide the model that the Balkans would follow throughout the century to break away from Ottoman sovereignty. This Russian action represented a new front in the European-Ottoman competition for land and economic trade.

French Invasion of Egypt

Napoleon Bonaparte invaded Egypt in 1798 and occupied this Ottoman province until 1801. When a combined Ottoman and British army and naval force defeated Napoleon's army, the ramifications of his incursion could be felt during the entire century. The action opened up new tactics in the European competition for the Ottoman Empire's resources. Up until this point, military conflict had occurred between the Ottomans, Austrians, and Russians while the British and French had used economic means for infiltrating Ottoman borders. After the incursion, the French and British became more directly involved in Ottoman governmental and economic affairs. European military officers trained new regiments and opened military academies; merchants bought increased amounts of raw materials from Ottoman producers while selling goods manufactured in European factories; and bankers loaned millions of dollars to the Ottoman and Egyptian governments.

By the end of the 19th century, Britain and France were in colonial control of almost all of North Africa, and their officials supervised governmental agencies in Istanbul. The Napoleonic invasion also brought to Egypt Mehmet Ali, a man who would lead the way toward innovation in Egypt and the Ottoman Empire at large, as he adopted the tactics already used by his rebellious predecessors throughout the empire and introduced European military, educational, and administrative institutions to Egyptian governance. His actions inaugurated a new phase of reform throughout the region that would change it economically, militarily, governmentally, and socially.

Mehmet Ali in Egypt

The Ottoman sultan declared Mehmet Ali governor of Egypt on July 9, 1805. This appointment was a spectacular achievement for a man who had arrived in the country five years earlier with no political connections at all. Either a Kurd or an Albanian in origin, he had come from Greece as commander of a small regiment in the Ottoman army fighting against the Napoleonic invasion; once in Egypt, he also took command of a unit of 4,000 Albanians who had been part of the Ottoman military force. In the aftermath of the French withdrawal in 1801, the economy came to a standstill, and in reaction demonstrations erupted continually over nonpayment of salaries for the army and increases in Ottoman taxation burdens for merchants and peasants.

Over the next few years, Mehmet Ali proved to be the most successful of all the many claimants to power in Egypt. He used the large army under his control to arrest and threaten Mamluk and Ottoman officials opposing his rising influence in Cairo. He also made alliances with the city's ulama and merchants by promising to bring security back to the streets and by publicly presenting himself as a defender of the local population. In making these moves, Mehmet Ali did not defy the Ottoman sultan; rather, he claimed to be working on his behalf against abusive local and Ottoman officials so that just governance could return. And with all of Cairo exploding in revolt by 1805, the ulama supported Mehmet Ali as the best possible protector of their interests and petitioned the Ottoman sultan to appoint Mehmet Ali as governor of Egypt. In so attaining the governorship in 1805, Mehmet Ali had won the loyalty of the Albanian troops, the ulama, the merchants, and Cairo's populace; he capped his victory by receiving Ottoman authorization for it.

FIGURE 2.3
A Mamluk from Aleppo, ca. 1816–1824.

In the years between 1805 and his death in 1849, Mehmet Ali harnessed the power of the Egyptian province in much the same way the rogue clients had done throughout the Ottoman Empire for the previous few decades. He transformed much of the Egyptian economy to supply revenues for the state treasury as the Levantine merchants had done on a smaller scale, he funneled those revenues into training and recruitment for a European-style military force, and he constructed a new administrative system to mobilize the population as no Egyptian governing force had done before. Along the way, he destroyed the vested interests that protected their privileges by opposing any reforms to their institutions. The difference between him and the previous rogues was one of degree; his policies were geared toward long-term change rather than ad hoc decision making. Because of the permanent nature of his reforms, Mehmet Ali succeeded in bequeathing a new kind of state and military to his family on his death. His descendants ruled Egypt until 1952.

Replacement of Elites

Mehmet Ali began the process of reform with the destruction of the old elites. His first targets were the Mamluks, who had served as the primary military force in Egypt since the 13th century and who had failed to defend Egypt against the Napoleonic army.

Mehmet Ali learned from the example of Sultan Selim III, who had tried to reform the Ottoman military in the 1790s but had failed because the Janissaries had stood in the way of such change. Mehmet Ali forestalled such opposition by attacking the Mamluks before he even began his reforms.

MAMLUKS

Mamluks were recruited for centuries through slave guilds from the Caucasus and Georgia. Emancipated Mamluks—grandees, or beys—bought new slaves to serve in their personal households; when these slaves reached maturity, they founded their own households, purchased slaves, and the cycle continued. Mamluk training and military service thus took place within numerous military households—not exclusively under the umbrella of one leader or sultan. As the last of the Ottoman devşirme levies ceased in 1704, Mamluk beys continued to purchase new slaves throughout the 18th century. By the turn of the 19th century, the Mamluks were not merely a military force but had become embedded in the economic life of Egypt through their control over rural and urban iltizam. Intermarriage within and between Mamluk households and their speaking Ottoman Turkish rather than Arabic separated this cadre from the native Egyptian Arab population.

Rarely did one Mamluk bey hold exclusive power in Egypt; in most centuries, Mamluk households competed with each other for influence. When a leader died, his competitors and his Mamluks fought over the right to take over his properties and position. For example, 'Ali Bey al-Kabir (r. 1760–1767; 1768–1772) began life as a Mamluk. When his patron died, he won the right to succeed him and eventually owned as many as 1,000 Mamluks himself. At the height of his power, he held more influence than any other Mamluk had for centuries, but when he chose to rebel against the sultan alongside Zahir al-'Umar of Akka, he failed. He died in 1773 in battle against the Ottoman army, and the rivalries between competing Mamluk beys were reignited.

Mehmet Ali made his move in 1811 when he accepted the sultan's request to send a military force to defeat the Saudi-Wahhab force that had captured Mecca and Medina in 1803. On the eve of his army's departure for the Hijaz on this sacred duty Mehmet Ali invited the Mamluk chiefs to the Citadel in Cairo for a ceremonial banquet. When they arrived, Mehmet Ali locked the doors behind them, and his troops massacred them, killing more than 450 in about an hour. Mehmet Ali finished the job by sending his son Ibrahim with the Albanian troops to kill about 1,000 more. In the aftermath, Mehmet Ali confiscated the Mamluks' tax farms, making it impossible for any of those who survived to establish economic or military bases separate from those of Mehmet Ali.

Weakening of the Ulama

By the early 19th century, the most influential ulama in Egypt controlled vast waqf properties and large numbers of iltizams and thus were largely independent from government control. Mehmet Ali, in his quest for con-

SULTAN SELIM III'S MILITARY REFORMS

In the 1790s, to defend against Russian and Austrian expansion, Ottoman Sultan Selim III (r. 1789–1807) attempted to construct a new kind of military force to offset the weakness of the Janissaries. He hired French officers to set the terms of the reforms, which replicated western European training and strategies. Engineering schools for the officer corps were opened and an infantry corps established, the Nizam-ı Cedid (New Order Army). It eventually included 23,000 soldiers from the Anatolian peasantry and urban unemployed. This move engendered opposition from the Janissaries, who did not want to undergo new types of training, be replaced by the new force, or have their new independent economic power weakened.

By the time Sultan Selim III began initiating his reforms, the Janissaries stood in the ambiguous position of wanting to maintain their accreditation with the Ottomans but opposing any efforts that would return full state control over their economic and military lives. In the Edirne Incident of 1806, the Janissaries successfully stopped the army from setting up camp near the town, forcing the Nizam-ı Cedid to retreat to Istanbul. In 1807, the Janissaries stationed along the Bosporus refused to wear the European uniforms of the new army, which would have symbolized their submission to the new force. They rebelled militarily instead; when they closed in on Istanbul, Sultan Selim III failed to organize an effective resistance so was forced to abdicate in favor of Mustafa IV (r. 1807–1808) and was later killed by the new sultan. Mustafa IV was in turn forced to abdicate by Selim III's brother Mahmoud II (r. 1808–1839). Sultan Mahmoud II took to heart the lesson that substantial reforms could not be successful unless the vested interests that opposed them were removed. He initiated wide-scale reforms against the Janissaries in the 1820s when he had sufficient force to destroy them as power brokers.

trol of Egypt's resources, did not kill the leading ulama as he had the Mamluks, but he weakened their independent economic power so they would not be an obstacle to the changes he planned. He confiscated many of their waqf lands and gradually eliminated the tax exemptions they had enjoyed as tax farmers. A new ministry for the collection of waqf took charge of Islamic donations so that the state rather than the ulama could direct the revenues. Henceforth, most ulama remained poorly paid state officials; a few who had connected themselves to Mehmet Ali and his family attained political power.

Economic Centralization

After appreciably weakening the old system involving the ulama and Mamluks, Mehmet Ali granted economic privileges to new players. He delivered the lands confiscated from the Mamluks and the ulama to his family, friends, and allies, making them a new landowning class beholden to his rule. These lands constituted approximately 50 percent of all the land of Egypt and possibly as much as 75 percent of the fertile land during the 19th century. Mehmet Ali made decisions about which crops would be grown and sold them to the Europeans directly, just as the 18th-century leaders such as Zahir al-'Umar had done earlier.

In 1808 Mehmet Ali signed an agreement with the British to sell grain via Alexandria, and the first transfers took place in 1810. As a second step, he officially monopolized cereal production in Upper Egypt in 1811, rice in the Delta in 1812, and sugar from Upper Egypt in 1815. He thus displaced the merchants, who no longer had control over the products moving into and out of Egypt. He used coerced peasant labor to enact his will, and when opposed, he adopted brutal techniques to punish any who refused to work as a warning to others who might consider the same tactics.

In 1820, Mehmet Ali began cultivating a long-staple cotton that subsequently gained fame around the world for its high quality. Cotton became the single most important product Egypt exported well into the mid-20th century. As a result of these policies, five times as much land was given over to cash crops by the 1820s than when Mehmet Ali came to power, and in most years cotton amounted to a third or a quarter of the government's overall income.

In the 1810s and 1820s, Mehmet Ali launched Egypt's first rudimentary factories for the production of uniforms and other textile products; by the 1830s, there were 30 cotton mills. He opened a gunpowder factory in 1815 and then a munitions foundry in Cairo. Together the factories employed between 30,000 and 40,000 workers by the 1830s. However, his factories were not particularly successful as an economic instrument because the country lacked sufficient numbers of skilled laborers, the internal market outside the military was too small to boost demand, and Egypt had a scarcity of natural power sources to exploit. Mehmet Ali imported a small number of steam engines, but the transition to a more mechanized source of energy was hampered because Egypt had no domestic sources of coal, wood, or workable iron.

Peasants also fought against the factories' obligatory and poorly paid labor requirements (corvée labor). The state resorted to tattooing the names of factories on workers' arms to keep track of who still owed labor duties on the factory floors. As a result of all these obstacles, by the early 1840s, Mehmet Ali was already starting to close his factories. Despite these setbacks, these economic changes collectively funneled more revenue into the state treasury than under the Ottoman governors and Mamluks of the past, in large measure because Mehmet Ali took revenues away from the nongovernmental actors who had dominated the economic scene for the previous decades.

Formation of Military and Professional Corps

The new revenue was spent primarily on the military. Mehmet Ali wanted to train a new officer corps and conscript large numbers of peasants so he could field an army comparable in strategy and strength to those of Britain and France. Although Mehmet Ali relied on his old connections—family members, Albanian soldiers, and Mamluk-like military slaves he had brought to Egypt—he placed them into new training regimens befitting the style of military he was constructing. He recruited French officers to open schools for his officer corps and sent several of his officers to Europe for further training. During the course of the 1810s and 1820s, European doctors and military officers set up military academies and medical and veterinary schools in Egypt to train even more officers and professionals.

Mehmet Ali opened a school of engineering in 1815 and, in 1825, a school for specialized training for the infantry; artillery and cavalry followed. To provide local editions of European scientific and military manuals, a school of translation opened in the 1820s and then expanded in 1835 to include study of Turkish, Persian, Italian, French, English, history, geography, literature, and Islamic law. Dr. Antoine Barthélemy Clot from France opened the Qasr al-'Ayni training hospital in 1827, followed in the 1840s by a series of provincial health clinics and hospitals. The new kind of training the students had undertaken in these schools made them stakeholders of the system Mehmet Ali was constructing.

While the graduates moved into leadership in the administration and military just as their Mamluk and Janissary predecessors had done after their specialized training, the era of slave recruitment into elite cadres had ended. These men leading Mehmet Ali's new institutions were free men choosing to work on his behalf; collectively, the men in the elite government and military circle around Mehmet Ali came to be grouped under the sobriquet "Turco-Circassians." "Turco" refers to the Turkish acculturation process the Mamluks, their households, and their families had undertaken to establish themselves as a separate social and military cadre within Egypt. "Circassians" recognizes the Caucasus region as the source for the vast majority of the Mamluks who had worked their way through the Egyptian system over the centuries. As they had done under Ottoman rule, these Turco-Circassians continued to serve in the top Egyptian military and administrative positions for much of the 19th century. They maintained cultural separation from the bulk of the population by speaking Ottoman Turkish rather than the local Arabic.

Mehmet Ali sent an army into the Sudan in 1820, hoping to capture enough men to fill out his new army with ranks of conscript soldiers, but these efforts failed because of poor logistical planning and the large mortality rate experienced by the Sudanese during the march back to Egypt. By 1824, of the 30,000 Sudanese slaves taken by the Egyptians, only 3,000 remained alive. As the problems with this route multiplied, Mehmet Ali decided to conscript Egyptian peasants; in February 1822, he instructed the provincial governors in Upper Egypt to supply the first 4,000 recruits, decreeing that they would all have to serve three-year tours of duty.

But Egyptian peasants did not acquiesce easily to these new obligations. Conditions in the military were harsh, and the time spent away from the fields endangered their families' livelihoods. In spring 1823 and again in 1824, tens of thousands of peasants revolted against the conscription efforts, and thousands died as officers and soldiers loyal to Mehmet Ali decimated the ranks of the mutineers. When these open rebellions failed, peasants resorted to maiming themselves by cutting off fingers and pouring poison in their eyes to induce temporary blindness. New methods of control against such rebellions involved the state issuing passports and certificates and stamping them when military service was completed.

The state also used force when such measures also failed, employing special guards and bedouin to patrol the routes around the military bases to keep peasants from escaping. Despite all these problems, Mehmet Ali built up an army of 130,000 troops within only a few years.

As the military grew and the economy expanded and required additional institutional support, the seeds of a new-style administration began to emerge. Peasants could not be conscripted into the new kind of military unless a state administration had the tools to count and capture them; the military could not buy weaponry and hire teachers without a proper treasury to collect taxes directly; and military tactics could not be incorporated into the new structure without knowledge of the

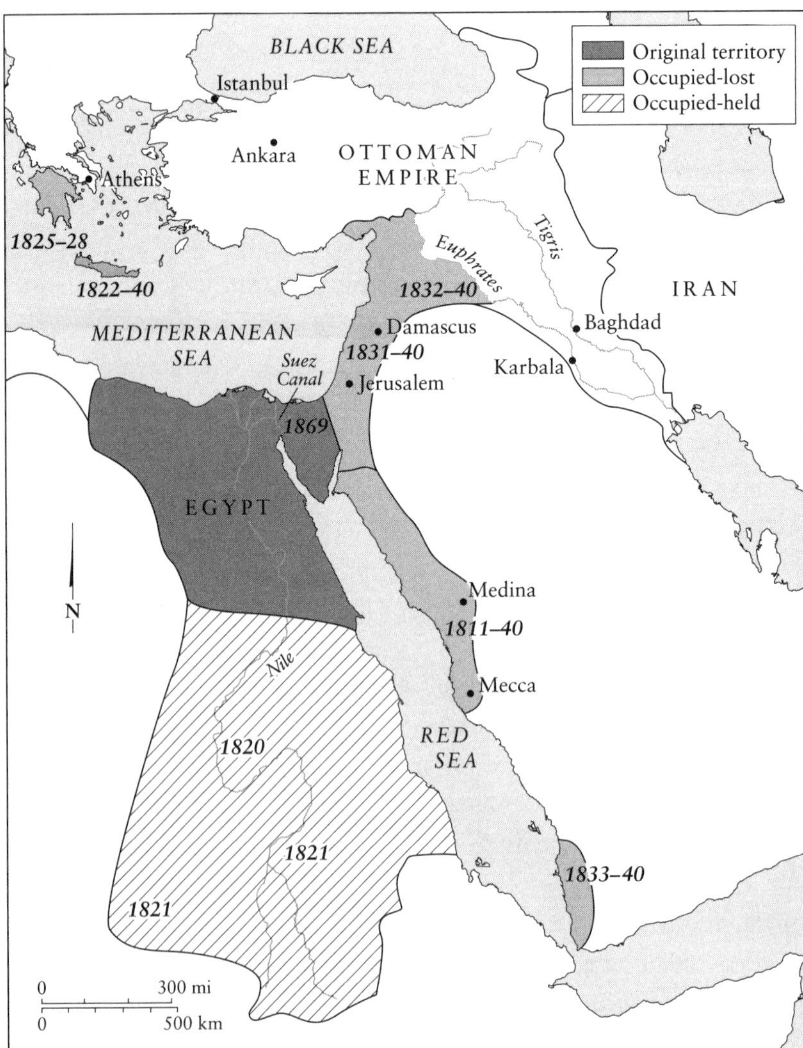

MAP 5. Territories Conquered by Mehmet Ali, 1811–1840. Mehmet Ali's military conquest of the Hijaz, the Sudan, Greece, and Syria and the track of the Suez Canal, opened in 1869.

languages used in European military manuals. Clearly, Mehmet Ali's plans did not depend merely on reforming the military forces in Egypt but also on adopting numerous western European administrative and educational institutions that could provide the needed infrastructure. Mehmet Ali went directly to the source: he hired European military officers, doctors, teachers, and administrators to bring their programs to Egypt, facilitating the further infiltration of western Europeans into the Middle East.

Mehmet Ali opened special departments for finance and for overseeing such agencies as the new navy and army. The state adapted madrasas to teach new curricula, opened primary and technical schools, and provided teachers' training, thus taking on tasks the ulama had monopolized in the past. For these new schools and new administrative positions, he attracted Egyptian Arabs who had been excluded from most realms of governance under the Ottomans and Mamluks but who had the skills necessary for assembling large numbers of people to work for the new projects. For example, Egyptian village shaykhs served as military recruiters because they knew the people in their regions and could mobilize local resources for the conscription effort. They gradually worked their way up the ranks of the state administration, gaining more benefits than they had ever accrued from Mamluk rule. In 1844, with the passage of a pension act, the civil service started to take on the attributes of a separate, professionalized state institution. At least as an ideal, promotion came through merit and retirement was tied to the period of time officials remained in office. By bringing Egyptian local elites into state agencies, Mehmet Ali's government began the process of tapping into the resources native Egyptians could offer the state.

Military Maneuvers

Building on these military, economic, and administrative changes, Mehmet Ali used his new army in warfare, both on behalf of the Ottoman sultan and in open rebellion against him. Generally, Mehmet Ali's army performed well when it fought against an army indigenous to the region, but it failed when presented with any combination of European armies and navies. For example, in 1818, his son Ibrahim finally defeated the Saudi-Wahhab alliance and regained Mecca and Medina for the Ottoman sultan. A more difficult task presented itself when the Greeks revolted against the Ottoman Empire in both the Danubian Provinces and the Peloponnese in 1821. The Ottoman army suppressed the former, but the latter continued

FIGURE 2.4. Mehmet Ali of Egypt interviews diplomats at his palace in Alexandria on May 12, 1839.

to grow in strength, despite strong military maneuvers by the sultan to end the Greek action.

As requested by the Ottoman sultan, Mehmet Ali sent his newly trained army and navy to the Peloponnese under the generalship of Ibrahim; after landing troops in 1825, Ibrahim was quickly en route to victory. But in 1827, Britain, France, and Russia chose to join forces in support of Greek independence, and the Europeans subsequently defeated the Egyptians and Ottomans at the Battle of Navarino in that same year, leading to the declaration of Greek independence in 1830 under European tutelage. This decision marked the moment when Britain and France joined Russia in actively shepherding the peoples of Greece and the Balkans into independence from the Ottoman Empire.

Rebellion against the Ottoman Empire

When defeat came at the hands of the Europeans, the sultan rescinded his previous offer to make Ibrahim a governor in Greece, and Ibrahim retaliated by taking control of Greater Syria, including present-day Syria, Lebanon, Jordan, and Israel-Palestine. Mehmet Ali and his son had an economic rationale for such an action because Syria represented both a market for Egypt's raw and manufactured goods and a source for foodstuffs for Egypt's markets. The Syria campaign to capture an economically viable province from the sultan was Mehmet Ali's only rebellion against the Ottoman Empire. He escalated his challenge to the sultan by having Ibrahim march his army from Syria into Anatolia. When the sultan recruited the Russians to move troops into the area for protection, Mehmet Ali chose to withdraw his army from Anatolia back to Syria, ending his most overt rebellion against the sultan. In the aftermath, the sultan recognized Ibrahim's position as governor over Greater Syria, a position he held between 1831 and 1840.

However, the sultan finally found a way to dislodge Mehmet Ali from his post in Syria through an alliance with the very Europeans he had just recently fought in Greece. The Europeans agreed to work with the Ottoman sultan because they considered Mehmet Ali a threat to their growing infiltration of the empire. In return for such aid, the Ottoman sultan signed a number of treaties with European powers trading in the empire that reduced import tariffs. The first was the Anglo-Ottoman Commercial Treaty in 1838 with Britain.

In summer 1840, the British bombarded Ibrahim's position from sea, and by October Ibrahim began his retreat. Soon thereafter Mehmet Ali accepted the terms of a European-Ottoman offer allowing him to become the hereditary governor of Egypt as long he limited his army to 18,000 men and agreed to pay Egypt's annual tribute to the sultan. The Ottomans and the British also forced him to sign the Anglo-Ottoman Commercial Treaty of 1838, which reduced import duties to 5 percent and ended Mehmet Ali's monopolies; even more of Mehmet Ali's factories shut down over the next few years.

Mehmet Ali ultimately lost his bid to control territory outside Egypt, but he did succeed in legitimizing his family's rule over everything inside Egypt's borders. He bequeathed to them a new kind of centralized state that enabled them to exploit revenues and mobilize the population in ways no Mamluk or Ottoman governor had ever succeeded in doing. Mehmet Ali's first successors—Ibrahim's son Abbas (r. 1848–1854) and his own son Sa'id (r. 1854–1863)—remained loyal Ottoman governors, albeit with more autonomous power than their counterparts in the other provinces. By the time of Isma'il (r. 1863–1879) a more independent polity began to form, epitomized by the shift from pasha as their official title to khedive (an Iranian term meaning "prince") in 1867.

Ottoman Military Reform and Balkan Independence

With Serbian autonomy granted in 1817 and in the midst of the Greek rebellion of the 1820s, Sultan Mehmet II (r. 1808–1839) and his closest advisers followed the military and administrative path of Mehmet Ali by reinstituting the reforms that had been cut short by Janissary opposition in the late 18th century. Sultan Mehmet II built up a new infantry regiment called the Trained Victorious Soldiers of Muhammad. He used it on June 17, 1826, in the "Auspicious Event," in which he abolished the Janissary corps, eliminating completely the biggest proven obstacle to the changes he wanted to launch. However, another war with Russia in 1828 erupted before the sultan could build a sufficiently powerful army in its place, and the Russians managed to advance through the two Danubian Provinces of Moldavia and Wallachia, where the war had begun, and past Edirne all the way to the outskirts of Istanbul. When it came time to negotiate the peace treaty, the Ottomans had little leverage so had to accept permanent Russian intervention in the Balkans. Under the terms of the Treaty of Adrianople (Edirne), Russia won the right to be the official protector of the two Danubian Provinces; these two later united as the autonomous state of Romania.

In an attempt to forestall further losses, in 1834 the Ottoman government expanded the new military-related schools that Sultan Selim III had opened in the late 18th century so officers could receive training from Prussian and French officers. A medical school had opened in 1826, and a school for surgeons, in 1831. For the rank and file, Sultan Mehmet II founded a reserve unit that recruited soldiers for weekly and yearly training sessions while allowing them to spend the remainder of the year at home on their farms and in their artisan shops. This reform increased the size of the military while maintaining the economic base throughout the empire.

In 1846, the state passed the first conscription law so the regular army could grow in size and provide for constant infusions of recruits. The law, however, exempted Islamic religious students and allowed non-Muslim subjects to pay a special tax to avoid military service, so the burden fell disproportionately on Muslim Anatolian and Balkan peasants. Like their Egyptian counterparts, the peasants being conscripted typically did whatever they could to avoid having to serve in the military. Despite these limitations, the post-1850 Ottoman army, along with its reserve force, was a dramatic improvement over those that had come before. The regular army amounted to about 125,000 well-trained soldiers, while another 350,000 were poorly trained reserves and irregulars.

To produce elite stakeholders for the reform program, the School for Military Science began instruction in 1837 and slowly graduated technically trained officers, the Mektepli (from the school). While they proved to be the staunchest supporters of the reforms overall during the course of the century, as of 1877 they amounted to only 1,600 officers. They faced numerous problems integrating into the army because they had no knowledge of or experience with actual combat conditions; they were experts instead in building fortifications, roads, bridges, and barracks. When the Mektepli were posted to combat regiments, they had little in common with the Alaylı officers (from the regiment) who had risen within the ranks, so proved ineffective in leadership. The Ottoman army also never created an effective administrative structure around the officers and soldiers that could produce detailed maps, plan the logistics around moving the empire's massive armies, and feed the soldiers. The officers on the line had to perform the tasks of the noncommissioned officers of other armies, keeping them from their combat duties and weakening the effectiveness of the army overall.

Crimean War and the Treaty of Paris

The one victory the Ottomans could claim with this new army in the 19th century was in the Crimean War (1853–1856), launched by the Russians when they demanded in 1853 that the Ottomans accept more Russian protection over the Orthodox Christians and the Christian Holy Places of the empire than the Treaty of Küçük Kaynarca of 1774 had granted. When the Ottoman sultan refused, war commenced between the two empires. But much of the Ottoman success came as a result of British and French intervention on its behalf. At the time of the cease-fire, the British, French, and Ottomans could claim a slight victory over the Russians but only after thousands died in warfare and more from disease.

In the Treaty of Paris, Russia returned the Ottoman land it had occupied in the Balkans during the course of the war; the signers agreed to a demilitarization of the Black Sea; and the European powers declared they would respect the territorial integrity of the Ottoman Empire. The last pledge, in particular, represented a significant Ottoman diplomatic victory. The Europeans had implicitly accepted this concept for a century, preferring a weak Ottoman Empire that all the powers could exploit to one in which one or more of the European powers could become dominant if the empire collapsed. The new treaty placed this pledge in writing; the Ottoman Empire, at least temporarily, retained control over key lands in the Balkans and along the shores of the Black Sea, backed by promises of security made by the British and French governments.

Balkan Crises and the Treaty of Berlin

This victory proved short-lived, however, because separatist movements in the Balkans continued to bring the Ottomans and Russians to war. With Bulgaria and Montenegro agitating for independence and bringing the Russians into new areas of the Balkans, another war broke out between 1877 and 1878. Without British and French aid this time, the Ottoman army lost to the Russians and had to accept the terms of the Treaty of Berlin, signed on July 13, 1878, which granted independence to Romania, Serbia, and Montenegro. The European powers divided Bulgaria into two provinces: the northern region became an autonomous tributary principality of the Ottomans, and the southern portion returned to Ottoman sovereignty as the semi-autonomous province of Eastern Rumelia. In 1885, the provinces united into one autonomous state of Bulgaria.

Russia acquired Ottoman territory in the Balkans and Eastern Anatolia, while Britain retained the island of Cyprus it had claimed just prior to the meeting in Berlin. The Austria-Hungary Empire earned the right to occupy Bosnia-Herzegovina. Overall, the Ottoman losses of 1878 amounted to almost two-fifths of the Ottoman landmass and one-

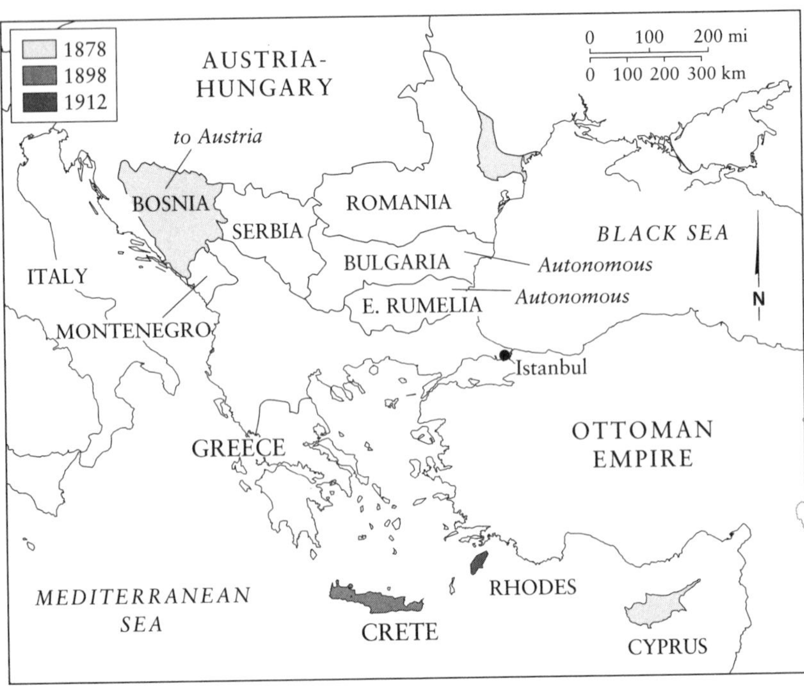

MAP 6. Ottoman Territorial Losses by 1878.

fifth of its subjects. In addition, the Treaty of Berlin nullified the promises of the 1856 treaty guaranteeing Ottoman sovereignty over its territory, providing avenues for increased infiltration by the European powers into Ottoman affairs. For example, the Ottoman government kept Macedonia, Albania, and Anatolia under its sovereign control but had to agree to institute reforms for the Christians living in those areas because of European pressure in this regard.

The losses in the Balkans disrupted the Ottoman Empire in innumerable ways. These provinces had supplied valuable resources to the Ottoman central treasury while serving as the most important postings for the officers newly trained and rising within the ranks of the army in the 19th century. Furthermore, the massacres that occurred in every battle for autonomy and independence in the Balkans killed hundreds of thousands of Muslims and Christians, forcing Muslim survivors to become refugees in Istanbul and many Christians to move from the empire into the new Balkan states. These events resulted in new identities for the combatants based on religion, language, and ethnicity that had never been elements of the Ottoman system before but now came out in bloody competitions for land and national identity.

Ottoman Tanzimat

The Ottoman sultans did not merely move to reform the military, the training of its officers, and the recruitment of its soldiers. The sultan and his allies in this reform effort wanted to direct revenues for institution building, train officials who could implement policies passed by the central administration, and codify law codes and regulations applicable across the breadth of the empire. The most influential officials advocating for the reforms came out of the Translation Bureau, which opened in 1821 to train replacements for the Greek translators who had traditionally worked with the Europeans and were now rebelling against the sultan. In addition to teaching the foreign languages necessary for an Ottoman Empire trying to introduce European institutions, the bureau trained the largest number of employees for the new Foreign Ministry, founded in 1834. This ministry housed the chief imperial diplomats, the initiators of most of the reforms passed throughout the century, and the authors of the primary Tanzimat documents and law codes. They based their reforms on the institutions they saw in Europe while stationed abroad. When they returned home, they enthusiastically lobbied to have the institutions replicated by the Ottoman government. Officials working within the Foreign Ministry as a result became the first and most influential of the administrative stakeholders for this model of modernity.

But all of their goals required the population to provide more services, in the form of conscription, corvée labor, and taxation, than the empire had ever envisioned. The approach chosen was to transform subjects into citizens and offer them rights in return for fulfilling a new list of obligations. Rather than the sultan working through intermediaries to project stability and just governance to the population, the state as a physical entity, with a standardized bureaucracy and newly trained military, would henceforth directly disseminate services and contract the necessary labor and financial resources. Authors of the new scheme saw in the reformed system a promise that the newly reformed state was not geared solely to enhancing the wealth and power of leaders but also to advancing the larger projects of its citizenry. It would also legalize the means by which non-Muslim communities could be transitioned out of the millet system and into citizenship in the state alongside Muslims. Falling into the new category of minorities, they would be given legal protections against discrimination by the state.

The process that came to be known as the Tanzimat (reorganization) began with the sultan's issuance of the Hatt-ı Şerif of Gülhane (Rose Chamber Edict, 1839) and Hatt-ı Hümayun (1856) regulating relations between government and its subjects. No longer would the millet system differentiate subjects based on religious affiliation; by law, all citizens would have the same rights and responsibilities toward the state. The documents abolished capital punishment without trial; guaranteed justice for all with respect to honor, life, and property; and set up mixed tribunals for Muslims and non-Muslims. They laid out the state's desire to eliminate tax farms in favor of direct taxation and called for military conscription of all citizens, irrespective of religion and for designated periods of time. According to these documents, all citizens had the potential to be trained through the new kinds of schools and military academies and become members of the new governing institutions. Concomitantly, all citizens owed new duties to the sultan. The foreign origins of the elite administrators went the way of the Janissaries; in order to bring citizens into the project of defending and enriching the state, the state in turn had to provide them services and social mobility within the governmental structure.

Law Code

Reinforcing these documents was an effort to codify a system of law that would help standardize legal adjudication throughout the empire and equalize the citizenry's legal status. Ottoman sultans had always adjudicated laws through imperial decree, and in the 16th century, Süleyman the Lawgiver codified these laws into the kanunname (book of law). These laws were all accredited by the shari'a, but the practice of imperial decrees granted the sultans much legal leeway to work outside the realm of clerical control. Completed in 1876, the new civil code, the Mecelle, technically fell under the purview of Islamic law, but most of its provisions were secularly oriented and copied from Europe. This new law slowly replaced the systems of laws that had developed during the centuries throughout all the provinces, organizing yet another element of Ottoman governance of the subjects.

In the transition taking place in the legal codes in the 19th century, personal status laws—marriage, divorce, custody, and inheritance—remained under the purview of the different religious laws recognized in the empire. However, any conflict in the public realm or between people from different religious groups came under the jurisdiction of this new Ottoman law code and was enforced by state officials. In implementing the Mecelle, the sultans turned to judges and lawyers trained in the new schools, not to the ulama and non-Muslim religious leaders who had monopolized the law for centuries. As a result, this process weakened religious figures by taking away an element of their authority over their co-religionists.

Land Code

The Land Code of 1858 revolutionized the legal definition of property, allowed for new taxation systems to be established, and encouraged the transition from subsistence agriculture. Up until this point, the sultan technically owned all the land of the empire by right of conquest; everyone else had the right to perform some function on that land. Different categories of land existed under this wide rubric, with much of it allotted to public use; small gardens, homesteads, and private groves could be held as private land. The vast majority of agricultural land, especially for vital goods such as wheat, was categorized as public land that Ottoman subjects had the right to cultivate or collect its revenue. Small farms, the çift-hanes, remained the dominant land-use structure. Over time peasants on these small farms had acquired rights that included allowances for bequeathing their cultivation rights to their heirs even though they did not technically own the land as private property.

In the 1858 code, the state designated individuals as the only entities with the right to own land; thus, the sultan agreed to transfer ownership of public lands to tax farmers, merchants, and peasants who were already farming and overseeing the land throughout the empire. Conflicts over land use and landownership also came under the authority of the central administration rather than being adjudicated through personalized ad hoc procedures in the provinces. By the end of the 19th century, the old distinctions between public and private lands had largely disappeared as peasants and large estate holders used their land as private property and as the Ottoman government passed laws recognizing this shift. In places like Jordan and Anatolia, the law aided small landowners who registered their property; in Palestine and Syria, wealthy merchants and tax farmers registered estates in their own names, becoming a new class of large landowners in much the same way that Mehmet Ali's allies and family were doing in Egypt.

The sultan and his government also envisioned this law as a tactic for more efficiently registering the land and assessing its taxes, not only for the produce grown but in the overall value of the land. Commercial agriculture was spreading rapidly throughout the empire, and the new legal code and accompanying tax scheme were designed to collect taxes on the revenue now being generated. The new rules promulgated from 1858 forward were designed to protect the security of tenure over the land so that additional profits could be eked out of it and then taxed by the state. A concomitant goal was the transfer of tax-collection processes from tax farmers to the central administration. However, throughout the 19th century tax farmers retained their dominant role in tax collection despite many efforts to prevent it, although the Ottoman state did collect more taxes and had more control over the tax farmers themselves.

Constitution

The last of the Tanzimat documents laid out the design for a participatory government, putting into institutional form the promises of liberty and equality articulated in the earlier documents. Promulgated by Sultan Abdülhamit II (r. 1876–1909) on December 23, 1876, the constitution was issued during the buildup to the 1877–1878 Russo-Ottoman war. It called for the creation of a bicameral legislature with an elected Chamber of Deputies and an appointed Senate. Although Islam was declared the religion of the state, the constitution reiterated the guarantee that all citizens were equal before the law regardless of religious affiliation. While retaining many of the liberal elements of its 1831 Belgian

FIGURE 2.5. Sultan Abdülhamit II visiting Balmoral Castle, Scotland, in 1867, before he ascended the Ottoman throne in 1876.

model, the finished product placed a great deal of power in the hands of the sultan, thus transforming an initially liberal document into a more conservative and authoritarian one. Sultans had the right to declare war, appoint and dismiss ministers, approve legislation, and convene and dismiss the Chamber of Deputies, making the executive branch far more powerful than its legislative counterpart. Furthermore, political parties were not allowed to form, cutting off yet another avenue for popular participation.

Per the provisions of the 1876 constitution, the first parliament convened on March 19, 1877, but it sat for only two sessions over the next year as war raged with Russia and in the Balkans. Sultan Abdülhamit II used the crisis in 1878 to dissolve parliament and prorogue the constitution on February 13, 1878. He ruled without this constitution or a parliamentary structure at all until forced to do so in the last year of his reign. In the intervening decades, Sultan Abdülhamit II presided over a governmental system that suppressed any attempt at opposition through an elaborate empirewide spy network. He also imposed heavy press censorship and arrested thousands who opposed his policies; many others fled to Europe or Egypt to avoid his attacks. Furthermore, his governing ethos privileged Muslim over Christian as he looked to strengthen the empire by highlighting its pan-Islamic qualities.

Conflicts were built into these documents from the very beginning, and the problems they created reverberated for decades. The Ottoman leadership cadres issuing the Tanzimat documents envisioned the reforms bringing the Ottoman state in line with western European governments and hoped that the Europeans, as a result of the changes, would invite the Ottomans to be an equal partner in determining the future of Europe and the Middle East. However, as the 19th century amply illustrated, the Europeans had designs on the empire's land and resources. The Tanzimat, instead of altering the balance of power in the Ottoman favor, tilted it even more strongly toward the Europeans in terms of their militaries, economic needs, and bankers.

Internally, the reformers wanted to bring the sultan's subjects under closer control of the central government, including the rebellious Christians of the Balkans. However, the rebellions in the Balkans moved enormous numbers of Christians outside Ottoman control while also creating and exacerbating conflicts between Christians and Muslims. Massacres between the two religious communities accompanied all the rebellions of the 19th century, followed by massive population transfers so the new

Balkan states could be as religiously homogeneous as possible. After the Treaty of Berlin of 1878, Muslims accounted for 73.3 percent of the total population of the empire.

The Christian audience for the Tanzimat promises diminished continually throughout the century, leaving only Armenian, Arab, and Macedonian Christians and those Greeks who chose not to move to the new state of Greece. And they fell into a problematic position in the empire because the European signers declared in the Treaty of Berlin of 1878 that they had the right and duty to protect these "minorities" of the Ottoman Empire. This designation for the Christians came with little tangible aid but made Ottoman leadership suspicious that the remaining Christians were further conduits for European infiltration against Ottoman sovereignty. From the Ottoman governmental perspective, the bulk of the Balkans had gained its independence primarily because of direct European aid; those Christians left behind in Ottoman territories could represent the vanguard for the next stage of European attacks.

Authoritarianism

The promise of equality before the law could be read as an inclusive Ottomanism that allowed all the empire's citizens to be part of the new project being undertaken. The state would ask more of its citizens and in return would grant them the right to vote, to express their opinions freely, to follow their religious practices without discrimination, and to obtain new kinds of jobs. However, Ottoman state leaders in the 19th century did not interpret Ottomanism as the mobilization of a politicized and engaged citizenry; to them it meant achieving the twin goals of centralization and standardization. They focused more on the enhanced extraction of economic resources and the conscription of people's labor services so they could prevail against the European powers. In 1876, when the sultan prorogued the constitution and dissolved the parliament, the authoritarian element of the Tanzimat documents came to the fore and allowed little room for most citizens to participate in any meaningful way in imperial governance. As had been the case since the first of the Tanzimat documents were issued, a small oligarchy of officials made the decisions, encircled around Sultan Abdülhamit II, who controlled them all.

Administration in the Ottoman Empire

To more efficiently catalogue, collect, and draft resources and labor, the Ottoman Empire professionalized and standardized administrative practices so that individual ministries handled specific tasks and recognizable hierarchies supervised the implementation of policies from the capital to the provinces. To take charge of waqf and weaken the ulama in another of its traditional realms, the state established the Ministry of Imperial Pious Foundations in 1826, the Ministry of Civil Affairs in 1835, and the Ministry of Finance in 1837.

FIGURE 2.6. Studio portrait, 1896, of a well-dressed Arab gentleman adorned with a fez.

Education of Civil Servants

In order for the Ottoman state to be able to employ civil servants capable of administering these laws, lands, and ministries in the newly introduced ways, the government allotted extensive resources to building primary and secondary schools as well as technical academies. The state established a Council of Education in 1845 and a Ministry of Education in 1857, followed by the promulgation of education laws in 1858 and 1869 throughout the territories. The goal of these institutions and laws was to gain state control over all educational institutions—state, private, and foreign missionary—to guarantee that the curricula across all the schools taught the skills necessary for new state offices while also instilling in students obedience to the Ottoman state. The moves also diminished the influence of the ulama who had previously monopolized Muslim schooling throughout the empire.

The three-tiered Ottoman educational structure mostly followed the French model. The rüştiye schools served as primary schools in villages and towns, idadiye were secondary schools in the larger towns and cities, and sultaniye were colleges opened in the provincial capitals. The premier secondary school, the Galatasaray Lycée in Istanbul, opened in 1868; its curriculum followed the French lycée system, with courses on natural sciences, law, philosophy, and classical European languages taught in French; religion, Islamic and Ottoman history, Arabic, Persian, Ottoman Turkish; and literature, geography, and calligraphy taught in Turkish or the languages under study. In 1909, the Imperial Civil Service School became a special university faculty. Since its founding in 1859, it had stood at the apex of the pyramid of administrative education with its primary goal to instill in its students the sacredness of their duty to the state. These schools produced educated stakeholders who applied their expertise in professional state positions. As the 19th century dawned, the Ottoman government employed 2,000 officials; at the beginning of the 20th, it employed between 35,000 and 50,000.

Young men became acculturated in the new schools and then entered the civil service, for it was one of the few career venues available to those with such a new and unique style of education; the remainder served as the core of the independent professional stratum of doctors, lawyers, and journalists. Collectively, they formed a new professional middle class that dressed differently from most of the population and used their new skills in new kinds of professions. The frock coat and fez became the uniform of choice as this new class strove to define itself by Western standards. The members used the burgeoning newspaper realm to debate political philosophies, science, and the attributes of modernity they considered most beneficial for strengthening Ottoman society, governance, and military might. They were stakeholders in both the actual reforms being implemented in their countries and in the idea of adopting Western institutions and ideas as a means for attaining the modernity that western Europe and, over time, America epitomized.

Entrenched Elite

After he dissolved parliament in 1878, Sultan Abdülhamit II created conflicts with this new class by privileging older elites in his administrative offices and keeping the newly educated out of positions of power. He gifted those in highest positions with ranks, decorations, and extravagant gifts while emphasizing that they were responsible to him alone rather to any state institution. The sultan followed a similar policy in appointing officers to military positions. He gave preference to Alaylı officers, on whose loyalty he could depend, and bypassed the Mektepli officers because he viewed them as potential rebels against his monopoly over appointments and decision making. The maintenance of the oligarchy around the sultan created disjunctions between those who held power and those trained in the new schools. Since the top positions remained in the hands of the sultan's allies, graduates could at best fill the lower ranks of the bureaucracy. As a result, the sultan was in fact molding an opposition force to his rule.

This tug-of-war between Ottoman authoritarianism and inclusiveness continued until the outbreak of World War I in 1914. Christians and Muslims alike demanded a diversity of voices in governmental decision making and a great deal of political autonomy for the many groups living within the provinces. By the last quarter of the 19th century, thousands of citizens had worked their way through the schools and the military academies to rise up within the ranks of their fields. They opposed the power held by the sultan and his favored officials because they believed the new class of civil servants was better suited to preside over the institution of further reforms.

Their training had made them stakeholders in the process of Westernized modernity that had defined the Tanzimat from the beginning. They bemoaned the glass ceiling that kept them from using their new skills to defend and strengthen their societal, military, and governmental institutions. The 1876 constitution became a rallying point for Muslims and Christians among the newly trained who saw in its tenets the way to equitably incorporate all the groups living under Ottoman sovereignty and continue the process of Westernized modernization. This was an inclusive Ottomanism in contrast to the authoritarianism presided over by Sultan Abdülhamit II.

Debt and European Control and Colonization

The Egyptian and Ottoman governments struggled with reorganizing their economies so they could more effectively harness economic production for their new state projects, but they suffered from a lack of natural resources, poor internal demand for manufactured goods, and weak monetary policies. European agreements like the Capitulation treaties and the Anglo-Ottoman Commercial Treaty made it difficult to post high tariffs and control monopolies over goods grown and produced within their borders. Mehmet Ali reorganized the economy to divert cash crop revenues and taxes to his state treasury, but the agreements making him the hereditary governor of Egypt forced him to shut down the monopolies that had proved so lucrative for a time. In the 1860s, faced with decreasing revenues from his cash crops and factories, his successors had to take out European loans to maintain their state structures and build the Suez Canal. The Ottoman government never succeeded in harnessing all

FIGURE 2.7. Interior of the Imperial Fez Factory, Istanbul, ca. 1880–1890.

the economic resources available within its borders, so it, too, had to take out loans to pay for the new army and the administrative institutions. By the last quarter of the 19th century, both governments were in debt and forced to cede governmental authority to their European creditors.

Ottoman Economic Challenges

The Ottoman leadership initiated many of the same programs as Mehmet Ali but found that the size and diversity of the empire negated the ability to truly centralize administrative and economic structures. In the 1830s and 1840s, Sultan Mehmet II tried to establish monopolies over such products as opium, silk, and cotton, but instead of bringing more revenues into the central treasury as Mehmet Ali had done, these measures encouraged black market smuggling to bypass state controls. Furthermore, the costs of waging almost constant warfare throughout the 19th century intensified financial demands on the Ottoman state and took valuable resources from potentially lucrative industries. The Tanzimat years saw more taxes remitted to the central treasury, but because agricultural yields were low, the net gain was not sufficient for paying the government's bills. Ottoman manufacturers continued to have their products taxed as their merchandise circulated throughout the empire; European manufacturers paid a tax only when their merchandise entered the empire. All these situations siphoned funds away from Istanbul or made it impossible to collect new revenues.

The Ottoman state invested in many industries, particularly textiles, in the late 18th and 19th centuries, but most manufacturers could not compete with European imports. To help alleviate these problems, the state instituted the first protectionist economic policies by raising customs tariffs from 5 to 8 percent in 1861 and granting new domestic factories 15-year tax exemptions starting in 1873. The Ottoman Empire thus saw a small industrial surge in the 1870s, but it did not by any means bring the empire in league with western Europe or substantially change the economic base of the country.

In the late 18th and early 19th centuries, the Ottoman sultan had taken out loans from internal sources—primarily from provincial leaders, ulama, and Greek Phanariot and Armenian Amira bankers—but these measures proved insufficient for the larger projects of the Tanzimat. To put more money into circulation, the Ottomans tried different strategies for moving more completely to a cash economy, such as demanding that taxes be paid in cash, but these efforts also failed. In another tactic, the state tried to issue paper currency in 1840 and 1850 but had to abandon these attempts when few people accepted the currency's legitimacy. Inflation rose for much of the century; in response the state resorted to debasing the currency on a number of occasions. By the middle of the 19th century, the coinage had been debased so often that coins with similar surface values contained different amounts of gold and silver, making it difficult to establish a stable currency for international trade.

When all these measures failed and while war raged in the Crimea, between 1853 and 1856 the Ottoman government took out the first loan from a European bank. In the following 27 years, the Ottoman state signed 15 loan agreements with other banks. Not only was the sheer number of loans indicative of the weak position of the Ottoman economy, but the loan terms themselves exacerbated the problems. The European loans came with low interest rates, but because of exorbitant fees and commissions collected prior to the money being dispersed to the Ottoman government, the state often received only about 50 percent of

FIGURE 2.8. Ships docked at Port Said, on the northern end of the Suez Canal, just one year after it opened in 1869.

the amount technically borrowed. Nonetheless, the entire amount of the loan had to be paid back.

In 1875, the empire declared bankruptcy; by that point 60 percent of the state's total revenues were servicing the debt. In 1881, European banks established the Ottoman Public Debt Administration (OPDA) with representatives from all major European creditors on the board, authorized to collect state revenues and use them to pay interest on the debt; these payments had priority over all other Ottoman expenditures. The OPDA supervised a quarter of all revenues brought into state coffers and even grew larger than the Ottoman Finance Ministry, eventually functioning as a state within a state because it held so much independent power.

Egyptian Economic Challenges

The Egyptian government might have held off the European bankers if not for the expenses accrued in building the Suez Canal; in the aftermath, Egypt found itself incapable of getting out of debt. Under Sa'id's rule (r. 1854–1863), French engineer Ferdinand de Lesseps negotiated the agreement for building the canal. He agreed to finance a little over half of the costs by selling shares in the Suez Canal Company to individual investors in Europe; Sa'id arranged for the Egyptian government to pay for and own the remaining part of the company. In the first part of the digging process, he had little trouble fronting the money needed because the US Civil War (1861–1865) curtailed the amount of cotton available on the world market. The result was a spike in prices because of the demand for Egyptian cotton. When the Civil War ended, prices plummeted with the flood of American cotton reaching the market. Furthermore, building the canal necessitated huge numbers of corvée laborers from the Egyptian peasantry. Approximately 60,000 Egyptian workers at a time, working in 20,000-man shifts, dug the canal. Tens of thousands died because of the horrific working conditions, and the loss to the Egyptian economy was equally enormous. Even those who lived through the ordeal were taken off their land for months at a time; a diminished number of crops could be grown given the dearth of workers available. By the time the canal opened to great fanfare in 1869, Egypt was heading toward bankruptcy.

The institutions remaining after Mehmet Ali's death also cost money to maintain, and the Egyptian economy rarely supplied enough resources even before the canal's costs began to escalate. Khedive Isma'il (r. 1863–1879) invested great resources into building and improving irrigation

FIGURE 2.9. Ship navigating the Suez Canal, ca. 1880.

canals, roads, harbors, and bridges, all of which required a heavy influx of cash. He also expanded the state educational structure and opened a national library. The state carried heavy annual expenses, while the prohibition on tariff duties and monopolies made it difficult for domestic goods to compete with inexpensive European industrial products, especially considering how many factories had been closed in the 1840s.

As a quick fix, the 1871 Exchange Law reduced taxes of the largest landowners as long as they agreed to pay six-years'-worth of taxes ahead of time. That act brought in an infusion of cash in the first year but weakened the government's leverage over the landowners over the long term. Khedive Isma'il tried to offset the combined losses from the canal and limitations in the economy by raising taxes on the peasants. As a result, peasants paid 75 percent more taxes in 1868 than in 1865. In 1875, Khedive Isma'il took the drastic step of selling the Egyptian government's 44 percent share in the Suez Canal Company to the British government, temporarily alleviating some of Egypt's debts but failing to improve its long-term ability to maintain its institutions. As a whole, none of these tactics succeeded in establishing long-term revenues sufficient for paying the Egyptian government's expenses.

When all these measures failed, the Egyptian government declared bankruptcy, and the European countries holding Egypt's loans formed the Debt Administration in 1876 to oversee repayment. Although banks in a number of European countries had supplied loans, the largest were provided by those in Britain and France. Egypt's Debt Administration came to be colloquially known as a system run by Dual Control. Technically, the khedive appointed the controllers from both countries, but in reality they were independent, supervising Egyptian state revenue and expenditure and gradually extending their hold over the treasury itself. From this position of strength, the controllers frequently used pressure against the khedive concerning cabinet appointments, and when Khedive Isma'il grew vocally critical of Dual Control, the controllers forced him from power in 1879 and replaced him with the far more pliable Tawfiq (r. 1879–1892). Economic intervention into Egypt had thereby translated into direct political power over governmental processes. No European country had physically taken control over Egypt by that point, but economic power served much the same purpose. In 1882, the British colonized Egypt and introduced what came to be called a "Veiled Protectorate," with British officials overseeing a local Egyptian government.

During the same period, European colonists conquered North Africa, with the French taking Algeria in 1830, Tunisia in 1881, and parts of Morocco in 1912. Italy started its conquest of Libya in 1911. These actions involved military conquest, followed by installation of a colonial administration to rule over the territories. The British had already established protectorates in Aden, Kuwait, and the Persian Gulf Emirates during the 18th century that served as naval bases protecting British shipping throughout the region. The Ottomans had no means to stop any of these losses because the reforms in the military had not produced the kind of disciplined officer corps and soldiery that could defeat the European powers. Debt to the Europeans curtailed Ottoman sovereignty; wars in the Balkans broke away lucrative provinces.

Qajar Iran

The Qajars were a Turkic nomadic tribe that moved into the Iranian region in the 13th century and allied themselves with the Safavids as part of the Qizilbash confederation. During the 18th-century breakdown in

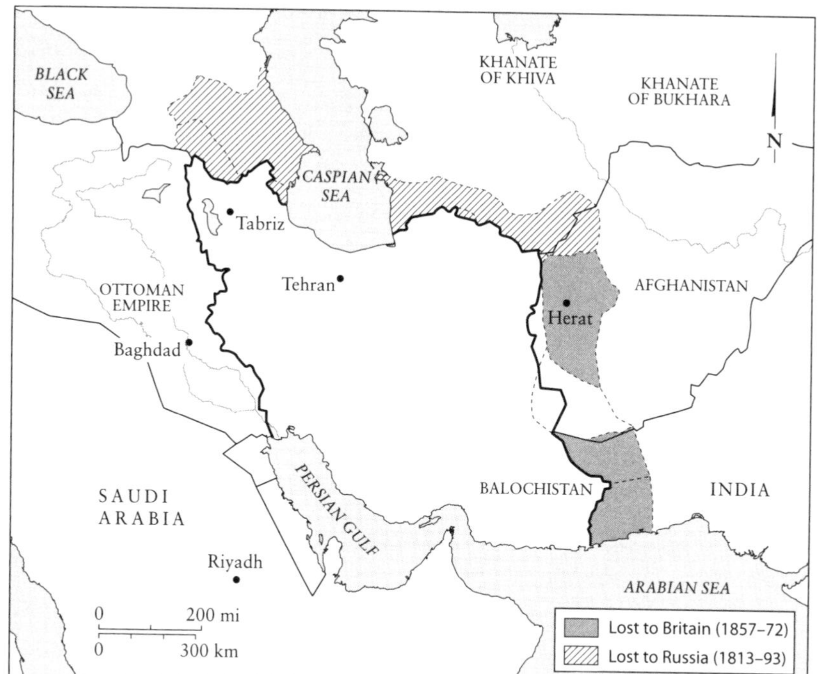

MAP 7. Qajar Territorial Losses, 19th Century.

central control within Iran, the Qajars battled for power, among factions within their own tribe, and against others controlling regions throughout the country. The Qajars began to come out ahead in this contest by the end of the 18th century when Agha Mohammad Khan (r. 1794–1797) led the tribe to victory, choosing to take the Safavid crown of Iran in 1796 when the country had been fully subdued. Agha Mohammad Khan, however, had little interest in shifting to settled governance after decades of military activity, and his governing system remained largely dependent on his nomadic tribesmen. His successors, Fath 'Ali Shah (r. 1797–1834), Muhammad Shah (r. 1834–1848), and Naser al-Din Shah (r. 1848–1896), took on the task of reestablishing a centralized, settled system for taking control of the country, its resources, and its people.

The Qajars followed the lead of the Ottomans in instituting reforms involving the military, administration, and education system during the 19th century, but they continued to struggle against the fragmentation that had marked recent Iranian history. The Qajar monarch centralized governance in ways Iran had not seen since the peak years of Safavid rule, but at no point could the Qajar state truly harness the financial and human resources of the country to build a strong military, control the court systems, or transform the educational system. Each successive shah and chief minister sought to curtail the independent power of the tribes, ulama, provincial governors, and royal princes (mirza), but entire sections of the country remained geographically outside effective Qajar authority, and entire segments of revenue remained under the aegis of independent groups. Under these pressures, their reforms never built up sufficient numbers of stakeholders to sustain the project.

Independence of the Ulama

Unlike the situation in the Ottoman regions, the ulama continued to maintain their economic independence from the state and close to a monopoly over its legal functions. During the various 19th-century reforms, the Qajar government tried to have shah-controlled ʻurf (common law) courts supervise the activities of the shariʻa courts, but its efforts never succeeded for any substantial periods of time. Strong shahs and chief ministers could, periodically, weaken the shariʻa courts but could never completely subsume them under state control. A key problem was that Iran had not, in the preceding centuries, instituted any kind of codified law, as Sultan Süleyman (the Lawgiver) had done in the Ottoman Empire. The demarcations between ʻurf and shariʻa had also never been set, so the Qajar 19th-century reform efforts led to a legal morass rather than submission of the ulama to Qajar legal jurisdiction.

In the 18th and 19th centuries, a number of Iranian clerics moved to the shrine cities of Najaf and Karbala in southern Iraq, fleeing the instability that accompanied the fall of the Safavid Empire to the Afghans and then the quest for power by the Qajars. Karbala, the location of the shrine to ʻAli's son Hussein, served as the most important religious post at first; that honor shifted to Najaf in the 1840s. In Najaf stands the shrine to ʻAli, the only caliph the Shiʻi recognize from the Rashidun era (632–661). By the turn of the 20th century, Najaf had 20 religious schools, and the most important of the Shiʻi mujtahids had established their centers there. Najaf also became an important conduit for the conversion of Arab tribes in the area to Shiʻism.

Although living outside Iranian jurisdiction, these mujtahids continued to maintain extensive influence among their countrymen. In particular, it was in southern Iraq that the Shiʻi mujtahids came to articulate the active political role for themselves that would eventually present challenges to Qajar sovereignty. In these cities, a theological debate erupted between the so-called Akhbari ulama who abjured political activity and the Usuli ulama who desired a more active political profile for religious clerics. Many of the latter were Iranian, and as they came to overshadow the influence of the Arab Shi'i clerics in these cities, their activist definition of Shi'ism came to the fore. They took charge of most of the religious endowments in the two cities, which augmented their influence and compensated for the fact that Iranians remained a small minority among the Shi'i believers in southern Iraq. These Iranian mujtahids acquired mass followings of devoted Shi'a from within Iran who revered their charismatic qualities and extensive knowledge of Islam. Throughout the century they served as important critics of the shahs' policies, especially of the Westernizing reforms that attempted to weaken the clerics' hold over society, and of the shahs' economic schemes, which privileged European over Iranian merchants.

Privileges of the Princes

Another powerful group pushing against centralization and reform were the many Qajar princes (mirza) who held privileges such as amnesty from taxation and access to politically influential positions. To give some idea of the numbers, Fath 'Ali Shah had 170 children, most of whom he married off into politically connected families. The extended Qajar family embedded themselves in all regions of the country and branches of government because their position at the head of the state provided them with the most largesse to distribute to their clients. Their positions around the country made many people beholden to a continuation of Qajar rule but also fragmented power to the various provinces where princes ruled autonomously during most of the century. As occurred with the Ottoman family, no group or coalition of forces in Iran questioned the legitimacy of Qajar rule; instead, they fought for autonomy over their realms and against any Qajar shah or official who sought to weaken their privileges.

Autonomy of Tribes

The tribes also remained independently strong in relation to the state because they kept most of their resources in their individual provinces and worked against the state to make sure it did not impinge on any of their rights. In the 1810s, the shah raised money by granting tribal leaders extensive rights to collect taxes in return for their military support in any wars against Iran. Thus, tribal leaders' lands became virtually hereditary and often out of the control of government tax assessors. Taxes on land where the state could collect the revenues remained excessively high throughout the 19th century and disadvantaged those who did not have state-granted privileges. Over time, the tribal militias existed solely to protect their territories from state intervention, not to defend the state from outside invasion.

Growth of Landowners

In the second half of the 19th century, Qajar princes, tribal shaykhs, merchants, and ulama all bought and registered lands in their names, making the vast majority of the peasantry landless sharecroppers and tenant farmers. On these large holdings, the owners collected taxes and kept as much of the revenue in their own regions and provinces as possible, passing little on to the central government in most years because the state meted out few punishments. Given this situation, peasants faced the brunt of high tax rates throughout the century. Large landowners also shifted great swaths of land to cash crops so they could sell cotton and opium to European merchants; these crops required extensive amounts of water,

THE GREAT GAME

The term "Great Game" was probably coined by a British officer in the aftermath of the First Anglo-Afghan War of 1839–1842, but its most famous enunciation came in Rudyard Kipling's *Kim* (1901). In the novel, Kim becomes embroiled in a British plan to keep the Russians from infiltrating India. The Russians had made plans for such an incursion in 1800, when Czar Paul I (r. 1754–1801) amassed troops in an alliance with Napoleon of France. The enterprise was aborted when Russian conspirators assassinated the czar in 1801. The Russians never again sought to force the British from India, but the Great Game was afoot, to use Kipling's terminology.

For the next century, Russia and Britain competed for military, diplomatic, and economic control over the Ottoman and Qajar Empires and areas of Central Asia such as Uzbekistan and Afghanistan. Britain's primary goal was to safeguard India; the Russians sought to gain territories along the Black and Caspian Seas. During the 19th century, Russia won control of substantial territories along the northern borders of the Ottoman and Qajar Empires and aided the Balkan states in gaining their independence from the Ottomans. The British fought wars such as those in Afghanistan and the Crimea but focused on increasing their influence over Ottoman and Qajar financial matters. In the process, both sides weakened the countries of the Middle East and Central Asia by instigating civil unrest and economic hardship.

The Great Game could be said to have ended with the signing of the Anglo-Russian Convention of 1907 concerning Iran, Afghanistan, and Tibet. This arrangement worked out respective spheres of influence in these areas. An alternative argument claims that the Great Game has never ended but just shifted players, as the United States and the Soviet Union took the place of Britain and Russia after World War II.

so only those with cash for irrigation projects could undertake their cultivation. In trying to keep up with these obligations, peasants were continually indebted to landowners and moneylenders who could supply sufficient cash for their upkeep.

British and Russian Pressure

From the 17th century forward, the Russians moved steadily south toward the Caspian Sea and Persian Gulf, and the British worked to guarantee that their colonial control over India remained secure. Afghanistan and Iran served as the primary playing fields for what came to be called the Great Game: Britain and Russia used trade agreements and military force to dominate the local powers and weaken each other's strategic position in these countries.

The various Capitulation treaties Iran signed with Britain and Russia increased the volume of Iran's international trade eight times during the course of the century, enriching those merchants who arranged trading contacts with the Europeans. Adaptations to manufacturing processing also occurred that allowed traditional merchants access to the world market. For example, the famous Persian carpets increased as a percentage of exports, but the higher volume resulted in large part because many of the weavers adapted to Western tastes. They also incorporated cheaper dyes and processes into the production process so they could better compete with carpets manufactured elsewhere in the world. Otherwise, Russian and British merchants handled most of the import-export trade going through their respective spheres of influence in the north and the south, and local middlemen emerged who facilitated the transfer of European and Iranian goods. A group largely disadvantaged by these changes were the bazaaris—local artisans and merchants working in the cities' marketplaces, or suqs—who were cut out of many of their traditional trading niches when they could not adapt their products to world tastes or reduce costs in order to price their products competitively.

Reform in Qajar Iran

As these players jockeyed to increase or retain their autonomous positions in Iranian society and politics, the Qajar shahs and their chief advisers attempted to bring Western-style institutions of governance on the model of the Ottoman Empire. While many of the same kinds of programs were begun in Iran, most reformers lost their positions long before their reforms had a chance to take effect because Iran's autonomous

FIGURE 2.10. Naser al-Din Shah standing at the foot of the bronze statue honoring him in Tehran, next to his son, Kamran Mirza.

players worked to oppose the reforms. Despite these obstacles, a small number of Iranians earned places in the new schools and upon graduation received jobs in the newly expanded bureaucracy. The reforms, however, were not substantial, sustained, or effective enough overall to create a social stratum that could pressure the government to transform society at all levels as had occurred in Ottoman and Egyptian territories. Thus, stakeholders in the reform program became another group growing in opposition to the shah's government; in this case, they were not working for more autonomy but for the expansion of the reform program.

Military Institutions

An aborted effort to construct a New Order Army in the early decades of the 19th century was reinvigorated when Naser al-Din Shah (r. 1848–1896) came to the throne and appointed Amir Kabir (the Great Lord) as lord of the army and prime minister tasked with overseeing reforms throughout the government. The catalysts for this effort were the military defeats to Russia that resulted in loss of territory in the Treaties of Gulistan (1813) and Turkmanchai (1828). Following in the footsteps of the Ottoman Empire, where he had served for a time in the Iranian diplomatic corps, Amir Kabir built a modern standing army, eventually enlarging it to over 137,000 men, more than 94,000 of whom were in the infantry. He opened 15 army supply factories and established the first official newspaper. The Dar al-Funun (House of the Arts), a school for the elites, offered a modern, Western education, modeled after the French polytechnic program. But his efforts engendered opposition from provincial notables when he called for raising taxes to pay for the new army and its associated institutions. He was forced from office in 1851 and executed soon thereafter.

Without any wars to fight after a defeat to Britain in Afghanistan in 1857, military leaders pocketed much of the pay that was supposed to be spent on their soldiers. Only in 1879 did the newly formed Cossack Brigade come to serve as the cornerstone of a modern army loyal to the Qajars. Officered and funded by Russians, the Cossack Brigade not only protected the shah and his government but also played a role in defending Russian interests throughout the country. But it comprised only 2,000 men at the dawn of the 20th century, so it did not have the ability to defend the entire country from outsiders, nor did it have the power to break down the autonomy of the many tribal militias existing in the provinces. Furthermore, few of the military-related factories built in midcentury remained open because of lack of commitment by the government and the poor road networks that existed for transporting men and materials.

Educational System

Except for Dar al-Funun and a few other schools that opened under state auspices, school expansion took place largely through the work of foreign missionaries. The Lazarist Catholic Mission, Alliance Française, and Alliance Israélite Universelle all opened schools during the 19th century; in the second half of the century, a French Catholic order opened girls' schools in four cities, including Tehran. American Protestants began opening schools for both boys and girls in the 1830s and steadily increased the number and quality of the schools during the course of the century. Christians and Jews attended them at first, but by the second half of the century Muslim students began to attend in increasing numbers when the value of this kind of education could be measured in the numbers of new jobs available to graduates. A professional middle class emerged who had been educated in these schools and who obtained jobs in the expanded bureaucracy. After graduation, they agitated for an expansion of the reforms so more could follow in their footsteps and be trained to bring additional changes to Iran.

They could be employed because more ministries came into existence during the course of these reforms, with specified and differentiated tasks. The change came with the promulgation of the Code of the Tanzimat-e Hasana (the Beneficent Reorganization) in the 1870s that laid out the duties of each state ministry. This rationalization and modernization of governance meant that officials were supposed to rule over just the tasks laid out in the ministerial portfolios for such ministries as education and finance. As part of this same process of centralization, the shah sent governors to newly reorganized provinces, and ministers laid out new tax-collection processes and new regulations for legal and educational institutions.

In reality, none of the new ministries held the full complement of bureaucrats necessary to fulfill their responsibilities, and the provincial governors sent from Tehran held little leverage against the religious, princely, and tribal power brokers in the provinces. The ministers also held their posts at the whim of the shah; he could dismiss them whenever pressure groups convinced him to do so. In addition, throughout the century, the shah continued selling government office as a way to bring in revenues to the central treasury; the people buying those positions had no special skills or preparation, and once in office they devoted most of their efforts to recouping their initial expense.

Conclusion

Nineteenth-century reforms transformed the type of governance used in the Ottoman Empire and Egypt from one based on contracts and ownership to one of central administrative control, standardized laws, and, at least on paper, equality for all. The old system of using individual contractors to govern limited areas in the sultan's stead kept too many people beyond the realm of direct governmental control. Using specially trained slaves in elite government positions no longer worked because the process was too slow and too narrow for educating elite cadres; more people with specialized training were required to implement government policies. State reforms began with destruction of old elites, moved into the phase of coercion to bring individuals into state service, and then slowly built up cadres of stakeholders who wanted the reforms to continue because they benefited from them. The states came into people's lives in more invasive ways than any seen prior to the 19th century because the new goals and the pressures of the changing world necessitated mobilizing all available resources.

In the Qajar realms, shahs and government officials instituted some reform programs, but the programs remained ad hoc and haphazard. As a result, the contours of the state had not changed appreciably by the end of the 19th century despite the attempted reforms, nor had the government become professionalized or Westernized. New administrative elements had been added to Qajar governance, but they could easily be superseded by personal connections and privileges. Professionalization and modernization were not considered inherently legitimate; they had to have the backing of a powerful individual or group. In Iran, no one individual or group stayed in power long enough to create a new constituency large enough to successfully battle for the reforms against the old vested interests. The late 19th century in Iran witnessed massive upheavals against the shah, not because his reforms were uneven but because state weakness led to European intervention into the economic and political spheres. Ulama, bazaaris, and the small cadres of new professionals protested against the shahs' selling off their nation.

In the midst of all these changes, Britain, France, and Russia came to hold great power over the economic affairs of these Middle Eastern governments. In the Ottoman Empire and Egypt, loans led to debt administrations that became states-within-states controlling a large percentage of the revenues coming into the central treasuries. The Ottoman Empire remained independent throughout the 19th century, but the sultans saw Greece and territories in the Balkans become independent and North Africa fall under European colonialism. The Qajar government, too, remained independent but had to contend with British and Russian rivalries over territory and economic influence to maintain that status. The western Europeans also represented for many new stakeholders in Middle Eastern society a new and modern way to organize political, military, and economic relations.

SOCIAL TRANSFORMATIONS 3

Workers and Nationalists in Egypt, Mount Lebanon, and the Ottoman Empire in the 19th Century

THE REFORMS initiated by Mehmet Ali, the Ottoman sultans, and the Qajar shahs were not the result of popular pressure. No rebellions or rogue actions were large or strong enough to truly challenge their governments; the Europeans were certainly banging on their doors by the early 19th century, but no action was sufficient to threaten the integrity of any of these states. Yet, as seen throughout the Ottoman Empire, many were looking for new ways to make money and gain local authority, while Sultan Selim III tried to reform the Ottoman military before being stopped by Janissary opposition.

European governance, society, and economic influence provided tantalizing new avenues for social and political change for those gaining access to these new opportunities. Once instituted, the reforms created a snowball effect, whereby the initial goal of reforming the military created the need for constructing associated institutions, which in turn produced stakeholders for the type of Westernized modernity that came along with the new institutions. Those stakeholders pushed for the reforms to spread more widely so that old elites and institutions could be replaced with the new and modern. Many found themselves working in new jobs; they frequently organized to fight for rights they never needed before.

These changes had unintended consequences for state leaders and those being swept up into the new institutions. The imperial machines still depended on intermediaries, but now the intermediaries increased in number and in the roles they could play. The timariot, mültizam, and religious clerics no longer had sufficient numbers or quality of skills necessary for the tasks being undertaken by state agencies. To conscript peasants into the military, monopolize cash crop exports, collect taxes for the central treasury, and standardize educational curricula, the intermediaries needed to be educated in the new administrative practices and fully embedded in their societies so they could identify the resources to be collected for the state. No longer could the empires rely on professional armies and administrators recruited from outside and trained as cadres separate and above society. Local landholders, merchants, and tribal shaykhs offered their services to their states because they could bring along members of their networks established in the provinces and the tribesmen who followed them in village and desert regions.

The state had to grant the new intermediaries additional authority to supervise and guide the people within their networks and tribes. In return for these services, state leaders had to recognize that these men were not just intermediaries but local notables. The most common title for this group in the Arab areas of the 19th century was a'yan (notable). The members were no longer merely tax farmers collecting revenues once a year but respected local authorities who could collect resources for the state and provide jobs, schooling, and loans to their allies from within the burgeoning state realm.

The traditional Ottoman reliance on divide-and-rule policies designed to forestall the emergence of a lineage that could challenge imperial legitimacy still paid dividends since none of these new notables sought out imperial authority. However, under the new conditions they could establish family lines that built up wealth and power over many generations in their home provinces, with networks that often included profits earned from land, commerce, manufacturing, and positions in local state governments. The 19th-century state required so many services from these notables that they had to be allowed to acquire local aristocratic privileges in return for providing as many resources to the state as possible.

But these new notables were not the only beneficiaries of the new reforms, nor were they the only group affected by them. In many regions, peasants registered the land they had worked for generations; in other areas they became sharecroppers or tenant farmers for large landowners.

FIGURE 3.1. Plaza in front of the Cairo railway station, early 20th century.

While soldiers conscripted into the Ottoman and Egyptian armies had maimed themselves to avoid military service at the beginning of the 19th century, their grandsons at the end of the century were demanding more rights of promotion within the military ranks.

Workers in the new railways and telegraph companies across the Middle East were among the first to organize unions to strike against poor working conditions and low pay. Women in Lebanese silk factories went on strike simultaneously; those women attending foreign missionary schools across the region were among the first to publish magazines addressing women's issues in the new societies forming around them. The magazines and newspapers that sprouted up in all the major cities included articles relating the history of the Arabs, Turks, and Armenians; they also all worked to standardize a language that everyone within the nation could speak.

Out of this work came the first stirrings of national identification and activism, complicating the already ambiguous definitions of Ottomanism put forth by Ottoman state leaders at the end of the 19th century and making Egyptian opposition to British colonialism a national cause. While these groups sought to construct new identities for themselves, they drew a line between those people who belonged and those who did not. A series of conflicts erupted throughout the century pitting newly defined national groups against each other; Islam, Christianity, and Judaism also came to be identifiers that acted as catalysts, prompting people to attack their neighbors. Everyone living in the Ottoman Empire and Egypt felt the effects of the reforms, and though most of the policies were imposed from the top down, many groups of individuals chose to organize themselves in new ways to tackle the problems and opportunities presented to them.

Turmoil in Egypt

In Egypt, the military and administrative elites in the early years of the reforms had been members of Mehmet Ali's family and the military slaves he had brought from Egypt, who together gradually came to form the free Turco-Circassian cadres. They manned the new administrative posts and on land confiscated from Egyptian Mamluks and the ulama they grew the cotton, wheat, and tobacco mandated by the state's monopolies. Under Mehmet Ali's successors, these cadres formed a new landowning elite that expanded to include Egyptian Arab village headmen who were useful to the governors because they supplied conscripts for the army and tax receipts for the state; in return, they acquired land as payment. Joining them over the next decades were Egyptian Arab families who had sufficient cash to pay taxes in advance on the land and, in the process, feed the immediate revenue needs of the state and become part of the landowning class.

Concentration of Landownership

The 1860s boom in cotton prices privileged those holdings that could supply world markets with the most cotton because they concentrated the necessary amounts of water, fertilizer, and labor in one place. Newly built roads and railways cut down transportation costs, making this trade even more profitable. In the late 1860s, when American cotton flooded onto the world market at the end of the Civil War and cotton prices crashed, small peasant farms went into bankruptcy at a higher rate than the large plantations, furthering the acquisition of land by those with cash and connections to the government.

The new needs of the state aided in the creation of landowning-bureaucratic networks that worked cooperatively to solidify the wealth and power the leaders were accumulating. As land became profitable for growing wheat, sugar, and other lucrative cash crops like cotton, it became the norm for bureaucratic officials to augment their salaries with money earned from land. The result was the accumulation of large plots of land by a relatively small number of landowners, while the vast majority of peasants became sharecroppers or migrated into the cities looking for alternative work. In this case, both Turco-Circassian and Egyptian Arab large landowners worked together to cement their privileges while the peasants lost their ownership stakes. By the end of the century, only about a quarter of all the land in the country was tilled as small peasant holdings.

Formation and Education of a New Bureaucracy

After Isma'il ascended to the governorship in 1863 and became khedive in 1867, a small number of Egyptian Arabs rose to the highest ranks of the administration. This shift was aided by the transition from Turkish to Arabic as the language of government as early as the Sa'id administration (1854–1863), which helped move the state from an instrument of outsiders personally loyal to or owned by the khedive to a more broad-based national concern. The number of civil servants increased from approximately 20,000 officials at the beginning of Isma'il's reign in 1863 to 50,000 on the eve of the British occupation in 1882. Egyptian Arabs, who represented the demographic majority, took on the largest share of the new bureaucratic jobs.

Key to all these appointments was the increasing number of missionary and state schools training Turco-Circassians and Egyptian Arabs for their new bureaucratic positions. The language of instruction was a combination of English and Arabic. The British Church Missionary Society (CMS) arrived in Egypt in 1825; the American Presbyterians set up a mission and schools in Egypt in 1854. Approximately 130 missionary schools opened, serving boys and girls from the elementary to secondary level; by the turn of the 20th century, American Protestant schools alone enrolled more than 11,000 students. Christian students predominated in these schools, but Muslims slowly began to see value in them so gradually increased their enrollment during the course of the century.

Egyptian official 'Ali Mubarak led the committee that passed the Primary School Law of 1868, which permitted the state to take over kuttab schools that had previously specialized in training students to recite the Quran. This move made the expansion of the elementary educational system quicker and easier because the state was able to transform existing institutions rather than construct costly new schools. The law also took advantage of the reservoir of respect that Egyptian society still maintained for the kuttab and the older style of education. It did not invalidate the older system but found ways to incorporate old and new through the medium of Arabic. The kuttab under this new system offered an expanded curriculum that covered reading, writing, and arithmetic in village schools. In larger towns and cities, it also offered courses such as botany, zoology, history, and geography. Approximately 4,500 such schools existed by 1882, paid for by a combination of state and waqf funds.

The Egyptian government established Dar al-'Ulum in Cairo as a teachers' training school in 1872, expanding it in 1880 under the name Central Teachers' College; in the early 20th century, a teachers' training college for women also opened. Under Khedive Isma'il, the School of Administration and Languages was reopened, having been closed by Abbas (r. 1848–1854). In the next years, schools for engineering, medicine, Egyptology, surveying, and accountancy were established. The first state girls' school opened its doors in 1873, initially under the patronage of Khedive Isma'il's wife, and its curriculum included, in addition to reading, writing, arithmetic, and religion, courses concerned with child rearing, the culinary arts, and needlework. Most of the graduates of these schools entered government service. Those who did not found new careers as journalists, doctors, lawyers, and teachers, forming a small but growing cadre of professionals.

By the time of the British occupation of Egypt in 1882, there were a number of avenues to state office. Landownership provided a strong base because the provincial notables were able to leverage their knowledge of the countryside into positions in the government. Turco-Circassian and Egyptian Arab landowners presided over extensive client networks of low-level bureaucrats who protected their interests in state offices and peasants who filled the conscription coffers and tax rolls. In return, these patrons supplied their clients with jobs, access to schooling, seeds, loans, irrigation tools, and protection. These patrons leveraged their client networks as a means for proving their continuing usefulness to the khedives. To gain access to more resources and labor throughout the country than it ever had before, the central government had to allow its intermediaries to hold more local power than the old contract holders of the Ottoman Empire did. The clients became dependent on their patrons in ways that the mültizam could never have achieved in the past.

Power Struggles during British Intervention

A split developed between elites in government who cultivated an alliance with the British and French debt controllers to augment their own influence and those who began to form a proto-nationalist movement calling for the end of European influence and advocating an "Egypt for the Egyptians" program. When Khedive Isma'il began to vocally oppose British and French dictates, the controllers worked to weaken his power by allying with sympathetic Turco-Circassian and Egyptian elites, passing decrees confiscating his lands, and placing him and his family on fixed salaries. Khedive Isma'il fought back by calling the elected Chamber of Deputies into session; over the years it had passed legislation concerning such domestic issues as taxation, education, and agricultural works. All the deputies were Egyptians, so the Chamber of Deputies became an institution in which specifically Egyptian demands could be made against the European controllers and the Turco-Circassians who held top positions within the government and military. In 1879, Khedive Isma'il hoped to mobilize the deputies against foreign intervention in Egypt, a tactic that worked briefly so Khedive Isma'il was able to regain a measure of his power in spring 1879. Nonetheless, he could not stop the forces allied against him; the controllers and their local allies replaced him with Tawfiq later that year.

'Urabi Revolution

The notables moving against British intervention in Egypt found allies among Egyptian Arab officers in the military. In the late 19th century after Egyptian Arabs realized that service in the state army could potentially provide an avenue for socioeconomic mobility. In the late 1870s, these officers directed their hostility toward the Turco-Circassian military leaders who dominated the top posts and treated the few Egyptian Arab officers and the rank and file with derision. Led by Colonel Ahmad 'Urabi, Arab officers sent repeated petitions to Khedive Tawfiq and his government ministers demanding changes to military policies to allow Arabs to rise to the highest ranks. Over the next months, this 'Urabi Revolution became a widespread call for an end to foreign control over Egypt and the establishment of constitutional limits on the power of the khedive. The Egyptian military officers were joined by landowners, professionals, bureaucrats, and students, many of whom wrote newspaper articles and petitions demanding indigenous control over the agencies of Egyptian governance. They were not acting as rogues seeking to gain positions of local power; they were rebels against the system because they wanted a radical transformation of Egyptian governance and leadership. In February 1882, the Chamber of Deputies ratified a constitution allowing parliament to take away many of the khedive's powers. For example, it designated the Chamber as the supervisory agency for the state's budget and treaties. The cabinet would no longer responsible to the khedive but to the Chamber.

Popular pressure grew so persuasive that in February 1882 Khedive Tawfiq appointed 'Urabi as minister of war. By this time, 'Urabi and his allies could bring thousands of people out into the streets to protest whenever Khedive Tawfiq, the Turco-Circassian officers, or the British and French tried to weaken the revolutionary movement that had spread throughout the country. Spurred on by the movement, peasants attacked Turco-Circassian landlords on whose land they worked.

By July, a revolutionary government ruled in Cairo, and by popular acclaim, 'Urabi became "Protector and Guardian of Egypt." His government's offices immediately began helping those who had been harmed by the exclusionary policies of Khedive Tawfiq's government and by the economic crisis that had accompanied the riots and shifts in government. Khedive Tawfiq's position became so tenuous he sought refuge in the Mediterranean port city of Alexandria under British and French protection. Soon thereafter, riots broke out throughout Alexandria, probably sparked by a local dispute, but the passions that had been ignited by 'Urabi over the previous few years caused them to spread throughout the city. To protect foreign citizens living in the city and to buttress Khedive Tawfiq's political position, the British began bombarding Alexandria's demonstrators from ships in the harbor. In order to destroy the revolutionary government in Cairo, the British began placing troops in Alexandria and moving toward Cairo throughout the summer of 1882. By September, the British had arrested 'Urabi and sent him into exile. Khedive Tawfiq returned to the governorship of the Egyptian government, but he was now in service to British colonialism.

The 'Urabi Revolution illustrates how the state transformations of the kind undertaken by Mehmet Ali, once launched, could not be entirely controlled. Stakeholders who had become integral to the success of the project because they helped implement the new strategies eventually also demanded commensurate decision-making positions within the state. Even people initially coerced into working at the lowest rungs of the state ladder began to organize over time so they could petition rights from the state. Mehmet Ali's successors still needed local officials as intermediaries, as in the contract system in the past, but since they had to gather so many more resources from the countryside than before, the local officials had to be granted more power than the previous contract holders. By bringing Egyptian notables and soldiers into state institutions, Mehmet Ali paved the way for a rising identification between Egyptian Arabs and the Egyptian state. Those Egyptian Arabs who had accessed the lower levels of the governmental ladder demanded to be promoted because they were Egyptian and had acquired skills in schools and on military bases. They viewed the European debt controllers, Khedive Tawfiq, and the Turco-Circassians as illegitimate rulers. By 1882 this was not a full-fledged national movement, but increasing numbers of Egyptians were starting to embrace it.

Civil War in Damascus and Mount Lebanon

In 1858, a civil war broke out between peasants and landlords in the Ottoman region of Mount Lebanon; by 1860, it was fought primarily between Maronites and Druze in Lebanon and between Christians and Muslims in Damascus. The numbers are impossible to calculate accurately, but approximately 11,000 died during the fighting in Mount Lebanon and maybe as many as 10,000 in Damascus. Most of the victims were Christians. Hundreds of thousands of residents of the region became refugees as they fled the fighting and destruction of their homes. Fighting ended only when a combined Ottoman and French force landed in Beirut, marched through Mount Lebanon, and arrived in Damascus in summer 1860.

Ottoman history rarely witnessed this kind of religious violence before the 19th century when it first appeared in the Balkans. The structure of the millet system had provided local influence for non-Muslim elites while maintaining separation between Ottoman government institutions and the non-Muslim population. This system did not eliminate all violence between religious groups living in the empire, but the conflicts often involved other causes, such as peasant revolts against oppressive mültizam, with religious affiliation playing little role. However, governmental changes in Syria and Mount Lebanon by the Ottoman Empire and during the decade of Egyptian control in the first half of the 19th century brought about a new scramble for jobs and opportunities as in Egypt. Muslims and Christians alike competed to gain control of the new institutions and take advantage of new opportunities.

Before 1800, Mount Lebanon was largely autonomous, aided by the geographic isolation of the region. As long as its elites kept local problems isolated from the larger empire, the Ottoman administration stayed

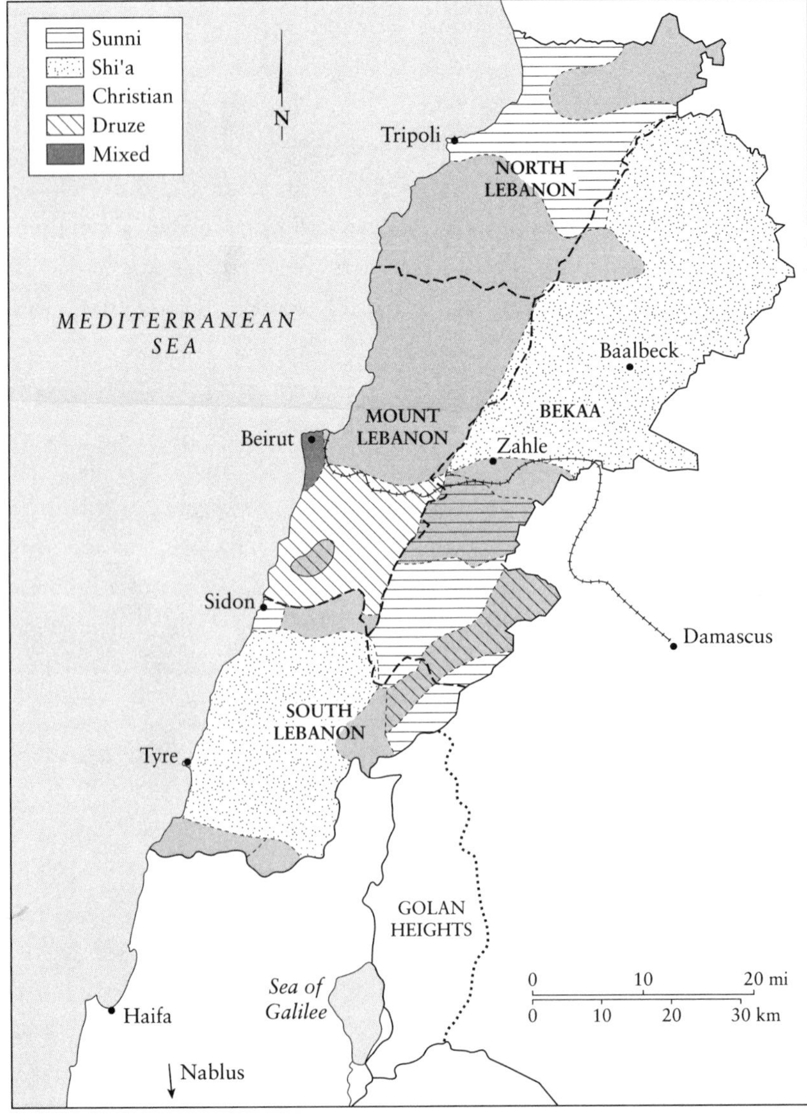

MAP 8. Mount Lebanon and the Surrounding Regions in the 19th Century. The primary locations for the Maronite, Druze, Sunni, and Shi'i populations.

clear. The Ottoman governor of Sidon or Tripoli technically appointed the emir (prince) from the most dominant family. This governorship was supposed to function the way it did in other regions, with the ruler continually appointed or replaced by Ottoman fiat. In reality, the most important family could use the title of emir and pass it on to descendants. The most powerful family in the region, the Shihabs, ruled as emirs from 1711 to 1841; Bashir II (r. 1788–1841) was the last emir in this family line. The dominant religious sects within Mount Lebanon in the 19th century were the Christian Maronites and the Druze, although the region also contained Eastern Orthodox, Greek Catholic, and other Christian sects as well as Sunni and Shi'i Muslims.

Mount Lebanon, where families held landed wealth and power over multiple generations, represented one of the few areas under the Ottoman aegis that maintained feudal practices. This custom survived because the Ottoman state had little influence in the relatively inaccessible mountainous area and the elites of all the religious faiths worked together to conserve their privileges. Elaborate rituals involving language, clothing, and rules for interacting separated elite from non-elite; peasants owed fealty and duties to the landholders and elites of their area. These elites, in turn, understood the reciprocal demands made on them and thus protected the peasants who worked their land. Only a few areas were divided along religious lines; in most areas, it was common to find a Druze landholder with mostly Christian workers or a Christian landholder with primarily Druze workers. It was just as common to have mixed religious groups of peasants working for a single landholder of one of the faiths. Although religious affiliation remained a potent identifier for the residents of Mount Lebanon, in daily interactions social strata

MARONITES

The Maronites were a recognizable group in Mount Lebanon by at least the 10th and 11th centuries. The name comes from Maron, a 5th-century hermit-priest who lived along the Orontes River in modern-day Syria. He preached that Jesus Christ had a divine nature only after the incarnation, which departs from the Catholic view that Jesus has both a human and a divine nature. Nevertheless, during the Crusades to Jerusalem in the 11th century, the Maronites affiliated themselves with the pope while continuing to reject aspects of Roman Catholicism. The Maronites followed their own patriarch and used Syriac as their liturgical language, yet they sent students to Rome to take the priestly orders and study Latin. The Shihab family served as leaders of the Maronites, although many members of the family were Sunni Muslims.

divided and distinguished people more than religion. In many regions, religious rituals were practiced across the faiths by people sharing the same social class.

Ibrahim's conquest of Greater Syria in 1831 disrupted this structure and paved the way for political identification through religion rather than socioeconomic status. The process began when the Shihabs and leaders of Christian sects in general allied with Ibrahim during his 10-year occupation, whereas the Druze revolted against Egyptian rule and many went into exile. By the late 1830s, however, Christians also began to oppose Ibrahim when he tried to curtail their privileges in his quest for centralized control. By the time the combined European-Ottoman forces dislodged Ibrahim in 1840, much of the region was in revolt. Relations between elites had always contained an element of rivalry, but when challenged by outsiders, they usually worked together to protect their shared privileges. Because Ibrahim's policies had pitted elites against elites in his quest to control Lebanon's resources, a rupture had been created between Druze and Christian elites that would not be healed even by the late 1830s when they had all joined the revolt against Egyptian rule.

DRUZE

The Druze consider Fatimid Caliph al-Hakim bi-amr Allah (996–1021) to be the final imam. Believers follow aspects of Shi'ism but diverge over who they recognize as the legitimate familial descendants of the Prophet Muhammad and, thus, the legitimate leaders of the Muslim community. In following Caliph al-Hakim, the Druze reject most aspects of Sunni and Shi'i practice and shari'a legal legitimacy; they consider al-Hakim, who disappeared in Cairo in 1022, a divine figure who will return on the Day of Judgment. The Druze settled the Mount Lebanon region in the 11th century when they left Egypt seeking refuge from persecution by the Fatimid caliphs who succeeded al-Hakim. The name Druze could have come from Muhammad ibn Isma'il al-Darazi, a controversial preacher killed in Cairo in 1019. Druze prefer to refer to themselves as Ma'shar al-Mustajibin (the acceptors' community).

Druze adopt theological elements from the Hebrew Bible, the New Testament, and the Quran, and followers elevate al-Hakim above Muhammad as a divine messenger, regarding the 106 letters and five decrees contained in the Rasa'il al-Hikma (Epistles of Wisdom) as the central documents of the faith. In the 11th century attempts were made to bring new followers into the movement, but as persecution escalated, the Druze closed their ranks permanently to protect the faith, their followers, and their sacred texts. The remaining Druze moved into the mountain regions of Lebanon and declared the security of their community a sacred obligation for all members. By the 19th century, they were the second most powerful group in Mount Lebanon, their new home, and the Jumblatts, the leading Druze family, were the wealthiest family in the region.

Partition

The Ottoman and European officials involved in the resulting negotiations regarding Mount Lebanon's political settlement rejected the option of returning the balance of power that had existed between the Maronite and Druze elite families before Ibrahim's invasion. Instead, on January 1, 1843, they formalized a separation between the two communities in the belief that the fighting between religious sects could be stopped only by partitioning Mount Lebanon into Christian southern and Druze northern districts. This decision was based on the misperception that Christians and Druze had always been hostile to each other, whereas the conflict had emerged as a result of the recent shifts in local power. As history would prove, the partition created new tensions because Mount Lebanon was now legally organized in sectarian fashion so that the peoples of the region would henceforth be politically identified by their religious

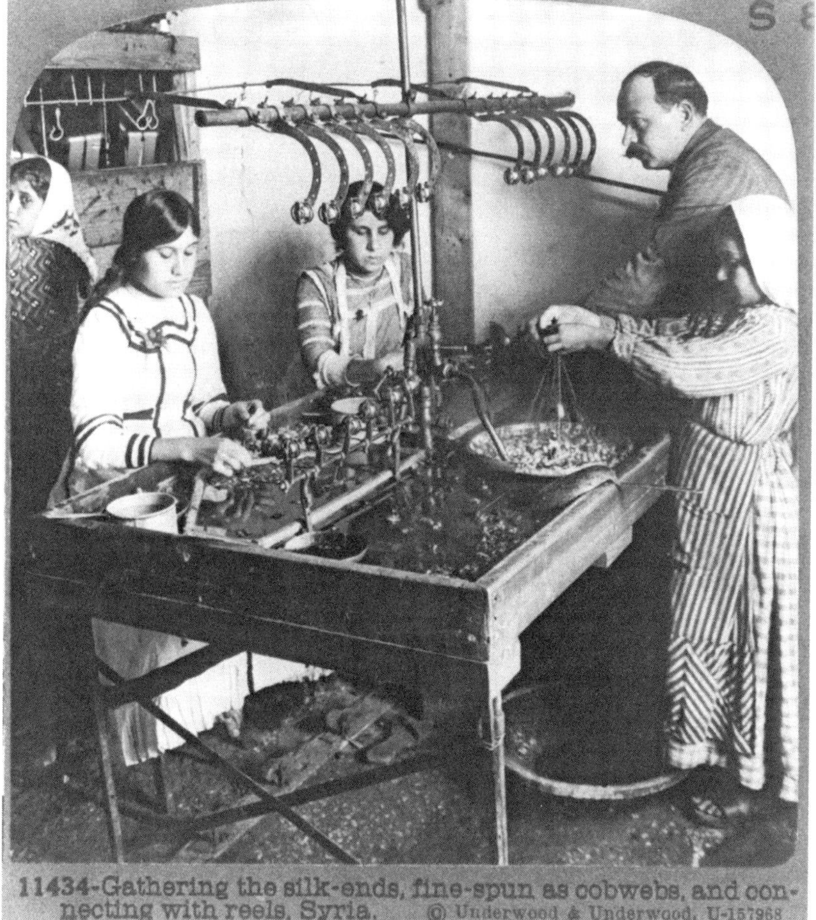

11434-Gathering the silk-ends, fine-spun as cobwebs, and connecting with reels, Syria. © Underwood & Underwood. U-157968

FIGURE 3.2. A family in Lebanon reeling (unwinding) silk ends to produce silk thread.

affiliation. To cement the separation still further, the British became the unofficial spokesmen for the Druze, and the French solidified their long-standing influence over Mount Lebanon by granting special protections for the Maronites. The Ottomans supervised the entire structure.

Muslim-Christian Tension

The rapid increase in production and export of silk in the mid-19th century favored the Christians aligned with French merchants. Mountain towns like Zahle and Dayr al-Qamar were already important way stations for the regional trade in grain and livestock; they grew prosperous in the 1840s as more trade in those goods headed toward the coast and as the export of silk expanded. Christian towns located along what would become the Beirut-Damascus road in 1863 funneled ever-increasing amounts of raw silk and thread toward the port of Beirut while Europeans imported the world's goods along the same routes. This shift toward Mount Lebanon and Beirut rerouted the most lucrative trade away from the Asian-European land route—the old Silk Road—where Muslim merchants in Aleppo and Damascus predominated.

Meanwhile, French missionaries had been in the region for centuries; American missionaries followed in 1820, and the British, in the 1840s. While facing initial opposition from the Christian religious clerics in the region who feared a loss of control over the young people of their faith, missionary schools eventually became key conduits for teaching Christians the linguistic, mathematical, and scientific skills they needed to work with foreign consulates and trading firms. All these missionary groups favored the Christian communities by educating their children in new elementary and secondary schools, first in Beirut and Mount Lebanon and then in Damascus in the 1830s when Ibrahim permitted them to set up schools. In this early stage, in the early 1800s, Muslims did not send their children to these schools nor did the Ottomans or local administrations provide a parallel kind of Westernized education. The Islamic kuttab and madrasas still predominated and could not impart the skills necessary for positions available in the expanding world economy. The Ottoman government had begun to recentralize its control over Greater Syria, but its institutions were too few at this stage to provide sufficient opportunities for socioeconomic advancement for Muslims.

Although Muslims in all regions of Syria and from all walks of life still held much of the land and power, these changes generated deep concern for the future of Muslim affairs in the Levant. Damascus in particular still served as a vital city within the Ottoman realm. It represented the most important annual gathering point for the Meccan pilgrimage caravan, and its markets served as the central location for selling wheat and other such staples grown throughout the province. Its artisans dominated manufacturing for the region, and its merchants moved goods from all over the Ottoman Arab provinces. Furthermore, the Ottoman military presence that remained in the city could be used to defend Ottoman interests and those of the dominant Muslim families. However, Christian merchants were increasing the share of wealth that could be obtained through new avenues, imperiling the traditional paths. Many Muslims began to define the situation as a zero-sum game in which gains for the Christians equaled losses for themselves. In the civil war of 1860, Muslims and Druze fought because they believed that Ottoman reforms and European intervention gave disproportionate benefits to Christians; Christians fought because they believed they were denied the equality promised them by the Ottoman sultans in the Tanzimat documents.

Peasant Unrest

The civil war also had elements of a popular uprising: peasants and urban workers attacked wealthy landlords and symbols of wealth—both Christian and Druze. Peasants had frequently revolted against landowners in the past, but now the promise of equality laid out in the Tanzimat documents rationalized their right to oppose the elites. For a brief period after 1858, Christian peasants took charge of 30 villages in Kisrawan and established a peasant republic, demanding repayment of the excessive taxes imposed in previous years. The immediate cause of this revolt had been a poor grain harvest and the peasants' economic difficulties, but the demand for equality grew out of two decades of discussions about citizen rights in the Tanzimat. This populist call in Mount Lebanon was a far more radical reading of the concept of equality than the Tanzimat writers had envisioned and incited a rebellion against the core leadership structure in the region.

Ottomanism as conceived in Istanbul continued to recognize the social hierarchies present within the religious and provincial groups in the empire; religious and notable leaders still maintained their privileged positions as the spokesmen for the people within their sect and region even as the millet structure technically dissolved. Equality as it was defined in Istanbul did not mean rights for the individual; it meant equality before the law for religious groups as collective entities. The rebelling peasants in Mount Lebanon wanted to dismantle social inequalities at the level of individuals; they did not want to stop at allowing one religious group to be equal to another. That form of equality would have no impact on peasants' lives. The settlement after the 1860 civil war, however, ignored their demands and reinstated elite rule in the new political structure.

Ottoman Centralization in Damascus Province

In the aftermath of the civil war, Damascus and Mount Lebanon both came under more centralized scrutiny of the Ottoman government than they had been for at least a century, with Damascus in particular increasing its importance in Ottoman provincial governance. The Ottoman government supervised the Damascus province through local councils that included Ottoman appointees from Istanbul and elected local representatives. The most important was the Administrative Council of the Province, which contained three imperial appointees and six elected positions allotted to the different religious groups of the province. Below that level were the Administrative Council of the District and the Municipal Council of Damascus. Damascene Sunni Muslim landowners and merchants dominated the seats with a few allotted to Christian merchants and to 'Alawi in proportion to their percentage in the population. Positions on the different councils enabled the holders to introduce legislation and regulations favoring their economic enterprises and acquisition of land.

Changes wrought by Egypt and the Ottoman Empire in Damascus in the 19th century displaced most of the old intermediaries from the contract system. Of the 12 most influential Muslim families in 1900, only al-'Azm had been powerful in the first half of the century. Local power had earlier been premised on control over tax farming, manufacturing, and

'ALAWI

Little is known about the early history of the 'Alawi. They are followers of Muhammad Ibn Nusair, who, in 9th-century Iraq, proclaimed himself the bab (door) to the knowledge of the imams who descended from the Prophet. 'Alawi also believed that 'Ali, cousin and son-in-law of Muhammad and the fourth Rashidun caliph, was the human embodiment of the divine, thus incorporating a concept from Christianity into their theology. Because Ibn Nusair and his followers faced persecution in Iraq for their ideas, they moved to the western mountains of Syria in the 11th century, where they were able to protect their community from attacks. By the end of the 19th century, they were a poor, marginalized group living primarily in the mountain regions of northwestern Syria.

AMERICAN COLONY, JERUSALEM.
848 Street Leading to Straight Street. Straße in Damaskus. Un Bazaar a Damas.

FIGURE 3.3. Street scene in the old city of Damascus.

trade. Through the 1858 Land Code, landownership became a potent means for establishing status from generation to generation within a family. Furthermore, the Ottomans still worked through intermediaries, but now the condition for such a relationship was that more resources could now be extracted from the people and the intermediaries could become more powerful than their provincial predecessors.

Everyone who benefited from Ottoman largesse—large landowners, urban merchants, and tribal shaykhs—established extensive client networks to protect their interests and proffer human and agricultural resources to the Ottoman state, in the process becoming more embedded in their communities than previous contract holders had been. These a'yan of Damascus grew wealthy owning land, investing in urban industry, and trading throughout the region and with the Europeans. They passed on their wealth and influence to their heirs, establishing themselves as local aristocrats with lineages that bequeathed wealth generation to generation. However, poorer merchants, small landholders, and weaker tribal shaykhs in the Damascus province were alienated by Ottoman policies because they did not have control over client networks useful to the sultans. After the introduction of new schools and court systems based on Western models, many ulama also lost the monopoly they had traditionally held in these venues.

The consolidation of landholdings by Muslims and Christians that resulted from these changes caused peasants to lose their hereditary rights to cultivation. In many instances, peasants gave up their rights for fear that registering their land would place them in the path of Ottoman conscription; notable families promised to protect them from this danger by registering the land in their own names. Furthermore, the law declared that land could be confiscated after three fallow years. Since many peasants could not afford the seeds and equipment necessary for farming year after year, they lost their land to the notables at auction. On that land, the vast majority of cultivation was for cereals, with lesser amounts devoted to cotton, tobacco, and silk; wool and hides from sheep served as important supplements.

While the Ottomans did not draw the strict sectarian separations in Damascus as they had done in Mount Lebanon, the changes of the preceding decades had established different Christian and Muslim paths to wealth and political power. The Muslims became the primary Tanzimat stakeholders. They acquired new positions of authority through the Ottoman governmental pathway to social mobility and continued to control internal trade routes throughout Greater Syria. Damascus served as a central focus for Ottoman governance, the annual hajj caravan, and regional trade; Muslim notables of the city and surrounding areas were thus able to prove their usefulness to the Ottoman leadership and obtain new positions of influence within the province.

The Muslim elites achieved such access because in the late 19th century, new Ottoman schools trained future administrators in Damascus and Istanbul. The Ottoman rüşdiyah primary schools began appearing in Damascus, Beirut, Aleppo, and Baghdad in the 1860s and then in small towns by the 1880s. Maktab al-'Anbar represented the premier secondary school of the Muslim elites in Damascus. It opened its doors in 1889 as a state school; a new academic level was added each new school year

FIGURE 3.4. Students stand at attention in the courtyard of an imperial high school in Baghdad, ca. 1880–1893.

until it reached its full seven-year curriculum in 1895–1896. The students studied Turkish, French, Arabic, economics, geometry, algebra, chemistry, physics, and history, as well as the Quran and Islamic jurisprudence.

Muslim students from elite families began their education in these state and private schools while typically completing higher professional and military education in Istanbul. The language of instruction was Ottoman Turkish, the language of governance and elite culture throughout the empire and the gateway to government influence for anyone seeking provincial office. Those who followed this educational trajectory returned to Damascus having learned the skills necessary for running a modern government and economy and acculturated to modern Ottoman society. By opening such schools for Damascene Arabs, the Ottoman leadership was, effectively, expanding the elite class by allowing graduates to enter their ranks and become influential stakeholders in the provinces.

The Christians of Damascus who traded European goods prospered, as they had done throughout the life of the Ottoman Empire. In the later

19th century they gained access to foreign missionary schools. Although most could not join their Muslim colleagues in the Ottoman administration, they had ample job offers to work in the schools where they had been educated and in European merchant and consular houses with which they had long worked. They continued and expanded their role as merchants by selling Damascene raw and finished products to Europe and by bringing European consumer items to the landowning bureaucratic elite within the city. Many used the cash earned in these exchanges to branch into moneylending for both Christian and Muslim enterprises. No Christian family of the Damascus province grew as wealthy or as powerful as the new Muslim notables because they could not use the state to their advantage, but their business and professional contacts with European concerns gave them leverage and wealth their predecessors had not been able to achieve.

Mount Lebanon, Beirut, and European Trade

As Damascus intensified its connections with the Ottoman state in the late 19th century, Mount Lebanon set up a different connection between state, power, and wealth at the resolution of the 1860 civil war. Accreditation by the Ottomans, through appointment to local councils, gave an advantage but did not provide the same levels of local influence achieved by elites in Damascus. As a result, a landowning and merchant elite emerged whose base of power came largely from the many private opportunities through trade with Europe and education in missionary schools. In particular, the Christian sects grew wealthy because they had the best connections with the Europeans, who were themselves increasing their trading contacts throughout the region. Beirut became the entrepôt for this new elite as the vast majority of the schools and jobs opened within the city and as the products of Mount Lebanon, Damascus, and Europe flowed through its docks. Its population reflected these changes; Beirut began the 19th century with a very small population of 6,000 but entered the 20th with possibly as many as 120,000 residents. The Ottomans acknowledged this change by declaring Beirut its own province in 1888.

The Règlement Organique of June 1861 made Mount Lebanon a privileged administrative region (mutasarrifate) internationally guaranteed and under the control of an Ottoman-appointed non-Lebanese Christian governor; the partition of 1843 was eliminated. Seats in a new advisory council were allotted based on religious affiliation: the Maronites received four seats; the Eastern Orthodox, two seats: and the Greek Catholics, Shi'a, and Sunni, one seat each. The Ottoman and European architects of this system faulted the Druze for causing the 1860 conflict, weakening their position politically; they received only three seats on the new advisory council. This sectarian agreement pointedly rejected the populist element of the civil war in favor of a reinvigoration of Mount Lebanon's hierarchical structure. In this case, the Ottoman government accredited sectarian leaders to rule over their co-religionists. Except for a few amendments made in 1864, this political system stayed in place until 1915, when the Ottoman government declared martial law and took direct military control of Lebanon during World War I.

As occurred in Egypt and Damascus, Western and Western-style schools provided the stepping-stone into new positions and professions; however, in the case of Mount Lebanon and Beirut, private entities played a much larger role than the state. The Ottomans established a branch of the Sultani Lycée in Beirut in 1883 and soon enrolled the sons of the most prominent and wealthy Lebanese families. In 1895, the Ottoman College offered all classes in Arabic; the curriculum ranged from religious studies to introductions to astronomy and the natural sciences. But most schools were opened by private act, not via the state. Butrus al-Bustani, a Maronite Christian convert to Protestantism, opened the National School in 1863, with the hopes of bringing all of Lebanon's religious groups under one educational umbrella.

Beginning in the late 19th century the Maqasid Islamic Benevolent Society, a group of Sunni Muslim notables in Beirut, organized a series of Arabic-language schools for girls and boys as a local alternative to the missionary schools. The Syrian Protestant College (SPC) opened with American backing in 1866 and used al-Bustani's school as its official preparatory school in its first years. In 1882, the Americans running the school shifted the language of instruction from Arabic to English. American missionaries also established the Beirut Female Seminary in 1835, renaming it the American School for Girls (ASG) in 1904. The French Catholic Jesuits opened St. Joseph University in 1875 with Maronite Christians the largest group of students.

Connected to these changes was the ever-increasing wealth accruing from the production of silk, benefiting the large Christian landowners and the merchants who transported their products to European buyers. Mount Lebanon had 3 million mulberry trees in the 1840s; that number grew to 28 million by World War I. When the French and Italian industry fell to blight in the 1860s, both countries focused on silk manufacturing rather than primary crop supply. The alteration meant that French factories needed to obtain increasing amounts of silk products from places like Mount Lebanon. French merchants and Lebanese Christians invested in mulberry trees and in the production of silk thread, using modern manufacturing techniques and machinery imported from France. At its height in 1873, the silk industry in Mount Lebanon accounted for 82.5 percent of the total exports from the region.

Beirut could be the primary exporter of these silk products because the late 19th century saw dramatic improvements in roads and railways. Frenchman Edmond de Perthuis opened the Beirut-Damascus road in 1863 with funds raised through the Compagnie Imperiale Ottomane de la Route de Beyrouth à Damas, based in Beirut and Paris. The first railway line between the two cities followed in 1894, again funded by a French company, with a later extension to the southern Syrian grain-producing hub of Hawran. Along the new silk road hotels and artisan

FIGURE 3.5. A segment of the Beirut-Damascus rail track running alongside the Barada River, outside Damascus, in the late 19th century.

shops opened, providing more avenues for the acquisition of wealth by residents of Mount Lebanon. Christians predominated in these industries because of their long-standing contacts with European firms, the skills they gained through the foreign missionary schools, and the consular protection afforded through the Capitulation treaties to thousands of workers and merchants.

Unlike in Damascus where about a dozen Muslim and a few Christian families dominated the economic and political scene in the second half of the 19th century, in Lebanon many individuals and families could become members of this upper stratum because money could be earned from several different venues. The wealthiest among them, about seven Christian families, combined land and trade within their family's property holdings, training members to be professionals such as doctors, teachers, bankers, journalists, and European consular aides while also often investing in such enterprises as railway and steamship companies throughout the Middle East. The Muslim families who managed to maintain their wealth through 1860 and those who joined them afterward did so because they captured a segment of the trade between Beirut and the hinterland of Greater Syria; a few managed to build up ties with European concerns as their Christian colleagues were doing. They could also, as their counterparts in Damascus were doing, leverage their positions on the local administrative councils to guarantee that Ottoman laws and decrees favored their businesses and landholdings.

Peasant and Worker Rebellions in the Empire

The economic, educational, and political changes in Egypt and Syria did not affect the elites alone but also transformed society below that economic level, as peasants and urban workers found themselves faced with new challenges. The influx of European-manufactured products forced guild workers to move into factory settings; urban expansion created transportation jobs; and foreign missionary schools opened their doors to even the poorest of peasants. These transitions made some of the participants wealthy in their new endeavors, but more often than not the changes disrupted people's lives.

Rural-to-urban migration in Egypt brought floods of peasants into Cairo, Alexandria, and the cities constructed to support the Suez Canal in the 1860s. By 1900, the largest employer in the country was the Egyptian State Railways, highlighting that the state was playing a new role in people's lives. Migrants who came into the cities for the jobs and schools

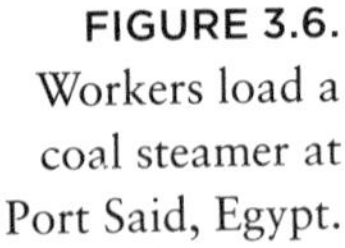

FIGURE 3.6. Workers load a coal steamer at Port Said, Egypt.

and were slowly transformed by the new cosmopolitan culture emerging in such major urban centers. They were joined by thousands of foreigners who wanted to be part of the larger Mediterranean trading and manufacturing zone expanding there; by 1907 almost 20 percent of Alexandria's population was foreign born. In such cities people organized labor unions, women's movements, and student political circles. Coffee shops provided venues for disseminating news; traveling theater groups told glorious tales of the Egyptian past and present. Much of this media was communicated in colloquial Egyptian Arabic, which helped create a shared sense of language, culture, and interests.

Cairo Cab Strike

Migration into cities provided the beginnings of a working class comprising tens of thousands of workers contributing in some aspect to the world economy. Quite quickly working conditions drove these workers to protest. After the British occupation in 1882, coal heavers in Port Said went on strike a number of times; the mostly Greek cigarette rollers in Cairo did the same in 1899 to demand better wages. Most of these strikes were only marginally successful, but one strike shows the potential power these strikers held.

In April 1907, approximately 2,000 Cairo cab drivers went on strike and paralyzed the city. The catalysts were the expansion of the city's tramline, with the potential to detour business away from the cabs, and a campaign by the British Society for the Prevention of Cruelty to Animals to regulate how the horses used in the cab trade were treated. No records exist about how the drivers organized the strike, but the institutions readily available to them in the city, such as coffee shops, afforded easy means for disseminating knowledge about the strike and for rallying supporters. The impact of the strike was so great that after only one day, the government acceded to the strikers' demands and eased restrictions on the use of animals. The high number of participants certainly played a role in this success, but many new newspapers in Cairo also carried the story, making it a far larger issue than the strike of just one group of workers. With success came imitators, and in the following weeks silk weavers, butchers, domestic servants, and other groups went on strike.

Damascus Textile Strike

In Damascus, cheap English textiles began to compete with Damascene products as early as the 1840s. While producers of expensive textiles could maintain their market share, those producing less exclusive products found themselves competing with cheap imported Manchester cotton. Guild masters could not keep newcomers out of the industry; anyone with money to buy machines and open a factory could potentially enter the newly competitive world of textile production. Masters could not protect their dependents because of the competition from Europe and from those local merchants who invested in textile factories. Spinners lost their business almost completely because the importation of new machines obviated the need for their work. The result of these changes was a breakdown in the guild structure that had guided and controlled textile production for centuries.

In the past, the guilds relied on personal relationships between members to facilitate cooperation; the guild structure was designed to protect all its members by maintaining quality, prices, and output. Except in periods of political or economic stress, the journeymen did well enough economically to sustain themselves. Under the new conditions, apprentices and journeymen could no longer rely on steady work within their guilds.

RAILWAYS

The first railway line in Egypt, between Alexandria and Cairo, opened in 1856, and new lines were extended along the Nile Valley, largely with British investment and technical expertise. In the 1860s, railway lines began to traverse Anatolia and the Balkans. In 1883, Istanbul became the southernmost terminus of the famed Orient Express, allowing rail passengers to travel from London to the Ottoman Empire and then throughout the Middle East. More than 2,600 kilometers of track existed in Egypt and 7,500 kilometers in the remaining Ottoman territories by the turn of the 20th century. On the eve of World War I, more than 13,000 people worked for Ottoman railroad companies, and about half of all products moving through Syria and Anatolia went via railway. Architectural gems such as Sirkeci Terminal in Istanbul (1890) and the Hijazi Railway Station in Damascus (1913) heralded rail lines as a symbol of Ottoman modernity and grandeur.

British, French, and German companies received most of the concessions from the sultan for building railways in the late 19th century. By World War I, the Ottoman government had invested only 10 percent in railways. The Great Powers competed particularly over the concession for the Baghdad Railway, designed to connect Baghdad with Basra and the Persian Gulf. A German company received a concession in 1903, and over the next decade Germany and Britain negotiated for rights of transport throughout that corridor.

The Hijazi Railway, the only line built solely with Ottoman financing, opened in 1908. Funds came from the treasury, the sultan and grand vizier, civil servants, and Muslims, making it also a pan-Islamic project. European contractors performed the most skilled work, but up to 10,000 Ottoman soldiers laid the rail bed and built much of the infrastructure in return for having their conscription contracts reduced from seven to five years. The line carried Muslim pilgrims along the 1,300-kilometer route from Damascus to Medina for the annual hajj and brought Islam's holiest sites under the direct control of Istanbul. The railway never reached Mecca as initially planned, but extensions into the grain-growing region of the Hawran in southern Syria and to Haifa on the Mediterranean coast added 2,000 kilometers to the line before World War I.

Faced with diminishing incomes, the journeymen in early 1879 chose to organize with their colleagues across the industry in the hopes that their complaints would be heard. After a four-week work stoppage by 3,000 journeymen, the masters agreed to rescind the proposed wage cut. Subsequent strikes were not so successful, but their continuance shows that workers no longer felt obligated to the masters or merchants controlling their economic lives. The Damascene textile industry eventually adapted to local and foreign pressures by producing cheaper products to compete with Europe or by choosing to maintain production of higher-end textiles that faced no such competition. Innovation, not the guild

MAP 9. Berlin-Baghdad and Hijazi Railways.

system, which had failed to maintain its influence under the new conditions, saved the industry.

Mount Lebanon Silk Workers

The silk industry in Mount Lebanon created wealth for large landowners and merchants involved and for peasants who found ways to take advantage of the opportunities offered. Money for investment could be earned and borrowed from a number of different private venues. It could be made through the cultivation of new mulberry trees or the opening of factories for weaving silk thread. For others, jobs with foreign consulates, at the new hotels along the Beirut-Damascus Road, or in merchant houses at the port, provided the investment cash. The factories primarily employed women, while the men of the families typically stayed home to work the family land and, in many cases, to tend to the new mulberry trees.

FIGURE 3.7. Women workers boil cocoons to loosen fiber ends in Mount Lebanon's largest silk reeling plant.

By one estimate 12,000 unmarried women were working in the Lebanese silk industry by the 1880s. By the 1890s, they had also begun to organize and strike for better pay and conditions. Increasingly, these strikes began to show results as women's demands for better pay and working conditions were slowly met. With the new earnings, paired often with the linguistic skills learned in missionary schools, thousands of Lebanese Christians immigrated to the Americas in the 50 years prior to World War I. The money sent home or brought back when they returned provided new lifestyles for these immigrants' families. They bought land and the luxury goods now readily available throughout Mount Lebanon via the port of Beirut.

Over the long term, these changes transformed the social hierarchies that had been present in Mount Lebanon for centuries. Before 1860, elaborate rituals and control over local resources constructed boundaries between elites and peasants. In the post-1860 period, cash could be earned by people well below the elite level, and that cash had the potential to buy middle-class homes and lifestyles. No longer could the elites hold themselves above those who served them. So many avenues to earning cash presented themselves that a peasant family could, in a couple of generations, buy not only the luxury items but also the educational credentials of the elite. Feudal dependencies that had marked many of the relationships in Mount Lebanon could not be sustained in this fast-moving economic and cultural milieu.

Nationalism in the Middle East

The process of reorganizing political, social, and economic relationships did not merely provide new skilled personnel for the Ottoman and Egyptian governments but generated questions about who had the right to speak on behalf of a nation and who had the right to decision-making power in the states of the region. Graduates of the new schools and administrators in the governments constructed narratives of national claims to their land. In Egypt, the state had evolved for more than a century; people lived within recognizable borders and were accustomed to working within Egyptian state institutions. People throughout the country were demanding that the Egyptian state represent the Egyptian nation. But for people in most areas of the world who sought to define a national identity at the end of the 19th century, the connection between history, language, religion, state institutions, and borders was not as clear-cut.

Arabs, Armenians, and Kurds all worked to write the narrative of history and culture defining their nations during the 19th century but struggled with how that nation could work within the confines of the Ottoman state. Arabs and Kurds received new positions of authority within the Ottoman state at the provincial level, but the sultan refused to grant political autonomy for the regions they controlled or to appoint Arabs and Kurds to positions with imperial influence. The Armenians found themselves by the end of the century threatened by Turkish and Kurdish national claims to the land on which they were living.

Nationalism: Egypt

The work of nationalist organizing in Egypt did not end with the 1882 British occupation. The next decades in fact saw the further institutionalization of concepts undergirding Egyptian identity; political parties formed, more newspapers were published, and more labor strikes took place. British actions hampered political activity while galvanizing the next generation to more fully orchestrate a political movement on the eve of the 20th century. The British under High Commissioner Lord Cromer (Evelyn Baring), who served during 1883–1907, took control of all strategic and imperial communications throughout the country and strengthened British hold over the Suez Canal Zone.

The British also used Egypt as a base for conquering the Sudan and for keeping the French from gaining important strategic positions in the sub-Saharan region. Domestically, the British chose to maintain the khedive and his state. Thus, the government still had internal decision-making power, but the British supervised all its policies and activities. As in the years before 1882, segments of the Egyptian population who agreed to work within the khedive's government benefited from business contacts with the British. Egypt's debt was paid off by 1900, but few Egyptians outside the landowning class saw tangible benefits. The military remained limited in number, which meant that the opportunities for advancement that 'Urabi had demanded were still not available.

Restive Professionals and Civil Servants

The students moving through the state and missionary schools in urban areas were able to obtain jobs in the state administration but could not advance to the level of the British officials in the government and the elites working with them. Many of these new professionals had come from the large landowning and urban merchant strata; once economic opportunities increased, a small number originated from poorer segments of society. Their educational experience formed them into a new professional middle stratum that had become stakeholders in the project of Westernized modernity that Mehmet Ali sparked in the early 19th century. The men dressed in the frock coat and fez, like their Ottoman counterparts in Istanbul, and the women were the first generation in the years after World War I to take off their veils and wear dresses like their European counterparts. Collectively, these cadres stood as a new and separate social group because of their educational experiences, professional positions, and unique ways in which they presented themselves to their countrymen.

Although some graduates worked in private professions, most could find only state employment. It was common for a civil servant to work by day for the government and by night in the political opposition movement. This conflict occurred because students and professionals could manifest attributes of a middle-class European lifestyle but were still not considered equal to British officials. High school and university graduates

FIGURE 3.8. Pedestrians walking along the old Gezira Bridge and in between two of Henri Alfred Jacquemart's lion sculptures in Cairo, Egypt.

learned about representative governmental models, but they saw few of those concepts put into practice in their own experience.

The British guided the education system to train middle- and lower-level officials for the Egyptian bureaucracy. Although the education minister was always an Egyptian, the British dictated the goals of the educational apparatus. They ensured that the budget for education never exceeded 1 percent of total government expenditures between 1882 and 1922. While graduates did move into their allotted positions in the bureaucracy and stay there, rising anger against British colonialism was bred within their ranks, and the British could not control it.

As a result, this professional middle stratum reinvigorated the nationalist movement, with political parties and newspapers again extolling "Egypt for the Egyptians." They viewed the government as a source for jobs but not of national legitimacy while the British remained in control. Writers and political activists from these groups engaged in a dynamic debate about Egypt's national weaknesses and how Egypt could grow strong enough to eliminate British colonialism. They founded political parties, secret societies, cultural associations, and schools as forums for their debates and as venues for disseminating their ideas. Women organized political salons, opened schools, and established newspapers to discuss women's issues and women's place as Egyptians in this moment of change. In the process, the national divisions between Egyptians and Turco-Circassians blurred as educated members of both groups teamed up to fight the British occupation.

Dinshaway Incident

Nevertheless, only a relatively small proportion of the population was engaged in the movement until the events of Dinshaway in June 1906 awakened national anger. Five British officers went pigeon hunting in the village of Dinshaway, as they had done in the past. This time, the villagers protested because these hunts targeted the pigeons that they were breeding for sale. During the protest, the villagers wounded two British officers. One of the officers and a female villager later died. Instead of recognizing this event as a spontaneous act of protest against localized British actions, the colonial court system tried 52 villagers on the charge of premeditated murder. In the end, 32 were convicted and sentenced to prison and flogging; 4 were publicly hanged. The British used this show of force as an attempt to forestall any more protests of this kind; in actuality, the opposite occurred, and anger against British rule became widespread. The large number of venues used to discuss and criticize the events of Dinshaway show how deep the anger against the British was in Egyptian society. Cartoons and political articles in a proliferating array of newspapers mobilized anger against the occupation. Popular songs written in commemoration of Dinshaway circulated around the country, and thousands sang them as they protested British actions.

People's Party and Al-Sayyid

In the aftermath of Dinshaway, civil servants and landowners formed political parties so they could better organize a national movement. Ahmad Lutfi al-Sayyid (1872–1963) edited *Al-Jarida* (The newspaper), founded in 1907 as the organ of the People's Party and operated largely by the Egyptian landowning elite. Al-Sayyid's writings focused on defining the unique elements making up Egyptian identity. For him, the national identifier was the territory of Egypt that had fed and sustained Egyptians for centuries. He believed that the Pharaonic era, when a unique civilization had been built, had provided a model of progress for modern Egyptians. Al-Sayyid often evoked the beauty of village life and the sights and sounds of the cotton fields in his writings to paint a picture of a centuries-long Egyptian connection to the soil and the land. In this narrative, Egyptians' shared bond to their land was far stronger than any bond they might share from religion, language, or education. Al-Sayyid also criticized his society for having become submissive to foreign rule but applauded the movement that had arisen around 'Urabi because it showed that Egyptians were starting to activate their national will.

National Party and Kamil

If al-Sayyid was an ideologue of this phase of the Egyptian national movement, Mustafa Kamil (1874–1908) was its activist. He organized the National Party (Hizb al-Watani) in 1907; its organ was *Al-Liwa'* (The standard). He lobbied the French and Ottoman governments to help Egypt gain its independence from British colonial control. In this quest, he benefited directly from the financial support that Khedive Abbas Hilmi (r. 1892–1914) extended to his nationalist activities. Together, they worked on using the power of the palace and the streets to influence Istanbul and Paris to oppose British occupation. Over time, however, their plans for mobilizing outside support failed, as the French and the Ottomans did not come to Egypt's aid.

By this time, France already had its own colonies in Algeria, Tunisia, and Morocco. When the British and French signed the Entente Cordiale in 1904, recognizing their respective positions in North Africa, Kamil no longer sought French support. He also failed to win any real aid from the sultan, who had no power to weaken the British hold over Egypt. Despite the failure of these alliances, Kamil's legacy was one of mobilization. His goal was not so much to analyze the nature of Egyptian society, as Lutfi al-Sayyid and others did, but to generate resources to oppose British rule. When he died at an early age in 1908, tens of thousands followed his coffin through the streets of Cairo, displaying their support for his actions and ideas. His funeral cortege can be considered the first tangible sign of mass support for the Egyptian nationalist idea.

By 1908 the Egyptian national movement had grown beyond its landowning-bureaucratic and professional middle-class leaders. Alongside the activities of the political parties and their associated newspapers was the increasing number of workers' strikes, like the one by Cairo cabbies in 1907. Egyptian workers joined the national movement by proving to its leaders that they were willing to organize in new ways to demand new rights. Their strikes were primarily against grievances peculiar to their occupations, but their mobilizing efforts showed that these workers could reach people the elite cadres could not. When the party leaders recognized how effective these workers could be, they began meeting with them to find common ground. As of 1910 nationalist leaders offered workers night school courses on literacy, history, and geography. All these actions expanded the message of Egyptian nationalism, which had become a mass movement on the eve of World War I.

Nationalism: Damascus, Mount Lebanon, and Beirut

In Egypt the state could easily be identified and equated with Egyptianness because of the clear connection between the state, its territorial boundaries, and, increasingly, its population and language. However, writers in the Ottoman Arab provinces had no such clear-cut parameters. The thorny question at the end of the 19th century pivoted around what it meant to be an Arab.

Nahda

For centuries, urban residents had typically used the term "Arab" to denote a backward nomad; for Arab nationalism to resonate with the population, the term had to become a source of pride. Several 19th-century Arab writers began to write about the impressive accomplishments of the Arab past and extol the integral connection between Islam and the Arabs from the religion's earliest days. They depicted the eras of the Rashidun and the Abbasid Empire as the pinnacles of Arab cultural, scientific, and political greatness to which Arabs could point with pride.

In the historical narratives, the fall of the Abbasids to the Mongols and the later imposition of Ottoman rule cut short Arab growth and development. During this period of weakness, European civilizations built their political and economic strength on the Arab foundations even as the Arabs themselves foundered. The 19th century witnessed a rebirth of Arab culture and the promise that the Arabs could regain their past glory. The writers of this Arab Nahda (Renaissance) sought out the best path for advancing Arab civilization, engaging in lively debates about how to properly mix Eastern and Western cultural attributes to form a strong Arab whole. Little dissension occurred between Muslim and Christian Nahda writers because they both wrote similar narratives of the Arab past, present, and future, in large part because they were being educated in similar ways and joining the professional middle stratum together.

Journalism

All these debates about nationalism took place in the many newspapers and journals appearing on the scene, in which writers diagnosed the problems they saw in their societies and then constructed paths to resolve them. Beirut served as the most important center of publishing between 1850 and the 1880s, with approximately 25 papers established during that time period, but after 1876, the center moved to the Egyptian cities. For example, Beirut saw the establishment of 42 private papers between 1880 and 1908, a large increase over the previous period, but 627 papers were established in Egypt during the same time period, especially as many Syrians moved to Cairo to avoid Sultan Abdülhamit II's censorship.

Activists wrote thousands of articles devoted to how readers could embrace the modernity represented by western Europe, while also taking pride in their national histories and cultures. Their papers covered the newest scientific discoveries, debates about the validity of Charles Darwin's theories, construction plans for modern homes, the shifting bases for gender relations, the proper etiquette at a Western-style dinner table, and the clothing to be worn to prove middle-class credentials. Papers like *al-Muqtataf* (Selections, or Digest) founded by two Syrian graduates of the Syrian Protestant College in Beirut, and published in Beirut and then Cairo, interspersed translated articles from such papers as *American Science* with philosophical analyses of current social problems and prescriptions for the Arab political future. *Al-Hilal* (The crescent), another Beirut paper transplanted to Cairo, published articles on Arab and Islamic history and culture as a way to elicit pride in the region's past. Women writers demanded the expansion of girls' education that would not only teach the students how to read and write but also prepare them to preside over a modern nuclear family home under the scientific guidelines set down by the new field of home economics.

However, the articles discussing these kinds of particulars largely failed to broach the larger issue of how an Arab state could be constructed to successfully include all the Arabs within its borders. If all the Arab provinces of the Ottoman Empire were taken into account, the Arab state would have to extend from Algeria to Iraq. Under what state agency could all of them be ruled together? Furthermore, European conquest in North Africa had broken many Arab territories away from Ottoman control during the course of the 19th century, so it would be difficult to form them into a single Arab state. The state structure modeled by the Ottomans also presented problems. Although Syrians gained posts in the Ottoman state, the language of that state was not Arabic; thus, the Ottoman state and the Arab nation could never fit neatly within the same borders or the same institutions. However, without an alternative institutional structure uniting the Arabs politically, the only rallying point for those Arabs remaining within the Ottoman Empire was the Ottoman state itself.

The new Arab professionals did not, before 1908 at least, call for Arab independence from Ottoman rule but of reform of its institutions. Since much of their schooling was in Ottoman Turkish, upon graduation many attained jobs in the Ottoman administration. They had thus built up natural affinities for Ottoman Turkish culture and had increased their local influence from their connections to Ottoman governance. When they organized against the state, they opposed the particular brand of authoritarian Ottomanism Sultan Abdülhamit II supported at the beginning of the 20th century, not the Ottoman system as a whole. Ottomanism for these activists meant equality for the different groups represented in the empire and fair access to positions of decision-making power. They demanded that the Ottoman state provide openings for Arab officials at the imperial level. They wanted political autonomy for the Arab provinces so they could determine their own internal policies without censorship and oppression from Sultan Abdülhamit II's spy network. These activists did not advocate the more radical populist concept of equality that emerged in some sectors in the 1860 civil war in Mount Lebanon and Damascus.

They wanted access to influential positions so they could use their new skills to bring the provinces into the modern age.

Islamic Modernism: Al-Afghani and 'Abduh

An important ideological strand in these discussions of Arabness was provided by the Islamic modernists, whose central tenet of empowerment addressed the quest to find answers to why the Arab and Muslim world had come under such attack from the West in the 19th century. Its leaders, Jamal al-Din al-Afghani and Muhammad 'Abduh, posited the need to reform Islam so its inherent strengths could unite Muslims and make them strong enough to stave off European intervention. Followers of al-Afghani and 'Abduh took up their call for action. They established political parties and newspapers and wrote magazine articles trying to mold public opinion about the proper actions Muslim Arabs and Egyptians could take to strengthen their society.

Jamal al-Din al-Afghani, born in 1839 in Iran, traveled extensively throughout the Muslim world, continually working to politicize Muslims so they would work to reform their societies and governments. Al-Afghani arrived in Cairo in the 1870s and immediately gathered a group of students around him, supporting himself for his eight-year stay through a government pension. By 1884, al-Afghani had been deported from Cairo, had moved to Paris, and was disseminating his ideas through his journal, *al-'Urwa al-Wuthqa* (The indissoluble bond). In 18 issues, he and Muhammad 'Abduh, joining him from Egypt, published their ideas about Islamic reform. In 1892, Sultan Abdülhamit II invited al-Afghani to Istanbul, where he enjoyed the sultan's favor for a while. But when al-Afghani was implicated in the assassination of Qajar Shah Naser al-Din (r. 1848–1896) in Iran in 1896, the sultan placed him under house arrest until his death in 1897.

Muhammad 'Abduh was born into a family of religious clerics in an Egyptian village in the Delta region in 1849. At the village school he memorized the Quran and then continued his studies at al-Azhar University in Cairo. 'Abduh became one of al-Afghani's most devoted students throughout the 1870s before he himself was deported first to Lebanon and then to Paris, where he rejoined his mentor. He returned to Egypt in 1888 and became the mufti of Egypt, the chief religious officer for the country. He used the remaining years before his death in 1905 to reform al-Azhar University and the educational system in general.

In articles for *al-'Urwa al-Wuthqa*, al-Afghani focused on how Islam could be a unifying belief system for Muslims fighting against European intrusion in their lives. He criticized the reform programs that defined the 19th-century Middle East because they had failed to stave off European intrusion while simultaneously rejecting the strengths inherent in Muslim society. But he did not advocate return to traditional interpretations of Islam because that path also led to weakness for Muslim governance in the face of European intervention. Instead, al-Afghani preached the twin themes of pan-Muslim unity and activism so that Muslims could break down the divisions the Europeans had established to weaken the Muslims. Muslims could work together to remove from power their own oppressive rulers. Islam as a civilization had to be regenerated, and all Muslims had to take an active part in the project so that Muslim society could be strengthened and its believers prepared to solve the problems of the modern age. More than anything, he worked to arouse Muslims to form political parties and write for newspapers and thus actively seek out ways to eliminate the foreign intrusions into their societies and build a strong Islamic state. The Quran was the guide, and by interpreting God's revelations for the modern age, Muslims could find constructive answers.

Muhammad ʻAbduh advocated reform of the educational system in Egypt. He believed that the options available to Egyptians were completely unsatisfactory for the modern world. The old Quranic schools and al-Azhar did not furnish students enough useful information about the sciences of the modern world. Yet the missionary and secular state schools followed only the European model and denigrated the Muslim style of life. The two systems produced two different classes of Egyptians: the one resisting change and the other accepting any and all things from Europe. Egyptians needed to accept change, but they had to link those changes to the fundamentals of Islam. In ʻAbduh's writings, Islam contained within itself the framework of a rational religion, as well as a moral code that could serve as the basis for modern life. Muslims needed to go back to the Quran and the traditions of the Prophet; they needed to reject Ottoman interpretations of Islam decreed during the centuries of Ottoman supremacy. A new type of ulama was needed who could reopen the gates of ijtihad to bring the strengths of Islam into the modern day by reinterpreting the Quran and the hadith of the Prophet. Islam, as a rational faith, could open the gateway for science and innovation; it could solve the problems the modern men and women of Egypt faced because the answers would be found in Egypt itself.

These men left a legacy of activism for their followers: to right the wrongs in Muslim and Egyptian society; to work to overthrow any institution that oppressed people's free will; and to interpret the faith themselves, eschewing the corrupting influences of the Ottoman Empire's religious education and legal adjudication. Their students came to serve as some of the most influential nationalist politicians in Egypt in the decades after their mentors died, and their influence spread across the Muslim world as intellectuals read their work and incorporated their ideas from Turkey to Iran.

Nationalism: Kurds

Anatolia served as another problematic nationalizing arena within the Ottoman realm. Kurds, Armenians, and Turks all claimed a portion of the land as their national home. From the last quarter of the 19th century through World War I, Anatolia became the site of battles and massacres as the three forces fought to control the land. The Kurds made a claim for Anatolia on the basis of residence there long before the Turkic nomads ever arrived; their tribesmen had patrolled and roamed the borders of the region for centuries. An Indo-European people, they possibly arrived in the Middle East as early as the 6th century BC, and though their language is related to Persian, it became uniquely Kurdish over the centuries. The largest groups of Kurds were nomadic, semi-nomadic, and settled farmers in the southeastern districts of Anatolia, but by the 19th century a substantial number of Kurds lived in Istanbul and throughout cities and towns in Anatolia.

MAP 10. Population Groups in Anatolia before World War I. The primary population zones shown are of the Turks, Kurds, Greeks, Arabs, and Armenians of Anatolia.

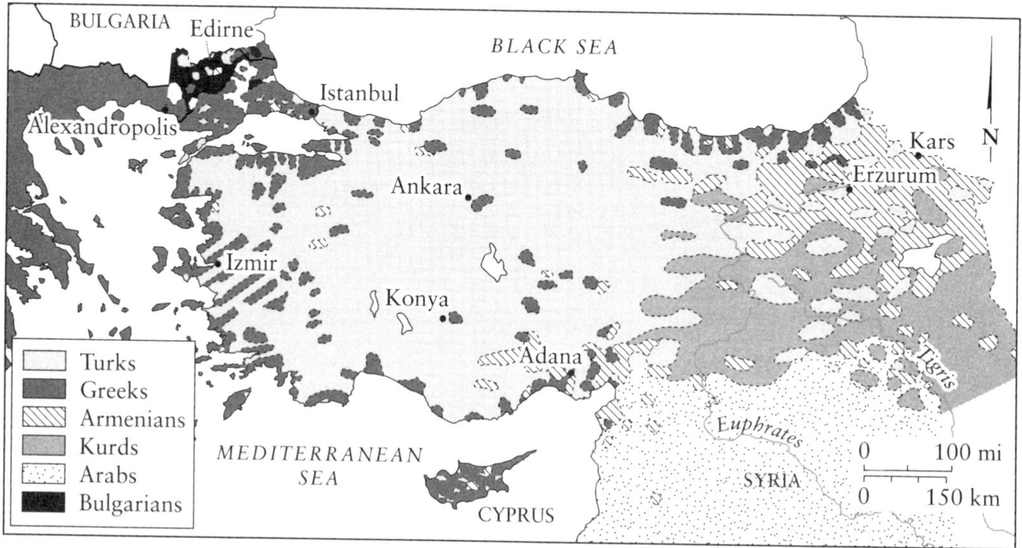

Shaykh Ubeydallah

In the early 19th century, the Kurds, led by princes (mirs), formed large tribal confederations that temporarily weakened Ottoman control over them. But by midcentury the confederations had broken apart, defeated by Ottoman military incursions into southeastern Anatolia. In the late 19th century, Kurds formed smaller tribal configurations, but this generation of leaders did not rely only on military power. The most successful tribal shaykhs were also Sufi religious leaders who augmented their military power with the authority that came with Islamic leadership. Shaykh Ubeydallah ascended to power in 1879 and became one of the most prominent Kurdish figures because he was able to use both religious symbolism and tribal affiliation to bring people under his rule. His actions marked the turning point after which religious shaykhs would dominate the Kurdish political arena in eastern Anatolia. Shaykh Ubeydallah made alliances through marriage, accumulated vast estates in his name per the 1858 Ottoman Land Law, and controlled extensive waqf lands in his position as a Sufi shaykh.

Kurdish shaykhs like Shaykh Ubeydallah began to perceive a threat to their land after the Russo-Ottoman War of 1877–1878 and the subsequent Treaty of Berlin, when Russia took over portions of Anatolia as part of the treaty provisions. Because of the European promise of protection for Ottoman minorities, rumors also spread that an Armenian state was to be declared in eastern Anatolia, cutting into land deemed by the shaykhs to be Kurdish. Shaykh Ubeydallah fought these threats by forming the Kurdish League, an alliance of Kurdish tribes. The Ottoman government initially supported this effort because of the threat of European encroachment into Ottoman land. However, Shaykh Ubeydallah lost Ottoman support when he led an invasion into Iran in 1880, extending his reach beyond what the Ottoman government deemed acceptable for a Kurdish shaykh. When the invasion failed, the Ottomans exiled Shaykh Ubeydallah to Mecca, where he died in 1883.

Hamidiye Light Cavalry Regiment

In 1890 Sultan Abdülhamit II organized the Hamidiye Light Cavalry Regiment to channel Kurdish military ambitions into aiding Ottoman policies. Exceeding 50,000 soldiers on the eve of World War I, the Hamidiye was never a well-trained force, but it did succeed in incorporating key Kurdish tribes into the Ottoman military structure. The Hamidiye empowered Kurdish participants because the act of training with new corps, wearing the Ottoman uniform, and displaying awards and insignias included the members in the collective identity of the Ottoman state. It also gave them implicit Ottoman authority for their raids against villages and Kurdish rivals. The losers in this arrangement were the Kurdish tribes who chose not to participate and the Kurdish and Armenian peasants who could no longer rely on Ottoman protection from Kurdish raids.

Kurds in Istanbul

Working in parallel organizations, an urban-based Kurdish nationalist movement simultaneously emerged in Istanbul, led by Kurdish bureaucrats and professionals who had been able to take advantage of the new schooling made available through the 19th-century Ottoman reform programs. The organizations they formed were generally made up of sons of the shaykhs and even some of the princes whose political power was destroyed in the 1840s but who understood the benefits of sending their sons to school in the capital. The organizations were cultural groups, focusing on modernizing the Kurdish language and identifying a shared history for the disparate tribes living along the borders of the empire. In Istanbul, Kurdish activists joined the opposition to Sultan Abdülhamit II, forming the Freedom and Accord Party and the Kurdish Society for Mutual Help and Progress and producing Kurdish magazines such as *Kurdistan*, *Roji Kurd* (Kurdish day), and *Hetawi Kurd* (Kurdish sun).

Kurdish National Identity

Like every other group now defining a national identity in the empire, these activists struggled against the fact that the Kurds had historically been divided between nomadic, settled, and urban areas. In addition, there were many Kurdish dialects, so the language could not be easily used to bring the disparate groups together. Because of the mountainous and desert terrain that marked many of their domains, over the centuries Kurds had established different types of leadership.

To counter these divisions, Kurdish national activists focused on the fact that Kurds had been in the region of what is now Iran, Turkey, Iraq, and Syria for thousands of years, long before the many Turkic-Mongol migrations. Its activists extolled the way of life that had kept the Kurds living separately and independent from others. A Kurd, Salah al-Din, successfully defeated the European Crusaders in Jerusalem in 1187. Their language, while divided into numerous dialects, had given rise to a distinctive Kurdish literary tradition, as evidenced by the Kurdish national epic of the 17th century, *Mem u Zin*. This epic love story of Mem and Zin opens with a prologue that exhorts Kurds to unite to fight their enemies and then describes the age-old characteristics of the Kurdish peoples. Kurdish poet Heci Qadire Koyi (1815–1892) built on this epic to demand that Kurds end their feuds, unite to fight for national rights, and come together using one shared Kurdish language. He called for revolution against foreign rule, feudal lords, and religious leaders.

While the narrative elements of the epic story aroused excitement in both rural and urban areas, much of the work of the urban activists did not translate well into the rural areas because the urban and rural populations had little in common. These nationalist activists could not compete for attention with the religious leaders like Shaykh Ubeydallah, who combined military power with spiritual leadership, or the shaykhs who made use of the Ottoman Hamidiye to dominate their local regions. Rural leaders understood how most Kurds lived and could literally speak their language. For these leaders, a key demand was the return of Islam as a legal and political force guiding the Muslims of the Ottoman Empire.

Although the urban Kurds, acculturated to the Tanzimat Ottoman world, favored a European, secular style of government, the two groups could agree on what role the empire should play in their lives. This one point of convergence was that neither group called for the outright independence of the Kurds. Instead, they lobbied for Kurdish autonomy in Anatolia and Kurdish inclusion into the halls of government under the large umbrella of Ottomanism. They were not a group in rebellion on the eve of World War I, but they did demand additional rights within the existing state structure. Eventually in the 20th century they would move into rebellion because this nascent movement had engendered in the Kurds a hunger and will to fight for national rights.

Nationalism: Balkans

Greece and the new Balkan states of Serbia, Romania, Bulgaria, and Montenegro gained autonomy and independence long before they had anything akin to a Serbian, Romanian, Bulgarian, Montenegrin, or Greek state structure. Those who had been exploited by Ottoman officials had formed bandit groups to successfully fight against the injustice of the Ottoman system. However, the new leaders did not, in the first half of the 19th century, have a way to harness the resources or mobilize the population over the long term as Mehmet Ali had done in Egypt. And there were no institutional structures to legitimize the states for which the new Greek and Balkan leaders claimed to speak. Institutions that were identifiably and uniquely Serbian, Romanian, and Greek had to be built from scratch. Furthermore, in none of these states did everyone speak the same dialect; few were aware of national histories that could bring them together as a people. Even after independence, all the new states fought their neighbors in order to extend their borders and include within them everyone they considered Serbian, Romanian, or Greek.

However, the 19th century witnessed the slow coming together of state and nation as old Ottoman intermediaries—the patriarch and the Phanariots—were removed from power and replaced with administrators capable of leading a modern state structure. Graduates of European and local schools wrote histories for their new countries and worked to develop national languages and dialects that could unite the citizenry. Particularly pivotal to these national projects were the Russians and then the British, French, and Italians, who worked to help these states gain independence and build up their administrative structures in the following decades.

Nationalism: Armenians

Armenian writers articulated a national historical narrative and worked to formulate one national language; they founded organizations that sidelined the Ottoman-era elites and promoted new revolutionary leaders. But they struggled to find roles within an Ottoman state structure that was inclusive in theory but authoritarian in practice; they faced a different set of obstacles to defining their national identity than their Greek and Balkan Christian co-religionists who had moved outside Ottoman control. They also found themselves competing for Anatolian land with the Kurds, the Turks, and the Muslims exiled from the Balkans and the southern borders of Russia. The result was a mobilized Armenian population but one facing massacres and expulsions from their land, with no clear path to statehood or even some type of political autonomy.

The Armenians had existed as a community in Anatolia and Central Asia since at least the 8th century BC, their language preserving evidence of their Indo-European roots. They were the first state to adopt, early in the 4th century, Christianity as the official state religion. In the 6th century, the Armenian Church broke with the Eastern Orthodox Christian Church based in the Byzantine Empire in Constantinople and constituted itself as a separate religious organization with its own Armenian liturgical language.

In southeastern Anatolia at the end of the 19th century, Armenians made up a significant segment of the population in six provinces, but only in the sanjak (subgovernorate) of Van did they reach 50 percent of the total, with the remainder of the population made up mostly of Kurds. Most Armenians in the late 19th century were peasants living in the Ottoman, Russian, and Iranian Empires. In the Ottoman Empire, the most educated and wealthy Armenians lived in cities such as Istanbul and Izmir, outside the predominantly Armenian provinces, and had little contact with Armenian peasants.

Vernacular Language

Armenian activists trained in cities such as Vienna and Venice, where their families had established trading houses and a series of schools. Many other Armenian youth stayed at home and attended the schools that American missionaries set up specifically for them throughout Anatolia, finishing their educations at Robert College in Istanbul, an American missionary institution established in 1863. Around the mid-19th century, hundreds of these expatriate and newly educated Armenians returned from study or entered into public life for the first time, imbued with the political ideas they had learned in these different venues. The graduates engaged in journalism, education, and literary criticism, in particular working to loosen the strictures of the Armenian classical language to write in a common vernacular. By the end of the 19th century, the western Armenian vernacular had evolved, growing out of exchanges in Istanbul and in European cities among the diasporic Armenian trading communities. This newly revamped language appeared in the journal *Hairenik* (Fatherland) in Istanbul in 1891. In the voice of this literary vernacular, authors and poets exhorted Armenians to recover their national collective memory and honor.

Esnafs

Armenian activists targeted the patriarchs in Istanbul and Jerusalem because they did not view them as capable of lobbying for state and national rights for the Armenian people of the Ottoman Empire. They also marginalized the merchant Amiras because they too had served the Ottoman Empire for many years. The young men who had been educated in Europe in the second half of the 19th century were particularly resentful of the power wielded by the patriarch, the Armenian Church, and the Amiras. Many of these men hailed from those Amira families, but their experience in Europe made them reject their families' authoritarian leadership positions. In their places they wanted to build new kinds of participatory agencies within the empire. They were joined by artisans and members of the working class who organized into unions (esnafs) and successfully challenged the Amiras as spokesmen for the Armenian urban communities. These players helped new schools, hospitals, and charitable organizations proliferate, breaking the social and economic monopoly of the patriarch, church, and Amiras.

National Assembly

Armenians officially began organizing in the late 1850s, and their political efforts culminated in the promulgation of the Regulations in 1863, often referred to as the Armenian National Constitution. This work established a National Assembly of 140 members, of whom 20 would be clergymen, 40 would represent Armenians of the interior provinces, and 80 would be elected by the Armenians of Istanbul. Simultaneously, Armenian organizations began lobbying the Europeans to aid their cause. Their chief tactic was to highlight the precarious place Armenians held in Ottoman society, hoping that by showing how weak the Armenians were against Ottomans, Kurds, and the Muslim migrants from Russia and the Balkans that the Ottoman government settled in Anatolia, the Europeans would extend them protection. Two reports issued by the Armenian National Assembly in Istanbul, in 1872 and 1876, detailed attacks against Armenians waged by the new Muslim migrants moving into Anatolia and by the Kurds expanding their landownership.

In addition to the new Muslim migrants, Kurdish shaykhs were legalizing their landholdings through the 1858 Ottoman Land Law. Ottoman centralization policies, in this case, favored Muslim claimants to the land and left most Armenians without the usual protections the millet structure had provided. Starting with the Zeytun district in 1862, Armenians in Anatolia rebelled on a number of occasions against Ottoman taxes and the repressive policies that accompanied Ottoman centralization. These actions failed to win any new rights for Armenians, but they did popularize the movement as thousands of Armenian were mobilized.

European Sympathy

Recognizing the severity of the Armenian case, the Treaty of Berlin included a provision demanding that the Ottoman government protect the civil rights of the Armenian minority. What would come to be known as the Armenian Question was thus internationalized, as many Armenian activists had hoped, meaning that governmental bodies outside the Ottoman Empire signaled their willingness to protect the Armenians. But none of the

European powers were willing to go so far as to midwife an Armenian state as they had done in Greece and the Balkans. All of the European powers took advantage of a weak Ottoman Empire to engage in trade and banking on their own terms, but none of the powers wanted to see the Ottoman Empire fall and open the way for one of their rivals to gain too much authority. Thus, the Europeans stopped short of intervening in Anatolia on behalf of the Armenians, which was territory at the core of the Empire.

Massacres against the Armenians occurred repeatedly from the 1890s forward, perpetrated by the Kurds, the new Muslim migrants, and increasingly members of the Hamidiye. For example, the massacres of 1895–1896 killed between 150,000 and 200,000 Armenians, with hundreds of towns looted and gutted. World press publicized the horrible conditions of the Armenians and blamed the "terrible Turk." The Europeans continued to pledge diplomatic support for the Armenian cause, but little aid was forthcoming. European rivalries over land and trade in the Ottoman Empire took precedence over extending protection to Armenians.

Revolutionary Organizations

By the late 19th century, with increasing threats against the Armenians and no aid coming from Europe or the Ottoman government, new revolutionary organizations formed to fight for the Armenian cause. Armenians established the Defense of the Fatherland in Erzurum in 1881, calling for "Liberty or Death" and advocating Armenian self-defense. It was the first mass Armenian movement, with about 5,000 members coming from the peasants and the working class. The Armenakan (1885), Hnchak (1887), and Dashnaktsutiun (the Armenian Revolutionary Federation [1890]) organizations followed, with the latter two by far the most influential. The Hnchaks, founded by Russian Armenian students, called for immediate Armenian independence and the construction of a socialist state. By the outbreak of World War I, this party's influence had diminished because national defense and independence, not a socialist agenda, were the priorities for activist Armenians. The Dashnaktsutiun was likewise founded by Armenian students from Russia, and it bypassed the Hnchaks in popularity in the 1890s because its founders and followers supported legal autonomy for the Armenians within an Ottoman framework, which was a much more popular idea within the Armenian community. It was revolutionary because it focused on violent action to achieve this goal, including the assassination of Ottoman officials and the killing of Kurdish leaders repressing Armenian peasants.

With these revolutionary organizations, the Armenians presented themselves as a political group demanding full political rights rather than as a religious millet subservient to the Ottoman Empire. The organizations used a combination of military attack against enemies and negotiation with potential allies. In 1905, the Dashnaktsutiun tried to kill Sultan Abdülhamit II by planting a bomb under his carriage on the way to Friday mosque. The sultan was delayed entering the carriage, however, and the attempt failed. Dashnaktsutiun guerrillas also frequently attacked Kurdish landlords and provincial Ottoman government officials who were exploiting Kurdish peasants.

Conclusion

The reforms in Egypt and the Arab areas of the Ottoman Empire were not driven only from the top, with the dictates of sultans and khedives providing the catalysts for change. Though many people were left out of positions of influence in the new systems—such as ulama, workers, and poorer merchants—they organized unions and literary societies as a means for coming together with like-minded colleagues and forging new kinds of horizontal relationships so they could traverse the new economic and political stages together. Stakeholders of all kinds did not remain content to implement the policies of monarchs and governors; rather, they pushed for an extension of reforms so that local populations could have power and the newly educated could be among the vanguard of government office. In other words, neither the stakeholders nor the disenfranchised remained the obedient tools of their governments; they all demanded a voice in their local realm and at the imperial and state levels.

In Anatolia, the nationalizing process that Kurds and Armenians undertook in the 19th century set the stage for violence between the two communities, with the Armenians largely the victims. In the 20th century, that conflict intensified when the Turks also came to identify Anatolia as their national homeland. Ottomanism came into the debate about who should control Anatolia and through what kinds of agencies. The Armenians supported the cause of federalism and autonomy for non-Turkish groups in the empire; the Turks increasingly came to view such a call as anathema to maintaining Ottoman strength in Anatolia. In the Arab provinces, writers articulated a conception of Arab nationalism for the first time while also demanding political autonomy from the Ottoman sultan.

THE GREAT WAR

Qajar Iran and the Ottoman Empire from Revolution to World War I

4

IRANIAN AND TURKISH NATIONALISMS were the last of the new identities to begin to form in the 19th-century Middle East. In the Ottoman Empire, Turks grappled with the same issues as the other new nationalist activists in their need to formulate a defining history and language. And like the nationalists in other parts of the empire, they articulated their views in newspapers, journals, poems, and stage productions. However, the unique problem they faced was how to reconcile their Turkish identity with Ottomanism. The Ottoman family was Turkish, but its elite cadres of officials were not of Turkish descent; being Turkish provided no special entrée into government and did not confer an elevated socioeconomic status. The Ottoman Empire had classified everyone by religion rather than nationality or ethnicity. Whereas the Armenians were distinguished by their Christianity, Turks were only one group within the diverse community of Muslims in the empire, and their claim that Turkishness provided them special insight into how the empire should be run was a challenge to substantiate.

The emerging Turkish nationalists were individuals who had benefited from the Tanzimat institutions. They were produced by the new schools and Westernized military training; as graduates they advanced the claim that their training gave them a unique skill base for modernizing and strengthening the empire. One such group took over the Ottoman government in the Young Turk Revolution of 1908, eliciting fervent enthusiasm all across the empire because the new government brought back the constitution and parliament and diminished the sultan's power. The glass ceiling that all had railed against for decades had been broken, and the new government ushered in rule by the newly educated and trained.

But conflicts quickly flared between the empire's constituent groups, each of which had different visions of governance. The Armenians, Kurds, and Arabs desired autonomy over their political affairs and thus a decentralized governing system; the civilians who had backed the Young Turk movement for years supported this position as well. These groups believed that the empire would grow strong again because the recently educated professionals could bring their skills to governance, and those with the most local knowledge would rule in the provinces. In contrast, the military officers who had taken the lead in the Revolution of 1908 favored a centralized government, believing it was the only way that all the empire's resources could be effectively harnessed to maintain its territorial integrity.

In the years after 1908 these opposing sides used the parliament and cabinet as the primary venues for their competition, with the centralizing faction of military officers gradually winning control. Despite the moniker of the Young Turks, the movement was not, for decades, focused on a uniquely Turkish solution to the empire's problems. A national component did enter into the discussion, however, as many of the Turks in the movement came to favor Turkish leadership over the empire, whereas the non-Turks advocated decentralization. By the time World War I broke out, three Turkish officers who monopolized Ottoman decision making redefined Ottomanism as distinctly Turkish and requiring centralized rule for the empire to remain strong.

The conflicts emerging in the late 19th century in Qajar Iran stemmed from factors reminiscent of both the Egyptian and Ottoman experiences. The reforms, however uneven, combined with the military losses to Russia and economic competition with the Europeans forced the Qajar shahs to take out loans to pay their expenses. Meanwhile, students, intellectuals, and professionals began to define an Iranian national narrative, celebrating Iranian civilizational preeminence in antiquity and projecting it into the present. These writers also debated about and experimented with different ways to modernize the Persian language to make it uniquely national and more useful for describing life in the modern world. Despite disagreements about how many Arabic and Turkish words to eliminate, these authors managed to create a simplified Persian that was closer to the vernacular spoken on the streets than to any previous literary versions of the language. But since the reform program of the Qajars was far less extensive than in Egypt or the Ottoman Empire, far fewer stakeholders were produced. As a result, neither the newly trained (those in the new army and educated in the new schools) nor the new intermediaries took the lead in mobilizing the population when conflicts emerged.

Instead, those groups joined with traditional societal leaders—the bazaaris and the ulama—in protesting against incompetence by the Qajar shahs and the infiltration of European economic interests. In the last quarter of the 19th century, the dire economic situation of the Qajar state led the shahs to sell concessions to foreign companies, thus allowing foreigners to monopolize the most lucrative industries inside Iran. The ulama and the bazaaris launched large protests against these concessions, proving they could mobilize thousands of followers, far outstripping what the new stakeholders were able to do. The ulama and the bazaaris leveraged their social position and their extensive client networks to get people out into the streets to support the many economic boycotts and strikes, presenting themselves as Iran's defenders against European imperialism and Qajar weakness. Their call for action tapped into the fear that the shahs were selling off Iran to the highest bidder. Their message had broad popular appeal because so many people had seen their livelihoods harmed by Qajar economic policies. "Iran for the Iranians" was not an explicit slogan, but Iran's experiences were similar to Egypt's during the 'Urabi revolution. Groups from across the social spectrum came out to defend Iran's independence because they had become conscious of the right to speak as Iranians on behalf of their country.

When Iran entered into the Constitutional Revolution of 1906, it did so as a mass movement; people organized all over the country to oppose decades of Qajar mismanagement. They succeeded in forcing the shah to institute a constitution modeled on the one from Belgium. However, the ulama, bazaaris, new Westernized stakeholders, workers in the new factories, tribal shaykhs, and Qajar princes all had different visions for the future of Qajar governance. As a result, the new parliament that formed after the revolution quickly devolved into factionalism, and little constructive legislation could be passed. The British and the Russians, the most formidable foreign powers in the country, took advantage of the factionalism to divide Iran into spheres of influence in the years immediately preceding the outbreak of World War I.

Iran remained neutral during the war; nonetheless, its territory became a battlefield for the British, Russians, Ottomans, and Germans. Under these pressures, the government remained weak and divided, and the entire country fractured along the old tribal and provincial lines. The Ottoman Empire did not remain neutral. The Turkish triumvirate in Istanbul chose to bring the empire into the war on the side of Germany and Austria. The Ottomans mobilized millions of soldiers and maintained a viable fighting force for four years, but they lost to the superior armies of the Entente Powers and also to the factionalization that resulted from the failure of Ottomanism to bring together all the new national groups of the empire.

Emerging Activism in Qajar Iran

The Qajars centralized the state as no shahs had done for about 200 years, but they still struggled against the independence of the tribes, landowning princes, bazaaris, and independent ulama. The state did not create opportunities for large groups of people to become new stakeholders, beholden to the Qajar rulers for the reforms they were initiating. In addition, Iran struggled with the fact that only about half the population spoke Persian, among them many dialects, with the rest speaking any number of Turkic and Arabic dialects. The majority of people were Shiʿa, following the state religion, but large segments of the population followed Sunni Islam, Christianity, Judaism, and a number of heterodox faiths. These societal fissures made establishing a nation-state out of the Qajar Empire a difficult undertaking.

However, among the many attributes that enabled Iranians to come together as a national entity, one of the most significant was their geographic continuity. The Safavids had united the Iranian plateau under their rule, and the borders they established have defined the state ever since, with only a few adjustments. Iran also had a long political and cultural legacy that could be tapped to unite modern Iranians.

Persian National Narratives

Persian had been the language of culture from Istanbul to Delhi for hundreds of years; Persian architects and artists who painted miniatures were esteemed members of all the courts of the Ottoman, Safavid, and Mughal Empires. It was not difficult for 19th-century writers to reveal the essence of Iranian culture because Iran had been the seat of powerful empires in the pre-Islamic period, and in the *Shahnama* Abu al-Qasem Ferdowsi had masterfully chronicled Persian kingship. In the centuries since Ferdowsi wrote the *Shahnama* it had become a symbol of kingly accreditation and Persian cultural prominence. Because the *Shahnama* was such a pivotal symbol of Persian national greatness, there was a revival of interest in the text in the 19th century, and new editions were printed.

The national narratives produced by 19th-century Iranian writers differed in some of their particulars, but most pinpointed Iranian greatness in the accomplishments of the pre-Islamic empires extolled in the *Shahnama*. According to these texts, Iran is an ancient land whose time-honored rituals and philosophies continue to define the people living within it; it is a unified land despite the many conquest states that have ruled over it since the rise of Islam. Myth narratives such as *Sharestan*, written in India in the early 17th century about Sufism, Hinduism, and the indigenous Persian religion of Zoroastrianism, circulated throughout the 19th century and became part of the project for finding Iran's cultural origins in the Iranian plateau and throughout regions where Persian culture had been influential. Manekji Limji Hataria's *Tarikh-e Parsian* (History of Persia) detailed the history of ancient Zoroastrianism in Iran. Mirza Fath 'Ali Akhundzade wrote numerous plays and social critiques that focused on Zoroastrianism and the grandeur of the ancient Iranian dynasties as the cornerstones of his conception of Iranian nationalism.

When these stories moved beyond ancient Iran, writers typically identified the Islamic conquest in 651 as the turning point when Iranian civilization weakened. Strength returned in the 16th century when the Safavid Empire revived Iran and built the cornerstone for the modern Persian state. The *Nameh-ye Khosravan* (Book of kings), written by Jalal al-Din Mirza Qajar in 1869, laid out much of this history and provided a narrative template for the authors who followed him. He mixed myth narratives of the kind that make up the early chapters of the *Shahnama* with more factually based studies of recent Iranian history. As a sign of how influential this work became, images of pre-Islamic Iran that appeared in the *Nameh-ye Khosravan* were reproduced repeatedly throughout the century on flags, maps, currency, and stamps.

Shi'ism was not a pivotal element of Iranian identity in these writings, but that component was not entirely lost in the cultural arena. The influential role the ulama played in Qajar politics reaffirmed the centrality of Shi'ism in Iranian daily life. In addition, the Qajar shahs found ways throughout the century to reaffirm that they ruled both the state and the Shi'i faith. For example, Naser al-Din Shah (r. 1848–1896) built a 20,000-

seat royal amphitheater in Tehran so he could stage large public ceremonies, the most important of which was the annual passion play commemorating the martyrdom of ʿAli, thus cementing the Safavid promotion of this Shiʿi ritual as an Iranian state event. One scholar calls this "royalist Shiʿism" because it combined religious and monarchical symbolism to illustrate that the shahs presided over the faith and the nation simultaneously. Through such events, the shah presented himself as the Shadow of God on earth as he played on his role as protector of Shiʿi Islam and the descendant of a long line of Persian kings. The spectators celebrated the Shiʿi religious rituals that had been appropriated as an Iranian national cultural form.

Bazaari Losses

For centuries the bazaar had been the economic and social focal point for manufacturing, trade, banking, religion, and education, with city dwellers and rural landowners relying on its services on a regular basis. The merchants and masters of the guilds provided those services and were therefore important interlocutors for the people working in their workshops and living in the quarters they dominated. Bazaari leaders presided over large client networks of workers, family members, and residents of the quarters. In return for the aid they provided their clients, they could rouse them to protest when the state threatened the bazaar.

World trade in the late 19th century brought both advantages and disadvantages to the Iranian bazaar. The increase in European trade through Iran brought unprecedented wealth to the merchants who had special connections with British or Russian traders or who were already wealthy and could invest in new industries and trade routes. The mid-19th century also witnessed an increased demand for raw materials such as silk and cotton, so many merchants bought up land and moved to production of cash crops. However, by the late 19th century a drop in prices for such raw materials left many bankrupt or struggling to maintain the lands they had just expanded. Some artisans and guild leaders innovated to manufacture products more conducive to world trade and contemporary tastes, while others found their livelihoods curtailed by the changes taking place locally and in the realm of global trade. Bazaaris lost their dominance over moneylending when agents for foreign companies muscled into that element of their business as well.

The new economic pressures from Britain and Russia created divisions within the bazaar between those who would protest the shah's policies and those who would keep quiet. Large merchants who benefited from European trade and official ulama who had positions in the Qajar government remained quiescent; landowners and smaller merchants who had fared badly in the shifting economic conditions took to the streets. The independent ulama, who had remained influential in society because they provided services, such as schooling and legal aid, that were not forthcoming from the state, took to the streets with the protesters.

Ulama and Bazaari Solidarity

The relationship between the ulama and bazaaris flourished because in the Iranian plateau, unlike in the Ottoman Empire, Muslims rather than Christians had always dominated manufacturing and trade. Except for the Armenians dealing in silk, Muslims provided the bulk of the work in the bazaars and for local trade. In addition, a long-standing ulama-bazaari relationship existed because bazaaris provided economic and political support for Shi'i clerics, particularly those that were not employees of the Qajar state or connected to the mujtahids living in Najaf and Karbala in southern Iraq. These ulama received tithes on bazaari profits while also controlling waqf property in the cities. In return for helping the ulama, the bazaaris were accorded the respect due to those who supported the religious establishment and guaranteed that their work and judgments received the stamp of the ulama.

From the 1880s forward, groups of ulama and the bazaaris forged a successful opposition to the shahs' policies and against European intervention, brought about by a series of concessions the shahs had granted to European companies. These were designed to bring revenues into the treasury and build up the country's infrastructure; instead, they channeled business away from bazaaris and local businessmen and placed national resources in foreign hands. Long-term economic deprivation, combined with the loss of lands to Russia in the early 19th century, undermined Naser al-Din Shah's claim that he was the protector of Shi'ism and the people of Iran. Because of this political vacuum, the independent bazaaris and the ulama were able to remake what had traditionally been a protective patronage over diverse local communities into a movement for the defense of Iran and its religious faith.

Qajar Economic Failings

Qajar rulers not only failed to alleviate the empire's economic problems but often exacerbated them. Inflation rose throughout the second half of the 19th century as debasement of the currency failed to generate economic growth. The government frequently sold offices to anyone who could pay the price, even including the positions of minister and ambassador; they also auctioned off titles, patents, and the right to collect taxes from crown lands. These transactions brought in immediate cash but generated little constructive work and fomented corruption as the purchasers recouped their initial payments. Furthermore, these tactics did not substantially alter the financial status of the Qajar government: it grew incapable of maintaining services or any semblance of a professional administrative staff amid rising budget deficits. Meanwhile, the British and Russian governments were expending extensive resources in their competition over the Iranian economy.

Tobacco Protests

Toward the end of the 19th century, economic crises and the Qajar practice of granting concessions to foreign companies brought out opposition elements in protest of the Qajar shah. In 1890, Naser al-Din Shah granted the Englishman Major G. F. Talbot a monopoly over the distribution and exportation of tobacco in Iran. Large protests broke out across the country against this concession, fronted by the ulama and the bazaaris who had already rallied their supporters and networks numerous times over the previous years. They were joined by the large landowners who were economically threatened by the concessions and by the still-small Western-educated professional middle class, who saw in these economic arrangements the first step toward a European takeover of Iran. All these groups formed societies (anjomen) to mobilize and organize their followers to get them out into the streets. In 1890, they engaged in a series of civil disobedience actions such as stopping the agents from gaining access to tobacco stock, burning it, and sending delegations to the shah to express their opposition to the concession.

These protests demonstrated how successful the ulama and bazaari networks were in rallying people throughout the country. The ulama gave them religious sanction, comparing the circumstances to other instances of Shi'i oppression and threat, such as the killing of 'Ali and Hussein, the ritual reenactment of which had become such an integral part of Iranian Shi'i practice. When threatened by authorities, protesters sought refuge in mosques, a Shi'i custom called bast (sanctuary), and this guarantee of safety gave further credence to the belief that Shi'ism sanctioned the protesters' work. Furthermore, some of the powerful mujtahids based in southern Iraq lent their religious and economic support to the many boycotts undertaken against the Qajar concession policy because they also considered Qajar actions anathema to Iranian independence.

Oil Concession

The tobacco protests grew so widespread they forced Nasr el-Din Shah to cancel the concession, but doing so meant the shah had to take out the first of the country's foreign loans, acquiring £500,000 from the British-owned Imperial Bank of Persia. After Naser el-Din Shah's assassination in 1896 by a man with ties to Jamal al-Din al-Afghani, Mozaffar al-Din Shah (r. 1896–1906) took out even more European loans and opened up the country to increased European investment. Belgian administrators took over the collection of customs duties throughout the country, making the process more efficient but also angering many Iranian merchants who felt disadvantaged by favors granted to European merchants.

In 1901, the Qajar government granted Englishman William Knox D'Arcy a concession to explore for oil; his efforts proved successful in 1908, and in 1909 he incorporated the Anglo-Persian Oil Company (APOC) to exploit the oil. When the British navy converted to oil as its primary energy resource on the eve of World War I, Iran became more than an arena for economic competition with Russia; Iran's territorial resource became pivotal to British ambitions to strengthen its own military reach.

APOC built pipelines to the Shatt al-'Arab waterway and constructed a refinery along its shores in Abadan so oil could be moved into the Persian

ANGLO-PERSIAN OIL COMPANY

Englishman William Knox D'Arcy made his fortune in the Australian gold fields in the late 19th century. He bid for the Iranian oil concession in 1901 after a meeting with Iranian general Antoine Kitabji in London convinced him of the economic viability of the oil. The concession granted D'Arcy the right to explore for oil in 500,000 square miles of southern Iran and to hold the monopoly over the concession and any possible profits for 60 years. In return, D'Arcy agreed to pay the Qajar government £20,000 and to deliver annual royalty payments worth 16 percent of the profits. In the first few years, D'Arcy failed to find oil, and in 1905, the British government, fearing the concession could be lost to Royal Dutch-Shell, helped him negotiate a partnership with Burmah Oil Limited, owned by Lord Strathcona and based in Glasgow, Scotland, so exploration could remain in English hands. The newly formed Concessions Syndicate Ltd. discovered oil in 1908 in Masjed-e Soleyman in western Iran near the Ottoman border. In 1909, D'Arcy assigned his concession to the new Anglo-Persian Oil Company (APOC) and became a member of its board of directors. Shares were sold to investors to raise the funds necessary to exploit the Iranian oil fields.

FIGURE 4.1. A parade and fireworks celebrating the Constitutional Revolution in Iran in 1906.

Gulf. APOC signed a treaty with the primary khans of the Bakhtiyari tribe to facilitate use of the land. The khans would receive 3 percent of the government's 16 percent share and were guaranteed that hundreds of their tribesmen would receive jobs with the company, especially as guards along the pipeline routes.

As early as 1905, the British Admiralty began investigating the option of fueling their naval ships with oil. Of particular concern was the British desire to maintain a fleet that would be faster and more cost efficient than German ships. But the Admiralty needed access to sufficient amounts of oil at prices low enough to rationalize shifting from coal. As the APOC oil fields expanded and after years of lobbying efforts by First Lord of the Admiralty, Winston Churchill, the British parliament decided to have the British government buy 51 percent of APOC in 1914.

Constitutional Revolution of 1906–1911

Fueled by the poor harvest in 1905 and the disruption of trade caused by the Russo-Japanese War, month after month enormous demonstrations took place in cities throughout the country, and strikes paralyzed the economy. As 1906 dawned, tens of thousands of ulama and bazaaris sought sanctuary in mosques and shrines in Tehran and other major cities, and even on the grounds of the British legation in Tehran, pledging to stay in place until the shah granted constitutional reforms. Bazaaris and bankers organized to bring food and resources to those seeking sanctuary while paying the workmen of the bazaar during the prolonged strikes as a show of solidarity with the protesters.

First Majles

When the Cossack Brigade, the strongest of the country's military units and protectors of the shah, hesitated to fire on protesting crowds in summer 1906, Muzaffar al-Din Shah had to accede to the pressure and grant the right to a National Assembly (majles). This First Majles convened in October 1906 and ratified the Fundamental Laws on December 30. After a failed coup attempt against this majles and the death of Muzaffar al-Din Shah, the members pressured Mohammad 'Ali Shah (r. 1907–1909) to issue another set of Fundamental Laws in 1907. It was modeled on the Belgian constitution, guaranteeing each citizen equality before the law; protection of life, property, and honor; safeguards from arbitrary arrest; and freedom to publish newspapers and organize associations. It also granted far more powers to the legislature than to the executive branch of government by allowing the members of the majles to appoint and dismiss ministers in the cabinet. In addition to these universal rights, the particular demands of the main players were also enshrined in the constitution. For example, the laws declared that Shi'ism was the official religion of the country. It also included protections against foreign economic encroachment into Iran, which had been the main catalyst for bazaari participation in the protests.

Factionalism

It proved much easier to bring crowds out into the streets to protest than to organize those forces to construct new policies. Factions appeared quickly within the majles and made governing difficult. The traditional and moderate group comprised ulama and bazaaris who held over 60 percent of the seats; landowners, civil servants, and a few independent professionals took most of the remainder of the seats. The dominant groups wanted to limit the power of the shah and the royal court but did not want to see a socioeconomic revolution change the fundamental structure of Iranian society. Specifically, they called for strengthening the constitutional monarchy, protecting the rights of landowners, assisting the middle class financially, and defending the family structure through religious education.

The more radical forces entering the protests and, in small numbers, the parliament supported universal male suffrage, separation of state and religion, equality for all citizens, free education for all—including women—child labor laws, and land redistribution. The strongest groups in this coalition were the Anjomens of the Mujtahidin (Councils of the Warriors of the Jihad), with the Tabriz Anjomen being the most influential among them. Their members were largely workers, craftsmen, and activists of merchant families; many were Armenians and members of the Turkic tribes of Azerbaijan (Azeris). They found common cause with Iranian expatriate workers who had moved to the Russian Caucasus to find work and had formed socialist and communist political parties in their new homes. The members of the Tabriz Anjomen challenged the majles to provide more services to the citizenry. They put their ideas into practice in Tabriz when they reduced bread prices, instituted land reform, and established a system of secular education.

By 1907, with parliamentary failures, continuing protests around the country, a weak but vocal radical element calling for dramatic changes, and an economy suffering from the chaos surrounding the revolution, many who had actively opposed the Qajar shahs turned again to the throne for resolutions to these problems. This newly formed faction contained ulama and bazaaris who feared the path that the revolution was taking and wanted to rebuild some semblance of stability. They were joined by those who had lost their jobs and been directly harmed in other ways by the weakening of the shahs. Many workers, artisans, and palace employees of the shah and the royal court faced parliamentary restrictions on their budgets, salaries, and pensions. Many in the poorer classes also came to back the royalist cause when none of their demands for lower taxes and access to landownership were met.

Disintegration of the Qajar State

When Mohammad ‘Ali Shah attempted to overthrow the majles with Russian aid, its members forced him to abdicate in favor of Ahmad Shah (r. 1909–1925), then still a minor and obligated to follow the wishes of the majles and a series of regents. But when the Second Majles convened in 1909, its members were so divided in their goals for the future of the country that little legislation could pass. Under this pressure the majles collapsed in 1911, and a new majles was not elected until 1914. The coalition that had brought the revolution to Iran in 1906 fell apart because the bazaaris and the ulama did not support the more revolutionary demands of the professionals and groups such as the Tabriz Anjomen. In 1911, in an effort to regain control over the country, the shah dissolved the anjomen, imposed press censorship, and allowed the British and Russians to supervise government activities.

As a result, Iran entered World War I as an independent, neutral country but in actuality was controlled by the British and Russians and with a majles elected in 1914 that survived only one year. When hostilities began, the British and Russians came to an agreement over the dispensation of Iranian territories so they could jointly defend their interests against a possible German invasion. Britain occupied the south, and Russia took over the northern provinces. The Ottomans used Iranian land in Azerbaijan as a battleground to fight Russian troops; meanwhile, the Germans maneuvered troops toward the southern Iranian oil fields.

In January 1916, the British organized an expedition from India that succeeded in dislodging the Germans from the areas they had infiltrated. In the midst of these battles, armies destroyed crops, farmland, and irrigation systems; foreign armies forced peasants to work on their behalf. A famine broke out in the country between 1918 and 1919 and may have killed as many as a quarter of the population. When the Russians pulled out of the war in early 1918 and the Germans lost in November 1918, the British became the dominant Great Power in Iran, controlling both the southern and northern regions once units from the British army had marched in from Baghdad. And whatever centralization the Qajars and the majles had achieved in the years before 1914 was largely rolled back as tribes, provincial governors, landowners, and ulama regained their regional and political autonomy.

Nationalism: Turks

Over the centuries, Europeans had used the term "Turk" in reference to Ottoman imperial leadership, and the royal family certainly hailed from the Turkic migrants who had founded the state so many centuries ago. But within the empire, Turks outside the royal family had not been especially esteemed. The Ottoman elite had for centuries been Christian subjects from the Balkans and along the Ottoman borders who converted to Islam and had been Turkified culturally in the devşirme system. Turks rarely achieved high rank because they were free-born Muslims and therefore ineligible to become participants in and beneficiaries of the devşirme system. Even when the devşirme system broke down, the new bureaucratic and military networks were largely built from descendants of the earlier child levies. Turks could advance within the religious bureaucracy, but being Turkish was not a particular qualification there either, since Arabic was the language of religion.

Ottoman elites typically used the term "Turk" to refer to a nomad or peasant in Anatolia. In the same way that the term "Arab" had to be redefined, the word "Turk" needed to be rehabilitated so that it was not merely a synonym for an uncivilized peasant. Turks needed to value their identity for Turkish nationalism to unify all the Turks of the empire and to justify their assuming the empire's leadership. The answer for the new Turkish national intellectuals of the late 19th century was to locate the strength of the empire in the qualities that Turks brought to it from the very beginning. In this way, the Turks were not doing anything the other nationalist activists were not; the difference was that the Turks hoped that Turkishness could restore the empire to its previous glory.

Historical Roots and Social Bonds

Turkish writers produced a new historiography that hypothesized a period of Turkish greatness prior to the Ottoman era, citing as examples the military success and cultural accomplishments of the migrating Turkic nomads. Writers explained that the Turkish people were not newcomers to the family of nations; thousands of years before the Islamic era Turks had already conquered regions in India, Iran, and Babylonia, and in these locations they had served as intermediaries between the great nations of the world. Throughout the centuries, they had contributed to the growth of civilization in these areas, proving that Turks were not the backward savages depicted by Europeans. Writers celebrated the many roles Turks had played in advancing Islamic civilization through the ages, documenting their achievements as Islamic jurists, poets, physicians, astronomers, mathematicians, historians, and geographers.

In 1897, poet Mehmet Emin published a collection of verse, *Poems in Turkish*, in which he proudly declared himself a Turk, possibly the first time the word had been used in such a positive way. Turkish Hearth associations appeared as of 1912 and had 35 branches and 1,200 members by the end of World War I. They sponsored talks and conferences about Turkish history and published articles discussing Turkish contributions to Asian civilization. Through these associations and their journal, *Turkish Homeland*, they sought to Turkify the peoples of Anatolia and awaken them to their identities as Turks. Ziya Gökalp, born in eastern Anatolia (1876–1924) and often considered the founding father of Turkish nationalism, advocated the Turkification of the empire by spreading the Turkish language and culture to all the citizenry.

Standardized Language

To make this shared history a tangible reality, Turkish intellectuals struggled to modernize and standardize Turkish so that it could truly serve as a national language. The 1876 Ottoman constitution stated for the first time in Ottoman history that Turkish was the official language of the state, and all subsequent governments reaffirmed this. But it was easier to make the statement than to enforce the policy since so many Turkish dialects existed, and the Ottoman Turkish of governance comprised more Arabic and Persian words than Turkish ones. The majority of reformers were in favor of establishing Istanbuli Turkish as the basis of the new literary language rather than reviving Çağatay, an eastern Turkish dialect, because a large number of writers had already adopted it, so it had undergone a process of modernization. The Academy of Learning issued the first Turkish grammar for the Istanbuli dialect in 1852. In the late 19th century, Ahmet Vefik Pasha, an Ottoman statesman, translated *The Genealogies of Turks* into Istanbuli Turkish and compiled a Turkish lexicon, *The Ottoman Dialect*. Many societies, such as the Ottoman Medical Society and the Ottoman Scientific Society, undertook the task of finding Turkish equivalents for modern scientific and technical terms.

In the 1890s and early 20th century, reformers went further and worked to purge Turkish of foreign loan words to make it a purer language, believing that earlier reformers were too accepting of Arabic and Persian words. Abandoning the Arabic script, however, was never seriously considered, since reformers believed that the alphabet, which was inextricably embedded in everyday life, bound together all Turkish Muslims. Paradoxically, the result of these reforms was a bifurcation of the Turkish language. By the time the empire entered World War I, Ottoman Turkish remained the language of state, while a shared vernacular Turkish was being used in literary journals and novels.

Pan-Turkism

Some Turkish writers, both those born in the empire and those in the Turkic areas outside it, expressed a desire to unite the millions of Turks living in the Ottoman, Russian, and Qajar Empires. This movement toward pan-Turkism encouraged all Turks, regardless of residence, to come together politically because of their shared history and language. For example, Yusuf Akçura published *Üç Tarz-ı Siyaset* (Three policies) in 1904, wherein he suggested that if the Turks from Europe to Central Asia united, they would form a pivotal civilization between the European and Asian worlds. Turkish intellectuals across this broad reach of territory read and built on each other's work, so this was by no means merely an Ottoman phenomenon. Nonetheless, while the cultural movement of Turkish nationalism within the Ottoman Empire did resonate across borders, no political organizations in any of the outlying areas were influential enough to devise a scheme for creating a pan-Turkish movement. Furthermore, the Turkic peoples of the Russian and Qajar Empires were also reinventing themselves at home and fighting for political rights under the unique conditions they faced. As a result, the focus of Turkism was restricted mainly to the Turkish people living inside the Ottoman borders, although cross-border affinities for the Turkish-speaking regions of Central Asia remained alive even as the Turkish Republic formed in the 1920s.

Young Ottomans and Young Turks

Groups also formed in the Ottoman Empire to work on ways that the state could better institute reform and grow strong in relation to the Europeans. One of the first was the secret society İttifak-ı Hamiyet (Alliance of Patriotism) founded in 1865; in 1867, it had a new name: Yeni Osmanlılar (New Ottomans). The typical participant, a Young Ottoman, was the son of a fairly highly placed family who had attended the new type of school and had encountered a glass ceiling in the bureaucracy since the old elites with traditional ties to the sultan held the top posts. The majority, because of their political activities, spent at least a few years in exile in Europe, fleeing the sultan's police. They criticized the policies of the Tanzimat as superficial imitations of European governance and faulted Ottoman officials for renouncing traditional Ottoman and Islamic values in their quest to replace all that was old with what was new and European. They derided the backers of the Tanzimat reforms in the grand vizier's office and Foreign Ministry for creating a bureaucratic despotism that had destroyed the older system of just governance requiring the sultan to protect his subjects. They also criticized the government for losing imperial territories despite implementing reforms allegedly designed to strengthen the empire.

Young Ottoman Constitutionalism

The Young Ottomans espoused a form of constitutionalism that built on the framework of Western parliamentarian representation but also incorporated Islamic notions such as al-amr bi-l-ma'ruf wa-l-nahy 'an al-munkar (commanding right and forbidding wrong) to curtail despotism and allow for mashwara (consultation) between ruler and ruled. They were trying to bridge the gap between traditional Islamic governance and modern western European statehood. Advocates wrote prolifically on constitutionalism, freedom, and patriotism, both in Istanbul and in European exile, where the London-based newspaper *Hürriyet* (Liberty) served as their principal organ. Despite their exile, many were able to persuade the Ottoman leadership to accept their ideas, which appear in provisions in the constitution that briefly regulated the government structure in 1876. Sultan Abdülhamit II's suppression of the constitution and the parliament in 1878 and his subsequent crackdown on dissent helped break apart this short-lived movement. The constitution of 1876 was a consummation, as well as an institutional end of, the Young Ottomans as an organization.

Ottoman Union

On May 21, 1889, four military students at the Imperial Medical Academy founded the Ottoman Union as a means for organizing those students and officers opposed to the policies of the Ottoman sultan. They quickly garnered new supporters by clandestinely distributing bulletins and newspapers to students throughout the empire. In accordance with an inclusive interpretation of Ottomanism, none of the founders were Turks: they were Albanians, Arabs, Kurds, and Circassians, most of them the Mektepli officers who had been trained in the new military academies of the Tanzimat era. The Ottoman Union attracted Turkish and non-Turkish Muslim civilians and military men who saw Ottomanism as a means for achieving equality of political access for the citizenry and by which they could make effective use of their skills in government office. The sultan tried to curtail the activities of the Ottoman Union by arresting large numbers of students during the 1890s; many others escaped to Egypt and Europe and continued their work from abroad. Those who remained in the empire worked clandestinely. As a result, civilians in the movement proved more influential in exile whereas military officers played a greater role in generating support from within the empire.

Members sought to break the glass ceiling so they could gain decision-making positions in government. They rallied around the 1876 constitution as the embodiment of the attributes they wanted to bring to Ottoman governance; they wanted to overthrow Sultan Abdülhamit II for proroguing the constitution and instituting an authoritarian government. They envisioned that once in office, they could bring their skills to the task of strengthening the Ottoman Empire. In the initial impulse for this movement, nationality per se was not an important element. Instead, the members presented themselves as the educated vanguard with the knowledge to rectify the Ottoman Empire's problems. They ascribed to a widely inclusive Ottomanism that would provide room in governance for all groups within the empire.

Congress of Ottoman Liberals

An attempt to bring together groups opposing the government of Sultan Abdülhamit II occurred in 1902 when the Congress of Ottoman Liberals met in Paris to devise a unified direction for the movement. With the military supporters largely confined to the empire, the meeting was dominated by the civilians who eventually called themselves the Young Turks. The founders and initial members included Turkish and non-Turkish Muslims as well as Christian Armenians who hoped the Young Turk program would forge a path toward Armenian autonomy. However, very quickly the collegiality disintegrated. The Armenian representatives found that their political ambitions were not supported by their colleagues, so they left the meeting. Furthermore, the organizers themselves broke into two opposing camps.

One group was led by Sabahattin Bey, a nephew of the sultan, who formed the League of Private Initiative and Decentralization. This group's primary objective was to overthrow the sultan, and to do so, its leaders lobbied the British government for assistance. In the end, all the group's plans came to naught and no such coup occurred, but the group maintained its cohesion over the next few years. The second group, which began calling itself the Committee of Union and Progress (CUP) in 1907, had branches throughout the Ottoman Empire and Europe, and its affiliated newspaper, *Meşveret* (Consultation), was the most important newspaper of Young Turk opposition in Europe.

Young Turk Revolution

While civilians worked in exile, Mektepli military officers organized within the empire, especially in the port city of Salonika, which was a major trading center and headquarters for Ottoman military activities in the Balkans. As the 20th century dawned, these newly educated military officers joined the Young Turk movement because they shared the same complaints about sultanic repressiveness and governmental ineffectiveness. They also had many grievances specific to their military role: the sultan's government frequently delayed paying salaries and rejected demands for improving conditions on military bases. Their military experience was largely in the lands still remaining in Ottoman hands after the 1878 Treaty of Berlin had granted independence to most of the Balkan states. Only Macedonia and Albania were still within Ottoman sovereignty, and while Albanians remained loyal to the Ottoman sultan, Macedonia was the site of repeated battles between the Ottomans, Greece, and all the newly independent Balkan states. In 1907, members of the military who had founded the Ottoman Freedom Society of Salonika

FIGURE 4.2. Young Turk leaders, Enver and Cemal Pasha, visiting the Dome of the Rock in the Old City of Jerusalem.

affiliated themselves with the CUP, effectively merging the civilian and military segments of the Young Turk movement.

On July 3, 1908, the Salonika military officers in the Second and Third Armies in Macedonia rebelled against the sultan, and on July 23 and 24, Sultan Abdülhamit II succumbed to the building pressure and issued a decree accepting their demands. He restored the 1876 constitution and called for elections to parliament. Excitement for what became known as the Young Turk Revolution reverberated around the empire, as it came to stand for "Liberty, Equality, Fraternity, and Justice." Newspapers proliferated as people jumped at the chance to write what they wanted without the sultan's censorship and his secret police hampering their activities.

CUP Leadership

CUP branches spread across the empire: whereas 83 existed before the revolution, there were 2,250 soon thereafter. They allied with organizations with shared goals for the Ottoman future, such as merchants' unions and professional associations. When elections were held for parliament in November and December 1908, deputies affiliated and in sympathy with CUP policies earned a strong majority in the new parliament, which convened in January 1909.

But the CUP leadership proved ineffective in turning success into a clear political path after the elections. For example, CUP leaders who led the revolt would not clarify the CUP's political function within the government, refusing to transition it from an opposition movement into an official political party. They claimed that the organization served to protect the new constitutional regime but failed to provide any details about how the CUP could legally or constitutionally fulfill this role. Leadership intransigence kept the CUP position ambiguous; no one working in government knew what role the CUP would play at any given moment. Amid contradictory and competing aims, more happened because of inaction than action; for example, repressive censorship eased in 1908 mostly because no single agency was in charge of policing publications.

At the same time, the general trend in CUP decision making came into conflict with the revolutionary slogan "Liberty, Equality, Fraternity, and Justice" that had rung out since the coup took place. The leadership consistently advocated the centralization and standardization of governmental processes rather than autonomous power for governmental and provincial agencies. They hewed to the belief that the only way to modernize the empire was through central planning and control. This stance created conflicts within CUP ranks, between CUP leaders pushing for centralization and those who wanted to establish a polity with more freedom of action for the provinces and a space for political contestation at the imperial center.

The CUP leadership worked to ensure that its preferences would prevail. The civilians who had worked in exile and others who had joined the revolution hoping to secure stronger regional autonomy—Young Turks who did not favor centralization—received almost no posts in the new government. The CUP members who had led the revolution of 1908 and taken power afterward had closed ranks, and only other military men based in Salonika could join the top circles of government.

CUP Factions

Sabahattin Bey organized his supporters into a CUP faction, the Osmanlı Ahrar Fırkası (Party of Ottoman Liberals), which called for decentralized rule from Istanbul. They found common cause with a wide range of groups, from the Islamists who were critical of the secular attributes

Lord Weardale and Turkish Delegates.
At the House of Commons July 21st 1909.
J. Benjamin Stone

FIGURE 4.3. Young Turk leader Talat Pasha standing with Philip James Stanhope, Baron Weardale, and two other Turkish delegates in front of the House of Commons, London.

of the new governing leadership to the socialists who took issue with CUP economic policies. They formally merged into a party called the İttihad-ı Muhammedi (Muhammadan Union) in April 1909.

April 1909 Countercoup

Alaylı soldiers were among the many who sympathized with the opposition cause. They were angry at the Mektepli officers of the CUP who had begun a massive purge as soon as they came to office. As many as 10,000 army officers and soldiers may have been purged in the years after the 1908 revolution to ensure that the army was unconditionally loyal to the CUP. Older members of the civil service who had served the empire for years were also alienated as younger men replaced those who had held positions under Sultan Abdülhamit II's government. Religious leaders and students who joined the opposition wanted a restoration of Islam in public life. In April 1909, these combined forces attempted a countercoup against the CUP government aimed at destroying the Young Turk government and returning Sultan Abdülhamit II to power. The attempt failed when the Third Army marched to Istanbul from Macedonia to end it.

Entente Libérale

In the aftermath, the CUP finally became an official political party in 1910 and from this position passed laws in parliament that gave progressively more power to the cabinet and especially to the military. Moving to further consolidate CUP power, the leadership used repressive and fraudulent tactics in the parliamentary elections of early 1912—colloquially known as the "election with the stick"—to keep oppositional candidates out of parliament. Only six opposition candidates managed to win in a 278-seat Chamber of Deputies, which was otherwise dominated by the military CUP leadership. Nevertheless, the new parliament survived for only a short time because of an Albanian uprising, the last group in the Balkans to remain loyal to the Ottomans. The Albanians rebelled out of fear that other Balkan states would not respect its territorial integrity and the knowledge that the Ottoman army was too weak to protect them.

After failing to end the uprising, the CUP leadership who had been in office since 1908 resigned. Between August 1912 and January 1913, the CUP served as the party in opposition, while the Entente Libérale (Party of Freedom and Understanding) dominated the cabinet. This party had been formed in November 1911 from those who had tried to bring Sultan Abdülhamit II back to the throne in 1909 and CUP members who desired more autonomy for the empire's constituents than the military officers permitted.

First Balkan War

However, this new government could not withstand the pressures coming from the outbreak of the first Balkan War in 1912. The Ottoman army at home was undermanned because a large number of troops had been moved to Libya in 1911 to fend off an Italian invasion. When Serbia, Bulgaria, Greece, and Montenegro formed the Balkan League and went to war against the Ottoman Empire over the lands of Macedonia in the fall of 1912, the Ottomans were ill prepared to fight. The Balkan states were the winners, and they divvied up the spoils in Macedonia. According to the Treaty of London, signed on May 30, 1913, Greece received southern Macedonia, including the port of Salonika. Bulgaria gained the remaining parts of Macedonia, including the city of Edirne. The Ottoman Empire fought so badly that it retained only a small strip of European land between Edirne and Istanbul.

MACEDONIA

Macedonia contained Salonika, the largest and most lucrative port in southeastern Europe, and its strong agricultural and industrial base had benefited from 19th-century Ottoman development policies. It also contained within its borders every national, linguistic, and religious group the Ottoman Empire had ever controlled in the Balkans. Thus, the new Greek and Balkan states wanted to extend their territories into Macedonia, while the Ottomans were determined to retain their sovereignty over it. Forces outside Macedonia commonly appealed to the population on the basis of nationalism. The Greeks and Bulgarians emphasized the ties of the Eastern Orthodox religion; the Serbs, the Slavic ethnicity of many of the residents; and the Ottomans, their centuries-long rule.

By the 1890s, numerous Balkan and Greek soldiers and militia groups were sent into Macedonia to conquer territory. Organizations such as the Bulgarian National Committee, Greek Association of Hellenistic Letters, and Serbian Society of Saint Sava set up schools to persuade Macedonians of each one's national claims. The goal was to mobilize the Macedonians who considered themselves Ottoman, Greek, Serbian, Romanian, or Bulgarian to give aid to the military forces sent from that particular state. Some did join outside forces, among them members of the External Macedonian Revolutionary Committee (EMRO), founded in Bulgaria in 1895. Others established institutions predicated on Macedonian national identity, such as the Internal Macedonian Revolutionary Organization (IMRO), founded in 1893 to use military means to gain Macedonian independence. By 1907, almost 200 armed bands roamed through Macedonia, and the struggle for land and hearts continued; these competing territorial ambitions initiated the Balkan Wars of 1912 and 1913.

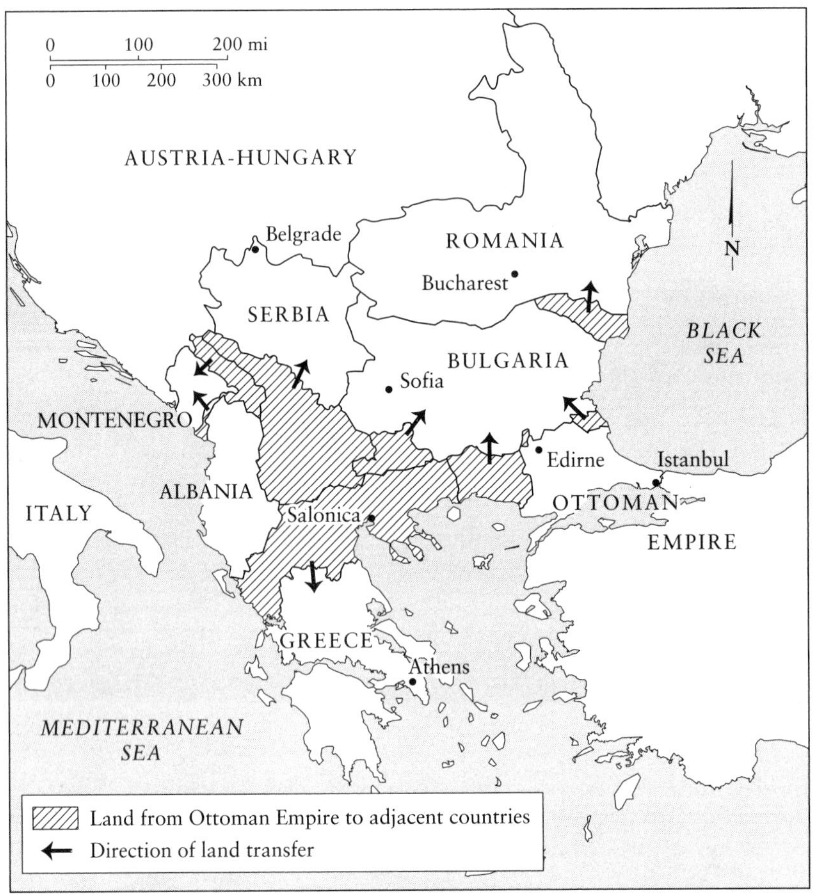

MAP 11. Land Transfers as a Result of the Balkan Wars of 1912 and 1913.

In the midst of the First Balkan War, when Edirne fell to the Bulgarians, the CUP had a perfect pretext for attacking the Entente Libérale government. The city was the first capital of the Ottoman Empire, before the conquest of Constantinople in 1453, and between the 17th and 18th centuries sultans lived in the palace there rather than in Topkapi in Istanbul. It was also one of the last remaining areas of Ottoman control in Europe and stood as a fortress protecting the path to Istanbul. For all these reasons, this amounted to a significant strategic and moral loss for the Ottoman government. In January 1913, CUP military officers staged a raid on the grand vizier's office and regained control of the Ottoman government.

Second Balkan War

Once back in office, the CUP immediately faced the Second Balkan War, which resulted from the dissolution of the Balkan League and the desire by Serbia, Greece, Montenegro, and Romania to take land in Macedonia that Bulgaria had received in the Treaty of London. Bulgaria attacked Serbian and Greek positions in Macedonia on June 29 and 30, 1913, igniting the new war. When the war ended, Serbia and Greece gained additional territories in Macedonia, while the Bulgarians lost much of what they had earned just a few months earlier. The Albanians declared independence during the war and in its aftermath received recognition by the European powers. Although the Ottomans were not key players in this second war, the CUP government took advantage of the circumstances to regain Edirne.

CUP Triumvirate

After 1913, CUP military officers grew increasingly authoritarian through their control of the government and parliament. The parliamentary elections of late 1913 returned a CUP majority, but by this point the CUP ruled largely without parliamentary input and directly through the cabinet. A triumvirate of officers took the reins of power: Enver, Cemal, and Talat Pasha became minister of war, the navy, and the interior, respectively.

FIGURE 4.4. Young Turk leader, Cemal Pasha, standing with members of the Ottoman parliament.

World War I Alliances

World War I began on June 28, 1914, in Sarajevo when Gavrilo Princip, a young Bosnian Serb revolutionary, assassinated Archduke Francis Ferdinand, heir to the Austria-Hungary throne. Members of the Black Hand Society had chosen this target because of Austria-Hungary's plans to keep the province of Bosnia-Herzegovina from coming under Serbian control. After the assassination, the Austrians accused the Serbian government of complicity in the attack, and the claims and counterclaims subsequently issued by the two governments led to a declaration of war between them. The domino effect brought the rest of Europe into war in the succeeding months. Germany, Austria-Hungary, Bulgaria, and Italy initially formed the Central Powers, fighting against the Entente Powers—Britain, France, Russia, and later Italy and the United States. The triumvirate of CUP officers made the decision to enter the war alongside the Central Powers, and by fall of 1914 the Ottoman Empire was at war. Although members of hostile alliances, the Ottoman Empire and the United States remained officially neutral toward each other throughout the war.

Bulgaria joined on the side of the Central Powers, though Greece and the other Balkan states chose the Entente alliance. When the war ended with an Entente victory, Bulgaria had to give up territory to Greece and Serbia and pay indemnities to both. The Romanians received Transylvania, Bessarabia, Crişana, and Bukovina. The newly established Kingdom of the Serbs, Croats, and Slovenes became Yugoslavia in 1929. Macedonia failed to gain independence, as Greece and Yugoslavia took its lands. Greece expanded its sovereign territory further by gaining islands in the Aegean and along the western coast of Anatolia from the Ottoman Empire. While Greece took its struggle for territory against the Ottoman Empire into the postwar period, the states of the Balkans ceased to be a Middle Eastern concern at this point.

Turks, Armenians, and Kurds and Their National Claims to Anatolia

The loss of soldiers and land in the Balkan wars and the launch of World War I further strained the inclusive Ottomanism that the Young Turk Revolution had promised. To retain control over the remaining territories, the CUP triumvirate became even more authoritarian as the leaders mobilized all available resources for the war effort. Any talk of autonomy not only conflicted with the centralization goals of the CUP but was now considered a sign of disloyalty to an empire struggling to survive.

Furthermore, the loss of the Balkans, and especially of Macedonia where so much of the CUP military leadership had served, had forced the Turkish leadership to look elsewhere for resources and national strength. On the eve of World War I, Anatolia became the focus for a Turkish leadership seeking to revive the empire. In Turkish writings and in CUP imperial policy, Anatolia became the central homeland for this national aspiration because it was here where the Turks had first begun to settle after their long migration and from where they conquered the rest of the empire. Turkish affection for Anatolia was enhanced by the fertility of its soil: Anatolia was an important breadbasket for the empire, not inconsequential at a time when resources were scarce.

By investing Anatolia with Turkish national claims, the CUP leaders accentuated the conflicts that had already erupted throughout the region because the Armenians and Kurds had both designated the region as central to their national claims. Armenians faced the brunt of this conflict in Anatolia because they paid the price for the anger arising from the loss of the Balkans. They were Christians like their Balkan counterparts and were also asking for the political autonomy that had led to independence for new Balkan states. Unlike their Balkan neighbors, however, they received no aid from the European powers. This came at a time when Turks, Kurds, and the new Muslim refugees were using violence to stop the Armenians from following the path of those in the Balkans.

Unified by the nationalizing process and radicalized by massacres in 1895 and 1896, the revolutionary organizations had fought for autonomy. But even under these conditions, the majority of Armenians remained loyal to the Ottoman leadership, and in 1902 the revolutionary parties had participated in the Congress of Ottoman Liberals alongside representatives of all the other nationalities of the empire. When the Young Turks gained power in 1908, many Armenian activists celebrated the event as the birth of a new era of inclusive Ottoman governance. In the first Ottoman parliament in 1908, 10 Armenians won seats, and their campaign speeches and platforms indicated that they believed in a definition of Ottomanism that saw all the peoples of the empire as equal partners.

Adana Massacre

However, in 1909, some 20,000 Armenians in the town of Adana in Cilicia were massacred. Local government officials and thousands of resident Muslims participated in the actions. Their anger grew out of the perception that Armenian Christians had prospered at the expense of their neighbors because they unfairly dominated cotton production for export and had acquired land by purchasing it from indebted Muslim peasants. The CUP government in Istanbul blamed the massacres on reactionaries in Adana who still supported the sultan, thereby eschewing responsibility. Few Armenian leaders accepted this explanation, and most organizations gave up hope that the CUP government could usher in any kind of agreement for Armenian autonomy. Only the Dashnaktsutiun among the major Armenian groups continued to work with the CUP. The result was a split within the Armenian leadership: most refused to work with the CUP government, but the Dashnaktsutiun kept open the possibility that Armenian autonomy could be achieved through negotiation.

Reform Act of February 8, 1914

In the years before World War I, the Dashnaktsutiun engaged in direct negotiations with the CUP government, hoping that reform could finally materialize. On the eve of World War I, this work resulted in the Ottoman government passing the Reform Act of February 8, 1914. Armenian areas of eastern Anatolia would be divided into two districts, with a foreign inspector-general as the supreme civil authority in each area. Additionally, the Ottoman government agreed to form administrative councils, establish a system of mixed Muslim-Christian police to patrol the Armenian areas, and issue official decrees in Turkish, Kurdish, and Armenian, with people legally entitled to use any of these languages in the courts. In return for these concessions, Armenians agreed to be eligible for conscription into the Ottoman military.

Ottomans and the Armenians held different views of this document. For the Ottoman leadership this document put the Armenians on the same path as the Balkan states; it represented the Armenians' first step toward independence. This was not reform: it was disloyalty. The Armenians were rebels opposing the right of the Ottoman government to rule them and the territory they claimed in Anatolia. For the Armenians, this agreement recognized their right to political autonomy under the umbrella of Ottomanism while protecting their status as citizens within the empire. In this view, they were rogues using military and diplomatic pressure against the sultan to achieve a better political position for themselves within the recognizable parameters of Ottoman governance. Soon after the war began, the Ottoman government suspended the Reform Act so few of its provisions were enacted.

World War I in Anatolia

In April 1915, the British and French launched a naval and amphibious attack in Western Anatolia at Gallipoli to gain unfettered sea and land access to Istanbul for the Entente Powers. The Ottoman army withstood the attack and by January 1916 had forced the British and French to retreat.

In eastern Anatolia and the Caucasus, however, the Ottoman army performed far more poorly. The Ottoman offensive that began on December 22, 1914, succeeded in pushing the Russian army back into the Caucasus temporarily, but the winter conditions soon negated territorial gains. At the Battle of Sarikamiş in January 1915 more than 60,000 Ottoman soldiers died, mostly from cold and disease and only a relatively few from battlefield wounds. As a result, the Russians forced the Ottoman army from the Caucasus and in February 1916 captured the strategic Anatolian city of Erzurum. From there they gained control over the Black Sea. Only when the Russian government fell in October 1917 to the Bolshevik Revolution did the pressure ease for the Ottomans on that front. With the signing of the Brest-Litovsk Treaty in early 1918, the Russian army withdrew from Anatolia, and the Ottomans recaptured Erzurum and provinces to the east.

FIGURE 4.5. An Ottoman battery stationed on the Gallipoli peninsula that repulsed the British attack in World War I between April 1915 and January 1916.

Armenian Deportations and Massacres of 1915

In between these two battle fronts, the long-term conflict between the Ottoman government, the Kurds, and the Armenians played out with devastating results. In 1915 the Russians, taking advantage of the Ottoman army's weakness, moved their forces toward Van, the city in eastern Anatolia with the largest number of Armenian inhabitants. A number of Armenians volunteered for the Russian army as it advanced, but the vast majority pledged their support for the Ottomans or at least did not impede the Ottoman war effort.

Nonetheless, the Ottoman government ordered the deportation of Armenians from the Anatolian towns most directly affected by the fighting, especially the provinces where the Armenian Reform Agreement of February 1914 was to be implemented. By June and July, the deportation orders expanded to include virtually all the Armenians in Anatolia and many from Istanbul; Armenians headed by the hundreds of thousands toward Syria, Russia, and Iran. Hundreds of thousands died in massacres in each of the towns and cities, and many thousands more died en route to their refuges. Those who remained were mostly women, girls, and boys who were adopted or forced to marry into Turkish Muslim families and converted to Islam. As many as 1.5 million Armenians died in the process: most of Anatolia was emptied of Armenians, and only 120,000 Armenians were left in Istanbul.

Armenian Genocide: Controversy and Accountability

Turks and Armenians have been in conflict since 1915 over how to characterize these events. A few conferences have taken place in Turkey over the last few years, where scholars have been allowed to discuss the fate of the Armenians who survived the massacres and were adopted and married into Turkish families. A number of descendants of these men and women have published memoirs of how they learned about their ancestors' lives and how the facts influenced their conception of national identity. Nonetheless, the Turkish government has not allowed the issue of accountability for the deportations and massacres to be discussed in a public forum.

The Turks characterize the deportations as a defensive action taken during a nationalist rebellion, when Armenians betrayed the Ottoman state to the invading Russians. From the Turkish perspective, the Armenians were another group in a long line of Christian aggressors intent on killing Muslims and forcing them out of their territory. The Turkish government has also consistently claimed that most of the attacks were undertaken by Kurds and local Muslim officials and were not initiated or supervised by officials in Istanbul. The Armenians characterize these events as a genocide and believe that they were planned at the highest level of government. They discount the claim that the Ottomans were acting in self-defense, pointing out that Armenians were not deported just from the war zones but from all over Anatolia and Istanbul.

Ottomans consistently removed Christians from their homelands during the many wars in the Balkans; forcible transfers of Christian populations from the empire had become Ottoman policy, according to the Armenians. The similarities in the ways the deportations and the killings took place from town to town indicated that the actions were being coordinated. Armenians also point out that the killings were undertaken not only by Kurds but also by the Special Organization, an irregular band formed by Minister of War Enver Pasha in November 1913 to attack behind enemy lines to weaken the enemy's regular forces and foment rebellion. The volunteers that made up the force were mostly recent Muslim refugees to Anatolia and one of the groups consistently attacking Armenians before the war.

No single "smoking gun" document has ever been found with a CUP leader's name authorizing a massacre of the Armenians, but evidence has accumulated that points to clear government intention. A series of documents issued immediately before World War I and in its first years indicate that the CUP leadership considered the Reform Agreement of 1914 a first step toward Armenians claiming independence, marking them as a threat to the empire's integrity. Documents also show that the deportation orders for most of the Armenians sent them into desert areas of southeastern Anatolia and the Syrian desert. The CUP government had already dismissed the Syrian desert as a possible site for the settlement of new Muslim migrants because of poor water resources and irrigation possibilities. Deliberately sending Armenians to these locations without any supporting aid was an implicit death sentence.

Ottoman Arabism

As did other peoples of the empire who had protested against Sultan Abdülhamit II's oppressive government for years, the politically active Arabs hoped the Young Turk Revolution of 1908 would usher in a new era of freedom and liberation and thus more rights for Arabs. A number of Arab military officers had joined the ranks of the CUP in the preceding years, adding their support to the broad-based Ottomanism advocated before the revolution. After 1908, the euphoria over the change in government slowly subsided as it became clear that Turks would monopolize the most prestigious posts throughout the empire and that Turks outnumbered Arabs in the newly elected parliament.

When the Young Turks' Ottomanism gave way to Turkish authoritarian centralization, Arabs in Damascus and Beirut began to slowly formulate an Arabism that had both political and cultural content. This Arabism, as it evolved in the years prior to World War I, focused on reforming the CUP to bring about a more inclusive Ottomanism, as promised in the restored 1876 constitution. Advocates of this position did not generally call for outright independence for the Arabs from the Ottoman Empire because they preferred reform and representation within it. Instead, they wanted guarantees that Arabs could hold influential government positions within the Arab provinces since they feared that CUP authoritarianism would curtail Arab freedom of political action.

A few societies made an explicit claim for independence, such as the Young Arab Society (al-Fatat) formed in Paris in 1911. The fraudulent elections of 1912 pushed many more Arab activists into political opposition; CUP censorship of the rising Arab activist press forced Arab writers to join their brethren in exile in Egypt and Europe so they could freely criticize CUP actions. In January 1913, Damascene and Lebanese Arab expatriates founded the Ottoman Party of Administrative Decentralization in Cairo, demanding greater administrative autonomy for Arabs within the Ottoman Empire. To gather supporters for both of these organizations, members established clandestine branches in Damascus and Beirut.

In June 1913, Arab Christians and Muslims from Syria and Lebanon convened the Arab Congress in Paris to assemble a comprehensive list of demands for the Ottoman government. Over the course of the six-day meeting, the participants declared they wanted the Ottoman Empire to remain sovereign over the Arab provinces. However, Arabs needed to be partners with, not subordinate to, the Turks. After the conference adjourned, a delegation met with CUP government representatives and demanded that Arabic be declared the language of instruction at all levels of education and administration in the Arab provinces and that Arabs receive guaranteed positions within the central government so they could supervise relations with the Arab provinces.

CUP officials responded by appointing six Arabs to the Senate, the upper house of parliament, and a number of others received high posts in the provincial administration; Arabic was made the language of instruction throughout the state schools in the region. The CUP motivation for granting such requests was to moderate Arab demands and forestall a call for more radical political changes in the Arab provinces. They were also easy concessions to make because they were cosmetic changes and did nothing to alter the balance of power between the Arabs and the CUP. The CUP leadership was mobilizing its resources to fight a world war, and Arab complaints were of little concern.

World War I in the Ottoman Arab Provinces

As soon as World War I broke out, Ottoman leaders made it clear that Arabs would be conscripted regardless of their particular political sentiments. Cemal Pasha left Istanbul, took up the post of military governor of Syria, and assumed command of the Fourth Army immediately after the war began. In Damascus and Beirut, he arrested hundreds of Arab notables, administrators, landowners, and journalists with little evidence that they had engaged in anti-CUP activity. In addition, Cemal Pasha hanged a Maronite priest for collusion with France; he tried and hanged 11 Beiruti political leaders on August 21, 1915. He executed 21 more Arab activists on May 6, 1916, many of them members of al-Fatat in Damascus and Beirut. Those who fled he tried in absentia, condemning to death 71 notables in this fashion. He also confiscated their property and deported as many as 5,000 others.

Economic Devastation

The Arabs suffered economic privation during the war. The Ottoman army conscripted most of the able-bodied men in the region, making them unavailable to harvest crops or manage their businesses; many thousands died or were wounded during the fighting. The Entente powers instituted a blockade of the Levant coast, and as a result exports and imports largely halted, food shortages became acute, and prices rose. The years of Ottoman devaluation of the currency had already severely weakened its viability as currency; wartime conditions increased the inflation exponentially. The wheat-producing areas of southern Syria—the Druze region of the Hawran—continued to cultivate wheat, but much of it was sold to the advancing army and denied to the local population.

People were weakened by nutritional deficiencies, and epidemics sped through the society, killing tens of thousands of people and forcing still more to move to cities such as Damascus and Beirut looking for jobs and assistance. According to one estimate, 100,000 people in Beirut and

Mount Lebanon died of famine during the war years, a famine brought on by the blockade, the fighting through the region, and a locust invasion that destroyed most of the crops. The massive move into the cities caused prices for housing and food to spike above even the already war-inflated prices. Furthermore, hundreds of thousands of soldiers deserted the Ottoman army, and the deserters who remained in Syria turned to brigandage as a way to survive, making cities and countryside dangerous even when not the site of battles.

Military Action

The Arabs suffered more than economic privations. The Levant became a battleground between the British and Ottomans. After suffering defeat in Gallipoli, the British held the Suez Canal against two attempts by the Ottoman Fourth Army in 1915 and 1916. The British then planned a series of offensives through the Arab provinces designed to weaken Ottoman forces and enable the British to take control of the strategic resources available there. Iraq and the Persian Gulf were of strategic importance because of the British navy's reliance on oil, which the British had been getting from Iran since 1908. British hopes for additional oil throughout the region had grown strong, with particular focus on the area that would become Iraq. British officials and soldiers from India landed in Basra in November 1914 and then advanced toward Baghdad. The Ottomans succeeded in stopping these forces in Kut in April 1916 and capturing 13,000 British soldiers in the process, but after receiving reinforcements from India, the British army conquered Baghdad in March 1917.

Arab Revolt

In the meantime, British officials moving toward Baghdad and those already headquartered in Cairo introduced the idea of fomenting an Arab revolt against the Ottomans, aimed at diverting Ottoman troops away from the British battle lines and cutting off access between Ottoman troops in the Middle East and German troops in Africa. British officials needed an Arab to lead this revolt, and the officers posted in Iraq favored Abdul Aziz ibn Abdul Rahman Al Saud, known as Ibn Saud. The leader of the Saud family of central Arabia, he had demonstrated his leadership and military potential by capturing huge swaths of the Arabian Peninsula in the years leading up to the war.

After retreating to Najd after the defeat by Mehmet Ali's forces in the Hijaz in 1818, the Saud family, in collaboration with the Wahhab religious group, regrouped and steadily conquered territory throughout the peninsula, including Riyadh (1902) and Hasa (1913). The Ottoman government recognized his victory by declaring Ibn Saud the wali (governor) of Najd in 1914. In 1915 the British signed the Anglo-Saudi Treaty in which they acknowledged Ibn Saud as the leader of Najd, Hasa, Qatif, and Jubayl. With the British material support that came along with this agreement, Ibn Saud was able to militarily chip away at rival territories during the war. Though Ibn Saud had his advocates, the British eventually determined that he would not be the proper conduit for an Arab revolt against the Ottomans because he focused his activities solely on the Arabian Peninsula and showed little interest in attacking the Ottoman army outside the region.

Hussein-McMahon Correspondence

Instead, the British Arab Bureau in Cairo took the lead in establishing a relationship with Sharif Hussein, the Ottoman official charged since 1908 with protecting the holy sites of Mecca and Medina. The family claimed descent from the Prophet, hailing from the Banu Hashim, or the Hashemites as the family called itself in the 20th century. Hussein's second son, Emir Abdullah, served in the Ottoman parliament as a representative for Mecca from 1909 to 1914; his third son, Emir Faysal, spent extended periods of time in Istanbul serving as the parliamentary representative from Jeddah. His oldest son and heir, Emir 'Ali, attended the Galatasary Lycée in Istanbul but otherwise served his father in Mecca. Because of this long-term affiliation with Ottoman governance, Sharif Hussein and his sons remained loyal officials of the Ottoman government and were not part of the Arab nationalist movement that had emerged in Damascus, Beirut, and Cairo.

But the Ottoman trend toward centralization in Sultan Abdülhamit II's day and under the CUP government threatened Sharif Hussein's autonomous power. In particular, the extension of the Hijazi Railway from Damascus to Medina, completed on September 1, 1908, meant that the government in Istanbul could more closely follow developments in the Hijaz. When the war erupted, Sharif Hussein decided to take advantage of the disruption to extend his influence and to align forces against the Ottoman Empire. Because Sharif Hussein was the official protector of the holy sites, his legitimacy for Arab Muslims was already established, and he could make the claim to being their natural leader.

Subsequent negotiations with the British produced what is called the Hussein-McMahon correspondence, named for Sharif Hussein and Sir Henry McMahon, the British high commissioner in Egypt. Over the course

FIGURE 4.6. Hijazi Railway station at Ma'an, Transjordan.

of 10 letters written between July 1915 and March 1916 the two men worked out an agreement that established the parameters for an Arab revolt. Sharif Hussein, claiming to represent the Arab people, asked the British to guarantee him leadership over an independent Arab state, which would include the Arabian Peninsula, the Levant, and Iraq, in exchange for his commitment to lead an armed rebellion against the Ottomans. The British countered by demanding that certain regions such as Iraq and the Syrian coast be kept under some type of British and French control. Sharif

Hussein agreed to these exclusions provisionally so the revolt could begin. The fate of Palestine remained equivocal, with Sharif Hussein believing it would come under Arab control after the war, and the British proposing it would be placed under French control. Sharif Hussein and McMahon made many compromises and accommodations during their exchange, and this was one of a number of the regions to be renegotiated after the war.

Faysal and the Arab Revolt

Regardless of the ambiguities embedded in these letters, the Arab revolt began in Mecca on June 10, 1916, under the leadership of Sharif Hussein's son, Emir Faysal, and with the aid of British liaison T. E. Lawrence,

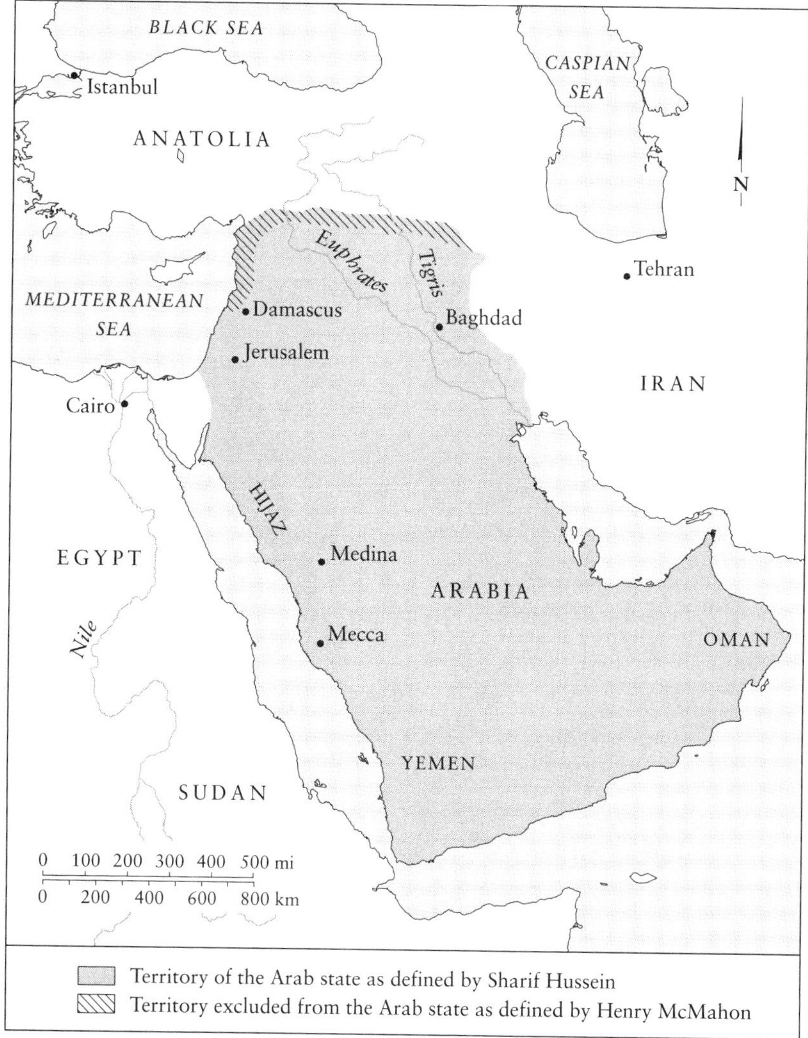

MAP 12. Territory of the Arab State as proposed by Sharif Hussein in the Hussein-McMahon correspondence, with exclusions defined by Henry McMahon.

known as "Lawrence of Arabia." As the army moved north, it attacked the Hijazi Railway while capturing towns from the Ottomans. Through their actions, the Arabs kept 30,000 Ottoman troops from linking up with German forces in Yemen and East Africa. In July 1917, the Arab revolt army captured the seaport of Aqaba, blocking the best possible inlet for German forces to land. From there, the army moved north through the future Transjordan toward Damascus.

During the move north, Emir Faysal had to continually negotiate with the tribes and families living along the attack route. In the move through the Hijaz, all the way to Aqaba and then to the town of Ma'an, now in modern-day southern Jordan, Emir Faysal used Islam as the rallying point to persuade the tribal leaders to help his cause. His father, in initiating the Arab revolt, had proclaimed the action a jihad (holy war) against the Ottomans. Influenced by pragmatic considerations and the respect the shaykhs held for the Hashemite family, some of the tribes along the route chose to fight alongside Emir Faysal while others at least allowed his army to travel through their territory. After the army moved north of Ma'an, Emir Faysal began to change his techniques. Because of

FIGURE 4.7. A snapshot taken by T. E. Lawrence of Emir Faysal (*in white*) and the Arab revolt army as it moved northward in the Hijaz, along the Red Sea, in 1917.

his proximity to Damascus and the influence of the Arab activists living there, he spoke in terms of Arab nationalism to attract followers. When he neared Damascus, he sent emissaries to the city's Arab leadership to gain their trust. Emir Faysal entered Damascus on October 1, 1918, and set up an Arab government under British supervision.

Mudros Armistice

Meanwhile, British forces under General Edmund Allenby were moving on a course parallel to that of the Arab revolt army, advancing up the Mediterranean coast. In 1914 the British had imposed martial law in Egypt, poured in thousands of troops, and made it a direct protectorate and headquarters for the combined offensive against the Ottoman army. To build their forces, the British recruited soldiers from around the British Empire and conscripted thousands of Egyptians. With this army, the British entered Jerusalem in December 1917, moved alongside Emir Faysal toward Damascus, and then defeated the Ottoman army in Aleppo on October 25.

The Ottoman Empire sued for peace by signing the Mudros Armistice on October 30, 1918. By that point, almost one million Ottoman officers and soldiers had died—most from disease—and almost one million more were wounded. Overall, less than a third of all Ottoman soldiers survived the war. To these statistics can be added the millions of civilians killed and displaced throughout the war.

Sykes-Picot Agreement and the Balfour Declaration

Complicating the postwar settlement, British officials in London parceled out Arab and Ottoman lands in contradictory ways in three separate agreements made after the Hussein-McMahon correspondence. In the Inter-Allied Constantinople Agreement of March 18, 1915, Britain promised that Russia would be allowed possession of Istanbul, the Straits connecting the Aegean and Black Seas, and the eastern provinces of Turkey at the end of the war. This agreement was never implemented, however, because Russia withdrew from the war before its end and signed the Treaty of Brest-Litovsk with the Central Powers, including the Ottoman Empire. This treaty restored to the Ottomans territory in eastern Anatolia that the Russians had captured in the 1877–1878 Russo-Ottoman War.

In the Sykes-Picot Agreement of May 1916, Englishman Sir Mark Sykes and Frenchman François Georges-Picot, anticipating Entente victory, divided up much of the Arab region into areas of direct and indirect influence, in the process contradicting many of the promises the British had made to Sharif Hussein in his correspondence with McMahon. According to this agreement, the British validated France's long-standing claims to Mount Lebanon and Damascus, and France was promised direct control over the coastal area and indirect control throughout the Syrian hinterland. Britain would assume direct control over the southern Iraqi provinces, while the remaining areas that would become Iraq would be under indirect control. The Arab state that had been promised to Sharif Hussein would be situated within the areas of indirect British and French control, with its borders and type of government to be determined after the war. Palestine was to be subject to an international governing structure.

In the Balfour Declaration of November 2, 1917, British Foreign Secretary Lord Balfour promised Zionist leader Lord Rothschild that "His Majesty's Government view with favour the establishment in Palestine of a national home for the Jewish people, and will use their best endeavours to facilitate the achievement of this object, it being clearly understood that nothing shall be done which may prejudice the civil and religious

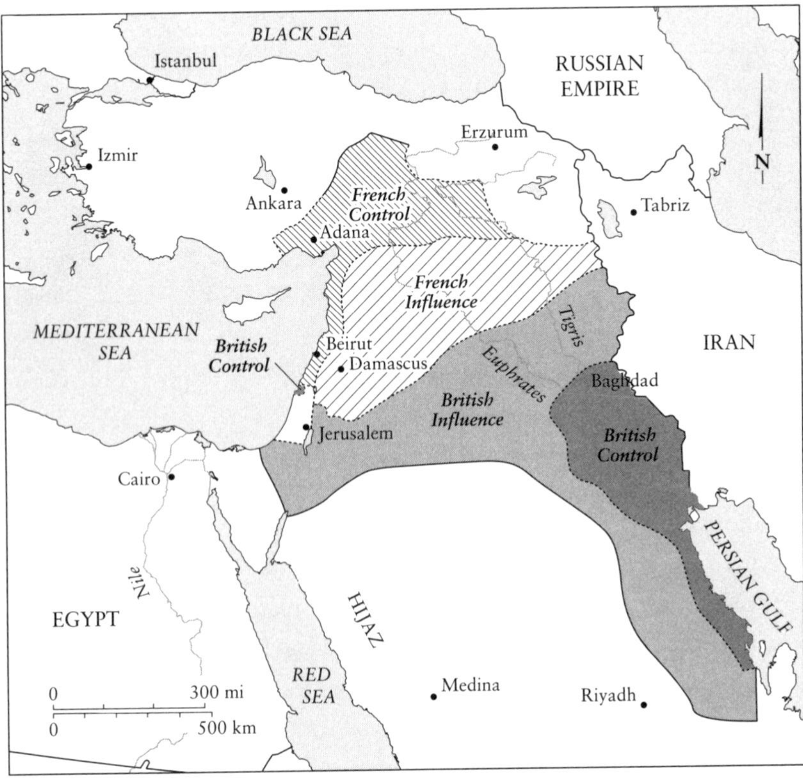

MAP 13. British and French Territories in the Inter-Allied Constantinople Agreement, 1915, and the Sykes-Picot Agreement, 1916. These agreements divided territory in the Arab world between direct and indirect zones of British and French control.

rights of the existing non-Jewish communities in Palestine, or the rights and political status enjoyed by Jews in any other country." The declaration was intended to garner international Jewish support for the British war effort, and it documented the British government's shift toward supporting Zionist claims to the lands of Ottoman Palestine.

While the Balfour Declaration directly addressed the interests of the Jews of Europe, it created a conundrum the British could never solve: How could a Jewish homeland be established in Palestine without compromising the civil and religious rights of the non-Jewish majority? This document brought more complications to an already fraught settlement over lands in the Middle East because in the many agreements the British signed as gambits to gain supporters in the war, Palestine had been promised to the Zionists as well as to the Arabs, the French, and to some never-defined international organization.

Roots of Zionism

For Jews the goal of returning to Jerusalem and reestablishing a Jewish homeland on territory from which they had been exiled by Roman act in AD 70 was not a new one. The Jews had conquered Palestine, or Canaan, in the 12th century BC and had established a united Israeli kingdom there for 70 years, between 1000 and 927 BC. The Babylonian Captivity exiled most of the Jews in the 6th century, but when the Persian kingdom of the Achaemenids conquered Babylon in 569 BC, many Jews were allowed to return to Israel. Jewish rule again emerged after Alexander's conquest of the region in 333 BC; however, it largely ended with the advent of Roman rule and the Jewish expulsion in AD 70. During the 19th century in Germany and eastern Europe, a number of Jewish organizations arose that called for reestablishing some kind of Jewish state or religious center in Palestine. They taught Hebrew as a national language and trained Jews for the agricultural work they would have to perform once they migrated. About 50,000 Jews took part in the first and second aliyahs (ascents), moving from Europe to Palestine, in the years between 1882 and 1903 and 1904 and 1914.

Although a number of societies advocated a return to Israel, Theodor Herzl is often considered the father of modern Zionism. His book *The Jewish State* was published in 1896, and he organized the first of the Zionist Conferences in 1897, which set in motion events that would eventually lead to the founding of Israel in May 1948. Herzl was born in Budapest in 1860 to a banking family and by the 1880s had received a

FIGURE 4.8. Theodor Herzl sailing on the Russian ship *Imperator Nikolai II* from Alexandria, Egypt, to Jaffa, Palestine, on October 26, 1898.

law degree and was working as a journalist. The trials of Jewish military officer Alfred Dreyfus for treason against the French state pushed Herzl to organize a political movement that could establish a refuge for Jews.

After two trials and two guilty verdicts, Dreyfus was finally vindicated in 1906. But in the meantime, his case generated controversy throughout Europe. Many believed that Dreyfus could not be unconditionally loyal to the French state because his Jewish identity superseded his French one. Herzl took away from the events the belief that Jews could never be completely safe from discrimination in Europe. Herzl wrote of the Jews' need for refuge from such persecution. He suggested Argentina and Ottoman Palestine as possible sites for settlement, while recognizing that the latter held the most emotional connection for the Jews. The delegates at the first Zionist Conference declared that Palestine would be the focus of efforts to establish a Jewish homeland.

Many Jews who had survived a series of late 19th-century pogroms in eastern Europe and Russia came to support Herzl's project because they knew they were not safe in their native terrain. Others supported his project because the Dreyfus Affair had shown that even in western Europe Jews were not safe from persecution. Herzl was an effective organizer of people and resources, so he guaranteed that his work could continue even after his death in 1904. He institutionalized the entire project by gaining support from powerful Europeans. In particular, he swayed many people in the British government, both Jewish and Christian, who came to support the idea of Zionism for religious reasons and also practical ones, because Jewish immigration to Palestine could populate it with allies protective of British interests. Zionism was not a mass movement in 1917, when the British government issued the Balfour Declaration, but it had powerful and wealthy allies willing to support the project. It had also attracted a great deal of passionate support from Jews throughout Europe who were willing to migrate to see their national ideal realized.

Palestinian National Awakening

Nevertheless, the Zionist movement ignored the fact that Arabs—Muslim, Christian, and Jewish—already lived in Palestine and were gradually forming their own national identity. The urban elite were undertaking the same nationalizing processes as their fellow Arabs in places like Damascus and Beirut. Palestinian Arabs took part in the movements protesting the authoritarianism of the governments of Sultan Abdülhamit II and the CUP. Their newspapers also extolled the uniqueness of Palestine and the special place it held in Arab culture, religion, and history.

By the time of the Balfour Declaration, Arab Muslims and Christians made up about 90 percent of the population, despite the preceding decades' migration of Jews from Europe. Palestinians were responsive to Westerners' preoccupation with the Holy Land because there had been tourists making pilgrimages to the region's holy sites since the early 19th century, highlighting the region's unique place in history. They were also aware of Zionism because Herzl had visited the region and requested that Sultan Abdülhamit II grant Palestinian land for his program. The sultan rejected Herzl's requests, but this attempt at political diplomacy had awakened Palestinian leaders to the threat that Zionism posed to their land. In the decade before World War I, Palestinian newspapers were filled with information about Zionism and warnings about how Zionists planned to transform the land of Palestine into their own national center.

Conclusion

The Ottoman and Qajar Empires both entered World War I having undergone revolutions in the preceding decade. In the former, a military coup brought to the surface conflicts over how inclusive or exclusive the concept of Ottomanism should be in determining the relationship between the Ottoman state and its varied citizenry. With restructuring and reforms, the Ottomans had tried in the 19th century to create new strata of loyal stakeholders, but instead it opened a Pandora's box of demands from those who sought greater autonomy because they perceived Ottomanism through the lens of their own national identity. The result was violence within the borders of the Ottoman Empire and defeat by the Western powers in World War I.

In Iran the Constitutional Revolution of 1906 began with the participation of the ulama, the bazaaris, and the many new anjomen, all the groups opposing the shahs' policies and European intervention in Iranian economic and political life. But it ended on the eve of World War I with the various groups incapable of working out a shared system for governance. In the years before the war the shahs and the groups in the majles had been unable stop the British and Russians from making Iran a virtual colony; the declaration of neutrality did not prevent Iran from serving as a battlefield for foreign conflicts. Iran exited World War I under British occupation, fragmented geographically and politically.

The years immediately after World War I brought the manifold conflicting desires for the Middle East into the open. Rebellions broke out across the Qajar and Ottoman Empires, while the British and the French began to implement their colonial designs on the region.

5 STATE FORMATION AND COLONIAL CONTROL

Turkey, Iran, Syria, Lebanon, Iraq, Transjordan, and Saudi Arabia in the 1920s and 1930s

BY THE TIME THE WAR ENDED in the Middle East in 1918, Britain held the largest military advantage of all the European powers. It maintained its protectorate over Egypt and during the war stationed troops in Palestine, Syria, Iraq, Anatolia, and Iran. After the war ended, in agreement with the Entente Powers, the British also became the dominant foreign power broker in Istanbul. French troops entered the Anatolian region of Cilicia, and French general Henri Gouraud landed troops in Beirut. Greece took control of the Anatolian port city of Izmir in May 1919. The subsequent Treaty of Sèvres of August 1920 gave Greece sovereignty over the European province of Thrace, including the old Ottoman capital of Edirne. The Italians moved into Anatolia via the port of Antalya. Russia was not included in the division of spoils because it had terminated its participation before the war's end. However, Russian troops remained along the Ottoman and Iranian borders, making it difficult to delineate clear borders between the three countries.

The years between 1918 and the early 1920s saw the emergence of the modern states of Iran, Iraq, Syria, Lebanon, Jordan, Saudi Arabia, and Egypt, ushered in by European fiat and local action. However, by no means did the process of state formation go smoothly in any of these new countries. The end of the war presented new opportunities for shaping the states being formed. With the defeat of the Ottoman Empire and the fragmentation and weakening of the Qajar Empire by the end of the war, many groups throughout this swath of territory rose up to defend their territories from the Europeans and other local leaders who were simultaneously moving into the political vacuum left by the war.

The rebels who emerged on the political scene in 1918 were those who had been marginalized by their governments before the war: small merchants, religious clerics, tribal shaykhs, urban workers, peasants, artisans, civil servants, and bazaaris who had been granted few positions of authority under the previous empires or who saw their local positions threatened by the configurations of states being designed by the Europeans. Some opposition groups, such as the Kurds in Turkey, sought to break away from their designated states altogether, but more often than not rebellions were led by men bidding for positions of power within the state being formed. The rebels rarely tried to coordinate their activities within the new state borders, but since a primary goal of most of the disparate groups was to keep European outsiders from colonizing their homelands, there was a proto-nationalist element in their actions. In Iran and Turkey, the rebels—led by Reza Shah and Mustafa Kemal, respectively—entered office and established authoritarian states independent of European colonial control.

In contrast, Iraq, Syria, Lebanon, Jordan, and Palestine came under European colonial control in the aftermath of World War I; Egypt and Saudi Arabia gained partial independence. In choosing state leaders for their new colonies, the Europeans looked not to the rebels they had to militarily defeat in the months after the war ended but to the large landowners, wealthy merchants, and tribal shaykhs who had served as intermediaries in the old empires. These notables had grown strong as a result of the changes wrought by the Ottoman government in the last half of the 19th century and maintained their influence by agreeing to work on behalf of the new post–World War I European-designed governments. In Egypt, the British allowed a greater measure of independence for the local government than before the war. But during the interwar period, British officials worked to keep all the political groups divided and thus incapable of threatening the British position. Saudi Arabian leaders spent the interwar years establishing a government that would span much of the Arabian Peninsula.

Across the region, new institutions of state brought increasing numbers of people into government orbit as civil servants, police and military forces, students, and tax payers. The problem of determining what would be a proper type of leadership for the new state and what type of government to form within it was not, however, resolved. New rebellions continued to break out throughout the decade and again in the 1930s as a result of the continuing divisions between those who had acquired and those who were excluded from positions of influence. The processes by which state formation between 1918 and the early 1930s took place in Turkey, Iran, Syria, Lebanon, Iraq, Transjordan, and Saudi Arabia illustrate these phenomena.

Rebellion and State Construction in Turkey

As the empire faced defeat in fall 1918, Ottoman CUP leaders fled the country, leaving a vacuum for junior-level CUP officials to form the Renovation Party. The Entente Libérale Party reemerged from underground, and one of its members, Ferid Pasha, served as grand vizier in five cabinets between March 1919 and October 1920. Sultan Mehmet VI sat on the Ottoman throne, succeeding Sultan Mehmet V, who had died a few months before the war ended. Together, these groups enabled the Ottoman government to continue to rule for the next few years. This government also signed the Treaty of Sèvres, which laid out arrangements for a postwar territorial settlement for the empire. Its provisions formally separated the Arab provinces from Ottoman control and granted the Kurds autonomy and the Armenians independence in the regions they

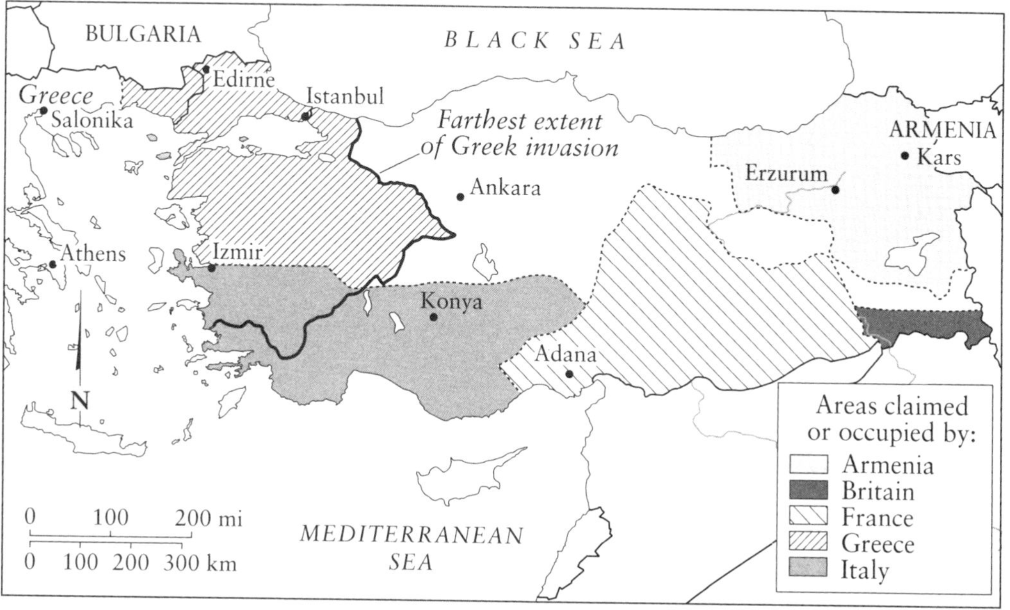

MAP 14. Spheres of Influence and Occupation in Anatolia in 1919.

dominated in Anatolia. The Ottoman government agreed to pay indemnities for the war, continue servicing the Ottoman debt, and maintain the low tariff duties contained within the old Capitulation treaties. France, Britain, Greece, and Italy all received the right to maintain the spheres of influence they had already established in Anatolia and Thrace.

While this government negotiated on the world stage concerning the division of the empire in the aftermath of the war, at home it struggled to regain direct control over an Anatolia that continued to be a national battleground for Turks, Armenians, and Kurds. Unlike the conflicts that had erupted since the late 19th century, now Greeks and Europeans also sought to control parts of the territory. The Treaty of Sèvres had delineated special zones for the Europeans as well as the Greeks, Kurds, and Armenians, making the division of the territory an international concern.

Defense of National Rights Societies

Because Istanbul has little effective control over Anatolia after the war, local Turkish groups calling themselves the Defense of National Rights Societies formed militias to defend their territories from the Europeans and from Armenians and Kurds who were being promised lands these Turks considered their national homeland. Local notables, former Ottoman army officers, ulama, and lower-level CUP leaders took advantage of the breakdown in governance to take command of their local regions. Although each society worked in only a small sector of Anatolia, so many groups were working in parallel that they were essentially forming a nationwide defense movement for the Turks of Anatolia.

Grand National Assembly

The sultan's government tried to organize a military force capable of defeating these societies by sending Mustafa Kemal, a hero of the Gallipoli campaign of 1916, as one of the officers. Instead of fighting against the Turkish societies, Kemal landed in Anatolia at the port of Samsun on May 19, 1919, and pledged to lead the Turks to independence. In July 1919, many of the societies' leaders met in a congress in Erzurum to coordinate their military activities against the Istanbul government. Kemal resigned his Ottoman military commission and took on chairmanship of the congress. Between September 4 and 11, 1919, a second congress met in Sivas, close to central Anatolia, and passed a series of resolutions collectively known as the National Pact. They declared that the Ottoman Arab provinces should hold plebiscites to determine sovereignty over their territories but that all other provinces within Anatolia and around Istanbul were indivisibly Turkish. This group constituted itself as the Grand National Assembly (GNA) on April 23, 1920, marking the moment when Turkey had two governments: one in Istanbul and one in Ankara.

Even with much popular enthusiasm for this government in Ankara, opposition arose as well, making its birth a difficult one, indicating that the GNA still had to gain legitimacy as the leading organization for Turkish defense. The national defense societies had from the beginning been independent organizations with very local concerns. A number had been included in the congresses, but many had been left out and resented the loss of power to the new government. Disparate rebels fought not only to maintain sovereignty over what they considered Turkish land but also to defend their own local hegemony. To discourage opposition, the GNA asserted that it had the legitimate right to punish even Turks who refused to accede to its authority. In summer 1920 a civil war broke out throughout Anatolia as recalcitrant rebels fought against the strictures being imposed on them from Ankara.

During late fall 1920 and into winter 1921, the GNA passed a series of laws designed to bring the rebels into line. One of the most influential was the Law on Fugitives, which required the GNA to punish deserters from the new national army. Another important measure was establishment of the Independence Tribunals, whose purpose was to put on trial anyone accused of treason against Ankara. Both legal strategies proved successful in defeating the rebellious societies, enabling the GNA to consolidate the disparate local forces into a new national army. In a further effort to establish its legitimacy, the GNA drafted the first constitution for republican Turkey—the Fundamental Law—and adopted it on January 20, 1921. It delineated the powers accorded the president and the assembly, while affirming the Turkish people's sovereignty over the government.

Turkish Military Victories

While battling the rebellious national defense societies and acquiring legitimacy by enacting a constitution for a new Turkish government, Kemal and the GNA turned their attention to the European powers occupying Turkish land and to the Kurds and Armenians, still struggling against the Turks as they had for decades. Throughout 1920, Turkish nationalist troops attacked the French position in southwestern Anatolia and forced the French to gradually retreat. Fighting against the French in the Battle of Marash in early 1920, the GNA massacred thousands of Armenians whom the French had repatriated after World War I and forced thousands more to flee, sending them into exile again. In October 1921, the GNA and the French government ratified the Ankara Agreement, which detailed the final French withdrawal from the region. Having also won a military victory over groups of rebellious Kurds, the Ankara government succeeded in destroying any possibility of an Armenian or Kurdish state in Anatolia in the 1920s. The competition for Anatolia that had begun in the late 19th century with the rise of Turkish, Kurdish, and Armenian national identities had ended with a victory for the Turks. The events of the war and the subsequent expulsion from Marash had forced almost all Armenians out of Anatolia. The centralizing Turkish state overpowered Kurdish efforts to rebel in the 1920s and 1930s.

The Ankara Turks then began an attack against the Greeks who had taken control over the western Anatolia coast in the aftermath of the war. The GNA rallied forces throughout Anatolia in defense of Turkish national land. In July 1922, the GNA army began its offensive against the Greeks in Izmir and succeeded in ending the occupation of the city and the surrounding province. The Mudanya Armistice was signed on September 11, 1922. The city of Izmir went up in flames during the campaign, thousands died in the fighting, and one million Greeks and half a million Turks were exchanged between Greek and Turkish lands.

Treaty of Lausanne

After taking full control of Anatolia, Kemal and the GNA brought the European powers back to the negotiating table. In the subsequent Treaty of Lausanne of 1923, the European spheres of influence were officially dismantled, and the signers recognized Turkish sovereignty over all territory under direct GNA control. The treaty also canceled the World War I debt and abolished the Capitulation treaties, but it maintained low import tariff duties until 1929 and required that the Turkish Republic pay a portion of the Ottoman public debt beginning in 1929. The Kurds and the Armenians lost their autonomous status and became Turkish citizens with special protections afforded them as minorities. The GNA followed ratification of the Lausanne Treaty with the proclamation of the Republic of Turkey on October 29, 1923. This new Turkish government had already abolished the Ottoman sultanate in 1922; on March 3, 1924, the GNA did the same for the caliphate and, with it, the last remaining authority of the Ottoman ruling family. Mustafa Kemal had harnessed a fragmented rebellion and transformed it into a Turkish War of Liberation to reclaim territorial

FIGURE 5.1. Turkish president Mustafa Kemal and his wife, Latife Hanım, 1923.

control over Anatolia. In the process, he secured international and domestic recognition for his particular leadership over the new Turkish state.

Authoritarianism in Turkey

From his position as president, Kemal pushed a series of laws through the Turkish parliament in the 1920s establishing institutions of state charged with disseminating his agenda throughout the country. Thus, Kemal defined an overarching identity for the Turkish Republic that would subsume religion under state control and look to the West for guidance on future political and cultural decisions. In place of the Ottoman identity that applauded cosmopolitanism and a centuries-long religious tolerance, Kemal substituted a new Turkish identity that harked back to the pre-Ottoman era of Turkic migrations and celebrated the distinctiveness of the Turkish language, culture, and history.

Legislation for Turkish Modernization

On March 3, 1924, the Turkish parliament passed the Law for the Unification of Education, which declared that henceforth all schools would be secular with the exception of a few Islamic Imam-Hatip schools and the Faculty of Divinity at the University of Istanbul. A month later, on April 8, the GNA abolished the shari'a courts; on November 30, 1925, it abolished all Sufi orders. The government adopted the Gregorian calendar in the place of the Islamic calendar on January 1, 1926. Over the next few months, the GNA voted to implement the Swiss Civil Code, the Italian Penal Code, and elements of the German and Italian Commercial Codes in the place of the shari'a and the Ottoman Mecelle. On November 1, 1928, the government declared that a new Turkish language, with Latin letters, would replace the Arabic alphabet beginning in 1929. Kemal used the new Republican People's Party (RPP), founded in August 1923, as his primary vehicle for these changes. In 1935, the RPP passed a resolution formally uniting state and party as one, making the decisions of one identical to the policies of the other. In 1934, the state had abolished the old titles of effendi and bey for men and hanım for women; in the same year, all citizens were required to select surnames, having for centuries used honorifics, fathers' names, occupations, and locales as monikers. Parliament bestowed on Kemal the surname Atatürk (father of the Turks), and he served as president with that name until his death in 1938.

Kemal capitalized on his triumphant leadership during the War of Liberation to push through radical and often contentious policies. He also took advantage of the fact that many of the Ottoman empire's elites had been discredited by the World War I defeat. Since Anatolia was made up of largely medium to small landowners, he did not have to contend with a powerful cadre of large landowners. In appointing the top officials for his government, Kemal favored the close advisers he had acquired from the War of Liberation. The vast majority of the national defense society leaders achieved a measure of local influence in the new provincial governments of Anatolia, but they did not have access to the halls of government in Ankara. Kemal also elevated to influential positions the Westernized partisans, such as administrators and professionals, who valued the modernization program he instituted and wanted to serve as its implementers.

The Six Principles of Kemalism

In 1931, at the Third Party Congress of the RPP, Kemal laid out the six principles of what became the cornerstone of Kemalism: republicanism, nationalism, populism, statism, secularism, and reformism. Republicanism rejected the monarchical Ottoman model and ushered in elements of popular sovereignty; nationalism integrated Turkish identity with Kemal's program; populism called for a wholesale mobilization of the population to accomplish state-defined projects; and statism identified the state as the leading investor in the economy. Kemalist secularism was in line with the tenets of the French concept of laicism by allowing for the practice of religion in private society but state control over its institutions in the public realm. Reformism encompassed all the changes that Kemal was initiating in Turkey. These elements became the backbone of Article 2 of the revised constitution of February 5, 1937.

The six elements of Kemalism defined a specific Turkish identity that differentiated the new Turks from the old Ottomans. This new polity could not completely divorce itself from its Ottoman legacy, but the institutions of republican Turkey were distinguished by being modern, uniquely Turkish, and reflective of Kemal's personal vision. The language reform measure is a good example of how this break with the Ottoman past was achieved. Not only was the alphabet changed but the Turkish Language Society as of 1932 took on the task of formulating a national language by eliminating Arabic and Persian words, finding Turkish substitutes, and inventing new words when no equivalents could be identified. In addition to the education provided in the expanding state school system, the state made available special classes for Turkish citizens of all ages to learn to read only the modern version of Turkish, with its Latin alphabet and its reformed vocabulary. Ottoman documents and records became inaccessible to the new generation of Turks as knowledge of Ottoman Turkish disappeared. The other new institutions of the 1920s may not have created such a clear-cut break with the past but still alienated the partisans of past institutions and brought in those beholden to Kemal, to the new republican Turkey, and to his combined vision for Turkishness and modernity.

Turkish National Narrative

The state recruited the Turkish Historical Society, which had been founded in 1931, to propose a scientifically sound thesis that explained the roots of Turkish history. Out of this work came the Turkish History Thesis, which highlighted the fact that Turks had migrated out of Central Asia long before the emergence of the Ottoman Empire. It was these early Turkish migrants who brought civilization to the peoples of China, India, the Middle East, North Africa, the Balkans, and parts of Europe. The affiliated Sun Language Theory stated that all these immigrants spoke an ancient form of Turkish, which contributed words to every language in the regions where Turks migrated. The Turkish Republic used these theories to subordinate its Ottoman past; they revealed that Turkish accomplishments predated the empire and represented a more lasting legacy. To disseminate this Turkish patriotic message, the RPP opened adult education centers called People's Houses and People's Rooms to bring movies, plays, libraries, dances, and schools to provincial towns so that the Turkish nationalist narrative could be understood and embraced by the population.

But even with these new institutions, along with their comprehensive ideology of nationalism and modernity, Kemal faced obstacles in embedding them into Turkish society in the interwar period. His government had acquired important new stakeholders, but there were many who had no voice in its decisions. The years after 1918 had brought many people out in support of defending Turks and their national claims, but by the 1920s, Mustafa Kemal was using the new state to curtail independent action by those same local leaders while imposing new regulations about how to live within his modern Turkish state.

Village Law

The Village Law, passed by parliament on March 8, 1924, was intended to modernize and standardize the villages of the country by requiring villages and villagers to fulfill a list of mandates. The list included the call to eliminate pools of standing water in the village, build a central water fountain, clean the village water supply, separate the living quarters of houses from their barns by a wall, and build covered toilets for every house. In addition, villages were supposed to build two roads that would run through the center of the community, inaugurate a Village Council room, build a school, and prohibit overloading an animal with a burden larger than it could carry.

Almost none of these mandates were carried out in the villages because the state lacked the resources to underwrite the expense, and the villages themselves could not afford it. Furthermore village leaders had no special ability or desire to bring about such reforms, nor did the central government expend many resources explaining the practical benefits the villages would accrue from these reforms. Vested groups such as the village leaders opposed the innovations, believing they would change the balance of power and weaken their positions. The villages tried to collect the taxes, fines, duties, and fees and supply the corvée labor the law required, but accomplishing these feats was just as difficult as it had been under the Ottomans. Even if all the taxes had been collected, the revenue would not have been enough to pay for the state-required projects. In this and similar cases, Kemal's popularity could not offset the government's lack of resources or its failure to deploy the extensive education efforts necessary to gain support for government policies.

Women's Rights

In another example of how the project of modernity under the Turkish Republic came up against societal obstacles, Mustafa Kemal tried to secure new legal rights for women, but he found here, too, that he had a dearth of stakeholders supporting his policies and a lack of institutional resources for their implementation.

Kemal focused particularly on legal and administrative reforms that would bring women out into the public sphere. On February 17, 1926, the Turkish parliament passed the Turkish Civil Code, overturning established shari'a precepts by making polygamy illegal, giving equal rights of divorce to men and women, granting custody of children to both parents, allowing equal inheritance to both men and women, according equal weight to testimony from men and women, and raising the legal age for marriage. In April 1930, Kemal's government passed a bill granting women the right to vote in municipal elections. Women did so for the first time in 1933. In December 1934, parliament voted unanimously to allow women to vote and run for candidacy to the parliament; in February 1935, 18 women won election.

While these measures granted women a degree of legal equality they had never had under the Ottomans, they did not immediately change most women's lives. Stakeholders in this project, members of the professional middle stratum who had already begun the process of Westernizing, observed the new code. Some attended international women's conferences to extol Turkish progress on women's issues. Villagers, however, largely ignored the laws, such as those regarding registration of marriages, because the process typically necessitated traveling to large administrative centers and spending time away from the farm or artisan shop. Also, birth records and medical certificates required to register marriages were hard to obtain in most areas. The Swiss Law Code on which Turkey's was modeled did not unconditionally support

WOMEN'S OPPORTUNITIES IN THE LATE OTTOMAN EMPIRE

In the Ottoman Empire, women and state leaders had already begun establishing institutions to address modern concerns about women. The 19th-century Ottoman school expansion program included schools for girls, although they were built at a slower rate than those for boys. A teacher's training college for women opened in 1863; in 1875, American missionaries opened the American College for Girls in Istanbul. The state made elementary education compulsory for girls in 1913 and opened a women's university in 1915. It merged with Istanbul University in 1920.

Between the Young Turk Revolution of 1908 and the beginning of World War I, women formed organizations to advance their cause: the Red-White Club, Association for the Betterment of Women, Ottoman Society for Women, and Ottoman Association for the Defense of Women's Rights, as well as the journal *Women's World*.

During World War I, the loss of male workers to the battlefields created job openings for women, and women's wage labor increased dramatically. Many Muslim women joined Christian and Jewish women who had long been working on the factory floor. During and immediately after the war, more than 20,000 women of all faiths became workers in food and ammunition factories and increased their representation in textile factories. Thousands more worked in banks, the postal services, and municipal administrations; still others volunteered to provide support along the battlefronts. The Islamic Society to Promote the Employment of Ottoman Women was founded in 1916 to aid these new workers, and a Women Merchants' Bazaar opened in Istanbul to aid small merchants. The years immediately after the collapse of the empire provided even more opportunities for women. As the war wound down, the Faculty of Philosophy opened courses for women. By 1921, not only could girls attend school in coeducational classrooms, but they could remove their veils during lectures. In 1922, Turkey's first female doctor established a clinic in Istanbul.

equal status for women. Men were still the legal heads of households, so women needed to be given permission from their husbands to work outside the home.

Even though these changes had been advocated and supported by the women who for decades had led the struggle for women's rights, Kemal subsumed their organizations within the larger modernizing and nationalizing project he was undertaking. Members of the independent Turkish Women's Union, founded in the 1920s, had enthusiastically supported his new policies, but Kemal dissolved the organization in mid-1935, declaring that it had achieved its goal of establishing political rights for women and was thus no longer necessary. Not even the women who were stakeholders in this process of reform and modernization were allowed to decide policy on their own issues. The Kemalist project was directed by dictates from the top; citizens were merely implementers.

Turkish Exclusivity

Kemal's exaltation of the particularly Turkish identity of his new state engendered complications for the non-Turks living within its borders, especially for those who had been in competition for Anatolian land. The Armenians who still remained in Turkey, including about 120,000 residents in Istanbul, received Turkish citizenship but faced prejudice because they did not meet all the criteria for citizenship in Kemal's republic. The definition of Turkish citizenship laid down in the 1924 constitution stated only that all the people of Turkey would receive citizenship regardless of religion and race. While providing an expansive definition for citizenship, this wording was sufficiently vague that the state was able to pass subsequent laws that discriminated against those who were not Muslim and did not speak Turkish as a mother tongue, adopt Turkish culture, and accept the ideals of Turkishness.

Minorities who did not fill all these criteria, such as the Armenians, received basic citizenship rights such as the right to vote and receive a passport but faced obstacles in other public realms. For example, in the 1920s the state passed laws privileging job seekers who had fought in the War of Liberation, specifically excluding Armenians who had been targets of Turkish military policies. The result was the mass firing of non-Turks, especially Armenians, from positions in the state bureaucracy and state-owned businesses in the 1920s. Nonetheless, Armenians did adapt to their new circumstances in the interwar period by finding ways to integrate publicly—by speaking only Turkish in public venues, for instance—while maintaining their traditions, religion, and language in private.

Kurdish Rebellions

Kurds also encountered difficulties as a result of Mustafa Kemal's designs for a newly defined Turkish identity. Although Kurdish leaders had agitated for autonomy within the Ottoman Empire, they remained loyal to the government throughout World War I in the hope that an expansive Ottomanism would respect their national identity. After the war, the Treaty of Sèvres, with its promise of regional autonomy, had given hope to the Kurdish nationalists. However, when the Treaty of Lausanne withdrew the promise and Kurds found themselves increasingly controlled by the centralizing Turkish state, they rebelled.

The issue of Kurdish citizenship was almost as fraught as it was for Armenians. In the new Kemalist national equation, Kurds represented Turks-in-the-making, or "mountain Turks," who could be fit into the Turkish historical lineage but needed guidance to become full-fledged Turks. Kurdish groups did not accept this designation and revolted at least 13 separate times between 1925 and 1930 alone. Their leaders frequently failed to coordinate their actions, which caused a good deal of fragmentation between different groups, but the repeated rebellions forced Ankara to expend great resources to subdue them. They also proved that Kurds would not easily be dismissed as inferior Turks.

The largest of the early revolts of the 1920s was led by the Sufi Shaykh Said of Piran in collaboration with a number of the tribal shaykhs in southeastern Anatolia and the urban-based Azadi (Freedom) Committee, which comprised intellectuals and professionals. Beginning in February 1925, the Turkish government sent 50,000 troops to crush the revolt, and in the ensuing battles, the leaders were killed and the uneasy alliance between tribal leaders, urban intellectuals, and a Sufi shaykh broke apart. In the following years, as smaller revolts flared, the Ankara government created a special legal structure for the Kurdish-dominated districts of southeastern Anatolia, with each district led by an Inspectorate-General vested with extensive powers. Each Inspectorate was granted funds for roads, schools, and police and administrative offices, all of which would help the central government in Ankara subdue the regions and bring the populations and resources under direct state control.

The largest Kurdish military revolt erupted between 1936 and 1938, when the Shi'i Alevi Kurds of Dersim rebelled once again. The Alevi had previously revolted in 1921 against the newly formed Ankara government but had been defeated. They remained quiet until the Turkish government announced in January 1936 that it had established a Fourth Inspectorate-General, this one for the region of Dersim. This Inspectorate-General began building roads and introducing Turkish state institutions into the region. Instead of accommodating this incursion, Dersim's tribes coordinated with a cadre of Kurdish urban intellectuals to oppose government efforts. The revolt began with a Kurdish military unit blowing up a bridge and attacking a party of Turkish officers in the spring of 1937.

The government moved 25,000 soldiers and 20 warplanes into the district and bombarded the Kurdish camps. However, the ongoing problem the government faced in its attempts to extend its reach was the lack of serviceable roads. This was particularly problematic in terrain as mountainous as that in southeastern Anatolia. Due to their inaccessibility, the Kurdish rebels were able to protect themselves from a frontal assault by the Turkish military. The Turkish government ultimately defeated the rebels by October 1938 by instituting a siege of the region and preventing food and supplies from entering. The government eventually succeeded in imposing the Inspectorate on Dersim and with it a strong measure of state control. However, the government was not able to put an end to Kurdish demands for national rights. Although the next few decades witnessed no new rebellions seriously threatening Turkish sovereignty, the

ALEVI

Alevi are the descendants of the Qizilbash tribes who served as the military force enabling the Safavid conquest of Iran in 1501. In the aftermath of their victory, Qizilbash tribesmen found themselves marginalized when the shahs established a centralized administration with Persian administrators and Shi'i clerics in the top positions. Instead of submitting to Safavid control, the Qizilbash retreated to Azerbaijan and took advantage of their position along the frontier between the Ottoman and Safavid Empires to maintain a great deal of independence. Neither empire had the military force to subdue all the tribes or conquer the territory they controlled, so the Qizilbash did not have to conform to either the Sunni or the Shi'i orthodoxies that the sultans and shahs endorsed. In this marginal zone, the Qizilbash maintained their heterodox belief systems. Once the name Qizilbash had become a liability, those who settled in Turkey took the name Alevi, and followers came from both Turkish and Kurdish communities. Their belief system combined Shi'i Islam with elements of Sufism. Eventually they closed the faith to anyone not born into an Alevi family as a means of protecting Alevi from persecution.

issue of Kurdish nationality within the larger Turkish polity had not been resolved, and later in the century Kurds again organized and rebelled.

Rebellion and State Construction in Iran

During and immediately after World War I, Qajar princes, tribal leaders, and religious clerics took advantage of the Qajar government's weakness to assert their political autonomy. A revolt in the northern province of Azerbaijan erupted immediately after the war ended, led by disparate groups of Turkic Azeris, Armenians, and local tribal forces, with the first two largely working through the local Communist Party with aid from the newly formed Soviet Union. Whereas the princes, shaykhs, and clerics sought to reconfirm the positions they had held leading up to and throughout the war, many rebels in the north were calling for a new kind of Iranian state that would incorporate elements of socialism and communism.

Anglo-Iranian Agreement of 1919

British officials tried to counter this fragmentation by strengthening Ahmad Shah's government in Tehran and thus solidifying their position as the dominant foreign power in the country. The Anglo-Iranian Agreement of 1919 offered the Qajar government a £2 million loan if it would grant the British a monopoly on the supply of arms, military training, and administrative advisers to the state. What the British wanted was continuing control over and access to Iranian oil; the shah needed the resources necessary for rebuilding Iran after years of warfare. The Qajar prime minister signed the treaty, but the majles refused to ratify it. Nonetheless, British officials assigned to Iran acted as if the treaty stood in force and began implementing its provisions.

Reza Khan and Sayyed Ziya' Tabataba'i

Out of the jockeying for local and national power, Reza Khan of the Cossack Brigade emerged as a new leader by marching 3,000 men from Qazvin near the Caspian Sea to take control of Tehran in early 1921. En route, he made an alliance with newspaper editor Sayyed Ziya' Tabataba'i, and the two orchestrated a bloodless coup against the Qajar government on February 2, 1921. The shah surrendered to the superior forces of Reza Khan and Tabataba'i without a fight. The shah was allowed to remain on his throne but had no access to real power. Tabataba'i became the new prime minister. Reza Khan, who served in the new position of army commander, established the foundation for a regular national army by merging the Cossacks with the gendarmerie. With this army, he gained control over one autonomous province after another during the 1920s and ended the fragmentation that had accompanied the events of World War I. He succeeded because he built on the centralization efforts of the Qajars, however incomplete they had been, and because he used his army to defeat the strongest of the princes and shaykhs who had reasserted their provincial autonomy during and after the war. The consolidation of power gave Reza Khan the leverage to abrogate the Anglo-Iranian Agreement and sign a treaty of friendship with the Soviet Union. Once the Soviet troops had withdrawn from Azerbaijan according to the terms of the treaty, Reza Khan had the requisite might to crush the rebellion there.

Constituent Assembly

Reza Khan used his military success to push Tabataba'i from power in May 1921 and began the process of acquiring allies for his bid to overthrow the Qajar shah. Even though his methods were authoritarian, he attracted a wide range of supporters because he was securing and centralizing the country, encouraging trade to flow. Among the conservative forces, large landowners and merchants favored the extra security his army provided; liberal Westernizing reformers saw in him the means by which the Iranian government could modernize. Even the bazaaris and the Shi'a ulama could find value in a leader who had reduced British and Soviet encroachment, just as they had so recently struggled to do. With this support behind him, Reza Shah convened a Constituent Assembly to examine the state's constitution. On April 26, 1926, the Assembly amended the constitution to end the Qajar dynasty and grant Reza Khan the title shah-in-shah. Ahmad Shah, the last Qajar ruler, had already left the country months before the vote; the day after, the crown prince followed. Reza Shah adopted the family name Pahlavi, an old Iranian name associated with pre-Islamic Persia, as a way to further legitimize his leadership over Iran.

Authoritarianism in Iran

Reza Shah established an authoritarian state with himself at the center using three key pillars of control: the army, the state bureaucracy, and the power he wielded over court patronage. By undermining local autonomy, he gained control over taxes he could use as revenues to build up his military and bureaucracy; his power over state offices translated

FIGURE 5.2. Reza Shah Pahlavi sitting on his new throne in Tehran, 1925.

into resources he could dispense as patronage. He confiscated land from all his opponents, making himself the largest landowner in the country and enriching his supply of resources with which to reward supporters. Reza Shah defeated tribal insurgencies, and by the mid-1930s his bureaucracy had managed to take on the tasks of the prior regime's provincial governors. His state and military effectively reached into every corner of the country, ending the endemic Iranian geographic and political fragmentation. Reza Shah's state attracted stakeholders from among the Qajar elites willing to work within the new political system, students and civil servants gaining new training and positions within the expanded state, and others who had been elevated by their personal relationships with Reza Shah.

Military Focus

The military, the cornerstone of Reza Shah's modernizing and centralizing project, increased its ranks from 40,000 in 1926 to 130,000 in 1941. To gain the support of its officer corps, Reza Shah spent the bulk of state revenue on the modernization and upkeep of the army and its small air force and navy. Officers received salaries far higher than those of civilian officials and were able to buy land at lower-than-market prices and gain access to special royal clubs and casinos. Reza Shah dressed in military uniform for public events to show his leadership of and solidarity with the military, and he organized every branch of the government according to a military system of hierarchy and discipline. Reza Shah established clear-cut divisions between the different ministries and distinct job descriptions within them, a task the Qajars had failed to complete. In 1926, a new civil service law was passed that defined employment ranks according to educational qualifications, declaring that positions and promotion would be determined, at least on paper, by merit rather than nepotism. By 1941, some 90,000 civil servants worked in the government, employing the vast majority of graduates from the secondary and higher educational institutions in the country. In a further social engineering project, the state eliminated all the old royal titles such as mirza to blur the divisions between the strata of society.

Legislation for Iranian Modernization

As was occurring in Turkey, Reza Shah worked to weaken the influence that the shari'a and thus the Shi'i clerics could have over the population. He passed into law the Commercial Code in 1925, an Italian-influenced Criminal Code in 1926, and the French-influenced Civil Code in 1928 that took legal and family issues out of the realm of shari'a law and placed it within a secular court system. The state went further in 1939–1940 by abolishing the shari'a courts completely so the ulama would no longer have a judicial role over Iranian citizens. From that point forward, only judges trained to adjudicate the new law codes could preside over the courts. Secular schools replaced many of the old religious schools, starting especially in 1926 when the majles voted to spend a portion of land-tax receipts on building up a secular elementary school system.

In 1929, the state decreed that all men in state office except the ulama must wear Western dress. Rather than sponsor Shi'i religious ceremonies such as the passion plays reenacting the betrayal of the Prophet's grandson Hussein, Reza Shah made his own birthday the focus of national celebrations. In this way, he linked his reign to the illustrious lineage of Persian monarchs, whose power source was temporal, not spiritual. In 1931, Reza Shah ended the right of theological students to avoid military conscription. As a final step in breaking down the independent power of the ulama, in 1939 the state took over collection and management of the religious endowments, the waqf.

In his project to modernize Iran following Western models, Reza Shah relied more on force than persuasion. Although the reforms did create new stakeholders, more members of the population were not brought into the new culture. The peasants were deprived of much of their land during the interwar period, and the ulama lost control of many of their traditional institutions.

Women's Rights

Reza Shah's modernity program, like Kemal's, expanded women's rights but eliminated their political organizations. The Patriotic Women's League had been founded in 1922, and the women activists working within it stood in the vanguard calling for political and economic rights for women. In the 1930s, Reza Shah opened the doors of the University of Tehran to women. In 1936, he prohibited women from wearing the veil in public. Both of these steps were supported by the activists in the Patriotic Women's League, yet after passing this legislation, Reza Shah shut down the league and allowed no women's organizations to exist outside state control. Furthermore, his secular law codes did little to improve women's legal position in society. For example, the Civil Code of 1936 endorsed polygamy, gave the right of divorce and custody of children to men, and prohibited women from traveling or entering educational and employment venues without their husbands' permission.

Similarities and Differences between Turkey and Iran

In the interwar period, both Reza Shah and Mustafa Kemal tried to impose on their states a top-down modernization and nationalizing project. Neither succeeded in fully controlling all the players and resources within their countries, but both established the groundwork for their successors to continue the process. Mustafa Kemal was able to rally stakeholders with the positions he offered them in the new state structure, and he attracted loyalty because of his unrivaled prestige as the preeminent leader defending Turkish rights. The Republic of Turkey could build on a century of change because the reforms of the Ottoman Empire had extended new kinds of state institutions across the territory the modern state claimed and had gained acceptance from many stakeholders in the society about the need for such reforms. As the Ottoman Empire gave way to republican Turkey, these same societal elements supported the new kinds of institutions Kemal was building. Kemal encountered obstacles when he shifted his focus away from Turkish national defense and pursued a policy of forced modernization. Projects for modernizing villages and schools met with opposition from local leaders wary of losing their influence and incapable of raising sufficient resources for their implementation. In imposing a specifically Turkish identity on the state, he antagonized the Kurds, who fought to determine their own kind of state in southeastern Anatolia.

Reza Shah could not rely on popular appeal to win supporters for his program. Because of the fragmented nature of state building under Qajar rule, he had to construct anew many of the central and provincial state institutions that had already been functioning in the Ottoman Empire before Kemal's arrival. Reza Shah had also not earned the national military acclaim that allowed Mustafa Kemal to push through policies that would otherwise generate sustained opposition. He depended heavily on force to remove opponents and to exploit all available resources. Although he largely succeeded in eliminating the old autonomous zones, he had difficulty building up sufficient numbers of stakeholders. Most of the population saw only the heavy hand of the state since few services emanated from the capital and few benefits compensated for the increasing number of obligations imposed by Tehran.

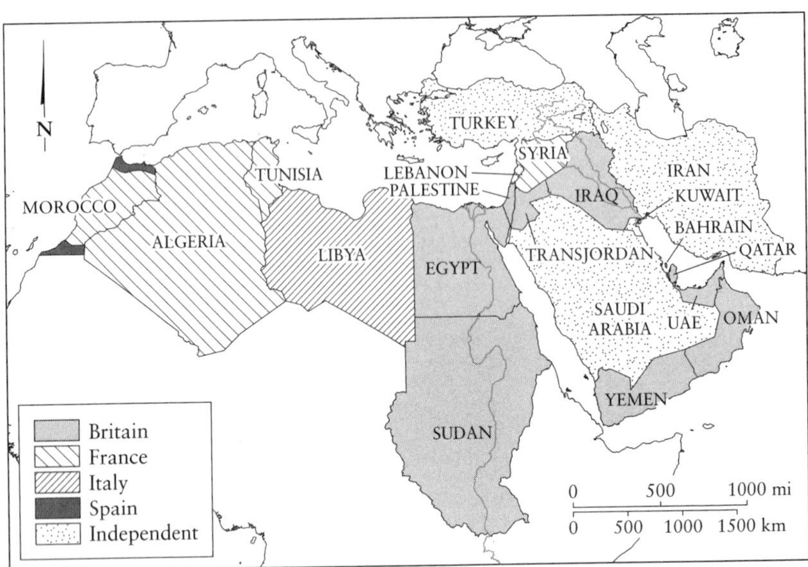

MAP 15. Colonial Control and Territorial Division of the Middle East after World War I. The British and French Mandate and colonies covered most of the Arab world, and Turkey, Iran, and Saudi Arabia became independent.

Rebellion and State Construction in Syria and Lebanon

When Emir Faysal entered Damascus on October 1, 1918, and inaugurated an Arab-led and British-financed government, he ruled it as part of the British-controlled OETA-East (Occupied Enemy Territory Administration) over modern-day Syria and Jordan. He appointed to the top posts officers who had fought alongside him in the Arab Revolt, collectively known as the Sharifian officers. The residents of Damascus and the Arab nationalists among them had been wary of his devotion to the Arab nationalist cause at the beginning of World War I, but his exploits during the war proved his Arab bona fides. Upon arrival in the city, Emir Faysal immediately received the support of the Arab Club, al-Fatat, and the Arab Independence Party, all of which were staffed by young Arab nationalists of the Western-educated and professional sectors. To bring people into the Faysali state project, these organizations repeatedly mobilized urban residents for marches and demonstrations in support of Emir Faysal and his government. On March 8, 1920, at the General Syrian Congress, these supporters declared Faysal the king of Syria.

The congress may have backed him in 1920, but King Faysal's governmental control was disintegrating by that time because of economic and administrative weaknesses and the clear French desire for colonial domination over Syria as expressed in the Sykes-Picot Agreement. The economy was in dire straits after the war, and the succeeding years produced poor harvests; the diminishing value of the British-imposed Egyptian pound forced merchants and farmers to revert to Ottoman gold when available and to barter when it was not. Outside the cities, brigandage along the roads made it difficult to transport food and goods from rural to urban areas, exacerbating food shortages and raising prices for all products. Tax collection proved difficult because King Faysal had little in the way of a governmental apparatus outside the cities. Exacerbating his difficulties, King Faysal failed to assign specific duties to each of his officials, so there were no clear-cut chains of authority for implementing orders that issued from his office and little effective governance.

Despite these problems, the system worked, albeit in an ad hoc fashion, until the British began curtailing funds for King Faysal's government in early 1920. Notwithstanding this added financial pressure, the government refused French aid because of the country's colonial designs on Syria. When the British began a pullout of troops in early 1920 and the French approached from Beirut, King Faysal sought support for Syrian

SHARIFIANS

The Sharifians were Arab officers from the Ottoman army trained in the new military academies opened by the sultans in the 19th century. A small percentage of the graduates continued their training at the War College in Istanbul. Lower-class Sunni Muslim students predominated because enrollment was free and study at the military academies provided social mobility. On the eve of World War I, about 1,200 Iraqis had graduated from the War College and become lieutenants in the Ottoman army, making up the largest contingent of Arab officers. About 15 percent of all officers were from the Arab provinces.

Some of these men supported Arab nationalism on the eve of World War I and opposed the authoritarian structure of the Young Turk government. They joined secret Arab nationalism societies in Baghdad, such as al-'Ahd (the Covenant), to discuss how Arabs could gain independence or political autonomy from Istanbul. However, the majority remained loyal to the Ottoman government throughout the war. When it became apparent by 1917 that the Ottoman Empire would lose the war, many army deserters returned home rather than join the Arab Revolt. Their long years of training and integration with soldiers and officers from every region of the empire provided them with an institutional loyalty that proved stronger than anything arising from a new Arab national identification.

A few army deserters did join the Arab Revolt army; another group joined after Faysal successfully entered Damascus in October 1918 and established an Arab government. The largest number chose enlistment with the Arab Revolt army as a path out of British prisoner-of-war camps. Those who fought alongside Faysal during the war and served him in Iraq received powerful political positions as a reward. Sharifians held top posts in the government throughout the interwar period; Nuri al-Sa'id, the most influential of them, held positions in government until it was overthrown by a military coup in 1958.

independence in the halls of government in Europe, presenting his case at Versailles and spending many months of his tenure lobbying in Europe. Yet support was not forthcoming. The Europeans also ignored the findings of the American-sponsored King-Crane Commission of 1919, which concluded that the majority of Syrian Arabs did not want French colonial control over their country and that Arabs throughout the region opposed Zionist plans for a state in Palestine.

Widespread Opposition

Meanwhile, by 1920 members of the Arab organizations that had worked to mobilize support for King Faysal's government since the beginning of his rule began to turn away, faulting him for failing to defend against French encroachment or resolve any of the country's internal problems. King Faysal also engendered hostility from the old Ottoman notables from the region—the large landowners, big urban merchants, and tribal shaykhs—when he favored the Sharifian officers and leaders of the local Arab organizations for top governmental posts. He had paid the notables regular subsidies from the moment he established his new government so he could placate and pacify them. But he had to cut those subsidies when his government ran into financial crisis; by 1920 their tolerance of his rule turned into active opposition.

Opposition also arose from new groups on the Syrian political scene, including smaller merchants and religious figures who for the most part had not received official positions under the Ottoman reforms but had established their own regional, trade, and family networks. These connections, independent of the Ottoman-supported local notables' range of authority, enabled the participants to sell products, intermarry, and aid each other in times of crisis. Suffering from postwar deprivations and discouraged by King Faysal's failing government, the people living in the popular quarters of the cities established a series of committees and militias to protect their zones of influence and trade routes.

Many called themselves national defense committees, although, as in Turkey, they rarely coordinated their activities across Syria. Different groups did attempt to do so within the Higher National Committee, which first met in February 1920, but the separate leaderships could not agree on a joint structure for working together. Nevertheless, they worked in parallel for the same goals: stopping the French from colonizing Syria while also making the country safe for cultivation, manufacturing, and trade. Tram and railway workers, printers, and workers in glass and textile factories and the Damascus electric company went on strike to protest the economic and political situation, continuing a pattern that workers had begun as early as the 1870s. These strikes were accompanied by bread riots in the cities. When the state voted conscription into law in December 1919, many of these new activists refused to comply because their local defensive work produced tangible results, and they did not want to divert their efforts for the sake of the Faysali state.

French Invasion

When French general Henri Gouraud marched from Beirut toward Damascus in summer 1920, all militias and opposition groups understood that national defense was at stake. Under this banner, the Faysali state and the national defense committees joined forces. However, the combined forces of Syria could not withstand the French army and were defeated in July 1920 at the Battle of Maysaloun. King Faysal fled to London, and Syria was put under direct French colonial jurisdiction. Within the year, Faysal and many of his Sharifian allies had decamped to Iraq, where the British engineered a plebiscite to make Faysal king.

The French occupied Syria with the imprimatur of the League of Nations. The Covenant of the League of Nations, signed on June 28, 1919, had established the concept of mandates, whereby the Great Powers would mentor former colonies and territories to help them achieve independence. The League of Nations officially designated the Arab provinces of the Ottoman Empire as class "A" mandates: they were nominally independent but subject to mandatory oversight until they reached political maturity. The League mandate commission charged Britain and France with establishing institutions that would enable the new states to achieve full sovereignty. Top diplomats from Britain, France, Italy, and Japan met at San Remo, Italy, in April 1920 and divided up the Arab world into British and French zones, mostly following the template of the Sykes-Picot Agreement.

French Imposition of the Syria Mandate

France divided the Syria Mandate into provincial segments, strategizing that these divisions would forestall Syrian unification to oppose French rule. Along the coast, France joined the Ottoman mutasarrifate of Mount Lebanon to the province of Beirut and areas of the coastal north and south to create Greater Lebanon. The majority of the Muslim political leaders in these areas opposed the plans for a separate Lebanon because they supported territorial and state unity between Syria and Lebanon. But with the fall of King Faysal's government and given the French desire to divide the regions within their new mandate, the region's leading Muslim notables failed to persuade the French to consider their desires. The Christian communities, however, largely favored the creation of a separate state for Lebanon and, with Maronite notables taking the lead, worked with the French to keep Lebanon outside the realm of Syrian sovereignty.

On May 23, 1926, Lebanese politicians ratified a constitution for the newly named Lebanese Republic. The Chamber of Deputies and Senate were elected on the basis of sectarian political identification so that each of the country's religious sects received designated numbers of seats in the parliament. The sectarian arrangement hewed to the practices established following the 1860 civil war in Mount Lebanon. The most powerful were those groups who had negotiated positions of influence in the war's aftermath, including the Maronite Christians, Sunni Muslim Arabs, and the Druze, who had regained a measure of influence in the country.

Parliament had little real power, while the French allowed the president authority only over domestic issues. One of the presidential powers was the right to appoint members to the Senate, but the Senate was dissolved by constitutional amendment in 1927, because the existence of an upper and lower house proved to be an ineffective tool for governance in a small country with a sectarian political structure. Henceforth, the president was allowed to appoint a third of the members to the Chamber of Deputies. By the mid-1930s, under pressure from the French high commissioner, it was established that the president of the country would always be a Maronite Christian. Although the French government negotiated a treaty with Lebanon in 1936 to grant it additional independence, the French parliament never ratified the document, so Lebanon remained a French-controlled mandate throughout the interwar period.

For the remaining portions of Syria, French officials continued their divide-and-rule policies by geographically and legally separating the residents from each other. The French initially sought to rule Damascus and Aleppo as separate provinces but found it more efficient to unite them within the state of Syria in 1924; the 'Alawi and Druze received their own autonomous provinces in the northwestern and southern regions, respectively. The bedouin of Syria came under a special administration called the Contrôle Bédouin, aimed at sedentarizing the nomads and enlisting the support of tribal shaykhs to serve as government intermediaries. To govern the regions and comply with the rules underlying the mandate structure, the French high commissioner established representative and federal councils for the different regions of Syria and elevated to positions of influence the original landowning and merchant elite who had been intermediaries under the Ottomans and had formed a key part of the opposition to Faysal's government.

The new system did stabilize under the French, who contributed more funds than King Faysal had been able to access, but the government was perceived as legitimate only by those who held positions within it. Sunni Arab urban notables were back in government service and could use their offices to benefit themselves and their lands, industries, and client networks. As before, in the last decades of Ottoman governance, these notables offered to serve as intermediaries for the French, guaranteeing that their clients served the new state. The French also gave privileged positions to rural notables so they would act as intermediaries throughout the country, providing a loyal bulwark against nationalist agitation in the urban areas. Members of the popular committees who had proved so pivotal in mobilizing much of the population in the postwar period were denied positions in the government because the French eschewed such leadership.

The French also created deeper social divisions by recruiting minorities such as the 'Alawi and Christians into their local military forces—the Troupes Spéciales and the Syrian Gendarmerie. Troops from their other colonies served in the Armée du Levant. As a result of these machinations, the majority Sunni Arab population, excepting the elite cadres, was excluded from participating in the state's governance.

Druze Revolt

Despite their careful calibrations in dividing up Syria and choosing their intermediaries, the French did not prevent unrest from igniting into violence. In 1925 a rebellion broke out in the area of Jabal (Mount) Druze in the Hawran region that encompassed much of the country over the next two years.

The Druze Revolt broke out because of a confluence of factors: high inflation that came with fluctuations in the French franc; high taxation at a time of poor harvests; French corvée labor demands imposed on the Druze peasantry; and French refusal to appoint local officials to the autonomous government in Jabal Druze. Sultan al-Atrash, chieftain of the most influential Druze family, became the revolt's leader and easily succeeded in mobilizing hundreds of fighters to stand up to the French and the Armée du Levant in the early days of the revolt.

FIGURE 5.3. After the failure of the Druze Revolt in Syria, Sultan al-Atrash (*seated third from right*) and his retinue found political refuge from French imprisonment in Transjordan. Here they are sitting in a bedouin tent in Wadi Sirhan, near the Transjordanian-Saudi border.

The Druze had never been completely isolated either before the war or after the French established the region as a separate district in 1920; thus, they were able to garner supporters outside the Hawran. Druze shaykhs and peasants had strong ties with the small merchants of the popular quarters of Damascus, many of whom had instigated revolts against King Faysal. During the last years of Ottoman rule these ties had expanded beyond relationships circumscribed by business contracts. For example, when young Druze men attended the Ottoman military secondary school outside Damascus, they often stayed in homes of Damascene merchants who conducted business with Druze shaykhs. These mostly Sunni Arab merchants had long-standing ties to the ulama community, enabling them to extend their networks even farther across the south and into Damascus. Members of these networks had no official power or influence under the Ottomans and the French, but they prospered by cooperating to further their familial, societal, and economic interests and mobilizing the popular quarters and allied rural areas against government policies.

When the Druze Revolt erupted in the Hawran, it immediately spread along these unofficial trade and network lines, and the Damascene popular quarters quickly joined in solidarity. Sultan al-Atrash's attempts to recruit support for the revolt from the notables of Damascus proved fruitless in the early months. Many of the notables, their sons, and Western-educated professionals held French colonial government jobs so were beholden to French rule. However, these notables had also formed political parties in the years after the French mandate, disseminating Arab nationalist and anti-imperialist platforms because they also wanted to achieve independence from colonialism. They burnished their nationalist credentials in this way but created the awkward situation of trying to serve two different masters: the French and the nationalists. Caught in this conundrum, Damascene elites refrained from supporting the revolt in the early months, waiting to see how it progressed.

An August 24, 1925, attempt to spread the revolt into Damascus failed in large part because so few Damascenes outside the popular quarters joined the fight along the barricades. Many people independently joined the militia bands roaming the city. A substantial number of women even organized marches in support of the revolt, but the elite groups held back. Not until 1926, when the revolt showed signs of strengthening, did

DRUZE IN SYRIA

In the post-1860 period, many of the Druze who felt persecuted after the civil war in Mount Lebanon moved to the Hawran, a grain-producing region of southern Syria. They were joined by Druze emigrating from Palestine and other parts of Syria before and during World War I. The migration into the Hawran required that the Druze militarily defeat the bedouin who had traditionally dominated the region, but over time the two groups came to an accommodation that benefited them both. The bedouin received the right to graze their animals on the lands after the grain harvest, and the Druze employed bedouin camel caravans to bring their grain to markets in Damascus. By clearing additional land for cultivation, the Druze newcomers brought the Hawran into the world market for grain and spread the wealth across all the families settling in the region. For centuries, the area's mountainous terrain had made it autonomous, but in the late 19th century, the Ottomans partially succeeded in reestablishing governmental control in the region. Druze revolts of 1896 and 1910 restored a measure of local autonomy; World War I accelerated the process since Hawran farms continued to grow substantial quantities of wheat while much of the surrounding area faced droughts.

the notables come to the fore to raise money throughout Damascus and central Syria, broadcast the events in their newspapers, and join in the military battles. With their widely disseminated newspaper articles and slogans, the elite helped define this revolt as a specifically Syrian nationalist movement against French colonization.

Despite the combined efforts of the elites and the populace, the revolt could not withstand the French indefinitely, and the rebels certainly did not have the military power to unseat the French completely. French officials brought in additional troops from their other colonies to augment those in the Armée du Levant and the Troupes Spéciales. By 1927 the revolt was over, and those who had led it were in jail, in exile, or in the most extreme cases executed by French order. The participants from the popular quarters faced the brunt of the punishment, while the elites received light punishment or none at all.

National Bloc

In the aftermath of the revolt, the notables of Damascus and the northern city of Aleppo joined together to revise their roles as intermediaries between the colonizing forces and the Syrian people. Forming the National Bloc, they offered to work with the French to establish pathways toward independence, a policy epitomized by their slogan of "honorable cooperation." They promised their Syrian constituents that they would demand of the French the right to draw up a constitution and form a representative government. They would also insist on clarification of the legal relationship between France and Syria and the addition of new positions for Syrians within the administration. The French rewarded their overtures by establishing a parliament and holding elections in August 1928. After the second parliament convened on June 7, 1932, its members elected Muhammad ʻAli al-ʻAbid as the first president of the Republic of Syria. In honor of the event, the new Syrian flag was unfurled atop the building, displaying the green, white, and black stripes that had constituted the flag of the Arab Revolt, with the addition of three stars in the center to symbolize Syria's separate national status.

Despite these French concessions, the National Bloc faced insurmountable obstacles in achieving any of the goals of "honorable cooperation." To be truly popular with voters, the members had to recommend policies that clearly defied French ambitions in Syria; yet to maintain their government positions, they had to appease the French mandate authorities. They had to also recognize that the French could rely on more loyal notables from different parts of the country to pass pro-French legislation through the parliament and cabinet. The French had obtained the support of shaykhs and landowners in the rural and nomadic areas by offering them a great deal of local autonomy in return for their loyalty.

In elections for the 1932 parliament, French authorities gerrymandered the districts to favor those who where nonpolitical and loyal, especially those from rural districts and among the religious minorities. In Damascus, where the National Bloc was strongest, the French placed prominent members under surveillance, suppressed opposition newspapers, and refused to allow nationalist manifestos to be printed and disseminated. On the days of voting in 1932, rumors of ballot stuffing ran rampant, and the French army moved into the streets of Damascus to control the demonstrations that broke out. The National Bloc still won the majority of parliamentary seats in the election, but it had to share power in the cabinet with pro-French politicians and was unable to pass much legislation. This pattern repeated itself throughout the 1930s, as the National Bloc continued to push for French concessions but received few. As in the case of Lebanon, members of parliament signed a new treaty with the French in 1936 granting Syria additional independence, but the French parliament failed to ratify it, so the political relationship between Syria and France did not change on the eve of World War II.

Geographically, however, Syria lost sovereignty over the sanjak (district) of Alexandretta, situated in the northwestern corner of the country astride the border with Turkey. This district had a multiethnic population of Turks, 'Alawi, Armenians, Sunni Arabs, Christian Arabs, Kurds, Circassians, and Jews. Turks made up the largest group, with about 39 percent of the population, but no one group held a demographic majority. The Turkish government renounced its claim to the district in the Treaty of Lausanne in 1923 but continued to demand that the French government grant special provisions to the Turkish population living there. The 1936 Franco-Syrian treaty reaffirmed Syrian control over the province, but the Turks declared that such an action would endanger the Turkish residents if specific protections for them were not included in the treaty. On November 29, 1937, the French brought the issue before the League of Nations, which subsequently voted to allow the sanjak to form an independent government. In June 1939, the new assembly for the district dissolved itself and Alexandretta became a formal province of the Turkish Republic.

Rebellion and State Construction in Iraq

When the British army occupied Iraq in 1917, many of the large landowners and tribal shaykhs who had emerged as local power brokers under late Ottoman rule endorsed the action and sought to gain positions within the new government, providing their services as intermediaries to the British in the same way they had done for the Ottomans. But others opposed British rule and rebelled in summer 1920.

The Ottomans had begun transforming the Iraqi provinces in the 19th century so they could better collect revenues and establish Tanzimat institutions. Midhat Pasha, the governor in Baghdad from 1869 to 1872 and one of the future authors of the 1876 Ottoman constitution, introduced municipal councils in Iraqi cities so that local notables could become part of the state project. The Ottomans cleaned out old canals and built new ones, while expanding the number of pumps for irrigation to increase the amount of agricultural land put into cultivation. The Ottoman Land Law of 1858 enticed tribal leaders, merchants, and tax farmers to register their lands as private property and invest in agricultural improvements. On large estates, owners moved over to cash cropping, particularly of wheat. They accelerated cultivation of this lucrative product after the Suez Canal opened in 1869 when more cost-effective means of shipping became available to Iraqi landowners. Although it had needed to import large quantities of grain at the beginning of the century, by the end of

SHI'ISM IN IRAQ

In the early 19th century, Shi'ism in Iraq was primarily an urban phenomenon centered on the two shrine cities of Najaf and Karbala; during the century, Arab tribesmen from the surrounding countryside began to convert in large numbers. These tribes had started migrating from the Arabian Peninsula to the southern regions of Iraq in the 17th century. In the late 18th and early 19th centuries, they began migrating to escape Saudi-Wahhab raids. Once in Iraq, they encountered the Ottoman administration's efforts to centralize its control over the Shi'i-dominated cities of Karbala and Najaf. The combined effects of migration and Ottoman pressure disrupted tribal cohesion and authority, forcing tribesmen to seek new relationships for protection. In Shi'ism converts found support and protection among the mujtahids and merchants of the shrine cities. Meanwhile, the mujtahids retained their influence and authority even under Ottoman centralization efforts, as evidenced by their intervention in Qajar political events throughout the 19th century. Due to the migration and conversions, Shi'ism expanded well beyond the urban areas, and Shi'a made up just over 50 percent of the population of the Ottoman Iraqi provinces when World War I ended in 1918.

the 19th century, Iraq was a net exporter of grain. While some tribal shaykhs lost influence under these new policies, other shaykhs and urban merchants performed vital intermediary functions for the Ottomans.

Ottoman centralization policies had produced stakeholders among the students who attended modern schools and who graduated into positions in the expanded administration, but the numbers were limited because the Ottomans tended to import officials from elsewhere rather than employ large numbers of local Iraqis. As a result, many felt disenfranchised.

The rebels in 1920 included the Shi'i tribal shaykhs who were closely aligned with the Shi'i mujtahids in and around the shrine cities. They opposed British control over Iraq and the formation of a secular government, which they assumed would follow. They were joined by Iraqi Sharifian officers who had returned home after the Arab Revolt and wanted Faysal to be Iraq's king. Iraqi Ottoman bureaucratic officials who had been refused positions by the British also numbered among the rebels. This was not an easy coalition, and the groups did not work to coordinate their activities. It was a case of disparate groups rebelling for their own regional reasons against a shared enemy. Just as in Turkey and Syria, local leaders sought to hold or gain positions in any kind of government being formed, but the rebellions acquired a nationalist patina because the one purpose the groups shared was to defend Iraq from British colonialism.

By October 1920, the rebellion was over, crushed by British troops and Royal Air Force (RAF) planes, and Faysal was appointed to the throne of this British-ruled region. Following this rebellion, Britain united the provinces of predominantly Shi'i Basra and Sunni Baghdad. In 1926, the British added the northern province of Mosul to the state of Iraq, including the towns of Erbil and al-Sulaymaniyya so that British oil companies could control any oil discovered in the region. The largest demographic group in most of these northern regions was Kurdish, although the population comprised large portions of Arabs and Turkomans—descendants of the Turkic tribes who had migrated to the region beginning in the 11th century.

King Faysal's Government

When King Faysal took the throne in 1921, the same questions about what kind of state would be formed and who would be leaders in the government came to the forefront as they had in Iraq's neighboring states. To create a government loyal to his throne, King Faysal elevated to top military and civilian positions the Sharifian officers who had rebelled on his behalf or followed him from Syria; he rehired the Ottoman Iraqi

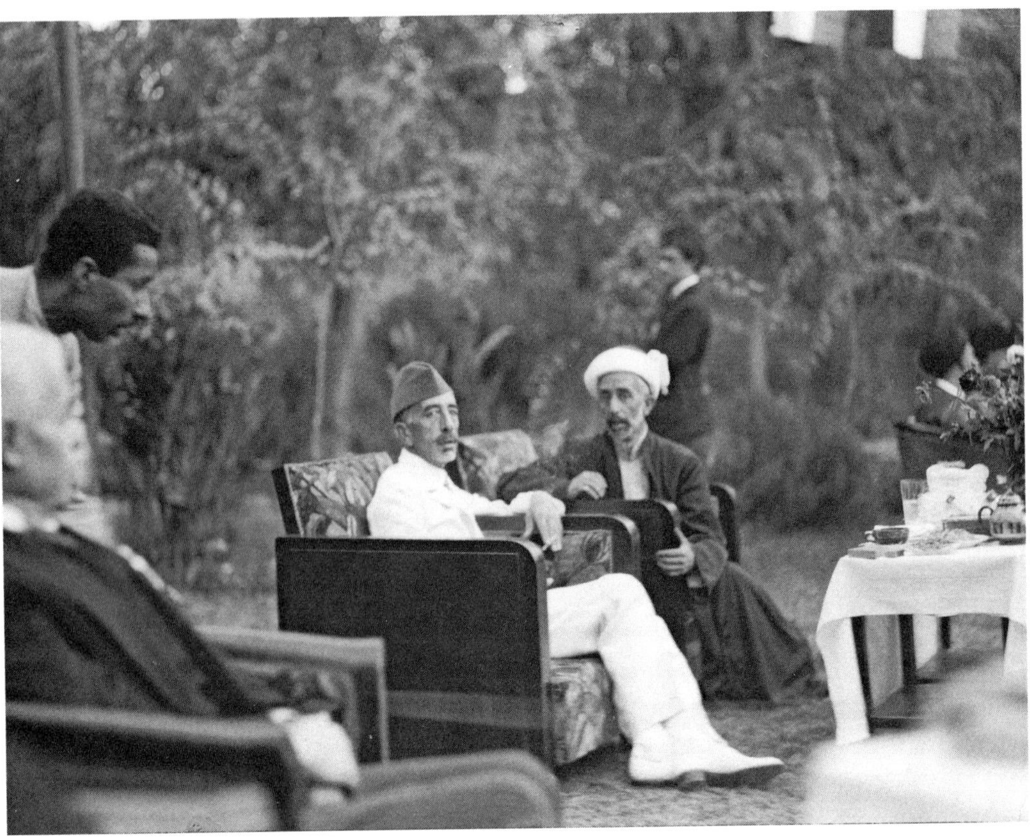

FIGURE 5.4. King Faysal of Iraq (*in white*) meeting with a visitor in the presidential palace in Baghdad, probably his brother, Emir Abdullah of Transjordan.

bureaucrats to preside over the expanding governmental apparatus and make them stakeholders for his leadership. The Sunni large landowners and merchants in and around Baghdad who had not participated in the rebellion were awarded positions in parliament and the cabinet.

Meanwhile, King Faysal and the British also worked to create divisions between the Shi'a, rewarding the tribal shaykhs who had chosen not to rebel against the British and punishing the shaykhs and mujtahids who had. The government courted select Shi'i shaykhs, believing they would respond to privileges by enforcing obedience among the tribesmen under their control. The British built favor with these rural tribal shaykhs to form a bulwark against the potentially rebellious urban areas and ensure that government institutions would be installed in the rural areas. The tribal areas in general came under a special Tribal Disputes Code that gave shaykhs power over legal issues among their tribesmen. Many shaykhs also moved into Baghdad to take up positions in the new parliament.

Over the next years, King Faysal proved adept at shifting these groups into and out of power in order to guarantee that no coalition could grow powerful enough to rise against him. He exploited the fact that these disparate groups did not necessarily agree on all elements of governance. The notables from the Ottoman era wanted to maintain their influential positions, and while King Faysal included them in his administration, he also obliged them to compete with each other for governmental influence. He elevated the Sharifians to many of the top posts so they would be pitted against the established Iraqi notables, who especially resented the Sharifians' elite status, given that these upstarts haled from lower- to medium-middle-class families, families that would have been social inferiors under the Ottomans. Rural landowners and shaykhs vied for positions against urban merchants.

Iraqi Constitution

The Iraqi constitution, ratified in 1924, gave King Faysal means to exert control over the process of elections. It provided for a bicameral legislature with a two-stage election process: the initial elections chose electors who, in the second phase, selected the representatives. The two stages allowed the king and British officials many opportunities for guaranteeing the election of a pliable parliament. The constitution reserved few legislative rights for the members of parliament because the king retained the power to confirm or veto all laws, call elections, and prorogue parliament at will; the cabinet answered to the king, not to parliament. The constitution included language promising equality for all before the law and freedom of speech, press, association, and religion, but the government recognized few of these rights in day-to-day practice.

As a result, only a small number of people held office in the cabinet or positions in parliament in the interwar years. In the 21 cabinets formed between 1920 and 1936, 57 men served, with only 14 holding any real influence. In parliament, a relatively small number of notable families provided the majority of the members of parliament and, as they had under the Ottomans, used their positions to pass laws giving them access to more land, more trade contracts, and—given Iraqi agriculture dependence on water from rivers and wells—the ever important water pumps.

Like their counterparts in Damascus, the notables who held the few positions in government also worked to establish nationalist credibility by forming political parties and associated newspapers. These parties lacked political platforms and failed to mobilize anyone outside the existing client networks. The politicians' papers repeated a nationalist mantra of anti-imperialism, but the politicians themselves benefited from their positions in the colonial government and from British protection for the system as a whole. The Iraqi notables occupied the same equivocal position as the notables in the National Bloc because they worked on behalf of Arab nationalist causes but were dependent on King Faysal and the British for their governmental power. Nonetheless, these papers did begin to politicize the urban educated population around ideas of fighting against British imperialism and for the establishment of a truly representative government.

Anglo-Iraqi Treaty of 1930

The 1930 signing of the Anglo-Iraqi Treaty and the country's subsequent admittance into the League of Nations granted the Iraqi government power over its own defense and state institutions. The Iraqi government, in exchange, agreed to allow the British to use all of the country's facilities in time of war and to move troops into the country if necessary. The RAF was given the right to maintain two major bases in Iraq in return for supplying the Iraqi military with equipment and advisers. The negotiations had taken place because the British government was fulfilling its duty to usher the Iraq Mandate into independence while also guaranteeing that British military interests would be protected. Although Iraq was granted independence before the neighboring mandates were, it was an independence severely circumscribed by continuing British control over Iraqi government and territory.

Rebellion and State Construction in Transjordan

At the San Remo Conference of 1920, Britain assumed control over the Palestine Mandate and soon divided it into two, with Palestine to the west of the River Jordan and Transjordan to the east. This division exempted the newly defined Transjordan region from the provisions of the Balfour Declaration of November 2, 1917, which now applied only to the Palestine region. Britain's colonial secretary, Winston Churchill, appointed Abdullah (r. 1921–1951), the second son of Sharif Hussein, as emir of the new state of Transjordan. At that point, members of the Hashemite family ruled both Transjordan and Iraq. Emir Abdullah and his British advisers chose the town of Amman as the capital of this new emirate because its small size and lack of importance prior to 1921 meant that it could be remade as a city inextricably connected to the new Hashemite project.

Initially, Transjordan's borders encompassed only what is now the northern districts of Jordan, but in November 1925 the Transjordanian-

Najd Agreement expanded the borders appreciably. Negotiations took place after repeated battles between Saudi and Transjordanian tribes over access to grazing lands and water sources. To end this conflict over land, Transjordan gave up the fertile Wadi Sirhan region on the Arabian Peninsula to Ibn Saud's new state but gained control over the town of Ma'an and the port of Aqaba, which had been traditionally considered part of the Hijaz.

In the Anglo-Transjordanian Treaty of 1928, Transjordan, once considered a region within the Palestine Mandate, was granted the status of a separate emirate, subject to British control over foreign affairs, defense, and finance. Britain retained the right to station troops in Transjordan and use Transjordanian troops to protect its strategic interests and military installations in the region. Further, Britain could exploit the natural resources of the country and veto any piece of legislation that hampered Britain's ability to fulfill its international obligations. In return, Britain pledged to give the government an annual subsidy to cover much of its operating costs. In the same year the treaty was signed, the Organic Law was passed, which proclaimed Emir Abdullah the head of state with hereditary rights and declared that the government would comprise an Executive and a Legislative Council. This law severely curtailed the powers accruing to the councils, however, as it gave Emir Abdullah the power, with few restrictions, to appoint members of the first and dismiss members of both.

Setting up a government and finding and training the stakeholders proved as difficult in Transjordan as in the surrounding mandates. Lieutenant Colonel Frederick Peake established the Arab Legion in 1923, and for the next two decades it served primarily as an internal police and gendarmerie force. This new force worked with the British RAF to subdue a number of tribal revolts that broke out in the early 1920s. Once order was restored, Emir Abdullah courted local shaykhs with outlays of cash, land, and cars to bring them into alliance with him personally and with the state he was creating under British supervision. The shaykhs and tribes were especially important building blocks of support in Transjordan because the country lacked the base of large landowners whose loyalty could have been ensured by granting them positions in the government. After the Ottoman Land Law, small and medium-sized farmers in Transjordan had registered the land in their own names, unlike in so many other regions where only large landowners had. In this situation, shaykhs were the only brokers who could bring large numbers of clients in service to the government.

FIGURE 5.5. A Pan-Islamic conference hosted by Emir Abdullah of Transjordan in a bedouin tent in Shunet Nimirn on December 12, 1931.

The groups left out of this state configuration in the interwar period were the urban merchants and the small but growing numbers of Western-educated Transjordanian students. Emir Abdullah and the British disenfranchised them by employing non-Transjordanians in the top positions in government from the very beginning of their project of state formation. Between 1921 and 1946, only eight men, all of whom came from Syria and Palestine, held the post of chief minister: not a single one was a Transjordanian. Although the bureaucracy expanded during the interwar period, Arab officials seconded from the Palestine Mandate dominated the available positions throughout the 1920s. The initial impetus for making such appointments was that Transjordan lacked the skilled officials to fill government positions. As the Western-educated stratum voiced its opposition to state policies in the 1930s, Palestinians maintained their leadership positions because of their loyalty to Emir Abdullah and the British.

To force the state to respect their rights, by 1928 Transjordanians had begun to organize, rallying to the slogan of "Transjordan for the Transjordanians" and opposing the provisions of the Anglo-Transjordanian Treaty and Organic Law. Strikes broke out in cities throughout the country, and 150 activists from among the tribal leaders and the urban merchant and educated class met in Amman on July 25 to draw up a list of demands for Emir Abdullah. They called for the adoption of a truly constitutional and representative government led by Transjordanians. When they won a large number of seats in parliament in 1928, they proved so vocal in their opposition to Emir Abdullah's policies that in all subsequent elections Emir Abdullah and the British worked to guarantee that only loyal followers, mostly tribal shaykhs, large merchants, and the small cadre of large landowners, won election. Parliament had initially shown signs of being a venue for debate about governance, but within months Emir Abdullah and the British had turned it into an agency for bringing elites into the state and excluding those who opposed state policies.

Rebellion and State Construction in Saudi Arabia

In the aftermath of World War I, Sharif Hussein lost British support because he opposed the division of the Arab territories into mandates. As a result, in the 1920s he had few means to defend the Hijaz against attacks from the forces of Ibn Saud. As a last effort to keep the Hashemite family in charge of the holy sites, he abdicated in favor of his son, Emir 'Ali, and went into exile in Cyprus in 1924. But this move did not shore up Emir 'Ali's position, and he was defeated by Ibn Saud's forces on December 5, 1924. In December 1925, Ibn Saud declared himself king of the Hijaz and sultan of Najd and its dependencies. In recognition of Ibn Saud's success, the British signed the Treaty of Jeddah with him in May 1927, declaring the complete independence of the dominions of His Majesty the King of the Hijaz and of Najd. Ibn Saud announced the Kingdom of Saudi Arabia on September 22, 1932. Although it was not a colony, the kingdom was dependent on British aid, making its position ambiguous in relation to the British Empire.

As of 1920, no government agencies existed, and few had been built by the time independence was declared in 1932. At that point, the Kingdom of Saudi Arabia's government consisted only of an eight-member Shura Council of the Hijaz, made up of posts filled by non-Saudi Arabs and Europeans. Other government branches remained similarly informal throughout the 1920s and 1930s, with the king convening a series of daily diwans (councils) to consult with his advisers and hear requests from his subjects. Meanwhile, the relationship between the Saudi royal family and the Wahhab clerics became more institutionalized. Since the 18th century, the Saudi-Wahhab alliance had led to many military victories, but it had been an informal relationship in which both parties had reciprocal duties. As the government structure evolved in the 1920s, the two parties recognized that they needed to remain loyal to each other to maintain their relative influence and their joint control over the country. The Wahhab clerics required Saudi funding and official recognition to spread their ideas, and the Saudi royal family needed the clerics' religious sanction to prove their legitimacy. As their alliance continued to evolve, the clerics issued fatwas rationalizing actions by the state while the royal family granted the clerics leeway to set the cultural agenda for the new state-in-formation.

As the Saudis sought to build up a national army, they found they had to destroy the tribal military force that had brought them to power. Ibn Saud had conquered the Arabian Peninsula with help from a group of bedouin calling themselves the Ikhwan (the Brothers). Initially the Ikhwan accepted the authority of Ibn Saud as imam of the Muslim community with a passion similar to that exhibited by the Qizilbash for Shah Isma'il of the Safavids in the 16th century. They not only defeated groups militarily but enforced on those they conquered the Wahhab interpretation of the shari'a in Ahasa' in 1913 and in Ta'if in 1924; they massacred those they considered nonbelievers. Ibn Saud's desire for settlement and centralization left little room for the autonomy of the Ikhwan because they were difficult to contain and control. Once Ibn Saud established his position as king in Riyadh, he worked to curtail their freedom, and the Ikhwan came out in open opposition to his leadership. To destroy this group, Ibn Saud recruited men from the Najd oases into a separate military force. With RAF aid, he succeeded in killing and exiling the Ikhwan and laying the groundwork for a national army.

Conclusion

The post–World War I period began with rebellions in every corner of the Ottoman and Qajar Empires, bringing down the royal families of both. These years represent a moment in Middle Eastern history when many possible state configurations could have been adopted and leaders were eager to participate in any government that emerged. These leaders mainly sought to defend their local positions against the infiltration of European or local challengers, but collectively, in one region after another, they also created a proto-nationalist movement, as all the different military organizations worked toward many of the same goals. However, European colonizers and their local collaborators quickly came to the fore and punished those who had rebelled. The window then closed on most of the state options. Most rebels found themselves losers in the new state configurations, but the winners were by no means guaranteed stable positions of governance.

In Turkey and Iran, Mustafa Kemal and Reza Shah turned from rebels into state leaders, with the former choosing to elevate a new elite into positions of power to implement his policies, while the latter subsumed the old landowners and tribes into a new centralized government. They both established authoritarian states where they dictated the parameters of institution building and the elements defining Turkish and Iranian identities. During the interwar years, both produced stakeholders for their programs, but both also struggled to impose on the citizenries what they envisioned as comprehensive programs of modernity.

The Europeans, who had been intervening in Middle Eastern politics for over a century, took the lead in drawing borders and establishing the state structures throughout the Arab world. The rebels in these areas failed to stop the Europeans or earn places in the new state governments being formed, but their opposition made state formation a fraught exercise. By choosing to fill their new state structures with the old elites, the Europeans and their allied local leaders created a conundrum that had lasting consequences. Integrating the former elites—whether merchants, landowners, or tribal leaders—into the new governments proved to be a successful tactic for gaining the largest number of supporters in the quickest fashion because these intermediaries brought along their tribesmen and client networks.

Yet by working with the European colonizers, these intermediaries placed themselves in an ambiguous position. Because they worked for the colonial governments, they benefited from the colonizers' largesse, but to retain client loyalty, they had to present themselves as nationalist leaders. Rarely were they able to effectively balance those contradictory roles. By the 1930s, leaders in all the Arab mandates faced new rebellions, not from the old tribal or religious sectors but from students, professionals, workers, and military officers who were trained by these new post–World War I states. These new groups challenged the legitimacy of the local intermediaries and the right of their European colonial overlords to speak on their behalf.

REBELS AND ROGUES

6

Egypt, Iraq, Transjordan, Palestine, and Israel in the Interwar Years

THE CONSTRUCTION OF NEW STATES throughout the Middle East did not end rebellions and rogue actions but in fact created new strata in society willing to come out in opposition to their state institutions. Student groups, paramilitary units, and labor unions organized into associations to fight against the Europeans holding a grip on politics and the economy and against local politicians whose members had increasingly shown themselves incapable of changing government policies. They fought to gain positions within governments and political parties, hoping to bring their educational expertise into governance. Still others organized into religious groups like the Muslim Brotherhood to voice their opposition to the secularization of society.

Meanwhile, economic developments throughout this period exacerbated the existing power divisions as the notables who won places in the new governments largely improved their economic status while the vast majority of the population suffered under European competition and deprivations wrought by the Great Depression. The Palestinians and Zionists fought to make national claims to the Palestine Mandate, culminating in the 1948 Arab-Israeli War that brought Israel into existence and the Palestinians under Israeli, Egyptian, and Jordanian control and as refugees throughout the region. The result for Palestine and the countries discussed in Chapter 5 was political upheaval for much of the 1930s and 1940s. The example of Egypt illustrates how new rebels and rogues emerged on the political scene and how their demands challenged the European and local political leadership.

Egypt after World War I

Immediately after World War I, a former Egyptian education minister, Sa'd Zaghlul, came forward as the leader of a new generation of Egyptian nationalist activists. He and his colleagues formed a delegation (wafd) and called on the British Resident to allow them to present the Egyptian case to the Great Powers at the Paris Peace Conference at Versailles. When the British government refused, members of this wafd and their allies fanned out around the country to rouse the population against the British decision. On March 10, 1919, a large demonstration of students from the Schools of Law, Medicine, and Engineering in Cairo marched in the streets to support the wafd action; the next day, secondary students joined them, and within days the revolt had spread throughout the country. This 1919 revolution was a truly national movement: all societal groups participated and stood in solidarity with the nationalist message disseminated by the wafd, in support of Egyptian self-determination and in opposition to continued British colonialism. The movement was widespread enough that the British were forced to rescind the ban on the wafd and allow its members to travel to Versailles. However, once there, they found that the Great Powers had as little interest in a truly independent Egypt as in Syria and Iraq. Back in Egypt, the British suppressed the revolt with military force, killing 800 and wounding 1,400 more.

In the aftermath of these events, the British made a unilateral declaration of Egypt's independence on February 28, 1922; Khedive Fu'ad became King Fu'ad (r. 1922–1936), followed by his son, King Farouk (r. 1936–1952). Britain reserved for itself four rights: control over Egyptian foreign policy, territorial rights to the Suez Canal, continuing governance over the Sudan, and protection for foreign nationals and minorities living in Egypt. These conditions modified the terms under which Britain had ruled Egypt since 1882 by granting additional domestic autonomy to the Egyptian government, but they did not constitute true independence, as evidenced by the fact that Egypt did not join the League of Nations after this declaration and Britain maintained extensive military and administrative forces in the country.

FIGURE 6.1. Women demonstrating in Cairo during the 1919 revolution.

Egyptian Constitutions

To set up a new kind of local Egyptian government, the constitution of 1923 vested legislative power in the king and a bicameral legislature. The king held the most power because he had the right to appoint the prime minister, dissolve parliament, and appoint two-fifths of the Senate. A two-stage electoral process gave the king the ability to manipulate the results in each election. When the king determined these protections were not sufficient for keeping opposition parties out of parliament, he issued a new constitution in 1931 granting him additional powers. It prohibited parliament from initiating legislation concerning financial issues reserved to the king; allowed the king to veto any law enacted by parliament; and gave the king the right to nominate half of the senators.

To weaken the electoral prospects of opposition parties, the king issued a new electoral law on October 22, 1930, that raised the voting age from 21 to 25; increased the qualifications necessary for voting; and returned the system of secondary electors that a cabinet of the 1920s had tried to eliminate. With these restrictions, coupled with the divisive positions taken by politicians, the political situation proved too fractious to maintain a stable government. The average lifespan of governments in the 1920s was only 16 months, as the king dismissed prime ministers for corruption or for trying to legislate in opposition to his wishes. Parliaments never lasted their constitutionally mandated four years. The underlying problem was that the system encouraged intraparty rivalries and competition with the king rather than cooperative action toward developing the country.

Wafd Party

Despite political manipulation, the Wafd Party, which had become an official political party in the aftermath of the 1919 revolution, won the largest number of parliamentary seats in elections in the 1920s. Once in office, however, the members proved ineffective in passing legislation. The primary problem was that the party could bring supporters out to the streets by the thousands as it had done in 1919, but ultimately that meant little in a system where the king held so much local power. Furthermore, as the decade progressed, the Wafd fractured into competing groups, with the top offices staffed by the large landowning and merchant strata. They stood in the same ambiguous position as their counterparts in Iraq and Syria in that they moved into and out of government positions and benefited from the sale of their products to the

British while also advocating anti-imperialist positions in their newspapers and political salons.

Meanwhile, younger professionals from both the notable class and lower economic strata rose up to demand decision-making power within the leadership cadres of the Wafd. They tended to push for more radical economic and political positions than the older members by the 1930s. Particularly after Zaghlul died on August 27, 1927, and Mustafa al-Nahhas became the Wafd's new leader, these fissures weakened the party in its struggles against the king. Al-Nahhas did not generate the same kind of loyalty as his predecessor; when he took over the party leadership, he had to compete against a number of new political parties, some openly supportive of the king and others established by former members of the Wafd who had broken with his policies.

Expansion of Education

Even more deleterious to the Wafd's position, the secondary and university students who were the most active supporters of the party and the largest segment of the demonstrators in the streets were also growing disillusioned with the Wafd leadership. They were aided in this endeavor because the Egyptian government supervised the expansion of the education system throughout the interwar period. In 1925, when the government made compulsory education the law of the land, about 15 of every 1,000 Egyptian youth were in school; in 1940 that number had jumped to 69. Those continuing through secondary education to the university level primarily attended the American University in Cairo (AUC), opened in 1920 by American missionaries, and Egyptian University, opened in 1908. This latter institution became a state university in 1925 under the same name and included four colleges: Arts from the original university; Science; Law; and Medicine, which had been incorporated as the School of Medicine and Pharmacy under Mehmet Ali in 1827. In 1935, the university added the School of Engineering, the Higher School of Agriculture, and the Higher School of Commerce. In 1940, the name changed to Fu'ad I University; enrollment in 1945–1946 stood at more than 10,000 students.

Green and Blue Shirts

Students joined the established parties in large numbers, while many also trained with paramilitary units as a way to express their frequent opposition to Wafd politicians, the British, and the king. The Green Shirts of the Young Egypt Society was inaugurated in 1933 as a patriotic association for youth, led by men in their 20s who had gone through the Westernized school system. It became a formal political party in late 1936; its successor after World War II, the Socialist Party, remained largely a youth movement. Its news organ, *Al-Sarkha*, covered the main political events of the day but also provided articles on the moral uplift to be found in Islam, patriotic pieces glorifying Egypt's past, and analyses of what might be learned from the historical experiences of other countries. The leaders also sent frequent petitions to the government opposing policy decisions and organizing events such as boycotts of foreign-owned products and companies. The group held marches and military drills, sometimes resulting in clashes with the police.

At times, the Green Shirts aligned with King Farouk, who had succeed his father in 1936, but more because they both opposed the Wafd Party than because of a shared ideology about Egypt's proper direction. At those times, especially in the post-1936 period, the number of members grew as the organization became aligned with top governmental officials and was thus able to hold large meetings without fear of police reprisal.

FIGURE 6.2. During riots in Cairo in 1936, students surround and climb on top of Prime Minister Nessim Pasha's car.

During the late 1930s, clashes broke out repeatedly between the Green Shirts and the Wafd's version of a paramilitary organization, the Blue Shirts, which had emerged out of the League of Wafdist Youth. An underlying complaint of all these participants was frustration with the older notables of all parties who held positions of power and kept the newcomers, often far more educated than themselves, from attaining positions of authority in the government, private practice, and political parties.

Muslim Brotherhood

Many of the same generation of urban educated youth turned to Muslim organizations as yet another path to political mobilization. Primary school teacher Hasan al-Banna founded the Muslim Brotherhood in the town of Ismailia in 1928. In the early years, it was just one of many such Islamic organizations but by the early 1930s was clearly becoming the largest and most influential in the country. In his many criticisms of Egypt's elite politicians, al-Banna frequently wrote about how they may express good ideas about changing Egyptian society yet did little but compete for positions of power once in office. The answer to Egypt's many problems for al-Banna was a return to Islam so the country's moral and social life could be renewed. The Brotherhood vision put forward Islam as a comprehensive system of values and governance, whereby religion and state (din wa-dawla) functioned interchangeably. The Islamic order that al-Banna spoke about would be based on the shari'a, which for him embodied all the virtues of democratic and socialist governmental systems but without the defects apparent in secularly oriented societies.

After the Brotherhood moved its headquarters to Cairo in 1932, the organization spread its institutional reach. The Third Conference of 1935 adopted the General Law of the Society, which gave extensive powers to an executive body appointed by al-Banna. The Brotherhood opened pharmacies, health clinics, hospitals, and schools to serve those in urban areas who were neglected by state institutions. Members spread the ideas of the organization through mosques and Islamic welfare societies in rural areas. By 1940, the Brotherhood had also established a paramilitary organization to compete with opponents on the streets.

The Brotherhood was not a cleric-led organization but a lay one, with leaders and members largely emerging from the same socioeconomic background as the students who followed the Wafd Party or joined paramilitary groups. Most of the young adherents were educated in new state schools through the university level, and many were first-generation immigrants into the cities. They were disenchanted with the breakdown of the political process and disappointed that so little was being done to alleviate the suffering most people experienced; they were frustrated by the lack of opportunities for advancement in their chosen fields. They looked to the many Brotherhood organizations throughout the country to provide services, a sense of community, and a philosophy for living in modern society.

Workers

Workers represented another mobilized urban group in Egypt, as they demonstrated along with the students and repeatedly went on strike to demand better working conditions throughout the 1930s. Workers had done so since the 1882 British occupation and participated in large numbers in the 1919 revolution. During the 1920s, the Wafd Party gradually consolidated the unions under its own control in the General Federation of Labor Unions in the Nile Valley. The union was empowered by the fact that between 1928 and 1937, almost 55,000 industrial establishments opened in Egypt, aided by the removal of the low tariffs that had accompanied the Capitulation treaty. By the 1930s, these new workers were available to participate in strikes. The government did pass laws protecting children and women, but implementation occurred slowly because of opposition by factory owners and urban merchants. Workers fought for those rights through strikes, while also trying to influence national policy by joining political parties, paramilitary organizations, and the Muslim Brotherhood.

Women

Egyptian women were very much a part of all these transformations in the interwar period, as activists on behalf of the parties, newly trained professionals, writers in the press, founders and teachers of girls' schools, and workers in the factories. They moved into the cities along with their families when the land no longer sustained them. A large number of women fronted organizations specifically designed to address and alleviate the political, social, and economic concerns of women. The most influential in the 1920s, the Egyptian Feminist Union (EFU), led by Huda Sha'rawi, opened day-care centers, clinics, and training centers in poor areas of the cities and later in rural areas to give women help while they worked and to teach them vocational skills to improve their economic status. Arab women joined their Iranian and Turkish counterparts in attending international women's conferences where they could rightfully boast of the number of girls and women in schools and the professions in Egypt. However, lobbying efforts gained no political rights for women, and little change came to the personal status laws concerning marriage, divorce, child custody, and inheritance, leaving women with few legal means of protection in the private realm.

Military

The last element emerging on the Egyptian political scene in the 1930s was the military, but this was still a force in evolution rather than one with a clear role to play in politics. One method the king used to rally every possible force to his side in his competition with the Wafd was to

WOMEN PERFORMERS IN CAIRO

Egyptian women had performed on the musical stage since of the turn of the 20th century, but a few made names for themselves throughout the Middle East during the interwar years. In the 1920s and 1930s, women singers and actresses were integral parts of a vibrant Egyptian entertainment scene. They formed a uniquely national style of Egyptian music by combining Egyptian lyrics and melodies with Western instruments. Political and societal elites flooded to their shows.

Munira al-Mahdiyya (1884–1965) was one of the first Egyptian women to record music at the turn of the 20th century. After World War I she opened her own theater hall where she staged Arabic versions of such operas as *Carmen* and *Madame Butterfly*. Badi'a Masabni (1892–1974), a Lebanese expatriate, began her career as a dancer and actress and in 1926 opened a music hall that featured cabaret acts with singers and comedy performers. Until it closed after World War II, it served as a gathering place for patrons from across Egypt's social spectrum and for European visitors.

The most famous singer at the time was undoubtedly Umm Kulthum (ca. 1904–1975), who first gained fame in Egypt and then attained regional and worldwide fame in the 1950s and 1960s. Her radio concerts on the first Thursday of every month were required appointments for hundreds of thousands of her followers. Her funeral in 1975 brought four million Egyptians out into the streets in mourning.

She began her life in a small village in the Nile Delta, the child of a mosque leader. When she was still young, her father took her around the area to sing religious songs for holidays and commemorations, often having her dress as a boy so she would not face the stigma of being a girl at the usually all-male events. By the 1920s, Umm Kulthum was in Cairo and slowly expanding her repertoire to include well-known poems put to music. Over time, she commissioned poets to write for her and worked with them and the composers so that the songs truly represented her style. In these years, she took advantage of the new technologies of recordings, radio, and film to spread her fame and gain followers who could not afford to see her live onstage. Her early training in Quranic recitation served her throughout her career because she was a brilliant vocalist and interpreter of lyrics.

open up the Military Academy to all ranks of society in 1936. Previously, only sons of rural landowners and urban merchants could attend, and the Egyptian military in general remained relatively small, per order of the British. As of 1936, the majority of new military and police officers rising through the system came from the lower- and middle-income brackets, both urban and rural. By bringing these newcomers into the military, the king was able to mold the army in the years before World War II into a branch loyal to his position and largely opposing the party politics that the Wafd represented.

Anglo-Egyptian Treaty of 1936

While the 1922 declaration had given Egypt only the weakest facade of independence, the Anglo-Egyptian Treaty of 1936 placed Egypt into a position similar to that of Iraq. Signed on August 26, 1936, the treaty admitted Egypt to the League of Nations on May 27, 1937. Per terms of the treaty, Egypt was charged with protecting the lives and properties of foreigners and received a guarantee that all British officials in the army and administration would be withdrawn. While these provisions granted Egyptians control over much local governance, the British retained the right to keep troops in the Suez Canal Zone on bases that were not subject to Egyptian authority. Britain was also allowed freedom over the skies of Egypt, and the Egyptian government agreed to build roads to facilitate British troop movements in case of emergency. A provision also allowed Britain to reenter Egypt in case of national emergency, a situation that arose just three years after the signing of the treaty when World War II broke out.

State Institutional Expansion: The Economy

The leaders of all of the states under study here struggled to expand, diversify, and improve their economic institutions during the interwar period. By World War II the region saw slow but steady economic growth but one that favored select groups in the society to the detriment of almost everyone else. The Great Depression of the 1930s brought to light the underdevelopment of the agricultural sectors and the disadvantageous position the region as a whole held in the world economy. With the exception of Turkey and Transjordan, which mostly maintained a base of small- to medium-sized landowners, the countries in the region moved more intensively during the interwar period to the dominance of large landowners. Hundreds of thousands of landless peasants moved into the cities; some found work in the new factories, while many more struggled to find jobs. Economic competition from abroad and state investment in modern industries forced the closure of many old artisan shops that had formed the foundation of manufacturing for centuries and the primary employment for urban workers.

During the Great Depression, these states struggled because their major exports were agricultural products that garnered few profits on the international market. Since the late 18th century and accelerating under the reforms of the 19th century, many regions in the Middle East had moved into cash cropping by selling cotton, silk, tobacco, and wheat in the world economy. With the world economic crash in 1929, many of these overseas markets dried up. The worst years occurred between 1929 and 1933, and then all the countries saw a measure of growth but not enough to employ the numbers or types of people needing jobs in agriculture or industry.

Agriculture

In the first years of the Great Depression, agricultural prices collapsed across the Middle East. In Turkey, overall prices dropped by as much as 50 percent. In Egypt, cotton prices dropped by half between 1929 and 1933, and Egypt's exports of this previously dominant product fell by a third overall in this same period. In the Levant, the situation was made even worse by infestations of locusts and low rainfall. In Turkey, the government instituted a system of subsidies by 1932 whereby the state bought wheat and other essential products at higher-than-market prices from the rural producers and then sold bread and other such manufactured goods at inflated prices in the urban areas. By 1936, when world agricultural prices rose, the state had thoroughly penetrated the agricultural market so reaped the revenues that accrued. In Egypt, the government restricted cotton production, calculating that a smaller harvest would raise prices, but the demand remained too low for this policy to sufficiently alleviate the crisis. Only in the late 1930s did prices rebound, and by then the market favored landowners who had consolidated the largest amount of land under their control in the previous years.

Landownership

The Iranian majles passed a number of laws protecting peasant rights during the 1930s, but the large landowners worked to impede their implementation. Because Reza Shah relied on the landowners as a pillar of his new state, he did not push for the changes. Between 95 and 98 percent of all peasants were landless in the 1930s, and with this body of cheap labor available, landowners did little to improve cultivation policies, so yield per acre saw little increase. French policies in Syria aided the absentee landlords living in the cities and those in the rural areas deemed loyal to the French, so by World War II, only 16 percent of the land around Aleppo and 45 percent near Homs was cultivated by small landholders.

On paper, the 1932 Land Settlement Law in Iraq granted landownership to tribesmen and peasants who had worked a given piece of land for 15 years or more. In reality, tribal shaykhs, large landowners, and urban merchants took advantage of the law to register the land in their own names. They were aided in this endeavor by the 1933 Law for the Rights and Duties of Cultivators, which many of them had passed as members in parliament. The law declared that tenants, not landowners, were responsible for crop failures. This law intensified the debt burden on the peasants and forced many to sell or lease their land to large landowners.

Cognizant of these problems, all the states tried to bring new resources into the rural areas to make improvements in cultivation. However, only a small percentage of the rural population benefited. New agricultural and credit banks opened across the region in the 1930s, but they provided little real help to the peasants in need of loans to buy seeds and equipment. In general, these financial institutions were located in the cities, far from the farming lands, or located in too few towns and villages for peasants to reach. They also frequently restricted those peasants who could obtain loans to those who already had land and capital, leaving most rural residents without access.

Land Reform in Transjordan

Three decades ahead of the surrounding countries, Emir Abdullah and the British officials posted to Transjordan instituted a land reform program in 1927 designed to register all the land in the country, make land more efficient, and improve taxation collection. Its benefits and problems would be replicated in the countries that followed their lead in the 1950s and 1960s. Islamic inheritance policies enshrined in the 1858 Ottoman Land Law provided for all heirs to receive a share of the land. By the interwar period, this policy meant that ever-increasing numbers of people lived off ever-smaller pieces of land. Even though many small farmers had been able to register their land, many of them fell into indebtedness during the 1930s. These were years of drought and overuse of the soil, so harvests were poor even as the state demanded more in taxation from its peasantry. The Agricultural Bank the government established in 1922 was of little help to the peasants because few could access it and it had relatively few funds to disperse in the economic crisis of the 1930s. While Transjordan remained a land of predominantly small- to medium-sized landholders by the time the reforms had been carried out, the program's provisions paradoxically provided for the expansion of the number of large landowners as smaller-sized holdings had to be sold off or leased out to pay the bills. This became particularly true in World War II when merchants in Amman made a profit selling products to the British army and thus had the resources to buy land.

Silk Industry in Lebanon

In Lebanon, emigration had served since the mid-19th century as an agricultural safety valve because it provided venues outside the country for excess labor and for those finding it difficult to live off the land in times of crisis. However, the silk industry that had brought profit to thousands in the 19th century was already in decline before World War I, was disrupted during the war, and was effectively destroyed in the aftermath because of blight so could no longer provide the revenues for costly migrations. In addition, new restrictions throughout the Americas in the 1920s made emigration difficult for even those with the resources to travel. The result was a dramatic decrease in remittances from immigrants and a surfeit of labor on the land in Lebanon, at the same time that prices for agricultural products had fallen drastically.

Infrastructure Projects

In an attempt to alleviate these economic crises, all the states built up their transportation infrastructures so that goods could be easily moved and civil servants and tax collectors could conduct business around the country. By the end of World War II, none succeeded in tying their countries together seamlessly, but many efforts were expended in extending road, railway, and telegraph networks. Reza Shah's government invested extensive resources into building up such networks with plans for the roads and railways to connect the ports of the Persian Gulf with producing cities like Tehran and Isfahan. The centerpiece was the Trans-Iranian Railway that began connecting cities within the country. In Lebanon, more improvements to the Port of Beirut quadrupled the amount of traffic moving through its facilities between 1920 and 1939. The road and railway network moving into and out of Baghdad helped make it the preeminent trading center in the country while bypassing older trading cities like Najaf and Karbala in the southern provinces of Iraq.

Industrial Development

Mustafa Kemal had the most comprehensive program for economic change, with statism as one of the six basic principles of his national project in the 1930s, but all of the states under study here focused on state intervention to build up infrastructure and modern industry. They all faced the endemic problem of too little investment money available in the private realm. A professional middle stratum emerged out of the changes of the 19th century but not an entrepreneurial class with funds to invest at the level needed to industrialize. The large landowners brought into local governance as intermediaries owned extensive landholdings and had investments in the small urban manufacturing sector but had little cash for large-scale investment. The only groups with sufficient resources for such investment were the large merchants in cities such as Beirut and Alexandria who traded with the Europeans.

In 1934, Ankara issued its first five-year plan modeled on those of the Soviet Union and made investments in factories for textiles, sugar, iron, steel, glassworks, cement, utilities, and mining. With little nongovernmental investment money available, the state came to control 80 percent of foreign trade by the mid-1930s. Iran followed the same policies of state investment in primarily import-substitution industries and transitioned from having only 20 modern factories in the mid-1920s to 350 by 1941, producing sugar, textiles, and electricity. In both countries, private capital remained a key component of urban industry, but it was largely based in small shops where the majority of goods were produced through World War II. Even when private capital moved into larger and more modern industries, it tended to be in partnership with the state because of the need for additional investments.

In the Arab mandates and Egypt, the relationship between state and industry was skewed by the fact that large industries, such as railways, tramlines, and electricity providers, were typically owned by foreign concerns. Members of the National Bloc in Syria invested in cement, food processing, cigarette production, cotton spinning, and textiles. These were all labor-intensive industries but could withstand foreign competition because they remained domestic and did not compete with French imports. At the same time, many other small artisan shops went bankrupt; by the mid-1930s, 300 of the 700 trades previously practiced in

Damascus had failed. By 1937, modern industry in Syria employed only 33,000 workers, and unemployment rose as weavers and silk spinners lost their jobs after the importation of modern machinery.

Oil Industry

Iraq and Saudi Arabia joined Iran as oil states, collectively adding jobs and bringing royalty payments into their central governments but still not earning enough to diversify their economies. In the case of Iran, by 1932, revenues fell so markedly because of the Great Depression that the Iranian government of Reza Shah chose to unilaterally end the Anglo-Persian Oil Company (APOC) concession. After much negotiation, the Iranian government and APOC came to a new agreement that increased the royalty payments from 16 to 20 percent and reduced the land of the concession to 100,000 square miles. In return for accepting these conditions, the Iranian government agreed to an extension of the oil concession from 1961 to 1993. In 1935, APOC became the Anglo-Iranian Oil Company (AIOC) and in 1954, British Petroleum (BP).

FIGURE 6.3. Oil wells and an oil driller tower in an Iraq Petroleum Company (IPC) camp, five miles south of Kirkuk.

After World War I, the Turkish Petroleum Company (TPC, founded in 1912) was made up by APOC, Royal Dutch Shell, Compagnie Française des Pétroles, a US-based consortium of Standard Oil of New Jersey and Mobil, and an independent company owned by Armenian businessman Calouste Gulbenkian. In 1925, the new Iraqi parliament granted TPC (renamed the Iraq Petroleum Company [IPC] in 1929) a new oil concession that was contracted to last 75 years. The Iraqi government agreed to relinquish its shares in return for enhanced royalty payments and the right to construct a refinery and pipeline. Over time, the concession included all the regions of Iraq except Basra in the south. That last segment went to the Basra Petroleum Company, a subsidiary of IPC. Drilling did not begin in any of these fields until 1927, but by 1934 four million tons of oil a year flowed through a pipeline to the port of Haifa in the Palestine Mandate.

Over the next few years, oil was pumped from Iraq toward the Mediterranean, through Transjordan, Palestine, Syria, and Lebanon, provid-

FIGURE 6.4. Iraq Petroleum Company oil tanks in Haifa, Palestine, where oil was stored after transshipment from Iraq.

ing royalty and rent payments to the oil-producing countries and to those countries along the pipeline routes. The associated industries employed thousands of workers and, along with workers on the railways and in telegraph offices, formed the largest group of modern workers in the region. However, even with the addition of new jobs and royalty payments disbursed along the pipeline routes, oil could not at this stage offset the lack of resources these countries otherwise faced when they looked to improve agriculture and industrialize in the 1930s. The bulk of the wealth left the region via the foreign companies who controlled the drilling, refinement, and overseas shipping.

In 1933, the Saudi government signed an agreement with Standard Oil of California (SOCAL) to start exploration for oil in the eastern provinces along the Persian Gulf. In signing this agreement, Ibn Saud received an immediate loan and the promise of annual rent. In 1933 SOCAL placed the oil concession with Saudi Arabia under a wholly owned subsidiary, California Arab Standard Oil Company (CASOC), which was the precursor to the Arabian American Oil Company (Aramco) established in 1944. Drilling for oil began in 1935, and on May 1, 1939, the first tanker with liquid fuel sailed from the port of Ras Tanura. Over the next few years, Aramco and the American government invested in roads, a railway, an airport, and port facilities to build up the oil industry in Saudi Arabia.

MAP 16. Oil Fields and Refineries in the Middle East.

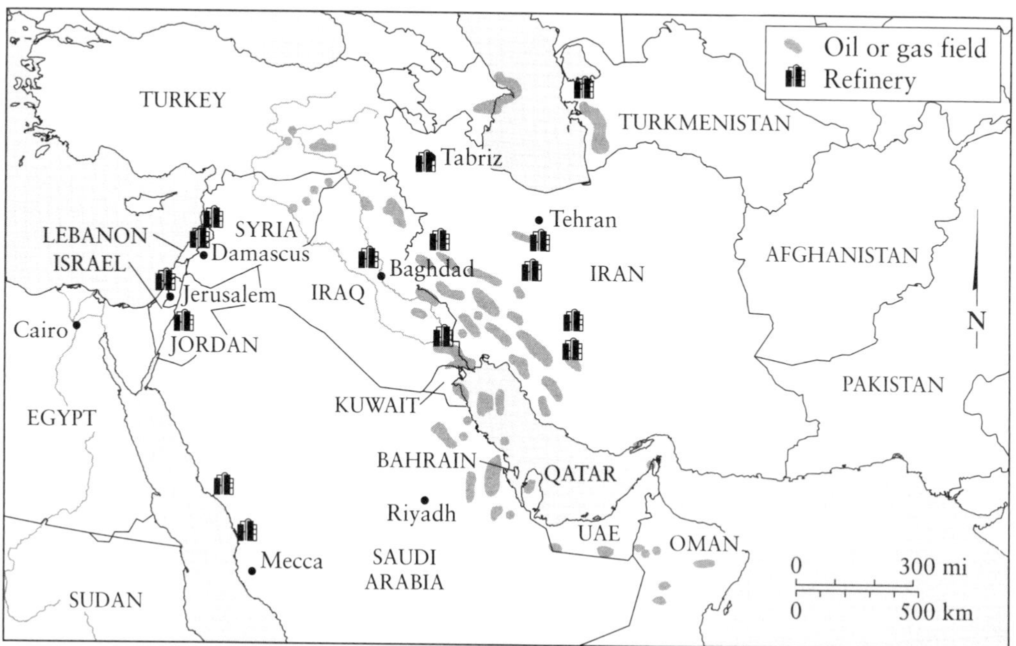

Worker Strikes

Workers in factories and large state-run utilities industries organized in the most sustained fashion during the interwar periods. In May 1929 in Iran, 11,000 workers at the Anglo-Persian Oil Company went on strike for better pay, an eight-hour workday, annual vacations, and the right to organize a union. The company agreed to the pay increases but nothing else and then arrested 500 of the workers involved. More than 800 workers on the Trans-Iranian Railway went on strike in the same year, and the pattern repeated itself: the company granted concessions about wages but jailed the organizers for many years afterward. In summer 1932, textile workers in Aleppo, Syria, undertook a massive strike, demanding the introduction of high tariffs to protect their products from foreign imports and higher wages. The French complied with the demand for the tariffs but did not raise wages. A 1931 strike at a textile factory in Isfahan, Iran, garnered the workers a 20 percent pay increase and the shift to a nine-hour workday.

State Institutional Expansion: Education

As in Egypt, opportunities for formal education increased across the Middle East, but none of the countries supplied universal education. Most educated during this time spent a few years at the primary level and reached a minimal level of literacy. A smaller group attended one of the few secondary schools in their country or universities serving the whole region. In Iraq, between 1920 and 1950, the public education system grew 10 to 15 times. By the end of World War II, almost 1,100 schools of all types enrolled approximately 140,000 students, but literacy remained at only 11 percent in 1947. In Turkey, the Kemalist government saw education as a pathway to inculcating modern Turkish values in the population. Thus, funds were put into all levels of education. The results were impressive, as the literacy rate stood at only 8 percent in 1928 but reached 30 percent by the end of World War II. In roughly the same time period, the number of elementary students expanded from 300,000 to 1.5 million. In Syria, literacy stood at 28 percent in 1931, a reflection of the relatively large amount of resources put into elementary education in the Ottoman and French eras.

Education in Iran

When Reza Shah took the Iranian throne in 1926, the country contained only 700 modern primary schools; by 1941, it had 2,500. Even with these changes, however, literacy remained at 10 percent in the 1940s and schooling was largely nonexistent in most rural areas. But in the schools he built, Reza Shah disseminated a clear narrative of Iranian history that traced its origins from the ancient period of Persian monarchical greatness to his leadership in the present. In 1934, the Ferdowsi Millennium celebrations commemorated the legacy of the *Shahnama* and praised Abu al-Qasem Ferdowsi for his beautiful prose and for choosing Persian words over Arabic loanwords. In this event, the text appeared as a Persian national epic and as a primer for how to reconstruct a pure Persian language.

The Ministry of Education and state-sponsored language institutions spent the 1930s and 1940s slowly standardizing the Persian language, eschewing the need for a complete break with the linguistic past that the Turks were doing at the same time. Language reformers made no attempt to eliminate the Arabic alphabet because that would have cut Iranians off from the national heritage as expressed in such texts as the *Shahnama*. Accompanying these efforts, the state established the Organization for the Cultivation of Intellectual Thought in 1939 to coordinate the dissemination of nationalist ideas in the press, in the theater, and through public lectures. The state's goal was to eliminate alternative Persian dialects and non-Persian languages still existing in Iran and to draw a chronological map for Iranian nationalism that connected the Iranian students to a glorious Persian past and Pahlavi present.

Education in Lebanon

Lebanon had the highest rate of literacy among the Arab states, with 70 to 75 percent of all children of primary-school age attending school by the end of World War II. In contrast to the situation of its neighbors, private groups played a larger role than the state in this endeavor. These facts reflect Lebanon's trajectory through the 19th century, where European and American schools opened in greater numbers than anywhere else; they were matched by the establishment of schools by sectarian groups within Lebanon in the 19th century and under the French mandate. This allowed more Lebanese students to attend schools than in any other region because the opportunities were so vast. By the end of World War II, Lebanon enrolled almost 145,000 students at all levels, but with only 21 percent in state schools. However, the emphasis on private school building eliminated an arena where the state could have worked to homogenize loyalty and national identity among large groups of boys and girls. Instead, each private school taught a history of Lebanon that accorded with the history of the particular sect organizing the school.

University Education

Growth was smaller at the university level across the region, but all the countries under study here except Saudi Arabia had schools of higher education in the interwar period. In Iran, about 700 students were enrolled in 1925 in the Colleges of Medicine, Agriculture, Teachers' Training, Law, Literature, and Political Sciences. In 1934, the University of Tehran combined these colleges and added to them the Colleges of Dentistry, Pharmacology, Veterinary Medicine, Fine Arts, and Science and Technology, with over 3,000 enrolled students by 1941. In Syria, the School of Medicine, founded in 1901, and the Institute of Law, founded in 1912, merged in 1923 to create Syrian University. The Syrian Protestant College (SPC) became the American University of Beirut (AUB) in 1920 and continued to educate students from around the region.

Student Political Activism

A focus on education is a useful case study for how the opportunities of urban living and state institution building produced new political actors. The sons and daughters of the wealthy continued to attend modern schools as their parents had done prior to World War I. But even more so than in the past, the young men and women heading through the newly expanded school systems were not from the wealthiest families but families that could manage to collect enough money to send at least one child to school or, in cases where state schooling was free, the families had enough resources to take their children out of work for periods of time. Still others received funding from their states: for example, the Iraqi and Transjordanian governments gave bursary scholarships for students to attend schools such as AUB on condition they return after graduation to serve in the government bureaucracy and state schools. For those who continued on past the primary level, the action necessitated moving into larger towns and into the capital city and beyond if university education became an option.

Even though larger numbers were on this educational trajectory by the 1930s, graduates of any of the schools were still a unique commodity in their countries. Because most upper-level schools opened in larger towns and cities, students congregated in the urban areas, available for organizing and mobilizing. These graduates formed a coterie because they experienced something relatively few else had: they graduated into careers, in state or private realms, as doctors, lawyers, journalists, teachers, and civil servants. After graduation, these young men and women maintained their connections by meeting in coffee shops and bookstores; they also joined and formed literary clubs. They could read debates about political ideas from the 180 new periodicals in Beirut and 50 in Damascus in the 1920s and 1930s, with comparable numbers in Cairo and many exported to Baghdad to join new ones being published there.

Memoirs of students from across the region in the interwar period credit their teachers as pivotal in their quest to find a role for themselves in the political world. Arab teachers consistently brought their students out into the streets to protest, such as on the November 2 anniversary of the Balfour Declaration. As educational records show in one country after another, ministries of education attempted to discipline teachers for discussing political issues in the classroom, but so few qualified teachers existed that they could not be removed from the classroom altogether. Particularly in the Arab world, teachers moved from country to country and province to province and, in the process, frequently spread the idea that students needed to be politically active. Many of the graduates became teachers themselves or maintained contacts with their fellow students and their teachers as they moved into government offices or the independent professions.

Collectively, these students at the secondary and university levels represented a recognizable social milieu in their countries, as they came out into the streets in protest or mobilized on behalf of political parties. These effendiyya (the Arabic term for men of the modern educated middle class) constituted a stratum that had been emerging in the 19th century and grew in size along with the expansion of school systems and state institutions in the early 20th century. They were joined by an increasing number of women who found expanded opportunities for education and access to modern professions. Collectively, they formed a stratum in all societies that had a stake in modernization and Westernization because they believed in the precepts underlying these programs. Instead of being welcomed into governance, they encountered obstacles to their advancement from an older generation that had the most respected late Ottoman educations and training but lagged behind the newer generation educationally.

Political Ideologies

The 1930s provided a wealth of political ideas and visions for these students to discuss and debate. Arabs, Turks, and Iranians had political systems such as liberalism, nationalism, communism, socialism, and fascism from which to choose. Rarely did they embrace one exclusively; rather, most favored a mixture of elements under offer. An author could include in one newspaper article an embrace of youth mobilization techniques of the European fascists while at the same time find the system of French liberalism the best means for electing government officials. Those calling for socialist answers to the region's economic problems could advocate nationalization of industries while also favoring the continuing existence of private property for farms and small shops. In other words, the new generation writing about the proper economic, social, and political futures for their countries did not adopt ideologies indiscriminately. Instead, they adapted and combined them to fit the circumstances under which they were living as they tried to define the societies and government they hoped to construct.

Nationalism

Of the "isms" coming under debate, nationalism elicited the most passionate discussion because old national identities had to be fit inside new state boundaries. In Turkey and Iran, at least for the Turks and Persians, the central state standardized a language and disseminated a historical narrative defining a national identity for the students. In a similar fashion, Egypt had been a recognized polity for much of the 19th century, and in the early 20th century the Egyptian state expended efforts to bring national identity into the newly built classrooms. The widespread recognition and popularity of activism in the interwar period attest to how well Egyptian teachers spread these national ideas to their students.

Arab Nationalism

The Arab mandate states faced a difficult path toward national identity because the states were too new and artificial within the borders drawn by the Europeans. Their 19th-century predecessors writing for the Arab Nahda had faced a similar conundrum about how the Ottoman state could accredit Arabness. The era had witnessed the burgeoning of an Arab nationalist movement focusing on the linguistic, cultural, and historical heritage of the Arabs. In these venues, little discussion centered on the types of state institutions necessary for ruling the Arabs and even less about specific borders. At the end of World War I, the Europeans created the states of Transjordan, Syria, Lebanon, and Iraq. These states were still too new and their apparatuses still too illegitimate in the interwar years to impose a cohesive national identity (wataniyya) on their citizenry or generate loyalty to it. But interaction between state institutions and the citizenry started to make new connections by the time independence came after World War II.

Students could not ignore the systems that provided their educational experiences and brought youth from across the new state together in the same classrooms. State institutions also registered their births, recorded the buying and selling of their land, and tasked them with guiding the new bureaucracies. In this last regard, the states held particular relevance to the lives of graduates because the majority of available jobs were in the civil service. Many activist students and professionals opposed such infiltration by their governments by reimagining Arab nationalism (qawmiyya) as a progressive identity that could erase the borders dividing and weakening the Arabs, end all types of imperialism, break the stranglehold elites held over state apparatuses, and bring in new officials

ARAB NATIONAL NARRATIVES IN HISTORY TEXTBOOKS

The Arab history textbooks of the interwar period present the same historical narrative from the ancient past into the present, regardless of their publishers. In these texts, Arab history is integrated into a larger world history template, starting with the birth of civilization in the Middle East, and continuing on to the Greeks, Romans, Chinese, and European Crusaders. The Arab sections extol the greatness of the Arab-Islamic empires of the Umayyads and Abbasids and point to a societal weakening that occurred under Ottoman control.

The texts locate an awakening of the Arabs in the 19th century, variably identified as occurring when Napoleon invaded Egypt in 1798; when Mehmet Ali reformed Egyptian governance and economy, as a result of Syrian intelligence and innovation during the Arab Nahda; or after the promulgation of the Ottoman constitution in 1878. In some texts, Islamist modernists such as Jamal al-Din al-Afghani and Muhammad ʻAbduh are praised for their insight into how Arabs could reform and modernize Islam and their society.

In the interwar period, Iraq under King Faysal saw the most comprehensive attempt to use schools to create national loyalty. Satiʻal-Husri served as director general for education. In his perspective, education was pivotal for instilling in students the elements of order, discipline, cooperation, love of fatherland, and the role individuals needed to play in the service of the nation. Under Faysal's kingship, students read about the heroes of Islam and the Arab past, with Iraq representing the national culmination point of their historical activities.

History textbooks specific to the history of Iraq's neighbors did not appear until the 1950s and 1960s, so in the interwar years, students could study only the Arab national narrative. Instead of being a tool for generating loyalty to the new states, schools were often incubators for Arab nationalist loyalty instead, especially as events throughout the region engaged students regardless of the borders within which they lived.

willing to enact revolutionary socioeconomic reforms. In this philosophy, local notables serving as government officials and intermediaries in Iraq and Syria stood as obstacles to the achievements that could be found on the pan-Arab stage.

During the interwar years, qawmiyya held a stronger emotional pull for many students because of their actual classroom experiences. The textbooks of the era, produced primarily in Damascus, Beirut, and Cairo, did not narrate the history of Syria or Transjordan; rather, they reported on the great events of the Arab past. The activism so many teachers encouraged among their students often came as a result of events taking place across the region. Arab students in all the countries demonstrated in solidarity with the Syrians in the Druze Revolt of 1925 and with the Palestinians whenever they resisted the terms of the Palestine Mandate. Students continuing their education through the university years frequently crossed borders to attend such schools as AUB, the American Junior College for Women in Beirut, and Syrian and Cairo Universities. There, the dominant national identity tended to be Arab rather than Transjordanian or Syrian, as students recognized the similarity of educational, cultural, and linguistic experience that had brought them together on the university campuses.

Political Parties in Syria and Lebanon

Despite failing to gain many concessions from the French under "honorable cooperation," the Syrian National Bloc was able to maintain a precarious hold as the most prominent national organization in the early 1930s. The bloc leaders had also founded the Nationalist Youth in 1929 to harness the energies of the new generation. However, the leaders were more successful in playing by the rules of the past than the present. The bloc presented itself as a nationalist organization, speaking on behalf of the Syrian people, but it was actually made up alliances built on traditional relationships that were, at their core, completely personal, albeit with a veneer of modern party politics on the surface. Rarely did leaders put forward complex agendas for political or socioeconomic change, focusing instead on the broader goal of gaining independence from France.

Communist and Syrian Social Nationalist Parties

When it became clear to the new generation politicized by the schools that the National Bloc would not be able to resolve the region's problems, Lebanese and Syrian activists formed a series of political parties designed to fill the political vacuum. The Syrian-Lebanese Communist Party was founded in the 1920s and grew in popularity in the 1930s. It might have had as many as 4,000 members from these two countries by 1939. Antun Sa'ada founded the Syrian Social Nationalist Party (SSNP) in 1932 while teaching at AUB. Quickly branches opened in Damascus, Tripoli, and other Syrian cities, with a membership of about 1,000 at the end of the decade. The first principle of the party was that "Syria belongs to the Syrians who constitute a nation complete in itself." This Syria did not stop at the borders of the French mandate but encompassed Greater Syria, extending from the Mediterranean to the Arabian Peninsula.

League of National Action

On August 20, 1933, a group of young men from throughout Greater Syria met at the Qurnayil Conference in Lebanon and founded the League of National Action ('Usbat al-'Amal al-Qawmi). In using the word "qawmi" to define their national designation, the founders were saying they looked to a pan-Arab solution to the region's problems. The basic tenets of the party were that the Arabs are one nation, Arabism forms the core of national consciousness, and Arabs are the masters of their own fate. For the founders, Syrian or Lebanese state nationalism (watani) divided and weakened the Arab world. The league's platform called instead for Arab sovereignty, independence, and unity and emphasized the need for economic development across the region to fight against the power of large landowners and foreign business interests.

Paramilitary Organizations

All the urban groups and the new and old political parties formed paramilitary counterparts to those in Egypt to directly fight for power on the streets. As part of their training, the young men learned about the history of Arab society, the greatness of their Arab national pasts, and the chivalry that must be reintegrated into the social fabric for society to grow strong again. These units extolled the honored position the young men were assuming in defending their nations and their societies from foreign control and elite corruption. Preaching a similar message were the many Boy Scout troops that emerged at the same time, either guided by the Baden-Powell organization from Britain or led by locals following the British template. In those cases, the training also often included survival training in the countryside and, in Palestine, the means by which the young boys could fight against British and Zionist encroachment on their land.

In Syria, the National Bloc founded the Iron Shirts in Damascus and Aleppo in 1936 as an attempt to gain control over a rising generation that was breaking away from its leadership. The twin goals of the movement were to spearhead battles in the streets and educate youth to the need for Syrian independence. By the end of 1936, the Iron Shirts may have had as many as 15,000 members. Soon thereafter, the League of National Action had its own paramilitary organization, the Lion Clubs of Arabism. In Lebanon, the Maronite patriarch sponsored the Party of Lebanese Unity and its paramilitary organization, the White Shirts. In November 1936, Pierre Gemayel founded the Kata'ib Lubnaniyya organization (also known as Les Phalange Libanaises) made up of Maronite Christian youth and following the model of the European fascists.

Urban Professionals

The differences between the old and new parties reflect the changing educational and professional landscape as well. The league's membership had an average age of 29, which was about 20 years younger than that of the National Bloc. All had received advanced Western-style education, while only 20 percent of the National Bloc membership had done so. A few of the league members came from the wealthiest notables, but most were from the poorer branches of those families or did not own property. An overwhelming majority of the league members, 70 percent, were lawyers with the rest engaged in other modern professions. In contrast, 60 percent of the National Bloc membership belonged to the absentee landlord class.

Even though the members of the parties represented a new generation in relation to the members of the older parties, they, too, failed to attract support outside the same urban cadres of students, workers, and young professionals mainly because none of these parties made serious forays into rural areas or the popular urban quarters. They also did not gain independence from the French or dislodge the older politicians from their positions in the upper rungs of the local governments, so could not rally nationalist support around any tangible victories. Their political ideas and their call for a new generation to challenge the old were not forgotten, however, because their program became the mantra of the new revolutionary movements after World War II.

Military Power in the Hashemite Kingdom of Iraq

In Egypt, the military was not yet an independent political actor; and in Turkey and Iran, the military served as a pillar of the government. In the

Arab mandates, the British and French used divide-and-rule policies to guarantee that no state military could potentially threaten the leadership structures they constructed. A common tactic was to employ religious and ethnic minorities in the ranks of the special forces while providing little in the way of resources to the main state army being formed. In this way, the military and associated police forces could provide defense for European advisers and state leaders but would not be powerful, united, or large enough to overthrow a government. With the exception of Iraq, only after World War II did the military in these countries enter into the political fray.

Iraqi Military

In Iraq, the military played a political role in the 1930s despite all British efforts to forestall such an eventuality. King Faysal continually pressed for a conscription law in the 1920s, but the British refused to allow it to pass. Instead, the army was divided: a small regular army officered by the Sharifians and manned mostly by Shi'a; and the Iraqi Levées made up mainly by Assyrians—ancient inhabitants of Iraq and followers of the Eastern rites of Christianity—and other Christian minorities. The result was a regular military force larger than any other tribal force in the country but one that was not strong enough to defeat any coalition of forces the tribes might form. However, with independence in 1932, the 1933 death of King Faysal, the transfer of leadership to King Ghazi (r. 1933–1939), and the 1934 conscription law, the military had the numbers and openings to become involved in political processes. King Faysal's death created a political vacuum that the politicians and military officers competed to fill because King Ghazi was not as astute a politician as his father, so he could not play the divide-and-rule game with the politicians with much precision.

Military Training

The shifts that made military action possible occurred simultaneously in both the military ranks and school classrooms. In Iraq in 1924, the government opened a new military academy and in the early 1930s lowered the entrance requirements to encourage more to enroll. After 1934, Shi'a, as the largest group in the country and statistically among the poorest, formed the bulk of the troops within this expanding military. But the changes also saw Sunni Arabs from families from the lower middle classes enlist; and a small number of Kurds joined and started moving up the ranks, allowing new social strata and groups to make a play for political influence. The state also decreed that military training had to become part of the school curriculum in the 1930s and thus founded the Futuwwa movement, which resurrected a medieval Islamic military concept that tapped into the same messages being taught among paramilitary units and Boy Scout troops around the Arab world. Army officers taught marksmanship and horsemanship to the students, and the teachers taught military terms and the history of war. The goal of the program was to instill in young Iraqi students the codes of manliness and chivalry prized by Iraqi Arab nationalism. The result was a militarization of the schools and a politicization of the newly expanded army ranks.

Assyrian and Tribal Revolts

This changing military institution came to national prominence for the first time over events that began in 1932 when the Assyrian Christians in the Iraqi Levées threatened to resign if the Iraqi government did not establish a special autonomous Assyrian enclave for their community. The Assyrian patriarch even made a plea to the League of Nations for international support for this idea. The Iraqi government reacted to these demands by deporting a large number of Assyrians into Syria. When the French government refused to accept them, they returned, and clashes broke out between the Assyrians and the Iraqi army in summer 1933. On August 11, 1933, an Iraqi military unit under the command of the Kurdish general Bakr al-Sidqi destroyed 40 to 50 Assyrian villages and killed more than 300 Assyrians.

These events took place when a series of tribal revolts between 1933 and 1935 proved that the rural Arab areas had also become destabilized. In the 1920s, many of the Sunni and Shi'i shaykhs had moved into Baghdad to enter parliament and take advantage of British support for their role in government. By the early 1930s, urban merchants and bureaucrats had succeeded in pushing back against this group and diminishing their membership in parliament. The 1934 conscription law promised to weaken them still further because they would no longer have the numbers to compete against an appreciably larger national army. Revolts broke out in Sunni and Shi'i tribal areas alike, as the shaykhs in these regions demanded more of a voice over local governance. With an army grown to 23,000 soldiers and with the aid of the British RAF, al-Sidqi managed to defeat the revolts by the end of 1936.

Leveraging the popularity gained because of his military successes against the Assyrians and the tribes, coupled with King Ghazi's weak control over the political process, al-Sidqi waged a military coup against the government in 1936. Instead of ruling directly, he and his colleagues chose to place in office allied civilian politicians. The bulk initially came from the Ahali group, founded in January 1932 and made up of young men in their 20s and 30s who had graduated from the Baghdad Law Faculty and AUB. By the mid-1930s, members were calling for redistributing land to peasants, establishing cooperative village organizations, providing free health care, and establishing educational and cultural institutions for all age groups.

Ahali Group

Ahali was part of the movement throughout the Arab world that saw a proliferation of cultural and nationalist clubs for the new effendiyya to come together as a cohesive social stratum. In Iraq, the Muthanna Club opened in 1935 with the goal of disseminating the spirit of Arab nationalism, preserving Arab traditions, strengthening Arab manhood, and creating a new Arab culture that would unite Arab and Western culture. The members were government employees and graduates of the new schools who regularly met in social venues to discuss poetry, literature, art, and politics. Like members of the Syrian League of National Action, the young people in these organizations were far more educated than the majority of government officials. They wanted to break through the glass ceiling and use their expertise in government leadership positions.

Once in office in 1936, the Ahali members in the cabinet immediately began to pass legislation annulling laws harmful to the peasants, encouraging the formation of trade unions, and stipulating the need for educational and cultural institutions for marginalized population groups. Al-Sidqi and his military colleagues quickly broke with Ahali because these policies did not help the military directly and threatened to destabilize Iraq's political scene. The military officers brought back to office the old notables who had just recently lost their posts in the coup. The Ahali politicians could do little to change this situation because they did not have an independent power base in the country and never approached the status of a mass party. Like their colleagues in the League of National Action, the rising generation had little contact with the popular quarters of the cities and in the rural agricultural areas so never created an organization that could truly challenge the old notables. When they lost military support, they had nowhere to turn. The old elites made a bargain with the military in which the former could return to their positions in government, while the military received sufficient resources to improve its fighting strength and remain an independent political actor.

Arab Legion in Transjordan

While the Iraqi military interceded to change governance in Iraq, the Hashemites of Transjordan found ways to make the military a pivotal supporter. The whole process took place during a years-long drought in the 1930s and a diminishing demand for rural products as a result of the Great Depression. The tribes were weakened still further by the transition from camel transport to movement of goods by railway and then automobile and truck. Even selling camels and sheep for meat proved less lucrative than in the past as regional and worldwide prices dropped along with prices for other raw goods. By 1933, most Transjordanian tribal areas were experiencing famine, and even many of the tribal shaykhs were suffering extreme poverty. Drawing borders between Transjordan, Saudi Arabia, Syria, and Palestine during the 1920s also cut into the tribes' seasonal movements and diminished their economic opportunities.

The result by 1933, the worst year of the drought, was the impoverishment of the tribes throughout the country, and many died from lack of food and proper nutrition. Livestock owned by the tribes fell by 70 percent between 1932 and 1936, and in the worst cases tribes with as many as 30 camels per tent in 1930 had only an average of 2.5 just a few years later. When General John Bagot Glubb took over the leadership of the Arab Legion in the 1930s from Frederick Peake, he recruited these Transjordanian bedouin into its ranks. By 1939 the Arab Legion had 300 men; in 1942 it employed 86 officers and 3,644 recruits. By the end of World War II, it had 8,000 men, 6,000 of whom were in combat units and the rest served as police and gendarmes.

By agreeing to work on behalf of the Hashemite state, the tribal shaykhs accrued new powers. Land reform measures allowed them to consolidate property under their control at a time when the nomadic economy no longer afforded them a lifestyle commensurate with their leadership positions. The shaykhs, in return for this land, had to pay taxes, but they had clear title and ownership over any profits from it. Shaykhs were rewarded with positions in the Legislative Council in Amman so had another venue from which to extract resources from the state. As a sign of how resilient the tribal system was, by and large the same families wielding power in

1921 maintained it at independence in 1946. But at the same time, they were increasingly dependent on the state for the largesse they distributed to their tribesmen.

Hashemite Military Conflict in World War II

World War II brought the two Hashemite armies into direct conflict when elements of the Iraqi army revolted against the British. The Transjordanian Arab Legion allied with the British to suppress the Iraqi action. King Ghazi died in an auto accident on April 4, 1939, and was succeeded by his young son Faysal II (r. 1939–1958). To push forward a staunchly pro-British policy, the king's uncle and regent, 'Abd al-Ilah, joined forces with Sharifian Nuri al-Sa'id. To end their governmental dominance, on April 1, 1941, politician Rashid 'Ali Kaylani staged a military coup in alliance with four colonels in the Iraqi military. This coup overthrew not only the cabinet but also the king and the regent, who both immediately fled the country.

When this new government would not declare war on Germany and Italy or honor the provisions of the 1930 Anglo-Iraqi treaty granting the British additional military rights in the country in times of crisis, the British re-invaded Iraq. British forces landed to the south in Basra and marched toward Baghdad while the Transjordanian Arab Legion proceeded across the desert. By June, both forces had reached the capital, Rashid 'Ali and his allies had fled the country, and the government had sentenced them to death in absentia. The British reinstated Nuri al-Sa'id as prime minister, invited the king and regent back, and maintained forces in the country for the remainder of the war. In 1945, British troops again withdrew and Iraq regained its independence but with a government firmly allied with British interests. The Transjordanian Arab Legion withdrew from Iraq after reinstating the king and regent on the throne. On May 25, 1946, Transjordan gained its independence as the Hashemite Kingdom of Jordan and Emir Abdullah became king.

Palestine Mandate

Palestine experienced all these phenomena—economic crises, illegitimacy of new leaderships, and rebellions by new groups—but in Transjordan, Syria, and the other states institution building was moving in the direction of independence. Notables in these areas competed to be the leaders when that independence materialized. The Palestine Mandate had no such clear trajectory since both Jews and Palestinian Arabs claimed the territory for their own national projects and the Balfour Declaration made conflicting promises to the two communities. The first British high commissioner, Herbert Samuels, attempted to set up an advisory council for Palestine when he arrived, but the Palestinian Arab community opposed these efforts because they gave credence to the promise of a Jewish homeland, provided too many seats for Jews in proportion to their percentage in the population, and retained too much power for British mandate officials.

Because of this opposition, British officials did not set up a local government but ruled Palestine directly during the mandate, building schools, a police force, and a civil bureaucracy. They also extended roads and transportation links throughout the country. Many Palestinians found positions in these new agencies, while the Jewish community largely established positions in the private realm outside British aegis. But these institutions were not building up a cohesive state structure for the resident communities, as in the surrounding states; they allowed the mandate merely to function. In the breach, the Palestinian and Jewish communities both created pseudo-state agencies serving their own particular communities, with little shared in common. As a result of the conflicting claims to the land of Palestine, rebellions broke out repeatedly between the two communities, with the Palestinians taking the lead for all of the 1930s and the Jewish community doing so in the 1940s.

Jewish State Building

The Jews in Palestine began to form their own government in 1920, with an elected National Assembly choosing the members of a National Council. The assembly met every year, held elections every three to six years, and received official status from the British. According to this schema, the council was empowered to make administrative decisions on behalf of the Jewish community. The Palestine Zionist Executive supervised Zionist organizations on behalf of the World Zionist Organization; in 1929, it became the Jewish Agency and received recognition by the British as an official representative for the Zionist community in Palestine. The Jewish National Fund sought to make the Jewish community self-sufficient by buying up land and making it available to Jewish migrants. Much of it was cultivated as collective farms (kibbutzim) where the families and individuals shared in the work together. Any land bought by the Jewish National Fund was made permanently unavailable to Palestinians because only Jews were allowed to work it. In the 1920s, the fund purchased land from absentee landlords living in Damascus and Beirut, but the Great Depression of the 1930s forced a small number of poor Palestinians to sell as well.

Histadrut and Labor Zionism

While large funds went into the development of agriculture, most new Jewish arrivals to Palestine in the 1920s lived in cities and towns, especially the new Mediterranean coastal city of Tel Aviv because of its expanding industrial sector. To organize those new workers, Histadrut (the Jewish Labor Federation of Palestine) was founded in Haifa in December 1920 and gradually expanded its role during the interwar years to engage in an extensive range of entrepreneurial activities, including shipping, agricultural marketing, road and housing construction, banking, and insurance. Histadrut's influence on the development of the Jewish community in Palestine was made all the more extensive by its control over the Jewish defense force, the Haganah, formed in 1920 in response to Palestinian attacks against Jewish settlements. It gradually evolved into a permanent underground reserve army protecting Jewish settlers throughout the mandate. The British authorities did not legalize the organization but made no concerted efforts to disband it during the mandate years.

In 1930, the Mapai (Palestine Workers') Party emerged from the Labor Zionist political wing, and in its different iterations it dominated Jewish political life and the state of Israel until 1977. David Ben-Gurion, a migrant from Poland in 1906, became the leader of the party from its earliest days and the movement associated with it, Labor Zionism. This concept had emerged from early 20th-century Jewish migrations, when new arrivals such as Ben-Gurion looked to socialist ideas and institutions as a way to build up the Jewish community in Palestine as a collective enterprise. Ben-Gurion and his allies in the 1920s led Histadrut and through that organization and its many subsidiary companies came to dominate the political scene in Palestine. They were strengthened still further when their many institutions and agencies came to the economic aid of the Jewish community during the worst years of the Great Depression. When few other options existed, the organizations associated with Mapai and Labor Zionism could provide jobs and assistance for those in need.

Palestinian State Building

The British employed Palestinian notables as intermediaries to help control and mobilize the population for state projects, as they did in their surrounding territories. These notables were large landowners and urban merchants; they sent their sons to the new schools in Palestinian cities to be trained for mandate administrative positions and professional careers. In the neighboring Arab states, such notables jockeyed for power in parliament so they could control as much of the state largesse as possible. But the contradictory promises made to the Palestinian and Jewish communities in the mandate curtailed the authority the British were willing to grant Palestinian notables on the national level. They could control waqf funds and deliver men for the new police and bureaucratic positions, but they had no venues for lobbying for such issues as the proper type of constitution or treaty that should govern Palestine.

Palestinian notable families built up numerous pseudo-state institutions but faced obstacles from the British in presenting their national claims. This occurred from the very beginning when notables met at the Palestine Arab Congress in Haifa in December 1920 and elected the Arab Executive, including representatives from all the influential urban families. Its platform included condemnation of the Balfour Declaration and support for the establishment of a national government in Palestine. The British, however, refused to accredit it as the official representative for the Palestinians because its members had not been elected by a nationwide vote. In Syria, the French recognized the National Bloc, which was made up of the same types of urban and landed notables as the Arab Executive, as speaking on behalf of the Syrian people.

Al-Husseini and al-Nashashibi Families

The British also followed divide-and-rule policies of assigning positions to members of rival families. In particular, mandate officials exploited the rivalry between the al-Husseini and al-Nashashibi families, the most influential among the Palestinians. The al-Husseini family took over leadership of the Supreme Muslim Council in January 1922 when Hajj Amin al-Husseini, the mufti of Jerusalem, took the post. The council was responsible for supervision of the shariʿa courts and appointment of court officials and judges; for management of waqfs; and for the system of Islamic religious schools, including selection of teachers. The council paid the salaries of these officials from an annual budget provided by the British mandatory government. Through this organization, the al-Husseinis were able to transform their religious authority into the most extensive Arab political organization in Palestine. The al-Nashashibi family controlled the mayorship of Jerusalem in most years and in this way gained control over a large number of new positions that could be doled out to supporters.

Palestinian National Institutions

Despite the obstacles, the Palestinians established new organizations that mobilized people from all social strata to fight for political independence. Palestinian notables opened a series of secondary schools in the urban areas so Palestinians could train as teachers and take the British baccalaureate exam in order to attend AUB and universities in Britain. These schools became vital politicization zones for students. Simultaneously, the Arab Bank provided loans for Palestinians while women's groups and Boy Scout troops organized among women and youth. In urban areas, societies aided the new rural migrants forced off the land because of Jewish land purchases. Artisan guilds organized to help their members.

Like their Arab neighbors, Palestinian notables also began to form political parties, although they were not based on a specific political platform but represented a new way for these notables to organize their networks. The only ideological party was a branch of the pan-Arab Independence (Istiqlal) Party that rallied the young educated generation to fight for independence as their colleagues were doing in the surrounding countries. All these parties fronted a secularly oriented national identity for Palestine, meaning that they envisioned eventually leading a state that would have a constitution and parliament rather than follow the shari'a law code.

The Palestinian national identity extolled in the newspapers and schools traced the nation's origins from the greatness of the Arab past to the fight the Palestinians were waging to save their land and nation from Zionism. Islam was a pivotal element of this identity, but it was not a guiding political force; it was a cultural element binding most of the Palestinians together and helping strengthen their society. In this configuration, Palestinian Christians could join the movement because they could stand with Muslims under a large national umbrella. And importantly, in the 1930s, this urban-led movement was largely not geared toward a military solution to the conflict but focused instead on lobbying British officials for increased Palestinian rights, similar to what the National Bloc was doing in Syria. And as occurred in surrounding mandates, the tactics of the Palestinian urban leaders failed to move Palestine toward independence during the interwar years.

Jewish Immigration and Palestinian Agriculture

A constant demand of the Palestinian notables was for the curtailment of Jewish immigration. Not only did the British not accede to this demand, but immigration increased in the mid-1930s with the ascendance of the Nazi Party to power in Germany in 1933. As a result, the Jewish population of Palestine doubled between 1933 and 1935. With new rules allowing Jews to take their property out of Germany, this influx of immigrants brought capital to invest in the Jewish Palestinian economy. Most moved into the cities, and the Tel Aviv population increased from 46,000 in 1931 to 135,000 in 1935, with comparable increases in Haifa and Jerusalem. As a result of this new funding and of institutions on the ground working for the Jewish community exclusively, the Jewish community in Palestine was able to separate itself from Palestinian life to an increasing degree.

The urban Palestinian population was less than 20 percent at the beginning of the mandate but rose to 33 percent at the end, in large measure because of the loss of land to Zionist land purchases. By 1930, of those remaining in rural areas, 30.7 percent owned no land at all but worked on the land of others, while another third worked partly on self-owned plots of less than five dunums (about 1.3 acres). A 1936 British report calculated that the majority of Palestinian peasants were living on plots of land far smaller than the minimum set by economists as viable. Additional British economic aid did flow in the 1930s but did not provide sufficient resources to dramatically alter the economic and political lives of most Palestinians.

Shaykh 'Izz al-Din al-Qassam

When the Palestinian urban notables failed to gain any concessions from the British and the socioeconomic situation continued to deteriorate because of the Great Depression and increased Jewish immigration in the 1930s, resistance organizations formed from among the rural and urban poor. Their primary targets were the British and the Zionist community, but their existence was also a challenge to the Palestinian urban notables. This alternative movement was initially led by Shaykh 'Izz al-Din al-Qassam, who came to Palestine from Syria to take charge of the Young Men's Muslim Association (YMMA) in Haifa in the 1920s. His followers were those who had largely migrated into Haifa quite recently after losing their jobs on the land and having little access to urban employment. He called on his supporters to follow God's message in their own lives while also helping the poor, feeding the hungry, and comforting the sick. The good character men could acquire through these acts would give them the dignity that the notables and the British were not allowing them.

This call was similar to what the Futuwwa movement of Iraq was preaching to the young men undergoing military training in that it was inculcating manliness and chivalry as the key elements to building up a successful resistance movement. Al-Qassam mobilized followers using personal contacts to meet with the men, gauge their knowledge and commitment to Islam, and teach them how to activate their ideas. Using the call for jihad against the British, he formed a paramilitary unit that fought against the British in the early 1930s. Although he died by British hands in November 1935, his merger of militant Islam and Palestinian nationalism was carried on by those influenced by his ideas. So important did he become for Palestinian history that in 1992 Hamas named its military unit the ‘Izz al-Din al-Qassam Brigade.

FIGURE 6.5. The Western Wall and Dome of the Rock on the Haram al-Sharif as seen from the Jewish quarter of the Old City of Jerusalem. The Moroccan quarter fills the area in front of the Western Wall.

Palestinian Revolts of the 1930s

The conflicting Jewish and Palestinian national desires for Palestine and the separate institution building they had undertaken caused sustained conflict beginning in 1929. The first revolt began when conflicts over Jewish prayer space at the Western Wall, or Wailing Wall, in Jerusalem erupted into fighting across the mandate, resulting in the deaths of more than 200 Palestinians and Jews. The British had followed Ottoman policies when taking over any contentious religious sites; in this case the Jews had very little access to the Western Wall of the Jewish Temple destroyed in AD 70 by the Romans. Efforts by Jewish men and women in the late 1920s to expand the site in front of the wall led to clashes with Palestinians trying to keep them from changing the religious arrangements.

OLD CITY OF JERUSALEM

The Old City of Jerusalem is a 4,000-year-old city that currently encompasses one square kilometer, surrounded on all sides by walls built in the 16th century by Ottoman Sultan Süleyman the Magnificent. The Romans, who ruled the city between 63 BC and AD 324, erected two roads bisecting the city east to west and north to south. Nineteenth-century maps designate the four quadrants separated by these roads as the Muslim, Christian, Armenian, and Jewish quarters, but this clear-cut delineation between religious groups does not represent the reality of life in the Old City when the maps were produced or even for decades thereafter. Census records indicate that no quarter was exclusive to only one religious group. For example, in the last years of the Ottoman Empire, only about 60 percent of the city's Muslims lived in the Muslim quarter, with the remaining families housed in the other three quarters.

The designations do coincide with holy sites important to the city's Muslims and Christians. The Muslim quarter includes the Haram al-Sharif (Noble Sanctuary) with the Dome of the Rock and the al-Aqsa Mosque; the Christian quarter, the Holy Sepulchre; and the Armenian quarter, the convent of St. James and the residence of the Armenian patriarch for Jerusalem. The Jewish quarter does not encompass the Western Wall, the holiest Jewish site in the city, because the Muslim empires prohibited Jews from building homes in the area. Instead, the Jewish quarter overlooks the Western Wall and includes within its zone synagogues and Jewish housing existing from at least the 13th century.

Situated between the Jewish quarter and the Western Wall was the Maghribi, or North African, neighborhood, built as a waqf endowment for North African Muslims in the aftermath of the Muslim expulsion of the Crusaders in the 12th century. Over succeeding centuries, additional endowments expanded the area, and the Ottomans invited Muslims expelled from Spain in the 15th century to live in it. Houses were built just a few feet from the Western Wall so provided little space for Jewish worshippers, resulting in a conflict over Jewish access in 1929. In June 1967, just days after the Israeli occupation of Jerusalem, the Israeli government leveled the Maghribi neighborhood and built the large plaza fronting the Western Wall today.

Great Arab Revolt of 1936–1939

Another Palestinian revolt broke out for a short period in 1933 but was eclipsed by the Great Arab Revolt that engulfed the mandate between 1936 and 1939. It began as a general strike led by the Arab Higher Committee (AHC), the successor to the Arab Executive, aimed at pressuring the British government to end Jewish immigration, ban land sales to Jews, and establish an independent national government in Palestine. The strike lasted six months, ending on October 10, 1936, through negotiation with the AHC, the British, and Arab leaders of the surrounding mandates.

While quieting for a while, the revolt erupted again in 1937, when it became a militia-dominated movement in which Palestinian paramilitary

FIGURE 6.6. An overview of the Old City of Jerusalem, with the Dome of the Rock on the Haram al-Sharif in the foreground.

units took over most of the country. At its peak in 1938, a core of 1,500 full-time fighters attracted tens of thousands of supporters and succeeded in gaining control of numerous towns and villages throughout the mandate. In the villages they ruled, militia leaders instituted legal and social changes as a way to offset the failure of the urban elite to initiate such programs. They canceled debts, barred debt collectors from entering the towns, and coerced wealthy landowners into donating money to the rebel cause. In most areas, they also set up judicial systems and courts to adjudicate local disputes. These groups were made up of those who had been marginalized by the urban notables as well as young educated men from the cities who had participated in paramilitary or Boy Scout training. Together these acts constituted a rebellion against the British colonizers and the Zionist project while also challenging the notable class to be more responsive to the needs of the mass of the population.

Notwithstanding the enthusiasm and solidarity exhibited by Palestinians in every stage of the revolt, the British and their allied paramilitary Jewish forces succeeded in defeating it in 1939. By the time it was over, about 5,000 Palestinians and 2,000 Jews had been killed, with approximately 14,000 wounded. In 1938 alone, 5,679 Palestinians were jailed. During the course of the revolt, much of the Palestinian urban leadership fled the country or were put under arrest by the British. Hajj Amin al-Husseini, for example, left for Cairo and then spent the war years in Germany.

British White Paper of 1939

In the end, neither the general strike of 1936 nor the rural militia movement of 1937 and 1938 could force the British to change policies dramatically, but they did bring the British to the negotiating table. In 1939, British officials invited Arab, Palestinian, and Jewish leaders to London to work out a settlement for the Palestine Mandate. When the parties would not negotiate together, the British delegation eventually chose to unilaterally issue the White Paper of 1939, stating that the Jewish national home was never meant to convert Palestine into a Jewish state. The British instead envisioned the establishment of an independent state in 10 years, with the two communities finding a way to share power. The British promised to limit the number of Jewish immigration certificates to 75,000 over the following five years and to curtail Jewish land purchases in most areas of the country. Both communities rejected the plan; the Jewish community did so because it went against all the promises the

British had ever made concerning a Jewish national homeland; and the Palestinians, because it delayed independence for too long and the leadership feared what might happen in the intervening years.

World War II

Soon after the issuance of the White Paper in London, the Middle East became involved in World War II, although it did not prove as momentous as World War I for long-term developments of the region. Turkey remained neutral for much of the war and only declared on the side of the Allied forces at the very end of the war. As Iran entered World War II, it faced the same problems it had in World War I: it was sitting on valuable oil wells and situated in a location strategically important to many different parties in the war. When Reza Shah hesitated to join the war on Britain's side and made contact with the Germans, Soviet and British forces invaded the country in August 1941. The goal was to keep Iran's oil installations open and provide a conduit for American Lend-Lease aid to travel from the Persian Gulf, through Iran, and to the Soviet Union. Within three weeks of the joint invasion, the shah abdicated in favor of his 21-year-old son, Mohammad Reza Shah. Reza Shah left the country for South Africa and died there on July 26, 1944.

Much of the fighting in the Middle East took place in North Africa and Iraq. Egypt, Transjordan, and Palestine served as military headquarters and supply depots for the British army and its allies, the United States and the Free French forces of Charles de Gaulle, who led the force opposing German occupation of northern France and the establishment of the German state of Vichy in the southern provinces of the country. Suez was a major conduit for goods reaching British forces in North Africa; Palestine was a training area for British-allied troops. Haifa, once its oil refinery was completed in June 1940 and with Iraqi and Iranian oil pumping through, became the major source of fuel for the British fleet in the Mediterranean.

In Syria and Lebanon, the French high commissioner took direct control of the governments as soon as the war began but could stay in this position only until summer 1940. During those intervening months, Germany occupied northern France, and the Vichy government took charge of the mandates of Syria and Lebanon. In July 1941, British and Free French forces marched from North Africa and liberated Syria and Lebanon from Vichy control. The new French officials held elections in both countries in summer and fall of 1943 but refused to withdraw the bulk of the troops stationed there. As a result, true independence came to Syria and Lebanon only in August 1946, when the final French troops withdrew under British pressure.

During World War II, the Jewish community in Palestine had an array of fighting forces at its disposal, but they rarely coordinated their activities because of the different missions attached to each. Chaim Weizmann, who led the World Zionist Organization (WZO), directed diplomatic endeavors in Europe and the United States and raised money for transmission to the Jewish community in Palestine. While political differences existed between Weizmann and Ben-Gurion, more often than not their respective organizations worked together. At the beginning of World War II, the Haganah established the Palmach as the elite element of the force; by 1948, it had about 7,000 members.

Labor Zionism's main challenge came from Vladimir Jabotinsky, who had founded the Revisionist Party in 1925. The party's primary goal was the creation of a Jewish state, favoring private investment and middle-class immigration as the best means for bringing funds and people to Palestine. Furthermore, in contrast to the WZO's early recognition of the creation of Transjordan to the east of the Jordan River, Jabotinsky considered that area an integral part of the land of Israel. To gain supporters, Jabotinsky formed youth groups throughout Europe and in Palestine itself in the late 1920s. In 1936, a Revisionist splinter group began military operations against Palestinians and the British as the Irgun Zvai Leumi. In 1940, Abraham Stern founded the Stern Gang (Lohamei Herut b'Yisrael [LEHI], Fighters for the Freedom of Israel). After Jabotinsky died in the same year, Menachem Begin took up leadership of the Irgun. By the last years of the war, both the Irgun and the Stern Gang were attacking British officials in Palestine.

Arab-Israeli War of 1948

When World War II ended in 1945, the situation in Palestine quickly grew unstable, with the 75,000 immigration certificates already issued, the Nazi concentration camps liberated, and the survivors of the Holocaust struggling to find new homes. The central focus of the conflict between the British and Zionists was the plight of the Jewish refugees in Europe. Zionist groups worked to bring them into Palestine, while the British intercepted as many as possible and rerouted them to camps in Cyprus and, when those filled up, back to camps in Europe. US president Harry Truman intervened in this conflict in August 1945 by calling on the British government to immediately allow 100,000 Jewish refugees into Palestine. This call came as US politicians were beginning to support the establishment of a Jewish state in Palestine. After WZO's intensive lobbying campaign of the US Congress and other US agencies and associations, both the Republican and Democratic platforms in 1944 endorsed the creation of a Jewish commonwealth in Palestine.

By 1946, all the Zionist military groups were attacking the British, killing dozens of soldiers and causing millions of dollars in damage to British installations. To try to stop these events, the British increased the army force in Palestine to 80,000 troops and moved into an offensive position by attacking Jewish governmental offices and arresting thousands of people. None of these efforts stemmed the tide of the fighting; on July 22, 1946, the Irgun initiated the largest of the Zionist attacks by blowing up the King David Hotel in Jerusalem because it housed British administrative offices. The action killed 99 British, Jewish, and Arab personnel and wounded dozens more.

United Nations Special Committee on Palestine

When such actions continued into 1947, and as Palestinian militia groups began initiating attacks again, the British government requested that the newly formed United Nations (UN) address the conflict. The United Nations Special Committee on Palestine (UNSCOP) visited Palestine throughout the summer of 1947 to interview the leaders of the communities to determine the proper solution to the crisis. In the fall, the committee issued a minority and a majority report. In the minority report, the committee recommended the establishment of a federal state after a three-year preparatory period of UN trusteeship, but this report never came up for a vote in the General Assembly.

The majority report called for a partition of the mandate into Arab and Jewish states and the creation of an international zone around Jerusalem and Bethlehem. This was not the first time partition had been suggested. The Royal (Peel) Commission Report of 1937 had called for the formation of a Jewish state, a Palestinian state allied with Transjordan, and an international zone around Jerusalem and Bethlehem with a corridor connecting those cities to the Mediterranean Sea. At that time, the Palestinian leadership rejected the recommendation outright, expressing outrage at the legitimation of Jewish claims. The Jewish community and their allies around the world had different reactions to the report but finally decided that partition was a good idea in principle but that the Peel

MAP 17. Peel Commission Report, 1937. The commission proposed the division of the Palestine Mandate into a Jewish state, an Arab state, and international enclaves surrounding major religious sites.

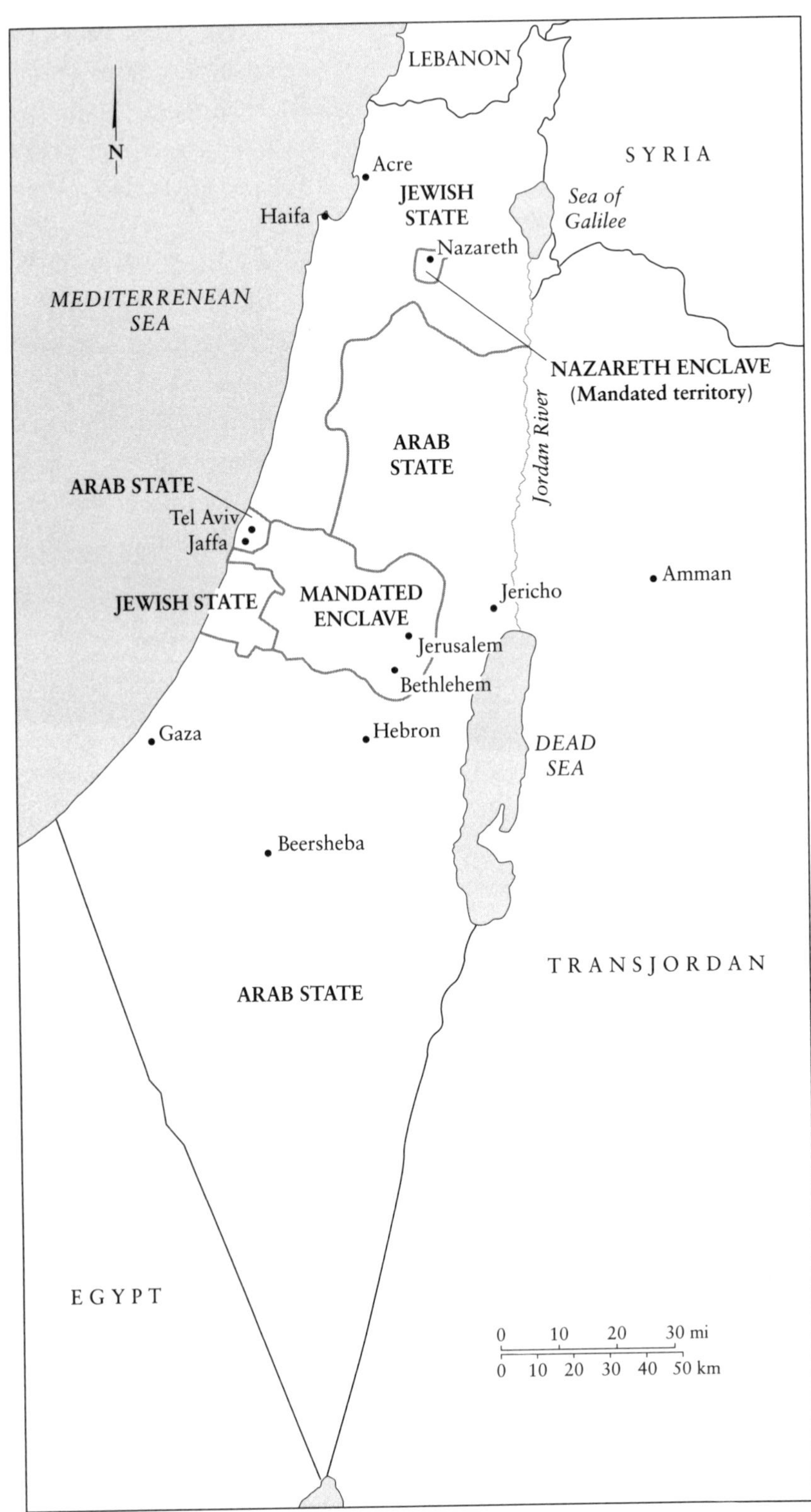

MAP 18.
UN Partition Plan for Palestine, 1947. The plan provided for a Jewish state, an Arab state, and an international enclave around Jerusalem.

Commission had not allowed for the creation of a viable Jewish state. The Peel partition plan was never implemented because of this opposition and because a renewal of the Great Arab Revolt made it impossible for the British to instigate such a political solution.

United Nations Partition Resolution 181

The partition plan was not implemented in 1937, but on November 29, 1947, the UN General Assembly voted for the majority report, with 33 states in favor, 13 opposed, and 10 abstentions. UN Partition Resolution 181 called for a Jewish state on 55 percent of the land of the Palestine Mandate; an Arab state on 42 percent; and an international zone comprising 3 percent. At this time, Palestine consisted of about 1.3 million Palestinians and 600,000 Jews. Jews owned about 20 percent of the cultivable land but only about 6 percent of the total land.

The period between November 29, 1947, and May 14, 1948, can be characterized as a civil war between the Palestinian and Jewish residents of the mandate, with the Jewish forces gaining most of the territory allotted to the Jewish state by the time the British withdrew their last troops and Ben-Gurion declared the establishment of the State of Israel on May 14, 1948. The United States and the Soviet Union were the first two countries to recognize it. On May 15, the Egyptian, Jordanian, Syrian, Lebanese, and Iraqi armies entered the territory to protect the Palestinian position. They organized their actions through the Arab League, founded in 1945 as a means for managing activities between the member states. From its earliest days, the organization highlighted Palestine as a territory in need of special protection by the Arabs. However, during the fighting, the Arab armies failed to coordinate their forces so performed poorly against the Israeli army.

Rhodes Armistice Agreements

By the time the fighting ended and the armistice agreements were signed on the island of Rhodes in 1949, the new State of Israel comprised about 78 percent of the Palestine Mandate. Jordan took control of the West Bank and East Jerusalem; in 1950 the Jordanian parliament voted to unite with the two Palestinian territories. Egypt took the Gaza Strip and heavily controlled the All-Palestine Government the Arab League had established in 1948 to provide Palestinian leadership over the state to be created. The Jordanian government prohibited the All-Palestine Government in East Jerusalem and the West Bank, so it functioned solely

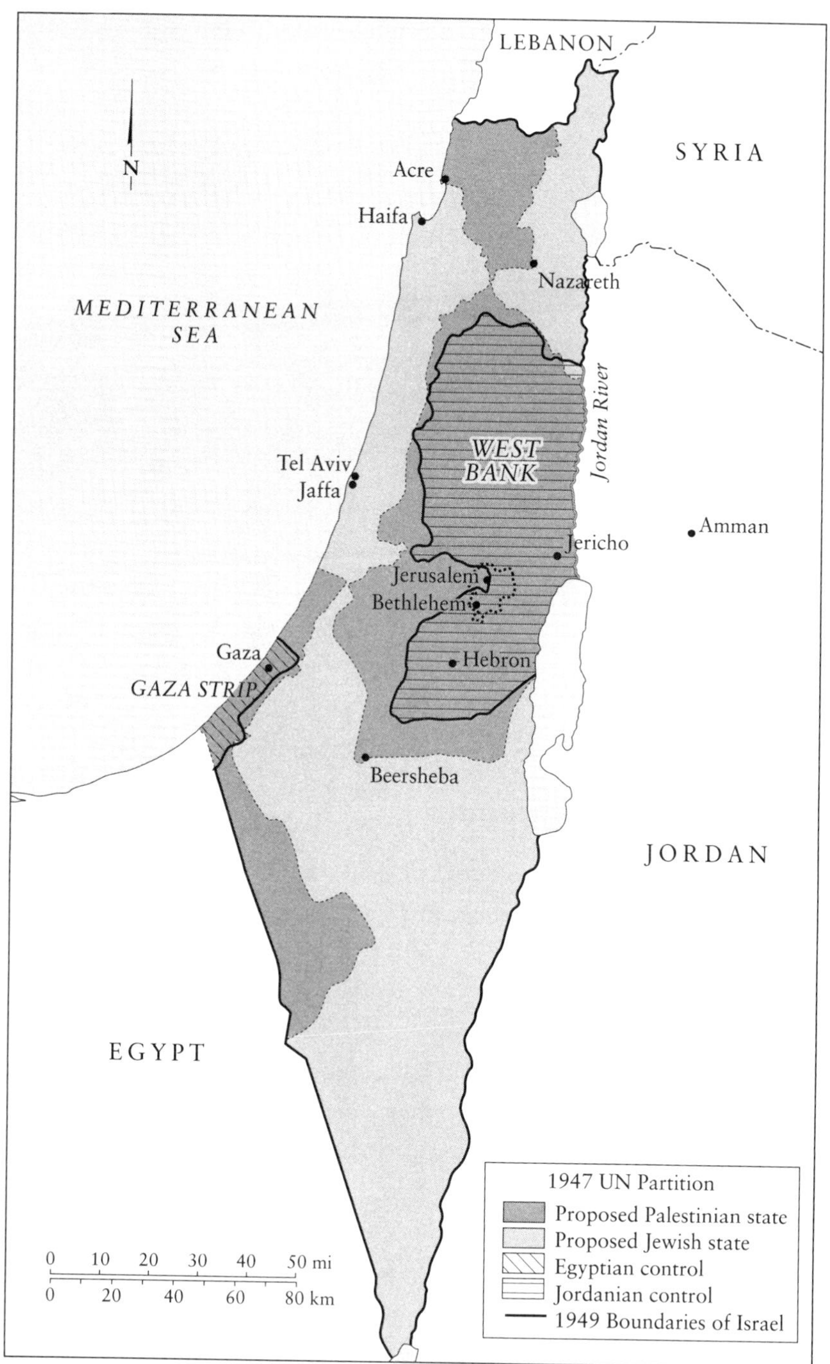

MAP 19. Israel, East Jerusalem, West Bank, and the Gaza Strip, 1949. After the 1948 Arab-Israeli War, Israel took control of approximately 78 percent of the Palestine Mandate; Jordan took over East Jerusalem and the West Bank; and Egypt gained control of the Gaza Strip.

within the Gaza Strip and with little authority granted it by the Egyptian government. Also formulated within the agreements were a series of demilitarized zones (DMZs), such as the one around Hebrew University in East Jerusalem and one along the Israel-Syrian border below the Golan Heights that provided ambiguous sovereignty over the territories and caused several conflicts between Israel and the surrounding Arab states over succeeding years.

Palestinian Refugees

When Ben-Gurion announced the establishment of Israel on May 14, approximately 300,000 Palestinians had already left the territories under Israeli control. Over the next months of fighting as many as 450,000 more joined them. They fled because of massacres in their villages and towns and from fear that a massacre would be replicated in their village. According to such policies as Plan Dalet, or Plan D, Israeli troops expelled Palestinians in strategic border areas and forced them to march toward areas in the surrounding states or into the West Bank or Gaza, which were under Jordanian and Egyptian military control. If the UN plan had gone through as envisioned, almost half of the population of the new Jewish state would have been made up of Palestinians. By the time the armistice agreements were signed, only 150,000 Palestinians resided in Israel. The rest were scattered throughout the remaining Palestinian territories and the surrounding Arab states.

Conclusion

Scholarly literature about the Arab regions of the Middle East in the interwar period often identifies the era as a liberal one in comparison to the military rule that came to most of these countries following independence after World War II. Certainly, most of these states codified constitutions to delineate the powers accruing to the different branches of government, political parties frequently vied for electoral office, and in some cases bills of rights laid out the rights guaranteed to the citizenry. However, the protections accorded to the Europeans, presidents, monarchs, and intermediaries in each of the countries counteracted the rights technically offered. To protest this imbalance in power, thousands went out into the streets repeatedly to demand that the provisions of the constitutions be fulfilled and that state agencies be more participatory.

These rogues particularly questioned the legitimacy of the old intermediaries to speak on their behalf; they considered themselves better educated and trained than those who held power. The intermediaries had entered governance after World War I because they had much to offer the new states being formed. By the 1930s, their usefulness had diminished because states provided many of the services of the old networks and more power flowed from the state than from those networks. No government before World War II could completely eliminate the independent power of the local elites, but the process had begun that would come to fruition under the authoritarian states of the 1950s and 1960s.

The establishment of Israel set up a conflict with the Arab states that influences developments even today. Israel and the Arab states fought several wars in succeeding decades and the US-USSR Cold War infiltrated into the Middle East as each superpower chose sides in their battles. At the same time, the Arab defeat in 1948 highlighted the failures of the Arab governments, not only militarily but in all aspects of governance. One government after another fell to a new generation of activists after 1948, organized under revolutionary slogans put forward by new political parties and units of junior officers in the military. And while the 1930s may have represented a failure to bring new voices into government office, despite the extensive politicizing and mobilizing efforts that took place in the urban areas, the long-term influence of these movements was momentous. When World War II ended, these same urban groupings reemerged in the streets and in electoral competitions. The ideas expressed by the groups of the 1930s provided incentive for political parties and junior military officers to take over their governments in the 1950s and 1960s.

MILITARY COUPS

Politics and Violence: Iran, Turkey, and the Arab States, 1952–1980

7

THE YEARS IMMEDIATELY AFTER WORLD WAR II witnessed another moment of political opportunity, comparable to what occurred after World War I. Syria, Lebanon, and Jordan joined Iraq, Egypt, Saudi Arabia, Turkey, and Iran as formally independent states, and all entered the United Nations as sovereign nations. Across the board, the men who held power in the post–World War II states were the successors to Reza Shah and Mustafa Kemal or those who had served as intermediaries and political players for the Europeans for decades. In the early months after the war, with the exception of the king of Saudi Arabia, these leaders initiated political liberalization programs that allowed political parties to form, elections to take place, and unions to organize, a period when the citizens of the new states could engage with national politics in unprecedented ways. A hopefulness marked these months because the war was over, European colonial officials had largely left the political scene, and many believed that with independence would come economic growth and new opportunities. Liberalization boded well for expanded political participation.

But this moment lasted for just a few short years in each of these countries because liberalization unleashed far more than its initiators had planned. The political forces forming under the terms of liberalization largely called for far more radical changes to governance and economic structures than any of the leadership was willing to undertake. The rebels and rogues of this new period were not the tribal shaykhs, militia leaders, and landowners of post–World War I, defending their territories against incursions from foreigners and domestic challengers. This era of the late 1940s and early 1950s was an extension of the work done in the 1930s to organize urban populations to fight for political rights and to articulate new visions for political independence. Many demanded such programs as land reform, expansion of education, and workers' rights, while a smaller number favored a more radical communist reordering of the economy. Implementing such programs would overturn the political, social, and economic hierarchies that kept leaders in power in these countries for decades, so none were willing to adopt them as government policy. To forestall such dramatic change, leaders used force to rein in the newly released passions exhibited on the streets, in the parliaments, and on factory floors. In the late 1940s and early 1950s, violence marked many of the encounters between the states and the new political forces and also those between the competing political forces created by the new opportunities.

In the Arab countries, Egypt, Jordan, Syria, and Iraq experienced vibrant political party activity in the post–World War II years. The Ba'th, Communist, and Arab Nationalist Parties failed to remove the old elites from government, but the leaders and members of the parties did succeed in dominating much of the discourse about the directions the newly independent countries should take, as they advocated land reform, workers' rights, industrialization, and, very importantly, a political break with the imperialist powers of the past and the US and Soviet superpowers of the present. Their ideas and ideologies came into political power, not through the ballot box but via a series of military coups in one country after another. Syria had three coups alone in 1949, one in 1954, another in 1961, and Ba'th-fronted coups in 1963, 1966, and 1970. The Iraqi Hashemites fell to a military coup in 1958, followed by those in 1963 and 1968 that brought the Ba'th to power. Jordan came close to following the same pattern in 1957, but King Hussein managed to forestall the military at that moment; Saudi Arabia even faced a coup attempt by army officers in 1969 that failed to overthrow the royal family.

While these actions were military coups performed by a small number of officers, the old elite political structure broke down and those who had been marginalized in the past, especially from the rural and poor urban sectors, rose to power. These officers then instituted policies that the parties of the 1930s and 1940s had demanded and thus ushered in political and socioeconomic revolutions in their countries. Even the Jordanian and Saudi kings had to broaden their base of support to forestall such upheaval in their own countries. Iran, Turkey, and Lebanon represent variations on these themes. In Iran, the military supported the shah in his fight against domestic opposition forces; in Turkey, the military instigated coups in 1960, 1971, and 1980 but then allowed political party competition to be renewed; and in Lebanon, the sectarian political structure has made it difficult for the army or political parties to be powerful. Regardless, these three countries saw dramatic changes in the makeup of the political elite because the decades between the 1950s and the 1980s brought new political pressures on the governments and new players into political competition.

Political Developments in Egypt

In Egypt, political liberalization lasted from 1945 to 1952 and allowed for political parties, unions, and urban militias to move on to the political stage in large numbers. Rising prices and a general downturn in the economy sparked calls for social and economic reform. Reformers wrote up plans for expanded educational options, public housing projects, health-care expansion, social insurance, and workers' compensation. Land reform came up for active debate since three-quarters of the peasants owned only a tiny plot or no land at all. None of these plans passed into law because parliament remained as fragmented as before the war. As a sign of the instability, eight minority governments ruled between October 1944 and January 1950. Two prime ministers were assassinated, and Muslim Brotherhood leader Hasan al-Banna was killed in February 1949.

In January 1950 the Wafd Party returned to power after a five-year hiatus, and supporters paraded in the streets for days. In the end, however, the promise of 1950 went unfulfilled. Mustafa al-Nahhas had pledged to reach an agreement on British troop withdrawal from the Suez Canal Zone, end martial law, lower the cost of living, and reorient the government bureaucracy around merit rather than patronage. Instead, corruption, intra-Wafd rivalries, and repression of parliamentary opponents made it impossible to pass legislation concerning any of the party's campaign promises. The climax of these tensions occurred on January 25, 1952, near the Suez Canal, when British troops surrounded the headquarters of the Ismailia gendarmerie and ordered the police to surrender their weapons. In the battle, dozens of Egyptian police and British officers died or were wounded. The following day, a large demonstration broke out in Cairo, during which the greater part of the city's business district was set aflame, with participants specifically targeting foreign businesses, airline offices, hotels, cinemas, bar, and clubs.

Revolution in 1952

On July 23, 1952, junior officers in the Egyptian military, calling themselves the Free Officers, led a bloodless coup against the government; King Farouk went into exile. The Free Officers of Egypt had attended the Military Academy when it opened to young men from lower-class backgrounds in 1936; the number of officers rose from 398 in 1936 to 982 only a few years later. They came of age during Egypt's political life after World War II when everyone from the Wafd to the Muslim Brotherhood vied for their support. They also fought in the Arab-Israeli War of 1948 and castigated their government for abandoning its soldiers on the battlefield by giving them poor-quality weapons and logistical support. A regiment that included a number of the future Free Officers found itself under siege in Falluja, in the northern Negev Desert, forced to spend the winter of 1948–1949 surrounded by Israeli forces. They were released only when Egypt and Israel signed an armistice agreement to end the hostilities. After they returned home, a small number of these politicized junior officers began making plans for overthrowing the government; they activated the plans as the streets exploded in 1952.

Immediately after the events of July 23, the instigators established the Revolutionary Command Council (RCC) as the chief executive instrument constructing a new kind of republican Egypt. Colonel Gamal Abdel Nasser was the most influential officer at this stage, but the Free Officers initially fronted an older, nationally known senior officer, Muhammad Naguib, as the first president of this new Egyptian Republic. In 1954 Nasser replaced him and served as president until his death in September 1970.

Free Officer Program

The core of the Free Officer program from the beginning was a nationalism that focused most of its attention on bringing Egypt into full independence from British control. The first victory came with the Anglo-Egyptian agreement in October 1954, which abrogated the treaty of 1936 and outlined terms for the complete removal of all British troops from the Suez Canal Zone by June 1956. The Free Officers passed a land reform program and then slowly nationalized banks and large industries.

The bulk of implementation efforts took place in the late 1950s and early 1960s, but the passage of such laws earlier signified that the government sought to break the power of the old elites while distributing services to a larger group than had ever been aided by the state. Economically, this program translated into state stimulation and development of the public and private sectors. Politically, the program had a populist element because the state called on the mass of the population to join in the Nasserite project for building a new and modern Egypt; no longer would the old notables monopolize all the state resources.

The new government also worked to weaken the old notables who had dominated the Egyptian political scene for decades and bring to office those who had been marginalized or had rebelled in the past. The Free Officers originated largely from modest social backgrounds, chiefly from the salaried middle class. They had more links to the rural and

THE NASSER FAMILY

Gamal Abdel Nasser was born on January 15, 1918, in a suburb of Alexandria. The story of his family is intertwined with the story of changes in Egypt in the 19th and 20th centuries. His grandfather, father, and Nasser took advantage of the new institutions and opportunities afforded by the Egyptian state to acquire land and an education and earn positions in the bureaucracy and military.

Nasser's grandfather, Hussein Khalil, owned five feddans of land in Bani Murr, in Upper Egypt, and earned enough to send two of his six sons to school, including Nasser's father—Abdel Nasser Hussein (1888–1968)—who attended the newly built kuttab in Bani Murr and then spent one year at an American Presbyterian mission high school in Assiut. His Primary Education Certificate in 1909 from a state school in Alexandria allowed him to enter the civil service in the Postal Administration, where he remained throughout his career.

In 1917, Abdel Nasser Hussein married Fahima Hammad, the daughter of a wealthy Alexandrian coal merchant. Gamal was the first of their four children, all sons. Before she died in 1926, Fahima used her monthly income from her father to pay for their schooling. Nasser began studying in the village schools in Assiut and Suez and completed secondary school at the al-Nahda al-Misriyya (Egyptian Rebirth) School in Cairo in 1936.

Nasser's schooling in Alexandria and Cairo coincided with the tumultuous political events of the 1930s. Nasser was a leader of the student movement in his school in Alexandria, and reportedly during his first demonstration he was struck by a policeman and spent a night in jail. In November 1935, Nasser was grazed by a bullet and saw two of his friends killed by gunfire during a demonstration. A newspaper article in *Al-Gihad* (The struggle) gave Nasser his first press notice. Nasser entered the military academy in March 1937. The men with whom he studied and served over the next few years formed the central cohort for the Free Officers.

poorer urban areas than to the economic and political centers of the past. They brought into office below them new technocrats from a much broader social milieu than any previous government had allowed, as people from various backgrounds attended the expanding school system and attained positions in expanding government agencies. The Free Officers were, in essence, answering the call made by the generations rebelling since the 1930s to open up positions of influence to the newly educated and skilled.

They banned political parties as soon as they came to power, but this dramatic step toward authoritarian rule generated little resistance. Instances of violence that had so wracked the country for decades decreased dramatically in the mid-1950s; workers' strikes stopped; and the students who had been the foundation of every demonstration since World War I no longer headed into the streets. These former rogues had been recruited into the Free Officer project, enticed by new governmental programs and hoping that their implementation would bring substantive improvements to the country.

Gamal Abdel Nasser

Leading this program unquestionably was Nasser, who positioned himself as standing above the political fray and uniquely qualified to speak on behalf of the Egyptian people. He could make such claims because his socioeconomic policies generated enormous enthusiasm among Egyptian citizens in the first years after the revolution. Nasser also distinguished himself by standing strong against the United States, the European powers, and Israel. Nasser employed extensive propaganda initiatives in the media, such as his new Sawt al-'Arab (Voice of the Arabs) radio station, and through the schools that affirmed and reaffirmed to Egyptians that he was the guardian of Egypt and the primary purveyor of the state's modernization program. The resocialization program (ta'wiya) in the schools and universities rewrote the textbooks so that Nasser appeared as the natural descendant of the Islamic and Arab heroes of the past. At the universities, students were required to take courses such as "Arab Society," "The July 23 Revolution," and "Socialism" so they could understand Nasserism and become his loyal followers. Tens of thousands of students enrolled in the youth groups Nasser initiated to bring them into his project.

But repression of any opposition also played a role: Nasser attacked any group who opposed his policies or challenged his leadership. He quickly sidelined any early political allies who disagreed with his acquisi-

FIGURE 7.1. Egypt's president Gamal Abdel Nasser greets fellow Egyptians during a stop at one of the stations en route from Alexandria to Cairo, July 28, 1956, on the day after he nationalized the Suez Canal.

tion of power; even the Free Officer leaders found themselves with little influence just a few years after the revolution. A major group not included in the Nasserite project was the Muslim Brotherhood, which had started out as a key ally in the coup of 1952 but quickly lost favor because it maintained its large organizational structure around the country. In 1954, after an alleged Brotherhood assassination attempt against Nasser, the government banned the organization, jailed many of its members, and exiled many more. These actions did not destroy the Brotherhood but forced it to work underground for the remainder of Nasser's presidency.

Egypt as a Revolutionary Model

The example of Egypt illustrates the vibrant but fragmented political life that existed across the region after World War II, with even more political viewpoints and more mobilizing than in the 1930s. Nasser became a model for Arabs throughout the region who wanted to bring revolutionary change to their societies, displace old elites, and shift their countries away from reliance on the old colonizing powers and the new US and Soviet superpowers. But as the example of Egypt also shows, civilian political forces were not the ones who would transform government offices and programs in most instances. Instead, junior military officers took up the platforms of the political parties and brought them into governance via military coups. They implemented the anti-imperialist and populist programs that would transform the government's leadership cadres, bringing new players into office while pushing those like the large landowners out, following the path trod by Nasser before them. Revolutionaries transformed the leadership in Syria, Iraq, and Turkey while forcing the monarchs of Iran, Saudi Arabia, and Transjordan to broaden their bases of support to retain their thrones.

Arab Political Parties

As in Egypt after World War II, party politics reignited in Jordan, Syria, and Iraq, because even though the state leaders were the elites from the pre-independence era, they initiated periods of political liberalization that lasted a few years. But as occurred in Egypt, the political process in Syria, Iraq, and Jordan in the postwar period proved no more successful in establishing participatory governance than in the past because the political parties struggled against the same problems as they had earlier. They were not mass parties; none sought to mobilize new constituencies, nor did they have the institutional structures had they wanted to do so. Given the divisions existing within the opposition groups, coupled with their inability to generate mass support, government leaders retained the ability to suppress their activities. The result by the end of the 1940s was a renewed instability as parties, paramilitary groups, and unions went out into the streets and as police forces worked on behalf of state governments to stop their activities.

The parties that put forward new visions for political power in Syria and found supporters in Jordan, Iraq, and Lebanon in the 1950s were the Communist, Ba'th, and a number of Arab Nationalist parties. Activists founded Communist Parties in Egypt, Iraq, Palestine, Syria, and Lebanon in the 1920s, which attracted increasing numbers decade after decade. Near the end of World War II, the Palestinian party split into its Jewish and Palestinian constituents, and the Syrian and Lebanese party became two separate state organizations. The Ba'th Party was founded in Damascus in 1941 by teachers Michel Aflaq and Salah al-Bitar, and branches organized in Iraq and Jordan in the 1950s. In 1945, Akram al-Hawrani founded the Socialist Party in Syria and merged it with the Ba'th in 1952 to create the Arab Ba'th Socialist Party. During the 1950s, Arab Nationalist parties, including the Arab Nationalist Movement (ANM) of George Habash and the National Socialist Party (NSP) in Jordan, the Progressive Socialist Party (PSP) of Kamal Jumblatt in Lebanon, and the Arab Nationalist Movement of Iraq, appealed for supporters as well. The Syrian Socialist Nationalist Party (SSNP) in Syria and Lebanon also continued to gain supporters with its own pan-Syrian ideology.

Like the League of National Action that had preceded them, these parties spoke in broad geographic terms about how to resolve the region's problems. Ba'th members framed their national discourse as pan-Arab (qawmiyya) with an emphasis on the need to erase the borders the Europeans had erected to divide and weaken the Arabs. Its structure mirrored this concept in that each country had a Regional Command that dealt with issues specific to that country, and each sent representatives to regular meetings of the National Committee, which was pan-Arab in construction. The Arab Nationalist parties called for Arab solidarity to fight imperialism and to work together on behalf of the Palestinians. The Communist Parties adopted a similar pan-Arab framework in the 1950s, but even earlier had spoken of worker and peasant rights irrespective of any state boundaries.

Party Platforms

The parties demanded that states protect the welfare of those who had been continually marginalized by the narrowly based elite governments of the Arab mandates and the newly independent governments. They were opposed to Western imperialism and to their countries' admittance into Western-dominated defense pacts connected to the Cold War; they protested against Israeli actions toward the Palestinians. Additionally, all the parties adopted elements of socialism to try to break down the power of the large landowners, provide aid to peasants, and industrialize so their countries could be independent of all imperialist control and fulfill the long-term desire to break the glass ceiling that kept their members from top government positions. For example, the Communists called for a sweeping nationalization of the countries' economies, while the Ba'th defined an Arab socialism that combined private ownership of small farms and workshops with state ownership of all large industries.

The parties were avowedly revolutionary because they did not want to merely win elections or take over governments but to overturn the power structures in their countries. For them the existence of individual Arab states made the Arabs weak and allowed imperialists and old notables to monopolize power. The Ba'th slogan was "Arab unity, liberty, and socialism," and the founders saw the need for a complete transformation of society to achieve these goals. Unity meant for the Ba'th a physical call for the boundaries to be erased so the Arab people could be ruled by one state and for the Arabs to work together to generate the awakening that needed to occur economically, culturally, and politically. Aflaq, the ideologue of the party, called for an upheaval (inqilab) of society so that it could be completely regenerated. The rebirth of the

STUDENT ACTIVISM AT THE AMERICAN UNIVERSITY OF BEIRUT

Student activism at the American University of Beirut (AUB) exemplifies the political passions at play throughout the Arab world in the years after the 1948 war. Students demonstrated for political causes on campus so often that the 1952 April Fool's Day issue of the school newspaper, *Outlook*, satirized the situation: "A School of Revolutionary Government" had been founded to teach students modern techniques of conspiracy and revolution. Laboratory hours would include street battles with police.

Students repeatedly protested on behalf of the Palestinians in their fight against the Israelis and for the Moroccans and Algerians as they struggled for independence from the French. The students opposed British and French imperialism and the growing US influence on the Arab states and societies. As the demonstrations spilled into the streets of Beirut, the Lebanese police attacked students outside the school gates and on several occasions stopped students from protesting on campus.

The AUB administration suspended the Student Council and shut down the most important student Arab nationalist organization, al-'Urwa al-Wuthqa. As *Outlook* reported, the Student Council president protested the suspension by declaring that "the Arab World is passing through another of history's decisive moments, but one no more critical than those the University has braved in the past. Yet we see our Administration reverse its course and, like an ostrich, hide its head in a mound of sand rather than face the challenge of the day." Students convened on the campus badminton courts and reminded members of the Tennis Court Oath of the French Revolution: "Let our meeting today be a new Badminton Oath—an oath to liberate and unite our nation; to fight for its independence and neutrality."

The AUB administration did not agree to the student demands. Al-'Urwa al-Wuthqa remained closed and the Student Council was suspended until 1969, but the arguments and passions expressed by the students were replicated across the Arab world in the 1950s.

Arabs (the meaning of the word Ba'th) would come as individual Arabs reformed their own attitudes and then worked collectively to improve life for their fellow Arabs.

Political Passions of the 1950s

These parties captured a moment in Arab history in the 1950s when people across the region were excited about independence and the possibility of real change and development. After many years of mandate and colonial rule, of the old notables dominating government to the detriment of everyone else, and of the 1948 defeat in Palestine, Arabs finally had a chance to define their own futures. This was a movement of a young generation of students, professionals, and military officers who considered themselves far better trained than the older people running their governments. It was a moment when countries needed to be built, when the most talented could see how to take the lead in such developments. It was a moment when Arabs struggled in solidarity with their fellow Arabs; when the Arabs in the Levant went out into the streets repeatedly to demonstrate on behalf of their brethren in Tunisia, Morocco, and Algeria against French colonialism; when Arabs in every country protested against the loss of Palestine in 1948. It was a moment when governments were changing so quickly, through election or military coup, that the new generation thought they could finally gain access to the halls of government and institute the revolution called for by the parties. And it was a moment that saw people's standard of living rising through the extension of new state institutions, health care, and career options. It was also a moment epitomized by Gamal Abdel Nasser in Egypt, who spent the decade standing up to the West and Israel and introducing revolutionary socioeconomic changes before any of his colleagues did in the other Arab states.

Political Party Weakness

However, these parties faced the same problems as their predecessors in the 1930s: they struggled to harness the political passions of the streets, factories, and classrooms into an arena that could truly challenge the power of state leaders. Although larger in number in the 1950s because of state institutional expansion, all these parties attracted essentially the same supporters: urban students, civil servants, professionals, and workers. The majority of the population in these countries was not mobilized and organized for the kinds of change the parties desired. The economic situation made rural life exceedingly difficult in the 1950s, so bedouin and peasants needed what few services the states provided and the aid they received from the old notables in their networks. The new parties, all based in the cities, did not have the means for alleviating these problems because they sat in weak positions in government. The party leaders made few moves to adjust their message for possible supporters outside the urban areas. Kings, presidents, old notables, and European and Cold War powers also worked together to offset the influence these new parties could wield. As proven year after year and in country after country in the 1950s, state leaders could repress the political parties because they held sufficient coercive power. They could silence, arrest, and fire young activists for speaking out against government policies.

Political Developments in Jordan

With the death of King Abdullah in 1950 at the hand of a Palestinian, Jordan saw the brief ascension of his son Talal and then the inauguration of his grandson Hussein's long reign in 1952. In the early years, King Hussein allowed political parties to compete for supporters and parliamentary seats, with the Ba'th, the NSP, the ANM, and the Communist Party gaining large numbers of supporters from among Jordanian and Palestinian urban students, professionals, and workers, and Palestinian refugees. While their political platforms exhibited some differences, their shared desire to weaken King Hussein's power, move Jordan away from an alliance with Britain and the United States in the Cold War, and move closer to Nasser's Egypt made them work together as part of a collective Jordanian National Movement (JNM). To counteract the enthusiasm these parties generated, King Hussein manipulated balloting in most years to guarantee that they did poorly in elections.

Only in 1956 did the king allow relatively free elections; with this opening the parties of the JNM received enough seats that the king allowed one of their leaders, Sulayman al-Nabulsi, to form a government in October. It remained in office until only April 1957. The king opposed the al-Nabulsi government because its members spent their months in office passing legislation weakening the prerogatives of the king and moving Jordan out of an alliance with the Western states. At the same time, the king countered rumors of a coup by a group of Free Officers by successfully calling on the majority of the army, those who had been a pillar of the state since the 1930s, to stand by him. By the dawn of the 1960s, King Hussein's experiment with political liberalization was over, and his authoritarian rule over the state had begun; the participants in the parties had to move underground or into exile.

Political Developments in Syria

In Syria immediately after World War II, longtime politician Shukri al-Quwatli became the first president of an independent Syria. The National Bloc members from Damascus reconstituted themselves as the National Party and found support among the same politicians and urban residents as in the past. The Aleppo notables of the National Bloc countered with the formation of the People's Party, which attracted large landowners and businessmen from the northern districts. In elections of the 1940s and 1950s, independent politicians and the People's Party won the majority of seats in parliament because they successfully mobilized their allies while putting forward a convincing argument that they could maintain stability better than the leaders of the upstart parties. However, none of these groups could set Syria on a new path, nor could they initiate much in the way of economic development. State institutions expanded slowly and unevenly throughout the country.

Military Coups in 1949 and 1954

Between 1949 and 1954, military officers forced their way into political office, in the same way the Free Officers had done in Egypt. The officers who led the three military coups in 1949 and the one in 1954 claimed to do so because they were better suited to protect the nation and move it beyond the narrow confines of elite governance. However, as the sheer number of coups indicates, military officers were no more united in their vision for Syria than the civilian politicians had been; the officer corps was riven with factions. The French had succeeded during the mandate years in keeping the armed forces small and divided; only after independence did it start to take on the attributes of a national army. The Homs military academy, founded in 1930 by the French, served as the primary training ground for shifting the Troupes Spéciales into a national army.

Before much work could even begin, the Arab-Israeli War of 1948 illustrated that the army was still poorly trained and supplied. When it became evident that the Syrian government had failed to support the army sufficiently in Palestine, military officers plotted to take charge. The first coup in 1949 was led by Husni al-Za'im, who had served under the French in the Troupes Spéciales and become chief of staff in May 1948. This initial action was followed by two others in 1949, the last of which brought to the presidency Colonel Adib Shishakli, who presided over an authoritarian government until a group of opposition politicians overthrew him in 1954.

Party Politics between 1954 and 1958

Between 1954 and 1958, the military withdrew to the political sidelines and Syria moved into an era of parliamentary politics. The People's Party and independent politicians formed the majority in most elections, but the Ba'th and Communist Parties began to gain supporters and votes. But, as in the previous eras of party politics in the 1930s and 1940s, party rivalries proved far more pervasive than the desire to work together to pass new types of legislation. The old notables repeatedly failed to alleviate Syria's many problems; new parties such as the Ba'th spent more time playing the game of politics in Damascus than they did in transforming their political platforms into real policy programs.

United Arab Republic

By 1958, the political process had reached a stalemate; to end it, the leaders of the Ba'th Party and a few sympathetic members of the officer corps worked together to find a radical solution to the problem. Ba'th leaders calculated that a union with Egypt would dilute the rising popularity of the Communist Party; the officer corps saw in such a merger the means for strengthening the Syrian military against Israel. However, after the merger of Syria and Egypt into the United Arab Republic (UAR) in 1958, the dominance of Egypt over Syria made the union less one of equals and more of one state taking control of the other. All UAR armed forces were subsumed under the direction of an Egyptian, Field Marshal 'Abd al-Hakim 'Amir. From that post, 'Amir purged any officer deemed supportive of the Communists or opposed to the Egyptianization of Syrian state structures. Factions within the Syrian military slowly began to organize in opposition to such moves because even early supporters of the union idea came to see the disadvantages the UAR had brought to Syria and to the military directly. In 1961, military officers staged a coup in Damascus and withdrew Syria from the UAR.

In the aftermath of the coup, it became clear that major shifts in the parties, the military, and the government had taken place during the three years of the UAR's existence. Ba'th Party leaders such as Michel Aflaq and Salah al-Bitar were discredited by the union because the great promise of pan-Arab unity and of Nasser's influence in Syria that 1958 represented failed to come to fruition. Furthermore, the price for union was the dissolution of all Syrian political parties, which contributed to the weakening of a Ba'th Party that had pushed so hard for the union to take place. The Communist Party that had begun to gather popular support throughout the country in the mid-1950s found itself besieged by UAR forces and the succeeding Syrian governments so lost its influence on the national stage.

Military Transformations

Societal shifts in the military, more than any other state institution, had changed the balance of power dramatically. Those officers who overthrew the government in 1961 did not represent the Syrian military as it stood at that moment because they were part of the small minority of urban Sunni Arab elites who had chosen the military as a career choice. But the ranks at all levels were filled with people from rural areas, many of them from minority groups within Syria. The 'Alawi, whom the French had elevated in the Troupes Spéciales during the mandate, continued to consider the military a path for social mobility, and a number of 'Alawi officers rose to the highest ranks by the early 1960s. They were joined by Druze tribesmen and lower- and lower-middle class Sunni Arabs. By 1961, 'Alawi, Druze, and poorer Sunni officers outnumbered those Sunni elites who had waged the coup.

The cause for this transformation was in large measure economic; young 'Alawi and Druze men had few resources to buy their way out of military service, while Sunni Arabs had more ability to do so. At the same time, those who rose to the officer ranks were not the poorest in their regions but tended to come from middle or lesser rural or village nobility, so their families were accustomed to a measure of local power if not access to national positions. Once in the upper ranks, the 'Alawi, Druze, and poorer Sunni Arab officers brought their own allies and family members along into the ranks. And there were a large number of possible positions because by 1963 the army comprised 63,000 soldiers.

Military Coups in 1963, 1966, and 1970

Many of these new officers joined the Ba'th Party because its political platform offered a path for bringing populist ideas such as land reform into the national political realm. Ba'th ideology also called for unity against foreign imperialism and the elites dominating the economic and political power centers. Ba'th officers waged coups in Syria in 1963, 1966, and 1970. On March 8, 1963, Major Ziyad al-Hariri, commander of the Syrian forces on the Israeli border, led a coup against the 1961 government. The participants were a mixture of various Ba'th factions, independent officers, and those with continuing support for a union with Nasser. Hundreds of officers, chiefly of the urban Sunni upper-middle and middle classes, were purged, and then as the Ba'th officers became dominant in the coalition, the Nasserite officers were pushed from office as well. Their places were filled by a wholesale recruitment of soldiers mainly from rural areas and often from minority religious groups, many the kinsmen of leading Ba'thist officers. The competition for power then devolved into intra-Ba'th rivalries between the various military units. In this situation, 'Alawi General Salah al-Jadid, a former chief of staff of the Syrian army and a leader of the Ba'th Military Command, overthrew the 1963 government on February 23, 1966. On November 13, air force general and Ba'th Military Command member 'Alawi Hafiz al-Asad overthrew the al-Jadid government. He held power until his death on June 10, 2000, when the presidency passed to his son, Bashar.

Ba'th Political Program

The new military leaders of the 1960s spoke the language of the era when they called for a revolution against the old elites. They privileged rural over urban, poor over wealthy, and to a large extent minority over majority. They passed land reform measures and nationalization orders that weakened the influence of large landowners and Sunni Arab merchant elites who had held power in Syria since the late Ottoman period. In their place, the new Ba'th leaders gave peasants of all faiths a stake in the system by extending state services around the country and by employing peasants in all offices of government.

This new Ba'th military leadership took advantage of the criticism waged against the civilian Ba'th leaders for initiating the union with Egypt in 1958 to push against the pan-Arab policies of the Ba'th Party. Ba'th military officers forced from power those members such as Aflaq and al-Bitar who still worked within the pan-Arab National Command and called for some kind of unity across borders. Under this pressure in the mid-1960s, Salah al-Bitar fled the country and was assassinated in Paris in 1980; Aflaq moved to Iraq, where military leaders had also adopted the Ba'th platform as their own. Al-Hawrani died in exile in Jordan in 1996. Any pretense of unity under the Ba'th National Command no longer existed as the Iraqi and Syrian Ba'th Parties functioned as separate national organizations even as union talks occasionally took place.

Political Developments in Iraq

The Hashemite Iraqi regent ʿAbd al-Ilah inaugurated a period of political liberalization in 1945 that provided for the licensing of new political parties made up of lawyers, journalists, and past supporters of Rashid Ali and the Ahali group. Their participants organized repeated street demonstrations and strikes to push the government to grant new freedoms and improve working conditions. In reaction to the passions that accompanied this display of popular opposition, the regent tried but failed to pull back on the liberalization process. On January 16, 1948, in an event that became known as al-Wathba (the Leap), students protested the failure of the government to sign a new treaty with Britain and to alleviate the dire economic circumstances most faced. The event quickly encompassed much of the country and spread to include people from every social strata. In April and May 1948, the Iraqi Communist Party organized a strike of 3,000 workers and clerical staff of the IPC pumping station K3 near Haditha.

Despite the numbers involved, these popular forces proved incapable of disrupting Hashemite power in any substantive way. Nuri al-Saʿid remained the dominant politician, and ʿAbd al-Ilah reigned as the regent. When Faysal II reached his maturity and took the throne on May 22, 1953, little changed and the country maintained its pro-British and pro-US stance. The king, the regent, and Nuri al-Saʿid controlled the political process so thoroughly that rarely could party politicians hold any national influence. The real competition was between the regent and al-Saʿid as they struggled to fill parliament with their own supporters. Any parties in opposition to the two men largely worked underground or found that their hard-won seats in parliament accorded them little room to enact their own policies.

Revolution of 1958

As occurred in Syria and Egypt, a military coup broke the logjam by introducing new types of leaders with new types of policies. As early as 1952, small cells of junior military officers began to form to discuss the political events and ideologies of the day. There was no coordination between them, but by 1956 the high command noticed their increasing numbers, so many participants were transferred or demoted. Cells re-formed almost immediately, and by 1957, Brigadier General ʿAbd al-Karim Qasim was in charge of a group calling itself the Free Officers in homage to Nasser. On July 14, 1958, Qasim coordinated his maneuvers with Colonel ʻAbd al-Salam al-ʻArif and overthrew the Hashemite government. Over the next few days their supporters killed the king, the regent, and Nuri al-Saʻid.

Al-ʻArif's allies included a small number of Baʻth military officers and a group of Arab nationalists who favored union with Egypt. The Baʻth had been founded in 1949 by university students and was still a weak party in 1958; the Arab Nationalists organized only in 1958 amid the enthusiasm for the formation of the UAR. Al-ʻArif, in particular, became an enthusiastic supporter of Nasser and his policies and hoped to unite Iraq and Egypt. Both parties attracted sympathetic military officers. Within weeks, however, the alliance between al-ʻArif and Qasim broke apart and Qasim pushed al-ʻArif and his allies from power. Qasim then instituted a divide-and-rule policy in which he brought allies into power for short periods and then forced them from office when they grew too influential.

With the Baʻth and Arab Nationalist factions weakened, Qasim entered into an alliance with the Communist Party because its popular base could help implement his new policies. But in calculating that the Communist Party could be a useful ally, Qasim underestimated the support the Communists had gained throughout the 1950s, with inroads not only

FIGURE 7.2. Iraqi President ʻAbd al-Karim Qasim cuts the tape at the inauguration of the Darbandikhan Dam on the Diyala River in al-Sulaymaniyya, Iraq, on November 27, 1961.

into the factories and campuses but also into rural areas since the party supported land reform. As the Communists increased their national influence by the early 1960s, Qasim made the decision to weaken the party and guarantee that it could not form a challenge to his leadership. The state forced Communist members from office, suppressed the Communist press, and curtailed the activities of two affiliated organizations, the Popular Resistance Force and the Peace Partisans.

Socioeconomic Development

In the midst of these political upheavals, Qasim instituted socioeconomic development projects that did not come to fruition under his rule but jump-started revolutionary changes over the next decade. The Agrarian Reform Law of September 30, 1958, restricted the extent of landholdings that any one person could control and provided for a compensation scheme for the peasants to pay the previous owners. His government enforced rent control laws and tried to lower prices on basic foodstuffs; it cut the working day from nine hours to eight and reduced income taxes for lower-income

ORGANIZATION OF PETROLEUM EXPORTING COUNTRIES

When the initial five countries founded the Organization of Petroleum Exporting Countries (OPEC) in 1960, none of them had any control over the drilling, refinement, or shipping of oil; they merely received royalty payments. The "seven sisters" of the oil industry—British Petroleum, Exxon, Gulf, Mobil, Royal Dutch/Shell, Standard Oil of California, and Texaco—dominated the industry within the countries joining OPEC. Oil consumption rose throughout the 1950s and 1960s faster than for any other energy source, as new oil fields came into production worldwide and need for oil increased in industrialized and developing countries. New companies entering the oil industry competed with the established transnational companies so kept prices low to maintain demand.

OPEC was initially established to stop a decrease in prices in August 1960. In reaction, oil companies did raise prices slightly but not high enough to bring new revenues into the exporting countries. OPEC gained more influence over the following years, and in its greatest success in the 1960s, OPEC successfully negotiated for higher royalty and taxation payments.

In the early 1970s, OPEC countries, working individually and collectively, reduced the amount of oil owned by international companies to 20 percent. These negotiations were made possible because exporting countries began to train their own oil engineers and managers so were no longer dependent on the expertise offered by the transnational oil companies. During the decade, Algeria, Iraq, and Libya nationalized the oil companies in their countries; Saudi Arabia, Kuwait, and the UAE negotiated new arrangements with the oil companies to allow for more local control and ownership. In 1973, OPEC countries exported 85 percent of the world's oil, and their oil revenues had risen at least sixfold since the 1960s.

groups. Housing in the slums around Baghdad was improved so that people now lived in simple brick houses rather than flimsy shacks. The largest such area was Madinat al-Thawra, or "City of the Revolution."

By eliminating the Tribal Disputes Code that had established a separate system of justice for tribe members, the government weakened the power of the shaykhs. Qasim also began negotiating with the Iraq Petroleum Company (IPC) for greater Iraqi control over the oil industry, but the parties failed to reach an agreement before his government fell in 1963. In the meantime, Iraq worked with Kuwait, Iran, Saudi Arabia, and Venezuela to form the Organization of Petroleum Exporting Countries (OPEC) in September 1960 to better coordinate the policies of the oil-producing countries. Qatar, Libya, the United Arab Emirates (UAE), and Algeria among the Arab states all joined the organization over the following decade.

While these measures garnered him popularity in the rural areas and among the urban poor, Qasim was simultaneously losing support from many others in the country because he proved militarily unsuccessful in defeating a Kurdish rebellion. He also generated collective Arab opposition to his project for incorporating Kuwait into Iraq when the former received its independence from Britain in 1961. With these failures on Qasim's tally sheet, al-'Arif succeeded in rallying independent officers and military and civilian members of the Arab Nationalist and Ba'th Parties to successfully overthrow and execute Qasim on February 8, 1963.

'Abd al-Salam al-'Arif's Government and the 1968 Military Coup

Al-'Arif initiated union talks with Egypt that ultimately failed, but he maintained many of the economic policies of Qasim's government because they paralleled those that Nasser was putting into place in Egypt in the early 1960s. In July 1964, the state passed laws to nationalize all banks, insurance companies, cement and cigarette companies, and some flour and textile industries. The goal of nationalization was to concentrate capital in the hands of the state so it could be reinvested in new industrial projects. A later piece of legislation made the import and distribution of pharmaceuticals, cars, tea, sugar, and other items a government monopoly. In terms of oil policy, al-'Arif gave into pressure from the IPC and granted the oil company increased access to all the important producing areas of Iraq. In return, the Iraqi government received a £20 million payment.

When al-ʻArif died in a helicopter crash on April 13, 1966, his brother, ʻAbd al-Rahman al-ʻArif, became president, but he was never as successful as his brother in holding the reins of power. Although ʻAbd al-Salam al-ʻArif had signed a cease-fire agreement with the major Kurdish factions, his brother found himself back at war with them. As happened under Qasim, the Iraqi military could use its superior weaponry and organizational structure to capture the cities of the region, but the Kurdish paramilitary forces maintained control over the rural and mountainous areas so could not be completely defeated. These military failures compounded the weaknesses the al-ʻArif government had shown in continuing negotiations with the IPC. By early 1968, many groups were organizing to overthrow his government. The victors were a coalition of Baʻthists and a small contingent of disaffected supporters of the al-ʻArif government. General Ahmad Hasan al-Bakr, who led them in overthrowing the government on July 17, 1968, became president of Iraq until July 16, 1979, when he handed the office to Saddam Hussein.

Political Developments in Iran

When Mohammad Reza Shah came to the throne in 1941 after his father's abdication, he lightened the authoritarianism his father had imposed during his reign. He decreed that parliament would choose the prime minister and that the bureaucracy would be answerable to the cabinet, both duties Reza Shah had reserved for himself. Furthermore, he released thousands of political prisoners and returned many of the waqf lands that his father had confiscated from religious clerics. Mohammad Reza Shah shifted much of the land his father had acquired during his reign to state control so it could be returned to previous owners or whose revenues could be funneled to state-generated projects. These decisions meant that the shah was giving away powerful tools his father had used to entice landowners into his service and to punish those who opposed him.

The shah did maintain a direct link to the military, so it remained answerable to him alone and not to the government. Because the officer corps was filled with royalist officers loyal to the Pahlavi throne and family, the shah refused to accede to pressure to bring officers to trial who had deserted their posts when British and Soviet forces invaded in 1941. Instead, the shah dramatically increased the ranks of the officer corps and continued paying them high salaries. Military officers maintained their privileged position in the country, and the shah made many personal appearances at military graduations and events to prove how integral he considered the military to his throne. With this support, the shah guaranteed that he could maintain the chief state pillar, even as he loosened the throne's hold over parliament and bureaucracy.

Political Parties

In the era of freedom allowed by the shah's political liberalization, several political movements emerged on the national scene but proved as incapable as their predecessors in 1906 of overcoming their different policy prescriptions and rivalries. The Communist Tudeh Party attracted those activists in the trade union movement, intellectuals and writers, and especially large populations in northern provinces such as Azerbaijan that had long been attracted to socialist and communist ideas.

The party also grew in strength and influence because the province became the first conflict zone of the Cold War. When the Soviet Union and Britain invaded Iran in 1941, each pledged to remove troops within six months of the end of hostilities. In 1945, tensions escalated as the Soviet Union disregarded that agreement by maintaining troops in the province of Azerbaijan and providing military support for "People's Democratic Republics" led by Azerbaijanis and Kurds. Simultaneously, the Soviets demanded that Turkey return lands the Ottoman Empire had captured along the northern borders and the Black Sea in the early 20th century. The United States and Britain considered both Turkey and Iran as lying within the Western sphere of influence so refused to cede the territories to Soviet intervention. Under US and British initiative, the United Nations Security Council successfully pressured the Soviets to withdraw and to rescind the demands for Turkish territories. In early 1946, the Soviets removed their troops from Azerbaijan; the Iranian government moved into the area in large numbers and militarily defeated the rebellions. The Tudeh Party, however, was not eliminated but managed to work clandestinely and even regain a public role by the early 1950s.

Large landowners, tribal chieftains, members of the clergy, and some bazaaris established political parties to better compete for seats in parliament and put forward shared governmental policies. These political groups varied in their support for the shah, depending on his particular policies at the moment, but all opposed radical change to the socioeconomic situation because of the potential threat to their own positions. The National Front, the last of the political movements of the mid-1940s, was a coalition of forces led by longtime politician Mohammad Mossadeq. The largest and most influential in the bloc was the Iran Party, formed in 1943, and filled with young, foreign-educated technocrats and professionals, government employees, and students. Under the umbrella of the National Front, the party entered into an uneasy coalition with ultranationalist supporters, progressive Muslims, and independent politicians.

Mohammed Mossadeq and Nationalization of Iranian Oil

The Iranian government and the Anglo-Iranian Oil Company began negotiations in 1951 to set up the same 50-50 division of profits that American companies had worked out with Saudi Arabia, but those negotiations failed. In reaction, the Iranian majles voted in 1951 to nationalize the Iranian oil industry and to establish the National Iranian Oil Company (NIOC) to take over all oil operations. A few months later, the shah asked Mohammed Mossadeq to serve as prime minister and form a government. Mossadeq, however, faced immediate problems in trying to control Iran's oil because ships from the AIOC set up a blockade so that no Iranian oil could be transferred out of the country. As Iran faced an economic crisis without the usual flow of oil revenues, the Tudeh Party

FIGURE 7.3. A demonstration by workers and peasants in Tehran led by the Tudeh Party in support of the nationalization of oil and against American interference on June 1, 1951.

led demonstrators into the streets to protest against the shah, the British, and the Americans, who had sided with the British in the conflict over Iranian oil.

With this support behind him, Mossadeq worked to weaken the power of the shah. He removed royal supporters from the cabinet, prohibited the shah from conferring directly with foreign diplomats, and placed the military under the authority of the cabinet rather than the shah. He also passed a land reform law that, if enacted, had the potential to break down the economic and political power of the large landowners. With the simultaneous cutting of the budget for the military, Mossadeq made clear that his policies were designed to break down the primary pillars of the Pahlavi state.

Under government pressure and increasing instability in the streets, the shah's position grew precarious enough that he left the country in August 1953. To bring him back, the US CIA, British intelligence, and Iranian military leaders worked together to wage a coup against Mossadeq and his allies. The resulting street demonstrations and show of force by the military succeeded in bringing down Mossadeq's government and returning the shah to Iran by the end of the summer. In the next two decades, the shah, with help from the United States and revenues from an oil industry that returned to foreign hands but provided more royalty payments to the Iranian government, built an authoritarian system that allowed little opposition. The military did not become an independent political organization but served as the shah's enforcement agency for the next 15 years.

Political Developments in Turkey

Turkey's post–World War II trajectory saw military coups in 1960, 1971, and 1980, and through them the military gained progressively more legal authority to intervene in Turkish governmental affairs. As a result, the military made itself independent, not beholden to any civilian institution. But Turkey's political history differs markedly from those of Iran and the Arab countries because the years between the coups saw vibrant political party competition and parliamentary rule. In these years, the military stood in the background, serving as guarantor that parliamentary governments did not impinge on military prerogatives or weaken the pillars of Kemalism. At the same time, parliamentary rule did not always guarantee the smooth functioning of government; economic crises and violence in the streets marked Turkey's political life in many years. These conditions, in turn, brought the military into political power to offset such problems.

Political Party Competition

The decade of the 1950s represented the moment when the Republican People's Party's (RPP) monopoly over the state ended forever. The Turkish political scene for the next decades usually involved two dominant parties competing for votes and leadership over the cabinet, alongside numerous small parties appealing to smaller constituencies. The RPP and its successors staked out a position to the political left, where they continued to espouse support for the Kemalist statist economic policies, state control over religion (laicism), and empowerment of the military. Starting with the Democrat Party's (DP) success in the election of 1950, the opposing parties supported private investment in the economy and a reinvigoration of Islam's role in the public sphere. Between the 1950s and the 1980s, neither the RPP nor the DP and its successor, the Justice Party, succeeded in winning a majority of votes in most elections. Passionate personality conflicts between the leaders of the two largest parties in any given election meant that the two parties refused to work together to form united cabinets. The result was the formation of coalition cabinets year after year, with one of the two parties working with a series of small parties to earn the right to form a government.

Despite the ideological split between the largest parties, and precisely because these cabinets proved so unstable, policies changed little regardless of which party formed a government. At the end of each decade,

FIGURE 7.4. During the military coup in Turkey on September 1, 1980, soldiers disperse demonstrators near the parliament building in Ankara.

double-digit inflation, immense rural-to-urban migration, high unemployment, and party rivalries gave rise to repeated street demonstrations and to paramilitary groups assassinating officials and attacking enemies. The military stepped onto the political stage in 1960, 1971, and 1980 to end the violence and reset the political arrangement. But soon after the return to civilian government, the same types of party politics resumed, the economy deteriorated again, and violence escalated; the military would respond again, repeating the pattern that began in the late 1950s and did not end until the late 1990s.

Military Coup of 1980

The events leading up to the September 1980 coup exemplify the conditions under which the military intervened in the previous two coups; the difference was the intensity of the violence and the political and economic instability the military sought to counteract. The oil crisis of 1973–1974 led to a quadrupling of the oil price on the international market, and by the end of the decade—with another oil price shock in 1979–1980—two-thirds of Turkey's foreign currency went to meeting the oil bill. The Turkish government responded by concluding costly short-term Euro-dollar loans and by printing money. Inflation began running at 20 percent a year during the early part of the 1970s; by 1979 it was at 90 percent and rising.

The biggest regional crisis Turkey faced in the 1970s occurred over the sovereignty of Cyprus. After the British granted independence to Cyprus in 1960, Greece repeatedly tried to unite the island under its own leadership. The Turkish government fought to keep that from happening because a substantial number of Turks lived there. The 1960s saw skirmishes over the island, which grew heated in 1967 when a military junta came to power in Athens. When the leadership then pushed for Cyprus to be united with Greece, Turkey opposed the measure. In 1974 the Greek military government engineered a coup d'état of the Cypriot government. Turkey immediately protested to the international community and demanded intervention to stop the takeover. When that did not take place, Turkey invaded northern Cyprus and in 1983 established the Turkish Republic of Northern Cyprus, with the Republic of Cyprus ruling over the remainder.

As a result of these military and economic crises, Turkey was near bankruptcy by the end of the 1970s, with high inflation, increasing unemployment, and widespread shortages of basic commodities. Turkish coffee had to be imported, but most could not afford it; many medicines were no longer available. Even staple foods like cooking oil and macaroni became only sporadically available. Small businesses faced bankruptcy; industrial workers and civil servants were not paid. The governments of the 1970s proved incapable of resolving these problems as they repeated the cycle of the past in which no single party won a clear majority so had to work with smaller parties to form cabinets. These cabinets, in turn, lasted for only short periods and often included unwieldy numbers of ministers because of all the deals that had to be made to form a majority. The ministers worked harder to place their own supporters in government offices than in trying to find solutions to Turkey's economic problems.

In the midst of these governmental problems, Turkey was wracked with violence perpetrated by groups on the political right and left. Youth groups on the left, such as the Revolutionary Left and the Revolutionary Way, tried to ignite a revolution by inspiring workers to undertake anti-Western and anticapitalist actions like kidnapping American soldiers and prominent Turkish corporate figures. Those on the right, such as the ultranationalist Grey Wolves, recruited young people who had few

FIGURE 7.5. The leaders of the September 1980 military coup in Turkey—Admiral Nejat Tumer, General Nurettin Ersin, General Kenan Evren, General Tahsin Sahinkaya, and General Sedat Celasun—celebrate their victory at Mustafa Kemal's mausoleum in Ankara on October 29, 1980.

job opportunities during Turkey's economic crisis. By the mid-1970s, the Grey Wolves were causing chaos and demoralization through demonstrations and bombings.

On September 12, 1980, army generals announced that the armed forces were taking over the government because state organs had ceased to function. Over the next days, the military dissolved parliament, dismissed the government, and suspended all political parties and trade union confederations. The army arrested all party leaders and dismissed all mayors and municipal councils. The generals decreed that the national politicians of the 1970s were prohibited from reentering the political arena. The National Security Council (NSC), formed after the coup of 1960, had gradually gained increasing legal right to intervene in government affairs and became the chief governing agency, codified by the 1982 constitution, which legalized this concentration of military power.

The military coup leaders of 1960 and 1971 had stepped back from direct governance within a few months; however, the leading military officers of 1980 held the reins of government within the NSC until the late 1980s. Only then were the national politicians of the 1970s allowed back into politics, as the generals allowed elections to take place at the municipal and then the national level. Even as the military receded from direct governance, the generals maintained a supervisory role over government decision making. As late as 1997, the military still retained enough independent power that it could wage a soft coup to bring down a government that appeared to be giving Islam too strong a public role. Every government formed in the decades after 1960 had to recognize that the military could return at any time.

Political Developments in Lebanon

Lebanon presents a variation on both party politics and military rule in the decades after World War II because of the sectarian political system evolving there. In September 1943, leading politicians in Lebanon agreed to the provisions of the National Pact, which declared that Lebanon had an "Arab face" but maintained its links with the West. This was a compromise between the Christians, who largely wanted Lebanon to remain a separate nation, and Muslim leaders, who preferred union with Syria but agreed to maintain Lebanon's distinctive national status and its economic links to the West. The pact also codified the unofficial demarcation of governmental positions each sect had held in the preceding years. The presidency henceforth went to a Maronite Christian; the prime minister's office, to a Sunni Muslim Arab; and the speaker of the house, to a Shi'i. In parliament, for every six seats allotted to a Christian, Muslims held five seats.

The sectarian system recognized the rule that no one sect represented a majority in the country, so positions needed to be allotted to each of the country's minorities according to their share of the population at the time of the 1932 census, the last one ever conducted in Lebanon. During the 20th century, the state recognized 18 separate religious sects. All were stakeholders in the country, but none were allowed to be considered the majority since no further census would determine if a shift in demographics had taken place. The entire structure relied on elites from the various sects negotiating power-sharing arrangements among themselves and thereby regulating political decision making under the umbrella of the government. Because of their demographic and economic positions in 1932, Maronite Christians and Sunni Arabs earned the right to hold the most important government positions. The Shi'a, who were fast becoming the largest sectarian group, struggled until the 1980s with establishing an organizational structure with enough political leverage to pressure the other sects to accord them power commensurate with their numbers.

Sectarian Organization

In a country with a strong central government, the Ministry of Interior provides health care, paved roads, schools, and access to jobs; bureaucrats serve in these institutions as state employees and revenues are collected and dispersed by the state. In Lebanon, the sect leaders frequently dispense what would normally be considered state services and do so in the name of the sect and of themselves personally. Instead of state-dominated courts handling personal status issues, the 18 separate sects adjudicate the legal conflicts among members of the sect. Since Lebanon did not move to a statist economic structure in the post–World War II period, as its neighbors did, the bulk of profits and revenues from state actions have remained in private hands, outside state control. Those resources, in turn, aid the sectarian leaders in maintaining their power while keeping the state weak because it has so few resources to disperse. The state thus exists as a table for negotiation between sect leaders while also providing services for those outside sectarian protection and patronage.

Sectarian leaders (zu'ama'; singular, za'im), in the Lebanese context, have played much the same role as the old notables who served as intermediaries between state and society in the late Ottoman era. In the other countries, state centralization and institutional expansion destroyed most remnants of the independent bases and networks that existed before the second half of the 20th century. Such players could increasingly hold their positions only because of their connection to the resources of the states, and often to the presidents and monarchs personally. But no Lebanese government emerged that could successfully weaken the zu'ama', who have held the most powerful national positions for decades.

Electoral System

The electoral system holds up the sectarian structure by directing votes to the sectarian leaders and those they select as their representatives. Everyone must vote in the town or village of his or her family's origins, helping cement the leadership of the long-term elites. Even though the vast majority of the population now lives in the cities, especially Beirut, they have no provision for voting on the bases of their interests in those locales. Furthermore, Lebanon follows a multi-member constituency system for voting, whereby every person in a given district votes as many times as there are allotted seats. To prepare for such a system, all the candidates establish lists of alliances they have made, pressuring voters to select from the prepared list of candidates. The seats allotted to each sect in the district have already been determined, so regardless of the number of raw votes, a certain number of Christians, Sunnis, and others will hold the seats; if the negotiations worked well beforehand, allies across the sects enter parliament together.

Independent candidates rarely win seats in this system because they do not have the patronage power to attract sufficient numbers of voters without the benefit of a list of alliances. Entrée to government provides access to economic privileges, making the sectarian elites wealthy and better able to maintain networks supportive of their continuing political leadership. Their supporters understand the importance of having connections to those elected to parliament and appointed to national office. Once in office, a successful member of parliament is expected to reward his supporters with services and privileges. Both the sect and individuals within it benefit from representatives in parliament.

Political Parties

Political parties have traditionally performed poorly in elections in Lebanon because the sectarian system favors the sects over any organization trying to construct an alliance across Lebanon's legal and political dividing lines. Voters make pragmatic decisions when voting because the outcome determines what aid they might receive from the winner. Parties lack such access so can offer little to their potential voters, even if their political platforms are especially appealing. Instead, parties in Lebanon have generally been extensions of the elite leaders of the sects even while they may also have formulated ideologies to attract additional supporters. In 1952 the Kata'ib organization of Pierre Gemayel became a full-fledged political party, the Phalanges Libanaises. Fellow Maronite Camille Chamoun challenged Gemayel while serving as president between 1952 and 1958 and when he formed the National Liberals' Party and its associated militia, the Tigers. Druze Kamal Jumblatt formed the Progressive Socialist Party (PSP) in 1949 with a nonsectarian socialist platform. It attracted a widespread membership far beyond the Druze community, but here too Jumblatt was able to position himself in part because of his leadership over the Druze community. The Communist Party cuts across sectarian lines by appealing to supporters based on its ideology, but it has failed to translate that support into electoral wins or substantial influence in national politics.

Shihabism

The most successful era for the parties was under the Fu'ad Shihab presidency (1958–1964). Shihab came to office pledging to enhance state power in relation to the sectarian leaders. In particular, the president sought to use state offices to spread socioeconomic development more evenly throughout the country, especially expansion of public utilities. His term extended the state into new areas in the country, and his efforts supplied services to those communities not well served by the sectarian hierarchies. But the measures largely failed to substantially alter the balance of power because the sectarian elites saw these changes as threatening to their own positions; the oligarchy of sectarian leaders fought to make sure they failed. No companies were nationalized, no land reform took place, and rarely did more than 35 to 40 percent of students attend state rather than private schools in the 20th century. Political parties won about a third of the seats in parliament in the 1960s but not enough to make dramatic changes to the sectarian system. By the end of the decade, party representation diminished yet again.

Military Role

The army followed much the same trajectory as in Syria, in that the French-controlled Troupes Spéciales evolved in 1945 into the national Lebanese army. The army has the duty of protecting the government and defending the nation from outside attack, as does any other national army, but it has not been able to take on the same domestic role as the neighboring armies. Domestic actions can take place only when the sects come to a consensus on a particular position. In other words, the army and the police frequently attacked student protesters in the 1950s and 1960s when they opposed British and American aid to the Lebanese government. In conflicts between the sects, the army has to remain neutral. Complicating the matter still further, the Lebanese army has not been the only military organization in the country since independence, as many of the sects constructed paramilitary organizations over the years to protect their interests and institutions. The result for Lebanon has been the construction of a weak government, a weak military, and a weak political party structure facing strong sectarian structures and leaders, but a government, a military, and a police force that can be activated when sectarian consensus reigns.

Conclusion

The post–World War II era ushered in new political parties with revolutionary ideologies about governance. In Turkey, the Democrat Party destroyed the monopoly of power the RPP had held since 1923 and set up a situation where two dominant parties competed for votes and positions in the cabinet. None could resolve the endemic economic problems in the country, and the military repeatedly stepped in to try to reset the parameters for governance. Until the 1990s, the military succeeded in legally establishing its supervisory role over the Turkish government but could not substantially ease the political instability that the parties helped generate.

In Jordan, Iran, and Lebanon the military failed to establish such an independent polity, as it became a pillar of the state in the first two countries and one of many power bases existing in the third. Otherwise, the rest of the countries experienced truly revolutionary changes in the aftermath of the many military coups. They removed from power the old elites who had dominated the political realm since the 19th century, opened up government office to professionals who had rebelled repeatedly against the old governments, and provided services to the long marginalized. But in trying to remain in power, these military leaders set up extensive security apparatuses to guarantee that no other military generals followed their lead; thus, they fronted increasingly authoritarian and repressive governing systems. Fear kept many from rebelling; incentives such as access to government office and economic opportunities stopped others.

None of these countries could formulate policies outside the confines of the Cold War because the United States and the USSR funneled weapons to their allies and competed with each other through proxy wars. State leaders articulated governing policies in accordance with their positions on the pro–United States and pro-USSR spectrum. Into this mix also came the continuation of the Arab-Israeli conflict that brought the parties to war repeatedly after 1948.

COLD WAR BATTLES

8

The Suez Crisis, Arab-Israeli Conflicts, and the Lebanese Civil War

OVER THE DECADES as military coups took place and as the domestic roles of the military and security forces evolved, the countries in the Middle East came into repeated conflict with each other. Also, none of these governments could avoid the pressures of the Cold War, as the United States and the USSR interceded in all the conflicts in their competition to weaken each other. The revolutionary ideology of Nasser demanded, in its essence, a break with all imperialist control that had supported the old notables. This meant that, as Nasser declared, the Arab countries should not be dependent on either of the superpowers. But this policy of neutrality was difficult to uphold in a region where the superpowers pushed their agendas with particular vehemence and opponents of Nasser welcomed the arms and aid funneled to them. Nasser negotiated the Cold War by trying to get the two superpowers to compete for his favors.

King Hussein of Jordan, Nuri al-Sa'id of Iraq, the kings of Saudi Arabia, the shah of Iran, and the military and civilian leaders in Turkey saw the military and economic aid that came along with an alliance with Britain and the United States as the best means for shoring up their rule. Israel, especially by the late 1960s, received far more military aid than any of the other countries; Egypt and Syria both turned to the Soviet Union to build up their military strength to counter that achieved by Israel. However, these leaders could not function in a political vacuum, and none could completely ignore the wishes of populations that frequently came out in support of the pan-Arab political parties and on behalf of Nasser's policies.

However, the conflicts were not merely proxy actions for the Cold War. As new leaders came into power, whether by military coup, the ballot box, or inheritance, they all wanted to make their mark on the region. Nasser achieved the mantle of regional leadership in the 1950s; in the following years, his competitors became rivals for his position, using aid from the superpowers to challenge his supremacy. And as new wars emerged in the Arab-Israeli crisis, none of the Arab state forces could retain or win back Palestinian land. A new force—the Palestinian fedayeen (those who sacrifice)—emerged that fought not only against Israel but also against the Arab state leaders who had failed in their promise to retake Palestine and who often opposed their activities in this regard. All these players converged on Lebanon between 1975 and 1990 as the sectarian political actors fought a civil war with aid from the surrounding states and the superpowers.

Cold War Polarization

The Cold War positions of the Middle Eastern players were clarified in 1954 and 1955 when all had a role to play on the regional and international stage through the agency of the Baghdad Pact, a defensive pact designed to bring the pro-Western countries together against a possible Soviet intervention in the Middle East. The process began with a Turco-Pakistan agreement on April 2, 1954, bringing into alliance two countries that had already pledged their support for the Western pole in the Cold War. Turkey, for example, had become a member of the North Atlantic Treaty Organization (NATO) in 1952. On February 24, 1955, Turkey and Iraq signed a mutual cooperation agreement, followed by the addition of Iran on September 23 and Pakistan on November 3, bringing them all into what was termed by then the Baghdad Pact. Britain officially joined in April 1955, taking the formal leadership position while the United States stood in the background. In return for signing, all the countries received British and US aid and weaponry.

As each new country signed on to the pact, little popular opposition had appeared. Conflict arose when the parties sought to entice other countries throughout the Arab world, hoping to forestall further Soviet infiltration into the region. Already moving toward a position of neutrality, Nasser immediately rejected the pact when Egypt was asked to join. At the Bandung Conference in Indonesia in April 1955, Nasser had stood with major world leaders such as Jawaharlal Nehru of India, declaring that he would take a position of nonalignment in the Cold War. The Baghdad Pact went against this pledge and against Nasser's opposition to colonialism, so he could not accept it. The parliamentary government in Syria in the 1950s contained many party members who agreed with Nasser's political views, so Syria also declined to join the Baghdad Pact.

To entice Jordan, members of the pact sent delegations to King Hussein in late 1955 and early 1956, laying out the aid his country would receive upon joining. Meanwhile, Nasser used his Sawt al-'Arab radio station to broadcast throughout the Arab world his denunciations of Nuri al-Sa'id for joining the pact and King Hussein for contemplating it. Jordan at that time had a highly politicized urban population that belonged in enormous numbers to the pan-Arab and leftist parties of the day. Thousands came out into the streets day after day between November 1955 and January 1956, bringing down four governments in just these two months and forcing King Hussein to recognize the extent of the opposition. He declined to join the pact, and from that point forward, with so much opposition mounted against it, the pact's usefulness stood in question. After Qasim and al-'Arif led the coup against the Hashemite government in Iraq in 1958, the new government withdrew the country from the pact and for all intents and purposes, it no longer existed. Turkey, Iran, Pakistan, and Jordan maintained alliances with the Western forces but henceforth through bilateral arrangements.

Suez Crisis

Throughout 1956, Cold War and regional politics encompassed the same players again, this time over the Egyptian nationalization of the Suez Canal. In February, the World Bank approved funds for building the Aswan Dam along the Nile River, with US and British financial backing. Before the funding could arrive and the project begin, Nasser recognized Communist China and received a substantial loan from the Soviet Union, having already received, in the previous year, a weapons shipment from Czechoslovakia, a member of the Soviet bloc. On July 19, 1956, the United States withdrew its promise of funding and Britain and the World Bank quickly followed suit. On July 26, Nasser nationalized the Canal Company so he could use its revenues to build the Aswan Dam. On that day, Egyptian engineers took over operation of the canal without a break in its services.

Britain and France opposed the action because they were the primary owners of the Canal Company; Israel wanted to attack because Nasser closed the canal to Israeli shipping. To end the nationalization, all three countries secretly planned a tripartite attack that would begin with an Israeli assault on the canal, to be followed by British and French actions in support of the Israeli maneuver. On October 29, Israel launched its attack across the Sinai Peninsula, and its troops quickly arrived at the canal. Per arrangement between the three, Britain and France demanded a cease-fire along the canal, hoping that with Israeli troops positioned so deep within its territory, Egypt would refuse. As anticipated, Egypt rejected such a concession and Britain and France immediately launched attacks against the canal. As fighting escalated, the war threatened to erupt into a larger Cold War event and potentially bring the United States and the Soviet Union into direct conflict, so the two superpowers worked together to end it, forcing a cease-fire on November 6. The parties subsequently negotiated the withdrawal of Israeli forces from the Sinai and the installation of a new UN force, the United Nations Emergency Force (UNEF), to create a buffer zone between Egypt and Israel in positions around the Suez Canal and in the Sinai Peninsula. Over the next years, Egypt continued to block Israeli shipping from the canal, but it did enter into successful negotiations over compensation for the British and French shareholders.

Nasser and the United States

The 1956 Suez Crisis made the United States the primary Western force in the region. Britain and France had already been discredited by decades of colonialism and continuing alliances with politicians such as Nuri al-Sa'id, who opposed the dominant political currents of the day. The events of Suez proved that Britain and France could no longer initiate policies without US support. Although Nasser's military could not withstand the tripartite attack, the Suez War was a political victory that changed his relationship with the Arabs in the region and with the superpowers. He could not defeat the combined forces of Britain, France, and Israel, but he still managed to hold on to the canal with superpower acquiescence. In the wake of this victory Nasser was viewed throughout the Arab world as a hero defending the Arab homeland from imperialists. Nasser also proved to the United States and the USSR that he was the most influential

Arab leader and, depending on the perspective, either the gateway or the obstacle to further superpower infiltration into the Middle East.

For two years after the 1956 events US officials decided that Nasser was an obstacle to their plans for the region, so they cut off funding for the Aswan Dam as well as promised food aid to Egypt. In January 1957, US president Dwight D. Eisenhower made a speech outlining a policy that came to be known as the Eisenhower Doctrine, ostensibly targeted at halting Communist expansion into the Middle East but primarily aimed at isolating Nasser. The United States supplied aid only to countries such as Jordan, Iraq, and Saudi Arabia that supported the US mission in the region. The US government tried to position the leaders of these countries as alternatives to Nasser, but none could match Nasser's popularity among the Arabs. In 1961, the new US administration of John F. Kennedy decided that Nasser was the best possible conduit for improving US relations in the Arab world. A couple of years of relatively warm US-Egyptian relations followed, and the United States sent millions of dollars in food and economic aid. In return, Nasser ceased attacking Israel from the Gaza Strip as he had done on several occasions throughout the 1950s.

Lebanon's Civil War of 1958

In the meantime, Lebanon, one of the staunchest allies of the United States, entered into a constitutional crisis when President Camille Chamoun tried to extend his term in office. Lebanon was strategically important for the United States because it stood at the terminus of oil pipelines and as a center for American firms conducting business in the region. Chamoun's government had received millions of dollars in US economic and military aid during the 1950s and in return had signed a preferential commercial treaty with the United States. Lebanon did not formally join the Baghdad Pact, but Chamoun's government gave tacit support, despite pressures from Egypt and Syria and from the thousands of Lebanese students and workers who marched in opposition to it.

When in 1957 Chamoun began talking about changing the constitution to allow himself a second six-year term in office, he set off crises within the Lebanese government because he was attempting to throw off the balance of power between the sects, privileging his Maronite Christian allies. In reaction, both Muslim forces and opposing Christian politicians armed themselves against Chamoun and his allies, signaling the beginning of a full-scale insurrection against the president and a civil war between sectarian alliances. Fu'ad Shihab, commander of the army, refused to allow the army to become involved in the conflict because this was not one of its defined tasks in the domestic political realm.

Lacking domestic military support, Chamoun asked for US assistance. On July 15, 1958, some 15,000 US marines landed in Lebanon, initially appearing to work on behalf of Chamoun's cause. In actuality, American government leaders had determined that Chamoun needed to be replaced and a new president elected because his tactics had destabilized Lebanon sufficiently to make the US position there precarious. The US government advocated for Fu'ad Shihab as a compromise candidate. Nasser came to the same conclusion, and his support for Shihab gave the decision added validity in the Arab world. Shihab was elected president by the parliament on July 31, 1958. Chamoun left office, and the United States withdrew its troops. Fighting continued in Lebanon for a few more months, but the political solution gradually calmed the country and returned the political balance between the sects.

Revolution in Yemen

After US-Egyptian relations had warmed in the early 1960s, the relationship began to deteriorate again in September 1962 when a military coup brought down the government in north Yemen and replaced it with a republic. The north of the country had been ruled as an independent monarchy under the Hamid al-Din family since 1918. In 1962, the Egyptian government came in on the side of the republican forces and the Saudis supported the royal family; both sides sent troops. After six years of fighting, the north became the Yemen Arab Republic. In the south, the British East India Company had colonized the port of Aden in 1839, and in the 20th century the British government extended its rule over all the provinces of south Yemen. After the formation of the Federation of South Arabia under British aegis in 1963, the region became embroiled in the civil war to the north and local nationalist forces attacked British installations. Under this pressure, the British withdrew from the region in 1967, and the south became an independent socialist state, the People's Democratic Republic of Yemen. North and south united to form one country on May 22, 1990.

In aiding both Egypt and Saudi Arabia at different times during the Yemeni revolution, the United States was in the awkward position of trying to improve relations with Egypt while maintaining its alliance with Saudi Arabia, threading a needle between a long-term ally and the most influential Arab leader. US leaders attempted to please both Egypt and Saudi Arabia, but their policies caused friction with both countries. The

United States exacerbated the problem with Egypt by strengthening its relationship with Israel. By the mid-1960s, the US government was selling and delivering heavy offensive weaponry to the Israeli government. The Soviet Union took advantage of the worsening US-Egyptian relations to increase weapons deliveries to Egypt, while expanding those to the Ba'th government in Syria. The Egyptian government accepted increasing numbers of Soviet advisers as it gravitated toward the Eastern bloc.

Arab-Israeli Conflicts

The borders between Israel and the surrounding Arab states were rarely calm after the end of the 1948 war, and Arab and Israeli skirmishes broke out on numerous occasions. In late 1966 and early 1967, tensions rose precipitously between Israel and the Arab states when Egypt and Syria signed a defense treaty and Israel blew up 125 homes during an attack on the West Bank town of Samu'. January 1967 brought clashes between Syrian and Israeli troops within the demilitarized zone that ran along the border of the Golan Heights. On April 7, 1967, Israeli planes flew over Damascus. On May 16, when Nasser demanded that the UNEF force be removed from Egyptian territory, he inserted his troops into the Sinai to replace them. Israel refused a request by the United Nations to place UNEF troops on Israeli land. On May 21, Nasser closed the Straits of Tiran, blocking Israeli shipping between the southern port of Eilat and the Red Sea. This effectively prevented Israel from shipping to the east since the Suez Canal was still closed to Israeli ships.

Six-Day War of June 1967

On June 5, 1967, the Israeli military launched a surprise attack against Egypt, destroying most of its air force in 170 minutes. By the end of the next day, Israeli forces had crossed the Sinai Peninsula without opposition, and on June 8, as a result of these defeats, Egypt accepted a UN-sponsored cease-fire. On June 7, the Israelis quickly captured the Old City of Jerusalem and gained complete control over the West Bank; King Hussein accepted a cease-fire on June 8. On June 9, the Israelis turned their attention to Syria and quickly occupied the Golan Heights; Syria accepted a cease-fire on June 10. As a result of this Six-Day War, Israel was in occupation of the Sinai Peninsula from Egypt, the Golan Heights from Syria, and the Palestinian territories of the West Bank, East Jerusalem, and the Gaza Strip.

In response, the UN Security Council unanimously passed Resolution 242 on November 22, 1967, calling for the withdrawal of Israeli armed

MAP 20. Areas Occupied by Israel in the June 1967 War. Israel took over occupation of East Jerusalem and the West Bank from Jordan, the Gaza Strip and the Sinai Peninsula from Egypt, and the Golan Heights from Syria.

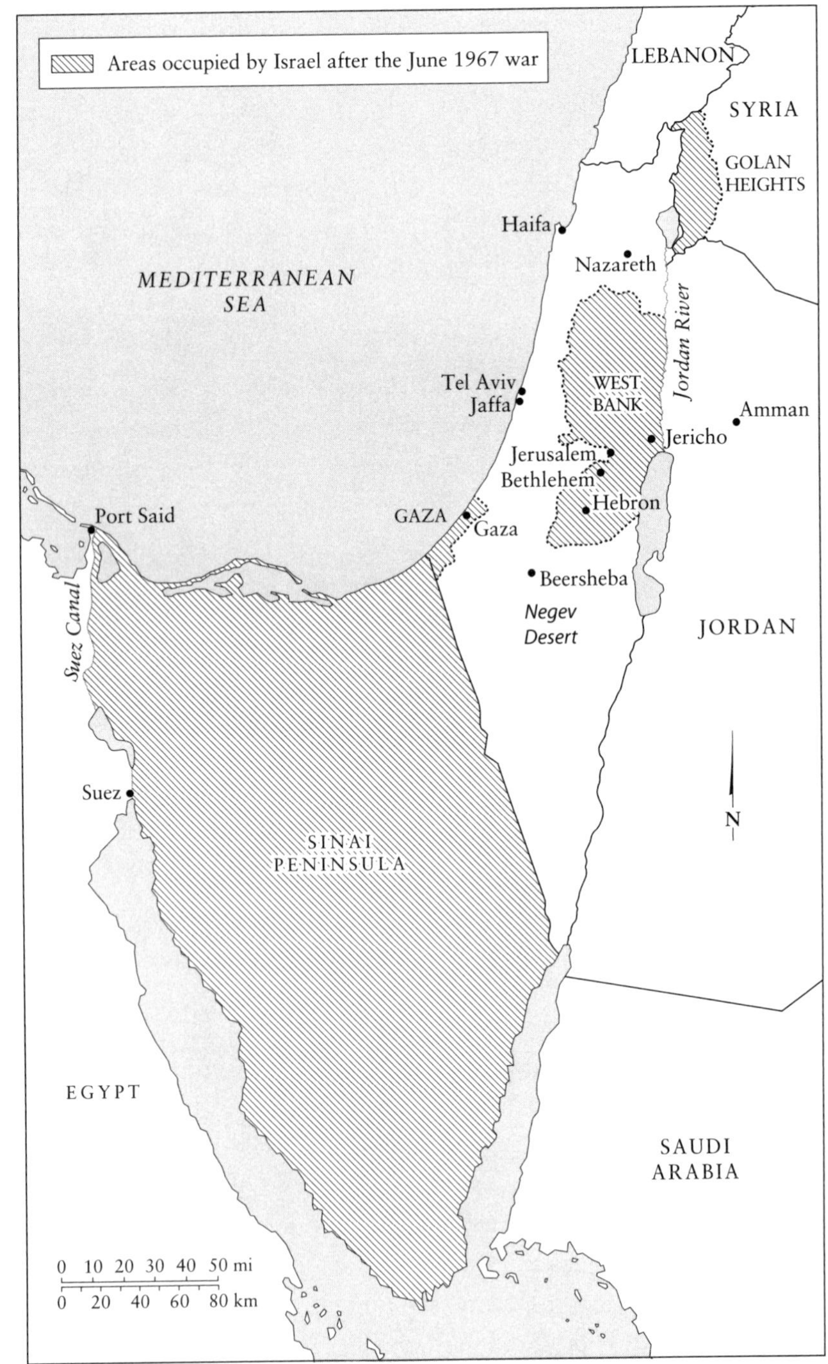

forces from territories occupied during the war and a complete end to the state of war between the belligerents. The resolution has been embedded in declarations concerning the Arab-Israeli peace process ever since. For example, UN Resolution 338, passed by the Security Council on October 22, 1973, to end the October 1973 war, called for the implementation of all of Resolution 242's provisions. Article I of the Oslo Accords signed between the Israeli government and the Palestine Liberation Organization on September 13, 1993, stated that the agreement was based on the provisions in Resolutions 242 and 338.

Despite its centrality to the documents issued since 1967, the ambiguous wording of UN Resolution 242 makes it a problematic document on which to base the Arab-Israeli peace process. The resolution does not indicate which provisions should be undertaken first or in what order they should be followed. The Israeli government has always called for ending the state of belligerence between the warring parties before withdrawal could take place, while the Arab states have emphasized the need for an Israeli withdrawal to precede negotiations about ending formal hostilities. Furthermore, Resolution 242 does not include any means for implementing its provisions besides calling on the UN to send a representative to assist the states in achieving peace.

In a final complication, the text calls for "achieving a just settlement of the refugee problem" as a necessity for the resolution to be imple-

FIGURE 8.1. A column of soldiers moves past a burned-out bus as paratroopers force open the Lion's Gate in Jerusalem during the Six-Day War, June 1967.

mented. At the time the resolution passed, its main provisions applied to the states involved in the conflict and acknowledged the Palestinians only as refugees and not possible claimants to a national land. In principle, if Israel withdrew from the Palestinian territories, they would be returned to Egypt and Jordan, not handed to a State of Palestine.

UN RESOLUTION 242

Disputes have arisen over how to interpret and implement the provisions of Resolution 242. One concern arises at the beginning of the text: "*Emphasizing* the inadmissibility of the acquisition of territory by war and the need to work for a just and lasting peace in which every State in the area can live in security," the UN seeks to find a means to resolve the crisis created by the 1967 war.

In achieving that peace, the resolution calls for the following:

> (i) Withdrawal of Israel armed forces from territories occupied in the recent conflict;
>
> (ii) Termination of all claims or states of belligerency and respect for and acknowledgment of the sovereignty, territorial integrity and political independence of every State in the area and their right to live in peace within secure and recognized boundaries free from threats or acts of force.

The first issue arises from the inadmissibility clause at the beginning of the text. This statement embeds an international principle, established in the 19th century and laid out in the UN Charter of 1945, that states have no legal right to gain territory through conquest. Provision is allowed in international law for temporary military control but does not permit the occupying state to establish communities, such as Israeli settlements, in the territory. The Israeli government has countered that since Egypt and Jordan did not have a valid legal title to the Gaza Strip, the West Bank, and East Jerusalem, it has not violated any national territorial claims in occupying the territories.

A second issue is the extent to which Israel is required to withdraw from the Occupied Territories. The lack of a definite article—*the*—from the English-language text allows for alternative readings and the possibility that Israel could retain territories occupied in 1967. A further complication is that the resolution was translated immediately into French, and that version includes the definite article, indicating that the resolution refers to all the Occupied Territories.

On the day the resolution passed the Security Council, the majority of member states expressed the opinion that the resolution included "all" the territories Israel had just captured. The US government representative made no statement during the debate over the vote, but the US position since then has been to interpret this omission to mean that only some of the territories would be involved. Israel has consistently emphasized the phrase that it has the right to live in peace within secure borders as part of the discussion of any possible withdrawal from the territories. In this reading, Israel claims that the 1949 borders were not defensible, so implementing this provision requires that Israel retain some territories captured in 1967.

However, in November 1974, the UN General Assembly passed Resolution 3236, which recognized the Palestinian people's inalienable right to self-determination; in 1988 the Jordanian government renounced its claim to the West Bank and East Jerusalem; and the Egyptian government regained the Sinai Peninsula in the Israel-Egyptian Treaty of 1979 and has made no national claim to the Gaza Strip. As a result, Resolution 242's provisions have been shifted over the decades since 1967 to identify the Palestinians as the natural possible recipients of lands from which the Israelis might withdraw. Since 1993, Resolution 242 has stood as the cornerstone of the peace process that is aimed at creating two states—Israeli and Palestinian—between the Mediterranean Sea and the border with Jordan.

October 1973 War

However, neither UN Resolution 242 nor the many peace plans put forward by the United States, the USSR, and the belligerents over the next years brought a resolution to the Arab-Israeli crisis. The years after 1967 bought more-intensified conflict between Egypt and Israel. Between March 1969 and August 1970, Israel and Egypt waged a war of attrition across the Suez Canal. Both the United States and the USSR augmented the weaponry available to their respective allies, but Israeli forces did not withdraw by the time the intensity of attacks began to level off. Nasser died on September 28, 1970, bringing Vice President Anwar Sadat to the presidency and a brief respite from the fighting but not a formal end to the hostilities.

The forces converged again in October 1973 in a new war, this time with Egypt and Syria waging a surprise attack against Israel. For two years before the war Egyptian popular pressure had been pushing Sadat to fulfill the promise he had made upon taking over the presidency to launch a new war as soon as possible. On October 6, Egyptian and Syrian forces attacked the Israelis on the Jewish Yom Kippur holiday by moving troops into the Sinai Peninsula and the Golan Heights. For the first week, the Arabs held the initiative and forced Israeli troops to retreat. However, on October 12 extra US aid enabled Israel to launch a counteroffensive that pushed the Egyptians and Syrians back to the pre–October 6 lines. Additional Soviet aid to Egypt and Syria was not sufficient to offset Israeli strength. By October 24, Syria, Egypt, and Israel had agreed to a cease-fire; little land changed hands as a result of the war.

Arab Oil Embargo

From the beginning of the October hostilities, the Arab oil producers in OPEC used oil as a weapon by immediately increasing the price of crude oil by 17 percent and declaring they would cut oil production 5 percent per month until Israel withdrew from the Occupied Territories. They augmented their action by placing an embargo on oil shipments to the United States for aiding Israel. The Arabs lifted the embargo in March 1974 even though the stated goals had not been met. The participants feared that prolonging the embargo could generate an economic crisis that could hurt the Arab producers over the long run. To rationalize the decision to end the boycott, the participants declared that the embargo had succeeded in showing the strength and unity of the Arab position toward Israel.

The embargo had not lasted long enough to truly upset oil supplies around the globe or weaken US government support for Israel, yet the consequences reverberated for years. For much of the mid-1970s the price of oil remained artificially high and brought unprecedented revenues to oil-producing countries. The Arab oil producers also used the event to renegotiate their contracts with the foreign oil companies operating on their soils. Saudi Arabia was set to take charge of its oil industry in 1999 but did so in 1977 under the new contract. Iraq had already nationalized its oil industry by 1972; Iran stayed aloof but took advantage of the rise in prices to accrue unprecedented revenues. Millions of Egyptians, Palestinians, Syrians, Lebanese, Jordanians, and Yemenis moved to the Persian Gulf States to work for the oil industry and the state structures that were expanding along with the new revenues. They returned billions of dollars of remittances back to their families in their resource-poor states, providing them with additional money to improve their homes, buy consumer goods, and send children to school for professional training.

Sinai I and II

Egypt militarily lost the 1973 October war, but Anwar Sadat won a political victory like Nasser's in 1956 because of the strength shown by the Egyptian military early on. At home, Sadat declared himself the "Hero of the Crossing" and used that status to distance himself from the Nasserite past. A key element in his new program was to move away from the Soviet Union and toward the United States as the primary supplier of weapons and economic aid. He initiated negotiations with Israel, cementing his alliance with the United States, recognizing that Egypt could not win back its territories through military means. As a result of this initiative, Egypt and Israel signed the Sinai I (1974) and Sinai II (1975) agreements, providing for a limited Israeli withdrawal from the Sinai Peninsula. In return for these concessions, Israel received a massive delivery of advanced weaponry from the United States and its promise to refrain from speaking to or negotiating with representatives of the Palestinians. As talks between Egypt and Israel continued, Anwar Sadat visited Jerusalem to speak at the Israeli Parliament (Knesset) on November 20, 1977.

Camp David Accords

The United States had been trying to arrange multilateral peace talks between the Israelis and Arab states in Geneva, but after Sadat's visit to Jerusalem, the focus turned to bilateral talks between Egypt and Israel. In September 1978 US president Jimmy Carter hosted negotiations between Anwar Sadat and Israeli prime minister Menachem Begin at Camp

FIGURE 8.2. Egyptian president Anwar Sadat (*standing*) shakes hands with Israeli prime minister Menachem Begin in the Israeli Knesset, on November 20, 1977. At right is chairman of the parliament, Yitzhak Shamir.

David. They first drew up the Framework for an Egyptian-Israeli Peace Treaty. Israel agreed to withdraw from the Sinai Peninsula in stages, while the United States pledged to bear the costs for the construction of two airfields in the Negev Desert to replace those lost to Egypt and for the relocation of the Israeli settlers who had been living in the Sinai Peninsula. In return, Israel would have unfettered access to the Suez Canal and the Straits of Tiran for shipping. Diplomatic relations would be established between the two countries, and a formal treaty would be signed within three months. This deadline was missed as the two sides continued to struggle over the details of the Camp David Accords, but in the end, Egypt and Israel signed the treaty on March 25, 1979, with the basic provisions from 1978 intact. Israel completed its withdrawal from the Sinai in 1982.

The Camp David Accords also attempted to open the door to a more comprehensive settlement to address the inevitable Arab backlash against Egypt for negotiating a separate peace. In the Framework for Peace in the Middle East, which pertained to the Palestinian situation, the Israeli leadership agreed to withdraw its military government and civilian administrations from the Occupied Territories and to replace them with an administrative council made up of Palestinians. After a five-year transition period, Israel would withdraw troops from unspecified sectors of the West Bank and Gaza Strip. This plan was never implemented, but if it had been, Palestinians would have attained a measure of control over their most immediate municipal arrangements even though ultimate jurisdiction over the Palestinian lands taken in 1967 would have remained with the Israelis. Furthermore, the nature of the administrative council was not specified, and Israel retained veto power over the form that any future Palestinian state might take. The status of Jerusalem and the Israeli settlers who had moved into the Occupied Territories after 1967 was left out of the proposal.

Ninth Arab Summit

Palestinian and Arab leaders, as expected, opposed both parts of the Camp David Accords and accused the Egyptian government of signing a separate peace with Israel. At the Ninth Arab Summit in Baghdad in November 1978, Arab leaders voted to expel Egypt from the Arab League and move its headquarters from Cairo to Tunis. Even Jordan and Saudi Arabia, who had been staunch US allies over the years, opposed the Egyptian action and agreed to the Arab League censure of Egypt. On October 6, 1981, during a military parade commemorating the crossing of the Suez Canal in 1973, soldiers adhering to a militant strand of Islamism assassinated Anwar Sadat for going to Jerusalem and for signing the peace treaty with Israel; Vice President Husni Mubarak entered office in his stead. Arab League headquarters did not return to Cairo until 1990 when Egypt was readmitted as a full member.

Palestinian Organizations

The 1967 war shifted the position of the Palestinians in relation to Israel and the Arab states because they could no longer rely on an Arab leader—even Nasser—to win back their land for them. Palestinian-run organizations took the cause into their own hands by initiating attacks against Israel and any Arab state that opposed their plans. They also set up state-like institutions to provide services for Palestinian refugees and recruit followers to their cause. They rejected any attempt by Arab leaders to speak on their behalf.

No Palestinian state had emerged from the 1948 war, as Israel, Egypt, and Jordan took control over territories that had been part of the Palestine Mandate; as many as 750,000 Palestinians fled the fighting or were forced out by Israeli troops during the war. They moved into the West Bank, the Gaza Strip, Lebanon, Syria, and Egypt. Many of the refugees lived in camps under the organizational structure of the United Nations Relief and Works Agency for Palestine Refugees (UNRWA); others moved into the surrounding Arab towns and cities. In 1949, the United Nations passed Resolution 194 affirming Palestinian refugees' right to repatriation and/or compensation for the loss of their property. In 1950, in order to become a member of the UN, Israel was required to agree to this resolution, but it has never implemented its provisions.

Among the Arab states, Lebanon imposed the most severe restrictions on the 100,000 to 130,000 refugees who arrived by 1949. Lebanese regulations placed limits on the Palestinian places of legal residence, freedom to travel in certain parts of the country or abroad, categories of private employment, and license to own property or conduct business. Predominantly Muslim, the Palestinian refugees would have upset the sectarian balance in Lebanon if they had been accorded national rights. Syria took in 85,000 to 100,000 refugees in 1949, and Egypt granted residency to about 7,000 Palestinians and took over jurisdiction of the Gaza Strip, with about 200,000 refugees and 88,000 original residents. The Gaza Strip remained subject to emergency law from 1949 to 1962. Under that system, a military administration headed by a governor-general held authority for virtually all local affairs and also controlled issuance of documents for foreign travel. The All-Palestine Government continued to function in the Gaza Strip until dissolved into the UAR in 1958, but it held little independent authority under Egyptian supervision. In all three countries, citizenship was granted to a negligible minority, with the majority of refugees issued residency permits and various types of travel documents. None of these documents offered much security in terms of residency, work, or travel.

On April 24, 1950, the Jordanian parliament, with representatives elected from the West Bank, East Jerusalem, and the original provinces of Jordan on the East Bank, ratified the union of these territories into the Hashemite Kingdom of Jordan. Palestinians received citizenship in this arrangement so had rights to enter the civil service and engage in commerce. The governing system nonetheless discriminated against Palestinians by underrepresenting their numbers in parliament. In addition, over the next two decades, the Jordanian government provided little development aid for the West Bank. As a result many Palestinians began moving to the East Bank to take advantage of additional opportunities emerging there; still others moved to Gulf States like Kuwait for jobs.

Palestine Liberation Organization

The Palestine Liberation Organization (PLO) arose from an Arab Summit meeting in Cairo convened in January 1964 to discuss how to stop Israel from diverting waters from Lake Tiberias (Sea of Galilee), a goal that was not achieved. After the summit, Ahmed Shuqayri, minister of the recently dissolved All-Palestine Government in Gaza, convened a Palestinian assembly in East Jerusalem in May 1964, where 422 Palestinian representatives declared the formation of the PLO, with the newly organized Palestinian National Council (PNC) empowered to serve as its highest authority. This new entity was dominated by members of established Palestinian families, those whose ancestors had held similar positions in the nascent state institutions of the Mandate era, joined by professionals who had been educated in the Arab host countries and abroad since 1948.

Led by Shuqayri, a smaller executive committee stood in the same position as any state cabinet, with members holding specialized ministerial portfolios. The PLO's founding charter declared that the boundaries of the state were those of the British Mandate. The Palestine Liberation Army (PLA) served as the PLO's armed force, but since its commander was Egyptian, King Hussein refused to allow its troops to be stationed on Jordanian soil. Thus, its effectiveness as a Palestinian force that could move around the region was limited. Nasser also tightly supervised the PLO so it had very little independent decision-making power.

Arab National Movement

It was not the PLO but Palestinian fedayeen groups, led by university graduates mainly from middle- and lower-middle-class backgrounds, who managed to mobilize the passions of the Palestinians. Throughout the Arab world in the 1950s and 1960s they found common cause at universities and while seeking work in their host Arab countries or the Persian Gulf states. They spoke most effectively to the Palestinians in the refugee camps and those impassioned by the Arab political arena and were the chief proponents of using force to retake Palestine. Their accession to leadership positions in the Palestinian community paralleled the shifts that took place in the surrounding countries after the military coups, when young and well-educated activists took leadership positions away from the old elites.

During the 1950s, many politically active Palestinians joined Arab nationalist parties because they believed that Arab unity provided the

FIGURE 8.3. PLO leaders Yasser Arafat, George Habash, and Nayif Hawatma, with Lebanese Communist leader George Hawi in Algiers, Algeria, on February 19, 1983.

best hope for regaining Palestine. Once Gamal Abdel Nasser had become an Arab hero for standing up to the West, many looked to him to lead the way. An example of such a party was the Arab Nationalist Movement (ANM), which coalesced in 1951 around George Habash and activists at the American University of Beirut. As they graduated with medical and engineering degrees and moved to Jordan to practice, they focused their political work on the liberation of Palestine. They slowly acquired a following, helped by their medical work and by publications they produced in Amman and Beirut. Throughout the 1950s and 1960s, the ANM hewed to Nasserism and the belief that only through the unity of the Arab peoples could Palestine be won back. In December 1967, the ANM merged with other newly established militia groups to become the Marxist-Leninist Popular Front for the Liberation of Palestine (PFLP). In December 1969, ideological differences created a split in the organization and Nayif Hawatma formed the Democratic Front for the Liberation of Palestine (DFLP).

Fatah

The organization Fatah ("Conquest," the reverse acronym for Harakat al-Tahrir al-Watani al-Filastini, or the Palestine Liberation Movement) was founded in Kuwait in the late 1950s by Yasser Arafat and colleagues who had been student activists in Cairo and had moved to Kuwait for work after graduation. Fatah occupied a unique space within the political spectrum because the organization declared it would not rely on the Arab states to take the lead in liberating Palestine but would do so itself. To accomplish this goal, Fatah called for armed struggle to liberate Palestine and began attracting support from pro-Soviet countries around the world as the cause became enmeshed in the movements of decolonization and superpower rivalries at the core of the Cold War. It also gained strength after the 1963 coup in Syria, where succeeding governments allowed the organization to set up training bases in the country. Fatah launched its first military attacks against Israel in the mid-1960s. They were ineffective as tools for influencing Israeli policy but garnered support from Palestinians desiring a more active policy to retake their national land.

Fedayeen in Jordan

After the war of 1967, Palestinian fedayeen from across the political spectrum made the decision to follow the path of Fatah and initiate military attacks against Israel. Jordan was the logical base for this strategy because it has the longest border with Israel and sits alongside the West Bank and its large Palestinian population. By early 1968, the Palestinian fedayeen forces and the Israeli military engaged in almost daily attacks across the Jordanian-Israeli border. The largest battle took place in the village of Karama on March 21, 1968, when Israel sent troops to attack this Fatah stronghold. During the raid, the Israeli forces destroyed much of the town, but in the end had to retreat in the face of the Palestinian and Jordanian defense. The unity shown between Palestinian and Jordanian forces at Karama, however, did not last long, and by the end of the year intense clashes between them were the norm. From the Jordanian perspective, the Palestinian fedayeen had set up a state-within-a-state along the West Bank that threatened the sovereignty of the Hashemite state. The Palestinians saw Jordan as the best location for militarily defeating the Israelis while also hoping they could weaken the pro-American King Hussein.

Black September

The tipping point came on September 6 and 9, 1970, when the PFLP hijacked four airplanes, landing three in Amman (American, British, and Swiss planes) and one in Cairo (an American plane). With this new provocation, King Hussein set up a military government on September 15 and commenced an attack against the fedayeen. Over the next months, the Jordanian army gained the upper hand in the fighting and succeeded in forcing the fedayeen to leave the country, killing thousands of fedayeen and civilians in what became known as Black September. The majority of the fighters left to set up base in southern Lebanon and Beirut. Palestinian organizations also took the fight to Europe with, for example, a group of Palestinian activists calling themselves Black September kidnapping Israeli athletes at the Olympics in Munich in 1972. The kidnapping was carried out to pressure Israel to release Palestinian prisoners held in its jails. It ended with a firefight between the kidnappers and German police that left all 11 Israeli athletes dead. None of the prisoners in Israel were released.

Arafat and the PLO

While taking the lead over the Arab states in attacking Israel, these fedayeen groups and their new members, led by Fatah, also wrested control of the PLO away from its original leadership and its Egyptian supervision. Yasser Arafat became chairman of the PLO on February 4, 1969, after which the PLO served as an umbrella organization for Palestinian-run organizations. The PLO, dominated by Fatah, became a state-in-exile as it built up institutions mostly in Beirut, addressing the needs of Palestinians throughout the region. In the process of shifting leadership and goals, the PLO grew increasingly authoritarian, with Arafat himself overseeing all policies, funding, and activities. The PLO and its associated groups provided many services but allowed only a tiny circle of top officials to participate in decision making.

The PLO under Arafat maintained the PNC and the Executive Committee of the old PLO as the legislative bodies and established other institutions to fulfill the needs of the organization: the Central Council as a subgroup of the PNC, a Political Department for foreign relations, and a Military Department to oversee the PLA. The PLO also began creating institutions to provide a social welfare net for the Palestinian refugees in the Arab host countries and under Israeli occupation. For example, in succeeding years the PLO established the Palestine National Fund (PNF); the Departments of Education, Information, and Popular Mobilization; a Social Affairs Institute; and a research center. During the 1970s, the United Nations accorded the PLO observer status, and several states granted the PLO diplomatic recognition.

Financing for the PLO came partly from taxes and remittances from Palestinians working in the Gulf, but the vast majority came as donations from international sources. At the 1974 Arab Summit in Rabat, Morocco, when the Arab ministers recognized the PLO as the sole representative of the Palestinian people, the oil states of the Gulf began sending yearly payments of hundreds of millions of dollars to the PLO to help in its resistance to Israel. Fatah and Jordan coordinated some of these "steadfast funds" to channel money directly into the Occupied Territories in the form of aid for agriculture, housing, education, and municipal activities. By the 1980s, PLO-affiliated organizations and institutions proliferated in the refugee camps and in the Territories, primarily supplying health care and educational services.

Palestinians under Israeli Occupation

After the 1967 war, approximately one million Palestinians came under Israeli occupation in East Jerusalem, the West Bank, and the Gaza Strip, and in the years that followed, many PLO-sponsored organizations were formed in the Territories. The fedayeen groups had already mobilized refugees and others to their organizations before 1967. The process continued apace in the Occupied Territories as young professionals took the lead in forming associations for aid and political activism, attracting support from merchants, manufacturers, and teachers. An increasing number of Palestinians graduated from universities throughout the Arab world and from the three new universities established in the West Bank—Birzeit, Bethlehem, and al-Najah Universities—and Islamic University in Gaza. Over time, many of the new organizations affiliated themselves with one or another of the fedayeen groups within the PLO according to whichever philosophy the organization's leadership favored.

Economic Development under Jordan and Egypt

Once the Israelis occupied the Territories, little economic development occurred, reflecting Israeli policies and a legacy of neglect under the Jordanian and Egyptian governments. Although Jordan had made promises that the East and West Banks would be treated equally when union took place in 1950, before 1967 the East Bank received the bulk of state revenues, and most government agencies were housed there. Thousands of Palestinians moved to the East Bank or migrated to the Gulf States for work during this period. In Gaza, a small minority of the population had lived and cultivated mostly citrus crops before 1948, and when the refugees poured into the Strip in 1948 and 1949, the economy could not sustain them. Most lived in refugee camps, served by UNRWA. Almost no development took place in Gaza under Egyptian control in the early 1950s, but after a brief Israeli occupation in 1955 and the events of the Suez Crisis of 1956, the Egyptian government increased the amount of development funds available but not enough to diversify and strengthen the economy substantially.

Israeli Economic Policies

In 1968, Israel banned independent Palestinian exports to European markets but allowed export to Arab countries where Israel could not conduct trade. Otherwise, Israel imposed heavy restrictions on production, cultivation, imports, and exports to guarantee that Palestinian products could not compete with those grown or produced in Israel. Under these conditions and with few local jobs available by the end of the 1970s, about a third of all Palestinian workers labored in Israel. By 1985, almost half of Gaza's labor force worked in Israel. In raw numbers, the Palestinians were making more money than they did before the occupation and could afford to buy more consumer goods than before.

The cost for this policy on the Palestinians, however, was increasing dependence on the Israeli economy, which provided uneven benefits for

Palestinian workers. In times of recession, such as the late 1970s and early 1980s, many Palestinians lost their jobs because of economic retraction. Furthermore, with relatively few products produced in the Territories, the bulk of consumer goods came from Israel, intensifying the Palestinian economic dependence on Israel. Palestinian workers also received lower salaries than Israelis, and few received the health care and social security benefits that Israeli workers did. Even so, Palestinian workers employed in Israel had to pay the social benefits tax as their Israeli counterparts did.

Israeli Settlements

In the immediate aftermath of the 1967 war, Israelis began establishing settlements in the West Bank, East Jerusalem, and Gaza. The first years saw the spread of primarily agricultural settlements in the Jordan Valley with the locations strategically chosen to take advantage of the fertility of the region and to enable fortifications to be built along the Jordanian border with Israel. By the late 1970s and early 1980s, the settlements had extended to the urban areas, becoming bedroom communities for such cities as West Jerusalem and Tel Aviv. In Gaza the settlements were agricultural, with settlers primarily cultivating citrus fruits. In the first decade after the 1967 war, the average number of new settlers throughout the Occupied Territories was about 770; in the second decade, the number increased to 5,400. By 1984, the number of settlers overall exceeded 10,000, living in more than 120 settlements.

Israeli settlers moving into the homes believed they were reclaiming the territories they called biblical Judea and Samaria, and others were enticed by the numerous economic incentives the Israeli state offered to those willing to live in a settlement. The initial settlements were built on state land but soon expanded to land owned by individual Palestinians. Almost no Palestinians were willing to sell land to Israelis, so the Israeli government confiscated it by declaring it military or green land, thus restricting residential development on it, or by claiming that the Palestinian owners did not have valid ownership papers.

Palestinian Resistance

Except for the 1976 Municipal Council elections that the Israeli government organized, no elections could take place; press censorship and banning of books were the norm. Infractions came with swift arrest and often administrative detention, which allowed the Israeli military to hold a prisoner without charge for extended periods of time. By 1985, almost a quarter of a million Palestinians had found themselves under interrogation or in detention. The Israeli authorities also used collective punishment against the Palestinian population in the Territories, including demolition of homes of suspected activists. To lead the resistance movement against the Israeli occupation, all the fedayeen groups formed an umbrella group called the Palestine National Front (PNF) in 1974, followed in the 1980s by the Fatah-dominated National Guidance Committee (NGC), which included organizations working on behalf of students, women, and workers and representing a wide spectrum of political ideologies. Through civil disobedience tactics, the affiliated associations organized to protest Israeli land confiscations, deportation of political leaders, and the treatment of political prisoners.

The electoral wins by the new Likud Party in 1978 ushered in new restrictions on organizing in the Territories; nonetheless, the 1980s witnessed a dramatic growth of mass organizations among Palestinians. When the Israeli government banned the NGC in the early part of the decade, Palestinians throughout the Territories filled in the vacuum by forming hundreds of popular committees that brought Palestinians together to provide health care and support for families and to address workers' rights issues. These committees had the advantage of providing real aid to the population while eschewing the outward marks of resistance that would have made them direct targets for Israeli repression. Over the years, they brought into the movement tens of thousands of young people who were politicized by the collective work they were doing. By the late 1980s, more than 400 local organizations, institutions, associations, and committees operated in all Palestinian towns, villages, and refugee camps. These organizations had local leadership who addressed local problems. But their sheer number and the fact that they were all, in different ways, mobilizing to empower Palestinians against the occupation nationalized and united their activities.

Intifada

The First Intifada (uprising) began on December 8, 1987, with a traffic accident between Israelis and Palestinians. But that event was just the spark causing the Palestinians to rise up against the occupation and their treatment by the Israeli government. The uprising included nearly all sectors of Palestinian society because of the extensive organizing that had taken place in the two decades before and, as a result, the movement was sustained for years. Popular committees joined the uprising in 1987 by

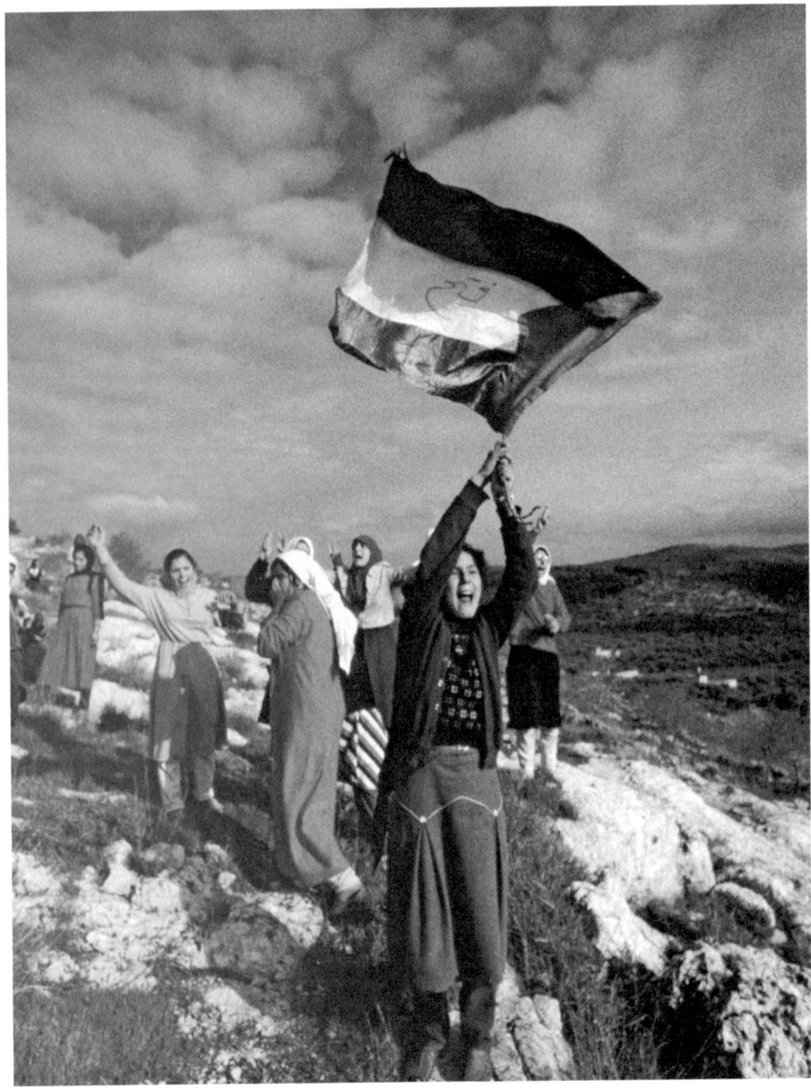

FIGURE 8.4. A young woman waves the outlawed Palestinian flag over a hilltop in the West Bank village of Beita during the First Palestinian Intifada in 1988.

organizing collective Palestinian actions throughout the Territories, supervised by the Unified National Leadership of the Uprising (UNLU) and led by the major political groups represented in the PLO.

UNLU issued communiqués that laid out weekly actions for the popular committees to undertake, including Palestinian boycotts of the Israeli economy and strikes against Israeli employers. Although the Israeli economy suffered, these measures hit the Palestinians harder, especially as they had become so dependent on the Israeli economy for jobs and products, with few other venues available to them since 1967. In addition to eliminating jobs and reducing wages, the Israelis also often cut phone lines and electricity and fuel supplies. Prolonged curfews particularly disrupted agricultural production in the villages where entire crops were lost because farmers were unable to irrigate or harvest their fields at the proper times.

Parallel to the UNLU and often in coordination with it was Hamas (Harakat al-Muqawama al-Islamiyya, or the Islamic Resistance Movement), founded in 1988 as an affiliate of the Muslim Brotherhood. Its first manifesto pledged that Hamas would work with the PLO in the Intifada, fighting for Palestinian nationalist goals but functioning independently of other Palestinian groups.

HAMAS

The Muslim Brotherhood founded its first Palestinian branch in Jerusalem in 1946. After 1948, Gamal Abdel Nasser banned the Brotherhood in Gaza as he had done in Egypt. Leaders were imprisoned for years, and the Brotherhood then had to function underground in Egypt. In the Palestinian territories under Jordanian rule, the Muslim Brotherhood had a good relationship with King Hussein so was able to function openly.

Under Israeli occupation, especially in Gaza, the Brotherhood initiated an era of institution building. The strongest, the Islamic Center, was run by 11 leaders of the Brotherhood, who used funds from Islamic charitable funds (zakat) to organize a mosque, medical clinic, sports club, and women's training center to cater to Palestinians who were not well served by the PLO. The Israelis recognized it as a charity, and it gradually took control over the many new mosques being built throughout the Gaza Strip in the 1970s and 1980s. The men leading the Islamic Center were not religious-trained clerics but engineers and doctors who wanted to spread ideas about how to live a pious Muslim life.

When the First Intifada broke out in December 1987, Brotherhood leaders decided to resist the occupation openly by forming Hamas as the political wing of the organization while Brotherhood institutions continued to maintain their services. These institutions aid Hamas in its ability to collect funds and to attract supporters for its activities in both the Gaza Strip and in the West Bank and East Jerusalem.

In January 1988, Hamas began to take on an institutional form and in August issued its Charter, which declares that Palestine is an Islamic endowment (waqf) and it is incumbent upon all Muslims to wage jihad to win back its independence. Once independence is achieved, Hamas's goal is to create an Islamic state for Palestine. The Charter rejects the path of negotiations that engaged the PLO and the Israeli government in the Oslo process in the 1990s because the Palestinians would have to give up part of the Islamic endowment.

Hamas named its military wing the 'Izz al-Din al-Qassam brigade in honor of the fighter for Palestine who had been killed in an attack by the British in 1935. Until 1994, the brigade's actions targeted the Israeli military. After Israeli Baruch Goldstein killed 17 Muslims praying in the Ibrahimi mosque in Hebron in 1994, Hamas began using suicide bombers to attack both civilian and military targets.

The Intifada continued until 1993, but the first Gulf War of 1990–1991eliminated much of the funding the PLO had received from Arab oil states as promised after the 1974 Rabat Summit. Arafat came out in support of Saddam Hussein's invasion of Kuwait in August 1992, and in retaliation the Gulf States cut their funding for the organization. The stress of the Intifada on the Palestinian communities inside the Territories, in terms of personal and economic losses, took its toll by the early 1990s as well.

Lebanese Civil War

While Palestinians forged a resistance movement inside the Israeli Occupied Territories, the PLO fedayeen groups converged on Lebanon in the 1970s and helped destabilize a Lebanese sectarian structure already teetering. After the majority of the fedayeen had moved from Jordan to Lebanon after Black September, fedayeen and Israeli attacks intensified across the Israeli-Lebanese border. These skirmishes contributed to the outbreak of the 1975 Lebanese civil war because some sects chose to ally with the Palestinian cause while others fought against the Palestinians. The Christian population largely opposed the PLO's activities since they brought Lebanon into an Arab fight. The Muslim and Druze forces largely supported the PLO's actions in the Arab fight for political unity and Palestinian liberation. Lebanon represents a case of a country devolving into a violent civil war between 1975 and 1990 because its precarious balance-of-power politics could not be maintained in the face of economic recession, a rising generation of youth disillusioned with old elites, the establishment of sectarian militias, and the arrival of the Palestinian fedayeen.

Economic Crises

Lebanon had twice the annual per capita GNP of any other country in the region besides those reliant on oil by the mid-1960s, the country continued to be the intermediary between Western markets and the Arab hinterland, and as early as 1948, some 30 percent of the world's gold transited through Beirut to the Gulf monarchies to pay for oil. In the 1950s, Lebanon benefited from the nationalization taking place in countries all around it, as world capital found the country's still private—and lightly regulated—banking system advantageous for business. Lebanon also prospered through services, tourism, construction, and the many foreign companies established in Beirut.

But under the surface stood stark economic inequalities where about 4 percent of the population controlled an enormous segment of the GNP. Furthermore, Lebanon instituted a regressive taxation system with duties imposed on fuel, salt, and tobacco but not on higher-end luxury goods. By the mid-1960s, these problems were coming to the surface with a series of labor strikes throughout the country, including workers in the oil industry, state schools, and the bureaucracy. Peasants waged a countrywide movement against the benefits accruing to large agribusinesses. In the early 1970s, more peasant and worker actions broke out as the economic situation remained discriminatory against them. The state in reaction frequently passed legislation to alleviate some of the problems, such as a minimum wage and a social security law, but the private owners of business and their allies in the parliament worked to guarantee that few laws were enforced. Given the realities of power in the country, the state did not have the coercive capacities to force them to accede to its legislation.

By 1975, the country was filled with thousands of university graduates frustrated by the glass ceiling, of workers poorly treated in factories, and of peasants finding their livelihoods threatened by economic change. With the Maronites and Sunnis dominating the system, many Lebanese, particularly the Shi'a, who formed the largest and poorest segment of the society, were largely left out of the largesse any group could dispense, and typically the state had only minimal resources to extend to them. As a result, a pivotal challenge to the system came not from the military or political parties but from below, as the society began to demand new kinds of leaders.

Shi'a in Lebanon

The challenge to sectarian leaders became particularly acute in the Shi'i community because the leading figures failed to give Shi'a an influential voice in the national system, despite their demographic growth throughout the 20th century. When Lebanon achieved independence after World War II, the Shi'a were officially recognized as the republic's third-largest community, but they remained relatively powerless well into the 1950s and 1960s. Only about 20 percent of the seats in the Chamber of Deputies were assigned to Shi'a, and they were allocated only the post of parliamentary speaker, which held little practical influence. To allow them a place at the government table commensurate with their numbers, the Maronites, Sunnis, and other groups would have had to give up a measure of their influence, and no Shi'i zu'ama put sufficient pressure on them to do so.

Over time, the Shi'i community also became economically and societally diverse, with many leaving the agricultural realm and finding new jobs in the cities. Some grew wealthy in the gold and diamond mines of West Africa; others migrated to North and South America. As state school building expanded into Shi'i areas in the 1960s under Fu'ad Shihab's guidance, graduates attained professional positions throughout Lebanon. These groups demanded patrons who could obtain jobs for Shi'a at home while improving the economic climate for their international investments.

By the mid-1960s, a number of political parties and movements competed for the support of the newly politicized Shi'a. Most were secular, such as the Lebanese Communist and Kamal Jumblatt's Progressive Socialist Parties. Sayyid Musa al-Sadr, however, appealed to them specifically as Shi'a. He was Iranian by birth but Lebanese by descent, a member of a prominent Shi'i religious family and trained in Islamic theology and jurisprudence. In the 15 years before the civil war, he employed the central symbols of Shi'ism, especially the martyrdom of Muhammad's grandson Hussein, to mobilize support among the Shi'a because those events provided a guide for rising up against oppressors of all kinds. He also attracted a dedicated cadre of Shi'i nouveaux riche who saw in him the means for reducing the power of the traditional Shi'i leadership and increasing their own role in politics.

Al-Sadr accepted the presidency of the Supreme Shi'i Council upon its establishment in 1969, guaranteeing that the old-time Shi'i zu'ama could not use the council for their own aggrandizement. The council had been authorized by the Chamber of Deputies and provided for the first time a representative body for the Shi'a independent of the Sunni Muslims. Through the council, al-Sadr made demands for the defense of the south from Israeli attack, provision of development funds for the Shi'i community, construction and improvement of schools and hospitals, and an increase in the number of Shi'a appointed to senior government positions. In 1974, he founded the Movement of the Deprived, whose militia over time took the name Amal ("hope" in Arabic). While popular with many segments of the Shi'i community, it had attracted only a portion of the Shi'a by the time the civil war erupted in 1975, while other parties, such as the PSP and the Communist Party, continued to siphon off others. In 1978, the situation changed when al-Sadr disappeared on a visit to Libya, never to been seen again. In the aftermath, al-Sadr became a powerful symbol for Shi'a and a focal point for mobilizing for the Amal movement.

Start of the Civil War

The Lebanese civil war broke out on April 13, 1975, with shootings of Lebanese Christian and Palestinian civilians. The fighting initially pitted the Christian militias (the Lebanese Front) that made up an uneasy coalition of Gemayel family's Kata'ib and a military force under the command of Samir Geagea against the Muslim- and Druze-affiliated forces (the Lebanese National Movement, LNM) led by Kamal Jumblatt. But these coalitions did not maintain their cohesion for long, and it was common for members to switch allegiances during the war. It was by no means solely a Christian versus Muslim fight, as intrasectarian fighting over territory and leadership over the sect frequently occurred. At the beginning of the war the Shi'a were mostly supportive of Palestinian goals; by the 1980s, some of the Shi'i groups were perpetrating attacks against Palestinians in retaliation for bringing Israeli violence to Lebanon. At times, Palestinian fedayeen even fought Palestinian fedayeen.

The war lasted 15 years but was made up of several discrete segments, with fighting frequently shifting to different parts of the country and away from others. The civil war also saw moments of quiet when all involved predicted that the war had come to an end, only for it to flare up again. The

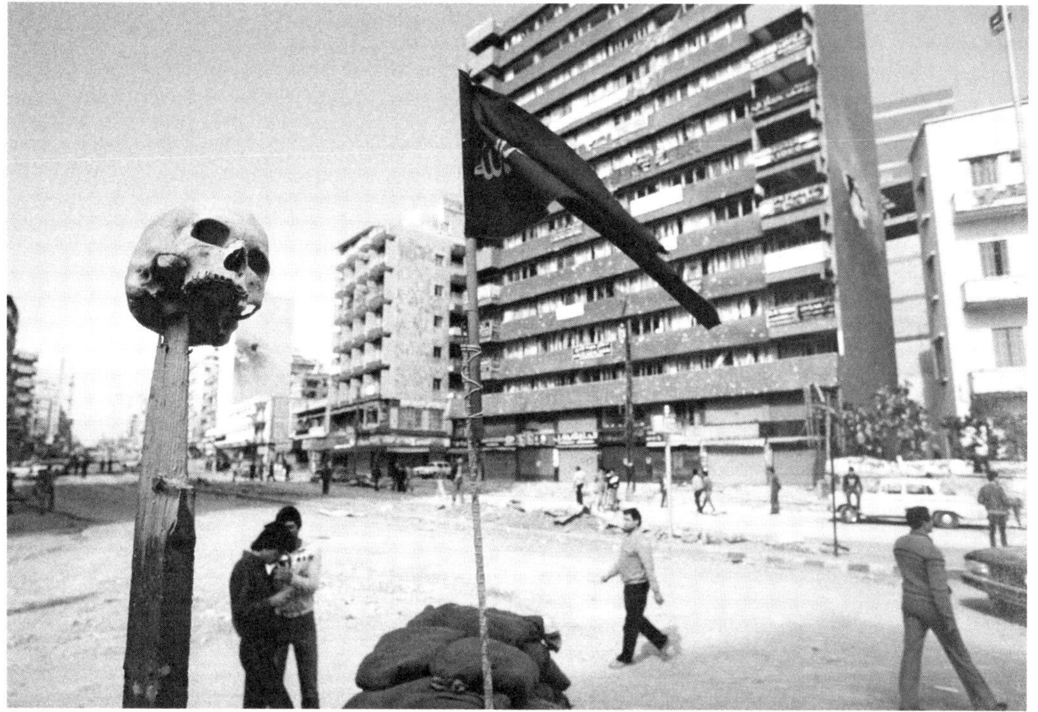

FIGURE 8.5. During the Lebanese civil war a human skull looks out over a checkpoint at the entrance of West Beirut during a lull in fighting in 1984.

fighting divided Beirut through most of the war and in the end destroyed the center of the city. All the surrounding states, as well as the United States, the USSR, and European nations played pivotal roles by providing weaponry, funds, troops, and training to the various militia organizations. With this aid, the fighting was prolonged still further. Tens of thousands died from aerial bombardments and street-to-street fighting; civilians were by no means protected. Most soldiers of the Lebanese Army defected to the militias, so the army almost ceased to exist as a national institution. Although Lebanon had a government throughout the war, it could do little to fight the actions of the militias and the intervening foreign powers.

Syrian Intervention

On June 1, 1976, the Syrian government sent three military detachments into Lebanon and by mid-October had taken control over much of central Lebanon and its urban centers. In October the Arab League met in Cairo and declared that an Arab Deterrence Force (ADF) would be sent to Lebanon to maintain peace between the warring sides. From the beginning, Syrians dominated the command structure and served as the majority of the soldiers, so, in essence, the Arab League decision provided cover for the Syrian intervention that had already taken place. Syria had entered Lebanon to prevent its partition and the possibility that Israel would take advantage of such an eventuality. Syria vacillated between supporting the Muslim, Druze, and the Christian forces, at all times working to guarantee that no group could grow powerful enough to control the entire country. When the war ended, Syrian military forces remained in place throughout Lebanon. They did not withdraw until spring 2005, pressured to do so because of massive anti-Syrian demonstrations following the assassination of former prime minister Rafiq Hariri.

Israeli Intervention

With relations improving between Israel and Egypt in the mid-1970s, Israel had a free hand to intervene in Lebanon because the threat of having to fight a war on two fronts had disappeared. Accordingly, as the Lebanese militias formed and Palestinians and Israelis attacked each other across the border, Israel began training and supplying portions of the Lebanese Christian forces and dissident units of the Lebanese army. Under the command of Major Sa‘d Haddad, these efforts established the Army of Free Lebanon, which evolved in 1980 into the South Lebanon Army (SLA).

In March 1978, Israel launched Operation Litani to invade southern

Lebanon and destroy the PLO's forces in the region south of the Litani River. The Israeli military failed in this endeavor, as the fedayeen maintained their organizational cohesion, but the destruction throughout southern Lebanon was widespread. Thousands of people died during the invasion, and hundreds of thousands fled north, most to the southern suburbs of Beirut. They included Lebanese Christians and Palestinians but mostly Shi'a, the demographic majority in the south. In late 1978, the United Nations Interim Force in Lebanon (UNIFIL) moved into southern Lebanon to confirm the withdrawal of Israeli forces from the country and act as a buffer between the Israeli and Palestinian forces. Neither force respected the UNIFIL mission, however, and fighting continued.

On June 6, 1982, the Israeli army invaded Lebanon again in the Peace for Galilee mission, but this time with more massive force than in 1978 and with more ambitious goals. Whereas Prime Minister Menachem Begin and Defense Minister Ariel Sharon characterized the attack using much the same language of 1978, by claiming they were aiming at PLO sites in southern Lebanon, they actually planned to quickly move on to Beirut so they could pacify all areas in between. Their goal was to completely destroy the PLO infrastructure in Lebanon and set up a 40-kilometer security zone in Lebanon along Israel's northern border. The first days of fighting saw a combination of a ground invasion and an enormous air battle with Syria over Beirut. Israel soon extended its reach to the Syrian Soviet-supplied surface-to-air (SAM) missile batteries in the Bekaa Valley. In the process, Israeli forces completely encircled the PLO and their allies inside West Beirut, cutting off food, water, and electricity supplies to all its residents and bombarding them from the air.

In August 1982, to defuse the crisis and protect civilians in West Beirut, a Multi-National Force (MNF) made up of American and French troops agreed to enter Beirut and supervise the departure of the PLO fighters from Lebanon. By September 1, the PLO fighters had left, and Fatah and the PLO set up headquarters in Tunisia. On September 10, MNF forces started to withdraw, leaving Lebanese army forces to protect the citizens of West Beirut. On September 15, Israeli forces moved into West Beirut in contravention of the agreement and occupied the PLO offices. On September 16 and for the next two days, the Maronite Kata'ib militia massacred Palestinian refugees in the Sabra and Shatila refugee camps in Beirut, while Israeli forces stationed outside prevented anyone from entering or leaving the camps during the attack. Possibly more than 3,000 Palestinians died before the Kata'ib left and rescuers could enter the camps.

In the meantime, the Israelis had worked with Kata'ib leader Bashir Gemayel to help get him elected as the new president of Lebanon with the hopes that his government would sign a peace treaty with Israel. On August 19, parliament elected Bashir Gemayel to the position, but on September 14 he was killed in a bomb attack perpetrated by a Maronite connected to the Syrian Socialist National Party. By the time Amin Gemayel, Bashir's brother, was elected president on September 23, he could no longer openly support an alliance with Israel because recent events had intensified Lebanese anger against Israeli actions across most sectors of Lebanese society.

Last Years of the Civil War

US and French troops of the MNF then returned to supervise the departure of Israeli troops from West Beirut. The Israelis withdrew their forces but maintained military control over land along the border in southern Lebanon until May 2000. The Syrians remained in control of the Bekaa Valley and along the Beirut-Damascus Road, and Shi'i and Druze forces captured West Beirut. Christian and Druze forces fought for territory in Mount Lebanon. Even the Palestinian fedayeen moved back into Lebanon over the next couple of years in contravention of the agreement. On October 23, 1983, two truck bombs organized by the new Shi'i group Hizballah simultaneously blew up the US and French military barracks near the Beirut airport, killing more than 300 soldiers and hastening the withdrawal of the remainder of MNF troops.

By the war's end, about 150,000 people had been killed, tens of thousands wounded, and hundreds of thousands displaced and left destitute. By fall 1989, the majority of the participants were willing to head to the negotiating table to work out a political settlement. The surviving members of the 1972 Lebanese parliament met in Ta'if, Saudi Arabia, between September 30 and October 22 under the auspices of the Arab League. The parliamentarians at Ta'if were split evenly between Christians and Muslims, as was a smaller group of 16 that conducted most of the discussions. The Ta'if Accords were the result, approved by 58 of the 62 deputies. They granted more power to the Sunni prime minister, weakened the authority of the Christian president, and equalized the number of representatives Christians and Muslims could elect to parliament but maintained the sectarian system intact. The civil war did not substantially changed the balance of power, but it had opened up political room for the Shi'a, particularly Hizballah, to join the established power brokers, the Maronites and the Sunnis.

Shi'i Allegiances and Hizballah

Whether working through Amal or one of the other parties and militias, the Shi'a generally began the civil war supporting the position of the LNM, which brought together Jumblatt's PSP and much of the Palestinian fedayeen in a predominantly Muslim and Druze fighting force. Eventually, however, the Shi'a split between those who continued to support the Palestinian parties and the LNM and those who blamed the Palestinians for bringing destruction upon the Shi'a in the southern districts by attracting the involvement of the Israeli forces. Amal staked out a position in active opposition to the Palestinians, as epitomized by its 1980s "War of the Camps" and the resulting massacres against Palestinian refugees. On the other side of this equation stood a new organization of Shi'a—Hizballah—formed in 1982 as a movement in resistance to Israeli and Western involvement in Lebanon.

Hizballah emerged out of the specific circumstances of the Lebanese civil war, as Shi'a came under repeated attack in the south and as they moved by the hundreds of thousands to the southern suburbs of Beirut to flee the fighting when Israel invaded in 1978 and 1982. The programmatic document of 1985, an open letter addressed to the "Downtrodden in Lebanon and in the World," laid out the program Hizballah's founders sought to implement in Lebanon. It rejected institutions modeled on the West; instead, it advocated Islam as the solution to the economic and political problems the Shi'a faced. It declared its opposition to both Communism and the polity advocated by the United States. In particular, it heavily criticized the United States for its support of Israel. The letter also rejected the Lebanese government because of its corruption and declared that it must be destroyed since no reform was possible within the system. In its place, Hizballah advocated the establishment in Lebanon of the type of ulama-controlled government Ayatollah Khomeini had just instituted in Iran after the 1979 Islamic Revolution. By the 1990s, however, this provision became less prominent in Hizballah statements.

In addition to the 1983 bombings against the US and French marines, in the mid- to late 1980s, groups linked to Hizballah kidnapped dozens of foreigners, holding some for several months and years. A number were transported to Iran for imprisonment, and the Iranian government succeeded in using them as leverage with the United States during its war with Iraq in the 1980s, in the Iran-Contra Affair in which the United States sold weapons to Iran and used the profits to aid the Contras fighting against their government in Nicaragua. The program did achieve the release of some hostages, but the process of hostage taking did not cease; the last of the hostages was released only in 1991.

After the end of the civil war in 1989, Hizballah stated as its primary task resistance to Israeli occupation of Lebanese territory along the southern border. Its actions helped facilitate the May 2000 withdrawal of Israeli forces from the strip of land they held in the south, with only the area of Shebaa Farms still under Israeli control. Since then, the two groups have frequently fought across the border, with the largest battle taking place for 34 days in summer 2006, resulting in 1,300 Lebanese and 165 Israeli deaths. Hizballah also expanded its institutional reach by providing schooling, health services, and military training in much the same way as the leaders of the other sects did. By the late 1990s, Hizballah was fielding candidates for political office in the Lebanese government, achieving its long-awaited entrée into the inner circle of elite politicians by the mid-2000s.

Post-Civil War Lebanon

Despite the civil war and despite continuing pressures from below against the sectarian system, the role of the zu'ama has remained largely unchanged. Hizballah joined the power brokers, and the Shi'a attained more influence, but otherwise the only real shift was to give Muslims in general and the office of prime minister in particular more institutionalized power. The presidency—held still by a Maronite politician—lost influence in this new configuration. The Ta'if Accords not only maintained the sectarian bargain intact in Lebanon but actually intensified the power and potential for corruption the elites could wield under the exigencies of reconstruction from the massive destruction of the civil war. The state has grown weaker than before the war, but the country continues to function because the sectarian elites supply much of what would normally be considered state services and the government continues to provide basic services and security functions.

To a greater degree than in the years before the war, Lebanon's economic structure has been privatized in favor of the sectarian elites and their allies outside the country. Before the civil war a number of public institutions had provided services to the Lebanese citizenry, but since that time public-sector money has been largely used for private-sector companies instead of for rebuilding public-sector institutions.

One of the most pivotal politicians in the postwar period was Rafiq Hariri, who first won the prime ministership in 1992. He was a Sunni

Arab from Lebanon but earned a fortune as the head of a construction firm in Saudi Arabia and, as a reward, Saudi citizenship for his activities. Immediately after the civil war ended, he used the Council of Development and Reconstruction (CDR), which had been established in 1977, as his agency for rebuilding Lebanon. In 1991 he also set up Solidere, a company in charge of rebuilding Beirut's downtown area, destroyed completely by fighting around the Green Line demarcation that had separated Muslim from Christian neighborhoods. Speaker of Parliament Nabih Berri established Elyssar, a company to rebuild the Shi'i suburbs of southern Beirut. Linord was the company charged with reconstructing the mainly Christian areas of Beirut. Smaller companies were led by other sectarian leaders.

The example of Solidere shows how the Lebanese citizenry paid for the country's rebuilding while private companies reaped the profits. Although Solidere was a private company, it was given public funds and took over responsibility for city planning and construction regulation. This type of public-to-private fund transfer took place in other realms as private companies took over such normally public-sector roles as the postal service, water delivery, and garbage collection. This economic structure opened up great wealth for the elites but increased the level of government corruption and made the Lebanese citizenry among the most indebted in the world.

Conclusion

The conflicts between the 1950s and 1990s brought the United States and the USSR into competition in the Middle East, and their intervention helped intensify conflicts among the states as well. Unresolved conflicts such as that between the Arabs and Israelis flared up repeatedly throughout these decades as Israel fought to retain its land and the Arab states and the Palestinian fedayeen fought to regain it for Palestine. The Yemeni revolution brought Egypt and Saudi Arabia into armed conflict, but this was just a foreshadowing of the involvement of all the regional states in the Lebanese civil war. Once the era of military coups was over by the 1970s, state leaders accrued great wealth and power and established long-term rule and authoritarian control over their countries and citizenries.

RULERS FOR LIFE

State Construction, Consolidation, and Collapse

9

BY THE 1980S, Husni Mubarak of Egypt (r. 1980–2011), Hafiz al-Asad of Syria (r. 1970–2000), and Saddam Hussein of Iraq (r. 1979–2003) seemed to have achieved the status of rulers for life because they successfully embedded themselves at the core of their state-societal structures and appeared invulnerable; by the 1990s, they were grooming their own sons to replace them. In 1975, a member of the royal family killed King Faysal of Saudi Arabia (r. 1964–1975), but the system altered not at all and kings could be assured of long terms on the throne in that country as well. After the death of King Hussein of Jordan in 1999, his throne was passed on to his son Abdullah II. Notwithstanding the means by which they gained or lost their positions, leaders in Egypt, Jordan, Syria, Saudi Arabia, and Iraq can be examined together because they maintained their positions for such long periods of time by instituting similar governmental structures. The political structure in Turkey included a competitive electoral process, but military coups of 1960, 1971, and 1980 legitimized the independent power of the military, and many socioeconomic changes occurring in the Arab countries were replicated in Turkey.

Whether they came to the presidency via a military coup or heredity, the leaders of Saudi Arabia, Egypt, Jordan, Syria, Turkey, and Iraq maintained their hold over their governing systems because of the military, security, and repressive power they had at their disposal. But such force was not sufficient for the longevity the leaders attained. Unlike the policies of previous governments in these countries, the national projects enunciated by these leaders could not allow for the marginalization of entire segments of society. A measure of populism defined each of these states, even the monarchies, as the leaders all called for mobilizing the population for the revolutionary changes they were undertaking. The massive modernization projects promised and pledged by these leaders could not rely merely on the old elites because more workers were required to build transportation networks, electricity grids, health systems, and schools. Furthermore, all the leaders pledged an element of their legitimacy on providing services to an expanded public, proclaiming that they led a nation, not just an elite few. They called on the citizenry to be part of the national projects and then had to provide the avenues for such participation and mobilization; failing to do so would mean their downfall. The difference in Turkey is that civilian politicians and military officers traded leadership posts, and both had to contend with fractious voting publics.

Populations were brought into the state projects in unprecedented ways in these decades, but all these leaders had to perform a balancing act between addressing public demands and managing any potential public mobilization that could threaten their positions. Land reform transformed the countryside by breaking the power of the large landowners, strengthening middle-level landowners, and extending state control into every village. Peasants came to own land while also serving as government officials implementing state agricultural policies. Those who did not gain land or who found the land could no longer sustain them moved into the cities. By the 1980s all the countries under study here were predominantly urban societies. An increasing number of migrants joined their urban brethren and received training as professionals. Others moved into the rapidly expanding working class and some into the urban slums because they had few opportunities for permanent jobs despite the efforts to diversify state economies. The new kinds of governments ushered in a social welfare net where the state took on the role of providing basic services of health care, education, and employment for the population. Thus, a paternalistic umbrella overlay the sophisticated systems of managed mobilization that were implemented.

Only the Pahlavi state system has been overthrown, with the ouster of Mohammad Reza Shah by Iranian revolutionary forces in 1979. In this case, oil profits did not generate sufficient support for the government and the shah; strict control over political institutions did not forestall the creation of a broad-based opposition movement. The hallmarks of managed mobilization existed in the shah's Iran, but he could not keep his population quiescent when economic crises wracked the country in the mid-1970s.

Governing Systems and Structures

The Safavid, Ottoman, and Qajar Empires organized layers of intermediaries who extracted resources from the population and brought the state into people's lives. Over the centuries, these systems proved to be fluid as they adapted to changing conditions and as they consistently attracted new groups of stakeholders. For example, the role of the intermediaries changed with the reforms of the 19th century as provincial actors became more powerful in their local realms because of additional responsibilities the states imposed on them. The interwar periods saw the same intermediaries move into state office under colonial and independent rule, but the transition had begun that would weaken their local influence. States became increasingly the purveyor of services and largesse, and fewer local resources were controllable by the intermediaries.

The state systems established in the 1960s and 1970s throughout the Middle East continued to use intermediaries to help govern, but the structures in which they worked were far more rigid than anything seen in the past. The president or monarch held the ultimate decision-making power and sustained connections to the various entities functioning within state borders because he stood at the central hub of governance. Surrounding him were the ministers, generals, state court justices, top religious clerics, and close advisers who held the top governmental and military positions and were the primary stakeholders in the system. Of lesser influence were those in an outer circle, comprising the rest of the religious clerics employed by the state, professional and labor unions, and municipal and village officials. Unlike in the past, when a measure of power flowed to the center because networks offered services to the state, this system redirected the bulk of the flow from the center to the outer circles, through the intermediaries who had to rely on the state for the funds, jobs, and resources to be disbursed to their networks. These intermediaries included technocrats newly trained for the next stage of state and infrastructure building and tribal shaykhs and village leaders who performed much the same function as they had in the past but were now more dependent on the state than their predecessors were. The outermost circle included the citizenry at large who had to receive services from the state but who also had to be managed to make sure that they did not revolt against the leadership.

The governing structures became powerful because the citizenry had to interact with the state so frequently. Attending school, acquiring a job, buying land, accessing subsidized products, and traveling outside the country all required state-issued national identification numbers and documents that could be withdrawn as punishment for oppositional activity. Furthermore, the population became more active with the state through elections, jobs, and military conscription and began to recognize these conduits as the means for gaining advantages in the system. They could vote for someone who had specifically promised to provide services to their family, tribe, or region; they could see how to move up through the hierarchy of a state agency or ministry through connections to those powerful individuals or through their own merit. At the same time, managed mobilization strategies worked to eliminate most independent action. To guarantee that the system was not disrupted, state leaders put into place control mechanisms, such as constraints on licenses for nongovernmental political parties and restrictions on who had the right to run in national elections.

While many of the relationships were controlled by the center, a degree of flexibility remained in each of these governing systems. The stakeholders of the states did not remain static even as presidents and kings settled in for long periods of governance. Leaders constantly found ways to shift new individuals and interest groups inside the central circle while pushing out others who had lost their usefulness or who had become too powerful and threatening. Such a shift can be seen in Syria in the transition from the al-Jadid government to that run by Hafiz al-Asad in 1970. The earlier Ba'th government had privileged the rural areas in the late 1960s, while the al-Asad government brought the Sunni Arab merchant elite of Damascus and Aleppo back into the halls of government to strengthen the economy and diversify the power base.

Regardless of how strong state leaders became, they could not fully control relationships in the outer circles. The new types of intermediaries maintained overlapping identities as members of tribes or of a given religious sect. What they could not do was use those other identities to build networks to challenge the leadership or the overall governing system. Individuals could be moved into or out of positions in any of the circles of influence, but the superstructure itself was not supposed to be changed as a result. Only in Iran in 1979 did the structure collapse completely, as

FIGURE 9.1. As in many towns throughout Syria, a statue of President Hafiz al-Asad stands in a plaza in Damascus.

groups from every region and social strata rose up to oppose the shah; in the vacuum, a new governmental system emerged. Only in Turkey did the electoral process open up opportunities for new leaders and political parties to compete for influence with the military.

Personality Cults and Centralization of Authority

At the very center of these governing systems over time stood one person—a king, shah, or president—who held ultimate authority. In the modern era, the precedent for this consolidation of power was Mustafa Kemal, who stood as the embodiment of the Turkish nation—Atatürk, father of the Turks—and the modernization process he initiated. Since his death in 1938, his image has been reproduced in every corner of the country, on everything from majestic statues to simple photographs of Kemal enjoying an evening at dinner. If anything, his likeness became more omnipresent after his death, as his successors used his legacy to legitimize their own leadership roles. Buildings throughout the country are emblazoned with Kemal's name, including the Istanbul Atatürk Airport. Visitors can inspect the room where Kemal died in Istanbul's Dolmabahçe palace in November 1938. This pattern of reference for Kemal has been upset only recently as the current president, Recep Tayyip Erdoğan, has been trying to usurp some of Kemal's national allegiance, but he has not succeeded in displacing Kemal completely. Kemal remains the most potent symbol of Turkish identity and leadership; since his death, no politician has been able to compete with his image.

In the post-Kemal era, Nasser in Egypt and the shah in Iran began the process of setting up such a system in the 1950s; King Hussein in Jor-

FIGURE 9.2. A memorial in Istanbul commemorating Mustafa Kemal's reform of the Turkish language and the introduction of the Latin alphabet.

dan followed in the 1960s; Hafiz al-Asad in Syria, Saddam Hussein, and Anwar Sadat did so in the 1970s, succeeded by Husni Mubarak in Egypt in the 1980s. They all acquired personality cults to greater and lesser degrees, with elaborate and national celebrations of their birthdays, student readings of their most famous speeches, songs of allegiance, and prayers for their health. Unlike in Turkey, when one president or king succeeded another, they either eliminated the images of their predecessor or relegated his iconography to a secondary position. In Iran and the Arab world, only one state leader could hold the political limelight at a time.

Nasser presented himself as the voice of the people, standing above the political fray so he could protect the nation and citizenry from reactionary politicians and imperialist aggression. Anwar Sadat took on the mantle of "Hero of the Crossing" after the 1973 October war and as part of his gambit to delegitimize Nasser's legacy. The shah of Iran threw a party for the 2,500th anniversary of the Persian throne in 1971 that cost tens of millions of dollars. Saddam Hussein portrayed himself as the inevitable end of a long line of ancient and powerful rulers over Iraq. Pictures

FIGURE 9.3. A likeness of Mustafa Kemal carved into a hillside in Izmir.

of King Hussein as the father of the country, the shaykh of shaykhs, appeared in just about every storefront and school in the country during his reign. His son initially presented images of his father handing over power to him, but now Abdullah and his own son dominate the iconography in Jordan. The takeaway for citizens was that the current king or the president personified the state and nation; loyalty and obedience to state equated with loyalty to the nation's leader.

In these personalized polities this did not meant that no one else held a degree of authority. A small coterie of advisers surrounded the king or president, usually from his family, clan, village, or military regiment, as well as from the most influential institutions in the religious establishment. A key tool of control the presidents and monarchs exerted was over entrance into this governmental elite. In a new version of the divide-and-rule game, presidents and kings brought allies into power for periods of time and then switched them out if they showed signs of growing too strong. While in power, these officials could maintain authority over their clients and dole out state largesse as they desired, but they could not challenge the leader and his policies in ways that could disrupt the overall

FIGURE 9.4. Thirty-foot-tall bronze sculptures of President Saddam Hussein of Iraq sit on the grounds of the Republican Palace in central Baghdad.

system. By the 1960s in Egypt and Jordan and the 1970s in the rest of the countries, these elites had little ability to move outside state-managed networks and mobilize large groups of citizens independently. Divide and rule, when it worked properly, also divided the coterie around the president and monarch. In more cases than not, intraelite competition for the resources emanating from the central institutions of the state became the most important realm for keeping top politicians from forging alliances against the monarch or president.

This system did not always work perfectly for any of the leaders. Saddam Hussein and King Hussein faced numerous attempts against their lives but were saved by others who chose not to ally with the plotters. Anwar Sadat was assassinated by someone outside the system of power, and though the presidency changed hands, the state system stayed intact with the inauguration of Husni Mubarak. In most cases, politicians and military generals in the inner circle gained great wealth and a modicum of influence. Bringing down a president or monarch had the potential to destroy the whole structure, so most of those who achieved positions in the innermost circle of government accepted the rules of the game.

State Control of Religious Establishments

Only Turkey formally eliminated the shari'a as the basis for law, and no other state leader used the term "laicism" to define the relationship between state and Islam, but state actions had the effect of subsuming the religious establishment under state control nonetheless The 19th-century Ottoman and Qajar Empires had codified the bifurcation of law between cases involving the private and public realms. Increasingly, commercial, economic, and penal codes came from Western sources, while personal status issues, such as marriage, divorce, inheritance, and child custody, were settled in religious courts, whether embedded in Muslim, Christian, or Jewish laws. The process continued into the 20th century as states strengthened the legal divisions. The exception is Saudi Arabia, which continues to use the shari'a for all legal issues.

Starting in the 1950s, state institutions began to take control of the religious establishment. Mosques, their preachers, and often the Friday sermons faced state regulations; religious charity organizations came under state supervision; religious schools had to incorporate state curricula; and those involved in these activities were often state employees. Judges adjudicated personal status issues within state courts, and religious clerics offered up their religious capital by granting legitimacy to the states through the issuance of fatwas and public support in times of crisis. In all, the religious institution served as another conduit of state power because its entities employed great numbers of people while often giving religious sanction for state acts.

State Control of Professional Organizations

These states also took control over other previously independent agencies, such as professional associations and labor unions. Engineering, architecture, and medical associations and the like had served as regulating agencies for their respective professions for decades. They established guidelines for entrance into the field and often provided a pension fund or other such services for members. Once the states passed restrictive laws, no engineer or doctor could practice without membership in the professional association; the state leadership could prevent the admittance of anyone considered a political opponent, regardless of his or her qualifications. Labor unions had shown their independent power decade after decade as members went on strike to demand better working conditions. Under state authoritarian control, labor unions could no longer go on strike but had to work with state employees to collectively lobby for rights. States also controlled annual elections to these associations and unions to keep tight hold over the decisions undertaken by their boards.

State Employment

As states initiated their economic policies, governments became the biggest employers. Hundreds of thousands to millions of people worked in some capacity for their states, whether in the bureaucracy, the military, or in the new state factories. In the process, women joined their male colleagues in these state offices at unprecedented levels because they were able to turn their educational opportunities into professional careers, and the populist policies of the leaders mandated that the entire population become part of the national projects. Workers in state positions did move beyond subsistence because they could rely on job security and pensions at retirement. Health-care options expanded and improved for all citizens; literacy rates rose markedly with expansion of the school systems. Within limits, state employees could afford the new consumer goods now available, especially if a member of the family migrated to the oil-rich Persian Gulf states or to the United States or Europe and sent remittances back. And into the 1960s and 1970s, standards of living rose, so parents could see their children fielding more opportunities than they themselves had had in their youth. These social welfare nets brought services to people who had rarely or ever seen them before, but in return, citizenries became largely dependent on the state for their livelihoods, education, and health care.

State Consolidation of National Identity

An additional outgrowth of this state expansion was the clarification of national identity. Turkey and Iran had used their educational systems since the interwar period to standardize their languages and write national narratives bringing at least the Turks and the Persians together within the nation-state. Egypt had seen the same process since the beginning of the 20th century. While the earlier nationalists had focused on Egypt's Pharaonic heritage, by the Nasser years, Egypt's Arab identity came into focus. Nasser's role as a pivotal leader in the Arab world translated into programs in school and at state holidays that narrated how Egyptians were historically connected to their Arab brethren.

In Syria, Iraq, and Jordan, the national identities being written under state guidance focused on the unique roles these countries had and were continuing to play in the Arab world. A fitting image for this narrative is a tree, with roots in Islam, the Prophet's life, and the era of the Rashidun in the Arabian Peninsula; the trunk encompasses the golden age of the Umayyad and Abbasid Empires; and branches delineate separate histories for the modern Arab nation-states. National histories taught in the new state schools and within the newly commissioned textbooks followed this trajectory to illustrate how Arabness formed the primordial origin for the new states but that each state had a unique history in the modern era. As one example, the narrative within the textbooks of the Hashemite Kingdom of Jordan retells the early history of the Arabs and their awakening in the 19th century. The pivotal moment of transition to a unique Jordanian history took place during World War I, according to the new texts, when Sharif Hussein and Emir Faysal led the Arab Revolt against the Ottoman Empire. The movements of Arab nationalism and Sharif Hussein's Arab Revolt merged and formed a natural progression from the Arab awakening to its culmination in the events of World War I, under the agency of the Hashemite family. Without Hashemite leadership, no such liberation could have taken place.

Along with these written histories over the decades after World War II were unique national claims to foods and Arab dialects, making Jordan different from Syria and different from Iraq, for example. The separate political structures formed in each of the countries further cemented national uniqueness; dependence on state institutions for jobs, health care, and education highlighted the different national lives people were living.

Constitutions and Parliaments

All of the military and royal leaders, with the exception of those in Saudi Arabia, commissioned constitutions that detailed the powers to be granted to the presidents, kings, cabinets, parliaments, and judiciaries. The bulk of power lay with the presidents and kings, who had the legal right, per the different constitutions, to appoint and dissolve governments, parliaments, and court judges. Judiciaries varied in their autonomy from country to country, with the Turkish judiciary holding the most independence. Judges more typically wielded authority in minor cases but with little right to interfere with the basic structure of their state or the decision-making power of its leadership cadres. In much the same fashion, parliaments usually had the right only to debate and vote on policies introduced by the king or president, with some limited influence granted to a prime minister when that position existed. Except in Turkey, no parliaments of this era initiated and passed legislation without executive guidance.

Property and education restrictions for men disappeared in the post–World War II era, and universal male suffrage for men over a designated age existed in each country conducting elections. Women's rights in this regard followed more slowly, but after the passage of a women's voting right law in Iraq in 1980, women across the region had the right to vote and run as candidates in all the countries except Saudi Arabia. Electoral laws provided rules for voting and establishing political parties, generally guaranteeing that no opposition parties had the chance to gain a majority of seats or even a substantial minority large enough to disrupt the delicate balance between populism and control that was the core of managed mobilization.

In the Arab countries and Iran, the existence of constitutions and parliaments meant voting on a regular basis for parliamentary, municipal, and village representatives. Many of these elections were relatively free on the day of voting, but typically state leaders had limited the candidates to those already vetted and approved. For the few opposition political parties licensed by the states, legal restrictions on holding public rallies and distributing campaign literature limited their ability to mobilize voters. Turkey has an election threshold of 10 percent that in most years precludes small parties from seating members in parliament, allowing the largest vote winner to take all the seats earned by those parties and enhancing its parliamentary influence.

Despite this threshold, Turkey did provide electoral competition and the possibility that new parties could gain seats in parliament and influence over legislation. However, in Iran and the Arab countries, institutions such as parliament or the judiciary could be venues for criticism but not for active mobilization for change at the leadership or national policy level. They were more often tools for elite recruitment into the system; for those already vetted and approved, winning electoral office meant gaining access to state largesse and contracts that could be distributed to supporters. Appointment to the ministerial level opened up even more access to state coffers and the opportunity for creating new kinds of networks that ultimately relied on the patron holding a top state position for an extended period of time. People frequently voted based on their practical concerns: members of their tribe, family, or local network who gained a position in government had the potential to provide access to university enrollment, jobs, and contracts. In this fashion, people throughout the country were connected to institutions and individuals who were in turn connected to the inner circles of governance. The services flowing out through these institutions made populations dependent on their governments and, concomitantly, raised the price of opposition to levels most people were not willing to pay. All became stakeholders in the system, even if to a minor degree, because any major changes could affect their ability to gain access to individuals and institutions doling out services.

The Kingdom of Saudi Arabia entered the postwar era with government institutions still being formalized and with family rivalries standing in for the intraelite competitions of the neighboring states. When Ibn Saud died in November 1953, his eldest son, Saud ibn Abdul Aziz (r. 1953–1964), took control over a government run through a new Council of Ministers. A measure of specialization and professionalization took place within government service through the establishment of the Ministries of Communications (1953), Agriculture and Water (1953), Education (1953), Petroleum and Mineral Resources (1960), Pilgrimage and Islamic Endowments (1960), Labor and Social Affairs (1962), and Information (1963). Regardless of the improved efficiency these ministries represented, power continued to lie exclusively with the king, who used the Council of Ministers to rule largely through royal decree.

Conflict emerged within the family itself as King Saud and Crown Prince Faysal fronted factions competing for national power. In 1964, Faysal forced Saud's abdication and took the throne himself (r. 1964–1975), replacing many of Saud's family allies with those of his own. Over the next decade King Faysal supervised the extension of state services throughout the country, bringing more Saudi citizens into contact with state institutions than ever before, but without providing any kind of participatory or advisory agencies for citizen engagement in the decision-making process. A nephew assassinated King Faysal in 1975, and the throne passed to Khalid (r. 1975–1982) with no shift in governmental authority outside the ruling circles of the family.

Military Rule

All of these governmental shifts occurred as the United States and the USSR repeatedly intervened in the region's political and economic realms. As part of their worldwide proxy war, both superpowers gifted and sold economic and military aid to their allies, with billions of dollars of military equipment provided over the years. The United States funded the Iranian, Lebanese, and Jordanian armies; the Soviet Union and the Eastern Bloc poured resources into the Egyptian, Syrian and, after 1958, the Iraqi armies. Turkey recognized Israel in 1949 and also received aid as a member of NATO. The Iranian government, before the 1979 Islamic Revolution, sold oil to Israel and consistently supported US policies during the Cold War.

The shah of Iran funneled his oil revenues toward military procurement as soon as he came back into office after the 1953 fall of Muhammad Mossadeq. After 1972, the Nixon administration in Washington agreed to underwrite the shah in his role as the chief American ally policing the Persian Gulf, granting him the right to buy large amounts of up-to-date and sophisticated US military equipment with little congressional oversight. By 1977, Iran had the largest navy in the Persian Gulf, an up-to-date air force, and the fifth-largest military force in the world. The United States also provided Israel with offensive weapons in the mid-1960s and an annual aid package after the 1967 war amounting to a minimum of $3 billion every year. The Israelis, who received more US aid than the Arabs did, constructed a military force that no conventional Arab army could defeat. The Soviet Union countered these moves by delivering the most sophisticated weapons in its arsenal to Egypt and Syria in the 1960s and 1970s, but never to the extent that the United States aided Israel.

The national armies in these countries fought wars—for example, Arab-Israeli conflicts in 1956, 1967, and 1973—but these militaries functioned more consistently as combatants for domestic power than as efficient offensive forces against a foreign enemy. The sheer number of military coups across the Middle East is indicative of the important domestic role militaries have played. Additionally, the militaries have provided employment agencies for the population and training for specialized fields; hundreds of thousands of men in each country passed through the ranks once conscription became the law of the land after independence. Many of the men serving beyond the conscription years or rising up in the ranks came from the lower to lower-middle classes, not from families who could make secure livings from land, business, or the professions. For the more fortunate, the military paid for their training as doctors and engineers; graduates spent a portion of their careers serving the military as payback for their schooling and then the remainder in private practice. The officer corps was privileged economically in terms of salaries and perks, with typically higher salaries than those of their counterparts in the civilian bureaucracy and with access to subsidized products, apartments, and land. They also had exclusive admission to clubs and commissaries that had no counterpart in the civilian realm. As a result, the military became the primary arena for schooling and national indoctrination for the rank and file and a path to socioeconomic privilege for those who rose in the officer ranks.

Turkey, Iran, and the Arab countries initiated new economic privatization policies that provided openings for military officers to buy into a new and potentially lucrative business world. In Egypt, the military had its hand in everything from shopping malls to the production of military hardware by the dawn of the 21st century. Still others became wealthy as intermediaries between the American, European, and Soviet suppliers of new weapons systems and the purchasers in the local militaries. As a result, military officers also became economic stakeholders in their governments.

Intelligence Agencies

Even as military officers gained economic benefits from their connections to state leaders, any leader who had come into office through a military coup knew that it could happen again at any time. State leaders protected themselves against such an eventuality by constructing massive security apparatuses (the mukhabarat in Arabic) to oversee the military and civilian branches of government. These many security forces took on the task of domestic surveillance, aided by special police units. For the task at hand, these irregular forces were better equipped than traditional military forces to watch the political and military elites and citizenry. They represented a supervisory element pervasive enough that the government could catch possible opposition plans and also make people too afraid to oppose the government.

In the 1950s, the shah of Iran established the Organization of Intelligence and National Security (SAVAK), and other countries' leaders followed suit, typically with more than one such agency. The rationale for such a proliferation of security forces was that if only one existed, its power could grow to such an extent that it could overthrow the government; the existence of two or more meant that they watched over each other. In the 1970s, Anwar Sadat of Egypt had three intelligence agencies under his control: the National Intelligence Service under the direct command of the president; the Defense Intelligence Service under the War Ministry; and the Secret Investigations Department under the Ministry of the Interior. Both Syria and Iraq, with Ba'th governments by the 1970s, infiltrated the military with party organizations that served as surveillance agencies watching over the military and answerable only to the presidents.

The most extensive such intelligence apparatus that scholars have studied is the one that Saddam Hussein set up as soon as his faction came to power in 1968. Over the following years, he used his personal control over the security forces as his means for acquiring the power he needed to become the president in 1979. The security bureaus infiltrated and controlled every aspect of military life, the goal being to guarantee that the military remained loyal to party and state. The many security services employed watchers throughout society so any statement of dissent could be reported. Televised trials illustrated the penalties to be paid for oppositional actions; attacks against family members of a person so tried dissuaded many from engaging in such activities. The Republican Guard had served since the 1960s as special protection for the state leadership against any possible military mutinies. In 1982, Hussein established the Special Republican Guard to protect the president, his palaces, and the strategic roads into and out of Baghdad.

Increasing with each decade as new leaders and governments consolidated their positions in the countries under study here, dissidents were arrested and often tortured. Their relatives frequently faced punishment in job placement and school admittance. Press censorship came in the form of restrictions on who could open a media outlet; once it was established, individual articles had to pass the rigors of state censors. Until the 1990s, state-run television and newspaper companies dominated the distribution of formal news. School curricula culled out any subjects deemed controversial or subversive by the Ministries of Education. Even the Turkish military imposed similar restrictions after the 1980 coup and took on political functions similar to those of Arab military leaders. Saudi Arabia employed religious police, or the Committee for the Promotion of Virtue and the Prevention of Vice, to guarantee that citizens in the streets followed Islamic dress codes and maintained proper separation between the sexes. Overall, the security apparatus became so pervasive in all of these countries that little opposition could succeed in challenging the state leadership.

One-Party Politics

Jordan experienced an era of vibrant party competition in the 1950s but went the route of closing down such political activities almost completely in the 1960s and 1970s. Leftist parties continued to exist but only underground since many of the former leaders lived in exile or were serving time in Jordanian jails. Party politics effectively ended in Jordan until their reemergence in the 1980s with a brief political liberalization inaugurated by King Hussein. Saudi Arabia held no elections until 2005, when municipal elections took place, and it continues to prohibit any political parties from forming. The shah of Iran experimented with different party configurations with the goal of funneling popular unrest into state-controlled venues. In preparation for the 1960 election, he orchestrated the pretense of a two-party system by establishing the Melliyun (Nationalist) Party and the nominal opposition Mardom (People's) Party, whose platforms were both the same. Scholars have come to call these parties the "yes" and the "yes, sir" parties because they could not challenge the shah's authority. But when voters nevertheless chose to adapt these parties to serve as vehicles for criticizing the government, the shah ended this experiment and ruled by decree for the rest of the decade.

In the 1970s, Syria, Iraq, and Iran—and to a certain extent Egypt—moved toward one-party systems, but unlike traditional parties, these and their affiliated organizations did not disseminate platforms to generate votes in national elections. Instead, they tried to provide a sense of community within the larger superstructure of the state, bringing people together by constituent group, such as youth or women or factory workers. In these associations, the parties frequently taught about the important services the state was providing, the role its leader was playing in its national success, and the overarching ideology of the party itself. These many associations and party organs also allowed select members to hold local leadership positions because they were called on to implement party policies and select new members. In essence, the parties harnessed people's interests into state-sanctioned organizations so they would not form independent societies instead. And, of course, at all times, these party organs served along with the security services as agents for monitoring the population for any breaches in loyalty.

Rastakhiz Party in Iran

In March 1975, the Iranian shah tried a one-party program with the establishment of the Rastakhiz (Resurgence) Party. The party spent much of 1975 building a statewide organization; it required most government and university employees, as well as many others the state wanted to control, to be members. Its leaders formed a Central Committee, set up a women's organization, convened a labor congress for state-controlled syndicates, held May Day parades, and founded newspapers. In its local branches, it enrolled millions of members, launched a campaign to register voters for the upcoming elections of the 24th majles, and in June 1975 shepherded to the polls as many as seven million voters. The Rastakhiz Party also took over the ministries that managed thousands of livelihoods and tightened state supervision over organizations dealing with communications and mass media. The party was supposed to be an all-purpose shop where party members could vote in elections, policies could be standardized across the ministries, and thousands of people could participate in state-managed popular associations.

The party also enabled infiltration into the bazaars and religious establishment. It opened branches in the bazaars, forced donations from small businessmen, introduced a minimum wage for workers in small plants, and required shopkeepers and workshop owners to register their employees with the Labor Ministry and pay monthly contributions for their medical insurance. Party leaders investigated the accounts of the religious endowments; declared that only state-controlled organizations of waqf could publish theology books; tried to recruit religious clerics into the ranks of SAVAK; and sent state-sanctioned religious teachers into the villages to counter the influence of local religious clerics. The party presented itself rather than the old patrons as the true protector of the people.

Ba'th Party in Syria and Iraq

The Ba'th Party in Syria and Iraq by the end of the 1970s linked to society through an array of party-controlled popular organizations and professional associations that enrolled hundreds of thousands of citizens from every sector of society. These associations mobilized groups that had not previously been incorporated into established party organs, including peasants, youth, scouting groups, artisans, workers, and women. Internally, party secretaries were responsible for party education, conducting elections, planning and coordinating meetings and conferences, implementing all party and leadership decrees, enforcing discipline, and making sure that the party played a significant role in every state institution and military unit. At the same time the party's most critical function was to be the eyes and ears of the state in every corner of the country.

One-Party Attempts in Egypt

Egyptian leaders struggled to provide overarching party control over state apparatuses and citizens. Nasser's government banned all political parties immediately after coming to office and in 1954 prohibited the Muslim Brotherhood from functioning legally. Nasser tried to replace political parties in 1953 with the Liberation Rally, but this organization failed to mobilize the population as the Free Officers hoped. It lacked strong leadership, experienced cadres, efficient organization, and a comprehensive ideology rationalizing its existence so that Egyptians could be enticed into becoming active members.

Between 1957 and 1961, the National Union represented the second attempt for mass mobilization on behalf of the state's program. In this case, the Union took on the position of a school teaching people about the benefits of the Nasserite program and the role the citizenry should play in it. But here, too, the program was not well thought out and did not have institutional structures sufficient for connecting people throughout the country. The last such attempt under Nasser occurred in 1962. The Arab Socialist Union (ASU) succeeded in recruiting millions of people and had a complex administrative structure that its predecessors had lacked. However, the innovations were not sufficient to make the ASU into an effective tool of state recruitment. Like the National Union, it had an unqualified leadership and a membership base that had been too quickly recruited to be well organized, trained, or vetted. As a result, it could not be efficiently used as a way to funnel people into the national project. Instead, Nasser's popularity served much the same function as the one-party systems elsewhere, for he was able to mobilize people around his personal policies.

Anwar Sadat became president in 1970 with few supporters and little of the charismatic appeal Nasser had so successfully wielded as a tool of personal power. In this situation, Sadat had to seek new supporters while also institutionalizing popular mobilization in ways that Nasser had not. He transformed the ASU into the National Democratic Party (NDP) in 1978, and from the 1980s forward it dominated parliamentary politics. Sadat and Mubarak allowed other parties to function for much of this time, but the NDP benefited from the resources of the state and the legal limitations the other parties faced in mobilizing supporters. Unlike in the Ba'thist countries of Syria and Iraq, state and party did not become one and the same in Egypt; rather, the party was merely another tool in Sadat and Mubarak's arsenal of managed mobilization, not the overarching umbrella for all state activities. The NDP lacked the all-encompassing party structure of the Ba'th in Iraq and Syria, as it did not have the support of numerous popular organizations. Thus, the NDP was a tool for recruitment into the elite ranks of the government, and its privileges guaranteed it overwhelming numbers of seats in every parliament, but it was a poor agency for mobilizing Egyptians for a comprehensive national project.

Land Reform

Iran, Syria, Egypt, and Iraq initiated land reform projects in the 1950s and 1960s, following the lead that Jordan had set in the 1920s and 1930s. These programs fit with the ethos of modernization that all the leaders of the era enunciated; the last major group, the peasantry, had to be made stakeholders for truly national policies to be instituted. This policy also complemented the fact that the new Arab leaders coming in to power were geographically and sympathetically closer to the rural areas themselves. In Egypt, Syria, and Iraq, they had proven their ability to move from the less privileged strata into the halls of government; they worked to displace the old elites in every other realm once they entered office. They pledged to weaken the large landowners as power brokers and replace them with those who had been marginalized in the past. Revolution in this instance meant overturning all aspects of the old society so that anyone with training and merit could rise to the upper reaches of government and in their professional fields. With the large landowners stripped of their local power, the peasantry could be mobilized in a controlled fashion to indicate the wishes of "the people," because it was through state offices that they received their land and the aid necessary for cultivation.

But there were also practical considerations underpinning land reform, just as there had been for Jordan earlier. The programs were geared toward weakening one social stratum while making sure that the citizens who benefited were grateful to the state but not empowered to push for an influential voice in its decision-making process. State leaders wanted to be able to infiltrate the villages with their own officials and bypass the old intermediaries. Thus, the impetus behind land reform was for new states to find ways to better tax and count the resources and the people, so they could control the rural areas. The new intermediaries implementing the process would have less independence than their predecessors and be more dependent on state largesse for their positions. Furthermore, the vast number of workers in the rural areas had to be freed from the control of the large landowners and brought into factories and infrastructure development projects. Even Turkey, which eschewed a comprehensive land reform program because the country was already filled with small- to medium-sized landholdings, used many of the same measures to infiltrate state institutions more thoroughly into the countryside.

Implementation

The results of these land reforms indicate that relatively little land actually changed hands. In Egypt between 1952 and 1970, the state transferred about 15 percent of the land to 11 percent of the population and reduced landlessness from 59 to 43 percent. In Iraq by 1971, almost all who lived off agriculture owned some land, but the process of land reform forced many into the cities and off the land altogether. Overall, the peasants who benefited were those with some land who succeeded in expanding their landholdings. Seasonal workers and landless peasants lost out in country after country and moved in enormous numbers into the cities to find work. And the land reform programs failed to make agriculture more efficient or profitable in any of the countries. The percentage of GDP devoted to agriculture continued to drop in relation to industry and services, and agricultural yield per acre diminished. By the 1970s, Iraq, Iran, and Egypt were net importers of basic foodstuffs.

Some categories of land were exempt from reform so could not be transferred to new owners. In Iran, the law did not include orchards, leaving whole swaths of land still under the control of large landowners. In still other countries, only those peasants with sharecropping agreements with landowners could register land, so a large number, if not the majority of rural residents, could not apply for ownership. In addition, the states initiating the programs lacked the resources necessary to see a thoroughgoing reform undertaken. Frequently, peasants received loans, seeds, and tools from a landowner at the beginning of the season, to be repaid after the harvest. The peasants could not work the land without that aid. All the countries established cooperatives that were supposed to replace the services previously provided by the landowners, but none had the resources to fully fund or staff them. Iran exacerbated the problems by putting a disproportionate amount of resources into supporting a small number of large agribusinesses and far less into institutions that could help the small- or medium-sized peasant holdings. Many peasants in all these countries quickly leased their newly registered land back to the former landowners because they were incapable of cultivating it.

Settlement of Bedouin

Accompanying land reform were policies for settling the remaining nomadic bedouin in countries such as Jordan and Saudi Arabia. In Jordan, the processes of drawing borders and shifting to motorized transport continued to weaken the economic base of the bedouin from the 1950s forward. In other cases, boundaries and private property claims destroyed seasonal migration routes. Many tribesmen were drawn into the military for their careers; their families settled along with them so that their children could attend school and follow their fathers into army careers. In Saudi Arabia, much of the work of settlement was completed in the interwar period; the king used both force and enticement to get at least a section of every tribal confederation settled by 1930. State leaders made another attempt in the 1960s when the state offered government-subsidized farms and the provision of technical training to teach the bedouin farming techniques. This settlement process worked less efficiently than in Jordan because Saudi agriculture was undeveloped and incapable of employing sufficient numbers of settled bedouin. As a result, large numbers of bedouin in Saudi Arabia remained at least seminomadic throughout the 1960s and 1970s.

Benefits to the State

Although agriculture did not become more profitable and large numbers of people did not receive land, at least aspects of the land reform's goals were achieved: these policies allowed each of the states to infiltrate the rural areas as never before, and as a corporate group the large landowners were generally stripped of their local power as intermediaries. Land reform required conducting cadastral surveys (determining and recording property boundaries) and setting up cooperatives and peasant societies, all controlled by the state. Schools, hospitals, military barracks, police stations, and tax collection systems followed on the heels of land reform. The employees of these organizations were state workers and represented the state to rural constituencies. At the beginning, these employees were former large landowners, but over time, they came more often from the poorer rural classes, peasants who won election to village councils, and those who earned positions after graduating from the state school systems and receiving appropriate training.

The various land reform and settlement policies succeeded in mobilizing the rural citizenry for state-directed projects in the countries with official programs and in Turkey, which instituted many of the same procedures. The state funded jobs, and the affiliated cooperatives and village councils provided local authority. The employees, as part of their mandates, could make local decisions based on their expertise but could not form countrywide village organizations to lobby for a voice in national government policies. Police, military, and party organizations stood as enforcement against such an eventuality, but the lure of resources kept the system working as well.

Industrial Development

While substantial resources were put into the agricultural areas to bring peasants into state projects, the vast majority of state funds were directed to urban industrialization. Import-substitution policies became the primary focus of these efforts, as these states sought to domestically produce the consumer and heavy goods that were currently imported. The oil states received steady amounts of royalty payments, fees, and profits. Saudi Arabia, Iraq, and Iran, with some of the largest known deposits of oil in the world, brought in the highest revenues, but by the 1960s and 1970s, Egypt and Syria produced small amounts of oil as well. However, for oil-rich and oil-poor countries alike, the quest for industrialization did not go smoothly because of lack of other natural resources, uneven revenue streams, and continuing competition with the industrialized powers.

The import-substitution policies initiated in an ad hoc way in the interwar period became state policy from the 1950s forward. Turkey, Iran, and the Arab countries initiated five-year economic plans in the 1960s, overseen by such agencies as the Egyptian Economic Development Organization. Nationalization of major resources, banks, and industries moved forward in the 1960s as a result of economic considerations, modernization desires, and the need to fulfill state revolutionary socioeconomic goals. This was true even for Saudi Arabia, which could rely on oil revenues but had poorly developed industrial and agricultural sectors. In 1965, King Faysal created the Central Planning Organization (CPO) to oversee the formulation of national development projects, coordinate with the ministries to shape a national vision, and help determine budgetary allocations for the individual projects.

Beginning in the 1950s these countries did expand their industrial bases, and growth in GNP resulted. However, as occurred during land reform, the policies had inherent contradictions that caused problems over the long term. These states did a relatively good job of expanding the necessary infrastructure, with massive expansion in transportation networks and energy grids that built on work already completed in the interwar period, but building this infrastructure and importing the machinery necessary for an industrial base proved enormously expensive. Achieving profitability in import-substitution industries was difficult because plans could not move forward without the hard currency that few countries could raise without the aid of foreign donors or through oil royalty payments. Also, the rise in the standard of living for the vast majority of the different populations increased demand for consumer goods. Few of those products could be easily produced domestically, so they, too, required heavy investment in imported products.

Rentier States and Structural Adjustment Policies

The policies of land reform and industrialization failed to bring in revenues sufficient for modernizing and sustaining the economies of Turkey, Iran, and the Arab countries. The problem was exacerbated by the fact that each of these states served as the largest employer in its country. A relatively small number of occupations were in industries that produced revenues and profits to be taxed by the states; the remainder of the workers served in the military, security services, schools, and civil bureaucracies, which required constant infusions of resources. Upholding the social welfare net of education, health care, and associated services, as well as national infrastructure needs, likewise put strains on state treasuries.

Taxes

Whereas in 1980, on average, countries outside the Middle East brought in 63 percent of state revenues via direct taxation of the citizenry, the Middle Eastern states had an average of only 11 percent. Turkey received 80 percent of revenues from the citizenry in 1980, but personal income tax amounted to only 1.3 percent of Syria's total revenues in 1985. The old saw of "taxation without representation" played out here because only in Turkey was there an ongoing participatory electoral process that engaged the citizenry, and the state could thus extract resources from the voters. The other countries mobilized their citizenries for national projects but failed to devolve authority sufficient to call on the citizenries to pay into the system. Furthermore, Arab leaders between the 1950s and 1970s based a large measure of their legitimacy on their ability to serve populations that had been marginalized by previous governments. Disseminating resources and revenues became an integral element in keeping populations obedient and mobilized but prohibited from taking part in the decision-making process. Without recourse to direct taxation, state leaders relied more heavily on indirect taxes in the form of customs revenues, fees, and commodity taxes. In this instance, only Lebanon succeeded in converting these types of taxes into a key element of its annual budget.

Expatriate Remittances

A valuable source of state revenues was the remittances sent from expatriate workers back to their families. For Turks, the primary foreign destination was Germany as early as the 1960s because of a bilateral Turkish-German agreement that facilitated the migration of skilled workers. Germany's booming industries had an acute labor shortage from the early 1950s forward, and Turks provided much of the workforce; by the end of the 1970s, about 2.5 million Turks were living in Germany and other Western European countries because of comparable agreements. In the case of the non-oil Arab states, hundreds of thousands of professionals and laborers moved to the Persian Gulf to take the jobs made available by the dramatic increase in oil wealth in the 1970s.

The remittances returned became a key pillar of the national economies, allowing people at home to buy imported products, build larger and better-quality homes, pay for advanced schooling for younger children, and in general put more money into circulation for the purchase of domestic and imported products. While the money largely went to individuals and families directly, state treasuries benefited from the indirect taxes citizens paid on consumer goods and imported items. Remittances, however, provide an uneven benefit for individuals and states alike because they are dependent on economic factors outside state control. By the 1980s, with a world recession and fluctuations in oil prices, the governments of the major employers of such labor pulled back on the number of work permits issued to Arabs and Turks. When workers returned home and the remittances decreased, unemployment soared and consumer industries faltered.

Sources of Revenue

For the oil states of Saudi Arabia, Iran, and Iraq the solution to these budget problems was to rely on the sale of oil and its associated industries as the basis for state revenues. For example, in Pahlavi Iran oil accounted for 84 percent of the total government budget in 1974. As of 2010, Saudi Arabia relied on oil for 90 percent of all state revenue. For the non-oil states, or those like Egypt and Syria with small amounts of oil for export, the intersection of colonialism, independence after World War II, and the onset of the Cold War made looking to Europe, the United States, and the Soviet Union the natural solution to their budget shortfalls.

The United States and the USSR provided economic, food, and military aid to their allies throughout the region as an element of their Cold War competition. Development would bring stability to the countries just gaining their independence while providing a conduit for selling US, Soviet, and European products to ever-growing markets. US programs such as Point IV provided aid in the 1950s, while the US Agency for International Aid (USAID) as of 1961 built everything from schools, bridges, dams, and electricity grids, to tourism outlets in its allied countries. The World Bank and the International Monetary Fund (IMF) doled out loans for development. In the 1970s, Saudi Arabia and Kuwait began disbursing funds not only to the PLO but to the so-called frontline states of Egypt, Jordan, Syria, and Lebanon confronting Israel.

Oil and Donor Rents

Because of the dominance of oil revenues, remittances, and foreign grants and loans, all but Turkey in this study can be considered rentier states, a concept derived from the "rent" that landowners—or in the case of much of Middle Eastern history, tax farmers—collected annually from the peasantry. This type of rent—and this is especially true for tax farmers—could be collected solely because the owner or the tax farmer had the right to that rent, not because he enhanced the property itself. In other words, this kind of rent comes without any demand for owners to prove they are engaged in a productive activity. In the modern sense, the recipients (state leaders) receive the rent from donors (foreign governments) because of the strategic interests of the recipients and donors and little to do with the needs or desires of the citizenry. In the oil states, leaders can disregard most demands of the citizenries because the advantage of geography gives them the privileges of economic independence.

The realities of the rentier state concern state power since dispensing such rent produces layers of dependency that cement state power. Oil and donor rents, by their very nature, go to the "owner" or, in this case, the state leader and his premier institutions. In real terms, this means that oil revenues or foreign funds are delivered directly to whoever sits at the center of governance; the president and king choose how to dispense them through state institutions. At every level, agencies and individuals become dependent on receiving a steady flow of those resources.

To keep this system intact, state leaders have to provide assistance to the foreign states dispensing funds to the country. Starting in the 1980s and 1990s, for example, Husni Mubarak of Egypt and King Hussein of Jordan provided military services on behalf of US policies in Israel and Iraq. Egypt received at least $2 billion annually from the United States after the Camp David Accords were signed in 1979. In turn, the donors also became dependent on state leaders because they guaranteed that donor interests would be protected in the country. For example, the US Obama administration stood by Mubarak in January and February 2011 long after it became clear that the mass of the Egyptian population wanted him to leave office precisely because Mubarak had been a vital conduit for US military and economic interests into the country for decades.

Rents provided to Middle Eastern leaders—whether from oil or foreign sources—strengthen control mechanisms because funds flow through state institutions regardless of most domestic dynamics. Citizenries can be "bought off" with services and jobs even when state leaders follow policies in opposition to domestic political views. Because little is being extracted directly from them, they have little leverage against the authoritarianism of their state leaders. At the same time, with funds flowing without a commensurate growth in economic production, individuals and agencies within the state have little incentive to improve on the local economic situation. Increasingly, technocratic expertise and educational experience become of little use in a system with so few incentives for growth; the winners are instead those with the proper political and family connections.

Privatization

Problems emerged in these states when rising populations and increasing pressures on the social welfare net exceeded the amounts flowing in as rent. Collectively, these factors created debts and inflation in all the countries under study here by the 1970s, except Saudi Arabia, which had far more oil wealth than the other countries. To offset this crisis, Egypt and Turkey took the lead in moving away from the statist policies of the past and began supporting the privatization of state industries. Both governments initiated programs before the surrounding countries followed suit: Anwar Sadat introduced the Infitah (Open Door) Policy of 1974, and Prime Minister Turgut Özal introduced similar policies under military supervision in the early 1980s. The policies involved loosening restrictions on imports and passing laws encouraging foreign donors and domestic investors to buy state industries or establish new consumer industries. In neither case did private ownership increase markedly in the early years because of the endemic problem of finding sufficient numbers of domestic and foreign donors with the funds and willingness to buy inefficient state companies. In most cases, the new industries that did open were joint private-public ventures because of the need for supplementary state investment.

Economies grew, even though the policies affected only a small segment of the economy overall in the early years. Turkey, for example, in the 1980s and especially in the early 1990s took advantage of increased trade with the Balkans, the collapse of the Soviet Union, and a new customs union with Europe. Turkey's markets, which had been empty in the 1970s, were now flooded with consumer products from around the world as import regulations disappeared. More important for long-term growth, the most dramatic achievement was the "export miracle" that saw earnings rise from the export of Turkish-made goods from $2.3 billion in 1979 to $11.7 billion in 1988. The Egyptian economy grew by almost 9 percent by the end of the 1970s, and those with a hand in the new enterprises grew wealthy. In this case, the economy was aided by an influx of US aid in response to Sadat's overtures to Israel and as the United States displaced the Soviet Union as the primary provider of Egyptian economic and military aid.

Large Turkish companies like those of Koç and Sabancı fared better than small companies, but the changes also presented opportunities for provincial businessmen running small companies to take advantage of the privatization efforts. This was particularly the case in the 1980s when previously powerful national politicians faced prohibitions on their political activities under military rule. Provincial businessmen filled the void and used their government offices to pass legislation aiding their ability to manufacture for the domestic market and export additional products. In Egypt, the economic shift was part of Sadat's larger program of displacing allies of Nasser with cadres dependent on him for their newly earned wealth. In this case, urban merchants and absentee landowners living in the cities had been weakened and stripped of their influence under Nasser but through the Infitah found places in government again. In both countries, the military also reaped new wealth because top officials received the right to bid on state contracts for constructing armaments locally and, over time, for investing in the consumer economy.

Structural Adjustment

Jordan and Syria followed a similar path of slow privatization in the 1980s and 1990s, respectively, and across the region the biggest economic changes occurred in the 1990s and into the first decade of the 2000s. When the Soviet Union fell and the United States and its allied agencies became the dominant foreign donors and investors in these new projects, the economies of the Middle East accelerated deregulation and privatization as part of what is called structural adjustment or neoliberal economic policies. Typical arrangements involved one of the countries signing an agreement with the IMF that would make loans and credit available but on condition that austerity measures be enacted, subsidies on basic goods be abolished, the currency be devalued to bring down inflation rates, and laws be passed deregulating business transactions and allowing a smoother process for foreign investment.

Under these new rules, privatization of state industries by the late 1990s included industrial firms as well as public utilities. Provisioning for militaries was contracted out to both local and foreign private concerns. New free trade zones in Turkey, Egypt, Syria, and Jordan—called Qualifying Industrial Zones (QIZs) in Jordan—provided space for the manufacture of such items as textiles and computer chips for export to the United States and elsewhere with low to zero tariff duties. Companies operating in such zones also frequently did not have to follow minimum wage and environmental legislation. In addition, foreign companies such as McDonald's and Nokia and every make and model of new and used cars gained access to Middle Eastern markets. The new businesses were aided by almost unlimited credit offered by the governments' state banks and by passage of laws providing incentives for such investments. They were accompanied by generous tax holidays of up to 15 years for anyone investing in a new company. States supported these efforts by providing cheap land for construction and building infrastructure necessary to access the property.

While this privatization process implies a devolution of economic resources from the states to private businessmen, in fact the shift into these neoliberal policies further cemented the role of the states in their national

QUALIFYING INDUSTRIAL ZONES IN JORDAN

In 1996, the US Congress expanded the US-Israel Free Trade Agreement (FTA) to include Jordan, Egypt, the West Bank, and the Gaza Strip so that joint Israeli-Jordanian, Israeli-Egyptian, and Israeli-Palestinian manufactured products could be imported to the United States duty-free. As part of the FTA, Jordan opened the first Qualifying Industrial Zone (QIZ) in 1998 and Egypt did so in 2005.

The inclusion of Jordan in 1996 resulted from the 1994 Jordanian-Israeli peace treaty. To export products to the United States duty-free, at least 35 percent of the appraised value must come from a combination of Jordanian and Israeli content. About seven QIZs were established in Jordan within the first decade, but much of the manufacturing, mostly clothing, that takes place within Jordanian QIZs does not fulfill the criteria laid out in 1996 and is destined for countries other than the United States. Only 3 of the 51 factories registered in the QIZs in 2004 were Jordanian owned. Many Asian companies have opened factories in the Jordanian QIZs in order to gain duty-free access to the US market, using fabrics from Asia and labor in Jordan.

One of the goals of the QIZ program was to provide jobs for Jordanians, but in 2004, only about 40 percent of workers were Jordanian; in 2010, about 25 percent; and in 2006, only about 1 percentof the total Jordanian labor force worked in a QIZ factory. The jobs provided to Jordanians have also done little to improve the economic status of the workers. In 1999, for example, the minimum monthly wage was about $113. Working a mandated 48-hour work week, Jordanians earned approximately 52 cents an hour. The highest pay any worker received in the textile industry was $1 an hour.

With few restrictions placed on them by the Jordanian government, the factories have little incentive to improve working conditions and pay. The Jordanian QIZ factories face competition from similar free-trade zones around the world, including new ones in Arab countries such as Egypt and Morocco. Many have closed in Jordan when opportunities for cheaper labor costs arise in other countries, with frequent instances of workers being left with unpaid back pay. The world economic crisis of 2008 closed even more, so the life span of many of the factories is less than five years.

economies. Presidents, kings, and their closest advisers continued to bring in rents from oil and foreign donors. Instead of moving the revenue into the social welfare net, they rerouted much of it to new businesses that now controlled privatized industries and served as intermediaries for foreign interests. As a result, the states remained just as strong because these new businessmen were still reliant on the state for economic opportunities and much of their financing.

In the Arab countries, the new business stratum worked to guarantee that the state continued to support their efforts; in turn, the states opened up new positions in government for them. In Egypt starting in the 1980s and in Jordan and Syria in the 1990s new businessmen were rewarded with a slight liberalization of the political process that allowed them to enter parliament and new government posts. For example, Egyptian businessmen increased their representation in parliament from 12 percent in 1995 to 22 percent in 2005. Syrian businessmen could be elected to such agencies as the People's Council, the Guidance Committee, and the boards of the Chambers of Commerce and Industry. In the 1990s, the Syrian government expanded the number of seats in parliament, and businessmen increased their percentage of representation. However, in none of these countries could these businessmen have political influence outside their own narrow economic concerns. Liberalization broadened the base of the elite but did not devolve authority to any of the new members of parliament or of the business councils.

These businessmen—and the attendant intermediaries—may have been the purveyors of "private business," but they derived power from their connections to the state. They were new interest groups in society but were not independent actors merely pressuring their states to ease regulation and allow new investments; they were in partnership with and dependent on state institutions. Divide-and-rule policies were maintained from the center because members within this new business stratum had to constantly compete with each other for government favors and vie with the military for contracts.

Only in Turkey did an independent business class emerge that had the power to influence national politics, which is a reflection of the different political context in which privatization took place. The military intervened in government repeatedly, but the state structure still allowed for the emergence and influence of independent political parties and interest groups. The Turkish business class, however, was not united because a small portion of it consisted of the large industrial, commercial, and import-export firms that benefited from state credit and legislation in the decades after World War II. A much larger segment that lived primarily outside the major cities, called the "Anatolian Tigers," were primarily small businessmen who relied on family or religious networks to guarantee markets for raw and manufactured goods. They did not depend on state financial support so could fund parties, such as the Islamist parties as of the 1970s, that favored their economic concerns over those of the larger businessmen. In 1990, these provincial businessmen formed the Independent Industrialists and Businessmen's Association (MÜSİAD) in competition with the Turkish Industrialist and Businessmen's Association (TÜSİAD) that catered to the interests of the largest businesses in the country.

Revolution in Iran

None of these measures attached to managed mobilization, divide and rule, and oil rent were fool-proof, as evidenced by the fall of the shah of Iran in 1979 and his replacement by Ayatollah Ruhollah Khomeini and a new Islamic government. The combined effects of economic crises in the mid-1970s, a national policy that focused on weapons acquisition rather than service provision, and a political system that provided no avenues for citizen grievance added up to a revolution that all sectors of society could join. The revolutionaries may not have agreed on what kind of leadership and government they wanted to see replace the shah, but they came together to force his ouster. In this case, all possible groups came out into the streets and by 1978 had coalesced around the symbols of Islam and the leadership of Khomeini. By January 1979, the shah could not rely on any of the pillars of the state as support for his throne.

The institutional and economic improvements of the 1960s and 1970s kept the shah in power and brought more people in as stakeholders but helped create the many layers of opposition that worked together in the late 1970s. Land reform had forced tens of thousands of agricultural workers from the land, who moved into the cities but struggled to find jobs. The cities themselves, especially Tehran, the destination for the majority of these migrants, provided better services than those in the countryside but still suffered from poor-quality electricity grids, transportation networks, health clinics, and schools. At the same time, the expansion of education overall greatly increased the number of secondary and university graduates, most of whom received state jobs on graduation, but also created a large population politically aware and frequently dissatisfied with the available opportunities for work.

The path of industrialization followed that of the surrounding countries, by producing an expanded working class but one that was unhappy with the decreasing value of wages by the mid-1970s. The state, in turn, became increasingly oppressive, symbolized by the work of SAVAK, the infiltration of the Rastakhiz Party throughout the country, and the complete lack of public venues for criticism to be aired against the shah and his government. As a result of the events of 1953, the shah could not rid himself of the label "puppet of the US government." The economic recession in the mid-1970s brought millions of people into the streets repeatedly in opposition to the shah and his government.

Westoxication

The work of Jalal Al-e Ahmad began the intellectual debate against the shah from among the educated urban cadres in the early 1960s by identifying gharbzadegi (Westoxication) as the reason why society had been weakened by state actions. Using this term, Al-e Ahmad expressed sadness at the loss of Iranian cultural identity that had come along with the state's modernization policies. Even those who had received educations and good jobs had come to understand that they had sacrificed much of what had defined cultural Iranianness. By the 1970s, ʻAli Shariʻati had taken up the intellectual debate by devoting his writings and speeches to presenting an Islamic response to the issues generated by the problems of the modern world. His most influential work was presented in a series of lectures at the Hosainiyeh Ershad Institute in Tehran in 1973, where he attracted secondary and university graduates who were seeking answers about how to be Iranian and Muslim in the modern world. To provide such guidance, Shariʻati spoke of an Islam that was not conservative but revolutionary, a religion that united believers so they could work toward equality and social justice. Shariʻati called on the modern Muslim to look to the era of the Prophet as a guide for knowing how to construct a dynamic community in constant motion toward progress. The Shiʻi imams like Hussein had raised the banner of revolt against corrupt leaders; according to Shariʻati, Shiʻa in every age had the duty to revolt against the oppressors in their lives.

Ayatollah Khomeini and Velayat-e Faqih

Ayatollah Khomeini became well known in Iran because he stood in constant opposition to the shahs, preaching about a dynamic Islam that stood in contradiction to the oppression presented by the shah's government. After being exiled from Iran in 1964 for such activities, he eventually moved to Iraq and lived in the Shi'i holy city of Najaf for almost 15 years. While there, in a series of lectures published as *Velayat-e Faqih: Hokumat-e Eslami* (The jurist's trusteeship: Islamic government), he articulated his view of an Islamic government led by clerics. He declared that the clerics needed to be active in all important spheres of society, interpreting and implementing the shari'a, guiding the community, and supervising the politicians. In practice, this meant that the ulama should control the state in order to implement the shari'a and create a truly Islamic community. This was not a new concept, but in the past the ulama spoke more often of a moral custodianship, not of political authority. For Khomeini and his followers, velayat-e faqih mandated the faqih, or the Supreme Leader, to render decisions on any matter affecting the welfare of the community. Khomeini was thus expressing the view that since God had intended the community to observe the shari'a and since governments had been created to implement the shari'a, the ulama were the only group qualified to interpret the shari'a and run the government.

In a series of speeches smuggled into Iran via cassette tape in the mid-1970s, Khomeini frequently attacked the shah's government for being un-Islamic, for selling the country out to the Americans, and for being allied with the Israelis against the Arabs. On socioeconomic issues, Khomeini accused the government of favoring the rich over the poor and of wasting Iran's precious resources without helping the majority of the country. He pointed to Islam as the means by which socioeconomic justice could be returned to Iran because it would help the peasants, protect the working classes, raise the standard of living, eliminate corruption, safeguard basic freedoms, give dignity to women, and establish a genuine Islamic state. Importantly, he spoke far more rarely about velayat-e faqih, which would have been rejected by many of the diverse groups protesting against the shah. Instead, Khomeini focused on those elements in Islam that had the effect of rallying people under a broad umbrella.

Demonstrations, Strikes, and Violence

Millions of people came out into the streets throughout 1977 and 1978. Students participated because they saw few returns on their educational investment; workers went out on strike when the economy slowed precipitously in 1978. Bazaaris took part in the demonstrations because the government had targeted them in the mid-1970s with price controls and with interventions by the Rastakhiz Party that broke up their community and guild organizations. The ulama participated as a way to regain their lost authority and fight against the secularization of society the state encouraged. Women enlisted because they had been politicized along with the male students, workers, and shopkeepers. In the midst of these demonstrations and strikes, paramilitary organizations perpetrated violent acts against government officials.

The participants in both the peaceful demonstrations and the violent attacks against the state did not join solely because they belonged to one particular group or for one particular reason. Participants joined as Iranians, workers, women, students—identities that overlapped—and all came with grievances against the government and hopes for a new system arising from its destruction. And since the shah had worked for almost two decades to subsume all independent political agencies such as workers' unions, professional unions, and opposition political parties under government aegis, there was no means by which distinct groups could be organized. The only major venues open for political debate over the decades of Pahlavi rule were mosques and other religious sites; they were augmented in 1977 by people organizing new and more ad hoc organizations in neighborhoods, schools, and factories. They all worked in parallel for a common cause and with little coordination between them; only Khomeini came to serve as a national leader that most of the groups could rally around.

Rex Cinema Fire and Black Friday

Throughout 1978, the numbers involved in the demonstrations increased and the number of violent attacks escalated. The shah vacillated between heavy repression against the participants and periods of appeasement; neither stopped the momentum of the revolution. A turning point for the demonstrations occurred on August 19, 1978, when almost 500 people died in a fire at the Rex Cinema in the city of Abadan. The government blamed the fire on oppositional activists, but the great majority of Iranians believed it to be the work of the shah via SAVAK. It was probably an accident, but perception was more influential. The next day, 10,000 relatives, friends, and sympathizers of those who were killed gathered for a mass funeral and blamed SAVAK for the attack. Demonstrators called for the shah to leave the country.

After this event, the intensity of demonstrations continued to increase. On September 4, in honor of 'Id-e Fetr (the festival at the end of Ramadan), hundreds of thousands of people returned to the streets. On September 7, a crowd of maybe a half a million people shouted slogans such as "death to the Pahlavis," "the shah is a bastard," "throw out America,"

"Hussein is our guide; Khomeini is our leader," "independence, freedom, and Islam," and "we want an Islamic republic." The government declared martial law in Tehran and 11 other cities in the hopes of quieting the streets. The protesters remained undaunted and returned to the streets on September 8 and in what became known as Black Friday possibly as many as 4,000 people died from police violence.

By December 20, street violence was a daily occurrence, with youth groups setting up barricades, taunting the military, and throwing Molotov cocktails at army trucks. On December 25, a series of general strikes brought the economy to a halt with strike committees occupying large factories, institutions associated with the oil industry, government ministries, and communication centers. By this time, army rank-and-file soldiers refused to shoot demonstrators. With none of the state pillars still intact and supportive of him, the shah left the country on January 16, 1979. He stayed briefly in the United States and then died of cancer on July 27, 1980, in Egypt.

Khomeini returned to Iran on February 1, and the fragmentary nature of the opposition became apparent in the ensuing political struggle. The leading actors envisioned a range of possible directions for the new state, from a secular republic to a cleric-led government on the model Khomeini presented. Khomeini won that battle in 1979 through a comprehensive campaign of taking over or founding new institutions at the local and national levels that successfully mobilized his widespread supporters. He at the same time marginalized any politician or institution

FIGURE 9.5. Crowds mass in front of Shahyad Tower (King's Memorial Tower) in support of overthrowing Mohammad Reza Shah during the Iranian Revolution, 1978. After the revolution, it was renamed Azadi Tower (Freedom Tower).

that did not accept his leadership and his vision for Iranian governance. He was further helped by the seizure of the US embassy in Tehran on November 4, 1979, by the Students Following the Line of the Imam. This act generated such enthusiasm in the country that Khomeini was able to take advantage of it to further weaken his opposition.

Islamic Republic Party and Constitution

To gain political power through parliament, Khomeini's followers founded the Islamic Republic Party (IRP), appealing especially to the bazaaris and the ulama who wanted an Islamic government established. The Foundation for the Dispossessed took control of the wealthy Pahlavi Foundation

US HOSTAGES IN IRAN

On November 4, 1979, Students Following the Line of the Imam stormed the US embassy in Tehran and took 66 hostages. Six embassy officials escaped on the day the hostage crisis began. The Canadian ambassador to Iran hid them for 10 weeks before a CIA mission could extract them under cover of producing a science fiction movie called *Argo*. On November 18 and 19, the students released 13 of the hostages, all black or female, and on July 11, 1980, one hostage was released for medical reasons. The remaining 52 hostages were released on January 20, 1981, two minutes after Ronald Reagan was inaugurated as the new US president.

Within days of the hostage taking, the Carter administration froze Iranian government assets (approximately $12 billion) held in US and foreign banks. This act was unprecedented because almost half the money frozen was held in banks outside the United States. The United States could impose such a restriction because much of the Iranian money was held as dollars and all international dollar transactions had to be processed through New York. The United States prohibited the purchase of oil from Iran within days of the embassy seizure. Over the next months, restrictions on trade increased, and as of April 1980, all imports from Iran and US exports to Iran had been blocked.

When US efforts at negotiations with the Iranian government failed, on April 7, 1980, the US government broke diplomatic relations with Iran. On April 24, a complex rescue attempt—code-named "Eagle Claw"—was made but had to be aborted because of bad weather and technical problems with the helicopters involved. While attempting to refuel, one helicopter crashed into a C-130 transport plane, killing eight US soldiers.

The release of the hostages came as a result of the Algiers Accords, signed on January 19, 1981, which stated that Iran would release the hostages and the United States would release Iranian assets. A complicated calculation was worked out for those Iranian assets, with many of them going to pay off loans the Iranian government owed to a large number of individuals and countries. In the end, Iran had its debts paid off and received about $3 billion in cash. The US government maintained sanctions against companies doing business with the Iranian government.

and distributed funds to supporters. The Reconstruction Jihad mobilized youth by sending them to rural areas to aid the poor to build housing. All of these institutions helped consolidate Khomeini's power and the institutions allied with him. As a result, when the new constitution for the Islamic Republic was presented for a vote, it received a 98 percent approval rating. Even accounting for a degree of fraud, these numbers represent overwhelming support.

This constitution enshrined velayat-e faqih as the system of governance for the new Islamic Republic of Iran. A provision in it gave extraordinary powers to Khomeini as the faqih, declaring that he was accountable only to God. Other articles list his specific powers, including control of the army and the right to disqualify presidential candidates and dismiss the president of the high court and the majles.

Guardian Council

Under the terms of the constitution, the faqih appoints six ulama for the Guardian Council and parliament selects six. The most basic function of the Guardian Council is to ensure that politicians follow the shari'a and that laws are in accord with it. Thus, the Guardian Council holds the right to supervise all elections, approves all candidates, and checks the compatibility of all laws with Islam. And while the Guardian Council enshrines clerical rule over the governing process in Iran, the constitution also provides for a president and parliament to hold designated powers. In this way, the Iranian government has participatory agencies, but they are constrained by control mechanisms that prohibit them from challenging the dominance of velayat-e faqih.

While Khomeini lived, he had unquestioning authority over the members of the Guardian Council and the state overall, but with his death in 1989, his successor, Ayatollah Ali Khamenei, has not been able to wield the same singular authority. In the breach, the Guardian Council has more power as an executive agency than it did under Khomeini.

Mohammad Khatami and Reform

The death of Khomeini also allowed for a shifting balance of power between the presidency and the council, with the former gaining influence in the 1990s as economic problems and questions about the role of Islam in public life gave birth to a rising popular movement for change. These issues came to light especially during the 1997 presidential election, when candidate Mohammad Khatami pledged to institute popular demands,

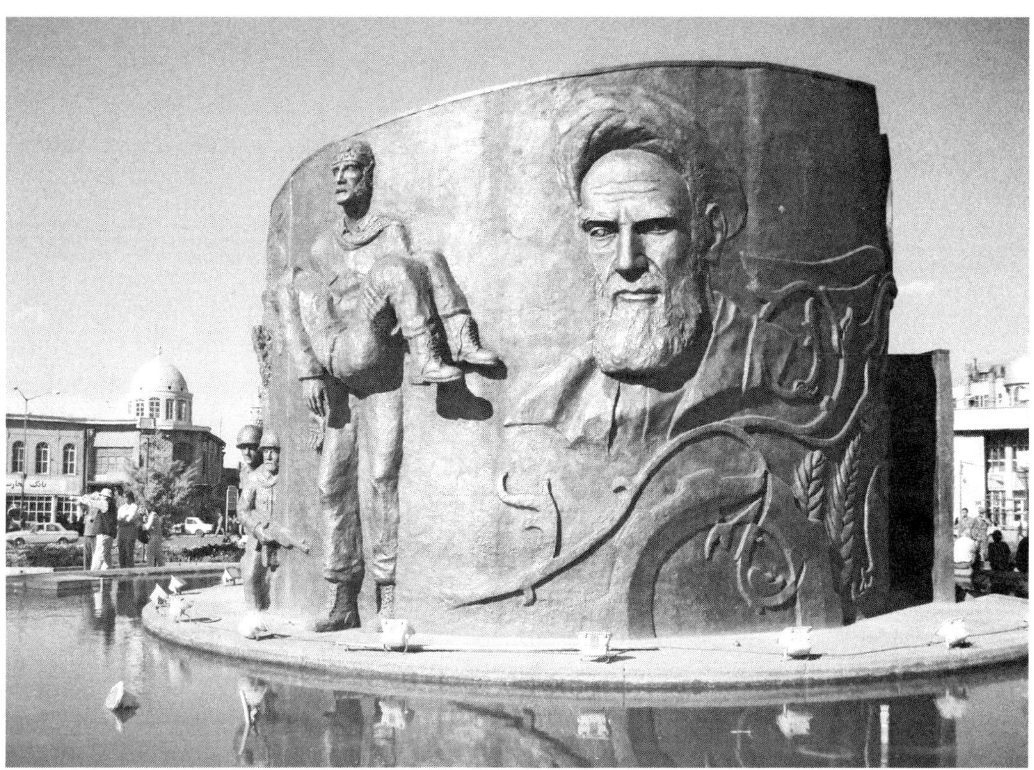

FIGURE 9.6. Monument to Ayatollah Khomeini and the Iranian martyrs of the Iran-Iraq War of 1980–1988 in Hamadan, Iran.

including enhanced legal rights for women and religious minorities, economic development, and the expansion of civil society. With strong backing from youth and students, women, the middle class, and the religious minorities, Khatami won 69 percent of the vote in May 1997. Newspapers proliferated in the political opening brought on by this victory, and their authors and editors engaged in a lively debate about the relationship between Islam and democracy, of the role women should play in public life, and of the need to weaken clerical supervision over the agencies of government. But for all his popularity, Khatami could not stand up to the clerics supervising the government. Few of his reforms passed through the parliament, and in 2005 Mahmoud Ahmadinejad won the presidency with a platform in opposition to the reforms of Khatami and in support of reinvigorating Islamic elements of governance.

Investment in Social Welfare

Many people left the country in the early 1980s because of the imposition of new morality codes and the repressive new government. Despite this exodus, the Islamic Republic has survived because it brought the socioeconomic improvements to Iranians that Egyptians, for example, had seen decades earlier. For all his oil wealth and for all his promises of change, the shah had done a poor job of extending the social welfare net as expansively as his colleagues across the borders had. In contrast, the Islamic Republic's constitution pledged to eliminate poverty, illiteracy, slums, and unemployment while also providing free education, accessible medical care, and decent housing.

Those pledges were largely fulfilled in the 1990s, after the country ended the Iran-Iraq War that had lasted throughout most of the 1980s. Illiteracy had stood at about 50 percent in 1979 but by the beginning of the 20th century had been reduced to 15 percent. Illiteracy among women, in particular, saw a drop from 65 percent to 20 percent. The state also extended services into the rural areas so people living there could enjoy the consumer goods and utilities that only the urban areas had seen under the shah. And rural areas, as a result, became the bastion of support for the Islamic Republic even as many urban residents came out in large numbers for the reformist Khatami and in opposition to continuing control by the clerics.

However, these improvements have come at the cost of many personal freedoms, for example, the change in the status of women. In March 1980, Khomeini ended the Family Protection Law (FPL) passed by the shah in 1967 and amended in 1975. The law's repeal returned women's legal status within the family to the laws of the 1930s and in the process eliminated family-planning programs and minimum marriage laws. The result was a revival of polygamy, temporary marriage, child marriage, public veiling, and an end to the FPL's equalization of women's rights in divorce and child custody. These laws remain in place in Iran, but the additional opportunities afforded to the entire society have meant that women are now in schools, universities, and professional positions in unprecedented numbers.

Conclusion

Between the 1950s and 1980s the experiences of Egypt, Syria, Iran, Jordan, and Saudi Arabia and the eras of Turkish military control show how effective control mechanisms were in keeping leaders in place and much of the population dependent on them. In cases where leaders did change, the system as a whole, as well as its constituent parts, remained intact, with few players working to destroy it. For a time citizenries did see a rise in their standards of living, but the improvements came at a cost as militaries, security forces, and associated governmental control mechanisms repressed true political participation and provided few avenues for the expression of opposing opinions. States imprisoned, executed, and fined opponents while curtailing freedom of the press and assembly. By the end of this era, control mechanisms were fraying and many people became marginalized from their states. The revolution in Iran demonstrated the underlying vulnerability shared by all the states.

UPHEAVAL

Islamism, Invasion, and Rebellion from the 1990s into the 21st Century

10

ALTHOUGH PAHLAVI IRAN had fallen to the Islamic Republic and Lebanon was in the process of reconstruction after 15 years of civil war, the rest of the states under study here appeared to be holding strong as the 1970s moved into the 1980s and beyond. The 21st century dawned on a Middle East with longtime state leaders still in office or successors maintaining the power bases of their fathers or predecessors. Saddam Hussein remained in power in Baghdad despite a decade of UN sanctions imposed against him after he invaded Kuwait on August 2, 1990. Jordan and Syria experienced peaceful transitions from King Hussein and Hafiz al-Asad to King Abdullah II and Bashar al-Asad, respectively. A soft coup by the military in Turkey in 1997 had pushed back a resurgent Islamist political party in favor of traditional Kemalist politicians.

But these state leaders had to contend with the ramifications of privatization and deregulation that funneled state funds away from the social welfare net. State jobs were less plentiful, schools at all levels deteriorated in quality, and health care weakened even as the state security mechanisms grew stronger. In the place of government employment, a parallel private, often foreign-financed, sector emerged that hired people with the linguistic and technical skills necessary for work in the new companies and that catered to those with the resources to pay for access to private institutions. At the same time, many people found that immigration to Europe or the Persian Gulf states or second and third jobs were necessary to raise sufficient money to get married, rent apartments, and buy consumer goods. Gaps between rich and poor grew wider and began to replicate and then surpass the numbers defining early 20th-century Middle Eastern economic systems, before the advent of the populist policies in midcentury.

To aid those most in need, voluntary associations opened to dole out funds for schoolbooks and uniforms, after-school tutoring to offset the weaknesses of the state school systems, food for holiday celebrations, and the like. People also turned to those communities with which they identified, whether by religious sect, family, kin, tribe, or neighborhood. These new associations filled the vacuum left by the states and helped families struggle through the economic crises, but their large number indicates how fragmented society had become in all these countries. Divisions between these groups frequently turned violent as they competed for resources and government access; and when that has not occurred, citizenries looked to separate organizations rather than their collective national institutions.

In the case of Turkey and Egypt, starting in the 1970s, and followed by the Arab countries in the decades thereafter, this fragmentation provided openings for the rise of an activist Sunni Islam that had both associational and militant elements. Organizations such as the Muslim Brotherhood in the Arab world and new Islamist political parties in Turkey attracted support from university students and professionals frustrated by the lack of jobs, rural migrants to the cities finding conditions little improved from those they had just left, and provincial and small urban merchants who were struggling economically. In many of the new organizations, the focus was on how individuals could mold their lifestyles in accordance with the shari'a. These Sunni Islamists can be considered rogues because overthrowing their governments was not the primary goal; they wanted to revitalize Islamic society and, as a grassroots movement, influence governmental policy from the inside. In Turkey, these parties became the dominant players in the government as of 2002; in Egypt and the Arab world, Islamists challenged their governments to change but failed to substantially alter their state structures.

Militant Islamists, however, were rebels working to destroy what they considered their irreligious governments and to eliminate the deleterious

Western influence in the Muslim world. Of the many organizations that formed, some functioned within state borders, such as the Islamic Jihad group that assassinated Anwar Sadat in 1981, and many others formed transnational organizations, such as al-Qa'ida (the Base), with units coalescing over time in places as far apart as Afghanistan, Iraq, and Syria. Their attacks affected an even larger geographic area and population, culminating in the 1993 attack against the World Trade Center in New York and the September 11, 2001, attacks on the World Trade Center and the Pentagon in Washington, D.C.

Fragmentation occurred in Iraq, not because of a shift in economic strategies but because of war and invasion. The Iraqi government could rely on oil wealth to maintain a guns-and-butter policy for much of the Iran-Iraq War of the 1980s, but the cumulative devastation of eight years of warfare, the subsequent Gulf War of 1990–1991, and the imposition of UN sanctions throughout the 1990s militated against economic growth. Saddam Hussein could maintain his strength because he monopolized the oil rent and the means of coercive power, but these events forced many people to look to alternatives to Iraqi state services. In particular, geographically, ethnically, and religiously, the country began to break apart along Shi'i, Sunni, and Kurdish lines, especially in the aftermath of the invasion by the US coalition forces in 2003. After the United States dismantled the government and the military, new institutions arose in their place with Shi'a displacing the Sunnis as the dominant political group, and the Kurds achieving political autonomy. Today, Iraq is structurally fragmented and wracked by violence. Millions have fled the country, and Iraq's sectarian battles have spilled over into a Syrian civil war that erupted in 2011.

The Israelis and the Palestinians are at a stalemate in their quest to find a solution to their ongoing conflict. The Oslo process initiated in 1993 has thus far failed to establish two states on the land of the Palestine Mandate. The years since have seen increasing numbers of Israeli settlements in the Occupied Territories and a split between the Fatah-led Palestinian Authority in the West Bank and Hamas control in the Gaza Strip. The Palestinian people struggled through a second Intifada between 2000 and 2005 but are no closer to achieving statehood.

Protest and Suppression

From at least the 1930s forward, a combination of students, professionals, and workers had repeatedly gone out into the streets to protest through party, union, and paramilitary organizations. Students and professionals had demanded that the glass ceiling be shattered so they could displace the old elites and colonial powers and bring their own expertise into government; the workers wanted better salaries and working conditions. Thus, in the interwar period, these groups were rogue actors trying to force change on their governments. By the 1950s, they became rebels who wanted to use such organizations as the Ba'th and the Communist Parties to revolutionize their societies and make a political and economic break with the old colonial powers and the new superpowers. They could not, however, in any of these countries turn their political passions into mass movements capable of overturning governments. Instead, military coups brought their ideas into the halls of government, or their protest actions slowly subsided under pressure from security forces and military repression.

In the late 1960s they emerged into the streets again after years of failed Turkish economic policies and the Arab defeat of 1967. In addition to the demonstrations and paramilitary attacks that took place between the late 1960s and late 1970s in Turkey, worker unions waged large strikes in support of better pay and conditions, with the Confederation of Revolutionary Trade Unions (DİSK) fronting many of them. One such event was the May Day 1977 protests, when DİSK organized a huge rally in Istanbul at the time of the national elections. Police came out in force, and 2 protesters died from bullet wounds, 34 were trampled or crushed to death, and hundreds were wounded. Starting in 1968, students at AUB came out repeatedly in protest against the school's administration and the governmental policies of Lebanon and the surrounding Arab countries. They focused their support not on Gamal Abdel Nasser as their predecessors had done but on the Palestinian fedayeen groups, who appeared to be more dynamic representatives of revolutionary ideas by that time. Underlying the specific calls for redress of grievances was an acknowledgment that the revolutionary politics of yore had evolved into the stale politics of the present.

Protests in Egypt

In Egypt in 1968, workers in the industrial suburb of Helwan in Cairo demonstrated against the light prison sentences meted out to senior military officers who had failed to protect Egypt's armed forces from Israeli planes in June 1967. They were quickly joined by university and secondary students who collectively demanded that the Nasserite project be more fully implemented so that economic resources could be equitably spread throughout the population. With the defeat in 1967, the death of

Nasser in 1970, and the arrival into office of a weak successor in Anwar Sadat, the vulnerability of the state made room for such political mobilization to emerge once again, which shows that tens of thousands of students and workers were no longer cowed by the fear of state violence or unquestionably loyal to an Egyptian leadership that had continually failed to reform the country. The focus of their attention in the early years of Sadat's presidency was on his unfulfilled promise that he would attack Israel to avenge the loss of 1967. But even after the October 1973 war, students and workers continued to protest and strike because the economy deteriorated year after year, with all of the groups coming together in the food riots in Cairo in 1977.

Demands of Protesters

In their protest actions, these leftist students and workers in Lebanon, Egypt, and Turkey, joined by similar groups in Jordan and Syria, did not call for a radically new national project to be instituted in the Middle East; rather, they largely spoke the populist and secularist language of Nasserism, Kemalism, and the many leftist parties of the 1950s and 1960s. They did not substantially question the paradigms of secular-oriented modernity that such figures as Gamal Abdel Nasser and Mustafa Kemal set as their models for state progress. Instead, they attacked the government for becoming ossified and for transferring power to politicians enmeshed in corruption and failed economic policies. They called for younger and more dynamic leaders who would institute the revolutionary changes required to further transform their societies. Many of these student and worker protesters saw in the Palestinian fedayeen the new political vanguard; others demanded that their leaders fulfill the promises of the past.

They fared no better politically in the 1970s than their predecessors had in the 1950s and 1960s. They did not alter government policy appreciably, although Sadat did have to return the food subsidies in 1977 he had threatened to eliminate. The military returned to Turkish political supremacy in 1980, and the parties that were allowed to lead the government in the aftermath initiated the economic privatization project that weakened the effectiveness of state services. Instead, Sadat, Mubarak, and the Turkish military moved decisively against the organizations these activists fronted to guarantee that they would not be able to grow into effective activist venues.

Political parties, student movements, and unions came under state attack, often identified by the leaderships as Communist organizations regardless of whether or not the label was true, because the label enabled political leaders to acquire increased funding and support from the United States as part of Cold War politics. Thousands were jailed, expelled from school, or fired from their jobs because of their political activism. By the 1980s few newcomers ventured into leftist political activism; to do so jeopardized their own freedom and often the occupations of their family members because the security forces targeted them as a means of discouraging all opposition activity.

Economic Crises in Egypt and Turkey

None of these actions appreciably altered the economic situation anywhere. In Egypt, for example, professionals, students, and the lower-middle and lower classes bore the brunt of the costs of Infitah, Sadat's economic opening. Peasants and urban workers paid for the new program through taxes and loss of the state services that had helped many alleviate the worst privations of poverty. By the mid-1970s, urban quarters saw few state services; in rural areas, the cooperatives that had accompanied land reform were neglected and irrigation networks deteriorated as agricultural investment stagnated. Unemployment soared, officially recorded as 12 percent in 1986 but unofficially much higher. Economic recession throughout the 1980s reduced the opportunities for labor migration to the Gulf States, so remittances declined markedly.

In 1964 Gamal Abdel Nasser had made into law that all graduates of a state university would receive a state job, but by the 1970s educational growth far exceeded state demand, so graduates had to wait years for the promised jobs. By one estimate, the country needed approximately 2,000 new engineers each year during the decade but was graduating as many 5,000. Despite these numbers, Anwar Sadat expanded the number of state universities by opening seven new provincial campuses between 1974 and 1978 while increasing the percentage of high school graduates admitted from 40 to 60 percent. The jobs, when obtained, came with security but low pay, few benefits, and few possibilities for professional achievement. Merit played little role in hiring and promotion, as positions within a given politician's network proved more influential. According to the 1986 census, the unemployment rate for intermediate-degree holders was 28.8 percent and for university graduates, 25.5 percent. For those who obtained jobs, by 1987 the salaries of government employees had fallen to slightly more than half the 1973 level. Many state employees began to take second and third jobs, as taxi drivers and tutors, for example, to pay for basic necessities and the consumer goods flooding the marketplace.

Rising prices and overcrowding changed the demographic makeup of old neighborhoods in Cairo and its new suburbs. The suburbs became heterogeneous areas where people of different socioeconomic strata lived in close proximity but without many of the old community ties binding

FIGURE 10.1. Bulaq neighborhood in Cairo, 1992.

them together. Residents were far from family and former institutional bonds and spent many hours of their day commuting to what jobs they could find. Even older but poorer neighborhoods closer to the city center of the city became more diverse because professionals could not afford to live in nicer, more middle-class neighborhoods. The diversity was also exhibited in the sha'bi (popular) neighborhoods of Cairo, as of the early 1990s, which were overcrowded and dilapidated.

In the late 1970s in Turkey, the government tried to offset the return of triple-digit inflation with extensive import restrictions and high tariffs designed to keep out American and European industrial products, but these efforts did little to shift toward domestic production. Turkish-made products, from cars to washing machines, were of such poor quality that an entire industry existed to fix them when they broke. Accompanying these crises was a decline in the value of wages and a dearth of products available on the legal market; luxury imports could be purchased at high prices for the few who could afford them. The main losers were the peasants and workers because they saw subsidies on basic foodstuffs reduced

FIGURE 10.2. Star Towers in Esenyurt, Istanbul, surrounded by a gecekondu neighborhood.

and state benefits diminished. Real wages declined by about 45 percent after 1980, while official unemployment hovered around 15 percent throughout the decade. The state abandoned its role as the guarantor of social and economic security.

In Turkish cities, the squatter towns of gecekondu (built at night) dwellings assumed gigantic proportions in the 1970s and 1980s. The first in Istanbul appeared in 1946; by 1983, some 55 percent of the city's population lived in these areas. The gecekondu neighborhoods at first lacked any kind of infrastructure; and the first homes were small and similar to those in villages the migrants had left behind. To alleviate these conditions, the inhabitants lobbied local politicians for aid in return for their votes, with the result that gradually the squatter towns became connected to the municipal electricity grids and water supplies, road systems, and sewers. Over time, the gecekondu areas became heterogeneous urban neighborhoods like those in Cairo, with a mix of old and new migrants, of those with good civil service and government jobs living next to those who had succeeded in finding only temporary or seasonal employment.

FIGURE 10.3. A gecekondu neighborhood in Seyrantepe, Istanbul.

Some families did well enough that they could build quite large homes, typically building upward because of the lack of space; others were living in temporary shacks. Overall, these were areas where people could hope to improve their lives, but economic conditions in Turkey fluctuated so much between the 1960s and 1980s that they could not rely on improving their standard of living consistently.

Sunni Islamism

With leftist opposition repressed and discredited, new Sunni political parties, community associations, student unions, and economic enterprises mobilized the discontent brewing among students and urban populations throughout the Middle East. In Iran, the mass movement in the late 1970s united around the figure of Ayatollah Khomeini as the best means for funneling anger against the shah and his government. However, even as the events of 1978 and 1979 became known as the Islamic Revolution, the participants envisioned very different types of state structures emerging from the destruction of the Pahlavi government. A large segment of the protesters supported a reinvigoration of Islam as a governing pivot, but only in the aftermath of Khomeini's success at consolidating his leadership position did a wholesale project of Islamizing governance and society take place. However, beginning in Egypt and Turkey in the 1970s and 1980s and spreading to the other Arab countries under study here, a grassroots Islamist movement caught the attention of many who no longer saw their governments as valid custodians of society.

The term "Islamism" encapsulates both the comprehensive ideology that "isms" in general exhibit and the active nature of the movement's supporters. The goal of Islamism was the establishment of a society where Islam was not a religion alone but a political ideology that shaped all aspects of society and governance and where the shari'a formed the basis for state structure and law. It was not a movement to convert non-Muslims to Islam but to convert passive Muslims into active ones. For believers, Islam provided guidance for the better functioning of governments and the means to live with dignity despite the many pressures of the modern world.

Islamism provided practical instruction on how Muslims could embrace a Muslim lifestyle rather than the modern Western lifestyle that their state institutions had advocated for decades. Followers donned Islamic clothing and attended mosque regularly to show they were not merely passive Muslims but active proponents of a pious way of life. Much of this movement was a bottom-up, grassroots phenomenon, in which individual Muslims sought to structure their lives around the ethical precepts laid out in the shari'a. Islamism reinvigorated the community connections that had never been fully wiped out by the secularism of the Middle Eastern sociopolitical structures of the 20th century. The movement's participants focused first and foremost on bringing Muslims together and teaching them how to live pious lives. Its associated organizations also provided the social services that the governments were neglecting by serving new economic priorities. By presenting themselves as a part of a social movement rather than a political one, Islamist activists escaped the worst of government interference, providing safe places where people could come together to attain the services they needed, feel connected to a larger community—especially in overcrowded cities filled with recent migrants—and be empowered by adhering to an indigenous cultural lifestyle.

The movement was also a protest against institutionalized Islam for failing to provide true guidance in times of crises and for choosing to shore up the legitimacy of oppressive leaders rather than address the needs of believers. Rather than focus on esoteric theology, much of the Islamist discourse addressed pragmatic issues, such as how to dress, how to behave morally in the modern world, what the proper elements of a Muslim marriage were, and which forms of entertainment were acceptable for pious Muslims. Much of the work was undertaken by laypeople rather than clerics. Adherents worked their regular jobs during the week and then preached in or attended private mosques on Fridays. A publishing industry arose to sell how-to books and cassettes detailing how to live a pious life in the modern world. Over time, television shows for children and adults preached much the same. This was a movement in which ordinary people taught ordinary people; Islamism gained followers primarily outside the halls of institutionalized Islam, and those ulama who did join had to adjust their message to fit the newly engaged audience.

The movement expanded in the 1980s alongside a vast building program by Islamic organizations in Turkey and Egypt. Private mosques, Islamic voluntary associations, and Islamic for-profit commercial and business enterprises opened across both countries. For example, all existing mosques in Egypt were subject to the jurisdiction of the Ministry of Religious Endowments, but private mosques, often just rooms in nondescript buildings, emerged too quickly for the ministry to regulate. These mosques and their associated voluntary institutions became focal points for community life in the city neighborhoods neglected by the state.

They sponsored religious lessons, after-school and day-care programs for young children, and competitions for reading the Quran and hadith on Islamic holy days. Their service organizations included health clinics, kindergartens, charity distribution centers, and bookstores for Islamic books and cassette tapes. In Egypt, one estimate puts the total number of private voluntary organizations in the early 1990s at between 14,000 and 15,000, although the number may have been much higher.

Funding for these many organizations in Egypt and Turkey came from businesses run according to the Quran's precepts governing economic transactions. Islamist businessmen had typically favored privatization because the weakening of state regulations provided an opportunity for Islamic rules to be implemented in their stead. Islamic banks refrained from charging usurious interest on loans and channeled profits into social welfare projects for less fortunate Egyptians and Turks; they thus turned a portion of the wealth into charitable giving, following the precepts of Islamic zakat. The activists and donors for the Islamist organizations and activities were independent of state control because they were volunteers or they used funds donated to them directly. The many welfare and educational groups could not be broken up because the state had little leverage over them. Meanwhile, they were providing vital welfare aid that the states no longer proffered.

Islamism in Egypt, Syria, Jordan, and Saudi Arabia

In 1970, when Sadat came to the presidency, he worked to construct cadres loyal to his leadership, so he allowed Brotherhood members to return to Egypt and released others from jail. The Brotherhood remained illegal, but Sadat encouraged its activities as a counterpoint to the Nasserites and especially as a buffer against students and workers protesting in the streets throughout the 1970s. Furthermore, as Sadat attacked the activist students for being too pro-Nasser, these organizations attracted fewer new students to their ranks. In their place, the Muslim Brotherhood, other Islamist organizations, and student-oriented Islamist associations began to gain followers on campuses across the country and then among graduates as they entered professional unions.

University and Professional Unions

Islamist activism at the universities began with the formation of small religious societies where participants discussed religion and engaged in such traditional practices as memorizing the Quran. Students sought a community structure that would tap into their Islamic identities and provide them aid in times of need. By the mid-1970s, the Brotherhood and a new organization, al-Gama'a al-Islamiyya (Islamic Society), which had no connections to the militant organization of the same name, were recruiting university students to their organizations. The latter group won elections to student unions at Cairo, Minya, and Alexandria Universities in 1976. From such positions, these and other Islamist societies offered aid to students, including cheap books, affordable accommodations, financial aid, and separate transportation for female students. The leftist students had never offered such aid when they controlled the student unions.

Professional unions also experienced a dramatic expansion between the mid-1970s and the mid-1980s, which reflected the swelling numbers of university graduates under Sadat and Mubarak. By the early 1990s, membership in Egypt's professional unions had grown to more than two million, most of whom held professional degrees in medicine, engineering, and law. The Muslim Brotherhood and other Islamist-oriented candidates were elected to and came to dominate the boards of these associations. These leaders followed the university model and organized subsidized health insurance and other types of aid for members of the union who did not make enough money to pay for such basic services.

Da'wa

Many students, graduates, and professionals took up the Da'wa (call to God), which promoted a new, activist conception of Islam, making it the duty of every Muslim to participate in the Islamic reform of state and society. Many began their study of Da'wa at the university, and afterward, as an outlet for their continuing activism, preached these ideas in Islamic institutions in suburbs and poor neighborhoods. Some worked full-time in the Islamic sector, but most worked part-time and held jobs elsewhere. Thus, young lawyers and engineers doubled as preachers in private mosques, delivering Friday sermons, offering religious lessons, and organizing special activities on holy days. Graduates also worked or volunteered in Islamic health clinics, day-care centers, kindergartens, and after-school programs.

Direct personal contact was the preferred and most prevalent method of outreach. Local preachers giving sermons in the private mosques proved to be a pivotal point of contact between the Da'wa movement and the people activists were trying to attract. Prayer leaders held question-and-answer sessions during which people could ask practical questions as they struggled to find ways to be committed Muslims. Little of this discourse was overtly political but focused largely on inspiring individuals to reform their daily activities and relationships. In an era when privatization brought new wealth to only a few, Da'wa extolled a society working together to help and uplift all.

Muslim Brotherhood in Egypt

The Da'wa movement itself was decentralized and diverse, but through the Muslim Brotherhood its ideas came to be part of an enormous national organization from the 1980s forward. Brotherhood followers dominated the boards of student and professional unions, and the national organization established systematized outreach to the community, with departments for social services, students, workers, teachers, families and the professional syndicates. In 1984, in a state-permitted alliance with the Wafd Party, Brotherhood members won 8 seats in parliament. In 1987, the number went up to 36, but members of the Brotherhood who sought to receive a license for their own Wasat (Center) Party throughout much of the 1990s failed on every occasion.

In the first decade of the 21st century, Brotherhood members won 17 seats in the 2000 election and 88 seats in 2005 but then won only a single seat in 2010 as a result of the fraudulent practices of the Mubarak government. Only in 2011, after Mubarak's ouster, did a Brotherhood-affiliated party, the Freedom and Justice Party, dominate the parliamentary and presidential elections. Muhammad Morsi, a Brotherhood leader, became president until his ouster by General 'Abd al-Fattah al-Sisi and the military on July 3, 2013.

Muslim Brotherhood in Syria and Jordan

In Syria the Muslim Brotherhood gained a foothold in the suqs of the provincial cities, those areas that were not given precedence by the Ba'thist governments of the 1960s and 1970s. Even when Hafiz al-Asad reincorporated the Sunni merchant elite of Damascus and Aleppo into government schema, smaller merchants remained independent of state control and had little access to government largesse. A number of these merchants formed a strong Muslim Brotherhood movement that provided the same social services as the organization in Egypt. By the late 1970s and early 1980s, some members also chose to attack government officials. In 1982, the state sent in a massive force of 12,000 armed with tanks, artillery, and helicopters to destroy the Brotherhood in its stronghold of Hama. Whole parts of the city were completely destroyed and possibly as many as 20,000 killed. These actions severely weakened the Brotherhood organization but did not eliminate it completely. When resistance to al-Asad's son, Bashar al-Asad, arose in 2011, the Muslim Brotherhood became an early leader.

The Hashemite monarchy of Jordan brought the Muslim Brotherhood into influential governmental positions, such as in the Ministry of Education, as a counter to the support garnered by leftist political parties in the 1950s. Only in the 1990s, when King Hussein initiated a political liberalization policy as a way to offset demonstrations against a 1989 IMF austerity program, did the Brotherhood shift into a more oppositional political stance. In the subsequent parliamentary elections, the Brotherhood's new political party, the Islamic Action Front (IAF), became the largest bloc of parliament members over the next few years. But when IAF members used this position to demand additional reforms and the Brotherhood opposed the 1994 peace treaty between Jordan and Israel, King Hussein backtracked on the reforms. In the late 1990s and then as Abdullah II took the throne in 1999, repressive measures returned, including arrests of dissidents, censorship of the press, and government control over the electoral process to guarantee the election of only loyal candidates, largely from tribal areas and those families gaining wealth through structural adjustment. Although the Brotherhood had spent decades supporting the Hashemite state, in the 1990s it became a key voice in opposition.

Islamism in Saudi Arabia

Even Saudi Arabia, with the deep state connections between the royal family and the Wahhab religious clerics, could not avoid Islamism from emerging on its soil. In 1979 a group of Islamists took over the Grand Mosque in Mecca and tried to overthrow the government. The siege ended with the death of the leader and the capture of most of his followers. The state could not defeat so easily the spread of ideas similar to those of the Da'wa in Egypt. New Islamist preachers denounced the West, materialism, corruption, and consumerism. The members of this movement were laypeople calling on their friends and fellow believers to return to authentic Islam. It meant, as in Egypt, adopting an Islamic lifestyle, following a strict moral code, dressing conservatively, and preaching a pious Islam to others. By the 1990s, as a sign of the enthusiasm for Islamism, about a quarter of all university students in Saudi Arabia were pursuing Islamic studies.

Islamist Parties in Turkey

Mustafa Kemal's Turkey had eschewed Islam as a public factor in governance, but starting in the 1950s, Turkey's leaders and opposition parties began to slowly bring Islam back into public dialogue. Despite the work of Kemal and his Republican People's Party successors, Islam had never diminished in most people's lives. Just as people earlier had ignored the dictates of modernization laws for their towns, they continued to give Islam pride of place in public life. As long as these observances did not gain national currency and did not threaten the powers in Ankara, they were allowed to exist alongside the laicist elements of Kemalism.

The Democrat Party of the 1950s opened the national arena to Islamic observance by making the call to prayer in Arabic legal again in 1950, expanding religious education, and allowing mosque building to increase. Muslim Sufi brotherhoods found the restrictions on their activities loosened. Every cleric still remained a civil servant, so the laicist relationship between church and state was maintained. However, by allowing Islam more visibility, the Democrat Party attracted supporters from the rural areas who had never agreed with the more secular elements of Kemalism. Long-term prime minister Süleyman Demirel, in reconstituting the Democrat Party as the Justice Party in the 1960s, emphasized its Islamic values as a way to hold together its unwieldy coalition of supporters. In 1970, influential businessmen, professors, and politicians worked to counter the cultural influence of the political left by founding the Hearths of the Enlightened organization. It put forward the Turkish-Islamic Synthesis, claiming Turkish culture was built on the two pillars of Turkish and Islamic culture. In the 1980s, this new historical-religious synthesis became embedded in school discourses on nationalism.

Anatolian Tigers

Turkey's economic growth in the 1980s and 1990s allowed the new Islamic-oriented Anatolian Tigers to flourish; they became political players when the military government prohibited the older politicians from engaging in politics. Unlike businessmen in countries like Egypt, who remained dependent on the state even as they grew wealthy under privatization and structural adjustment, those in Turkey in the 1980s formed a distinctly independent class that could pool resources to lobby government to pass legislation in its favor. This group of businessmen had always favored economic privatization because it allowed them to apply Islamic rules; they had voted over the decades for parties that had supported breaking apart statist regulations. As they were largely made up of artisans, traders, shopkeepers, and small merchants, they opposed the dominance of the large commercial and industrial firms of Istanbul.

Gülen Movement

Fethullah Gülen and his movement became key financial supporters of the Islamist parties, using resources acquired through schools, media outlets, and businesses throughout Turkey and Central Asia. From 1970 to 1983, Gülen worked to build a movement from the town of Izmir, where he opened a local Quran school and held summer camps for the religious education of young men. The economic privatization efforts of the 1980s provided Gülen's followers with the space to open businesses across the economic spectrum. The movement also founded its own business association, the Association for Solidarity in Business Life (İŞHAD). Particularly successful are the schools and dormitories that exist in Turkey as well as throughout Central Asia, the Middle East, Africa, and even the United States. They have excellent reputations for academic quality while also being arenas for teaching about the reformist Islam that underpins the movement. When the state ended its monopoly in the 1980s, supporters of Gülen made *Zaman* (Time) into one of the most dominant newspapers in Turkey.

Erbakan and the Rise of Islamist Parties

Necmettin Erbakan established the Islamist National Order Party (NOP) in January 1970. It immediately attracted the support of the Anatolian merchants when Erbakan called for rapid industrialization and a "factory for each city" aimed at disbursing economic resources beyond the small cadre of large industrialists, manufacturers, and importers favored by Ankara. When the government shut it down in 1971 after the military coup, Erbakan reconstituted it as the National Salvation Party (NSP) in October 1972. The aim of the party was to encourage growth of heavy industry in Turkey while also providing encouragement for small businessmen. By January 1974, the NSP had positions within a number of coalition governments, although it typically garnered only a small minority of votes in each of the elections in the 1970s. The military banned the party after the 1980 coup, along with all other national parties, declaring that the leadership could no longer participate in national politics.

The NSP was able to reemerge as the Welfare Party (Refah Partisi) in March 1984, as a result of the National Assembly's decision to allow some of the banned parties to reconstitute themselves for the municipal elections that year. The military-supported Motherland Party (MP) of Prime Minister Özal took the largest number of seats, while the Welfare Party received 4.5 percent of the vote. As a sign of the Welfare Party's growing influence in this changing milieu, it won 17 percent of the vote in the National Assembly elections of October 20, 1991, and 30 percent in 1996. The party earned enough of a share of the vote that Erbakan served as prime minister between June 1996 and June 1997, but tension was rising between the overtly public Islamic activities of party members and the traditional military opposition to such a role for Islam. On February 28, 1997, the military presented the cabinet with a long list of demands aimed at curbing the influence of the Islamists in the economy, in education, and inside the state apparatus.

While Erbakan withstood the military pressure for months, he resigned the prime ministership on June 18, 1997, after the army mobilized supporters throughout the country. This amounted to a soft coup by the military against the government, removing a prime minister but not reasserting itself in the same direct way as in the earlier coups of 1960, 1971, and 1980. On January 16, 1998, the constitutional court banned the Welfare Party and prohibited Erbakan from ever entering political life again. In February, the court turned to the Welfare Party mayor of Istanbul, Recep Tayyip Erdoğan, and accused him of inciting religious hatred for reciting an old Ziya Gökalp poem comparing Turkey's mosque minarets with bayonets. Two months later Erdoğan was sentenced to 10 months in prison. A number of other Welfare Party mayors were also prosecuted, and a case was opened against MÜSİAD, the society for Muslim businessmen.

Justice and Development Party

Despite the political persecution, the Islamists reorganized. On February 23, 1998, members of parliament who had been associated with the Welfare Party formed the Virtue Party and immediately became the largest group in parliament with 140 seats. Soon thereafter, leaders in the party split over ideology, with the moderates breaking away and forming the Justice and Development Party (Adalet ve Kalkınma Partisi, or the AKP) on August 14, 2001. Erdoğan's jail term had been served, and he could assume leadership of the party along with Abdullah Gül, a parliament member for both the Welfare and Virtue Parties. In the general elections of 2002, the AKP won more than 34 percent of the vote and an overwhelming 363 seats because it earned the seats of those parties that did not reach the 10 percent threshold required to seat their own candidates. The reconstituted Kemalist Republican People's Party (RPP) won only half as many seats, as the only other party winning enough votes to take a place in parliament. In the 2007 elections the AKP won almost 47 percent of the vote, and in 2011 the number went up to 50 percent. Gül was prime minister for a short period before being elected president; Erdoğan stepped in as prime minister in March 2003.

Islamist Party Supporters

By the 1980s, the parties that were the descendants of Kemal's RPP continued to declaim their support for economic policies that would distribute wealth and protect the social welfare net, but in office they did little to bring those promises into action. In elections, they expected that their historic support from workers and urban migrants would continue because they saw little chance that these voters would turn to the parties that served the wealthier sectors of society. But from the 1990s forward, the various Islamic parties took those votes away, finding supporters particularly among the urban poor, including small shopkeepers and recent migrants in the gecekondu areas. By this time the Anatolian Tigers and the Gülen movement also served as a strong voting bloc on behalf of less state control over the economy, less foreign interference in it, and more focus on Islamic values. The Welfare Party was a perfect fit for these groups because it took on issues no other party discussed by attacking the poverty, inequality, and injustice present within Turkish society. Some voters found the idea of pious Muslims leading government appealing; others preferred the economic protections Islam afforded; others liked the AKP promise to end governmental corruption; and still others could appreciate the economic boom enabled by an AKP government that made Turkey the 18th-largest economy in the world by the early 21st century.

The AKP government also began negotiations with the largest of the Kurdish parties, the Kurdish Workers' Party (PKK), led by Abdullah Öcalan. The Kurdish resistance had been reignited in the late 1970s and resulted, over the next decades, in tens of thousands of Kurds and Turks being killed. In 1999, Turkish security forces captured Öcalan, and after he issued calls for reconciliation with the Turkish government, the AKP initiated openings for Kurds to express their cultural rights, garnering support from those tired of warfare.

Members of the Virtue, Welfare, and Justice and Development Parties went out into the gecekondus and villages to actively seek votes. They declared themselves vanguards of a social and political movement that would bring comprehensive improvement to people's lives regardless of whether or not their party won electoral office. Members had informal discussions with potential followers to hear about the problems they faced and provided aid, such as money for school books and fees when people were in need. It did not matter that the government banned the actual parties on several occasions; the parties had established sustained grassroots connections and associations that continued to function.

In its platform, the AKP did not call for the establishment of an Islamic state or the return of the shari'a; instead, the party presented itself as led by pious Muslims who would bring their Islamic identity

TURKEY AND THE EUROPEAN UNION

On November 1, 1993, the Maastrich Treaty formally established the European Union (EU); currently 28 countries belong, and 7 countries, including Turkey, are candidates for membership. Turkey became an associate member in 1963 and formally applied for full membership on April 14, 1987. But the EU only agreed to establish a Customs Union between Turkey and the European Community beginning January 1, 1996.

Turkey must fulfill the Copenhagen criteria to be admitted: proof that Turkey has stable institutions supporting democracy, the rule of law, and respect for human rights; a functioning market economy; and a willingness to accept the obligations of EU membership. In December 12, 1997, the European Council, which steers the EU's political direction, announced that the EU would open official discussions with all the candidate states, but Turkey was not on the list because of failure to fulfill all the listed criteria. Turkey subsequently developed a functioning market economy, but the other demands have proved more daunting.

In 1997, the EU Commission proposed that all outstanding conflicts over Cyprus be resolved before Turkey could enter the EU and demanded that Turkey recognize the Republic of Cyprus before entering into further negotiations for membership. Since the 1990s, the Turkish government has made reforms to address human rights violations, but the changes have not been sufficient to sway the EU. Kurds have more rights to use their language in official forums and schools, and Kurdish political parties have been legalized and have run in elections, but the Kurdish community still faces restrictions on its national rights. Rights to freedom of press and assembly for all citizens have also been severely curtailed over the last years, despite new laws providing protections for these activities.

When the AKP government came to office in 2002, Prime Minister Recep Tayyip Erdoğan and his colleagues were initially enthusiastic supporters of Turkey entering the EU. The comparable economic policies and the AKP government's support of protections for minorities fit with the avowed return to Ottoman cosmopolitanism. But the obstacles and demands placed on Turkey have turned much of that early enthusiasm , including that of the population, against the idea, so the Turkish government is not pursuing new negotiations.

to their decision making in office. Kemalist Turkish nationalism was predicated on a veneration of the pre-Ottoman era of Turkish supremacy, whereas the AKP reintegrated Ottoman achievements into Turkish nationalism. Following Ottoman precedent, the AKP found ways to allow non-Turkish Muslims and even non-Muslims to form associations that supported their distinctive cultures, replicating the protective function of the Ottoman millet system and embracing a more cosmopolitan approach to governance. The AKP challenged the laicist nature of Kemalism, not by calling for an Islamic state to be established in Turkey but by reconfiguring how the state controls and manages the Islamic sphere. For example, the military and Kemalist politicians of the past enforced laws banning women wearing headscarves from entering state institutions such as universities and parliament. The AKP's definition of laicism, rather, allowed individuals to practice Islam as he or she preferred, without interference from state agencies; thus, women could wear headscarves in state institutions.

Militant Sunni Islamism

Unlike the Sunni Islamist political activists involved in the Da'wa movement and with Turkish political parties, militant Islamists focus their attention on overthrowing governments and establishing Islamic states in their stead. To achieve their goals, they work within national borders and transnationally by bringing together Muslims throughout the world who oppose the Western countries for supporting irreligious governments. By the late 20th century, militant Islamists came to see the need for attacks against those government leaders who were taking sovereignty away from God and against the West, especially the United States, which funded and influenced such governments.

This militant trend includes Muslims who call themselves Salafs, those who want to return to the example set by the companions (salafs) of the Prophet. In their view, in the centuries since the Rashidun period, innovations have been added to the faith by politicians and social leaders that go against the pure message preached by the Prophet. The activist Islamists working within their societies and governments believe in this need for purification, but the militant Islamists also subscribe to tenets of Wahhabism that emerged in the Arabian Peninsula in the 18th century and became the cornerstone of the Saudi state in the 20th century. This merger of ideas could take place because many Arabs migrated to Saudi Arabia to work in the 1970s and 1980s and came into contact with Saudi-sponsored Wahhabism. As a result of its great oil wealth, the Saudi state also began exporting its ideas throughout the Muslim world by building mosques and schools and expanding its publication of religious books, satellite stations, and television shows.

Sayyid al-Qutb, Jahiliyya, and Jihad

An influential writer in this era was Sayyid al-Qutb (1906–1966), who gave a rationale for the actions of militant Islamists. Like many of the Islamists who followed him, he was not an Islamic cleric but a layperson writing to his fellow Egyptians. After he had served years in jail for his ideas, the Egyptian government executed him in 1966. While in prison he wrote his most influential work, *Milestones along the Path* (*Ma'alim fi al-Tariq*). In this book, he used the concept of jahiliyya (the era of ignorance before the coming of Islam) as a way to describe the Egyptian government. Jahiliyya meant the willful rejection by government and societal leaders of God's sovereign power over them. He faulted modern governments for relying on human-made laws rather than those prescribed by God. He called instead for hakimiyyat Allah (the absolute sovereignty of God), meaning the establishment of a system of Islamic law derived from the texts of the Quran and sunna of the Prophet. Al-Qutb called on Muslim youth to form a vanguard ready to launch holy war (jihad) against the modern jahili system and all who support it so they could establish a government and society based on the laws of God.

The definition of and role for jihad has become a hallmark of the intellectual discussions by and the actions of various Islamists. Islamist reformers focus on the definition of jihad as a personal struggle to understand the faith and live by its precepts; in this perspective, fighting is a collective rather than an individual duty imposed on all Muslims when the community is threatened. Many interpreted al-Qutb's words to mean that the community needed to struggle to live by God's laws and hence viewed his prescriptions as a call for reform rather than rebellion. For militant Islamists, al-Qutb's words triggered a belief that a permanent duty of individual Muslims was to defend the faith and its people by fighting against leaders who claim to be Muslim but are leading their societies as in the era of jahiliyya.

Groups of militant Islamists in Egypt, calling themselves the Military Academy Group, the Society of Muslims, and al-Jihad, perpetrated attacks against the state, its leaders, and its institutions from the 1970s forward. State police arrested a large number of them in the 1970s, and their activities subsided for a time. But by 1979, a new al-Jihad had formed, which merged with the group of militant students from Upper Egypt who assassinated Anwar Sadat on October 6, 1981. The Mubarak government spent much of the 1980s and 1990s attacking this group throughout Egypt, but not until the end of the 1990s did such attacks diminish substantially.

Afghanistan

In the 1980s, Afghanistan became an epicenter for militant Islamist activism. When the Soviet Union invaded the country on December 24, 1979, to shore up a Communist government in Kabul, a decade of fighting ensued, involving the countries surrounding Afghanistan, the United States, and Saudi Arabia, as well as thousands of foreign fighters.

Mujahidin

The majority of Afghans who fought the Soviet and Afghan Communist governments were the mujahidin (fighters on behalf of Islam). The mujahidin had started as a small group opposing the government in the 1970s, dedicated to a revivalist Islam, but grew quickly with foreign military aid. The group's movement attracted thousands of Muslims from around the world, especially Arabs, who wanted to defend Islam from a Communist invasion. The mujahidin were funded and armed by the United States and Saudi Arabia with the assistance of Pakistan, with billions of dollars in aid and weaponry flowing to them during the decade. Under such pressure, the Soviet Union withdrew its forces in 1989.

Taliban

The local forces were united only in their opposition to the Soviet Union: when the Soviets withdrew, and the United States shortly thereafter, the various groups that had fought on the same side for years went to war against each other and against the still-standing Communist government in Kabul. The Taliban ultimately overthrew the Kabul government and took control of the capital in 1996. The name means "students" and refers to the fact that the organization emerged from madrasas in Pakistan that educated young Afghan refugees during the years of fighting. By the early 1990s, the leadership under Mullah Muhammad Omar had set up in Kandahar, Afghanistan, and from there militarily worked their way to Kabul in 1996. In the late 1990s, the Taliban government gained control over most of the country.

Al-Qa'ida

In the meantime, after 1989, the thousands of Arab volunteers who had fought with the mujahidin returned to their countries, trained in heavy weaponry and imbued with the ideas of militant Islam. The group al-Qa'ida was under the leadership of Saudi Osama bin Laden, who brought his followers to train in camps in Afghanistan, Pakistan, and around the Arab world in the 1990s. Over the following years, these Arab veterans of the Afghan war and the subsequent followers who were influenced by ideas expressed by Salafs, Wahhabism, and Sayyid al-Qutb joined al-Qa'ida. Although these Islamists had worked with the United States in Afghanistan, a turning point in this relationship was the positioning of US troops in Saudi Arabia in 1990 in preparation for the attack against the Iraqi invasion of Kuwait. Although the Americans had worked with militant Islamists to oust the Soviet Union, when the United States staged troops on sacred Muslim soil, they became the primary target of al-Qa'ida in the war against the West.

The rationale for targeting the West was that by so doing, al-Qa'ida could gain popular followers throughout the Muslim world who would then rise up against their own governments. Despite this call and despite the large amount of anti-Americanism that permeated many parts of the Muslim world, this international jihadi cause never at any point became a mass movement among Muslims. At best, al-Qa'ida and associated groups could boast of a few hundred followers at any one time in the 1990s. Although those numbers increased after September 11, 2001, and the subsequent US-allied invasions of Afghanistan and Iraq, they failed to attract substantial support in any Muslim nation.

Nineteen members of al-Qa'ida on the morning of September 11, 2011, hijacked two planes from Boston's Logan Airport, one from Newark International Airport, and one from Washington Dulles International Airport. The two from Boston flew into and destroyed the twin towers of the World Trade Center in New York City; the one from Washington flew into the Pentagon; and passengers on the fourth plane subdued the hijackers, and the plane crashed in Shanksville, Pennsylvania. More than 3,000 people died.

On September 20, 2001, US president George W. Bush made a statement declaring that the United States would pursue nations that provided a safe haven for terrorists, the initial call for what would be termed the "War on Terror" over the next years. As Bush said in the statement, "Either you are with us, or you are with the terrorists." The same day, the US government issued an ultimatum to the Taliban in Afghanistan, demanding that they turn over Osama bin Laden, expel al-Qa'ida from Afghanistan, and shut down terrorist training bases. The Taliban called on the US government to provide evidence of bin Laden's involvement in the 9/11 attacks before extraditing him. The US government refused and invaded Afghani-

PLANNING FOR SEPTEMBER 11, 2001

Khalid Sheikh Mohammed of Pakistan suggested to Osama bin Laden in 1996 that al-Qa'ida could hijack as many as 10 American planes to attack cities throughout the country. At the time, bin Laden rejected the plan, but after the al-Qa'ida bombings against the US embassies in Kenya and Tanzania on August 7, 1998, and the US retaliation against al-Qa'ida bases in Afghanistan, bin Laden decided to revisit the plan, and al-Qa'ida members began training at US flight schools.

A goal of 9/11 was to prove that the United States was vulnerable, that it could be attacked at its financial, military, and political heart. Leaders in the Muslim world who relied on US aid to maintain their positions would understand that the United States was not strong enough to support them; Muslim publics dissatisfied with their rulers could rise up without fear of US retaliation. The result would be the fall of leaders who primarily served the United States rather than their Muslim populations; the United States would pull out its troops, dismantle its bases, and end funding for puppet leaders in the Muslim world.

After the US invasion of Afghanistan in 2001 and the dismantling of its headquarters there, relatively small-sized al-Qa'ida branches proliferated around the Muslim world but with little coordination between them. Others in places such as Iraq and Syria established organizations with the al-Qa'ida name but with little to no institutional connection, only a shared belief in the ideas expressed by bin Laden and his closest advisers. Although they follow the basic ideological underpinnings of al-Qa'ida, they functionally work on their own and react to events taking place in the particular country in which they are working. The United States and its allies in Europe and the Middle East countered this movement with its War on Terror, which has brought US troops, bombs, and drones to areas as far apart as Somalia and Pakistan and Libya. These attacks have done little to diminish the appeal of international jihadism among those favoring this position.

Bin Laden repeatedly criticized US policies, including US support for the Israeli occupation of Palestine, the stationing of US troops in Saudi Arabia, and US military attacks against Muslims in places such as Somalia. These criticisms resonated with Muslim publics in many countries because they believed US policies were geared toward weakening the Muslim community, but the 9/11 attacks did not elicit mass support for the al-Qa'ida program. Al-Qa'ida- influenced groups such as the Islamic State of Iraq and Sham (ISIS) have continued to form and gain supporters, but they have little support within the communities in which they function.

The United States initially failed to capture bin Laden in 2001, who fled to Pakistan, but over the next years did capture many top al-Qa'ida leaders, including Khalid Sheikh Mohammed, who is being held at Guantanamo prison. US forces killed bin Laden on May 2, 2011, after locating him in Pakistan.

stan with a coalition of forces on October 7, 2001, and quickly drove the Taliban from power. On March 19, 2003, the United States and a coalition of allied forces invaded Iraq under the claim that Saddam Hussein had weapons of mass destruction and that the United States must invade to prevent him from using them against the United States or its allies.

Operation Enduring Freedom in Afghanistan forced the fall of the Taliban government within weeks, and the United States and its allies set up a new government in Kabul led by a transitional administration. Then followed elections to the Loya Jirga (Council of Advisers) in 2003 and the election of Hamid Karzai as president in 2004. On May 2, 2012, the US and Afghan governments signed the Strategic Partnership Agreement, which called for the removal of most military troops by the end of 2014. In fall 2014, however, the two governments returned to the negotiating table and worked out an arrangement whereby the United States could maintain approximately 10,000 troops in the country after that deadline.

Shi'i Resistance in Iraq

Just as Sunni Muslims found ways to resist the political and social structures of their governments, so, too, have the Shi'a around the region. In Bahrain since independence from Britain in 1971, Shi'a have been in the demographic majority; in Saudi Arabia they are a minority mostly living in the Eastern Province along the Persian Gulf. Both communities have organized opposition movements to their governments but thus far have not succeeded in achieving their national goals. In Iraq Shi'a waged an opposition movement to the government decade after decade and finally took over the Iraqi government after the US invasion of the country in 2003.

Because the majority of people in Iraq are Shi'a, their opposition to the Iraqi state has been sustained and large in scope. In 1958, six of the seven largest landowners in the entire country were Shi'a. Shi'i youth represented the largest bloc of soldiers in the Iraqi army every year, and the 1950s and 1960s in particular saw enormous Shi'i migration to Baghdad, changing the composition of the capital markedly. While a small number of Shi'a held leadership positions in every government of the 20th century and in the municipalities in the southern part where they predominate, Sunni Arab Muslims controlled the most important positions once the British left after World War II, especially following the 1958 revolution and the formation of the Ba'thist government in 1968.

When organized opposition rose in the 1950s, the leaders were not the old tribal shaykhs of the 1930s but religious clerics and laypeople putting forward a religious message of empowerment and resistance. In the 1950s, cleric Muhammad Baqir al-Sadr established the Da'wa Party as a vehicle for reviving Shi'i religious life amid the secularizing influences embedded in Iraqi society. When it started, it was not a challenge to the Iraqi government as much as to the Shi'i older elite who were opposed to allowing young ulama and laypeople to direct the community's religious life. The movement continued to grow, with followers especially energized by the arrival of Ayatollah Khomeini in Najaf in the mid-1960s, who preached a similarly activist politico-religious message.

The resistance to the Ba'thist state became stronger in the 1970s and continued for the next decades, as part of the long-term conflict between Iraq and Iran and the result of increased aid by Iran after the establishment of the Islamic Republic in 1979. Starting in 1969, the Iraqi state instituted regular waves of arrests of Iranian religious students, deportations of thousands of people of alleged Iranian descent, and closures of religious schools and universities and the confiscation of their waqf religious endowments. After the Iranian Revolution of 1979, the Iraqi government increased the number of regulations it imposed on Shi'a and took charge of the collection, allocation, and distribution of income from all the Shi'i shrines.

Iran-Iraq War

In the 20th century, many conflicts between Iran and Iraq broke out across their long, shared border. The modern state of Iraq is at a geographic disadvantage along the Persian Gulf because it lacks a deep-water port easily navigable by large ships. In trying to rectify that problem, the Iraqis have frequently negotiated and, at times, used force to pressure Kuwait to allow access via islands along the coast. Conflict also occurred over the Shatt al-'Arab waterway dividing Iraq and Iran, especially because it discharges into the Gulf and the oil industries of both countries sit astride it. Throughout the 20th century, the two countries disputed the location of the border, whether along the deepest part in the center (Iran's position) or along the low-water mark along the eastern shore (Iraq's position). Exacerbating the conflict still further, Kurds live along both sides of the Iran-Iraq border, and whenever relations were tense between Tehran and Baghdad, the leadership of each supported the Kurds of the opposing country as they rebelled in the hopes of gaining independence. Furthermore, the Iraqi holy cities of Najaf and Karbala brought many Iranian Shi'a across the border for study and pilgrimage; many Iraqi Shi'a crossed into Iran to study at the seminaries in Qom.

Iran and Iraq came to a brief rapprochement in the Algiers Agreement in 1975 concerning the border and aid for the Kurds, but the fall of the shah in January 1979 and subsequent establishment of the Islamic Republic reignited tensions. The new Islamic government in Iran immediately began to proclaim its desire to spread its revolutionary ideas throughout the Middle East, starting with the Shi'a living in Iraq. From Baghdad's perspective, there was a danger that the Shi'a of Iraq would become fifth columnists for Iran. However, Iraq saw that in the aftermath of the Islamic Revolution, Iran was militarily weak and its western oil fields vulnerable to takeover.

In September 1980, Saddam Hussein launched the Iran-Iraq War by invading Iran, but over the next few years he discovered that many of the assumptions leading up to the war did not prove to be correct. The majority of Iraqi Shi'a remained loyal to the Iraqi state and served in enormous numbers in the military, while only a relatively small number established a political opposition movement in Iran. Iraq had the military advantage early in the war and took substantial territory in Iran at the beginning, but in 1982 the Iranian army successfully counterattacked.

In July 1987 the UN Security Council passed Resolution 598 calling for a cease-fire, and the war ended in July 1988 when the Iranian government accepted the resolution. More than a million soldiers and civilians died during the war, the infrastructure of both countries was devastated, and ultimately the border changed very little. Before it ended, the Iraqi government used chemical weapons against Iranian towns and against the Kurds living within its borders, such as in the al-Anfal campaign in 1988, which killed as many as 100,000 Kurds. The United States became heavily invested in the outcome and, as result, deeply embedded in Persian Gulf politics. Even though Iraq had aligned itself with the Soviet Union since the 1960s, especially after signing a treaty of friendship in the 1970s, the United States chose to support Iraq in this conflict, calculating that the Islamic Republic of Iran was a larger threat to US interests than Iraq was. The United States provided arms and strategic plans to Iraq, while also reflagging Kuwait oil tankers as American tankers when they came under attack from the combatants. For a brief time in the mid-1980s, the United States offered weapons to Iran in exchange for releasing American hostages captured by Iran-allied Hizballah during the Lebanese civil war.

When the Iran-Iraq War began, and for much of the 1980s, Hussein's government followed carrot-and-stick policies in regard to the Shi'a at home, repressing any activity that might be construed as supportive of Iran but funneling new resources to the southern, Shi'i-dominated districts to enhance loyalty to the state. While the majority of Iraqi Shi'a remained loyal during the war, the Da'wa leadership and many of its members went into exile in Iran because of the attacks against them by the Iraqi state. In Iran, however, a new rivalry emerged among the activist Shi'i parties in 1982 after establishment of the Supreme Council for the Islamic Revolution in Iraq (SCIRI). Heavily subsidized by the Iranian government, SCIRI had resources Da'wa lacked, and the two organizations came into conflict over the type of government they hoped for Iraq. SCIRI ascribed to Khomeini's velayat-e faqih, while Da'wa was wary of the Iranian influence that would follow in the wake of such a government.

Gulf War of 1990–1991

When the war ended in 1988, the United States was the most important foreign power involved in the Persian Gulf because of the aid it had supplied during the war and because the Soviet Union was beginning to collapse, officially dissolving in 1991. In keeping with its strategy of supporting Iraq as a strong force within the Persian Gulf, the US government provided food and financial aid to Iraq in the aftermath of the war. The relationship began fraying, however, as Iraqi attacks against the Kurds continued, and it broke apart completely when Iraq invaded Kuwait on August 2, 1990, quickly overrunning the country and forcing the royal Al Sabah family to flee.

The motive for the invasion related to the huge debt Iraq had accumulated during the Iran-Iraq War. Saudi Arabia, Kuwait, and the neighboring Arab Gulf countries had loaned large sums to Iraq so it could wage the war, and none of the countries was willing to forgive the debt. Neither would these countries—or any of the other OPEC states—decrease oil production and increase the price of oil so that Iraqi revenues could increase. Saddam Hussein invaded Kuwait to alleviate this economic crisis and pressure the Arab Gulf States to accede to Iraqi demands.

The UN Security Council immediately issued a resolution condemning the invasion and imposing sanctions on Iraq. Within days, the US government initiated Operation Desert Shield to build up military forces in the region to prevent Iraq from crossing the border from Kuwait into Saudi Arabia. Throughout the fall of 1990, an international coalition, mostly made up of troops from the United States and Britain but with units from Arab and non-Arab countries, threatened war if Iraq did not pull out of Kuwait. For the first time since World War II, Cold War strategy did not complicate decision making, since the Soviet Union was no longer a counterforce to the United States. On January 17, 1991, when the ultimatum for Iraqi troops to withdraw from Kuwait had expired with no change on the ground, the United States and its allies began Operation Desert Storm with an intensive air-bombing campaign; the following month the allies' ground forces invaded Kuwait and forced the Iraqi troops to evacuate. The fighting ended on March 1.

With strong US support, the UN imposed sanctions on the Iraqi government to pressure Saddam Hussein to recognize Kuwaiti sovereignty, pay war reparations, and open up all sites in Iraq for inspection by UN teams searching for evidence of Iraq's nuclear, chemical, and biological weapons. In 1992, the UN passed a resolution allowing an oil-for-food exchange whereby Iraq could sell a set amount of oil on the world market and use the profits to pay for imported food and medicine. Saddam Hussein accepted the provisions in 1996. But even with the infusion of money and supplies coming into the country, hundreds of thousands of people died from treatable diseases, professionals left the country in droves for better opportunities abroad, and the quality of schooling deteriorated to the point where a generation of children was denied an education. The sanctions never weakened Saddam Hussein's hold over the government and society because he controlled the bulk of the revenues flowing into the country.

In the aftermath of the Gulf War the Shi'a revolted against the Iraqi government, calculating that Western coalition aid would materialize and that a weakened Iraqi government could be pressured to grant local rights to its community. But coalition aid did not materialize, and Saddam Hussein, who had held back the Republican Guards during the fighting in Kuwait, crushed the rebellion quickly. When the fighting ended within a few weeks, tens of thousands of Shi'i refugees poured across the border into Iran and Saudi Arabia, and thousands more were killed by Iraqi guns. At that point, the UN established a no-fly zone over the Shi'i-dominated districts in the south to prevent future Iraqi military attacks from the air. Nonetheless, the Iraqi government maintained control over the region and over the next years drained most of the swamps in the Shi'i regions farthest to the south, destroying many people's livelihoods. Ayatollah Muhammad Sadiq al-Sadr and two of his sons were killed in 1999, and the senior Shi'i mujtahid, Grand Ayatollah Ali al-Sistani, was placed under house arrest in 1994 to limit his contacts with the Shi'i community.

Kurdish Resistance in Iraq

While Shi'a were rebelling against the Iraqi government from the south in 1991, the Kurds based in the north rebelled, continuing a decades-long process of resistance. Kurdish leader Mustafa Barzani began fighting against the Iraqi state in 1931 when he established a small guerrilla force. In 1945, he and his colleagues formed the Kurdish Democratic Party (KDP), modeled after the Iraqi Communist Party. It maintained cohesion for decades, but at a KDP congress in June 1964, the party split into two wings after a group led by Jalal Talabani was expelled.

Barzani had always attracted followers among the Kurds of the northern mountains and Talabani from the more urbanized southern regions. Over the decades, the two sides had forged an uneasy alliance to fight against the Iraqi government, but the tensions grew in 1964 when Barzani's faction allied with the Iranian government to receive weapons and aid and Talabani's side made common cause with the Iraqi government. When the Iraqi and Iranian governments signed the Algiers Agreement in 1975, the Iraqi government agreed to border adjustments favoring Iran and the Iranian government agreed to withdraw support from Barzani and his Kurdish forces. Barzani could no longer sustain his military opposition to the Iraqi government so had to surrender, and he and many of his followers moved to Iran. With this defeat, Talabani formally broke with Barzani and the KDP and formed the Patriotic Union of Kurdistan (PUK).

Between the 1930s and 1990s, the conflict between the Kurdish resistance and the Iraqi government followed a similar pattern year after year. At times, the two forces signed a cease-fire agreement and the Iraqi government promised and even initiated autonomy measures, but before long those agreements broke down because the Iraqi government refused to implement policies introducing true autonomy. From the governmental perspective, the agreements were solely designed to end the fighting and facilitate greater Iraqi control over the Kurdish-dominated provinces; Kurds quickly grew frustrated by the failure of the government to implement the promised autonomy. In eras of fighting, the Iraqi military usually succeeded in gaining control over the cities in the Kurdish provinces, but the Kurdish irregular forces maintained their military positions in the mountainous regions.

The years of fighting saw hundreds of thousands killed and frequent Kurdish refugee flows into Iran or Turkey, but never did these conflicts produce a clear victory for either side. At times, the Iranian and US governments supported the Kurdish rebels, but whenever these governments' relations with the Iraqi government improved, aid to the Kurds was withdrawn. During the Iran-Iraq War, the Kurdish rebellion emerged again with aid from the Iranian government, and when the war ended in 1988, the Iraqi government used chemical weapons against the Kurds in an attempt to tip the balance of power and subdue them for good. However, just as in the past, the Kurdish rebellion was not destroyed, just temporarily weakened and displaced.

Kurds after the Gulf War

In the midst of the Iraqi withdrawal from Kuwait in 1991, the Kurds relaunched their rebellion with a more efficient organizational structure than the Shi'a had fronted because the Kurds had rebelled so often against the Iraqi government that they were well trained. Initially, the combined forces of the Kurdish militia groups performed well and took over the city of Kirkuk on March 19. However, without aid from outside to protect the Kurds, the Iraqi military crushed the revolt and possibly as many as two million Kurds fled across the border into Turkey. As a result of the defeat and the exodus of much of the population, the UN Security Council passed Resolution 688 establishing a no-fly zone north of the 36th parallel to protect the Kurds from Iraqi air attacks.

Within this zone and under coalition protection, the Kurds received more autonomy than ever before, with the KDP the power broker in the northern region and the PUK controlling most of the southern districts. After years of competition between the two organizations, only in the Washington Agreement of September 1998 did Barzani and Talabani commit themselves to power sharing in the region. During this period, a new Kurdish order began to take shape: Kurdish institutions were established, school curricula were revised, and the Kurdish language was given prominence. Between the two parties, they controlled armed forces amounting to 80,000 men who were now starting to take on the attributes of a national army.

Iraqi National Council

The Iraqi National Council (INC), made up of parties opposing Saddam Hussein's continuing leadership and led by longtime Iraqi exile Ahmad Chalabi, was based in the Kurdish areas between 1992 and 1996. The US government funded the INC in those years in the hopes it would overthrow the Iraqi government. However, the INC had difficulty finding supporters inside Iraq since most of the participants had spent years outside the country and lacked the necessary connections, so it never attained such a victory. By the mid-1990s, its leaders had fled the area and the US government had pulled back much of its support.

US Invasion of Iraq

A US-led coalition invaded Iraq in spring 2003 and established the Coalition Provisional Authority (CPA) in April, which supervised the dismantlement of the Ba'th Party, the Iraqi military, and most offices of the Iraqi government. The CPA turned over authority to the Iraqi Interim Government between 2004 and 2005, and elections were held for a constituent assembly in January 2005. In the voting system, the Shi'a as the majority in the population received the largest number of seats, with the Sunnis relegated to a number befitting their 20 percent representation in the total population.

The US advisers designing this new structure favored the Shi'a because of their long-standing opposition to the Sunni-dominated government. This rapid shift to Shi'i political empowerment caused Sunnis to lose jobs and positions of authority at all levels of the government and military. By summer 2003, Sunni insurgents began to retaliate by attacking people working with the United States in the new government, from which they were largely excluded. These actions quickly devolved into Sunni and Shi'i attacks against each other and the exodus of millions of Iraqis from their homes and from Iraq altogether. To protest the disposition of seats within the constituent assembly, Sunni groups also boycotted the elections of 2005, so the returns brought into the assembly primarily members of Shi'i political parties, Kurdish leaders, and Sunni independents.

The biggest winner in 2005 with almost 50 percent of the vote was a coalition called the United Iraqi Alliance (UIA), including the Shi'i-based Islamist parties, SCIRI, and Da'wa, and endorsed by Ayatollah al-Sistani. The second-largest bloc came from the Democratic Patriotic Alliance of Kurdistan, which included KDP and PUK candidates. UIA member Nouri al-Maliki was sworn in as prime minister in May 2006. This government tried and executed Saddam Hussein for the use of chemical weapons in the al-Anfal campaign. The United States signed the Status of Forces Agreement (SOFA) with the new government in 2008 and under its provisions withdrew the vast majority of its forces by the end of 2011. On September 8, 2014, Haidar al-Abadi succeeded al-Maliki as prime minister.

Kurdish Regional Government

But even as the United States and its allies pulled out and the new Iraqi government appeared to be taking charge, problems persisted throughout the country. The Kurdish regions received a large degree of autonomy as part of the reconstruction of the Iraqi government after 2003. The Kurdish Regional Government (KRG) maintains its representation in parliament and espouses support for Iraqi unity. However, because the Kurdish regions contain large oil deposits, Kurdish leaders have been able to acquire far more functional independence than the post-2003 Iraqi constitution allows. On its own independent authority, the KRG has negotiated oil and trade agreements with oil companies and surrounding states.

Al-Qa'ida in Iraq

The KRG has thus far confirmed its desire to remain part of the Iraqi federation, but the Sunni quest for political power is a more destabilizing factor in the country. Joining the local Sunni insurgents by 2005 were foreign Sunni fighters who brought to Iraq the transnational organization and ideology of militant Islamism associated with al-Qa'ida. Local and foreign fighters attacked the United States, coalition allies, and the newly formed Iraqi government. By 2007, conflict erupted between the local and foreign Sunni fighters because of concerns that al-Qa'ida in Iraq (AQI) was causing more problems than they were solving for the local Sunnis. To counteract al-Qa'ida's influence, local Sunni groups formed the Awakening Councils (Sahwa) as an organizational tool to bring together local Sunni forces in the Sunni-dominated districts. The United States helped support these groups financially and militarily because they were a strong force opposing al-Qa'ida.

By 2010, AQI was a depleted force, with many fighters in jail, killed, or having left Iraq because of the strength of the Sahwa movement. While the worst of the violence subsided for a time, conflicts between the Shi'i government and marginalized Sunnis continued. Former Ba'thist military officers and tribal leaders were forced, because of the lack of support from the government, to provide much aid to their constituencies. In addition, both the Iraqi government and Iranian-backed militias attacked Sunni leaders and necessitated continuation of the Sahwa units for protection of the Sunni community. By 2013, AQI was growing in size and influence again because its leaders had been released from prison and the local Sunni leaders were beginning to see value in establishing a broad-based

Sunni alliance against the Iraqi government and its associated militias. In February 2014, this combined group, now calling itself the Islamic State in Iraq, captured the Sunni-dominated city of Fallujah; in June these forces took control of the city of Mosul and began the process of setting up an Islamic state in most of the Sunni-dominated provinces of Iraq.

The Oslo Process

While these events were happening in Iraq, the Israelis and Palestinians appeared to be heading toward a solution to their conflict. The Gulf War of 1990–1991 altered the rhythm of the First Intifada and gave an impetus for the PLO, the Israelis, and the Americans to push for the start of a new peace process. Egypt and Syria had agreed to contribute troops to the US coalition against Iraq based in part on the condition that the United States accelerate efforts to bring about peace negotiations between the Arabs and Israelis. Furthermore, when Chairman of the PLO Yasser Arafat supported Iraq's invasion of Kuwait, the Gulf States withdrew their funding. The move weakened the PLO in the 1990s, and the Intifada had shown that the PLO was not the only organization capable of mobilizing large groups of Palestinians. The PLO looked to a peace conference as a means for strengthening its position.

That conference, a multinational undertaking under the auspices of the United States and the Soviet Union, began in Madrid on October 30, 1991. The Palestinians and diplomats from Lebanon, Syria, and Jordan all agreed to participate, but the Israelis stipulated that the Palestinians could be represented only as part of the Jordanian delegation, not as a separate state organization. After the opening session in Madrid, negotiations shifted to bilateral talks in Washington, D.C., between December 1991 and spring 1992. Out of these talks came the Israeli-Jordanian Treaty, signed in 1994 marking the second time an Arab state had negotiated peace with Israel. Israel and Syria also came relatively close to an agreement but were hamstrung on differences over the positioning of the international border between their two countries and the conditions by which the Israeli forces would withdraw settler and military forces from the Golan Heights.

Oslo Declaration of Principles

The Israeli-Palestinian track broke away from Jordanian supervision once the participants moved to Washington. Then participants entered into secret negotiations in Oslo under the aegis of the Norwegian government.

Their talks resulted in the Oslo Declaration of Principles (DOP), signed on September 13, 1993, on the White House lawn and presided over by US president Bill Clinton. As a final step to enable the agreement, Yasser Arafat sent a letter to Israeli prime minister Yitzhak Rabin acknowledging Israel's right to exist in peace and security and renouncing terrorism as a PLO tactic. The next day, Rabin sent a letter to Arafat recognizing the PLO as the representative of the Palestinian people.

The DOP was not a peace treaty but an interim agreement laying out the timetable and tasks to be undertaken by the Israeli government and the Palestinians over a period of five years. It called for a two-state solution to the conflict: Israel would keep the area it established in 1948, and a Palestinian state would be formed in Territories captured by Israel in the 1967 war, following the terms of UN Resolution 242. Israel agreed to withdraw from most of the Gaza Strip and the West Bank town of Jericho by April 1994 so the Palestinians could set up a government in those two areas. Elections would be held within nine months for positions to a Palestinian council that would govern the Gaza Strip and West Bank for a transitional period not exceeding five years. During that time, Israel would turn over elements of governance to this new Palestinian authority in the spheres of education, health, social welfare, taxation, and tourism.

After withdrawing from Gaza and Jericho, the Israeli army would redeploy outside Palestinian population areas in the West Bank, while retaining authority for internal security even in areas from which the military had withdrawn. Two years into this so-called empowerment phase, final-status negotiations would begin concerning Jerusalem, borders, refugees, settlements, and security arrangements. The Israelis and Palestinians have not made it to the final-status phase, but the years after 1993 did see the establishment of the first Palestinian government in the Territories and the slow redeployment of Israeli forces from areas in the West Bank and Gaza.

The Palestinian Authority (PA) was established in 1994 in Gaza and Jericho, and with this government came thousands of Palestinians who had been working for the PLO in the diaspora for the previous two decades. Presidential and legislative elections took place in 1996, and Arafat was elected president. However, many of the Palestinian organizations, from Hamas to the PFLP, boycotted the elections because of opposition to the Oslo framework. As a result, the Legislative Council came to be filled with those loyal to Arafat and Fatah.

Oslo II

Since the Oslo Accords did not outline the specific areas for Israeli redeployment, Israeli and Palestinian negotiators worked throughout the 1990s to ratify a series of accords on this issue. The most comprehensive agreement was the Interim Agreement on the West Bank and the Gaza Strip, colloquially known as Oslo II, signed on September 28, 1995. It was followed by agreements on smaller pieces of territory. Overall, the West Bank was divided into three areas. Area A encompassed the municipal areas of the six largest Palestinian cities. The PA took responsibility for all internal affairs and overall security in this area, which by the end of the decade included about 3 percent of the West Bank. Area B, which by the 1990s amounted to 27 percent of the West Bank, covered the areas of about 450 Palestinian villages. In these areas, the PA took charge of jurisdiction for civil affairs and public order, while Israel maintained authority over security issues. The remaining territory of Area C, 70 percent, came under complete Israeli control. It included Israeli settlements and the border areas with Jordan.

Economic Crises

In 1993, just months before signing the DOP, Israel began instituting checkpoints between the Territories and the areas inside the 1948 borders of Israel, and it blocked many Palestinians from moving between the two. Thousands of Palestinians lost their jobs in Israel as a result, and the two economies began to separate under the provisions of Oslo. Because the Palestinian economy had not developed much since 1967, there were high unemployment rates for most years of the 1990s, particularly in the Gaza Strip, which had been more dependent on Israeli jobs than had the workers of the West Bank. The Israeli government accelerated the settlement-building project, increasing from about 200,000 settlers in 1993 to about 400,000 in 2000. The Israelis also imposed a closure policy on the Territories whenever Palestinian groups attacked Israelis or Israeli installations, some years closing borders for three months overall. Economic crises ensued, and millions of dollars in donor aid from the European Union and the United States could not completely alleviate the situation.

The PA was now the most concrete manifestation of a state the Palestinians had achieved since 1948, and its institutions covered a slowly increasing amount of territory in the West Bank and the Gaza Strip. The establishment of the PA opened up new jobs for Palestinians as police, teachers, and bureaucrats; new infrastructure projects employed construc-

MAP 21. Oslo–West Bank Areas A, B, and C as of 2000. In accordance with the Oslo II Accords of 1995, the West Bank was divided into Area A (under full Palestinian Authority control), Area B (Palestinian control over civil affairs and Israel over security), and Area C (full Israeli control).

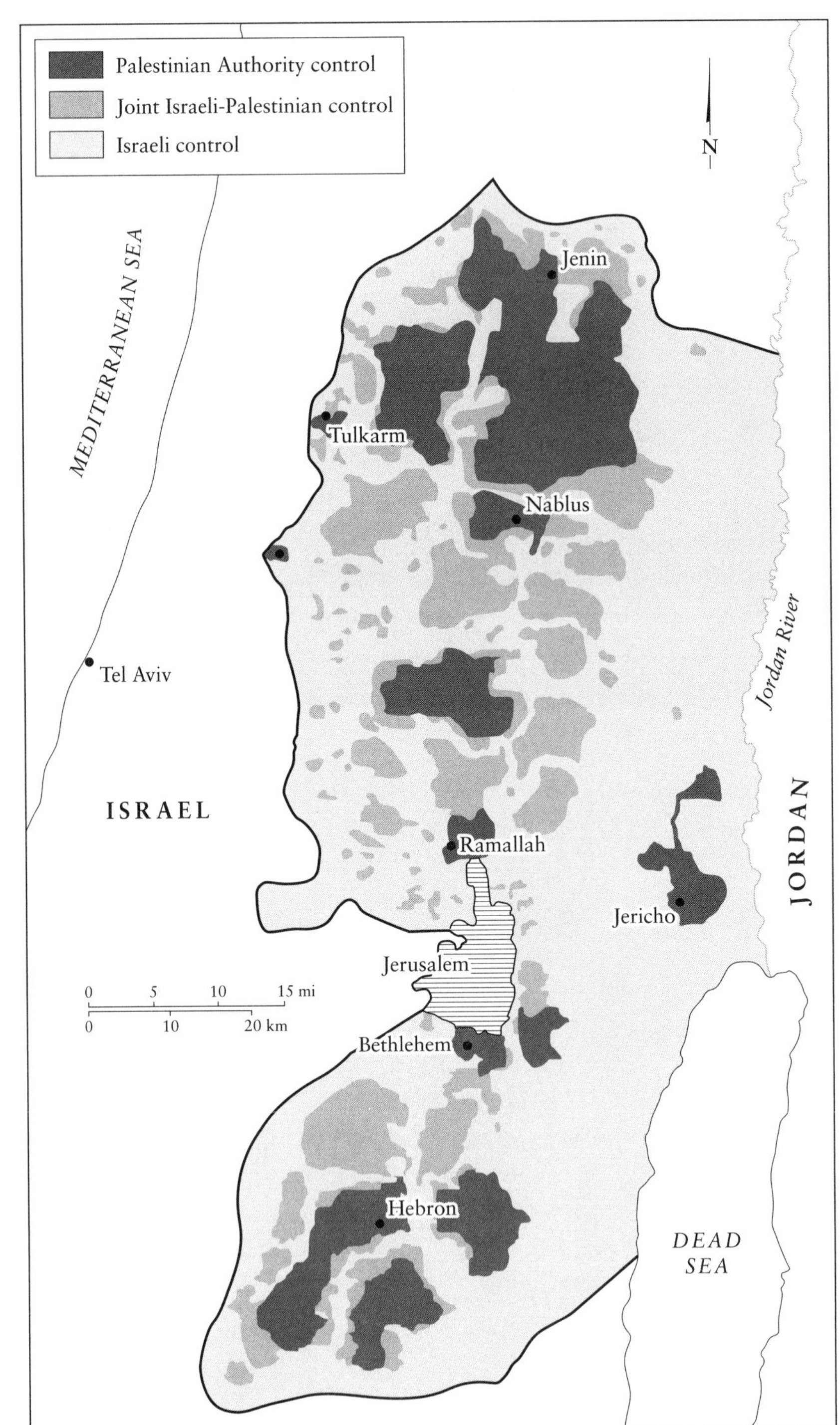

tion workers who could no longer work in Israel. These new positions could not completely offset the job losses to Israel, nor could the new infusions of cash work to diversify the economy enough to make the Palestinians self-sufficient. But these new jobs increased the numbers of people dependent on PA salaries and thus the PA itself. The PA leadership also worked to guarantee that no political opposition force could threaten its authority. By the mid-1990s, the PA controlled about 13 separate security agencies, and people suspected of anti-PA activities were jailed and often tortured for their activities.

Although it has a state apparatus, Palestine is not a sovereign state since its borders are controlled by Israel, and Israel still legally occupies all of the lands taken in 1967 despite the redeployments negotiated under the Oslo framework. Under the terms of Oslo, goods coming into and going out of the Territories still pass through Israeli controls and are not allowed to compete with those produced by Israelis. Just as the PLO and its fedayeen constituencies received funding from foreign sources in the 1960s, the PA receives the bulk of its revenues from the European Union, United States, and Gulf States, as well as from customs taxes Israel collects and is obligated to pass on to the PA. This funding is unstable, increasing and decreasing depending on how well the PA complies with the pressure the donors apply.

Each Israeli redeployment required painstaking negotiations, delaying the PA's ability to take charge of new territories. Meanwhile, Israel confiscated additional Palestinian land, building settlements and roads in new areas. As the economic situation grew worse for many Palestinians, the PA proved incapable of moving the Oslo process forward or of establishing institutions with real popular participation. Thus, Palestinian resistance intensified in the late 1990s, sponsored by an array of new and old paramilitary organizations. Hamas's Shaykh 'Izz al-Din al-Qassam Brigade attacked numerous Israeli targets inside and outside the Territories, frequently employing suicide bombers at checkpoints and settlements. Fatah relied on the al-Aqsa Martyrs' Brigade.

It was under these conditions that President Bill Clinton invited Arafat and Israeli prime minister Ehud Barak to Camp David in July 2000 to work out final-status issues. Those efforts failed, but in January 2001 all the players met again at the Egyptian resort town of Taba, and the two sides came closer than ever before to agreeing on the issue of Palestinian refugees, on the possible division of Jerusalem into capitals for both Israel and Palestine, and on establishing a Palestinian state in the West

Bank and Gaza, but there was no political leader available to ratify its provisions. The agreement was achieved just as Clinton was leaving office to be replaced by George W. Bush, Ehud Barak was turning power over to Ariel Sharon, and Arafat was preoccupied with the Second Intifada, which broke out in September 2000.

The Second Intifada

The Second Intifada erupted in September 2000 because of the Palestinians' frustration with the Oslo process. Over the next years, the Israelis and Palestinians used far more firepower than in the First Intifada. Israel employed F-16 fighters and targeted assassinations against Palestinian leaders, and the Palestinian groups relied on suicide bombers and attacks against Israeli military personnel and settlers. Far fewer grassroots Palestinian organizations participated in this new fight than in the First Intifada because most had been weakened and eliminated by the PA in the 1990s. Unlike the First Intifada, which was characterized by unity among the vast array of Palestinian organizations, the Second Intifada was complicated by a rivalry between the PA, dominated by Fatah controlling the West Bank, and Hamas with its headquarters in the Gaza Strip.

Between March 28 and April 4, 2002, the Israeli military reinvaded the areas of the West Bank from which it had redeployed during the 1990s. The PA still held control over civil matters in Areas A and B, but Israel took complete control of the security situation. In the aftermath of the attack, the Israelis kept Arafat under house arrest in his headquarters in Ramallah, where he remained until removed to Paris in 2004 because of a life-threatening illness. After Arafat's death, Mahmoud Abbas succeeded him as president of the PA in 2005. The Second Intifada had ended for the most part, and Israel began building a wall to block Palestinian attackers from entering Israeli territories, in the process bringing additional Palestinian lands under direct Israeli control.

Israeli Withdrawal from Gaza

In August 2005, Israel withdrew all its 9,000 settlers from Gaza but maintained its occupation of the territory. Israel enclosed the Strip in a wall, provided few permits to Palestinians to enter or leave, and heavily restricted the amount and types of goods that could be imported and exported. In 2006, Hamas won 56 percent of the seats in the second legislative elections across Palestinian territories. Immediately, the United States, the European Union, and the UN announced that they would

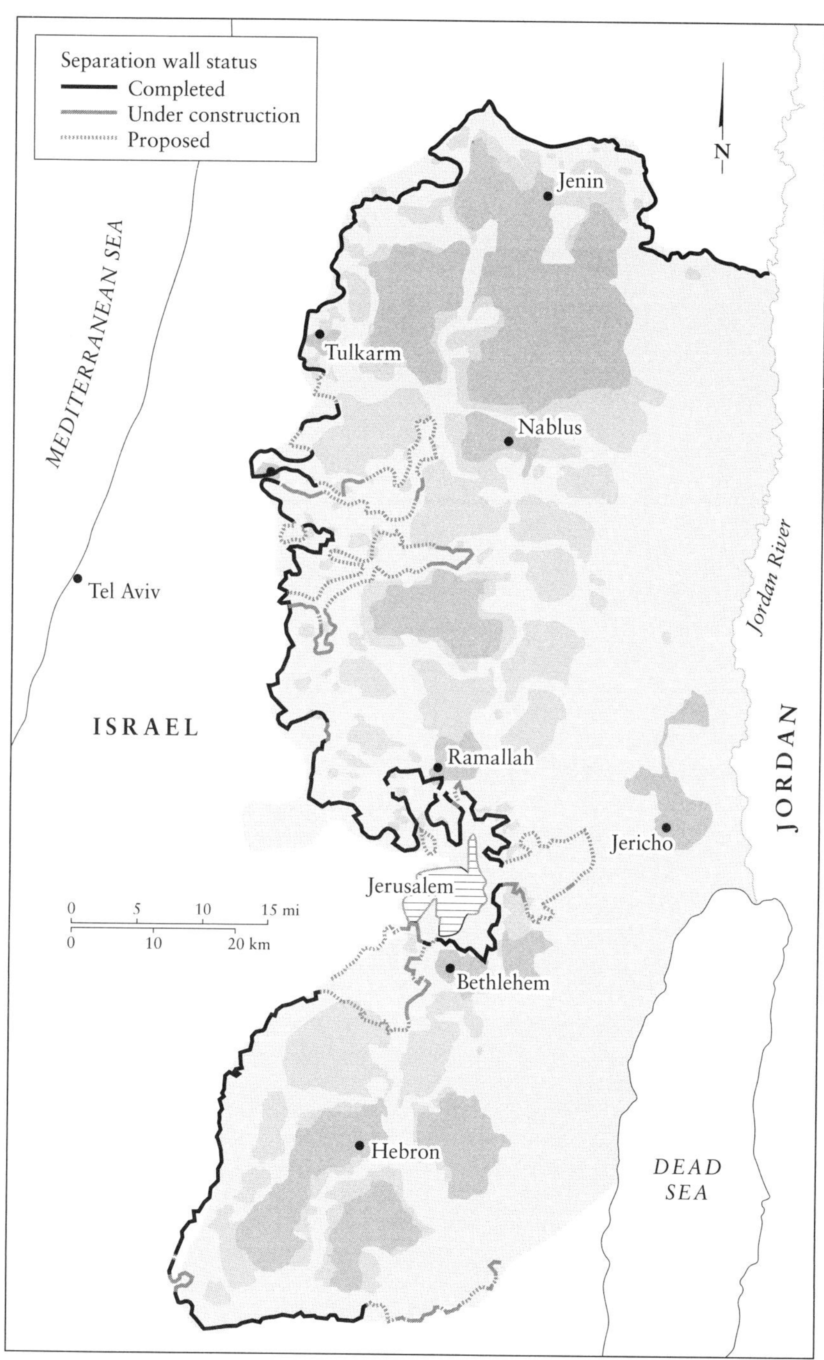

MAP 22. Israeli Separation Wall in the West Bank, 2011. The path of the Israeli Separation Wall was built along the Green Line in some places and within the West Bank and East Jerusalem in others.

accept Hamas's victory only if it renounced violence, recognized Israel, and agreed to the terms of the previous agreements signed between Israel and the PA. Hamas refused, and the legislature could not convene.

The Gaza Strip and the West Bank have functionally separate governments, with Hamas dominating the former and the PA the latter, although unity negotiations have taken place on numerous occasions. In January 2009, the Israeli military initiated Operation Cast Lead aimed at ending rocket fire from Gaza and into Israel. More than 1,000 Palestinians died in the bombardment. Operation Protective Edge in July 2014 repeated the process, with the Israeli deaths of civilians and soldiers totaling about 70 people and the Palestinians over 2,000. Israel continues to impose a blockade around Gaza instituted in 2005, and the people of Gaza are struggling to rebuild from the recent conflicts and acquire the necessities for life. The wall around the West Bank is almost complete, and few Palestinians hold permits allowing them to leave the Territories. As of 2015, some 500,000 settlers lived in the West Bank and East Jerusalem, with more settlements being built and planned throughout the year.

No Palestinian elections have been held since 2006, meaning that PA leaders have exceeded their legal mandate. The latest arena for negotiating Palestinian statehood is through international institutions. In 2012, the UN General Assembly upgraded Palestine's position from an Observer status to Non-Member Observer State status. On April 1, 2015, Palestine became a member of the International Criminal Court (ICC), and the Palestinian-Israeli conflict may go before the court in the next few years.

Conclusion

These conflicts in Iraq and Israel-Palestine have overflowed their borders. Many foreign fighters who gained experience in Iraq after 2003 initiated violence in their countries after they returned. The intransigence of the Israeli-Palestinian conflict has had ripple effects across the entire region because of the large number of Palestinian refugees and the passions the Palestinian plight elicit. Leaders and citizenries across the region must also contend with endemic economic problems and continuing interference from other countries—the United States, Britain, France, Russia, and now also Iran, Saudi Arabia, and Qatar—into their economic, political, and military structures, compromising their sovereignty. The instability in the region has made it a difficult place for investment, exacerbating the economic difficulties already present. Religious polarization has led to armed conflicts within and across borders. In reaction to these crises, millions of people mobilized through professional, party, union, and sectarian organizations to protest against the conditions under which they were living. These actions have brought down longtime government leaders and have destabilized state governments. The relationship between the region's rulers, rebels, and rogues continues to change and define the Middle East.

EPILOGUE

Revolution, Reaction, and Civil War

ARAB FRUSTRATION over the failure of the peace process between the Israelis and the Palestinians, the ramifications of the US invasion of Iraq, and dissatisfaction with leadership from Iran to Turkey to the Arab countries sparked the revolts that exploded in 2005 and reemerged in 2011 in the form of the anti-Syrian protests in Lebanon, the Green Revolution in Iran, the Arab Spring uprisings, and the Gezi protests in Turkey. By the 21st century, youth unemployment in these countries was far higher than the general unemployment rate, ranging as high as 30 percent in some countries and particularly affecting those with secondary and university degrees. As of January 2011, more than 20 percent of the Egyptian population lived below the poverty line, and comparable figures could be found for the surrounding countries. Almost half of all Egyptian farms consisted of less than one feddan, or around one acre. When Syria's uprisings began in 2011, they erupted along the northern and southern borders, in regions hit hardest by a years-long drought and by the government's repressive policies.

The demonstrations across the region over the last few years had a spontaneous element in that thousands and then hundreds of thousands appeared to be involved almost immediately as soon as the outbreak

MAP 23. Upheaval in the Middle East and North Africa since 2005.
The countries in which demonstrations broke out against governments and leaders in the Middle East, beginning in 2005.

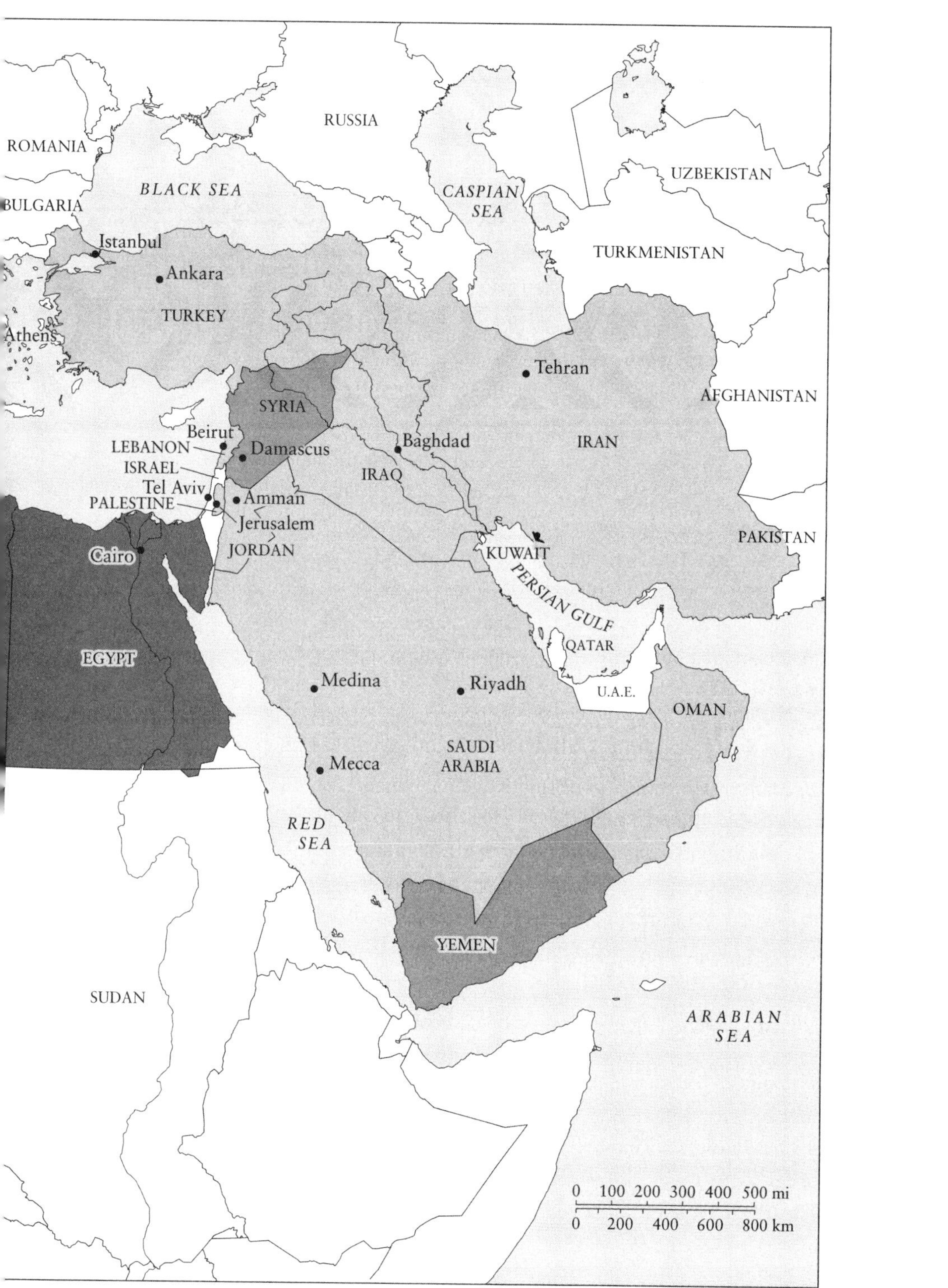

RUSSIA
ROMANIA
BULGARIA
BLACK SEA
CASPIAN SEA
UZBEKISTAN
TURKMENISTAN
Istanbul
Ankara
TURKEY
Athens
Tehran
SYRIA
AFGHANISTAN
Beirut
LEBANON
Damascus
Baghdad
IRAN
ISRAEL
IRAQ
Tel Aviv
PALESTINE
Amman
Jerusalem
JORDAN
Cairo
KUWAIT
PAKISTAN
PERSIAN GULF
QATAR
EGYPT
U.A.E.
Medina
Riyadh
OMAN
SAUDI ARABIA
Mecca
RED SEA
YEMEN
SUDAN
ARABIAN SEA
0 100 200 300 400 500 mi
0 200 400 600 800 km

began. However, they could not have succeeded without years of organizing that had the effect of mobilizing people across the socioeconomic spectrum. These early efforts managed to bring people out into the streets and to diverse political arenas to discuss the problems of the day so they could seek solutions collectively. They also, in a more pragmatic way, established lists of phone numbers and names that could be easily activated for new events. In 2005 in Lebanon, in 2009 in Iran, and in 2011 in the much of the Arab world and Turkey these early maneuvers brought all the actors together.

One means for organizing in the early 21st century was through the establishment of political parties that were not legalized by the states but that mobilized large numbers of people into street demonstrations. One of the largest independent political groups to arise was the Kefaya (Enough) movement in Cairo, which organized demonstrations in 2005 calling for Mubarak to leave office. It emerged out of the foundation of the Egyptian Popular Committee in Solidarity with the (Palestinian) Intifada (EPSCI) in 2000, which later organized protests against the US invasion of Iraq. However, prohibitions on party organizing meant that Kefaya and similar parties throughout the region faced a difficult time in moving from the mobilization phase into one that could effectively lobby agencies for governmental change.

Newly organized independent labor movements also waged strike after strike for better wages and working conditions across the region. This rise was in stark contrast to many governmental efforts to abolish unions in favor of non-union shops. Between 2004 and 2008, Egypt alone experienced almost 2,000 strikes. The strikers came from all sectors of the economy, from health and textile workers, pharmacists, doctors, lawyers, judges, transportation and postal workers, real estate tax collectors, and the new free-trade factories. The strikes did little to improve the situation for workers, as state governments brutally suppressed them, but the very act of mobilizing so many thousands of workers meant that they were also available for the events of 2005 and beyond.

Mobilization occurred also because more media outlets broadcast the events of the day and connected people across their countries and the region at large. Public information about strikes and demonstrations could not be censored as effectively as in the past, because wide-scale privatization efforts across the region broke down state control of the media in all these countries. As recently as the Gulf War of 1990–1991, no Arab satellite broadcasts existed, but by the beginning of the 21st century, at least 20 different regional satellites had been launched. Satellite station Al Jazeera dominated the airwaves for the 1990s and into the 21st century, but it has since been challenged by al-Arabiya, owned by a Saudi businessman, al-Manar, disseminated by Hizballah in Lebanon, and others.

Newspapers such as *Al-Hayat*, *Al-Sharq al-Awsat*, and *Al-Quds al-'Arabi*, aimed at a pan-Arab audience, flooded the Arab world with opposing political viewpoints. This proliferation of media outlets has increased the amount of news Arabs receive and also created a shared space in which Arabs throughout the region can understand the difficulties encountered by their brethren across the borders. In Turkey, Erdoğan has had difficulty suppressing critical analyses of his government in such forums as the Gülen-owned *Zaman* newspaper. Under these conditions, state leaders can no longer mold and monopolize the public narrative of their policies and their actions as they could in the past when only state-sponsored media existed in each country. In one such example, a Reuters photographer captured the moment when a Turkish policeman tear-gassed a woman dressed in red at the Gezi protests in 2013, and it reverberated around the country. The image of a peaceful protester being attacked by police quickly became a touchstone for Turkish grievances against the Erdoğan government.

FIGURE E.1. A Turkish riot policeman uses tear gas against a woman in a red dress during protests against the destruction of trees in a park in Taksim Square, Istanbul, on May 28, 2013. Widely shared on social media and replicated as a cartoon on posters and stickers, the image of the woman in red became a leitmotif for female protesters during days of violent antigovernment demonstrations in Istanbul.

These years also saw Internet organizing spread quickly throughout the region: for example, Facebook came to attract three million followers in Egypt by 2011 alone. The numbers were small relative to the population, but the images and YouTube videos easily available for watching on many different platforms documented the brutality of state security agencies across the region. The availability of cheap smartphones, access to affordable data plans, and many venues for free Wi-Fi have facilitated the dissemination of information in much wider and faster fashion than ever before. The bloggers who present these images and demand political change represent positions across the political spectrum in the Middle East, but some common demands can be determined. In general, they have called for the end to the longtime state leaderships under which they had struggled; the expansion of political freedoms and the creation of democratic institutions; and an immediate end to state violence. Attempts to block this transmission of information have largely failed, for example, when Turkish prime minister Erdoğan unsuccessfully tried to ban Twitter in 2014.

These new political and media venues sparked enthusiasm for the changes that collective actions could generate. The demonstrations of 2011 forced the fall of the Tunisian and Egyptian presidents, generated by the hope that the age of dictatorial oppression and economic inequality could be alleviated. However, except for possibly Tunisia, which is still undergoing political change, the other countries involved in the upheavals have seen little real change to their state power structures. Demonstrators returned again to Tahrir Square in January 2012 to celebrate the one-year anniversary of the tumultuous events that had toppled Husni Mubarak, but the hopes of most of the participants in 2011 have not been met. The new Egyptian political parties that emerged on the scene in 2011 in the aftermath of Mubarak's ouster could not compete with the Muslim Brotherhood's national reach; the Muslim Brotherhood soon fell to an authoritarian military state. King Abdullah II's "reform game" in Jordan moves players onto and off the political chessboard but does little to change the balance of power. The governments in Bahrain and Saudi Arabia have largely repressed the movements calling for change. None of these governments have been able to alleviate the economic crises or improve the effectiveness of state institutions such as schools and hospitals.

Millions have become refugees within their own countries or have been forced to move into the surrounding ones, with Syrians, Iraqis, and Palestinians facing the brunt of these crises. Jordan, Lebanon, and Tur-

FIGURE E.2. People gather in Tahrir Square, Cairo, on January 25, 2012, for the one-year anniversary of the events that toppled Husni Mubarak.

key continue to struggle to find the resources to house these refugees after many years of displacement. The fragmentation of society in the decades leading up to these recent upheavals directed people to religious, clan, and tribal structures because they provided aid in a world where the states could no longer do so. These divisions exist between Muslim sects, between Christians and Muslims, between tribes, between religiosity and secularism, and between areas of the country or the capital city. At the end of the 20th century and beginning of the 21st these divisions have become a starker element of societal discourse and organization than in decades past. The sectarianism that defined Lebanese political life has spread across the borders and throughout the region. Sectarian allegiances have divided formerly united citizenries, and societies have become polarized by religious identification.

Syria has become the epicenter for the phenomena seen around the region because the protests over authoritarian state policies that began in 2011 evolved into a countrywide civil war within only a few months. The Muslim Brotherhood and provincial and tribal leaders organized their followers to meet Syrian government repression with military attacks of their own. Over subsequent years, the United States, Turkey, Saudi Arabia, and Qatar became the main foreign supporters of the rebels, loosely organized around the Syrian National Council (SNC) and the Free Syrian Army (FSA), while the Syrian government received aid from Russia, Iran, and Hizballah in Lebanon. As the war grew more violent and widespread in 2012, local Sunni militia groups on the ground proliferated, with the Kurds of the northeastern provinces also organizing for protection, and al-Qa'ida groups establishing themselves as powerful militia groups in the country.

In 2013, the Islamic State in Iraq gave aid to Syrian al-Qa'ida-affiliated units such as al-Nusra Front. Although that alliance ruptured by the end of the year, the Islamic State had such strong supporters in Syria and among the hundreds of foreign fighters flooding into the country that it was able to move across the border into Syria in summer 2014. The Islamic State of Iraq and Sham (ISIS) under the leadership of Abu Bakr al-Baghdadi subsequently declared the establishment of a caliphate in the captured areas of Syria and Iraq. In late 2014, the United States, Britain, Jordan, Saudi Arabia, and the UAE, among other states, began operations designed to push ISIS back from territories taken in Iraq and Syria while also aiming to topple the Syrian government of Bashar al-Asad. These acts have included bombings of ISIS units and aid to those forces that oppose ISIS, including Kurdish groups in Syria and Iraq, the Iraqi government, and Syrian rebel organizations. As of summer 2015, ISIS has been forced from Kurdish areas along the northern Syrian border with Turkey and small cities such as Tikrit in Iraq but has otherwise consolidated its hold over territory captured in early 2014 in both countries and has expanded in Sunni-dominated areas of Iraq and Syria. Russian forces began bombing ISIS and the Syrian rebel groups in October 2015 to shore up the Syrian government.

This civil war in Syria has not been contained within the borders but has affected people in the region and also in Europe. With no end to the conflict in sight and with diminishing resources for the refugee camps in Turkey, Lebanon, and Jordan, Syrians headed by the hundreds of thousands to Europe in the summer and fall of 2015. They arrived in countries such as Greece and Serbia, which had economic crises of their own, and to those such as Germany and Sweden that were initially welcoming but are now overwhelmed. ISIS affiliates have initiated attacks against civilians in Egypt, Libya, Lebanon, and France, killing hundreds of people. The Turkish government has grown increasingly authoritarian because it is embroiled in the Syrian conflict and because Erdoğan seeks to cement his hold over the institutions of government. Negotiations between the Turkish government and the PKK have ended, and violent attacks by the two sides have begun again.

In the current day, groups such as ISIS in Syria and Iraq are working to change the foundational elements of their respective governing bodies. The Syrian and Iraqi governmental leaders are trying to stave off such dramatic change but are losing control over increasing amounts of territory, so it is unclear if they can hold the line. The millions of refugees throughout the region struggle to gain access to basic foodstuffs, jobs, health care, housing, and education. Because of these conflicts and crises, it is difficult to determine in what direction the Middle East might go in the next decades.

Note on Transliteration

Transliterations of Arabic words largely follow the rules laid out in the *International Journal of Middle East Studies* (*IJMES*), while those in Persian have been modified from *IJMES* in order to simplify them. Ottoman and Turkish words obey the rules of modern Turkish. Names of people and places recognizable to the reader and those that appear in *Merriam-Webster's Dictionary* have been replicated here using the most common spelling. Linguistic and regional variations have been taken into account, so the Prophet Muhammad appears in this text as does Mohammad Reza Shah of Iran. The Egyptian spelling for Gamal Abdel Nasser has been retained while Jamal al-Din al-Afghani's spelling follows the more traditional Arabic transliteration. Words transliterated from other languages recognize differences in practice but have also been simplified to allow the reader to see the similarities in word usage.

Acknowledgments

No book, and certainly no book as large as this one, can be truly produced and written by just one person. I want to thank Kate Wahl, Gigi Mark, and Nora Spiegel at Stanford University Press for their shepherding of this book to completion. Allison Brown took on the task of creating a system for transliterating words from five different languages. Michelle Woodward found the wonderful images on the cover and included within each of the chapters. Cynthia Lindlof has done an excellent job copyediting the text. The Center for the Humanities and the Dean's Office of the College of Arts and Sciences of Boston University provided funds to pay production costs. I thank you all for your gracious help. As usual, any errors included in the text are entirely my own.

Photo Credits

Prologue

Figure 0.1: Seventeenth-century fritware with underglaze painting. Iznik, Turkey. 24 9/16 × 14 1/8 × 1 3/8 in. Courtesy of the Walters Art Museum, Baltimore.

Chapter 1

Figure 1.1: A detail from the diorama of the conquest of Constantinople by Sultan Ahmet II in 1453 in the Askeri Müze (Military Museum), Istanbul. Photo by Dick Osseman.

Figure 1.2: Keith Turner after Fanny Davis. Courtesy of the MIT Libraries, Aga Khan Visual Archive.

Figure 1.3: Ink, opaque watercolor, and gold on paper. 6 1/2 × 5 3/8 in. (16.51 × 13.65 cm). Courtesy of The Edwin Binney, 3rd Collection of Turkish Art at the Los Angeles County Museum of Art.

Figure 1.4: Author: Bijan. Artist: Mu'in Musavvir. Opaque watercolor and ink on paper. 14 1/8 × 9 1/4 in. (35.9 × 23.5 cm). Courtesy of the Freer Gallery of Art, Smithsonian Institution, Washington, D.C.: Gift of Martha Mayor Smith and Alfred Mayor in memory of A. Hyatt Mayor, F2000.3

Figure 1.5: Opaque watercolor, ink, silver, and gold on paper. Painting: H. 10 15/16 in. (27.9 cm). W. 7 1/8 in. (18.1 cm). Circa 1525. Courtesy of The Metropolitan Museum of Art.

Figure 1.6: Figure on page 191 of Renata Holod and Darl Rastorfer, "Restoration of Ali Qapu, Chehel Sutun and Hasht Behesht," in *Architecture and Community*, edited by Renata Holod and Darl Rastorfer (New York: Aperture, 1983). © The Aga Khan Award for Architecture.

Chapter 2

Figure 2.1: Courtesy of Library of Congress, LC-DIG-ppmsca-10669.

Figure 2.2: By Francis Frith. Albumen silver print from glass plate negative. Courtesy of The Metropolitan Museum of Art.

Figure 2.3: By William Page. Watercolor over pencil, touched with white. © Victoria and Albert Museum, London.

Figure 2.4: Illustration in *Egypt & Nubia: From Drawings Made on the Spot by David Roberts*, vol. 3, pt. 1. (London: F. G. Moon, 1846–1849). Lithographed by Louis Haghe. Courtesy of the Library of Congress, LC-USZC4-4053.

Figure 2.5: Courtesy of the Library of Congress, LC-USZ62-77295.

Figure 2.6: Yvonne Sursock Collection. Courtesy of the Arab Image Foundation.

Figure 2.7: Abdul-Hamid II Collection. Courtesy of the Library of Congress, LC-USZ62-78328.

Figure 2.8: Ken and Jenny Jacobson Orientalist Photography Collection. Digital image courtesy of the Getty's Open Content Program.

Figure 2.9: Ken and Jenny Jacobson Orientalist Photography Collection. Digital image courtesy of the Getty's Open Content Program.

Figure 2.10: The Myron Bement Smith Collection. Courtesy of the Freer Gallery of Art and Arthur M. Sackler Gallery Archives. Smithsonian Institution, Washington, D.C., FSA_A.4_2.12.GN.48.03.

Chapter 3

Figure 3.1: Courtesy of the Library of Congress, LC-DIG-matpc-01458.

Figure 3.2: Courtesy of the Library of Congress, LC-USZ62-69085.

Figure 3.3: Courtesy of the Library of Congress, LC-DIG-matpc-07047.

Figure 3.4: Abdul-Hamid II Collection. Courtesy of the Library of Congress, LC-USZ62-81321.

Figure 3.5: Photo by Maison Bonfils. IAA100858 © Ecochard Collection/Aga Khan Trust for Culture.

Figure 3.6: Courtesy of the Library of Congress, LC-DIG-matpc-01456.

Figure 3.7: Courtesy of the Library of Congress, LC-DIG-ppmsca-10721.

Figure 3.8: By Photo Zürich. Photochrom (photolithograph), 28 × 35 cm. Digital image courtesy of the Getty's Open Content Program.

Chapter 4

Figure 4.1: A Crowd of Men and Women Gathered to Celebrate the Granting of a Constitution III. One of 274 Vintage Photographs, late 19th–early 20th century. Albumen silver photograph, 6 3/16 × 11 in. (15.7 × 27.9 cm). Courtesy of the Brooklyn Museum, Purchase gift of Leona Soudavar in memory of Ahmad Soudavar, 1997.3.247.

Figure 4.2: Courtesy of the Library of Congress, LC-DIG-matpc-11599.

Figure 4.3: Mehmed Talat Pasha, Philip James Stanhope, and Baron Weardale with two other Turkish delegates. By Sir (John) Benjamin Stone. July 21, 1909. Platinum print, 6 1/8 × 8 in. (155 × 202 mm). © National Portrait Gallery, London

Figure 4.4: Courtesy of the Library of Congress, LC-DIG-ppmsca-13709-00109.

Figure 4.5: Courtesy of the Library of Congress, LC-DIG-ggbain-20341.

Figure 4.6: Courtesy of the Library of Congress, LC-DIG-matpc-01625.

Figure 4.7: Courtesy of Imperial War Museums. © IWM (Q 58863)

Figure 4.8: Courtesy of the Herzl Museum.

Chapter 5

Figure 5.1: Photo © Tallandier/Bridgeman Images.
Figure 5.2: Courtesy of the Library of Congress, LC-USZ62-139361.
Figure 5.3: Courtesy of the Library of Congress, LC-DIG-matpc-06442.
Figure 5.4: Courtesy of the Library of Congress, LC-DIG-matpc-13171.
Figure 5.5: Courtesy of the Library of Congress, LC-DIG-matpc-03058.

Chapter 6

Figure 6.1: Photographer unknown. Source: Wikipedia.
Figure 6.2: Photo by Imagno/Hulton Archive/Getty Images.
Figure 6.3: Courtesy of the Library of Congress, LC-DIG-matpc-13164.
Figure 6.4: Courtesy of the Library of Congress, LC-DIG-matpc-17057.
Figure 6.5: Courtesy of the Library of Congress, LC-DIG-matpc-15160.
Figure 6.6: Courtesy of the Library of Congress, LC-DIG-matpc-22134.

Chapter 7

Figure 7.1: Photo by Stringer/AP Photo. © AP Images.
Figure 7.2: Photo by Paul Popper/Popperfoto/Getty Images.
Figure 7.3: © Bettmann/Corbis/AP Images.
Figure 7.4: Photo by AP Photo/Burhan Ozbilci. © AP Images.
Figure 7.5: Photo by AP Photo/Burhan Ozbilci. © AP Images.

Chapter 8

Figure 8.1: Photo by unknown photographer/AP Photo. © AP Images.
Figure 8.2: Photo by unknown photographer/AP Photo. © AP Images.
Figure 8.3: Photo by Alain MINGAM/Gamma-Rapho/Getty Images.
Figure 8.4: © George Azar.
Figure 8.5: © George Azar.

Chapter 9

Figure 9.1: Photo by Talal Foz. Licensed under Creative Commons Attribution-Share Alike 3.0 Unported license.
Figure 9.2: Photo by Wikimedia Commons User: Darwinek. Licensed under Creative Commons Attribution-Share Alike 3.0 Unported license.
Figure 9.3: Photo by Ed Kohler. Licensed under Creative Commons Attribution 2.0 Generic license.
Figure 9.4: Photo by Jim Gordon, CIV. Courtesy of the US Department of Defense.
Figure 9.5: Photographer unknown. Public domain image from Wikipedia Commons.
Figure 9.6: Photo by David Holt. Licensed under Creative Commons Attribution-Share Alike 2.0 license.

Chapter 10

Figure 10.1: Photo by AP Photo/Norbert Schiller. © AP Images.
Figure 10.2: Photo by Wikimedia Commons Author: buzkozan. Licensed under Creative Commons Attribution-Share Alike 3.0 Unported license.
Figure 10.3: Photo by Vincent Teeuwen. Licensed under Creative Commons Attribution 2.0 Generic license.
Figure 10.4: Photo by Gigi Ibrahim. Licensed under Creative Commons Attribution 2.0 license.
Figure 10.5: © REUTERS/Osman Orsal.

Bibliography

Preface

Achcar, Gilbert. *The People Want: A Radical Exploration of the Arab Uprising*. Translated by G. M. Goshgarian. Berkeley: University of California Press, 2013.

Ali, Tariq. "What Is a Revolution?" *Guernica*, September 14, 2013. http://www.guernicamag.com/daily/tariq-ali-what-is-a-revolution/.

Amar, Paul. "Why Mubarak Is Out." In *The Dawn of the Arab Uprisings: End of an Old Order?*, edited by Bassam Haddad, Rosie Bsheer, and Ziad Abu-Rish, 83–90. London: Pluto Press, 2012.

Armbrust, Walter. "The Revolution against Neoliberalism." In *The Dawn of the Arab Uprisings: End of an Old Order?*, edited by Bassam Haddad, Rosie Bsheer, and Ziad Abu-Rish, 113–123. London: Pluto Press, 2012.

Bamyeh, Mohammed. "The Tunisian Revolution: Initial Reflections." In *The Dawn of the Arab Uprisings: End of an Old Order?*, edited by Bassam Haddad, Rosie Bsheer, and Ziad Abu-Rish, 49–58. London: Pluto Press, 2012.

Barkey, Karen. *Empire of Difference: The Ottomans in Comparative Perspective*. Cambridge: Cambridge University Press, 2008.

Bayat, Asef. *Life as Politics: How Ordinary People Change the Middle East*. Stanford, CA: Stanford University Press, 2010.

———. "Paradoxes of Arab Refo-lutions." In *The Dawn of the Arab Uprisings: End of an Old Order?*, edited by Bassam Haddad, Rosie Bsheer, and Ziad Abu-Rish, 28–32. London: Pluto Press, 2012.

Beinin, Joel. "Neo-liberal Structural Adjustment, Political Demobilization and Neo-authoritarianism in Egypt." In *The Arab State and Neo-liberal Globalization: The Restructuring of State Power in the Middle East*, edited by Laura Guazzone and Daniela Pioppi, 19–46. Reading, UK: Ithaca Press, 2009.

Cammett, Melani, and Ishac Diwan. "Toward a Political Economy of the Arab Uprisings (Part One)." Jadaliyya.com, December 26, 2013. http://www.jadaliyya.com/pages/index/15754/toward-a-political-economy-of-the-arab-uprisings-%28.

———. "Toward a Political Economy of the Arab Uprisings (Part Two)." Jadaliyya.com, December 27, 2013. http://www.jadaliyya.com/pages/index/15755/toward-a-political-economy-of-the-arab-uprisings-%28.

Eng, Brent, and José Ciro Martinez. "Starvation, Submission and Survival: Syria's War through the Prism of War." *Middle East Report* 273 (Winter 2014): 28–32.

Gershoni, Israel. "Rethinking the Formation of Arab Nationalism in the Middle East,1920–1945: Old and New Narratives." In *Rethinking Nationalism in the Arab Middle East*, edited by James Jankowski and Israel Gershoni, 3–25. New York: Columbia University Press, 1997.

Hudson, Michael. "Awakening, Cataclysm, or Just a Series of Events? Reflections on the Current Wave of Protest in the Arab World." In *The Dawn of the Arab Uprisings: End of an Old Order?*, edited by Bassam Haddad, Rosie Bsheer, and Ziad Abu-Rish, 17–27. London: Pluto Press, 2012.

Jankowski, James, and Israel Gershoni, eds. *Rethinking Nationalism in the Arab Middle East*. New York: Columbia University Press, 1997.

Lesch, David W. "The Uprising That Wasn't Supposed to Happen: Syria and the Arab

Spring." In *The Arab Spring: Change and Resistance in the Middle East*, edited by Mark L. Haas and David W. Lesch, 79–96. Boulder, CO: Westview Press, 2013.

Lynch, Marc. *The Arab Uprising: The Unfinished Revolution of the New Middle East*. New York: PublicAffairs, 2012.

Mahmoud, Saba. "The Architects of the Egyptian Uprising and the Challenges Ahead." In *The Dawn of the Arab Uprisings: End of an Old Order?*, edited by Bassam Haddad, Rosie Bsheer, and Ziad Abu-Rish, 104–112. London: Pluto Press, 2012.

Rabbani, Mouin. "The Year of the Citizen." In *The Dawn of the Arab Uprisings: End of an Old Order?*, edited by Bassam Haddad, Rosie Bsheer, and Ziad Abu-Rish, 33–36. London: Pluto Press, 2012.

Rutherford, Bruce K. "Egypt: The Origins and Consequences of the January 25 Uprising." In *The Arab Spring: Change and Resistance in the Middle East*, edited by Mark L. Haas and David W. Lesch, 35–63. Boulder, CO: Westview Press, 2013.

Ryan, Curtis R. "Jordan and the Arab Spring." In *The Arab Spring: Change and Resistance in the Middle East*, edited by Mark L. Haas and David W. Lesch, 116–130. Boulder, CO: Westview Press, 2013.

Thompson, Elizabeth F. *Justice Interrupted: The Struggle for Constitutional Government in the Middle East*. Cambridge, MA: Harvard University Press, 2013.

Prologue: Islam and the Prophet's Successors

Berkey, Jonathan P. *The Formation of Islam: Religion and Society in the Near East, 600–1800*. Cambridge: Cambridge University Press, 2003.

———. "Madrasa, Medieval and Modern: Politics, Education, and the Problem of Muslim Identity." In *Schooling Islam: The Culture and Politics of Modern Muslim Education*, edited by Robert W. Hefner and Muhammad Qasim Zaman 40–60. Princeton, NJ: Princeton University Press, 2007.

Donner, Fred M. *Muhammad and the Believers: At the Origins of Islam*. Cambridge, MA: Belknap Press of Harvard University Press, 2010.

Hefner, Robert W. "Introduction: The Culture, Politics, and Future of Muslim Education." In *Schooling Islam: The Culture and Politics of Modern Muslim Education*, edited by Robert W. Hefner and Muhammad Qasim Zaman, 1–39. Princeton, NJ: Princeton University Press, 2007.

Hodgson, Marshall G. S. *The Venture of Islam: Conscience and History in a World Civilization*. 2 vols. Chicago: University of Chicago Press, 1974.

Lapidus, Ira M. *A History of Islamic Societies*. Cambridge: Cambridge University Press, 1988.

Watt, W. Montgomery. *Muhammad at Medina*. Karachi, Pakistan: Oxford University Press, 1981.

Chapter 1. Birth of Empires

Anooshahr, Ali. "The Rise of the Safavids according to Their Old Veterans: Amini Haravi's *Futuhat-e Shahi*." *Iranian Studies* 48, no. 2 (February 25, 2014): 1–19.

Anscombe, Frederick F. *State, Faith, and Nation in Ottoman and Post-Ottoman Lands*. Cambridge: Cambridge University Press, 2014.

Babayan, Kathryn. "Sufis, Dervishes and Mullas: The Controversy over Spiritual and Temporal Dominion in Seventeenth-Century Iran." In *Safavid Persia: The History and Politics of an Islamic Society*, edited by Charles Melville, 117–138. London: I. B. Tauris, 1996.

Barfield, Thomas J. *Afghanistan: A Cultural and Political History*. Princeton, NJ: Princeton University Press, 2010.

———. "Turk, Persian, and Arab: Changing Relations between Tribes and States in Iran and along Its Frontiers." In *Iran and the Surrounding World: Interactions in Culture and Cultural Politics*, edited by Nikki R. Keddie and Rudi Matthee, 61–86. Seattle: University of Washington Press, 2002.

Barkey, Karen. *Empire of Difference: The Ottomans in Comparative Perspective.* Cambridge: Cambridge University Press, 2008.

Beinin, Joel. *Workers and Peasants in the Modern Middle East.* Cambridge: Cambridge University Press, 2001.

Crecelius, Daniel. "The Mamluk Beylicate of Egypt in the Last Decades before Its Destruction by Muhammad 'Ali Pasha in 1811." In *The Mamluks in Egyptian Politics and Society*, edited by Thomas Philipp and Ulrich Haarman, 128–149. Cambridge: Cambridge University Press, 1998.

Dale, Stephen Frederic. *The Muslim Empires of the Ottomans, Safavids, and Mughals.* Cambridge: Cambridge University Press, 2010.

Findley, Carter Vaughn. *Bureaucratic Reform in the Ottoman Empire: The Sublime Porte, 1789–1922.* Princeton, NJ: Princeton University Press, 1980.

———. *Turkey, Islam, Nationalism, and Modernity: A History, 1789–2007.* New Haven, CT: Yale University Press, 2010.

Goffman, Daniel. *The Ottoman Empire and Early Modern Europe.* Cambridge: Cambridge University Press, 2002.

Goodwin, Godfrey. *The Janissaries.* London: Saqi Books, 1994.

Hanioğlu, M. Şükrü. *A Brief History of the Late Ottoman Empire.* Princeton, NJ: Princeton University Press, 2008.

Imber, Colin. "The Ottoman Dynastic Myth." *Turcica* 19 (1987): 7–27.

Inalcik, Halil, ed., with Donald Quartaert. *An Economic and Social History of the Ottoman Empire.* Cambridge: Cambridge University Press, 1994.

Kafadar, Cemal. *Between Two Worlds: The Construction of the Ottoman State.* Berkeley: University of California Press, 1995.

Kasaba, Reşat. *A Moveable Empire: Ottoman Nomads, Migrants, and Refugees.* Seattle: University of Washington Press, 2009.

Keddie, Nikki R. "Introduction." In *Iran and the Surrounding World: Interactions in Culture and Cultural Politics*, edited by Nikki R. Keddie and Rudi Matthee, 3–11. Seattle: University of Washington Press, 2002.

Kitromilides, Paschalis M. "The Orthodox Church in Modern State Formation in South-East Europe." In *Ottomans into Europeans: State and Institution Building in South-East Europe*, edited by Alina Mungiu-Pippidi and Wim Van Meurs, 31–50. London: Hurst, 2010.

Manz, Beatrice Forbes. *Power, Politics and Religion in Timurid Iran.* Cambridge: Cambridge University Press, 2007.

McCarthy, Justin. *The Ottoman Turks: An Introductory History to 1923.* London: Addison Wesley Longman, 1997.

Mélikoff, Irène. "Bektashi/*Kizilbaş*: Historical Bipartition and Its Consequences." In *Alevi Identity: Cultural, Religious and Social Perspectives*, edited by Tord Olsson, Elisabeth Özdalga, and Catharina Raudvere, 1–10. Swedish Research Institute in Istanbul, *Transactions* vol. 8. Richmond, UK: Curzon Press, 1998.

Morgan, David. *The Mongols.* 2nd ed. Malden, MA: Blackwell Publishing, 2007.

Necipoğlu, Gülru. *Architecture, Ceremonial, and Power: The Topkapi Palace in the Fifteenth and Sixteenth Centuries.* New York: Architectural History Foundation; Cambridge, MA: MIT Press, 1991.

———. "Framing the Gaze in Ottoman, Safavid, and Mughal Palaces." In "Pre-modern Islamic Palaces," special issue, *Ars Orientalis* 23 (1993): 303– 342.

Peirce, Leslie P. *The Imperial Harem: Women and Sovereignty in the Ottoman Empire.* New York: Oxford University Press, 1993.

Philliou, Christine M. *Biography of an Empire: Governing Ottomans in an Age of Revolution.* Berkeley: University of California Press, 2011.

Quartaert, Donald. *The Ottoman Empire, 1700–1922.* Cambridge: Cambridge University Press, 2005.

Quinn, Sholeh A. "Notes on Timurid Legitimacy in Three Safavid Chronicles." *Iranian Studies* 31, no. 2 (Spring 1998): 149–158.

Rafeq, Abdul-Karim. "Damascus and the Pilgrim Caravan." In *Modernity and Culture: From the Mediterranean to the Indian Ocean*, edited by Leila Tarazi Fawaz and C. A. Bayly, 130–143. New York: Columbia University Press, 2002.

Soudavar, Abolala. "The Early Safavids and Their Cultural Interactions with Surrounding States." In *Iran and the Surrounding World: Interactions in Culture and Cultural Politics*, edited by Nikki R. Keddie and Rudi Matthee, 89–120. Seattle: University of Washington Press, 2002.

Streusand, Douglas E. *Islamic Gunpowder Empires: Ottomans, Safavids, and Mughals*. Philadelphia: Westview Press, 2011.

Thompson, Elizabeth F. *Justice Interrupted: The Struggle for Constitutional Government in the Middle East*. Cambridge, MA: Harvard University Press, 2013.

Tolan, John, Gilles Veinstein, and Henry Laurens. *Europe and the Islamic World: A History*. Princeton, NJ: Princeton University Press, 2013.

Uyar, Mesut, and Edward J. Erickson. *A Military History of the Ottomans: From Osman to Atatürk*. Santa Barbara, CA: Praeger Security International, 2009.

Voll, John Obert. *Islam: Continuity and Change in the Modern World*. Boulder, CO: Westview Press, 1982.

White, Sam. *The Climate Rebellion in the Early Modern Ottoman Empire*. Cambridge: Cambridge University Press, 2011.

Winter, Michael. "The Re-emergence of the Mamluks following the Ottoman Conquest." In *The Mamluks in Egyptian Politics and Society*, edited by Thomas Philipp and Ulrich Haarman, 87–106. Cambridge: Cambridge University Press, 1998.

Zürcher, Erik J. *Turkey: A Modern History*. London: I. B. Tauris, 2009.

Chapter 2. Reform and Rebellion

Abrahamian, Ervand. *Iran between Two Revolutions*. Princeton, NJ: Princeton University Press, 1982.

Ayalon, Ami. *The Press in the Arab Middle East: A History*. New York: Oxford University Press, 1995.

Aytekin, E. Attila. "Agrarian Relations, Property and Law: An Analysis of the Land Code of 1858 in the Ottoman Empire." *Middle Eastern Studies* 45, no. 6 (November 2009): 935–951.

Bechev, Dimitar. "The State and Local Authorities in the Balkans, 1804–1939." In *Ottomans into Europeans: State and Institution Building in South-East Europe*, edited by Alina Mungiu-Pippidi and Wim Van Meurs, 135–151. London: Hurst, 2010.

Beinin, Joel. *Workers and Peasants in the Modern Middle East*. Cambridge: Cambridge University Press, 2001.

Boyar, Ebru, and Kate Fleet. *A Social History of Ottoman Istanbul*. Cambridge: Cambridge University Press, 2010.

Cioeta, Donald J. "Islamic Benevolent Societies and Public Education in Ottoman Syria,1875–1882." *Islamic Quarterly* 26, no. 1 (1982): 40–55.

Crecelius, Daniel. "The Mamluk Beylicate of Egypt in the Last Decades before Its Destruction by Muhammad 'Ali Pasha in 1811." In *The Mamluks in Egyptian Politics and Society*, edited by Thomas Philipp and Ulrich Haarman, 128–149. Cambridge: Cambridge University Press, 1998.

Dale, Stephen Frederic. *The Muslim Empires of the Ottomans, Safavids, and Mughals*. Cambridge: Cambridge University Press, 2010.

Deringil, Selim. *The Well-Protected Domains: Ideology and the Legitimation of Power in the Ottoman Empire 1876–1909*. London: I. B. Tauris, 1998.

Doumani, Beshara. *Rediscovering Palestine Merchants and Peasants in Jabal Nablus, 1700–1900*. Berkeley: University of California Press, 1995.

Fahmy, Khaled. *All the Pasha's Men: Mehmed Ali, His Army and the Making of Modern Egypt*. Cambridge: Cambridge University Press, 1997.

———. *Mehmed Ali: From Ottoman Governor to Ruler of Egypt*. Oxford: Oneworld, 2009.

Findley, Carter Vaughn. *Bureaucratic Reform in the Ottoman Empire: The Sublime Porte, 1789–1922*. Princeton, NJ: Princeton University Press, 1980.

———. *Turkey, Islam, Nationalism, and Modernity: A History, 1789–2007*. New Haven, CT: Yale University Press, 2010.

Fromkin, David. "The Great Game in Asia." *Foreign Affairs* 58, no. 4 (Spring 1980): 936–951.

Gledhill, John, and Charles King. "Institution, Violence, and Captive States in Balkan History." In *Ottomans into Europeans: State and Institution Building in South-East Europe*, edited by Alina Mungiu-Pippidi and Wim Van Meurs, 245–275. London: Hurst, 2010.

Göçek, Fatma Müge. *Rise of the Bourgeoisie, Demise of Empire: Ottoman Westernization and Social Change*. New York: Oxford University Press, 1996.

Hanioğlu, M. Şükrü. *A Brief History of the Late Ottoman Empire*. Princeton, NJ: Princeton University Press, 2008.

Hauner, Milan. "The Last Great Game." *Middle East Journal* 38, no. 1 (Winter 1984): 72–84.

Hunter, F. Robert. *Egypt under the Khedives 1805–1879: From Household Government to Modern Bureaucracy*. Pittsburgh: University of Pittsburgh Press, 1984.

Inalcik, Halil, ed., with Donald Quartaert. *An Economic and Social History of the Ottoman Empire*. Cambridge: Cambridge University Press, 1994.

Islamoglu, Huri. "Property as a Contested Domain: A Reevaluation of the Ottoman Land Code of 1858." In *New Perspectives on Property and Land in the Middle East*, edited by Roger Owen, 3–62. Harvard Middle East Monographs 34. Cambridge, MA: Harvard University Press, 2000.

Jelavich, Barbara. *History of the Balkans*. 2 vols. Cambridge: Cambridge University Press, 1983.

Kasaba, Reşat. *A Moveable Empire: Ottoman Nomads, Migrants, and Refugees*. Seattle: University of Washington Press, 2009.

———. *The Ottoman Empire and the World Economy: The Nineteenth Century*. Albany: State University of New York, 1988.

Kitromilides, Paschalis M. "The Orthodox Church in Modern State Formation in South-East Europe." In *Ottomans into Europeans: State and Institution Building in South-East Europe*, edited by Alina Mungiu-Pippidi and Wim Van Meurs, 31–50. London: Hurst, 2010.

Lawson, Fred H. *The Social Origins of Egyptian Expansionism during the Muhammad 'Ali Period*. New York: Columbia University Press, 1992.

Marsot, Afaf Lutfi al-Sayyid. *Egypt in the Reign of Muhammad Ali*. Cambridge: Cambridge University Press, 1984.

McCarthy, Justin. *The Ottoman Turks: An Introductory History to 1923*. London: Addison Wesley Longman, 1997.

Owen, Roger. "Introduction." In *New Perspectives on Property and Land in the Middle East*, edited by Roger Owen, ix–xxiv. Harvard Middle East Monographs 34. Cambridge, MA: Harvard University Press, 2000.

———. *The Middle East in the World Economy: 1800–1914*. London: Methuen, 1981.

———. *State, Power and Politics in the Making of the Modern Middle East*. London: Routledge, 1992.

Pelt, Mogens. "Organized Violence in the Service of Nation Building." In *Ottomans into Europeans: State and Institution Building in South-East Europe*, edited by Alina Mungiu-Pippidi and Wim Van Meurs, 221–244. London: Hurst, 2010.

Philipp, Thomas. *Acre: The Rise and Fall of a Palestinian City, 1730–1831*. New York: Columbia University Press, 2001.

———. "Personal Loyalty and Political Power of the Mamluks in the Eighteenth Century." In *The Mamluks in Egyptian Politics and Society*, edited by Thomas Philipp and Ulrich Haarman, 118–127. Cambridge: Cambridge University Press, 1998.

Philliou, Christine M. *Biography of an Empire: Governing Ottomans in an Age of Revolution*. Berkeley: University of California Press, 2011.

Quartaert, Donald. *The Ottoman Empire, 1700–1922*. Cambridge: Cambridge University Press, 2005.

Rezun, Miron. "The Great Game Revisited." In "Southwest Asia," special issue, *International Journal* 41, no. 2 (Spring 1986): 324–341.

Rubin, Barnett R., and Ahmed Rashid. "From Great Game to Grand Bargain: Ending Chaos in Afghanistan and Pakistan." *Foreign Affairs* 87, no. 6 (November–December 2008): 30–44.

Rugh, William A. "A Tale of Two Houses." *Wilson Quarterly* 3, no. 1 (Winter 1979): 58–72.

Steppat, Fritz. "National Education Projects in Egypt before the British Occupation." In *Beginnings of Modernization in the Middle East: The Nineteenth Century*, edited by William R. Polk and Richard L. Chambers, 281–297. Chicago: University of Chicago Press, 1968.

Streusand, Douglas E. *Islamic Gunpowder Empires: Ottomans, Safavids, and Mughals*. Philadelphia: Westview Press, 2011.

Thompson, Jason. *A History of Egypt: From Earliest Times to the Present*. Cairo: American University in Cairo Press, 2008.

Tignor, Robert L. *Egypt: A Short History*. Princeton, NJ: Princeton University Press, 2010.

Toledano, Ehud. *State and Society in Mid-Nineteenth-Century Egypt*. Cambridge: Cambridge University Press, 1990.

Uyar, Mesut, and Edward J. Erickson. *A Military History of the Ottomans: From Osman to Atatürk*. Santa Barbara, CA: Praeger Security International, 2009.

Voll, John Obert. *Islam: Continuity and Change in the Modern World*. Boulder, CO: Westview Press, 1982.

Zürcher, Erik J. *Turkey: A Modern History*. London: I. B. Tauris, 2009.

Chapter 3. Social Transformations

Akarli, Engin Deniz. "The Administrative Council of Mount Lebanon." In *Lebanon: A History of Conflict and Consensus*, edited by Nadim Shehadi and Dana Haffar Mills, 79–100. London: I. B. Tauris, 1988.

———. *The Long Peace: Ottoman Lebanon, 1861–1920*. Berkeley: University of California Press, 1993.

Anderson, Betty S. *The American University of Beirut: Arab Nationalism and Liberal Education*. Austin: University of Texas Press, 2011.

Aringberg-Laanatza, Marianne. "Alevis in Turkey—Alawites in Syria: Similarities and Differences." In *Alevi Identity: Cultural, Religious and Social Perspectives*, edited by Tord Olsson, Elisabeth Özdalga, and Catharina Raudvere, 200–222. Swedish Research Institute in Istanbul, *Transactions* vol. 8. Richmond, UK: Curzon Press, 1998.

Astourian, Stephan H. "The Silence of the Land: Agrarian Relations, Ethnicity, and Power." In *A Question of Genocide: Armenians and Turks at the End of the Ottoman Empire*, edited by Ronald Grigor Suny, Fatma Müge Göçek, and Norman M. Naimark, 55–81. Oxford: Oxford University Press, 2011.

Ayalon, Ami. *The Press in the Arab Middle East: A History*. New York: Oxford University Press, 1995.

Badran, Margot. "Independent Women: More Than a Century of Feminism in Egypt."

In *Arab Women: Old Boundaries, New Frontiers*, edited by Judith E. Tucker, 129–148. Bloomington: Indiana University Press, 1993.

Baron, Beth. *The Women's Awakening in Egypt: Culture, Society, and the Press*. New Haven, CT: Yale University Press, 1994.

Barsoumian, Hagop. "The Eastern Question and the Tanzimat Era." In *The Armenian People from Ancient to Modern Times*, vol. 2, *Foreign Dominion to Statehood: The Fifteenth Century to the Twentieth Century*, edited by Richard G. Hovannisian, 175–201. New York: St. Martin's Press, 1997.

Bechev, Dimitar. "The State and Local Authorities in the Balkans, 1804–1939." In *Ottomans into Europeans: State and Institution Building in South-East Europe*, edited by Alina Mungiu-Pippidi and Wim Van Meurs, 135–151. London: Hurst, 2010.

Beinin, Joel. *Workers and Peasants in the Modern Middle East*. Cambridge: Cambridge University Press, 2001.

Beinin, Joel, and Zachary Lockman. *Workers on the Nile: Nationalism, Communism, Islam, and the Egyptian Working Class, 1882–1954*. Princeton, NJ: Princeton University Press, 1987.

Binder-Iijima, Edda, and Ekkehard Kraft. "The Making of States: Constitutional Monarchies in the Balkans." In *Ottomans into Europeans: State and Institution Building in South-East Europe*, edited by Alina Mungiu-Pippidi and Wim Van Meurs, 1–29. London: Hurst, 2010.

Biondich, Mark. *The Balkans: Revolution, War, and Political Violence since 1878*. Oxford: Oxford University Press, 2011.

Bonine, Michael E. "The Introduction of Railroads in the Eastern Mediterranean: Economic and Social Impacts." In *The Syrian Land: Processes of Integration and Fragmentation. Bilad al-Sham from the 18th to the 20th Century*, edited by Thomas Philipp and Birgit Schäbler, 53–78. Stuttgart: Franz Steiner Verlag, 1998.

Boyar, Ebru, and Kate Fleet. *A Social History of Ottoman Istanbul*. Cambridge: Cambridge University Press, 2010.

Castellan, Georges. *History of the Balkans: From Mohammed the Conqueror to Stalin*. Translated by Nicholas Bradley. Boulder, CO: East European Monographs, 1992.

Chalcroft, John T. *The Striking Cabbies of Cairo and Other Stories: Crafts and Guilds in Egypt, 1863–1914*. Albany: State University of New York, 2004.

Cioeta, Donald J. "Islamic Benevolent Societies and Public Education in Ottoman Syria,1875–1882." *Islamic Quarterly* 26, no. 1 (1982): 40–55.

Cole, Juan R. I. *Colonialism and Revolution in the Middle East: Social and Cultural Origins of Egypt's 'Urabi Movement*. Cairo: American University in Cairo Press, 1999.

Commins, David Dean. *Islamic Reform: Politics and Social Change in Late Ottoman Syria*. New York: Oxford University Press, 1990.

Dawn, C. Ernest. *From Ottomanism to Arabism: Essays on the Origins of Arab Nationalism*. Urbana: University of Illinois Press, 1973.

Deguilhem, Randi. "State Civil Education in Late Ottoman Damascus: A Unifying or a Separating Force?" In *The Syrian Land: Processes of Integration and Fragmentation. Bilad al-Sham from the 18th to the 20th Century*, edited by Thomas Philipp and Birgit Schäbler, 221–250. Stuttgart: Franz Steiner Verlag, 1998.

Der Matossian, Bedross. *Shattered Dreams of Revolution: From Liberty to Violence in the Late Ottoman Empire*. Stanford, CA: Stanford University Press, 2014.

Deringil, Selim. *The Well-Protected Domains: Ideology and the Legitimation of Power in the Ottoman Empire 1876–1909*. London: I. B. Tauris, 1998.

Di-Capua, Yoav. *Gatekeepers of the Arab Past: Historians and History Writing in Twentieth-Century Egypt*. Berkeley: University of California Press, 2009.

Doumani, Beshara. *Rediscovering Palestine Merchants and Peasants in Jabal Nablus, 1700–1900*. Berkeley: University of California Press, 1995.

Edmonds, C. J. "Kurdish Nationalism." In "Nationalism and Separatism," special issue, *Journal of Contemporary History* 6, no. 1 (1971): 87–97, 99–107.

Fahmy, Khaled. *All the Pasha's Men: Mehmed Ali, His Army and the Making of Modern Egypt*. Cambridge: Cambridge University Press, 1997.

Fahmy, Ziad. *Ordinary Egyptians: Creating the Modern Nation through Popular Culture*. Stanford, CA: Stanford University Press, 2011.

Fawaz, Leila Tarazi. *Merchants and Migrants in Nineteenth-Century Beirut*. Cambridge, MA: Harvard University Press, 1983.

———. *An Occasion for War: Civil Conflict in Lebanon and Damascus in 1860*. Berkeley: University of California Press, 1994.

Freely, John. *A History of Robert College: The American College for Girls, and Boğaziçi (Bosphorus University)*. Vol. 1. Istanbul: Yapi Kredi Yayınları, 2000.

Gelvin, James L. "Post Hoc Ergo Propter Hoc? Reassessing the Lineages of Nationalism in Bilad al-Sham." In *From the Syrian Land to the States of Syria and Lebanon*, edited by Thomas Philipp and Christoph Schumann, 127–142. Würzburg: Ergon in Kommission, 2004.

Gerolymatos, André. *The Balkan Wars: Conquest, Revolution, and Retribution from the Ottoman Era to the Twentieth Century and Beyond*. New York: Basic Books, 2002.

Gershoni, Israel, and James P. Jankowski. *Egypt, Islam, and the Arabs: The Search for Nationhood, 1900–1930*. New York: Oxford University Press, 1987.

Göçek, Fatma Müge. "The Decline of the Ottoman Empire and the Emergence of Greek,Armenian, Turkish, and Arab Nationalisms." In *Social Constructions of Nationalism in the Middle East*, edited by Fatma Müge Göçek, 15–84. Albany: State University of New York, 2002.

———. "Ethnic Segmentation, Western Education, and Political Outcomes: Nineteenth-Century Ottoman Society." *Poetics Today* 14, no. 3 (Autumn 1993): 507–538.

———. *Rise of the Bourgeoisie, Demise of Empire: Ottoman Westernization and Social Change*. New York: Oxford University Press, 1996.

Haddad, Mahmoud. "The Rise of Arab Nationalism Reconsidered." *International Journal of Middle East Studies* 26, no. 2 (May 1994): 201–222.

Hourani, Albert. *Arabic Thought in the Liberal Age, 1798–1939*. Cambridge: Cambridge University Press, 1983.

Hovannisian, Richard G. "The Armenian Question in the Ottoman Empire, 1876–1915," "Armenia's Road to Independence," and "The Republic of Armenia." In *The Armenian People from Ancient to Modern Times*, vol. 2, *Foreign Dominion to Statehood: The Fifteenth Century to the Twentieth Century*, edited by Richard G. Hovannisian, 203–238, 275–346. New York: St. Martin's Press, 1997.

Hovannisian, Richard, and Simon Payaslian, eds. *Armenian Constantinople*. Costa Mesa, CA: Mazda Publishers, 2010.

Hunter, F. Robert. *Egypt under the Khedives 1805–1879: From Household Government to Modern Bureaucracy*. Pittsburgh: University of Pittsburgh Press, 1984.

Jelavich, Barbara. *History of the Balkans*. 2 vols. Cambridge: Cambridge University Press, 1983.

Jongerden, Joost. "Elite Encounters of a Violent Kind: Milli Ibrahim Paşa, Ziya Gökalp and Political Struggle in Diyarbekir at the Turn of the 20th Century." In *Social Relations in Ottoman Diyarbekir, 1870–1915*, edited by Joost Jongerden and Jelle Verheij, 55–84. Leiden, Netherlands: Brill, 2012.

Kasaba, Reşat. *The Ottoman Empire and the World Economy: The Nineteenth Century*. Albany: State University of New York, 1988.

Kassab, Elizabeth Suzanne. *Contemporary Arab Thought: Cultural Critique in Comparative Perspective*. New York: Columbia University Press, 2010.

Keddie, Nikki R. *Sayyid Jamil ad-Din "al-Afghani": A Political Biography*. Berkeley: University of California Press, 1972.

Khater, Akram Fouad. *Inventing Home: Emigration, Gender, and the Middle Class in Lebanon, 1870–1920*. Berkeley: University of California Press, 2001.

Khoury, Philip S. *Urban Notables and Arab Nationalism: The Politics of Damascus 1860–1920*. Cambridge: Cambridge University Press, 1983.

Khuri, Fuad I. *Being a Druze*. London: Druze Heritage Foundation, 2004.

Klein, Janet. *The Margins of Empire: Kurdish Militias in the Ottoman Tribal Zone*. Stanford, CA: Stanford University Press, 2011.

Lawson, Fred H. *The Social Origins of Egyptian Expansionism during the Muhammad 'Ali Period*. New York: Columbia University Press, 1992.

Laycock, Jo. *Imagining Armenia: Orientalism, Ambiguity and Intervention*. Manchester, UK: Manchester University Press, 2009.

Libaridian, Gerard J. "What Was Revolutionary about Armenian Revolutionary Parties in the Ottoman Empire?" In *A Question of Genocide: Armenians and Turks at the End of the Ottoman Empire*, edited by Ronald Grigor Suny, Fatma Müge Göçek, and Norman M. Naimark, 82–112. Oxford: Oxford University Press, 2011.

Makarem, Sami Nasib. *The Druze Faith*. Delmark, NY: Caravan Books, 1974.

Makdisi, Ussama. "After 1860: Debating Religion, Reform, and Nationalism in the Ottoman Empire." *International Journal of Middle East Studies* 34 (2002): 601–617.

———. *The Culture of Sectarianism: Community, History, and Violence in Nineteenth-Century Ottoman Lebanon*. Berkeley: University of California Press, 2000.

Mazower, Mark. *The Balkans: A Short History*. New York: Modern Library, 2000.

McCarthy, Justin. *The Ottoman Turks: An Introductory History to 1923*. London: Addison Wesley Longman, 1997.

Mungiu-Pippidi, Alina, and Wim Van Meurs, eds. *Ottomans into Europeans: State and Institution Building in South-East Europe*. London: Hurst, 2010.

Nalbandian, Louise. *The Armenian Revolutionary Movement: The Development of Armenian Political Parties through the Nineteenth Century*. Berkeley: University of California Press, 1963.

Nisan, Mordechai. *Minorities in the Middle East: A History of Struggle and Self-Expression*. 2nd ed. Jefferson, NC: McFarland , 2002.

Ochsenwald, William. "The Financing of the Hijaz Railroad." *Die Welt des Islams*, n.s., 14, no. 1/4 (1973): 129–149.

Olson, Robert. *The Emergence of Kurdish Nationalism and the Sheikh Said Rebellion, 1880–1925*. Austin: University of Texas Press, 1989.

Mehmet Orhan, Mehmet. "Kurdish Rebellions and Conflict Groups in Turkey during the 1920s and 1930s." *Journal of Muslim Minority Affairs* 32, no. 3 (September 2012): 339–358.

Oshagan, Vahé. "Modern Armenian Literature and Intellectual History from 1700 to 1915." In *The Armenian People from Ancient to Modern* Times, vol. 2, *Foreign Dominion to Statehood: The Fifteenth Century to the Twentieth Century*, edited by Richard G. Hovannisian, 139–174. New York: St. Martin's Press, 1997.

Owen, Roger. *The Middle East in the World Economy: 1800–1914*. London: Methuen, 1981.

———. *State, Power and Politics in the Making of the Modern Middle East*. London: Routledge, 1992.

Özoğlu, Hakan. "'Nationalism' and Kurdish Notables in the Late Ottoman–Early Republican Era." *International Journal of Middle East Studies* 33, no. 3 (August 2001): 383–409.

Panossian, Razmik. *The Armenians: From Kings and Priests to Merchants and Commissars*. New York: Columbia University Press, 2006.

Piterberg, Gabriel. "The Tropes of Stagnation and Awakening in Nationalist Historical Consciousness: The Egyptian Case." In *Rethinking Nationalism in the Arab*

Middle East, edited by James Jankowski and Israel Gershoni, 42–61. New York: Columbia University Press, 1997.

Pollard, Lisa. *Nurturing the Nation: The Family Politics of Modernizing, Colonizing, and Liberating Egypt, 1805–1923*. Berkeley: University of California Press, 2005.

Quartaert, Donald. "The Age of Reform, 1812–1914." In *An Economic and Social History of the Ottoman Empire: 1300–1914*, edited by Halil Inalcik with Donald Quartaert, 759–943. Cambridge: Cambridge University Press, 1994.

———. *The Ottoman Empire, 1700–1922*. Cambridge: Cambridge University Press, 2005.

Rafeq, Abdul-Karim. "Damascus and the Pilgrim Caravan." In *Modernity and Culture: From the Mediterranean to the Indian Ocean*, edited by Leila Tarazi Fawaz and C. A. Bayly, 130–143. New York: Columbia University Press, 2002.

———. *The Province of Damascus, 1723–1783*. Beirut: Khayats, 1966.

Rogan, Eugene. "The Political Significance of an Ottoman Education: Maktab 'Anbar Revisited." In *From the Syrian Land to the States of Syria and Lebanon*, edited by Thomas Philipp and Christoph Schumann, 77–94. Würzburg: Ergon in Kommission, 2004.

Salibi, Kamal. *A House of Many Mansions: The History of Lebanon Reconsidered*. Berkeley: University of California Press, 1988.

———. *The Modern History of Lebanon*. New York: Frederick A. Praeger, 1965.

Sbaiti, Nadya. "Lessons in History: Education and the Formation of National Society in Beirut, Lebanon, 1920–1960s." PhD diss., Georgetown University, 2008.

Schoenberg, Philip Ernest. "The Evolution of Transport in Turkey (Eastern Thrace and Asia Minor) under Ottoman Rule, 1856–1918." *Middle Eastern Studies* 13, no. 3 (October 1977): 359–372.

Scott, Rachel Marion. "Education and Arabism in Damascus at the Turn of the Twentieth Century." *Islamic Culture* 72, no. 3 (July 1998): 17–64.

Starrett, Gregory. *Putting Islam to Work: Education, Politics, and Religious Transformation in Egypt*. Berkeley: University of California Press, 1998.

Steppat, Fritz. "National Education Projects in Egypt before the British Occupation." In *Beginnings of Modernization in the Middle East: The Nineteenth Century*, edited by William R. Polk and Richard L. Chambers, 281–297. Chicago: University of Chicago Press, 1968.

Strohmeier, Martin. *Crucial Images in the Presentation of a Kurdish National Identity: Heroes and Patriots, Traitors and Foes*. Leiden, Netherlands: Brill Academic Publishers, 2003.

Thompson, Elizabeth F. *Justice Interrupted: The Struggle for Constitutional Government in the Middle East*. Cambridge, MA: Harvard University Press, 2013.

Thompson, Jason. *A History of Egypt: From Earliest Times to the Present*. Cairo: American University in Cairo Press, 2008.

Tignor, Robert L. *Egypt: A Short History*. Princeton, NJ: Princeton University Press, 2010.

Toledano, Ehud. *State and Society in Mid-Nineteenth-Century Egypt*. Cambridge: Cambridge University Press, 1990.

Vatter, Sherry. "Journeymen Textile Weavers in Nineteenth-Century Damascus: A Collective Biography." In *Struggle and Survival in the Modern Middle East*, edited by Edmund Burke III, 75–90. Berkeley: University of California Press, 1993.

Zeidner, Robert F. "Britain and the Launching of the Armenian Question." *International Journal of Middle East Studies* 7, no. 4 (October 1976): 465–483.

Zürcher, Erik J. *Turkey: A Modern History*. London: I. B. Tauris, 2009.

Chapter 4. The Great War

Abdullah, Thabit A. J. *A Short History of Iraq*. 2nd ed. Edinburgh Gate: Pearson Education, 2011.

Abrahamian, Ervand. *Iran between Two Revolutions*. Princeton, NJ: Princeton University Press, 1982.

Adanir, Fikret. "Non-Muslims in the Ottoman Army and the Ottoman Defeat in the Balkan War of 1912–1913." In *A Question of Genocide: Armenians and Turks at the End of the Ottoman Empire*, edited by Ronald Grigor Suny, Fatma Müge Göçek, and Norman M. Naimark, 113–125. Oxford: Oxford University Press, 2011.

Afary, Janet. "Social Democracy and the Iranian Constitutional Revolution of 1906–11." In *A Century of Revolution Social Movements in Iran*, edited by John Foran, 21–43. Minneapolis: University of Minnesota Press, 1994.

Ahmad, Feroz. *The Making of Modern Turkey*. London: Routledge, 1993.

Akçam, Taner. *The Young Turks' Crimes against Humanity: The Armenian Genocide and Ethnic Cleansing in the Ottoman Empire*. Princeton, NJ: Princeton University Press, 2012.

Aksakal, Mustafa. *The Ottoman Road to War in 1914: The Ottoman Empire and the First World War*. Cambridge: Cambridge University Press, 2008.

Akşin, Sina. *Turkey from Empire to Revolutionary Republic: The Emergence of the Turkish Nation from 1789 to the Present*. New York: New York University Press, 2007.

Algar, Hamid. *Religion and State in Iran, 1785–1906: The Role of the Ulama in the Qajar Period*. Berkeley: University of California Press, 1969.

Amerie, Sultan M. "Addenda: The Three Major Commodities of Persia." In "The Far East," special issue, *Annals of the American Academy of Political and Social Science* 122 (November 1925): 247–264.

Ansari, Ali M. *Modern Iran: The Pahlavis and After*. 2nd ed. Harlow, UK: Pearson Longman, 2007.

Ashraf, Ahmad. "Bazaar-Mosque Alliance: The Social Basis of Revolts and Revolutions." *International Journal of Politics, Culture, and Society* 1, no. 4 (Summer 1988): 538–567.

Astourian, Stephan H. "The Silence of the Land: Agrarian Relations, Ethnicity, and Power." In *A Question of Genocide: Armenians and Turks at the End of the Ottoman Empire*, edited by Ronald Grigor Suny, Fatma Müge Göçek, and Norman M. Naimark, 55–81. Oxford: Oxford University Press, 2011.

Aydin, Suavi, and Jelle Verheij. "Confusion in the Cauldron: Some Notes on Ethno-religious Groups, Local Powers and the Ottoman State in Diyabekir Province, 1800–1870." In *Social Relations in Ottoman Diyarbekir, 1870–1915*, edited by Joost Jongerden and Jelle Verheij, 15–54. Ottoman Empire and Its Heritage, vol. 51. Leiden, Netherlands: Brill, 2012.

Bakhash, Shaul. "The Failure of Reform: The Prime Ministership of Amin al-Dawla, 1897–8." In *Qajar Iran: Political, Social and Cultural Change 1800–1925*, edited by Edmund Bosworth and Carole Hillenbrand, 14–33. Edinburgh: Edinburgh University Press, 1983.

Barsoumian, Hagop. "The Eastern Question and the Tanzimat Era." In *The Armenian People from Ancient to Modern Times*, vol. 2, *Foreign Dominion to Statehood: The Fifteenth Century to the Twentieth Century*, edited by Richard G. Hovannisian, 175–201. New York: St. Martin's Press, 1997.

Beck, Peter J. "The Anglo-Persian Oil Dispute 1932–33." *Journal of Contemporary History* 9, no. 4 (October 1974): 123–151.

Berberian, Houri. *Armenians and the Iranian Constitutional Revolution of 1905–1911*. Boulder, CO: Westview Press, 2001.

Biondich, Mark. *The Balkans: Revolution, War, and Political Violence since 1878*. Oxford: Oxford University Press, 2011.

Boyar, Ebru, and Kate Fleet. *A Social History of Ottoman Istanbul*. Cambridge: Cambridge University Press, 2010.

Bozarslan, Hamit. "Kurds and the Turkish State." In *The Cambridge History of Turkey*, vol. 4, *Turkey in the Modern World*, edited by Reşat Kasaba, 333–356. Cambridge: Cambridge University Press, 2008.

Brysac, Shareen Blair. "A Very British Coup: How Reza Shah Won and Lost His Throne." *World Policy Journal* 24, no. 2 (Summer 2007): 90–103.

Cadman, John. "The Development of the Petroleum Industry in Persia." *Journal of the Royal Society of Arts* 75, no. 3878 (March 18, 1927): 430–435.

Cagapatay, Soner. *Islam, Secularism, and Nationalism in Modern Turkey: Who Is a Turk?* London: Routledge, 2006.

Castellan, Georges. *History of the Balkans: From Mohammed the Conqueror to Stalin.* Translated by Nicholas Bradley. Boulder, CO: East European Monographs, 1992.

Cole, Juan R. I. "Marking Boundaries, Marking Time: The Iranian Past and the Construction of the Self by Qajar Thinkers." *Iranian Studies* 29, no. 1/2 (Winter–Spring 1996): 35–56.

Cronin, Stephanie. "The Politics of Debt: The Anglo-Persian Oil Company and the Bakhtiyari Khans." *Middle Eastern Studies* 40, no. 4 (2004): 1–31.

Der Matossian, Bedross. *Shattered Dreams of Revolution: From Liberty to Violence in the Late Ottoman Empire*. Stanford, CA: Stanford University Press, 2014.

Deringil, Selim. *The Well-Protected Domains: Ideology and the Legitimation of Power in the Ottoman Empire 1876–1909*. London: I. B. Tauris, 1998.

Duggan, Stephen P. "The Syrian Question." *Journal of International Relations* 11, no. 4 (April 1921): 571–588.

Dündar, Fuat. "Pouring a People into the Desert: The 'Definitive Solution' of the Unionists to the Armenian Question." In *A Question of Genocide: Armenians and Turks at the End of the Ottoman Empire*, edited by Ronald Grigor Suny, Fatma Müge Göçek, and Norman M. Naimark, 276–284. Oxford: Oxford University Press, 2011.

Edmonds, C. J. "Kurdish Nationalism." In "Nationalism and Separatism," special issue, *Journal of Contemporary History* 6, no. 1 (1971): 87–97, 99–107.

Ettehadieh, Mansoureh. "The Origins and Development of the Women's Movement in Iran,1906–41." In *Women in Iran from 1800 to the Islamic Republic*, edited by Lois Beck and Guity Nashat, 85–106. Urbana: University of Illinois Press, 2004.

Ferrier, R. W. *The History of the British Petroleum Company*. Vol. 1, *The Developing Years, 1901–1932*. Cambridge: Cambridge University Press, 1982.

Findley, Carter Vaughn. *Turkey, Islam, Nationalism, and Modernity: A History, 1789–2007*. New Haven, CT: Yale University Press, 2010.

Gelvin, James L. "Post Hoc Ergo Propter Hoc? Reassessing the Lineages of Nationalism in Bilad al-Sham." In *From the Syrian Land to the States of Syria and Lebanon*, edited by Thomas Philipp and Christoph Schumann, 127–142. Würzburg: Ergon in Kommission, 2004.

Gerolymatos, André. *The Balkan Wars: Conquest, Revolution, and Retribution from the Ottoman Era to the Twentieth Century and Beyond*. New York: Basic Books, 2002.

Gingeras, Ryan. *Sorrowful Shores: Violence, Ethnicity, and the End of the Ottoman Empire, 1912–1923*. Oxford: Oxford University Press, 2009.

Göçek, Fatma Müge. "The Decline of the Ottoman Empire and the Emergence of Greek,Armenian, Turkish, and Arab Nationalisms." In *Social Constructions of Nationalism in the Middle East*, edited by Fatma Müge Göçek, 15–84. Albany: State University of New York, 2002.

———. "Ethnic Segmentation, Western Education, and Political Outcomes: Nineteenth-Century Ottoman Society." *Poetics Today* 14, no. 3 (Autumn 1993): 507–538.

———. *Rise of the Bourgeoisie, Demise of Empire: Ottoman Westernization and Social Change*. New York: Oxford University Press, 1996.

Haddad, Mahmoud. "The Rise of Arab Nationalism Reconsidered." *International Journal of Middle East Studies* 26, no. 2 (May 1994): 201–222.

Hanioğlu, M. Şükrü. *A Brief History of the Late Ottoman Empire*. Princeton, NJ: Princeton University Press, 2008.

Hourani, Albert. *Arabic Thought in the Liberal Age, 1798–1939*. Cambridge: Cambridge University Press, 1983.

Hovannisian, Richard G. "The Armenian Question in the Ottoman Empire, 1876–1915," "Armenia's Road to Independence," and "The Republic of Armenia." In *The Armenian People from Ancient to Modern Times*, vol. 2, *Foreign Dominion to Statehood: The Fifteenth Century to the Twentieth Century*, edited by Richard G. Hovannisian, 203-238, 275–346. New York: St. Martin's Press, 1997.

Hovannisian, Richard, and Simon Payaslian, eds. *Armenian Constantinople*. Costa Mesa, CA: Mazda Publishers, 2010.

Iordachi, Constantin. "The Making of Citizenship in the Post-Ottoman Balkans: State Building, Foreign Models, and Legal-Political Transfers." In *Ottomans into Europeans: State and Institution Building in South-East Europe*, edited by Alina Mungiu-Pippidi and Wim Van Meurs, 179–220. London: Hurst, 2010.

Jack, Marian. "The Purchase of the British Government's Share in the British Petroleum Company 1912–1914." *Past & Present* 39 (April 1968): 139–168.

Jelavich, Barbara. *History of the Balkans*. 2 vols. Cambridge: Cambridge University Press, 1983.

Jongerden, Joost. "Elite Encounters of a Violent Kind: Milli Ibrahim Paşa, Ziya Gökalp and Political Struggle in Diyarbekir at the Turn of the 20th Century." In *Social Relations in Ottoman Diyarbekir, 1870–1915*, edited by Joost Jongerden and Jelle Verheij, 55–84. Ottoman Empire and Its Heritage, vol. 51. Leiden, Netherlands: Brill, 2012.

Kamrava, Mehran. *The Political History of Modern Iran: From Tribalism to Theocracy*. Westport, CT: Praeger, 1992.

Kasaba, Reşat. *The Ottoman Empire and the World Economy: The Nineteenth Century*. Albany: State University of New York, 1988.

Kashani-Sabet, Firoozeh. "Cultures of Iranianness: The Evolving Polemic of Iranian Nationalism." In *Iran and the Surrounding World: Interactions in Culture and Cultural Politics*, edited by Nikki R. Keddie and Rudi Matthee, 162–181. Seattle: University of Washington Press, 2002.

Kayali, Hasan. *Arabs and Young Turks: Ottomanism, Arabism, and Islamism in the Ottoman Empire, 1908–1918*. Berkeley: University of California Press, 1997.

———. "The Struggle for Independence." In *The Cambridge History of Turkey*, vol. 4, *Turkey in the Modern World*, edited by Reşat Kasaba, 112–146. Cambridge: Cambridge University Press, 2008.

Keddie, Nikki R., with Yann Richard. *Modern Iran: Roots and Results of Revolution*. New Haven, CT: Yale University Press, 2003.

———. *Roots of Revolution: An Interpretive History of Modern Iran*. New Haven, CT: Yale University Press, 1981.

Khoury, Philip S. *Urban Notables and Arab Nationalism: The Politics of Damascus 1860–1920*. Cambridge: Cambridge University Press, 1983.

Kia, Mehrdad. "Persian Nationalism and the Campaign for Language Purification." *Middle Eastern Studies* 34, no. 2 (April 1998): 9–36.

Kushner, David. *The Rise of Turkish Nationalism: 1876–1908*. London: Frank Cass, 1977.

Lenczowski, George. "Foreign Powers' Intervention in Iran during World War I." In *Qajar Iran: Political, Social and Cultural Change 1800–1925*, edited by Edmund Bosworth and Carole Hillenbrand, 76–92. Edinburgh: Edinburgh University Press, 1983.

Libaridian, Gerard J. "What Was Revolutionary about Armenian Revolutionary Parties in the Ottoman Empire?" In *A Question of Genocide: Armenians and Turks at the End of the Ottoman Empire*, edited by Ronald Grigor Suny, Fatma Müge Göçek, and Norman M. Naimark, 82–112. Oxford: Oxford University Press, 2011.

Mahdavi, Shireen. "Social Mobility in Qajar Iran: Haj Muhammad Hassan Amin al-Zarb." *Middle Eastern Studies* 26, no. 4 (October 1990): 582–595.

Marashi, Afshin. *Nationalizing Iran: Culture, Power, and the State, 1870–1940*. Seattle: University of Washington Press, 2008.

Mazower, Mark. *The Balkans: A Short History*. New York: Modern Library, 2000.

———. *Salonica: City of Ghosts: Christians, Muslims and Jews 1450–1950*. London: HarperCollins Publishers, 2004.

McCarthy, Justin. *The Ottoman Turks: An Introductory History to 1923*. London: Addison Wesley Longman, 1997.

Moaddel, Mansoor. "Shi'i Political Discourse and Class Mobilization in the Tobacco Movement of 1890–92." In *A Century of Revolution Social Movements in Iran*, edited by John Foran, 1–20. Minneapolis: University of Minnesota Press, 1994.

Mungiu-Pippidi, Alina, and Wim Van Meurs, eds. *Ottomans into Europeans: State and Institution Building in South-East Europe*. London: Hurst, 2010.

Nalbandian, Louise. *The Armenian Revolutionary Movement: The Development of Armenian Political Parties through the Nineteenth Century*. Berkeley: University of California Press, 1963.

Nashat, Guity. "From Bazaar to Market: Foreign Trade and Economic Development in Nineteenth-Century Iran." *Iranian Studies* 14, no. 1/2 (Winter–Spring 1981): 53–85.

———. *The Origins of Modern Reform in Iran, 1870–80*. Urbana: University of Illinois Press, 1982.

Oshagan, Vahé. "Modern Armenian Literature and Intellectual History from 1700 to 1915." In *The Armenian People from Ancient to Modern Times*, vol. 2, *Foreign Dominion to Statehood: The Fifteenth Century to the Twentieth Century*, edited by Richard G. Hovannisian, 139–174. New York: St. Martin's Press, 1997.

Owen, Roger. *The Middle East in the World Economy: 1800–1914*. London: Methuen, 1981.

Özkirimli, Umat, and Spyros A. Sofos. *Tormented by History: Nationalism in Greece and Turkey*. New York: Columbia University Press, 2008.

Özoğlu, Hakan. "'Nationalism' and Kurdish Notables in the Late Ottoman–Early Republican Era." *International Journal of Middle East Studies* 33, no. 3 (August 2001): 383–409.

Panossian, Razmik. *The Armenians: From Kings and Priests to Merchants and Commissars*. New York: Columbia University Press, 2006.

Quartaert, Donald. *The Ottoman Empire, 1700–1922*. Cambridge: Cambridge University Press, 2005.

al-Rasheed, Madawi. *A History of Saudi Arabia*. Cambridge: Cambridge University Press, 2002.

Reguer, Sara. "Persian Oil and the First Lord: A Chapter in the Career of Winston Churchill." *Military Affairs* 46, no. 3 (October 1982): 134–138.

Reynolds, Michael A. *Shattering Empires: The Clash and Collapse of the Ottoman and Russian Empires, 1908–1918*. Cambridge: Cambridge University Press, 2011.

Rugh, William A. "A Tale of Two Houses." *Wilson Quarterly* 3, no. 1 (Winter 1979): 58–72.

Sachar, Howard M. *A History of Israel: From the Rise of Zionism to Our Time*. 2nd ed. New York: Alfred A. Knopf, 1996.

Schneer, Jonathan. *The Balfour Declaration: The Origins of the Arab-Israeli Conflict*. New York: Random House, 2010.

Scott, Rachel Marion. "Education and Arabism in Damascus at the Turn of the Twentieth Century." *Islamic Culture* 72, no. 3 (July 1998): 17–64.

Smith, Charles D. *Palestine and the Arab-Israeli Conflict.* 8th ed. Boston: Bedford/St. Martin's, 2013.

Sultan, Shabana. "The West Asian Oil and the Great Powers." *Indian Journal of Political Science* 68, no. 3 (July–September 2007): 615–628.

Thompson, Elizabeth F. *Justice Interrupted: The Struggle for Constitutional Government in the Middle East.* Cambridge, MA: Harvard University Press, 2013.

Üngor, Uğur Ümit. "Disastrous Decade: Armenians and Kurds in the Young Turk Era: 1915–1925." In *Social Relations in Ottoman Diyarbekir, 1870–1915*, edited by Joost Jongerden and Jelle Verheij, 267–296. Ottoman Empire and Its Heritage, vol. 51. Leiden, Netherlands: Brill, 2012.

———. *The Making of Modern Turkey: Nation and State in Eastern Anatolia, 1913–1950.* Oxford: Oxford University Press, 2011.

———. "'Turkey for the Turks': Demographic Engineering in Eastern Anatolia, 1914–1945." In *A Question of Genocide: Armenians and Turks at the End of the Ottoman Empire*, edited by Ronald Grigor Suny, Fatma Müge Göçek, and Norman M. Naimark, 287–305. Oxford: Oxford University Press, 2011.

Uyar, Mesut, and Edward J. Erickson. *A Military History of the Ottomans: From Osman to Atatürk.* Santa Barbara, CA: Praeger Security International, 2009.

Wilson, Mary C. "The Hashemites, the Arab Revolt, and Arab Nationalism." In *The Origins of Arab Nationalism*, edited by Rashid Khalidi, Lisa Anderson, Muhammad Muslih, and Reeva S. Simon, 204–221. New York: Columbia University Press, 1991.

Yarshater, E. "Observations of Nasir al-Din Shah." In *Qajar Iran: Political, Social and Cultural Change 1800–1925*, edited by Edmund Bosworth and Carole Hillenbrand, 3–13. Edinburgh: Edinburgh University Press, 1983.

Zürcher, Erik J. *Turkey: A Modern History.* London: I. B. Tauris, 2009.

Chapter 5. State Formation and Colonial Control

Abadan-Unat, Nermin. "Social Change and Turkish Women." In *Women in Turkish Society*, edited by Nermin Abadan-Unat, 5–31. Leiden, Netherlands: E. J. Brill, 1981.

Abdullah, Thabit A. J. *A Short History of Iraq.* 2nd ed. Edinburgh Gate: Pearson Education, 2011.

Abrahamian, Ervand. *Iran between Two Revolutions.* Princeton, NJ: Princeton University Press, 1982.

Ahmad, Feroz. *The Making of Modern Turkey.* London: Routledge, 1993.

Akrawi, Matta, and A. A. El-Koussy. "Recent Trends in Arab Education." In "Educational Trends in Some Developing Countries," special issue, *International Review of Education* 17, no. 2 (1971): 181–197.

Akşin, Sina. *Turkey from Empire to Revolutionary Republic: The Emergence of the Turkish Nation from 1789 to the Present.* New York: New York University Press, 2007.

Alon, Yoav. *The Making of Jordan: Tribes, Colonialism and the Modern State.* London: I. B. Tauris, 2007.

Anderson, Betty. *Nationalist Voices in Jordan: The Street and the State.* Austin: University of Texas Press, 2005.

Ansari, Ali M. *Modern Iran: The Pahlavis and After.* 2nd ed. Harlow, UK: Pearson Longman, 2007.

Ari, Eyal. "The People's Houses and the Theatre in Turkey." *Middle Eastern Studies* 40, no. 4 (July 2004): 32–58.

Aringberg-Laanatza, Marianne. "Alevis in Turkey—Alawites in Syria: Similarities and Differences." In *Alevi Identity: Cultural, Religious and Social Perspectives*, edited by Tord Olsson, Elisabeth Özdalga, and Catharina Raudvere, 200–222. Swedish Research Institute in Istanbul, *Transactions* vol. 8. Richmond, UK: Curzon Press, 1998.

Aytürk, Ilker. "The First Episode of Language Reform in Republican Turkey: The Language Council from 1926 to 1931." *Journal of the Royal Asiatic Society*, 3rd ser., 18, no. 3 (July 2008): 275–293.

Bashkin, Orit. *The Other Iraq: Pluralism and Culture in Hashemite Iraq*. Stanford, CA: Stanford University Press, 2009.

Batatu, Hanna. "Iraq's Underground Shi'i Movements." In "Islam and Politics," special issue, *MERIP Reports* 102 (January 1982): 3–9.

———. *The Old Social Classes and the Revolutionary Movements of Iraq: A Study of Iraq's Old Landed and Commercial Classes and of Its Communists, Ba'thists, and Free Officers*. Princeton, NJ: Princeton University Press, 1978.

Benglo, Ofra. "Shi'is and Politics in Ba'thi Iraq." *Middle Eastern Studies* 21, no. 1 (January 1985): 1–14.

Bozarslan, Hamit. "Kurds and the Turkish State." In *The Cambridge History of Turkey*, vol. 4, *Turkey in the Modern World*, edited by Reşat Kasaba, 333–356. Cambridge: Cambridge University Press, 2008.

Brockett, Gavin D. "Collective Action and the Turkish Revolution: Towards a Framework for the Social History of the Atatürk Era, 1923–1938." In "Turkey before and after Atatürk: Internal and External Affairs," special issue, *Middle Eastern Studies* 34, no. 4 (October 1998): 44–66.

Cagapatay, Soner. *Islam, Secularism, and Nationalism in Modern Turkey: Who Is a Turk?* London: Routledge, 2006.

Davis, Eric. *Memories of State: Politics, History, and Collective Identity in Modern Iraq*. Berkeley: University of California Press, 2005.

Edmonds, C. J. "Kurdish Nationalism." In "Nationalism and Separatism," special issue, *Journal of Contemporary History* 6, no. 1 (1971): 87–97, 99–107.

Ekmekcioglu, Lerna. "A Climate for Abduction, a Climate for Redemption: The Politics of Inclusion during and after the Armenian Genocide." *Comparative Studies in Society and History* 55, no. 3 (2013): 522–553.

———. "A Republic of Paradox: The League of Nations Minority Protection Regime and the New Turkey's Step-Citizens." In "World War I," special issue, *International Journal of Middle East Studies* 46, no. 4 (November 2014): 657–679.

Ettehadieh, Mansoureh. "The Origins and Development of the Women's Movement in Iran,1906–41." In *Women in Iran from 1800 to the Islamic Republic*, edited by Lois Beck and Guity Nashat, 85–106. Urbana: University of Illinois Press, 2004.

Farouk-Sluglett, Marion, and Peter Sluglett. "The Transformation of Land Tenure and Rural Social Structure in Central and Southern Iraq, c. 1870–1958." *International Journal of Middle East Studies* 15, no. 4 (November 1983): 491–505.

Findley, Carter Vaughn. *Turkey, Islam, Nationalism, and Modernity: A History, 1789–2007*. New Haven, CT: Yale University Press, 2010.

Gelvin, James L. *Divided Loyalties: Nationalism and Mass Politics in Syria at the Close of Empire*. Berkeley: University of California Press, 1998.

———. "The Ironic Legacy of the King-Crane Commission." In *The Middle East and the United States: History, Politics, and Ideologies*, edited by David W. Lesch, 15–32. Boulder, CO: Westview Press, 2013.

Gershoni, Israel. "Rethinking the Formation of Arab Nationalism in the Middle East,1920–1945: Old and New Narratives." In *Rethinking Nationalism in the Arab Middle East*, edited by James Jankowski and Israel Gershoni, 3–25. New York: Columbia University Press, 1997.

Gingeras, Ryan. *Sorrowful Shores: Violence, Ethnicity, and the End of the Ottoman Empire, 1912–1923*. Oxford: Oxford University Press, 2009.

Güçlü, Yücel. "The Role of Ottoman-Trained Officers in Independent Iraq." *Oriente Moderno*, n.s., 82, no. 2 (2002): 441–458.

———. "The Struggle for Mastery in Cilicia: Turkey, France, and the Ankara Agreement of 1921." *International History Review* 23, no. 3 (September 2001): 580–603.

Habachy, Saba. "The Republican Institutions of Lebanon: Its Constitution." *American Journal of Comparative Law* 13, no. 4 (Autumn 1964): 594–604.

Hadar, Gila. "Jewish Tobacco Workers in Salonika: Gender and Family in the Context of Social and Ethnic Strife." In *Women in the Ottoman Balkans: Gender, Culture and History*, edited by Amila Buturovi? and Irvin Cemal Schick, 127–152. London: I. B. Tauris, 2007.

Jones, Toby Craig. *Desert Kingdom: How Oil and Water Forged Modern Saudi Arabia.* Cambridge, MA: Harvard University Press, 2010.

Kamrava, Mehran. *The Political History of Modern Iran: From Tribalism to Theocracy.* Westport, CT: Praeger, 1992.

Kayali, Hasan. "The Struggle for Independence." In *The Cambridge History of Turkey*, vol. 4, *Turkey in the Modern World*, edited by Reşat Kasaba, 112–146. Cambridge: Cambridge University Press, 2008.

Keddie, Nikki R., with Yann Richard. *Modern Iran: Roots and Results of Revolution.* New Haven, CT: Yale University Press, 2003.

———. *Roots of Revolution: An Interpretive History of Modern Iran.* New Haven, CT: Yale University Press, 1981.

Khoury, Philip S. "Factionalism among Syrian Nationalists during the French Mandate." *International Journal of Middle East Studies* 13, no. 4 (November 1981): 441–469.

———. *Syria and the French Mandate: The Politics of Arab Nationalism 1920–1945.* Princeton, NJ: Princeton University Press, 1987.

———. *Urban Notables and Arab Nationalism: The Politics of Damascus 1860–1920.* Cambridge: Cambridge University Press, 1983.

Mango, Andrew. "Atatürk and the Kurds." In "Seventy-Five Years of the Turkish Republic," special issue, *Middle Eastern Studies* 35, no. 4 (October 1999): 1–25.

Marr, Phebe. *The Modern History of Iraq.* Boulder, CO: Westview Press, 1985.

Massad, Joseph A. *Colonial Effects: The Making of National Identity in Jordan.* New York: Columbia University Press, 2001.

McCarthy, Justin. *The Ottoman Turks: An Introductory History to 1923.* London: Addison Wesley Longman, 1997.

Mélikoff, Irène. "Bektashi/*Kizilbaş*: Historical Bipartition and Its Consequences." In *Alevi Identity: Cultural, Religious and Social Perspectives*, edited by Tord Olsson, Elisabeth Özdalga, and Catharina Raudvere, 1–10. Swedish Research Institute in Istanbul, *Transactions* vol. 8. Richmond, UK: Curzon Press, 1998.

Moubayed, Sami, M. *The Politics of Damascus, 1920–1946: Urban Notables and the French Mandate.* Damascus: Tlass House, 1999.

Nakash, Yitzhak. *Shi'is of Iraq.* Princeton, NJ: Princeton University Press, 1994.

Nisan, Mordechai. *Minorities in the Middle East: A History of Struggle and Self-Expression.* 2nd ed. Jefferson, NC: McFarland, 2002.

Özkirimli, Umat, and Spyros A. Sofos. *Tormented by History: Nationalism in Greece and Turkey.* New York: Columbia University Press, 2008.

Pakizegi, Behnaz. "Legal and Social Positions of Iranian Women." In *Women in the Muslim World*, edited by Lois Beck and Nikki Keddie, 216–226. Cambridge, MA: Harvard University Press,1978.

Perry, John, R. "Language Reform in Turkey and Iran." *International Journal of Middle East Studies* 17, no. 3 (August 1985): 295–311.

Pool, David. "From Elite to Class: The Transformation of Iraqi Leadership, 1920–1939." *International Journal of Middle East Studies* 12, no. 3 (November 1980): 331–350.

Provence, Michael. *The Great Syrian Arab Revolt and the Rise of Arab Nationalism.* Austin: University of Texas Press, 2005.

———. "Ottoman Modernity, Colonialism, and Insurgency in the Interwar Arab East." *International Journal of Middle East Studies* 4 (2011): 205–225.

Quartaert, Donald. *The Ottoman Empire, 1700–1922*. Cambridge: Cambridge University Press, 2005.

al-Rasheed, Madawi. *A History of Saudi Arabia*. Cambridge: Cambridge University Press, 2002.

Robins, Philip. *A History of Jordan*. Cambridge: Cambridge University Press, 2004.

Rogan, Eugene. *Frontiers of the State in the Late Ottoman Empire: Transjordan, 1850–1921*. Cambridge: Cambridge University Press, 1999.

Rugh, William A. "A Tale of Two Houses." *Wilson Quarterly* 3, no. 1 (Winter 1979): 58–72.

Salibi, Kamal. *A House of Many Mansions: The History of Lebanon Reconsidered*. Berkeley: University of California Press, 1988.

———. *The Modern History of Lebanon*. New York: Frederick A. Praeger, 1965.

Sanasarian, Eliz. *The Women's Rights Movement in Iran: Mutiny, Appeasement, and Repression from 1900 to Khomeini*. New York: Praeger Publishers, 1982.

Seale, Patrick. *The Struggle for Arab Independence: Riad el-Solh and the Makers of the Modern Middle East*. Cambridge: Cambridge University Press, 2010.

Simon, James J. "The Role of the Administrative Council of Mount Lebanon in the Creation of Greater Lebanon: 1918–1920." *Journal of Third World Studies* 13, no. 2 (Fall 1996): 119–171.

Simon, Reeva S. "The Imposition of Nationalism on a Non-nation State: The Case of Iraq during the Interwar Period, 1921–1941." In *Rethinking Nationalism in the Arab Middle East*, edited by James Jankowski and Israel Gershoni, 87–104. New York: Columbia University Press, 1997.

———. *Iraq between the Two World Wars: The Creation and Implementation of a Nationalist Ideology*. New York: Columbia University Press, 1986.

Tachau, Frank. "Language and Politics: Turkish Language Reform." *Review of Politics* 26, no. 2 (April 1964): 191–204.

Thompson, Elizabeth F. *Colonial Citizens: Republican Rights, Paternal Privilege, and Gender in French Syria and Lebanon*. New York: Columbia University Press, 2000.

———. *Justice Interrupted: The Struggle for Constitutional Government in the Middle East*. Cambridge, MA: Harvard University Press, 2013.

Traboulsi, Fawwaz. *A History of Modern Lebanon*. London: Pluto Press, 2007.

Tripp, Charles. *A History of Iraq*. 3rd ed. Cambridge: Cambridge University Press, 2007.

Üngor, Uğur Ümit. "Disastrous Decade: Armenians and Kurds in the Young Turk Era: 1915–1925." In *Social Relations in Ottoman Diyarbekir, 1870–1915*, edited by Joost Jongerden and Jelle Verheij, 267–296. Ottoman Empire and Its Heritage, vol. 51. Leiden, Netherlands: Brill, 2012.

———. *The Making of Modern Turkey: Nation and State in Eastern Anatolia, 1913–1950*. Oxford: Oxford University Press, 2011.

———. "'Turkey for the Turks': Demographic Engineering in Eastern Anatolia, 1914–1945." In *A Question of Genocide: Armenians and Turks at the End of the Ottoman Empire*, edited by Ronald Grigor Suny, Fatma Müge Göçek, and Norman M. Naimark, 287–305. Oxford: Oxford University Press, 2011.

Uyar, Mesut. "Ottoman Arab Officers between Nationalism and Loyalty during the First World War." *War in History* 20, no. 4 (2013): 526–544.

Uyar, Mesut, and Edward J. Erickson. *A Military History of the Ottomans: From Osman to Atatürk*. Santa Barbara, CA: Praeger Security International, 2009.

Wein, Peter. *Iraqi Arab Nationalism: Authoritarian, Totalitarian, and Pro-Fascist Inclinations, 1932–1941*. London: Routledge, 2006.

White, Jenny B. "State Feminism, Modernization, and the Turkish Republican Women." In "Gender and Modernism between the Wars, 1981–1939," special issue, *NWSA Journal* 15, no. 3 (Autumn 2003): 145–149.

———. "Tin Towns to Fanatics: Turkey's Rural to Urban Migration from 1923 to the Present." In *Turkey's Engagement with Modernity: Conflict and Change in the Twentieth Century*, edited by Celia Kerslake, Kerem Öktem, and Philip Robins, 425–442. London: Palgrave Macmillan, 2010.

Wilson, Mary C. *King Abdullah, Britain and the Making of Jordan*. Cambridge: Cambridge University Press, 1987.

Yeganeh, Nahd. "Women, Nationalism and Islam in Contemporary Political Discourse in Iran." In "Nationalisms and National Identities," special issue, *Feminist Review* 44 (Summer 1993): 3–18.

Zirinsky, Michael P. "The Rise of Reza Khan." In *A Century of Revolution Social Movements in Iran*, edited by John Foran, 44–77. Minneapolis: University of Minnesota Press, 1994.

Zürcher, Erik J. *Turkey: A Modern History*. London: I. B. Tauris, 2009.

Chapter 6. Rebels and Rogues

Abdalla, Ahmed. *The Student Movement and National Politics in Egypt: 1923–1973*. London: Al Saqi Books, 1985.

Abdullah, Thabit A. J. *A Short History of Iraq*. 2nd ed. Edinburgh Gate: Pearson Education, 2011.

Abrahamian, Ervand. *Iran between Two Revolutions*. Princeton, NJ: Princeton University Press, 1982.

Ahmed, Jamal Mohammed. *The Intellectual Origins of Egyptian Nationalism*. London: Oxford University Press, 1960.

Akrawi, Matta, and A. A. El-Koussy. "Recent Trends in Arab Education." In "Educational Trends in Some Developing Countries," special issue, *International Review of Education* 17, no. 2 (1971): 181–197.

Alon, Yoav. *The Making of Jordan: Tribes, Colonialism and the Modern State*. London: I. B. Tauris, 2007.

Anderson, Betty. *Nationalist Voices in Jordan: The Street and the State*. Austin: University of Texas Press, 2005.

———. "Writing the Nation: Textbooks of the Hashemite Kingdom of Jordan." *Comparative Studies of South Asia, Africa and the Middle East* 21, no. 1–2 (2001): 5–14.

Ansari, Ali M. *Modern Iran: The Pahlavis and After*. 2nd ed. Harlow, UK: Pearson Longman, 2007.

Arnon, Adar. "The Quarters of Jerusalem in the Ottoman Period." *Middle Eastern Studies* 28, no. 1 (January 1992): 1–65.

Badran, Margot. "Independent Women: More Than a Century of Feminism in Egypt." In *Arab Women: Old Boundaries, New Frontiers*, edited by Judith E. Tucker, 129–148. Bloomington: Indiana University Press, 1993.

Baron, Beth. *The Women's Awakening in Egypt: Culture, Society, and the Press*. New Haven, CT: Yale University Press, 1994.

Barth, Hans Karl, and Friedrich Quiel. "Development and Changes in the Eastern Province of Saudi Arabia." In "The Arab Gulf States," special issue, *GeoJournal* 13, no. 3 (October 1986): 251–259.

Bashkin, Orit. *The Other Iraq: Pluralism and Culture in Hashemite Iraq*. Stanford, CA: Stanford University Press, 2009.

Batatu, Hanna. *The Old Social Classes and the Revolutionary Movements of Iraq: A Study of Iraq's Old Landed and Commercial Classes and of Its Communists, Ba'thists, and Free Officers*. Princeton, NJ: Princeton University Press, 1978.

Beinin, Joel, and Zachary Lockman. *Workers on the Nile: Nationalism, Communism, Islam, and the Egyptian Working Class, 1882–1954*. Princeton, NJ: Princeton University Press, 1987.

Ben-Arieh, Y. "The Growth of Jerusalem in the Nineteenth Century." *Annals of the Association of American Geographers* 65, no. 2 (June 1975): 252–269.

Benglo, Ofra. "Shi'is and Politics in Ba'thi Iraq." *Middle Eastern Studies* 21, no. 1 (January 1985): 1–14.

Brockett, Gavin D. "Collective Action and the Turkish Revolution: Towards a Framework for the Social History of the Atatürk Era, 1923–1938." In "Turkey before and after Atatürk: Internal and External Affairs," special issue, *Middle Eastern Studies* 34, no. 4 (October 1998): 44–66.

Cesarani, David. "The War on Terror That Failed: British Counter-insurgency in Palestine 1945–1947 and the 'Farran Affair.'" *Small Wars & Insurgencies* 23, no. 4–5 (October–December 2012): 648–670.

Danielson, Virginia. *The Voice of Egypt: Umm Kulthum, Arabic Song, and Egyptian Society in the Twentieth Century*. Chicago: University of Chicago Press, 1997.

Davis, Eric. *Memories of State: Politics, History, and Collective Identity in Modern Iraq*. Berkeley: University of California Press, 2005.

Di-Capua, Yoav. *Gatekeepers of the Arab Past: Historians and History Writing in Twentieth-Century Egypt*. Berkeley: University of California Press, 2009.

El-Eini, Roza I. M. "The Implementation of British Agricultural Policy in Palestine in the 1930s." *Middle Eastern Studies* 32, no. 4 (October 1996): 211–250.

Fahmy, Ziad. *Ordinary Egyptians: Creating the Modern Nation through Popular Culture*. Stanford, CA: Stanford University Press, 2011.

Farouk-Sluglett, Marion, and Peter Sluglett. "The Transformation of Land Tenure and Rural Social Structure in Central and Southern Iraq, c. 1870–1958." *International Journal of Middle East Studies* 15, no. 4 (November 1983): 491–505.

Farsoun, Samih K., with Christina E. Zacharia. *Palestine and the Palestinians*. Boulder, CO: Westview Press, 1997.

Fischbach, Michael R. *State, Society and Land in Jordan*. Leiden, Netherlands: Brill, 2000.

Gershoni, Israel. "Rethinking the Formation of Arab Nationalism in the Middle East,1920–1945: Old and New Narratives." In *Rethinking Nationalism in the Arab Middle East*, edited by James Jankowski and Israel Gershoni, 3–25. New York: Columbia University Press, 1997.

Gershoni, Israel, and James P. Jankowski. *Egypt, Islam, and the Arabs: The Search for Nationhood, 1900–1930*. New York: Oxford University Press, 1987.

———. *Redefining the Egyptian Nation, 1930–1945*. Cambridge: Cambridge University Press, 1995.

Gitler, Inbal Ben-Asher. "'Marrying Modern Progress with Treasured Antiquity': Jerusalem City Plans during the British Mandate, 1917–1948." *Traditional Dwellings and Settlement Review* 15, no. 1 (Fall 2003): 39–58.

Halevi, Nadav. "The Political Economy of Absorptive Capacity: Growth and Cycles in Jewish Palestine under Mandate." *Middle Eastern Studies* 19, no. 4 (October 1983): 456–469.

Jankowski, James. *Egypt's Young Rebels: 'Young Egypt': 1933–1952*. Stanford, CA: Hoover Institution Press, Stanford University, 1975.

Jones, Toby Craig. *Desert Kingdom: How Oil and Water Forged Modern Saudi Arabia*. Cambridge, MA: Harvard University Press, 2010.

Kamrava, Mehran. *The Political History of Modern Iran: From Tribalism to Theocracy*. Westport, CT: Praeger, 1992.

Khalaf, Issa. "The Effect of Socioeconomic Change on Arab Societal Collapse in Mandate Palestine." *International Journal of Middle East Studies* 29, no. 1 (February 1997): 93–112.

Khalidi, Rashid. *Palestinian Identity: The Construction of Modern National Consciousness*. New York: Columbia University Press, 1997.

Khoury, Philip S. "Factionalism among Syrian Nationalists during the French Mandate." *International Journal of Middle East Studies* 13, no. 4 (November 1981): 441–469.

———. *Syria and the French Mandate: The Politics of Arab Nationalism 1920–1945*. Princeton, NJ: Princeton University Press, 1987.

Lia, Brynjar. *The Society of the Muslim Brothers in Egypt: The Rise of an Islamic Mass Movement 1928–1942*. Reading, UK: Ithaca Press, 1998.

Marr, Phebe. *The Modern History of Iraq*. Boulder, CO: Westview Press, 1985.

Marsot, Afaf Lutfi al-Sayyid. *Egypt's Liberal Experiment: 1922–1936*. Berkeley: University of California Press, 1977.

Massad, Joseph A. *Colonial Effects: The Making of National Identity in Jordan*. New York: Columbia University Press, 2001.

Matthews, Roderic D., and Matta Akrawi. *Education in Arab Countries of the Near East*. Washington, DC: American Council on Education, 1949.

Moubayed, Sami, M. *The Politics of Damascus, 1920–1946: Urban Notables and the French Mandate*. Damascus: Tlass House, 1999.

Nadan, Amos. "No Holy Statistics for the Holy Land: The Fallacy of Growth in the Palestinian Rural Economy, 1920s–1930s." In *Britain, Palestine and Empire: The Mandate Years*, edited by Rory Miller, 101–118. Surrey, UK: Ashgate Publishing, 2010.

———. *The Palestinian Peasant Economy under the Mandate: A Story of Colonial Bungling*. Cambridge, MA: Center for Middle Eastern Studies of Harvard University, 2006.

Nakash, Yitzhak. *Shi'is of Iraq*. Princeton, NJ: Princeton University Press, 1994.

Nordbruch, Götz. *Nazism in Syria and Lebanon: The Ambivalence of the German Option, 1933–1945*. London: Routledge, 2009.

Pappé, Ilan. *A History of Modern Palestine: One Land, Two Peoples*. 2nd ed. Cambridge: Cambridge University Press, 2006.

Perry, John R. "Language Reform in Turkey and Iran." *International Journal of Middle East Studies* 17, no. 3 (August 1985): 295–311.

Piterberg, Gabriel. "The Tropes of Stagnation and Awakening in Nationalist Historical Consciousness: The Egyptian Case." In *Rethinking Nationalism in the Arab Middle East*, edited by James Jankowski and Israel Gershoni, 42–61. New York: Columbia University Press, 1997.

Provence, Michael. "Ottoman Modernity, Colonialism, and Insurgency in the Interwar Arab East." *International Journal of Middle East Studies* 43 (2011): 205–225.

al-Rasheed, Madawi. *A History of Saudi Arabia*. Cambridge: Cambridge University Press, 2002.

Robins, Philip. *A History of Jordan*. Cambridge: Cambridge University Press, 2004.

Roy, Delwin A. "The Educational System of Iraq." *Middle Eastern Studies* 29, no. 2 (April 1993): 167–197.

Rugh, William A. "A Tale of Two Houses." *Wilson Quarterly* 3, no. 1 (Winter 1979): 58–72.

Sachar, Howard M. *A History of Israel: From the Rise of Zionism to Our Time*. 2nd ed. New York: Alfred A. Knopf, 1996.

Sayigh, Rosemary. *Palestinians: From Peasants to Revolutionaries*. London: Zed Press, 1979.

Sbaiti, Nadya. "Lessons in History: Education and the Formation of National Society in Beirut, Lebanon, 1920–1960s." PhD diss., Georgetown University, 2008.

Schliefer, Abdullah. "Izz al-Din al-Qassam: Preacher and Mujahid." In *Struggle and Survival in the Modern Middle East*, edited by Edmund Burke III, 164–178. Berkeley: University of California Press, 1993.

Seale, Patrick. *The Struggle for Arab Independence: Riad el-Solh and the Makers of the Modern Middle East*. Cambridge: Cambridge University Press, 2010.

Simon, Reeva S. "The Imposition of Nationalism on a Non-nation State: The Case of Iraq during the Interwar Period, 1921–1941." In *Rethinking Nationalism in the*

Arab Middle East, edited by James Jankowski and Israel Gershoni, 87–104. New York: Columbia University Press, 1997.

———. *Iraq between the Two World Wars: The Creation and Implementation of a Nationalist Ideology*. New York: Columbia University Press, 1986.

Smith, Charles D. *Palestine and the Arab-Israeli Conflict*. 8th ed. Boston: Bedford/St. Martin's, 2013.

Stein, Kenneth W. "The Intifada and the 1936–39 Uprising: A Comparison." *Journal of Palestine Studies* 19, no. 4 (Summer 1990): 64–85.

Swedenburg, Ted. "The Palestinian Peasant as National Signifier." In "Tendentious Revisions of the Past in the Construction of Community," special issue, *Anthropological Quarterly* 63, no. 1 (January 1990): 18–30.

———. "The Role of the Palestinian Peasantry in the Great Revolt (1936–1939)." In *The Modern Middle East: A Reader*, edited by Albert Hourani, Philip S. Khoury, and Mary C. Wilson, 467–502. Berkeley: University of California Press, 1993.

Thompson, Elizabeth F. "The Climax and Crisis of the Colonial Welfare State in Syria and Lebanon during World War II." In *War, Institutions, and Social Change in the Middle East*, edited by Steven Heydemann, 59–99. Berkeley: University of California Press, 2000.

———. *Colonial Citizens: Republican Rights, Paternal Privilege, and Gender in French Syria and Lebanon*. New York: Columbia University Press, 2000.

———. *Justice Interrupted: The Struggle for Constitutional Government in the Middle East*. Cambridge, MA: Harvard University Press, 2013.

Thompson, Jason. *A History of Egypt: From Earliest Times to the Present*. Cairo: American University in Cairo Press, 2008.

Tignor, Robert L. *Egypt: A Short History*. Princeton, NJ: Princeton University Press, 2010.

Traboulsi, Fawwaz. *A History of Modern Lebanon*. London: Pluto Press, 2007.

Tripp, Charles. *A History of Iraq*. 3rd ed. Cambridge: Cambridge University Press, 2007.

Üngor, Uğur Ümit. *The Making of Modern Turkey: Nation and State in Eastern Anatolia, 1913–1950*. Oxford: Oxford University Press, 2011.

———. "'Turkey for the Turks': Demographic Engineering in Eastern Anatolia, 1914–1945." In *A Question of Genocide: Armenians and Turks at the End of the Ottoman Empire*, edited by Ronald Grigor Suny, Fatma Müge Göçek, and Norman M. Naimark, 287–305. Oxford: Oxford University Press, 2011.

Vitalis, Robert. *America's Kingdom: Mythmaking on the Saudi Oil Frontier*. Stanford, CA: Stanford University Press, 2007.

Wein, Peter. *Iraqi Arab Nationalism: Authoritarian, Totalitarian, and Pro-Fascist Inclinations, 1932–1941*. London: Routledge, 2006.

Whidden, James. "The Generation of 1919." In *Re-envisioning Egypt: 1919–1952*, edited by Arthur Goldschmidt, Amy J. Johnson, and Barak A. Salmoni, 19–45. Cairo: American University in Cairo Press, 2005.

White, Jenny B. "Tin Towns to Fanatics: Turkey's Rural to Urban Migration from 1923 to the Present." In *Turkey's Engagement with Modernity: Conflict and Change in the Twentieth Century*, edited by Celia Kerslake, Kerem Öktem, and Philip Robins, 425–442. London: Palgrave Macmillan, 2010.

Wickham, Carrie Rosefsky. *The Muslim Brotherhood: Evolution of an Islamist Movement*. Princeton, NJ: Princeton University Press, 2013.

Wilson, Mary C. *King Abdullah, Britain and the Making of Jordan*. Cambridge: Cambridge University Press, 1987.

Zuhur, Sherifa. *Asmahan's Secrets: Woman, War, and Song*. Austin: Center for Middle Eastern Studies, University of Texas at Austin, 2000.

Zürcher, Erik J. *Turkey: A Modern History*. London: I. B. Tauris, 2009.

Chapter 7. Military Coups

Abdullah, Thabit A. J. *A Short History of Iraq*. 2nd ed. Edinburgh Gate: Pearson Education, 2011.

Abrahamian, Ervand. *Iran between Two Revolutions*. Princeton, NJ: Princeton University Press, 1982.

Abu-Laban, Baha. "The National Charter in the Egyptian Revolution." *Journal of Developing Areas* 1, no. 2 (January 1967): 179–198.

———. "Social Change and Local Politics in Sidon, Lebanon." *Journal of Developing Areas* 5, no. 1 (October 1970): 27–42.

Aburish, Saïd K. *Nasser: The Last Arab*. New York: Thomas Dunne Books, St. Martin's Press, 2004.

Ahmed, Jamal Mohammed. *The Intellectual Origins of Egyptian Nationalism*. London: Oxford University Press, 1960.

Anderson, Betty S. *The American University of Beirut: Arab Nationalism and Liberal Education*. Austin: University of Texas Press, 2011.

———. *Nationalist Voices in Jordan: The Street and the State*. Austin: University of Texas Press, 2005.

Batatu, Hanna. *The Old Social Classes and the Revolutionary Movements of Iraq: A Study of Iraq's Old Landed and Commercial Classes and of Its Communists, Ba'thists, and Free Officers*. Princeton, NJ: Princeton University Press, 1978.

———. *Syria's Peasantry, the Descendants of Its Lesser Rural Notables, and Their Politics*. Princeton, NJ: Princeton University Press, 1999.

Beinin, Joel, and Zachary Lockman. *Workers on the Nile: Nationalism, Communism, Islam, and the Egyptian Working Class, 1882–1954*. Princeton, NJ: Princeton University Press, 1987.

Benglo, Ofra. "Shi'is and Politics in Ba'thi Iraq." *Middle Eastern Studies* 21, no. 1 (January 1985): 1–14.

Bier, Laura. *Revolutionary Womanhood: Feminisms, Modernity, and the State in Nasser's Egypt*. Stanford, CA: Stanford University Press, 2011.

C. B. "OPEC Thirty Years On." *Economic and Political Weekly* 25, no. 45 (November 10, 1990): 2476–2477.

Cobban, Helena. *The Making of Modern Lebanon*. Boulder, CO: Westview Press, 1985.

———. *The Palestinian Liberation Organization: People, Power and Politics*. Cambridge: Cambridge University Press, 1984.

Cook, Steven A. *The Struggle for Egypt: From Nasser to Tahrir Square*. Oxford: Oxford University Press, 2012.

Dam, Nikolaos van. *The Struggle for Power in Syria: Politics and Society under Asad and the Ba'th Party*. London: I. B. Tauris, 2011.

Dann, Uriel. *Iraq under Qassem: A Political History, 1958–1963*. New York: Frederick A. Praeger, 1969.

Davis, Eric. *Memories of State: Politics, History, and Collective Identity in Modern Iraq*. Berkeley: University of California Press, 2005.

Dekmejian, R. Hrair. *Egypt under Nasir: A Study in Political Dynamics*. Albany: State University of New York Press, 1971.

Erlich, Haggai. *Students and University in 20th Century Egyptian Politics*. London: Frank Cass, 1989.

Farouk-Sluglett, Marion, and Peter Sluglett. *Iraq since 1958: From Revolution to Dictatorship*. London: I. B. Tauris, 1990.

———. "The Transformation of Land Tenure and Rural Social Structure in Central and Southern Iraq, c. 1870–1958." *International Journal of Middle East Studies* 15, no. 4 (November 1983): 491–505.

Fawaz, Leila Tarazi. "Contemporary History—Understanding Lebanon." *American Scholar* 54, no. 3 (Summer 1985): 377–384.

Gaspard, Toufic K. *A Political Economy of Lebanon 1948–2002: The Limits of Laissez-Faire*. Leiden, Netherlands: Brill, 2004.

Gates, Carolyn L. *The Merchant Republic of Lebanon: Rise of an Open Economy*. London: I. B. Tauris, 1998.

Gordon, Joel. *Nasser: Hero of the Arab Nation*. Oxford: Oneworld Publications, 2006.

———. *Nasser's Blessed Movement: Egypt's Free Officers and the July Revolution*. Oxford: Oxford University Press, 1992.

Hamzeh, A. Nizar. "Clientelism, Lebanon: Roots and Trends." *Middle Eastern Studies* 37, no. 3 (July 2001): 167–178.

Harik, Iliya. "Continuity and Change in Local Development Policies in Egypt: From Nasser to Sadat." *International Journal of Middle East Studies* 16, no. 1 (March 1984): 43–66.

Hertog, Steffen. *Princes, Brokers, and Bureaucrats: Oil and the State in Saudi Arabia*. Ithaca, NY: Cornell University Press, 2010.

Hinnebusch, Raymond A. *Authoritarian Power and State Formation in Ba'thist Syria: Army, Party, and Peasant*. Boulder, CO: Westview Press, 1990.

———. "Local Politics in Syria: Organization and Mobilization in Four Village Cases." *Middle East Journal* 30, no. 1 (Winter 1976): 1–24.

———. "Party Activists in Syria and Egypt: Political Participation in Authoritarian Modernizing States." In "Party Activists in Comparative Perspective," special issue, *International Political Science Review* 4, no. 1 (1983): 84–93.

Holbik, Karel, and Edward Drachman. "Egypt as Recipient of Soviet Aid, 1955–1970." *Journal of Institutional and Theoretical Economics* 127, no. 1 (January 1971): 137–165.

Hopwood, Derek. *Syria 1945–1986: Politics and Society*. London: Unwin Hyman, 1988.

Issawi, Charles. "Economic Development and Liberalism in Lebanon." *Middle East Journal* 18, no. 3 (Summer 1964): 279–292.

Jankowski, James. *Egypt's Young Rebels: 'Young Egypt': 1933–1952*. Stanford, CA: Hoover Institution Press, Stanford University, 1975.

———. *Nasser's Egypt, Arab Nationalism, and the United Arab Republic*. Boulder, CO: Lynne Rienner Publishers, 2002.

Joesten, Joachim. *Nasser: The Rise to Power*. Westport, CT: Greenwood Press, 1974.

Kamrava, Mehran. *The Political History of Modern Iran: From Tribalism to Theocracy*. Westport, CT: Praeger, 1992.

Keddie, Nikki R., with Yann Richard. *Modern Iran: Roots and Results of Revolution*. New Haven, CT: Yale University Press, 2003.

———. *Roots of Revolution: An Interpretive History of Modern Iran*. New Haven, CT: Yale University Press, 1981.

Keilany, Ziad. "Economic Planning in Syria, 1960–1965: An Evaluation." *Journal of Developing Areas* 4, no. 3 (April 1970): 361–374.

———. "Socialism and Economic Change in Syria." *Middle Eastern Studies* 9, no. 1 (January 1973): 61–72.

Khuri, Fuad I. "The Changing Class Structure in Lebanon." *Middle East Journal* 23, no. 1 (Winter 1969): 29–44.

Landau, Jacob M. "Elections in Lebanon." *Western Political Quarterly* 14, no. 1, pt. 1 (March 1961): 120–147.

———. *Radical Politics in Modern Turkey*. Leiden, Netherlands: E. J. Brill, 1974.

Mansfield, Peter. "Nasser and Nasserism." In "The Arab States and Israel," special issue, *International Journal* 28, no. 4 (Autumn 1973): 670–688.

Marr, Phebe. *The Modern History of Iraq*. Boulder, CO: Westview Press, 1985.

Meo, Leila M. T. *Lebanon Improbable Nation: A Study in Political Development*. Westport, CT: Greenwood Press, 1976.

Mikdashi, Zuhayr. "Cooperating among Oil Exporting Countries with Special Reference to Arab Countries: A Political Economy Analysis." *International Organization* 28, no. 1 (Winter 1974): 1–30.

———. "The OPEC Process." In "The Oil Crisis: In Perspective," special issue, *Daedalus* 104, no. 4e (Fall 1975): 203–215.

Najmabadi, Afsaneh. *Land Reform and Social Change in Iran.* Salt Lake City: University of Utah Press, 1987.

Olson, Robert. "The Ba'th in Syria 1947–1949: An Interpretative Historical Essay (Part One)." *Oriente Moderno* 58, no. 12 (December 1978): 645–681.

———. "The Ba'th in Syria 1947–1949: An Interpretative Historical Essay (Part Two)." *Oriente Moderno* 59, no. 6 (June 1979): 439–474.

———. *The Ba'th Party and Syria, 1947 to 1982: The Evolution of Ideology, Party, and State.* Princeton, NJ: Kingston Press, 1982.

Penrose, Edith. "OPEC's Importance in the World Oil Industry." *International Affairs* 55, no. 1 (January 1979): 18–32.

al-Rasheed, Madawi. *A History of Saudi Arabia.* Cambridge: Cambridge University Press, 2002.

Roberts, David. *The Ba'th and the Creation of Modern Syria.* New York: St. Martin's Press, 1987.

Robins, Philip. *A History of Jordan.* Cambridge: Cambridge University Press, 2004.

Rugh, William A. "Emergence of a New Middle Class in Saudi Arabia." *Middle East Journal* 27, no. 1 (Winter 1973): 7–20.

Russell, Tom. "A Lebanon Primer." *MERIP Reports* 133 (June 1985): 17–19.

Seale, Patrick. *The Struggle for Arab Independence: Riad el-Solh and the Makers of the Modern Middle East.* Cambridge: Cambridge University Press, 2010.

———. *The Struggle for Syria: A Study of Post-war Arab Politics 1945–1958.* New Haven, CT: Yale University Press, 1987.

Springborg, Robert. "Baathism in Practice: Agriculture, Politics, and Political Culture in Syria and Iraq." *Middle Eastern Studies* 17, no. 2 (April 1981): 191–209.

Suleiman, Michael W. *Political Parties in Lebanon: The Challenge of a Fragmented Political Culture.* Ithaca, NY: Cornell University Press, 1967.

Szyliowicz, Joseph S. *Political Change in Rural Turkey: Erdemli.* The Hague: Mouton, 1966.

Thompson, Elizabeth F. *Justice Interrupted: The Struggle for Constitutional Government in the Middle East.* Cambridge, MA: Harvard University Press, 2013.

Thompson, Jason. *A History of Egypt: From Earliest Times to the Present.* Cairo: American University in Cairo Press, 2008.

Tignor, Robert L. *Egypt: A Short History.* Princeton, NJ: Princeton University Press, 2010.

Torrey, Gordon H. *Syrian Politics and the Military: 1945–1958.* Columbus: Ohio State University Press, 1964.

Traboulsi, Fawwaz. *A History of Modern Lebanon.* London: Pluto Press, 2007.

Tripp, Charles. *A History of Iraq.* 3rd ed. Cambridge: Cambridge University Press, 2007.

Üngor, Uğur Ümit. *The Making of Modern Turkey: Nation and State in Eastern Anatolia, 1913–1950.* Oxford: Oxford University Press, 2011.

Van Dusen, Michael H. "Political Integration and Regionalism in Syria." *Middle East Journal* 26, no. 2 (Spring 1972): 123–136.

Waterbury, John. *The Egypt of Nasser and Sadat: The Political Economy of Two Regimes.* Princeton, NJ: Princeton University Press, 1983.

White, Jenny B. "Tin Towns to Fanatics: Turkey's Rural to Urban Migration from 1923 to the Present." In *Turkey's Engagement with Modernity: Conflict and Change in the Twentieth Century*, edited by Celia Kerslake, Kerem Öktem, and Philip Robins, 425–442. London: Palgrave Macmillan, 2010.

Yodfat, Aryeh. "The End of Syria's Isolation?" *World Today* 27, no. 8 (August 1971): 329–339.

Zürcher, Erik J. *Turkey: A Modern History*. London: I. B. Tauris, 2009.

Chapter 8. Cold War Battles

Abdullah, Thabit A. J. *A Short History of Iraq*. 2nd ed. Edinburgh Gate: Pearson Education, 2011.

Abrahamian, Ervand. *Iran between Two Revolutions*. Princeton, NJ: Princeton University Press, 1982.

Abu-Amr, Ziad. "Hamas: A Historical and Political Background." *Journal of Palestine Studies* 22, no. 4 (Summer 1993): 5–19.

Batatu, Hanna. *The Old Social Classes and the Revolutionary Movements of Iraq: A Study of Iraq's Old Landed and Commercial Classes and of Its Communists, Ba'thists, and Free Officers*. Princeton, NJ: Princeton University Press, 1978.

Baumgarten, Helga. "The Three Faces/Phases of Palestinian Nationalism, 1948–2005." *Journal of Palestine Studies* 34, no. 4 (Summer 2005): 25–48.

Cobban, Helena. "Lebanon's Chinese Puzzle." *Foreign Policy* 53 (Winter 1983–1984): 34–48.

———. *The Making of Modern Lebanon*. Boulder, CO: Westview Press,1985.

———. *The Palestinian Liberation Organization: People, Power and Politics*. Cambridge: Cambridge University Press, 1984.

Cook, Steven A. *The Struggle for Egypt: From Nasser to Tahrir Square*. Oxford: Oxford University Press, 2012.

Dajani, Omar M. "Forty Years without Resolve: Tracing the Influence of Security Council Resolution 242 on the Middle East Peace Process." *Journal of Palestine Studies* 37, no. 1 (Autumn 2007): 24–38.

Dam, Nikolaos van. *The Struggle for Power in Syria: Politics and Society under Asad and the Ba'th Party*. London: I. B. Tauris, 2011.

Davis, Eric. *Memories of State: Politics, History, and Collective Identity in Modern Iraq*. Berkeley: University of California Press, 2005.

Dekmejian, R. Hrair. *Egypt under Nasir: A Study in Political Dynamics*. Albany: State University of New York Press, 1971.

Falk, Richard. "Forty Years after 242: A 'Canonical' Text in Disrepute?" *Journal of Palestine Studies* 37, no. 1 (Autumn 2007): 39–48.

Farouk-Sluglett, Marion, and Peter Sluglett. *Iraq since 1958: From Revolution to Dictatorship*. London: I. B. Tauris, 1990.

Fawaz, Leila Tarazi. "Contemporary History—Understanding Lebanon." *American Scholar* 54, no. 3 (Summer 1985): 377–384.

Filiu, Jean-Pierre. "The Origins of Hamas: Militant Legacy or Israeli Tool?" *Journal of Palestine Studies* 41, no. 3 (Spring 2012): 54–70.

Fruchter-Ronen, Iris. "Black September: The 1970–71 Events and Their Impact on the Formation of Jordanian National Identity." *Civil Wars* 10, no. 3 (September 2008): 244–260.

Gaspard, Toufic K. *A Political Economy of Lebanon 1948–2002: The Limits of Laissez-Faire*. Leiden, Netherlands: Brill, 2004.

Gates, Carolyn L. *The Merchant Republic of Lebanon: Rise of an Open Economy*. London: I. B. Tauris, 1998.

Gerges, Fawaz A. "The 1967 Arab-Israeli War: US Actions and Arab Perceptions." In *The Middle East and the United States: A Historical and Political Reassessment*, 4th ed., edited by David W. Lesch and Mark L. Haas, 163–181. Boulder, CO: Westview Press, 2007.

Gilmour, David. *Lebanon: The Fractured Country*. New York: St. Martin's Press, 1983.

Graf, Rüdiger. "Making Use of the 'Oil Weapon': Western Industrialized Countries and Arab Petropolitics in 1973–1974." *Diplomatic History* 36, no. 1 (January 2012): 185–208.

Graham-Brown, Sarah. "The West Bank and Gaza: The Structural Impact of Israeli Colonization." *MERIP Reports* 74 (January 1979): 9–20.

Haddad, Bassam. "Business Associations and the New Nexus of Power in Syria." In *Civil Society in Syria and Iran: Activism in Authoritarian Contexts*, edited by Paul Aarts and Francesco Cavatorta, 69–92. Boulder, CO: Lynne Rienner Publishers, 2013.

———. *Business Networks in Syria: The Political Economy of Authoritarian Resilience.* Stanford, CA: Stanford University Press, 2012.

Hamzeh, A. Nizar. "Clientelism, Lebanon: Roots and Trends." *Middle Eastern Studies* 37, no. 3 (July 2001): 167–178.

Harik, Iliya. "Continuity and Change in Local Development Policies in Egypt: From Nasser to Sadat." *International Journal of Middle East Studies* 16, no. 1 (March 1984): 43–66.

Harrington, Craig A. "The Colonial Office and the Retreat from Aden: Great Britain in South Arabia, 1957–1967." *Mediterranean Quarterly* 25, no. 3 (Summer 2014): 5–26.

Hilal, Jamil. "Class Transformation in the West Bank and Gaza." *MERIP Reports* 53 (December 1976): 9–15.

Hinnebusch, Raymond A. *Authoritarian Power and State Formation in Ba'thist Syria: Army, Party, and Peasant.* Boulder, CO: Westview Press, 1990.

Holbik, Karel, and Edward Drachman. "Egypt as Recipient of Soviet Aid, 1955–1970." *Journal of Institutional and Theoretical Economics* 127, no. 1 (January 1971): 137–165.

Hopwood, Derek. *Syria 1945–1986: Politics and Society.* London: Unwin Hyman, 1988.

el-Husseini, Rola. *Pax Syriana: Elite Politics in Postwar Lebanon.* Syracuse, NY: Syracuse University Press, 2012.

Issawi, Charles. "Economic Development and Liberalism in Lebanon." *Middle East Journal* 18, no. 3 (Summer 1964): 279–292.

Jankowski, James. *Nasser's Egypt, Arab Nationalism, and the United Arab Republic.* Boulder, CO: Lynne Rienner Publishers, 2002.

Kamrava, Mehran. *The Political History of Modern Iran: From Tribalism to Theocracy.* Westport, CT: Praeger, 1992.

Karawan, Ibrahim A. "Sadat and the Egyptian-Israeli Peace Revisited." *International Journal of Middle East Studies* 26, no. 2 (May 1994): 249–266.

Keddie, Nikki R., with Yann Richard. *Modern Iran: Roots and Results of Revolution.* New Haven, CT: Yale University Press, 2003.

———. *Roots of Revolution: An Interpretive History of Modern Iran.* New Haven, CT: Yale University Press, 1981.

Kerr, Malcolm. "'Coming to Terms with Nasser': Attempts and Failures." *International Affairs* 43, no. 1 (January 1967): 65–84.

Khuri, Fuad I. "The Changing Class Structure in Lebanon." *Middle East Journal* 23, no. 1 (Winter 1969): 29–44.

Knudsen, Are. "Crescent and Sword: The Hamas Enigma." *Third World Quarterly* 26, no. 8 (2005): 1373–1388.

Kristianasen, Wendy. "Challenge and Counterchallenge: Hamas' Response to Oslo." *Journal of Palestine Studies* 28, no. 3 (Spring 1999): 19–36.

Landau, Jacob M. "Elections in Lebanon." *Western Political Quarterly* 14, no. 1, pt. 1 (March 1961): 120–147.

Lawson, Fred H. "Syria's Intervention in the Lebanese Civil War, 1976: A Domestic Conflict Explanation." *International Organization* 38, no. 3 (Summer 1984): 451–480.

Lesch, David W. "The 1957 American-Syrian Crisis: Globalist Policy in a Regional Reality." In *The Middle East and the United States: A Historical and Political*

Reassessment, 4th ed., edited by David W. Lesch and Mark L. Haas, 106–121. Boulder, CO: Westview Press, 2007.

Lucas, Russell. "Side Effects of Regime Building in Jordan: The State and the Nation." *Civil Wars* 10, no. 3 (September 2008): 281–293.

Lynk, Michael. "Conceived in Law: The Legal Foundations of Resolution 242." *Journal of Palestine Studies* 37, no. 1 (Autumn 2007): 7–23.

Mansfield, Peter. "Nasser and Nasserism." In "The Arab States and Israel," special issue, *International Journal* 28, no. 4 (Autumn 1973): 670–688.

Marr, Phebe. *The Modern History of Iraq*. Boulder, CO: Westview Press, 1985.

Meo, Leila M. T. *Lebanon Improbable Nation: A Study in Political Development.* Westport, CT: Greenwood Press, Publishers, 1976.

MERIP Staff. "Why Syria Invaded Lebanon." *MERIP Report* 51 (October 1976): 3–10.

Mufti, Malik. "The United States and Nasserist Pan-Arabism." In *The Middle East and the United States: A Historical and Political Reassessment*, 4th ed., edited by David W. Lesch and Mark L. Haas, 141–161. Boulder, CO: Westview Press, 2007.

Norton, Augustus Richard. "Changing Actors and Leadership among the Shiites of Lebanon." In "Changing Patterns of Power in the Middle East," special issue, *Annals of the American Academy of Political and Social Science* 482 (November 1985): 109–121.

———. *Hezbollah: A Short History*. Princeton, NJ: Princeton University Press, 2007.

———. "Lebanon after Ta'if: Is the Civil War Over?" *Middle East Journal* 45, no. 3 (Summer 1991): 457–473.

Olson, Robert. *The Ba'th Party and Syria, 1947 to 1982: The Evolution of Ideology, Party, and State*. Princeton, NJ: Kingston Press, 1982.

Pappé, Ilan. *A History of Modern Palestine: One Land, Two Peoples*. 2nd ed. Cambridge: Cambridge University Press, 2006.

Perry, Glenn. "Security Council 242: The Withdrawal Clause." *Middle East Journal* 31, no. 4 (Autumn 1977): 413–433.

Podeh, Elie. "The Perils of Ambiguity: The United States and the Baghdad Pact." In *The Middle East and the United States: A Historical and Political Reassessment*, 4th ed., edited by David W. Lesch and Mark L. Haas, 86–105. Boulder, CO: Westview Press, 2012.

Pressberg, Gail. "The Uprising: Causes and Consequences." *Journal of Palestine Studies* 17, no. 3 (Spring 1988): 38–50.

Roberts, David. *The Ba'th and the Creation of Modern Syria*. New York: St. Martin's Press, 1987.

Robins, Philip. *A History of Jordan*. Cambridge: Cambridge University Press, 2004.

Roy, Sara. "The Gaza Strip: Critical Effects of the Occupation." In *Occupation: Israel over Palestine*, edited by Naseer H. Aruri, 249–296. Belmont, MA: Association of Arab-American University Graduates, 1989.

Russell, Tom. "A Lebanon Primer." *MERIP Reports* 133 (June 1985): 17–19.

Sachar, Howard M. *A History of Israel: From the Rise of Zionism to Our Time*. 2nd ed. New York: Alfred A. Knopf, 1996.

Saleh, Hassan Abdul Kadir. "Jewish Settlement and Its Economic Impact on the West Bank, 1967–1987." In "Some Geographical Aspects of the Israeli-Palestinian Conflict," special issue, *GeoJournal* 21, no. 4 (August 1990): 337–348.

Sayigh, Rosemary. *Palestinians: From Peasants to Revolutionaries*. London: Zed Press, 1979.

Sayigh, Yezid. *Armed Struggle and the Search for State: The Palestinian Movement, 1949–1993*. Oxford: Oxford University Press, 1997.

Schayegh, Cyrus. "1958 Reconsidered: State Formation and the Cold War in the Early Postcolonial Arab Middle East." *International Journal of Middle East Studies* 45 (2013): 421–443.

Seale, Patrick. *The Struggle for Syria: A Study of Post-war Arab Politics 1945–1958.* New Haven, CT: Yale University Press, 1987.
Shemesh, Moshe. "The Origins of Sadat's Strategic Volte-Face (Marking 30 Years since Sadat's Historic Visit to Israel, November 1977)." *Israel Studies* 13, no. 2 (Summer 2008): 28–53.
Smith, Charles D. *Palestine and the Arab-Israeli Conflict.* 8th ed. Boston: Bedford/St. Martin's, 2013.
Stein, Kenneth W. "The Intifada and the 1936–39 Uprising: A Comparison." *Journal of Palestine Studies* 19, no. 4 (Summer 1990): 64–85.
Stork, Joe. "Report from Lebanon." In "Lebanon: The State and the Opposition," special issue, *MERIP Reports* 118 (October 1983): 3–13, 22.
Suleiman, Michael W. *Political Parties in Lebanon: The Challenge of a Fragmented Political Culture.* Ithaca, NY: Cornell University Press, 1967.
Swedenburg, Ted. "The Palestinian Peasant as National Signifier." In "Tendentious Revisions of the Past in the Construction of Community," special issue, *Anthropological Quarterly* 63, no. 1 (January 1990): 18–30.
Tal, David. "A Tested Alliance: The American Airlift to Israel in the 1973 Yom Kippur War." *Israel Studies* 19, no. 3 (Fall 2014): 29–54.
Tamari, Salim. "The Palestinian Movement in Transition: Historical Reversals and the Uprising." *Journal of Palestine Studies* 20, no. 2 (Winter 1991): 57–70.
Taraki, Lisa. "The Islamic Resistance Movement in the Palestinian Uprising." In "Iran's Revolution Turns Ten," special issue, *Middle East Report* 156 (January–February 1989): 30–32.
Thompson, Elizabeth F. *Justice Interrupted: The Struggle for Constitutional Government in the Middle East.* Cambridge, MA: Harvard University Press, 2013.
Thompson, Jason. *A History of Egypt: From Earliest Times to the Present.* Cairo: American University in Cairo Press, 2008.
Tignor, Robert L. *Egypt: A Short History.* Princeton, NJ: Princeton University Press, 2010.
Torrey, Gordon H. *Syrian Politics and the Military: 1945–1958.* Columbus: Ohio State University Press, 1964.
Traboulsi, Fawwaz. *A History of Modern Lebanon.* London: Pluto Press, 2007.
Tripp, Charles. *A History of Iraq.* 3rd ed. Cambridge: Cambridge University Press, 2007.
Usher, Graham. "What Kind of Nation? The Rise of Hamas in the Occupied Territories." *Race & Class* 37, no. 2 (1995): 65–80.
Van Arkadie, Brian. "The Impact of the Israeli Occupation on the Economies of the West Bank and Gaza." *Journal of Palestine Studies* 6, no. 2 (Winter 1977): 103–129.
Waterbury, John. *The Egypt of Nasser and Sadat: The Political Economy of Two Regimes.* Princeton, NJ: Princeton University Press, 1983.
Wenger, Martha, and Julie Denney. "Lebanon's Fifteen-Year War 1975–1990." In "Lebanon's War," special issue, *Middle East Report* 162 (January–February 1990): 23–25.
Yodfat, Aryeh. "The End of Syria's Isolation?" *World Today* 27, no. 8 (August 1971): 329–339.
Younger, Sam. "The Syrian Stake in Lebanon." *World Today* 32, no. 11 (November 1976): 399–406.
Zürcher, Erik J. *Turkey: A Modern History.* London: I. B. Tauris, 2009.

Chapter 9. Rulers for Life

Abrahamian, Ervand. "The Crowd in the Persian Revolution." *Iranian Studies* 2, no. 4 (Autumn 1969): 128–150.
———. *Iran between Two Revolutions.* Princeton, NJ: Princeton University Press, 1982.
———. "Why the Islamic Republic Has Survived." *Middle East Report* 250 (Spring 2009): 11–14, 16.

Albrecht, Holger. "Authoritarian Opposition and the Politics of Challenge in Egypt." In *Debating Arab Authoritarianism: Dynamics and Durability in Nondemocratic Regimes*, edited by Oliver Schlumberger, 59–74. Stanford, CA: Stanford University Press, 2007.

Anderson, Betty. "Writing the Nation: Textbooks of the Hashemite Kingdom of Jordan." *Comparative Studies of South Asia, Africa and the Middle East* 21, no. 1–2 (2001): 5–14.

Arjomand, Said Amir. "Iran's Islamic Revolution in Comparative Perspective." *World Politics* 38, no. 3 (April 1986): 383–414.

Ashraf, Ahmad. "Bazaar-Mosque Alliance: The Social Basis of Revolts and Revolutions." *International Journal of Politics, Culture, and Society* 1, no. 4 (Summer 1988): 538–567.

Aziz-al Ahsan, Syed. "Economic Policy and Class Structure in Syria: 1958–1980." *International Journal of Middle East Studies* 16, no. 3 (August 1984): 301–323.

Azmeh, Shamel. "Labour in Global Production Networks: Workers in the Qualifying Industrial Zones (QIZs) of Egypt and Jordan." *Global Networks* 14, no. 4 (2014): 495–513.

Bahramitash, Roksana. "Islamic Fundamentalism and Women's Economic Role: The Case of Iran." *International Journal of Politics, Culture, and Society* 16, no. 4 (Summer 2003): 551–568.

Beinin, Joel. "Neo-liberal Structural Adjustment, Political Demobilization and Neo-authoritarianism In Egypt." In *The Arab State and Neo-liberal Globalization: The Restructuring of State Power in the Middle East*, edited by Laura Guazzone and Daniela Pioppi, 19–46. Reading, UK: Ithaca Press, 2009.

Bellin, Eva. "The Robustness of Authoritarianism in the Middle East: Exceptionalism in Comparative Perspective." *Comparative Politics* 36, no. 2 (January 2004): 139–157.

Bolle, Mary Jane, Alfred B. Prados, and Jeremy M. Sharp. *Qualifying Industrial Zones in Jordan and Egypt*. CRS Report for Congress, July 7, 2006. http://www.au.af.mil/au/awc/awcgate/crs/rs22002.pdf.

Brynen, Rex. "The Politics of Monarchical Liberalism: Jordan." In *Political Liberalization and Democratization in the Arab World*, vol. 2, *Comparative Experiences*, edited by Bahgat Korany, Rex Brynen, and Paul Noble, 71–100. Boulder, CO: Lynne Rienner Publishers, 1998.

Çandar, Cengiz. "Atatürk's' Ambitious Legacy." *Wilson Quarterly* 24, no. 4 (Autumn 2000): 88–96.

Carswell, Robert. "Economic Sanctions and the Iran Experience." *Foreign Affairs* 60, no. 2 (Winter 1981): 247–265.

Chehabi, H. E. *Iranian Politics and Religious Modernism: The Liberation Movement of Iran under the Shah and Khomeini*. Ithaca, NY: Cornell University Press, 1990.

Cogan, Charles G. "Desert One and Its Disorders." *Journal of Military History* 67, no. 1 (January 2003): 201–216.

Cook, Steven A. *The Struggle for Egypt: From Nasser to Tahrir Square*. Oxford: Oxford University Press, 2012.

Dam, Nikolaos van. *The Struggle for Power in Syria: Politics and Society under Asad and the Ba'th Party*. London: I. B. Tauris, 2011.

Daugherty, William J. "Argo/Our Man in Tehran." *International Journal of Intelligence and Counterintelligence* 28, no. 1 (2015): 156–165.

Davis, Eric. *Memories of State: Politics, History, and Collective Identity in Modern Iraq*. Berkeley: University of California Press, 2005.

Dawn, C. Ernest. *From Ottomanism to Arabism: Essays on the Origins of Arab Nationalism*. Urbana: University of Illinois Press, 1973.

Dekmejian, R. Hrair. *Egypt under Nasir: A Study in Political Dynamics*. Albany: State University of New York Press, 1971.

———. "Saudi Arabia's Consultative Council." *Middle East Journal* 52, no. 2 (Spring 1998): 204–218.

Drysdale, Alasdair. "The Regional Equalization of Health Care and Education in Syria since the Ba'thi Revolution." *International Journal of Middle East Studies* 13, no.1 (February 1981): 93–111.

Ehteshami, Anoushiravan, and Emma C. Murphy. "Transformation of the Corporatist State in the Middle East." in "The Developmental State? Democracy, Reform and Economic Prosperity in the Third World in the Nineties," special issue, *Third World Quarterly* 17, no. 4 (1996): 753–772.

Erlich, Haggai. *Students and University in 20th Century Egyptian Politics.* London: Frank Cass, 1989.

Farouk-Sluglett, Marion, and Peter Sluglett. *Iraq since 1958: From Revolution to Dictatorship.* London: I. B. Tauris, 1990.

al-Gabbani, Mohammed. "Growth Trends and Changes in Small Towns in Saudi Arabia (1974–1993)." In "The Muslim World," special issue, *GeoJournal* 37, no. 1 (September 1995): 105–112.

Gaspard, Toufic K. *A Political Economy of Lebanon 1948–2002: The Limits of Laissez-Faire.* Leiden, Netherlands: Brill, 2004.

Gates, Carolyn L. *The Merchant Republic of Lebanon: Rise of an Open Economy.* London: I. B. Tauris, 1998.

Guazzone, Laura, and Daniela Pioppi. "Interpreting Change in the Arab World." In *The Arab State and Neo-liberal Globalization: The Restructuring of State Power in the Middle East*, edited by Laura Guazzone and Daniela Pioppi, 1–15. Reading, UK: Ithaca Press, 2009.

Harik, Iliya. "Continuity and Change in Local Development Policies in Egypt: From Nasser to Sadat." *International Journal of Middle East Studies* 16, no. 1 (March 1984): 43–66.

Hertog, Steffen. *Princes, Brokers, and Bureaucrats: Oil and the State in Saudi Arabia.* Ithaca, NY: Cornell University Press, 2010.

Heydemann, Steven. "Social Pacts and the Persistence of Authoritarianism in the Middle East." In *Debating Arab Authoritarianism: Dynamics and Durability in Nondemocratic Regimes*, edited by Oliver Schlumberger, 21–38. Stanford, CA: Stanford University Press, 2007.

Hinnebusch, Raymond A. *Authoritarian Power and State Formation in Ba'thist Syria: Army, Party, and Peasant.* Boulder, CO: Westview Press, 1990.

———. "Calculated Decompression as a Substitute for Democratization: Syria." In *Political Liberalization and Democratization in the Arab World*, vol. 2, *Comparative Experiences*, edited by Bahgat Korany, Rex Brynen, and Paul Noble, 223–240. Boulder, CO: Lynne Rienner Publishers, 1998.

———. *Egyptian Politics under Sadat: The Post-populist Development of an Authoritarian-Modernizing State.* Boulder, CO: Lynne Rienner Publishers, 1988.

———. "Local Politics in Syria: Organization and Mobilization in Four Village Cases." *Middle East Journal* 30, no. 1 (Winter 1976): 1–24.

———. "Party Activists in Syria and Egypt: Political Participation in Authoritarian Modernizing States." In "Party Activists in Comparative Perspective," special issue, *International Political Science Review* 4, no. 1 (1983): 84–93.

———. "State and Civil Society in Syria." *Middle East Journal* 47, no. 2 (Spring 1993): 243–257.

Holbik, Karel, and Edward Drachman. "Egypt as Recipient of Soviet Aid, 1955–1970." *Journal of Institutional and Theoretical Economics* 127, no. 1 (January 1971): 137–165.

Hooglund, Eric. *Land and Revolution in Iran, 1960–1980.* Austin: University of Texas Press, 1982.

———. "Rural Participation in the Revolution." In "Iran's Revolution: The Rural Dimension," special issue, *MERIP Reports* 87 (May 1980): 3–6.

———. "The Shi'i Clergy of Iran and the Conception of an Islamic State." *State, Culture, and Society* 1, no. 3 (Spring 1985): 102–117.

Hopwood, Derek. *Syria 1945–1986: Politics and Society*. London: Unwin Hyman, 1988.

Jafari, Peyman. "The Ambiguous Role of Entrepreneurs in Iran." In *Civil Society in Syria and Iran: Activism in Authoritarian Contexts*, edited by Paul Aarts and Francesco Cavatorta, 93–118. Boulder, CO: Lynne Rienner Publishers, 2013.

Jeffrey, Anthea. "The American Hostages in Tehran: The I.C.J. and the Legality of Rescue Missions." *The International and Comparative Law Quarterly* 30, no. 3 (July 1981): 717–729.

Kamrava, Mehran. *The Political History of Modern Iran: From Tribalism to Theocracy*. Westport, CT: Praeger, 1992.

Kandeel, Amal A. "The US-Market-Oriented Qualifying Industrial Zones: Economic Realities and Scope of Benefits (1996–2006)." *Arab Studies Quarterly* 30, no. 3 (Summer 2008): 25–39.

Keddie, Nikki R., with Yann Richard. *Modern Iran: Roots and Results of Revolution*. New Haven, CT: Yale University Press, 2003.

———. *Roots of Revolution: An Interpretive History of Modern Iran*. New Haven, CT: Yale University Press, 1981.

Keilany, Ziad. "Economic Planning in Syria, 1960–1965: An Evaluation." *Journal of Developing Areas* 4, no. 3 (April 1970): 361–374.

———. "Socialism and Economic Change in Syria." *Middle Eastern Studies* 9, no. 1 (January 1973): 61–72.

Khatib, Lina. "Syria's Civil Society as a Tool for Regime Legitimacy." In *Civil Society in Syria and Iran: Activism in Authoritarian Contexts*, edited by Paul Aarts and Francesco Cavatorta, 19–38. Boulder, CO: Lynne Rienner Publishers, 2013.

Lawson, Fred H. "Intraregime Dynamics, Uncertainty, and the Persistence of Authoritarianism in the Contemporary Arab World." In *Debating Arab Authoritarianism: Dynamics and Durability in Nondemocratic Regimes*, edited by Oliver Schlumberger, 109–128. Stanford, CA: Stanford University Press, 2007.

Losman, Donald L. "The Rentier State and National Oil Companies: An Economic and Political Perspective." *Middle East Journal* 64, no. 3 (Summer 2010): 427–445.

Lust-Okar, Ellen. "The Management of Opposition: Formal Structures of Contestation and Informal Political Manipulation in Egypt, Jordan, and Morocco." In *Debating Arab Authoritarianism: Dynamics and Durability in Nondemocratic Regimes*, edited by Oliver Schlumberger, 39–58. Stanford, CA: Stanford University Press, 2007.

Marr, Phebe. *The Modern History of Iraq*. Boulder, CO: Westview Press, 1985.

McDermott, Rose. "Prospect Theory in International Relations: The Iranian Hostage Rescue Mission." In "Prospect Theory and Political Psychology," special issue, *Political Psychology* 13, no. 2 (June 1992): 237–263.

Moore, Pete W. "QIZs, FTAs, USAID, and the MEFTA: A Political Economy of Acronyms." *Middle East Report* 234 (Spring 2005): 18–23.

Najmabadi, Afsaneh. *Land Reform and Social Change in Iran*. Salt Lake City: University of Utah Press, 1987.

Olson, Robert. *The Ba'th Party and Syria, 1947 to 1982: The Evolution of Ideology, Party, and State*. Princeton, NJ: Kingston Press, 1982.

Owen, Roger. *The Rise and Fall of Arab Presidents for Life*. Cambridge, MA: Harvard University Press, 2012.

Özyürek, Esra. "Miniaturizing Atatürk: Privatization of State Imagery and Ideology in Turkey." *American Ethnologist* 31, no. 3 (August 2004): 374–391.

Perthes, Volker. *The Political Economy of Syria under Asad*. London: I. B. Tauris, 1995.

Potter, Willis N. "Modern Education in Syria." *Comparative Education Review* 5, no. 1 (June 1961): 35–38.

Raphaeli, Nimrod. "Demands for Reform in Saudi Arabia." *Middle Eastern Studies* 41, no. 4 (July 2005): 517–532.

al-Rasheed, Madawi. *A History of Saudi Arabia.* Cambridge: Cambridge University Press, 2002.

Roberts, David. *The Ba'th and the Creation of Modern Syria.* New York: St. Martin's Press, 1987.

Robins, Philip. *A History of Jordan.* Cambridge: Cambridge University Press, 2004.

Robinson, Leonard. "Rentierism and Foreign Policy in Syria." *Arab Studies Journal* 4, no. 1 (Spring 1996): 34–54.

Rugh, William A. "Emergence of a New Middle Class in Saudi Arabia." *Middle East Journal* 27, no. 1 (Winter 1973): 7–20.

———. "A Tale of Two Houses." *Wilson Quarterly* 3, no. 1 (Winter 1979): 58–72.

Ryan, Curtis R. *Jordan in Transition: From Hussein to Abdullah.* Boulder, CO: Lynne Rienner Publishers, 2002.

Saleh, Mahmoud Abdullah. "Development of Higher Education in Saudi Arabia." *Higher Education* 15, no. 1–2 (1986): 17–23.

Sassoon, Joseph. *Saddam Hussein's Ba'th Party: Inside an Authoritarian Regime.* Cambridge: Cambridge University Press, 2012.

Shambayati, Hootan. "The Rentier State, Interest Groups, and the Paradox of Autonomy: State and Business in Turkey and Iran." *Comparative Politics* 26, no. 3 (April 1994): 307–331.

Springborg, Robert. "Baathism in Practice: Agriculture, Politics, and Political Culture in Syria and Iraq." *Middle Eastern Studies* 17, no. 2 (April 1981): 191–209.

Szyliowicz, Joseph S. *Political Change in Rural Turkey: Erdemli.* The Hague: Mouton, 1966.

Thompson, Elizabeth F. *Justice Interrupted: Historical Perspectives on Promoting Democracy in the Middle East.* Special Report 225. Washington, DC: United States Institute of Peace, 2009.

Tripp, Charles. *A History of Iraq.* 3rd ed. Cambridge: Cambridge University Press, 2007.

Van Dusen, Michael H. "Political Integration and Regionalism in Syria." *Middle East Journal* 26, no. 2 (Spring 1972): 123–136.

Waterbury, John. *The Egypt of Nasser and Sadat: The Political Economy of Two Regimes.* Princeton, NJ: Princeton University Press, 1983.

White, Jenny B. "Tin Towns to Fanatics: Turkey's Rural to Urban Migration from 1923 to the Present." In *Turkey's Engagement with Modernity: Conflict and Change in the Twentieth Century*, edited by Celia Kerslake, Kerem Öktem, and Philip Robins, 425–442. London: Palgrave Macmillan, 2010.

Wilson, Christopher S. "Representing National Identity and Memory in the Mausoleum of Mustafa Kemal Atatürk." *Journal of the Society of Architectural Historians* 68, no. 2 (June 2009): 224–253.

Wurzel, Ulrich G. "The Political Economy of Authoritarianism in Egypt: Insufficient Structural Reforms, Limited Outcomes and a Lack of New Actors." In *The Arab State and Neo-liberal Globalization: The Restructuring of State Power in the Middle East*, edited by Laura Guazzone and Daniela Pioppi, 97–124. Reading, UK: Ithaca Press, 2009.

Yeganeh, Nahd. "Women, Nationalism and Islam in Contemporary Political Discourse in Iran." In "Nationalisms and National Identities," special issue, *Feminist Review* 44 (Summer 1993): 3–18.

Ziadeh, Radwan. *Power and Policy in Syria: The Intelligence Services, Foreign Relations and Democracy in the Modern Middle East.* London: I. B. Tauris, 2011.

Zürcher, Erik J. *Turkey: A Modern History.* London: I. B. Tauris, 2009.

Chapter 10. Upheaval

Aarts, Paul. "The Longevity of the House of Saud: Looking outside the Box." In *Debating Arab Authoritarianism: Dynamics and Durability in Nondemocratic Regimes*, edited by Oliver Schlumberger, 251–270. Stanford, CA: Stanford University Press, 2007.

Abdalla, Ahmed. *The Student Movement and National Politics in Egypt: 1923–1973*. London: Al Saqi Books, 1985.

Abdo, Geneive. *No God but God: Egypt and the Triumph of Islam*. Oxford: Oxford University Press, 2000.

Abdullah, Thabit A. J. *A Short History of Iraq*. 2nd ed. Edinburgh Gate: Pearson Education, 2011.

Abrahamian, Ervand. *Iran between Two Revolutions*. Princeton, NJ: Princeton University Press, 1982.

al-Alawdi, Hesham. *In Pursuit of Legitimacy: The Muslim Brothers and Mubarak, 1982–2000*. London: Tauris Academic Studies, 2004.

Albrecht, Holger. "Authoritarian Opposition and the Politics of Challenge in Egypt." In *Debating Arab Authoritarianism: Dynamics and Durability in Nondemocratic Regimes*, edited by Oliver Schlumberger, 59–74. Stanford, CA: Stanford University Press, 2007.

Anderson, Betty S. *The American University of Beirut: Arab Nationalism and Liberal Education*. Austin: University of Texas Press, 2011.

Batatu, Hanna. "Iraq's Underground Shi'i Movements." In "Islam and Politics," special issue, *MERIP Reports* 102 (January 1982): 3–9.

Beinin, Joel. "Neo-liberal Structural Adjustment, Political Demobilization and Neo-authoritarianism In Egypt." In *The Arab State and Neo-liberal Globalization: The Restructuring of State Power in the Middle East*, edited by Laura Guazzone and Daniela Pioppi, 19–46. Reading, UK: Ithaca Press, 2009.

Benglo, Ofra. "Shi'is and Politics in Ba'thi Iraq." *Middle Eastern Studies* 21, no. 1 (January 1985): 1–14.

Brynen, Rex. "The Politics of Monarchical Liberalism: Jordan." In *Political Liberalization and Democratization in the Arab World*, vol. 2, *Comparative Experiences*, edited by Bahgat Korany, Rex Brynen, and Paul Noble, 71–100. Boulder, CO: Lynne Rienner Publishers, 1998.

Cook, Steven A. *The Struggle for Egypt: From Nasser to Tahrir Square*. Oxford: Oxford University Press, 2012.

Ehteshami, Anoushiravan, and Emma C. Murphy. "Transformation of the Corporatist State in the Middle East." In "The Developmental State? Democracy, Reform and Economic Prosperity in the Third World in the Nineties," special issue, *Third World Quarterly* 17, no. 4 (1996): 753–772.

Eickelman, Dale F. "Mass Higher Education and the Religious Imagination in Contemporary Arab Societies." *American Ethnologist* 19, no. 4 (November 1992): 643–655.

Elver, Hilal. "Reluctant Partners: Turkey and the European Union." In "Middle East Research & Information Project," special issue, *Middle East Report* 235 (Summer 2005): 24–29.

Entessar, Nader. "The Kurds in Post-revolutionary Iran and Iraq." *Third World Quarterly* 6. no. 4 (October 1984): 911–933.

Ergin, Murat. "The Racialization of Kurdish Identity in Turkey." *Ethnic and Racial Studies* 37, no. 2 (2012): 1–20.

Erlich, Haggai. *Students and University in 20th Century Egyptian Politics*. London: Frank Cass, 1989.

Farouk-Sluglett, Marion, and Peter Sluglett. "Iraq since 1986: The Strengthening of Saddam." In "On the Edge of War," special issue, *Middle East Report* 167 (November–December 1990): 19–24.

Farsoun, Samih K., with Christina E. Zacharia. *Palestine and the Palestinians*. Boulder, CO: Westview Press, 1997.
Gerges, Fawaz A. *The Rise and Fall of al-Qaeda*. Oxford: Oxford University Press, 2011.
Gökalp, Deniz, and Seda Ünsar. "From the Myth of European Union Ascension to Disillusion: Implications for Religious and Ethnic Politicization in Turkey." *Middle East Journal* 62, no. 1 (Winter 2008): 93–116.
Guazzone, Laura, and Daniela Pioppi. "Interpreting Change in the Arab World." In *The Arab State and Neo-liberal Globalization: The Restructuring of State Power in the Middle East*, edited by Laura Guazzone and Daniela Pioppi, 1–15. Reading, UK: Ithaca Press, 2009.
Gunter, Michael M. "The KDP-PUK Conflict in Northern Iraq." *Middle East Journal* 50, no. 2 (Spring 1996): 224–241.
Haddad, Bassam. "Business Associations and the New Nexus of Power in Syria." In *Civil Society in Syria and Iran: Activism in Authoritarian Contexts*, edited by Paul Aarts and Francesco Cavatorta, 69–92. Boulder, CO: Lynne Rienner Publishers, 2013.
———. *Business Networks in Syria: The Political Economy of Authoritarian Resilience*. Stanford, CA: Stanford University Press, 2012.
Hinnebusch, Raymond A. "Calculated Decompression as a Substitute for Democratization: Syria." In *Political Liberalization and Democratization in the Arab World*, vol. 2, *Comparative Experiences*, edited by Bahgat Korany, Rex Brynen, and Paul Noble, 223–240. Boulder, CO: Lynne Rienner Publishers, 1998.
Honari, Ali. "From Virtual to Tangible Social Movements in Iran." In *Civil Society in Syria and Iran: Activism in Authoritarian Contexts*, edited by Paul Aarts and Francesco Cavatorta, 143–168. Boulder, CO: Lynne Rienner Publishers, 2013.
Jafari, Peyman. "The Ambiguous Role of Entrepreneurs in Iran." In *Civil Society in Syria and Iran: Activism in Authoritarian Contexts*, edited by Paul Aarts and Francesco Cavatorta, 93–118. Boulder, CO: Lynne Rienner Publishers, 2013.
Jones, Toby Craig. "Seeking a 'Social Contract' for Saudi Arabia." *Middle East Report* 228 (Autumn 2003): 42–48.
Kamrava, Mehran. *Qatar: Small State, Big Politics*. Ithaca, NY: Cornell University Press, 2013.
Kepel, Gilles. *Jihad: The Trail of Political Islam*. Translated by Anthony F. Roberts. Cambridge: Belknap Press of Harvard University Press, 2002.
———. "A Line in the Sand." *RSA Journal* 154, no. 5536 (Winter 2008): 28–33.
Langohr, Vickie. "Too Much Civil Society, Too Little Politics: Egypt and Liberalizing Arab Regimes." *Comparative Politics* 36, no. 2 (January 2004): 181–204.
Lawson, Fred H. "Intraregime Dynamics, Uncertainty, and the Persistence of Authoritarianism in the Contemporary Arab World." In *Debating Arab Authoritarianism: Dynamics and Durability in Nondemocratic Regimes*, edited by Oliver Schlumberger, 109–128. Stanford, CA: Stanford University Press, 2007.
Lust-Okar, Ellen. "The Management of Opposition: Formal Structures of Contestation and Informal Political Manipulation in Egypt, Jordan, and Morocco." In *Debating Arab Authoritarianism: Dynamics and Durability in Nondemocratic Regimes*, edited by Oliver Schlumberger, 39–58. Stanford, CA: Stanford University Press, 2007.
Lynch, Marc. *Voices of the New Arab Public: Iraq, al-Jazeera, and Middle East Politics Today*. New York: Columbia University Press, 2006.
Mahmoud, Saba. *Politics of Piety: The Islamic Revival and the Feminist Subject*. Princeton, NJ: Princeton University Press, 2005.
Moon, John Ellis van Courtland. "The Death of Distinctions: From 9/11 to Abu Ghraib." *Politics and the Life Sciences* 23, no. 2 (September 2004): 2–12.
Müftüler-Bac, Meltem. "The Never-Ending Story: Turkey and the European Union."

In “Turkey before and after Atatürk: Internal and External Affairs,” special issue, *Middle Eastern Studies* 34, no. 4 (October 1998): 240–258.
Nakash, Yitzhak. *Shi'is of Iraq*. Princeton, NJ: Princeton University Press, 1994.
Ochsenwald, William. “Saudi Arabia and the Islamic Revival.” *International Journal of Middle East Studies* 13, no. 3 (August 1981): 271–286.
Pamuk, Şevket. “Economic Change in Twentieth-Century Turkey: Is the Glass More Than Half Full?” In *The Cambridge History of Turkey*, Vol. 4, *Turkey in the Modern World*, edited by Reşat Kasaba, 266–300. Cambridge: Cambridge University Press, 2008.
Peretz, Don. “The Impact of the Gulf War on Israeli and Palestinian Political Attitudes.” *Journal of Palestine Studies* 21, no. 1 (Autumn 1991): 17–35.
Perthes, Volker. *The Political Economy of Syria under Asad*. London: I. B. Tauris, 1995.
———. *Syria under Bashar al-Asad: Modernisation and the Limits of Change*. Adelphi Paper 366. Oxford: Oxford University Press, 2004.
Prokop, Michaela. “Saudi Arabia: The Politics of Education.” *International Affairs (Royal Institute of International Affairs 1944–)* 79, no. 1 (January 2003): 77–89.
Redmond, John. “Turkey and the European Union: Troubled European or European Trouble?” In “Europe at 50,” special issue, *International Affairs* 83, no. 2 (March 2007): 305–317.
Robins, Philip. *A History of Jordan*. Cambridge: Cambridge University Press, 2004.
Robinson, Leonard. “Rentierism and Foreign Policy in Syria.” *Arab Studies Journal* 4, no. 1 (Spring 1996): 34–54.
Roy, Olivier. *Globalised Islam: The Search for a New Ummah*. London: Hurst, 2002.
Ryan, Curtis R. *Jordan in Transition: From Hussein to Abdullah*. Boulder, CO: Lynne Rienner Publishers, 2002.
Schwedler, Jillian. *Faith in Moderation: Islamist Parties in Jordan and Yemen*. Cambridge: Cambridge University Press, 2006.
Shambayati, Hootan. “The Rentier State, Interest Groups, and the Paradox of Autonomy: State and Business in Turkey and Iran.” *Comparative Politics* 26, no. 3 (April 1994): 307–331.
Singerman, Diane. “The Networked World of Islamist Social Movements.” In *Islamic Activism: A Social Movement Theory Approach*, edited by Quintan Wiktorowicz, 143–163. Bloomington: Indiana University Press, 2004.
Smith, Charles D. *Palestine and the Arab-Israeli Conflict*. 8th ed. Boston: Bedford/St. Martin's, 2013.
Starrett, Gregory. *Putting Islam to Work: Education, Politics, and Religious Transformation in Egypt*. Berkeley: University of California Press, 1998.
Thompson, Elizabeth F. *Justice Interrupted: Historical Perspectives on Promoting Democracy in the Middle East*. Special Report 225. Washington, DC: United States Institute of Peace, 2009.
———. *Justice Interrupted: The Struggle for Constitutional Government in the Middle East*. Cambridge: Harvard University Press, 2013.
Tripp, Charles. *A History of Iraq*. 3rd ed. Cambridge: Cambridge University Press, 2007.
White, Jenny B. *Islamist Mobilization in Turkey: A Study in Vernacular Politics*. Seattle: University of Washington Press, 2002.
———. “The Islamist Paradox.” In *Fragments of Culture: The Everyday of Modern Turkey*, edited by Deniz Kandiyoti and Ayşe Saktanber, 191–217. New Brunswick, NJ: Rutgers University Press, 2002.
———. *Money Makes Us Relatives: Women's Labor in Urban Turkey*. Austin: University of Texas Press, 1994.
———. *Muslim Nationalism and the New Turks*. Princeton, NJ: Princeton University Press, 2013.

———. "Tin Towns to Fanatics: Turkey's Rural to Urban Migration from 1923 to the Present." In *Turkey's Engagement with Modernity: Conflict and Change in the Twentieth Century*, edited by Celia Kerslake, Kerem Öktem, and Philip Robins, 425–442. London: Palgrave Macmillan, 2010.

Wickham, Carrie Rosefsky. *Mobilizing Islam: Religion, Activism, and Political Change in Egypt*. New York: Columbia University Press, 2002.

———. *The Muslim Brotherhood: Evolution of an Islamist Movement*. Princeton, NJ: Princeton University Press, 2013.

Wiktorowicz, Quintan. "A Genealogy of Radical Islam." *Studies in Conflict & Terrorism* 28, no. 2 (2005): 75–97.

Wurzel, Ulrich G. "The Political Economy of Authoritarianism in Egypt: Insufficient Structural Reforms, Limited Outcomes and a Lack of New Actors." In *The Arab State and Neo-liberal Globalization: The Restructuring of State Power in the Middle East*, edited by Laura Guazzone and Daniela Pioppi, 97–124. Reading, UK: Ithaca Press, 2009.

Yavuz, M. Hakan. "The Gülen Movement: The Turkish Puritans." In *Turkish Islam and the Secular State: The Gülen Movement*, edited by M. Hakan Yavuz and John L. Esposito, 19–47. Syracuse, NY: Syracuse University Press, 2003.

———. *Toward an Islamic Enlightenment: The Gülen Movement*. Oxford: Oxford University Press, 2013.

Zubaida, Sami. "Islam, the State and Democracy: Contrasting Conceptions in Egypt." In "Islam, the State and Democracy," special issue, *Middle East Report* 179 (November–December 1992): 2–10.

Zürcher, Erik J. *Turkey: A Modern History*. London: I. B. Tauris, 2009.

Epilogue: Revolution, Reaction, and Civil War

Achcar, Gilbert. *The People Want: A Radical Exploration of the Arab Uprising*. Translated by G. M. Goshgarian. Berkeley: University of California Press, 2013.

Ali, Tariq. "What Is a Revolution?" *Guernica*, September 14, 2013. http://www.guernicamag.com/daily/tariq-ali-what-is-a-revolution/.

Amar, Paul. "Why Mubarak Is Out." In *The Dawn of the Arab Uprisings: End of an Old Order?*, edited by Bassam Haddad, Rosie Bsheer, and Ziad Abu-Rish, 83–90. London: Pluto Press, 2012.

Armbrust, Walter. "The Revolution against Neoliberalism." In *The Dawn of the Arab Uprisings: End of an Old Order?*, edited by Bassam Haddad, Rosie Bsheer, and Ziad Abu-Rish, 113–123. London: Pluto Press, 2012.

Ayeb, Habib, and Ray Bush. "Small Farmer Uprisings and Rural Neglect in Egypt and Tunisia." *Middle East Report* 272 (Fall 2014): 2–10.

Bamyeh, Mohammed. "The Tunisian Revolution: Initial Reflections." In *The Dawn of the Arab Uprisings: End of an Old Order?*, edited by Bassam Haddad, Rosie Bsheer, and Ziad Abu-Rish, 49–58. London: Pluto Press, 2012.

Bayat, Asef. *Life as Politics: How Ordinary People Change the Middle East*. Stanford, CA: Stanford University Press, 2010.

———. "Paradoxes of Arab Refo-lutions." In *The Dawn of the Arab Uprisings: End of an Old Order?*, edited by Bassam Haddad, Rosie Bsheer, and Ziad Abu-Rish, 28–32. London: Pluto Press, 2012.

Cammett, Melani, and Ishac Diwan. "Toward a Political Economy of the Arab Uprisings (Part One)." Jadaliyya.com, December 26, 2013. http://www.jadaliyya.com/pages/index/15754/toward-a-political-economy-of-the-arab-uprisings-%28.

———. "Toward a Political Economy of the Arab Uprisings (Part Two)." Jadaliyya.com, December 27, 2013. http://www.jadaliyya.com/pages/index/15755/toward-a-political-economy-of-the-arab-uprisings-%28.

Eng, Brent, and José Ciro Martinez. "Starvation, Submission and Survival: Syria's War through the Prism of War." *Middle East Report* 273 (Winter 2014): 28–32.

Hudson, Michael. "Awakening, Cataclysm, or Just a Series of Events? Reflections on the Current Wave of Protest in the Arab World." In *The Dawn of the Arab Uprisings: End of an Old Order?*, edited by Bassam Haddad, Rosie Bsheer, and Ziad Abu-Rish, 17–27. London: Pluto Press, 2012.

Lesch, David W. "The Uprising That Wasn't Supposed to Happen: Syria and the Arab Spring." In *The Arab Spring: Change and Resistance in the Middle East*, edited by Mark L. Haas and David W. Lesch, 79–96. Boulder, CO: Westview Press, 2013.

Lynch, Marc. *The Arab Uprising: The Unfinished Revolution of the New Middle East.* New York: PublicAffairs, 2012.

Mahmoud, Saba. "The Architects of the Egyptian Uprising and the Challenges Ahead." In *The Dawn of the Arab Uprisings: End of an Old Order?*, edited by Bassam Haddad, Rosie Bsheer, and Ziad Abu-Rish, 104–112. London: Pluto Press, 2012.

McCormick, Jared. "The Whispers of WhatsApp: Beyond Facebook and Twitter in the Middle East." Jadaliyya.com, December 9, 2013. http://www.jadaliyya.com/pages/index/15495/the-whispers-of-whatsapp_beyond-facebook-and-twitt.

Rutherford, Bruce K. "Egypt: The Origins and Consequences of the January 25 Uprising." In *The Arab Spring: Change and Resistance in the Middle East*, edited by Mark L. Haas and David W. Lesch, 35–63. Boulder, CO: Westview Press, 2013.

Ryan, Curtis R. "Jordan and the Arab Spring." In *The Arab Spring: Change and Resistance in the Middle East*, edited by Mark L. Haas and David W. Lesch, 116–130. Boulder, CO: Westview Press, 2013.

Index

Page numbers in italics refer to figures and maps.